State & National Parks

ALSO AVAILABLE IN THE COMPLEAT TRAVELER SERIES

□ Europe by Eurail: *How to Tour Europe by Train*

□ Britain by Britrail: *How to Tour Britain by Train*

□ America by Train: *How to Tour America by Rail*

□ Bed & Breakfast America: *Great American Guest House Book*

□ National & State Parks: *Lodges, Cabins, & Resorts*

□ **Country Inns** & Historic Hotels of Great Britain

□ **Country Inns** & Historic Hotels of Canada

□ **Country Inns** & Historic Hotels of Ireland

□ **Country** New England **Inns**

□ **Country Inns** & Historic Hotels of the Middle Atlantic States

□ **Country Inns** & Historic Hotels of the South

□ **Country Inns** & Historic Hotels of the Midwest & Rocky Mts.

□ **Country Inns** & Historic Hotels of California & the Northwest

□ Guide to Country New England

□ Guide to California & Pacific N.W.

□ Guide to Texas and the Southwest

□ *Scheer's* Guide to Virginia

□ *Scheer's* Guide to North Carolina

□ *Scheer's* Guide to Tennessee

□ *Scheer's* Guide to Florida

If your local bookseller, gift shop, or country inn does not stock a particular title, ask them to order directly from Burt Franklin & Co., Inc., P.O. Box 856, New York 10014, U.S.A. Telephone orders are accepted from recognized retailers and credit-card holders. In the U.S.A., call, toll-free, 1-800-223-0766 during regular business hours. (In New York State, call 212-627-0027.)

John Thaxton

Lodges Cabins

State & National Parks

Resorts

89/90

BURT FRANKLIN & COMPANY, INC.

Published by
BURT FRANKLIN & COMPANY
P.O. Box 856
New York, New York 10014

FIFTH EDITION

ISBN 0-89102-414-X

Manufactured in the United States of America

1   3   4   2

Acknowledgments

I want to thank the many people who have helped me in preparing this volume.
My appreciation goes especially to the many park personnel who have shared their
knowledge, and I only regret that space does not permit my mentioning each by
name. My thanks go also to the National Park Service for its help in locating
photographs.

I want to thank, as well, Bonnie Stylides, whose preliminary research made
writing this book easier; Jodie Gould and Maura Milligan for their help in double-
and triple-checking the many details that make a book like this useful; Nancy
Landau for her editing; and Katharita Lamoza for her careful proofreading.

This book would not have been possible without the guidance and energy of
my publisher, Tom Franklin.

Most of all, I want to acknowledge my wife, who endured with grace everything
from mountains to rain forests, as well as my exhausting work schedule.

Introduction

This book describes cabins, lodges, and resorts located in state and national parks, recreation areas, monuments, and forests. The text is arranged alphabetically by state and, within each state, alphabetically by park. Each park, recreation area, monument or forest is described individually, and each entry consists of two sections. The first describes the essential characteristics of a particular park, such as its location, its size, its predominant flora and fauna, its terrain, its distinctive geographical features and its major recreational facilities. The distances given are "as the crow flies"—they are meant to enable readers to find quickly a park on a map and are supplemented by specific driving instructions, which appear at the end of each entry.

The second section describes overnight accommodations, other than campsites, available at a particular park. The accommodations available in state and national parks are as varied as the parks themselves, ranging from primitive log cabins with no plumbing, no electricity, and no furnishings other than an ax for cutting firewood to a palatial first-class hotel listed in the National Register of Historic Places. Most of the accommodations fall somewhere in between these two extremes, and the basic features of each are described, giving such information as whether or not a cabin has a private bath, a telephone, a fireplace, cooking facilities and eating utensils, a porch or a deck, or a nearby restaurant.

At the beginning of each state is a map keyed to each entry in the state and an explanation of general state-park rules and reservation procedures. I can't stress enough the importance of following reservation procedures: Some of the accommodations are reserved as much as a year in advance. In several cases reservations are given out by means of a lottery; in others, on a first-come, first-served basis. Familiarizing yourself with reservation procedures is the surest way to avoid unnecessary disappointments. Additional information about particular parks or accommodations is available from the parks or from state and national park bureaus, which usually send out literature on request.

Many people are unaware that parks are a relatively recent

phenomenon, the world's first national park having been Yellowstone National Park, which was designated in 1872. Since then hundreds of state and national parks have been set aside for public enjoyment. The nation owes a debt to the Civilian Conservation Corps. CCC workers built roads, dams, trails, and thousands of cabins, most of which are still in use today. An attempt to create jobs during a period of economic hardship, the Civilian Conservation Corps created more than that—it created a rich natural heritage that's still here for all of us to enjoy.

JOHN THAXTON

Contents

How to Use This Book

• Each park listed in this book appears on a map at the beginning of its state chapter. The number that appears within the little box on the map is keyed to the park heading in the text. The maps have been provided to help locate a park on a full-size state map.

• While most parks are open all year, many facilities may be closed during the off season. The opening and closing dates listed at the end of each entry refer specifically to the opening and closing dates of the lodges or cabins, not the park itself.

• The telephone numbers and addresses that appear at the end of each entry are those of the park accommodations. If the park has a separate phone number, this generally has been listed just before the information about the lodge or cabins.

• Information concerning state-park reservations, state-park restrictions, and state tourist information is given at the beginning of each state. (National Park information varies from park to park and should be requested directly from the individual park.)

• It is recommended that reservations be made as far in advance as possible. Several states have a lottery system that requires that an application be submitted to enter the lottery for a cabin. This information has been provided at the beginning of each state.

• Most parks permit fishing, although most are subject to state regulations, which generally require a license. These are usually obtainable at local sporting-goods stores for a nominal fee.

• Many states prohibit hunting within park boundaries. This has been mentioned at the beginning of each state.

• Information about towels, linens, utensils, stoves, and refrigerators refers to facilities in cabins or in a lodge that has no dining facilities.

Alabama

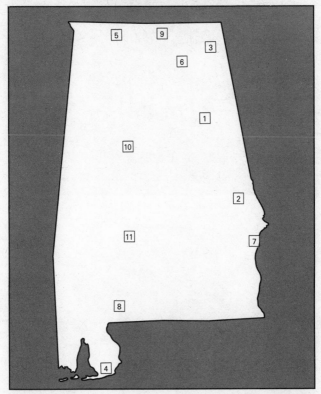

State map and tourist information: Bureau of Publicity and Information, 532 S. Perry St., Montgomery, AL 36104; 800-ALA-BAMA (out-of-state), 800-392-8096 (Alabama only), 205-261-4169 (Alaska and Hawaii). **State parks:** *Information and Reservations:* Alabama Dept. of Conservation, Parks Div., 64 N. Union St., Montgomery, AL 36130; 800-ALA-PARK (Alabama only), 205-261-3333. *Entrance fees:* nominal; waived for lodgers. *Reservations:* Reservations required with deposit for first night's lodging to be received at least 7 days in advance; or call to use credit cards. Minimum stay, 2 days; 3 days on holiday weekends (Mem. Day, July 4, and Labor Day). Advance reservations recommended April—Labor Day. *Restrictions:* No hunting. No alcoholic beverages in dry counties. Dogs must be leashed (not permitted in lodgings). *Facilities:* Swimming, late May—early September. ·

Cheaha State Park Resort is in eastern Alabama, roughly 70 miles east of Birmingham and about 100 miles west of Atlanta, Georgia. The 2,719-acre park is surrounded by Talladega National Forest and takes its name from Cheaha Mountain, at 2,407 feet the highest point in the state. There's an observation tower on top of the mountain, with panoramic views of mountains and valleys wooded with oaks, maples, hickories, pines, and beeches. The park is prettiest in spring, when it is full of wildflowers, and in fall, when the leaves turn color.

Popular activities include swimming (the park has both a pool and a lake), hiking, fishing, boating, and miniature golf. The park also has picnic facilities and playground areas for children. *Park mailing address:* Lineville, AL 36266. *Park phone:* (205) 488-5111.

Cheaha Lodge, Chalets, and Cottages

A rustic stone lodge of modern design, Cheaha has thirty guest rooms, a gift shop, and a large restaurant with exposed-beam ceilings and a series of picture windows overlooking the forest. Each guest room has two double beds, wall-to-wall carpeting, color television, and a telephone.

The lodge, operated by an independent concessionaire, also administers thirteen A-frame chalets and ten stone cottages. The chalets have hardwood floors, fireplaces, kitchens, and private baths with showers and can accommodate six people each. The stone cottages come in two sizes and have either one room (that serves as a combination living room, bedroom, and kitchen) or two rooms. The cabins can accommodate from four to eight people and have hardwood floors. The smaller cabins have fireplaces. The cabins and chalets have complete kitchen facilities but neither television nor telephones.

The park also includes a rustic-style group lodge built of stone by the Civilian Conservation Corps in the 1930s. This lodge can accommodate up to fifty people and has its own kitchen and a large dining area. Some guest rooms have two single beds, while others have bunk-style beds. The three-story lodge is situated along the ridge of Cheaha Mountain.

Accommodations: 30 lodge rooms and 13 chalets, and 10 cottages, all with private bath; 1 group lodge with 6 shared baths.

Cheaha Mountain

Towels and linens: Provided. *Cooking and eating utensils:* In chalets, cottages, and group lodge. *Stove and refrigerator:* In chalets, cottages, and group lodge. *Pets:* Permitted if leashed. *Open:* All year. *Mailing address:* Cheaha State Park Resort, PO Box 546, Lineville, AL 36266. *Phone:* (205) 488-5115. *Driving instructions:* Cheaha State Park is off Route 49 about 17 miles north of Lineville.

4

Chewacla State Park is in southeastern Alabama about 55 miles east of Montgomery, 35 miles west of Columbus, Georgia, and about 5 miles northeast of Tuskegee National Forest. The 696-acre park is on the edge of a piedmont, in a rugged little valley wooded with oaks, hickories, maples, dogwoods, and redbuds. Four main hiking trails meander through the park. One of them follows a creek and winds around Chewacla Lake. Another trail leads to the spillway of Chewacla Dam, known to locals as Chewacla Falls. In spring the area is full of wildflowers, as well as mountain laurel, which lines the basin of the creek.

Popular activities include picnicking, swimming, boating, and fishing. The park has a beach·with a bathhouse, plus rowboat, paddleboat, and canoe rentals. Anglers fish the 26-acre Chewacla Lake for bass, bream, crappies, and catfishes. For children there are several playground areas.

The park has available five stone-and-wood cabins in a wooded area overlooking the lake. Four have one room for up to four people in each, and the fifth cabin is a one-bedroom unit that can comfortably accommodate six. All cabins have a fully equipped kitchenette, a private bath, and a porch. One has a fireplace.

Accommodations: 5 cabins with private bath. *Towels and linens:* Provided. *Cooking and eating utensils:* Provided. *Stove and refrigerator:* Provided. *Pets:* Permitted. *Open:* All year. *Mailing address:* Chewacla, PO Box 447, Auburn, AL 36830. *Phone:* (205) 887-5621. *Driving instructions:* Chewacla State Park is off U.S. 29, roughly 3 miles south of Auburn.

Desoto State Park is in northeastern Alabama about 110 miles northeast of Birmingham and roughly 50 miles southwest of Chattanooga, Tennessee. The 5,067-acre park is 40 miles long and runs beside the Little River Canyon, the deepest gorge east of the Mississippi. The terrain is hilly, with elevations as high as 1,835 feet, and wooded with oaks, maples, hickories, and pines. The park has a large amount of rhododendrons and laurels, which makes for a colorful spring, as well as 22 miles of hiking trails, several of which skirt the canyon and run past Desoto Falls and Little River Falls. A 20-mile scenic road runs along the rim of the gorge.

Popular activities in the park include swimming (in either the park's pool or the river), hiking, tennis, and field sports. There's a golf course a few minutes' drive from the park. The park is open all year, and winter visitors frequently visit Cloudmont Resort, which has snowmaking equipment. *Park mailing address:* Route 1, Box 210, Fort Payne, AL, 35967. *Park phone:* (205) 845-0051.

Desoto Lodge, Chalets, and Cabins

A hybrid, Desoto Lodge consists of a 1930s stone building constructed by the Civilian Conservation Corps (CCC) and a 25-bedroom motel unit connected by a walkway. The main lodge has several dining rooms, a large lobby, and a gift shop. The main dining room has an exposed-beam ceiling, stone walls, and a large stone fireplace.

The guest rooms in the adjacent motel have wall-to-wall carpeting, two double beds, a private bath, color television, a telephone, air-conditioning, and heat. Several of the rooms have porches overlooking a stream.

The lodge also administers eleven A-frame chalets and twelve rustic cabins. The chalets, which are on a bluff near the river (some have river views), have hardwood floors, fireplaces, complete kitchens, two downstairs rooms, and a sleeping loft. They can accommodate as many as six people each.

The cabins, also constructed by the CCC, vary in size and can accommodate from four to ten people. They are a combination wood-frame and log design and have hardwood floors and complete kitchens. All but three have fireplaces.

Accommodations: 25 lodge rooms, 11 chalets, and 12 cabins, all with private bath. *Towels and linens:* Provided. *Cooking and eating utensils:* In chalets and cabins. *Stove and refrigerator:* In chalets and cabins. *Pets:* Permitted on leashes. *Open:* All year. *Mailing address:* Route 1, Box 205, Fort Payne, AL 35967. *Phone:* (205) 845-5380. *Driving instructions:* Desoto State Park is on Route 89 roughly 8 miles northeast of Fort Payne.

Gulf State Park is 45 miles southeast of Mobile on the Gulf of Mexico. The 6,000-acre park has 2½ miles of white-sand beachfront, along with all manner of waterfowl congregating in and around the park, especially during migrations. Visitors will almost surely see little and great blue herons, great and snowy egrets, seven species of gull, eight species of tern, ducks, geese, anhingas, and ospreys. The terrain is relatively flat, and much of the vegetation is slightly mutated because of all the salt in the air. Plant life includes seven species of pine and thirteen of oak, plus myrtles, palmettos, magnolias, and hollies.

The beach has bathhouse facilities and an 825-foot fishing pier that juts out into the Gulf of Mexico. Swimming, boating, and waterskiing are popular, and the facilities include tennis courts and an eighteen-hole golf course with rentals, a pro shop, and a clubhouse.

Gulf State Park Cabins and Group Lodge

The park has twenty-one cabins, seventeen of which are along an inland lake and feature screened porches, private baths, and fully equipped kitchenettes. Of wood-frame construction, these cabins are supported by 12-foot-tall pylons. (Two of the cabins are completely equipped for the handicapped.) There are also four rustic cabins built in the 1930s by the Civilian Conservation Corps. These shingled wood-frame cabins are in the woods and have private baths and kitchenettes. Two have screened porches.

The park also includes a new group lodge with fifteen rooms that can accommodate up to fifty people. Modern in design, the lodge has a kitchen, a dining area, and a recreation room as well as electric, hot-air heat and air conditioning. Each guest room has four bunk beds and its own bath. The lodge is located 2½ miles from the beach, adjacent to the fresh-water lake, and has its own private beach for swimming.

Accommodations: 21 cabins with private bath; 1 group lodge with bunk rooms and shared baths. *Towels and linens:* Provided. *Cooking and eating utensils:* Provided. *Stove and refrigerator:* Provided. *Pets:* Not permitted. *Open:* All year. *Mailing address:* Route 2, Box 9, Gulf Shores, AL 36542. *Phone:* (205) 968-7531 for lodge, (205) 968-7544 for cabins, (205) 968-7544 for group lodge. *Driving instructions:* See below.

Gulf State Park Resort Inn

A group of modern buildings directly on the beach, Gulf State Park Resort Inn consists of 144 guest rooms, a restaurant, a lounge, and meeting and banquet facilities, all run by an independent concessionaire. Each guest room has wall-to-wall carpeting, color television, a telephone, a private bath, and a private balcony overlooking the Gulf of Mexico. The restaurant and the lounge also overlook the Gulf.

Accommodations: 144 rooms with private bath. *Pets:* Not permitted. *Open:* All year. *Mailing address:* Gulf State Park Resort (ARA Services), PO Box 437, Gulf Shores, AL 36542. *Phone:* (205) 968-7531. *Driving instructions:* Gulf State Park is off Route 182, about 3 miles east of Gulf Shores.

Joe Wheeler State Park is in northern Alabama about 110 miles
north of Birmingham and 30 miles south of the Tennessee border.
The 2,550-acre heavily wooded park is along the banks of the
Tennessee River, where fishing, boating, and swimming are
popular. The park takes its name from "Fighting Joe" Wheeler,
a general in both the Confederate and U.S. armies who later
served in the House of Representatives. The park has bicycle
and hiking trails, tennis courts, boat-launching and rental
facilities, a beach complex, a swimming pool, a 134-slip marina,
basketball courts, and an eighteen-hole golf course. The park
is divided into three areas, one near Wheeler Dam, one near
First Creek, and one near Elk River. *Park phone:* (205) 247-5466
or (205) 247-5467.

Joe Wheeler Park Cottages and Group Lodges

The park has accommodations in all three sections of the
park, two of which are operated by the state. At the Wheeler
Dam area are twenty-five vacation cottages in a wooded area.
The cottages, which can accommodate from four to eight people, are of wood-frame construction, fully furnished, and complete with kitchens and private baths.

Also in the Wheeler Dam section, overlooking the dam, is
a modern, brick lodge with its own kitchen, dining area, and
two shared baths. The rooms can accommodate up to twenty
people, several with two single beds each, the rest with bunk-
style beds. The lodge is popular with church, scouting, and family groups, and there's a boat ramp about a quarter of a mile
away.

In the Elk River section of the park, about 15 miles west
of Athens, is another modern group lodge with room for up
to twenty-six people. Some rooms have two single beds each,
while the balance have four bunk beds each, all sharing 3
bathrooms. The lodge is adjacent to a small lake, making the
lodge popular with fishermen and families. (Rowboats are
available for rent, but no motors are permitted.)

Accommodations: 25 cottages with private bath; 2 lodges
with shared baths. *Towels and linens:* Provided. *Cooking and
eating utensils:* Provided. *Stove and refrigerator:* Provided.
Pets: Not permitted. *Open:* All year. *Mailing address:* Wheeler

Dam section: Route 2, Town Creek, AL 35672; Elk River section: Route 5, Athens, AL 35611. *Phone:* Wheeler Dam section: (205) 685-3306; Elk River section: (205) 729-8228. *Driving instructions:* Joe Wheeler State Park is off U.S. 72. The Wheeler Dam section is about 10 miles west of Rogersville; the Elk River section is about 4 miles east of Rogersville, about 15 miles west of Athens.

Joe Wheeler Resort Lodge

At the First Creek section of the park, Joe Wheeler Resort consists of a 74-bedroom, stone-and-wood motel-type lodge overlooking the Tennessee River. The lodge, operated by an independent concessionaire, has a restaurant and a coffee shop, both of which overlook the river, and a gift shop, as well as meeting and banquet facilities. Each lodge room has wall-to-wall carpeting, color television, a telephone, a private bath, and a private balcony overlooking the water.

Accommodations: 74 rooms with private bath. *Pets:* Not permitted. *Open:* All year. *Mailing address:* ARA Services, PO Drawer K, Rogersville, AL 35652. *Phone:* (205) 247-5461. *Driving instructions:* The First Creek section of the park is off U.S. 72, in Rogersville.

Lake Guntersville State Park is in northeastern Alabama in the Tennessee River Valley, about 90 miles northeast of Birmingham. The park consists of 5,559 acres, most of which overlook the 66,470-acre Guntersville Reservoir. The terrain is hilly and wooded, broken by patches of meadow. The park has been fully developed as a resort: Its facilities include a swimming pool, lighted tennis courts, an art gallery, a playground, saunas, hiking and interpretative trails, picnic areas, 322 campsites with hookups, a fishing center, an eighteen-hole golf course, and a beach with a bathhouse, boat-launching facilities and boat rentals. *Park mailing address:* Star Route 63, Box 224, Guntersville, AL 35976. *Park phone:* (205) 582-3666.

Lake Guntersville State Park Lodge and Convention Center

The park lodge and convention center is a rustic stone-and-wood structure of modern design built with a great deal of glass. The lodge has a restaurant and coffee shop overlooking the reservoir, a game room, meeting rooms that can hold as many as 1,800, and lounging areas.

Various buildings offer three different types of accommodations—a hundred-room motel, thirty-four cottages, and eighteen chalets. Each motel room has color television, a telephone, background music, two lavatories, wall-to-wall carpeting, and a balcony or patio. The motel is on a bluff that overlooks the reservoir, of which some rooms have views. (Some view the parking lot.) Suites, equipped with refrigerators and wet bars, bedrooms with king-size beds, and living rooms, are also available.

The lodge also administers eighteen chalets, each having two bedrooms, a living room with a fireplace, a kitchen, a dressing room, color television, a telephone, and a sun deck overlooking the reservoir.

Also available are sixteen two-bedroom, two-bath cottages directly on the water. Each of these has carpeting, a kitchen, and a telephone but no television or fireplace.

Accommodations: 100 lodge rooms, 34 cottages, and 18 chalets, all with private bath. *Towels and linens:* Provided. *Cooking and eating utensils:* In cottages and chalets. *Stove and*

refrigerator: In cottages, chalets, and lodge suites. *Pets:* Not permitted. *Open:* All year. *Mailing address:* Star Route 63, Box 232, Guntersville, AL 35976. *Phone:* (205) 582-2061. *Driving instructions:* Lake Guntersville State Park is on Route 227 about 8 miles northeast of Guntersville.

Lakepoint Resort State Park is in southeastern Alabama about 7 miles north of Eufaula. The 1,220-acre park is along the shore of Lake Eufaula, a 45,200-acre impoundment of the Chattahoochee River, which forms the southern part of Alabama's border with Georgia. The terrain is relatively flat and thickly wooded with pines, and the lake is a popular boating and fishing site particularly noted for its population of bass. The lake's sandy beach has a bathhouse, plus a full-service marina with launch facilities, boats for rent, and fishing supplies. Activities include tennis (lighted courts), hiking, horseback riding, picnicking, and golf on an eighteen-hole course, which has a pro shop and a clubhouse. *Park phone:* (205) 687-6676. *Park mailing address:* Route 2, Box 94, Eufaula, AL 36027.

Lakepoint Lodge and Cabins

Lakepoint Lodge, operated by an independent concessionaire, is a modern rectilinear stone-and-glass building with ninety guest rooms, a restaurant, a lounge, an indoor and an outdoor swimming pool, and banquet facilities for five hundred. Each guest room has wall-to-wall carpeting, color television, a telephone, a private bath, and a private balcony. About half of the rooms overlook the lake.

The park also administers twenty-two modern wood-frame cabins in the woods. Each has either two or four bedrooms, a fully equipped kitchen, a fireplace, a porch, and a private bath.

Accommodations: 90 lodge rooms and 22 cabins, all with private bath. *Towels and linens:* Provided. *Cooking and eating utensils:* In cabins. *Stove and refrigerator:* In cabins. *Pets:* Permitted in cabins only. *Open:* All year. *Mailing address:* Lakepoint Resort State Park, Route 2, Box 294, Eufaula, AL 36027. *Phone:* (205) 687-8011. *Driving instructions:* Lakepoint Resort State Park is off U.S. 431 about 7 miles north of Eufaula.

Little River State Park is in southwestern Alabama about 60 miles northeast of Mobile. The 960-acre park is in an area of gently rolling hills wooded primarily with oaks, hickories, pines, sweetgums, dogwoods, tulip trees, and cypresses. The Little River runs through the park, which has a 25-acre lake formed by a dam across Chitlin Creek. Boating, fishing, and swimming from the beach are popular at the lake, where visitors can rent fishing boats and go after channel catfish, bream, and bass. Although there are no designated hiking trails, a system of old logging roads runs through the area. The park has a substantial variety of bird life, including quail, wild turkeys, bluebirds, jays, red-tailed hawks, and many species of duck and goose, which appear here in large numbers during migrations.

The park has two wood-frame cabins in a wooded area beside the lake. Each cabin can accommodate four people and has a kitchenette and private bath. One has a porch, and the other a deck.

Accommodations: 2 cabins with private bath. *Towels and linens:* Not provided. *Cooking and eating utensils:* Not provided. *Stove and refrigerator:* Provided. *Pets:* Permitted. *Open:* All year. *Mailing address:* Route 2, Box 77, Atmore, AL 36502. *Phone:* (205) 862-2511. *Driving instructions:* From Atmore take Route 21 north to the park entrance (follow the signs).

Monte Sano State Park is in northern Alabama about 3 miles east of Huntsville and 20 miles south of the Tennessee border. The 2,140-acre park is nestled around Monte Sano Mountain, which rises 1,650 feet above the surrounding terrain. The area is wooded primarily with oaks, pines, cedars, maples, and dogwoods, and one hiking trail runs through an area full of wildflowers. Other hiking trails, varying in length from half a mile to 8 miles, run along cliffs to the summit of the mountain and then loop their way down again. The view from the peak is scenic—even at night, when the lights of Huntsville sparkle, illuminating the bottoms of any clouds that happen to be passing.

The park includes a phenomenon called the Natural Well, a circular hole that extends 186 feet straight down to something of a platform where it then continues its descent. Spelunkers have descended 325 feet into the hole and come up with reports of stalactites and stone columns. Hiking, picnicking, and camping are the most popular park activities. There are playground facilities as well.

The park has fourteen cabins along the rim of a cliff that overlooks Huntsville. Three of them are of wood-frame construction, and the other eleven were built of native stone. All have kitchens, three have fireplaces, and each has a private bath as well as expansive views.

Accommodations: 14 cabins with private bath. *Towels and linens:* Provided. *Cooking and eating utensils:* Provided. *Stove and refrigerator:* Provided. *Pets:* Permitted. *Open:* All year. *Mailing address:* Huntsville, AL 35801. *Phone:* (205) 534-3757. *Driving instructions:* Monte Sano State Park is on the Bankhead Parkway north of U.S. 431 and about 5 miles east of Huntsville.

Oak Mountain State Park is in central Alabama about 15 miles south of Birmingham in the foothills of the Appalachian Mountains. The 9,940-acre park, Alabama's largest, is situated around the summit of Oak Mountain, which has an elevation of just under 1,000 feet, overlooking the surrounding valleys. The area is heavily wooded, primarily with oaks, hickories, and pines, as well as scattered stands of dogwoods and redbuds. The park has 30 miles of hiking trails, including an 8½ mile trail that leads to Peavine Falls, which drops over a 40-foot precipice, varying from a slow trickle to a swift cataract depending on the time of year and the amount of rainfall.

The park has an 85-acre lake stocked with bream, bass, and catfish, plus a marina with launch facilities (electric trolling motors only), boat rentals, a snack bar, and a store that sells fishing supplies. Also along the lake are a 400-foot boardwalk and a sandy beach with a bathhouse. The park has an eighteen-hole golf course (with a pro shop, cart and club rentals, a lounge, and a snack bar) as well as lighted tennis courts, stables for those who bring their own horses, and a BMX track also used for organized bicycle racing.

The park has ten two-bedroom wood-frame cabins that overlook Lake Tranquility and can accommodate up to eight people. Each cabin has a fully equipped kitchen, a screened porch, a living room with a sofa, central air-conditioning and heat, a private bath, an outdoor barbecue grill, and a picnic table.

Accommodations: 10 cabins with private bath. *Towels and linens:* Provided. *Cooking and eating utensils:* Provided. *Stove and refrigerator:* Provided. *Pets:* Permitted with advance notice. *Open:* All year. *Mailing address:* PO Box 278, Pelham, AL 35124. *Phone:* (205) 663-6783. *Driving instructions:* Oak Mountain State Park is off U.S. 31 about 2 miles east of Pelham.

Roland Cooper State Park is in southwestern Alabama about 70 miles southwest of Montgomery, on the southern shore of the William Dannelly Reservoir, a 22,000-acre impoundment of the Alabama River. The terrain is nearly level and is wooded almost entirely with pines. Migrating and resident waterfowl paddle around in the reservoir, red-tailed and red-shouldered hawks soar overhead, and white-tailed deer and wild turkeys roam the forest.

Popular activities include bicycling, fishing, boating, picnicking, and golf. The park has a nine-hole golf course with a clubhouse, and by the reservoir it has launching facilities for visitors who bring their own boats (no rentals available). There's also a playground, a laundry, and a store that sells groceries and sundries.

The park has five brick-and-wood cabins that overlook the reservoir from a stand of 80-foot-tall pines. Each cabin can accommodate six people in two bedrooms, and each has a fully equipped kitchenette, a living room with a sofa bed, central heating and air-conditioning, and a private bath. Outside the cabins are patios with barbecue grills.

Accommodations: 5 cabins with private bath. *Towels and linens:* Provided. *Cooking and eating utensils:* Provided. *Stove and refrigerator:* Provided. *Pets:* Permitted. *Open:* All year. *Mailing address:* PO Box 301, Camden, AL 36726. *Phone:* (205) 682-4838. *Driving instructions:* Roland Cooper State Park is off Route 41, roughly 6 miles northeast of Camden.

Alaska

State map and tourist information: Division of Tourism, Pouch E, Juneau, AK 99811; 907-465-2010. **State parks:** *Information:* Dept. of Natural Resources, Division of Parks, Pouch 7001, Anchorage, AK 99510; 907-265-4518. **National parks:** Contact park directly.

The 1980 Alaska National Interest Lands Conservation Act increased the size of Mount McKinley National Park from 2 million to 6 million acres—creating a reserve slightly larger than Massachusetts—and changed its name to Denali National Park and Preserve. In the language of the Athabascan native people *denali* means "the high one" — Mount McKinley. At 20,320 feet, it is the tallest mountain in North America. To those who measure mountains by their vertical relief—the distance they rise from the surrounding terrain—Mount McKinley is the tallest in the world as well.

Mount McKinley was formed roughly 65 million years ago, when two sections of the earth's crust collided and created the Denali Fault, which to this day generates frequent earth tremors. The cataclysm caused the formation of a 600-mile-long chain of mountains—the Alaska Range, where glaciers cover the higher elevations. There are almost a dozen within 20 miles of Mount McKinley, the centerpiece of this ruggedly beautiful national park and preserve.

Snow covers the summit of Mount McKinley the year round, and clouds obscure it completely three-quarters of the time. Below the timberline white and black spruces predominate in the wooded areas, which are sprinkled with quaking aspens, paper birches, balsam poplars, and dwarf willows and birches. Among the rocks and spruces of the tundra, colorful wildflowers proliferate during the short summer, when temperatures vary from 35° to 75°F.

Although indigenous plants are prepared for such radical shifts in temperature, visitors frequently are not. Traveling unprepared here can ruin your appreciation of the environment. Regardless of how delightful a morning appears, always carry a heavy sweater and a pair of gloves while exploring Denali. Rain gear is also recommended.

Denali's wildlife is spectacular—golden eagles, northern harriers, and gyrfalcons soar here; Dall sheep, moose, timber wolves, caribou, and grizzly bears roam. The northern boundary of Denali was, in fact, partly determined by the migratory range of caribou. Officials placed radio transmitters around their necks to find out the northern limits of their wanderings.

Mount McKinley Village, adjacent to the park entrance, in-

cludes the Alaska Railroad depot—which offers access from Fairbanks and Anchorage—an airstrip, the Riley Creek Information Center, a post office, and a general store. This is the main access point for the accommodations listed below. *Park mailing address:* Superintendent, Denali National Park, Box 9, McKinley Park, AK 99755. *Park phone:* (907) 683-2294.

Denali National Park Hotel

A complex of buildings and converted railroad cars, adjacent to the Alaska Railroad depot, the Denali National Park Hotel has two types of accommodations. Each "luxury" room has wood-paneled walls, wall-to-wall carpeting, a desk-dresser combination, and a private bath. The "economy" rooms are in actual Pullman sleeper cars, each with two single bunk beds, upper and lower. Roomettes, with only a single bed, are also available in the Pullman cars. The sleeper cars and the roomettes share baths and are quite small, but they are reasonable.

The hotel dining room specializes in steak, crab legs, halibut, and salmon. Other facilities include a snack bar for more casual eating; a gift shop specializing in Alaskan arts and crafts; and in one of the Pullman cars, a cocktail lounge.

A 300-seat auditorium, where the National Parks Service presents slide shows and talks, is at the hotel. The Park Service also conducts nature walks that depart from here. The hotel staff will help guests arrange their activities. Some of the more popular are raft trips on the Nenana River and "flightseeing." The raft trips last from two to four hours and range from leisurely twilight floats to rough-and-tumble white-water journeys. There are two standard flightseeing runs: One of them, weather permitting, is a cruise around Mount McKinley; and the other is a flight over Denali's glaciers, lakes, and rivers. Organized two-hour horseback trips are also easily arranged.

Accommodations: 140 rooms, 100 with private bath. *Pets:* Not permitted. *Open:* Late May to mid-September. *Mailing address:* McKinley Park, AK 99755. *Phone:* (907) 278-1122. *Driving instructions:* Denali National Park Hotel is off the George Parks Highway, 238 miles north of Anchorage and 120 miles south of Fairbanks.

McKinley Chalets

The McKinley Chalets are owned and operated by the same company that manages the nearby Denali National Park Hotel (Outdoor World, Ltd.). At the eastern border of the park and overlooking the Nenana River, of which most of the rooms have views, the McKinley Chalets are Swiss-style cedar buildings consisting of 144 two-room suites in all. Larger suites are also available, as are executive suites with kitchens and sitting rooms. The decor of the rooms features rust-colored wall-to-wall carpeting and coordinated bedspreads and draperies.

The chalet complex includes a full-service restaurant, a snack bar, a cocktail lounge, and a gift shop. The hotel staff will assist guests in arranging their activities.

Accommodations: 144 2-room suites (plus several executive suites) with private bath. *Pets:* Not permitted. *Open:* Mid-May to mid-September. *Mailing address:* McKinley Park, AK 99755. *Phone:* (907) 683-2215. *Driving instructions:* The McKinley Chalets are off the George Parks Highway, 238 miles north of Anchorage and 120 miles south of Fairbanks.

Camp Denali

Ninety miles west of the Alaska Railroad depot which is at the Denali National Park entrance, Camp Denali is 3 miles from the Wonder Lake Ranger Station. You can get here via the National Park Service's shuttle bus or by one of Camp Denali's Mercedes-Benz sightseeing vehicles. The Park Service shuttle bus is free, and Camp Denali arranges to pick you up at the ranger station for a small charge, which includes dinner en route.

Camp Denali consists of individual cabins on a hillside that affords a view of Mount McKinley and overlooks a pond, and a central lodge with a dining room and a large library full of books about Alaska. The cabins have cold spring water, propane lights, hot plates, and wood stoves for heat. Guests take showers in a central facility. The rates include all meals, which are served family style in the dining room. The camp offers several special packages such as workshops on wildflowers and nesting birds or wildlife and fall-color photography, as well as guided backpacking trips.

Also available are "hawk's nest housekeeping vacations." A "hawk's nest" is a two-cabin unit equipped with a wood stove for heating, a propane range, a refrigerator, fuel, and cold water. These units are on the park road between the main camp and Wonder Lake.

Accommodations: 16 cabins with shared bath. *Towels and linens:* Provided. *Cooking and eating utensils:* Provided. *Stove:* Provided. *Refrigerator:* Not provided except in dual units. *Pets:* Not permitted. *Open:* Early June to early September. *Mailing address:* PO Box 67, Denali National Park, AK 99755. *Phone:* (907) 683-2290; (907) 683-2302 off season. *Driving instructions:* Camp Denali is accessible by the Denali National Park and Preserve's free shuttle bus, or by Camp Denali's own vehicle for a fee, from the Alaska Railroad depot.

North Face Lodge

On the northern border of Denali National Park and Preserve, North Face Lodge is, as its name implies, almost directly north of Mount McKinley, about 25 miles distant. The modern motel-style lodge is between Moose Creek and Wonder Lake and offers views of the mountain. The lodge management arranges to pick up guests at Mount McKinley Village, at the entrance to the park. An experienced driver and a snack served en route liven up the 100-mile trip.

The lodge is at once rustic and modern, and each guest room has a private bath. The dining room serves guests three meals a day, which are included in the room rates (steak and king salmon are frequent entrées).

Accommodations: 15 rooms with private bath. *Pets:* Not permitted. *Children:* Discouraged. *Open:* Early June through early September. *Mailing address:* Mt. McKinley Village, Inc., PO Box 66, Denali National Park, AK 99755. *Phone:* (907) 683-2265. *Driving instructions:* The management will arrange to pick up guests at the Alaska Railroad depot.

Glacier Bay National Park is in southeastern Alaska, about 90 miles west of Juneau, at the northern end of the Alexander Archipelago. The park encompasses some 3.22 million acres and contains more than a dozen tidewater glaciers, several of which front on the bay and rise 150 feet. As active glaciers, they are either in the process of advancing or of receding; and when a huge chunk of ice breaks off one of those fronting on the bay, it can boom like thunder and create 30-foot waves and hundreds or even thousands of icebergs. Visitors can watch ice falling off the glacial cliffs from cruise ships that remain at least ½ mile from these massive walls of ice.

The park also contains Mount Fairweather, at 15,320 feet the highest in southeastern Alaska, and a wide range of plant communities, ranging from moss and lichen-covered areas recently evacuated by receding glaciers, to alpine meadows full of wildflowers, spruce and hemlock forests, and lush temperate rain forests. The wildlife includes grizzly, black, and glacier bears, as well as red foxes, wolverines, mountain goats, whales, seals, eagles, loons, and puffins. Kayak, raft, and cruise-ship tours are popular, as are hiking, backpacking, and fishing. Many concessions in the park provide services and charters, and visitors should inquire about clothing appropriate to the cold, wet climate. *Park mailing address:* Superintendent, Glacier Bay National Park, Gustavus, AK 99826. *Park Phone:* (907) 697-2231.

Glacier Bay Lodge and Cabins

Glacier Bay Lodge consists of a rustic wooden two-story building with a great deal of glass and fifty-four wood-frame cabins. The main lodge and the cabins are at Bartlett Cove, and some of the cabins, as well as the main lodge, have views of the bay. The main lodge has a restaurant, a bar, and meeting and banquet facilities and is the starting point for daily tours and interpretive programs run by park naturalists.

Some of the cabins have private baths; all have two double beds each, hardwood floors, and sleeping lofts. They are centrally heated but have no kitchen facilities.

Accommodations: 54 cabins with private bath. *Towels and linens:* Provided. *Cooking and eating utensils:* Not provided.

Stove and refrigerator: Not provided. *Pets:* Not permitted. *Open:* Late May to late September. *Mailing address:* PO Box 31, Gustavus, AK 99826; off season: 1500 Metropolitan Park Building, Seattle, WA 98101. *Phone:* (907) 697-3221; (206) 624-8551 off season. *Driving instructions:* Glacier Bay Lodge is accessible only by boat or seaplane. Alaska Airlines operates a jet service once a day during the summer season. Guests must make travel arrangements with the lodge.

Katmai National Park is in southwestern Alaska, about 250 miles southwest of Anchorage, at the beginning of the Alaska Peninsula. The park, which consists of 3.96 million acres and contains a section of the Alagnak Wild River, is named for the crater formed when Mount Katmai erupted in 1912 and then collapsed. The shock waves sent out by the explosion and collapse are among the strongest ever recorded by seismographs. The official version has it that Katmai drained its lava into Nova Rupta Volcano, slightly to its west, and then caved in as Nova Rupta exploded. Kodiak Island, 100 miles southeast, was covered with an inch of ash after the blast. More than seventy years later, a few fumaroles—holes in and around a volcano from which heat escapes—are still smoking.

The valley beneath Katmai was filled with ash and fumaroles and came to be called the Valley of Ten Thousand Smokes, while the crater now contains a deep jade-green lake. The terrain in the park varies from the rugged and fjordlike coastal sections to 7,000-foot mountains. It includes thick forests of spruce, birch, and poplar, as well as an extensive system of rivers and streams, lakes, ponds, and stretches of swamp. Wildlife thrives; and one can observe Alaska brown bears (the world's largest carnivores), bald eagles along the coast, moose, lynxes, sea lions, and whistling swans, to name a few.

Activities in the park and the adjacent national preserve include hiking, sightseeing, and fishing. The myriad waterways offer anglers Dolly Varden and lake trout; chinook, pink, and sockeye salmon; northern pike, and more. *Park mailing address:* Superintendent, Katmai National Park, Box 7, King Salmon, AK 99613. *Park phone:* (907) 246-3305.

Brooks River Lodge

The Brooks River Lodge is a group of log buildings beside Naknek Lake near the Brooks River. The main lodge has a dining room where all meals are served to guests, a lounge with a stone fireplace, and a bar—all of which overlook Naknek Lake. The complex also has a small store that sells souvenirs, fishing supplies, and sundries. The guest rooms here are either in individual cabins or in an eight-unit building. All have private baths, and about a quarter have views of the lake. The lodge

29

offers a three day, two night package that includes a bus tour to the Valley of Ten Thousand Smokes. Sightseeing and fishing are the two main activities.

Accommodations: 16 rooms with private bath. *Pets:* Not permitted. *Open:* June 1 through September 10. *Mailing address:* Katmailand, 455 H Street, Anchorage, AK 99501. *Phone:* (907) 277-4314. *Driving instructions:* Brooks Lodge is accessible only by airplane, and visitors should make prior arrangements with Katmailand for transportation from King Salmon or Anchorage.

Grosvenor Camp

Primarily used by sport fishermen, Grosvenor Lodge is more rustic than Brooks River Lodge. It is a group of log buildings that includes three cabins, a kitchen-dining building, and a main lodge building that has a bar, a lounge with a wood stove, and a small store that sells fishing equipment and sundries. The lodge is on a narrow strip of land between Lakes Coville and Grosvenor, and its cabins can accommodate a maximum of two each. The cabins have no running water and share a central lavatory and shower facility. Room rates include all meals and transportation, and arrangements are made for three-, four- or seven-day stays.

Accommodations: 3 cabins with shared bath. *Open:* Late May through late September. *Mailing address:* Katmailand, 455 H Street, Anchorage, AK 99501. *Phone:* (907) 277-4314. *Driving instructions:* Grosvenor Lodge is accessible only by airplane, and guests must make travel arrangements with Katmailand.

In south-central Alaska, bordered to the east by Cook Inlet, Lake Clark National Park and Preserve encompasses more than 3 million acres, 2.4 million of them designated wilderness. The area is accessible almost exclusively by airplanes, which land, for the most part, on the park's many beautiful lakes. The Alaska and Aleutian mountain ranges approach each other here, where they are divided by the Chigmit Range, a rugged product of volcanic action and glacial erosion. Two volcanoes, Iliamna and Redoubt, both more than 10,000 feet high, haven't finished letting off steam yet. When clouds gather around the Chigmits (in some parts of the park the sun is almost never visible), air access becomes severely limited.

Lake Clark National Park includes three designated wild rivers, which rush through open tundra forests of black and white spruce. Rafting and fishing, often done in combination, are popular. The average king salmon here weighs about 30 pounds; a trophy-size rainbow trout, about 10 pounds. Many species of mammals inhabit the park and its immediate environs—seals, caribou, grizzly and black bears, moose, Dall sheep, wolves, whales, lynxes, foxes; and bird life includes puffins, swans, cormorants, kittiwakes, and eagles. Wildflowers (lupine, fireweed, blueberry, and bearberry) are rife in summer, and the tundra turns the color of burgundy in the fall.

The park attracts artists and photographers the year round to its glacier-covered mountains reflected in smooth blue lakes dotted with spruce-covered islands. The weather here, as elsewhere in Alaska, can turn rough even in summer; so on any journeys to this part of the world, visitors should bring warm clothing and wet-weather gear. *Park phone:* (907) 271-3751. *Park mailing address:* Superintendent, Lake Clark National Park, 701 C Street, Box 61, Anchorage, AK 99513.

The Farm Lodge and Cabin

Originally a homestead, the Farm Lodge consists of three buildings, all of which were painted red and trimmed in white. The main lodge, a gambrel-roofed three-story, barn-like building, contains two guest rooms, as well as a kitchen and dining room. The lodge also has a wood-frame duplex that sleeps eight and is set into a hillside wooded with white birch

and black spruce. The third building is a small tongue-and-groove log cabin that sleeps four. All of the guest rooms are carpeted, and the duplex and the main lodge have baths with showers. The cabin has no shower but is next to a sauna that has shower heads. All of the buildings contain rustic cedar furniture made by the owner's father, for whom the town of Port Alsworth was named.

The rates include all meals; and several types of packages are available, including fishing packages where guests fly to a new fishing spot each day. Access to the lodge is by airplane only, and the owners also operate the Lake Clark Air Service, which shuttles guests between here and Anchorage.

Meals at the Farm Lodge are served to guests family style and include fresh vegetables in summer and fresh eggs and chickens from the hen house. The hosts pack lunches for those going hiking or fishing.

Accommodations: 2 guest rooms and 1 duplex with private bath and 1 cabin. *Open:* All year. *Mailing address:* Port Alsworth, AK 99653. *Phone:* (907) 781-2211. *Driving instructions:* The Farm Lodge is accessible only by plane. Guests must make travel arrangements with the lodge.

Van Valin's Island Lodge and Cabins

Van Valin's Island Lodge is a log A-frame on the shore of Lake Clark, surrounded by a forest of white spruce. The main lodge has exposed rough-hewn timbers, a wood stove, vaulted ceilings, and a large picture window overlooking the lake. This building contains the dining room, where meals are served to guests family style.

There are also five log cabins, each with wall-to-wall carpeting, individual heating, and a bath with shower. The cabins are set in a wooded area, and the complex of buildings includes a steam bath beside the lake.

The lodge has various packages, the most popular offering planes that transport guests to remote fishing spots each day and wilderness raft trips, one of which includes a ride down both the Chilikadrotna and Mulchatna Rivers.

Accommodations: 5 cabins with private bath. *Open:* June through September. *Mailing address:* Port Alsworth, AK 99653. *Telephone:* (907) 781-2230. *Driving instructions:* The lodge is accessible only by plane. Guests are advised to make travel arrangements with the lodge.

Arizona

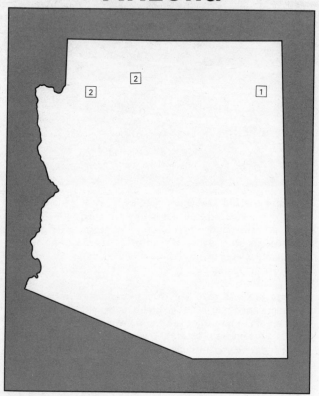

State map and tourist information: Department of Tourism, 3507 N. Central, Suite 506, Phoenix, 85012; 602-255-3618. **State parks:** *Information:* Arizona State Parks, 1688 West Adams, Phoenix, 85007; 602-255-4174. **National parks:** Contact parks directly.

Canyon de Chelly National Monument is in northeastern Arizona, just west of the New Mexico border, in the Navaho Indian reservation. The monument consists of 83,840 acres, mostly canyons with reddish brown, precipitous walls. The area was inhabited by prehistoric peoples, and the monument preserves many ancient cliff dwellings and pictographs, which probably date from between A.D. 350 and 1300. Some of the most extensive of these ruins are accessible via a self-guiding trail that leads to the White House ruin, so named because of a long plaster-covered wall along the canyon.

Observation of other ruins requires the permission of park rangers, and visitors should remember that most of the canyon and its valley are on an indian reservation where Navaho live and farm. Rim Drive runs along the canyon edge and affords several scenic views, including an overview of Spider Rock—a thin sandstone column that rises 800 feet from the canyon floor. The park service offers interpretative talks and guided hikes. *Monument mailing address:* Box 588, Chinle, AZ 86503. *Monument phone:* (602) 674-5436.

Thunderbird Lodge

Thunderbird Lodge is a group of eight buildings, some older and constructed of stone and others that are new, more like motels. The complex includes seventy-five guest rooms, a cafeteria-style restaurant, and a gift shop that specializes in Navaho arts and crafts. The lodge is staffed primarily by Navaho.

The guest rooms, which offer wall-to-wall carpeting, color television and private baths, are in several buildings, each of which contains from one to twelve rooms. The center of the complex is a landscaped area outfitted with lawn furniture in summer. The lodge offers daily guided jeep tours of the canyon floor from mid-April through October.

Accommodations: 75 rooms with private bath. *Pets:* Permitted if leashed. *Open:* All year. *Mailing address:* Box 548, Chinle, AZ 86503. *Phone:* (602) 674-5443. *Driving instructions:* The monument headquarters and Thunderbird Lodge are in Chinle, 3 miles east of Route 191.

The Grand Canyon changes from minute to minute. Shifting sunlight and clouds transform its colors even as you watch: Dark reds become vermilions; deep greens turn a dusty pale. It's red, gray, and pink along its summits; charcoal, brown, and violet below. Among the colors, the shadows of the rocks move constantly, changing shapes, forming and reforming the view.

The canyon is about 277 miles long, from one-tenth of a mile to 18 miles across, and plunges as deep as 5,300 feet at a spot aptly called Awesome Abyss. The Colorado River—tumultuous, fast, and almost saturated with abrasive minerals—continues cutting into the canyon, which encompasses 140,000 square miles and is formed, for the most part, of limestone, sandstone, shale, and Vishnu schist with granite intrusions. From its lowest point to its highest, climates range from subtropical to subarctic, terrain from desert to forest, flora from cacti to ponderosa pines, and fauna from iguanas to deer.

Stretching across northwestern Arizona, the park is bordered on the northeast by Lake Powell (an impoundment of the Colorado River) and Glen Canyon National Recreation Area, and on the west by Lake Mead National Recreation Area. The South Rim of the canyon, where elevations are near 7,000 feet, is open all year. The North Rim, colder and wetter and as high as 8,900 feet, is open from mid-May through mid-October. The canyon is also accessible by a combination of train and bus: Amtrak stops in Flagstaff (80 miles away), and Nava-Hopi tours—(602) 774-5003—runs buses to the park.

The South Rim: Grand Canyon National Park Lodges operates six lodge and cabin complexes at the South Rim of the canyon, in and around Grand Canyon Village, which is about 4 miles north of the south entrance. This entrance to the park is on Route 64, roughly 60 miles north of Williams, Arizona. Grand Canyon Village has a health clinic, a dental clinic, and a visitors' center, with all the information one needs about guided tours and interpretative programs. *Mailing address:* For all South Rim accommodations, write to Grand Canyon National Park Lodges, Grand Canyon, AZ 86023. *Phone:* (602) 638-2401.

El Tovar Hotel

Listed in the National Register of Historic Places, El Tovar Hotel has the park's most luxurious accommodations. It was built in 1905 of pine logs and local stone. Exposed logs appear everywhere in the hotel's public rooms, which include a large lobby with couches and a stone fireplace, a bar, a gift shop, and a dining room where meals are served. The last, fitted with a great deal of glass, overlooks the canyon.

Each of the hotel's seventy-seven guest rooms has wall-to-wall carpeting, color television, a telephone, and a private bath. Ten of the rooms have private balconies, four of which overlook the canyon.

Accommodations: 77 rooms with private bath. *Pets:* Not permitted (Grand Canyon Village has a kennel). *Open:* All year. *Mailing address, phone, and driving instructions:* See above.

Bright Angel Lodge and Cabins

Slightly west of El Tovar Hotel, Bright Angel Lodge and Cabins consist of a rustic stone-and-wood, fifty-bedroom lodge and fourteen cabins. The lodge has exposed log walls, several stone fireplaces, and a restaurant and a coffee shop that overlook the canyon. The main building also has a beauty shop, a barbershop, a gift shop, a newsstand, and an information booth.

Each guest room has wall-to-wall carpeting, a telephone, and two double beds. Twenty-five of the rooms have private baths, and fourteen have views of the canyon. The cabins, west of the lodge, are of wood-frame construction, and five of them have fireplaces. (One of the cabins with a fireplace has two bedrooms.) The cabins have private baths but no cooking facilities.

Accommodations: 50 lodge rooms, 25 with private bath, and 14 cabins with private bath. *Towels and linens:* Provided. *Cooking and eating utensils:* Not provided. *Stove and refrigerator:* Not provided. *Pets:* Not permitted (Grand Canyon Village has a kennel). *Open:* All year. *Mailing address, phone, and driving instructions:* See above.

Thunderbird Lodge and Kachina Lodge

Thunderbird and Kachina are sister lodges at the rim of the canyon that were built in the 1970s of light-colored brick and stone. Contemporary in design and with a Southwestern feeling, the lodges were built with a great deal of glass. Half the rooms have a view of the canyon. The lodges have no restaurant or gift shop and provide no cooking facilities, but are close enough to El Tovar and the Bright Angel complex to make dining no problem.

Thunderbird Lodge has fifty-five guest rooms, and Kachina has forty-nine. Each room has wall-to-wall carpeting, color television, a telephone, and a private bath.

Accommodations: 104 rooms with private bath. *Pets:* Not permitted (Grand Canyon Village has a kennel). *Open:* All year. *Mailing address, phone, and driving instructions:* See above.

Yavapai Lodge

Yavapai Lodge consists of two motel-type buildings at the eastern end of Grand Canyon Village. The older of the two, built in the 1950s of brick and much glass, has 157 guest rooms. The newer, built in the 1970s, is two stories tall and has 198 guest rooms. The complex is about three-quarters of a mile from the canyon rim and includes a cafeteria, a bar, and lounge and a gift shop. The rooms, which overlook a wooded area, have wall-to-wall carpeting, color television, telephones, and private baths.

Accommodations: 355 rooms with private bath. *Pets:* Not permitted (Grand Canyon Village has a kennel). *Open:* All year. *Mailing address, phone, and driving instructions:* See above.

Maswik Lodge

A quarter mile from the canyon rim and behind the Bright Angel complex, Grand Canyon Motor Lodge consists of a ninety-bedroom motel-type building; a 160 bedroom, eight-building complex built of stone and wood; a lodge with 12 bedrooms especially designed for the handicapped; and thirty-five wood-frame cabins. The complex has a cafeteria, a lounge, and a gift shop. Each guest bedroom has wall-to-wall carpeting, color television, a telephone, and a private bath. The cabins, which accommodate four each, have carpeting, telephones, and private baths.

Accommodations: 250 bedrooms and 35 cabins, all with private bath. *Towels and linens:* Provided. *Cooking and eating utensils:* Not provided. *Stove and refrigerator:* Not provided. *Pets:* Not permitted (Grand Canyon Village has a kennel). *Open:* All year. *Mailing address, phone, and driving instructions:* See above.

Phantom Ranch

At the bottom of the canyon, about a half mile from the Colorado River, Phantom Ranch has eleven stone-and-wood cabins and four wood-frame bunkhouses. The cabins are rustic and fitted out with bunk beds. Nine of them sleep four, and two sleep ten. Each has a sink and a toilet, but guests have to shower in a central lavatory facility. Each bunkhouse has ten bunks, a toilet, and a shower. The bunks are rented individually, and the bunkhouses accommodate either male or female groups.

Getting to Phantom Ranch involves an 8-mile hike, and the temperature toward the bottom can get very high. You can also ride a mule to the ranch, but those who wish to do so are advised to make arrangments at least six months in advance. The mule trip is restricted to those who speak and understand English and who weigh less than 200 pounds. The cabins and bunkhouses are air-conditioned, and the ranch has a snack bar and a dining hall.

Accommodations: 11 cabins with toilet and sink; 4 bunkhouses with shared baths. *Towels and linens:* Not provided. *Cooking and eating utensils:* Not provided. *Stove and refrigerator:* Not provided. *Pets:* Not permitted (Grand Canyon Village has a kennel). *Mailing address, phone, and driving instructions:* See above.

Grand Canyon Lodge (North Rim)

Accommodations at the North Rim of the canyon, at an elevation of 8,200 feet, consist of 174 log cabins and a 40-unit motel. The complex has a main lodge, built of native stone and peeled logs, that includes a dining room, a sun parlor, a Western-style saloon, and a "buffeteria." The dining room has exposed-log ceilings and a great deal of glass overlooking the canyon. The sun parlor, enclosed entirely with glass, also overlooks the canyon and is flanked by outdoor patios.

Each "Western" cabin has wall-to-wall carpeting, individually controlled heat, a telephone, a porch, and a private bath with tub and shower and can accommodate five. These cabins have no cooking facilities; but there is a dressing and vanity area in each, and they overlook the canyon.

The "frontier" cabins can accommodate three. Each is carpeted and has a double bed, a single bed, and a private bath with shower.

42

Lake Powell

The "pioneer" cabins were designed for families and have four single beds in each. Individually heated, each has a private bath with shower.

Each room in the motel unit has carpeting, a private bath, and oaken ranch furniture, but no telephone or television.

Accommodations: 40 motel rooms, 174 cabins, all with private bath. *Towels and linens:* Provided. *Cooking and eating utensils:* Not provided. *Stove and refrigerator:* Not provided. *Pets:* Not permitted. *Open:* Mid-May to mid-October. *Mailing address:* TW Services, Inc., PO Box 400, Cedar City, UT 84720. *Phone:* (801) 586-7686. *Driving instructions:* The lodge is near the end of Route 67.

Arkansas

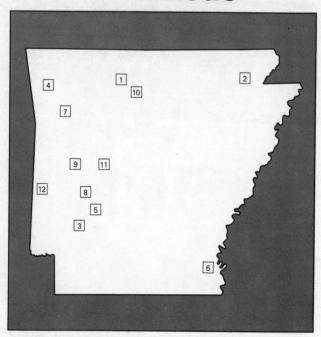

State map, tourist, and **State parks** *information:* Office of Tourism & Parks, One Capitol Mall, Little Rock, AR 72201; 800-643-8383 (out-of-state), 800-482-8999 (in-state). *Entrance fees:* None. *Reservations:* Contact individual park and send check for first night's lodgings or use credit card, where permitted. Reservations recommended at least 2 months in advance for mid June—Labor Day. *Restrictions:* No hunting. No alcoholic beverages. Dogs must be leashed (not allowed in lodgings). *Facilities:* Swimming and interpretative programs, Mem. Day—Labor Day. Tennis, golf, and hiking trails, open all year.

From an elevation of 2,385 feet in the Boston Mountains to one of 375 feet where it merges with the White River, the Buffalo River flows for 148 miles without interruption—no dams, no tunnels, no bridges, no hydroelectric turbines. It is one of the few remaining rivers in the forty-eight contiguous states to have escaped development and pollution. In places swiftly, in others slowly, the river flows through the Ozarks, winding between multicolored sandstone bluffs. Congress designated the Buffalo a national river on March 1, 1972, a hundred years to the day after a previous congress had designated Yellowstone as the first national park.

The Buffalo Valley boasts upward of eight hundred species of flowering plants, and the bluffs the river courses through rise as high as 500 feet. Ferns cascade like verdant waterfalls from the sides of the moister bluffs, and meadows, forests, and sheer rock faces line the shore.

The 95,000-acre reserve is in northwestern Arkansas, about 125 miles from Little Rock. Popular activities here are hiking and canoeing. The park has several developed hiking trails, including one that passes through a natural bridge. Canoes can be rented from various concessions at Ponca, Yellville, Cotter, St. Joe, Jasper, Pruitt, Gilbert, and Mountain Home. *Park mailing address:* PO Box 1173, Harrison AR, 72602-1173. *Park phone:* (501) 741-5443.

Buffalo Point Concession

Although information and ranger stations are located in three places in the park—Silver Hill, Pruitt, and Buffalo Point—Buffalo Point is the major center of activities. Here, on a wooded ridge beside the river, Buffalo Point Concession administers a restaurant and thirteen cabins. Five of the cabins, classified as "rustic," are of wood-frame construction and were built during the 1930s. These are one-bedroom units with fireplaces, handmade furniture, kitchens, and screened porches. The other eight cabins are designated as "duplex" and are also of wood-frame construction, 1950s vintage. Each of these has a large living room, electric heating, a separate bedroom, a kitchen, and a deck. Two of the duplex cabins have a view of the river, as does the forty-seat restaurant.

Buffalo River

Accommodations: 13 cabins with private bath. *Towels and linens:* Provided. *Cooking and eating utensils:* Not provided. *Stove and refrigerator:* Provided. *Pets:* Not permitted. *Open:* April through November. *Mailing address:* Route A, Box 214-0, Yellville, AR 72687. *Phone:* (501) 449-6206. *Driving instructions:* Buffalo Point is off Route 14, about 17 miles south of Yellville.

Crowley's Ridge State Park, 271 acres in size, is in northeastern Arkansas, roughly 15 miles north of Jonesboro and 50 miles west of the Mississippi River. The park, named for an early settler, Benjamin F. Crowley, is the only elevated section of land in the Mississippi alluvial delta—bottomlands formed by sand, gravel, and clay deposits left by the flooding of the Arkansas, White, St. Francis, and Mississippi rivers, as well as the Ohio River, which once flowed through this area. A 200-mile stretch of 100- to 200-foot-high land, the ridge runs northward from Helena, Arkansas, in the east-central part of the state, on the Mississippi bank, up into Missouri. The ridge is a unique geological formation containing some of the oldest fossils in America and is heavily mantled with loess (a loamy soil believed to be deposited by the wind).

The park, perched on the western slope of the ridge, is wooded with oaks, hickories, and pines. There are two lakes, one used for fishing and the other for swimming and boating. Visitors can rent paddleboats or canoes or hike the local trails. Other facilities include a playground, a baseball field, and picnic areas. The park is open all year, but facilities are limited in winter.

Crowley's Ridge State Park has four concrete-block cabins in an area wooded with pines and oaks. Each can accommodate as many as six with a bedroom, a living area with a couch and a rocking chair, a kitchen, a bath with a shower, and a porch.

Accommodations: 4 cabins with private bath. *Towels and linens:* Provided. *Cooking and eating utensils:* Provided. *Stove and refrigerator:* Provided. *Pets:* Permitted. *Open:* All year. *Mailing address:* PO Box 97, Walcott, AR 72474. *Phone:* (501) 573-6751. *Driving instructions:* Crowley's Ridge State Park is at Walcott on Route 141 about 15 miles north of Jonesboro.

On the northeastern shore of the 13,400-acre DeGray Lake, DeGray State Park is in southwestern Arkansas about 20 miles south of Hot Springs. The park, in the foothills of the Ouachita Mountains, a little less than 10 miles east of Ouachita National Forest, has been developed after the fashion of a resort. Facilities include a 7,200-yard, eighteen-hole golf course with complete clubhouse amenities (rentals, refreshments, sales), plus tennis courts, swimming areas, hiking trails, picnic areas, interpretative programs, and a full-service marina where one can rent motorboats, party barges, docking slips, and mooring buoys. The marina also sells fishing gear to those who have come to pursue striped bass, pike, catfishes, bream, and crappies. *Park mailing address:* Route 1, Box 144, Bismarck, AR 71929. *Park phone:* (501) 865-4501.

DeGray Lodge

A rustic 96-bedroom lodge of modern design, DeGray is on an island in DeGray Lake. It has a restaurant that overlooks the lake, meeting and banquet facilities, a gift shop, and a lobby with a fireplace.

Each of the guest rooms has wall-to-wall carpeting, color television, a telephone, and a private bath. Half have views of the lake, and the others face trees.

Accommodations: 96 rooms with private bath. *Pets:* Not permitted. *Open:* All year except for three weeks from late December to early January. *Mailing address:* PO Box 375, Arkadelphia, AR 71923. *Phone:* (501) 865-4591. *Driving instructions:* DeGray State Park is 21 miles south of Hot Springs on Route 7.

On 2,280 acres in the Ozark National Forest, Devil's Den State Park is in northwestern Arkansas, roughly 25 miles south of Fayetteville, in the Lee Creek Valley, bordered by sandstone cliffs. The area is thickly wooded with oaks, hickories, and maples, and contains several caves (one called the Devil's Icebox). The park was developed by the Civilian Conservation Corps, which built many of its structures of stones from Lee Creek.

Activities include fishing and boating in a small lake formed by a stone dam in the creek, swimming in the park's pool, and hiking. There are 22 miles of hiking trails, including the 15-mile Butterfield Hiking Trail, named after an old stagecoach route. The park also offers picnic areas, playgrounds, interpretative programs, and guided hikes. The park restaurant is open in summer only.

Devil's Den State Park has thirteen stone cabins near Lee Creek, of which about half have a view. They vary in size from one- to three-bedroom units, and each has a stone fireplace, a porch, a living area furnished with couches and chairs, a kitchen, and a private bath with a shower. All have knotty-pine paneling.

Accommodations: 13 cabins with private bath. *Towels and linens:* Provided. *Cooking and eating utensils:* Provided. *Stove and refrigerator:* Provided. *Pets:* Not permitted. *Open:* All year. *Mailing address:* West Fork, AR 72774. *Phone:* (501) 761-3325. *Driving instructions:* From Fayetteville take U.S. 71 south 8 miles to West Fork, then take Route 170 south 18 miles to the park.

On 2,180 acres, Lake Catherine State Park is in southwestern Arkansas about 10 miles south of Hot Springs in the Ouachita Mountains. The park has several national recreation trails, which range in length from 2½ to 4½ miles and run through mountainous tracts wooded with oaks, hickories, pines, and hemlocks. Visitors can rent motorboats or paddle boats, launch their own craft, and acquire bait, fuel, and other such necessities. The park has a beach for swimming, a grocery store, many picnic sites, a playground, as well as a restaurant with views of the lake and the beach. The park naturalist service provides guided walks and interpretative programs.

Lake Catherine State Park has seventeen cabins along the shore of the lake—one-bedroom units that can accommodate six each and are constructed of either concrete blocks or wood. Five of the cabins are rustic. These were built in the 1930s by the Civilian Conservation Corps, and each has carpeting, a stone fireplace supplied with free firewood, a kitchen, a porch, air-conditioning, heat, a barbecue grill in front, and a private dock in back.

The concrete-block cabins are duplexes (side by side rather than above and below), and each pair of units shares a private dock. Each of these cabins has paneling, a porch, a kitchen, and a private bath but no fireplace. All the cabins have couches and easy chairs in the living areas.

Accommodations: 17 cabins with private bath. *Towels and linens:* Provided. *Cooking and eating utensils:* Provided. *Stove and refrigerator:* Provided. *Pets:* Not permitted. *Open:* All year. *Mailing address:* Route 19, Box 360, Hot Springs, AR 71913. *Phone:* (501) 844-4176. *Driving instructions:* Lake Catherine State Park is on Route 171, 12 miles north of exit 97 from I-30.

Horseshoe-shaped and just west of the Mississippi River in southeastern Arkansas, Lake Chicot, the largest natural lake in Arkansas, is surrounded by mature cypresses and an extensive stand of pecan trees. The 132-acre park is, as one of its rangers described it, a "fisherman's park," and anglers go after crappies, bass, and catfishes, all of which, apparently, make no great effort to avoid park visitors. The fully equipped marina rents out boats, has launching facilities, and sells bait, fuel, and other marine items.

The park's naturalist service offers year-round interpretative programs that range from films to barge tours of the lake. The park has many picnic areas, a swimming pool, and a playground.

The park has fourteen cabins, all of which overlook the lake. The cabins are one-bedroom units with kitchens, living areas fitted out with sofa beds and easy chairs, and private baths with showers. Six of the cabins are of wood-frame construction, and the other eight were built of stone. All have electric heat and carpeted bedrooms.

Accommodations: 14 cabins with private bath. *Towels and linens:* Provided. *Cooking and eating utensils:* Provided. *Stove and refrigerator:* Provided. *Pets:* Not permitted. *Open:* All year. *Mailing address:* Route 1, Box 648, Lake Village, AR 71653. *Phone:* (501) 265-5480. *Driving instructions:* Lake Chicot State Park is on Route 144 about 8 miles northeast of Lake Village.

Lake Fort Smith State Park is in northwestern Arkansas, about 20 miles south of Fayetville in the Boston Mountains, which are, in turn, in the Ozark National Forest. The area is wooded primarily with hardwoods—oak, sycamore, hickory, elm, and black walnut—and offers a scenic panorama at just about any season. The terrain is hilly, wooded, and broken up by the 900-acre Lake Fort Smith. The 125-acre park, below the dam that impounds the lake, has an Olympic-size swimming pool, tennis courts, launching facilities, boat rentals, picnic grounds, a playground, and a group camping area.

Lake Fort Smith State Park has five stone cabins on a hill overlooking the spillway of the dam. Each has a stone fireplace and either one or two bedrooms and can accommodate from four to six. Each also has a small porch, a living area furnished with a sofa and easy chairs, a kitchen, and a private bath with a shower.

Accommodations: 5 cabins with private bath. *Towels and linens:* Provided. *Cooking and eating utensils:* Provided. *Stove and refrigerator:* Provided. *Pets:* Not permitted. *Open:* All year. *Mailing address:* PO Box 4, Mountainburg, AR 72946. *Phone:* (501) 369-2469. *Driving instructions:* Lake Fort Smith is off U.S. 71, just north of Mountainburg.

At the eastern end of Lake Ouachita, the largest man-made lake in the Hot Springs area, Lake Ouachita State Park comprises 370 acres surrounded by the Ouachita Mountains, which are composed for the most part of sandstone and shale and run east and west. The 48,300-acre lake, created by flooding nearby lowlands, produced a terrain that is rife with dells and valleys, as well as numerous islands where visitors are allowed to camp.

The park offers various interpretative programs, a café, a grocery store, many hiking trails, and a marina with boat rentals, slips, and fuel.

The park has five modern A-frame cabins on a wooded hillside overlooking the lake. The cabins have two levels: The downstairs part contains a bedroom, a living room with a couch and easy chairs, and a kitchen; upstairs there's a sleeping loft. Each cabin can accommodate six and has a private bath with a shower, wood paneling, and a balcony overlooking the lake.

Accommodations: 5 cabins with private bath. *Towels and linens:* Provided. *Cooking and eating utensils:* Provided. *Stove and refrigerator:* Provided. *Pets:* Not permitted. *Open:* All year. *Mailing address:* Star Route 1, Box 1160, Mountain Pines, AR 71956. *Phone:* (501) 767-9366. *Driving instructions:* From Hot Springs take U.S. 270 about 3 miles west, then take Route 227 north 12 miles.

Mount Nebo State Park has 3,404 acres in northwestern Arkansas, roughly 70 miles north of Hot Springs, 5 miles south of Lake Dardanelle, and 5 miles east of the southern section of Ozark National Forest. At 1,775 feet above sea level, the park overlooks the Arkansas River; and when the weather's right, vast panoramas of the Ouachita and Ozark national forests and the 34,000-acre Lake Dardanelle open up.

Mount Nebo is a mountain plateau, and the surrounding area is wooded with hardwoods—oaks, hickories, maples, and poplars for the most part—as well as some scattered pines. The park has a swimming pool, lighted tennis courts, seven hiking trails (including a self-guided nature trail) that total 14 ½ miles, picnic facilities, a playground, a ball field, and a visitors' center with interpretative displays and a store that sells groceries and souvenirs.

The park has fourteen cabins. Ten were built in the 1930s by the Civilian Conservation Corps, and these are of wood-frame construction with stone foundations. These cabins are either one- or two-bedroom units, each having a porch, carpeting, a kitchen, and a private bath. Eight of the ten have stone fireplaces, and a few are perched on a bluff overlooking a valley. The park also has four modern A-frame cabins, each with carpeting, wood-paneled walls, a kitchen, a private bath, and a fireplace.

Accommodations: 14 cabins with private bath. *Towels and linens:* Provided. *Cooking and eating utensils:* Provided. *Stove and refrigerator:* Provided. *Pets:* Not permitted. *Open:* All year. *Mailing address:* Route 3, Box 374, Dardanelle, AR 72834. *Phone:* (501) 229-3655. *Driving instructions:* Mount Nebo State Park is on Route 155 about 7 miles west of Dardanelle.

Ozark Folk Center   **ARKANSAS**

A park dedicated to preserving and demonstrating the traditional crafts and music of the Ozarks, the Ozark Folk Center is in north-central Arkansas, about 100 miles north of Little Rock. The White River, which borders the Ozark National Forest on the east, is about 3 miles north of here. The park is elevated at about 2,000 feet and consists of a complex of buildings set in an area wooded with oaks, hickories, maples, beeches, and poplars. The complex includes a thousand-seat auditorium that features traditional Ozark music nightly from May through October. The instruments most likely to be heard are banjos, fiddles, guitars, dulcimers, mandolins, hammered dulcimers and picking bows.

The "Craft Forum" is a group of twenty-five buildings, each of which preserves a traditional Ozark craft. Blacksmithing, printing, weaving, and woodworking are a few examples. In each building demonstrations of traditional craft techniques are given. Prospective visitors should check the park's schedule in advance.

The Ozark Folk Center has sixty rooms—two in each of thirty hexagonal buildings. Each room has wall-to-wall carpeting, color television, a telephone, two double beds, and a private bath. The rooms also have sliding glass doors that lead onto patios that overlook wooded areas. Guests are served meals in a 165-seat dining room in a modern stone building that also houses a meeting, banquet, and conference center. *Folk Center phone:* (501) 269-3851.

Accommodations: 60 rooms with private bath. *Pets:* Not permitted. *Open:* All year. *Mailing address:* Mountain View, AR 72560. *Phone:* (501) 269-3871. *Driving instructions:* The Ozark Folk Center is near the junction of Routes 9, 14, and 66, about a mile north of Mountain View.

Petit Jean State Park, 3,471 acres in size, is in western Arkansas, about 70 miles northwest of Little Rock and between the two largest sections of Ouachita National Forest. Situated along a mountain plateau, the park is the oldest in the Arkansas system. It was named for a Frenchwoman who, disguised as a cabin boy, followed her fiancé to the New World. Petit Jean Mountain has high bluffs, intricate rock formations, precipitous valleys, and a flat top. The area around the mountain is wooded with a great deal of virgin hardwood, and the park contains one of the highest water-falls in the south, Cedar Falls, which drops 96 feet. There are many overlooks that afford panoramas of the Arkansas River Valley.

Popular activites include swimming in the park's two pools, hiking along its network of trails, fishing, boating, and tennis. Visitors can rent canoes or paddleboats, and the park naturalist service offers guided hikes and other interpretative programs. *Park phone* (501) 727-5441.

Mather Lodge and Cabins

Petit Jean State Park has three types of accommodations—lodge rooms, cabins, and "duplexes." Mather Lodge is a rustic 24-room log-and-stone building of modern design. Its rooms have carpeting and two double beds, a private bath, and television, and several have views of the valley. The lodge is connected to the restaurant by a roofed stone breezeway with benches. The restaurant itself is another log-and-stone building, with exposed logs inside, a seating capacity of two hundred, and a wall of glass overlooking the valley. It is closed on weekdays from December through mid-March.

The park's eighteen cabins—six of which are in attached pairs—have views of either the valley or the woods. Each has carpeting, a kitchen, a living room, a bedroom, and a fireplace. (Some of the fireplaces are stone; some, brick.) Some of the cabins were built of logs, some are of wood-frame construction.

There are also twelve "duplexes." Six of these have fireplaces; and each of the twelve has a single room with carpeting and two double beds but no cooking facilities. These are wood-frame buildings approached via stone walkways.

Accommodations: 24 lodge rooms, 18 cabins, and 12

duplexes, all with private bath. *Towels and linens:* Provided. *Cooking and eating utensils:* In cabins. *Stove and refrigerator:* In cabins. *Pets:* Not permitted. *Open:* Cabins all year; lodge and duplexes April 1 through November 1. *Mailing address:* Petit Jean State Park, Route 3, Box 164, Morrilton, AR 72110. *Phone:* (501) 727-5431. *Driving instructions:* From Morrilton take Route 9 south 6 miles, then take Route 154 west about 15 miles.

Queen Wilhelmina State Park is in western Arkansas about 85 miles west of Hot Springs and 5 miles east of the Oklahoma border, in Ouachita National Forest. Situated around the top of Rich Mountain at approximately 2,500 feet above sea level, the 820-acre park is just off the Talimena Scenic Highway, a 55-mile road that runs through Arkansas and Oklahoma. The park takes its name from the Queen Wilhelmina Inn, which a group of Dutch railroad people built in anticipation of a visit by their queen. The park has several hiking trails and scenic overlooks that afford panoramic views of Ouachita National Forest.

The most popular activities in the park are hiking and sightseeing, and the facilities include a petting zoo, a miniature scenic railway, and a miniature-golf course. A store in the park sells groceries, ice, and souvenirs.

Queen Wilhelmina Inn

The Queen Wilhelmina Inn was built in 1896, and rebuilt in 1963 and again in 1976, after it was destroyed by a fire. The current inn is a rustic stone-and-maple building with thirty-eight guest rooms, a large lobby with a stone fireplace, a restaurant with another stone fireplace, and a gift shop. The restaurant, which overlooks the valley, has a great deal of glass and features traditional Arkansas cuisine.

The guest rooms have wall-to-wall carpeting, color television, and private baths. Two of the rooms have fireplaces. Views from the rooms are of either the valley, the mountains, or the petting zoo and the miniature scenic railway.

Accommodations: 38 rooms with private bath. *Pets:* Not permitted. *Open:* All year. *Mailing address:* Route 7, Box 53A, Mena, AR 71953. *Phone:* (501) 394-2863. *Driving instructions:* Queen Wilhelmina State Park is off Route 88 roughly 13 miles west of Mena.

California

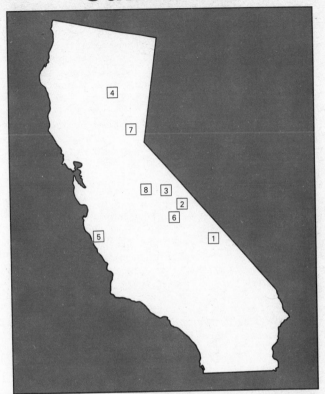

State map and tourist information: Office of Tourism, Dept. of Economic Development, 1030 13th St., Suite 200, Sacramento, CA 95814; 916-322-1396. Send self-addressed, stamped (54¢), 6″ × 9″ envelope. **State parks:** Information: Dept. of Parks, Box 2390, Sacramento, CA 95811; 916-445-6477. Entrance fees: $2 per vehicle; waived for lodgers. Reservations: Contact individual park and mail deposit for first night's lodgings. At Pfeiffer S.P., 3 month's advance reservations needed for mid June—early September; 4 weeks notice rest of year. Restrictions (Pfeiffer S.P.): No hunting. No loaded firearms. No camping vehicles longer than 27 feet. (Dogs must have proof of current rabies vaccination and be leashed, not allowed in lodgings). Facilities: Swimming not recommended December—March. Interpretative programs on weekends only mid June—September.

The largest section of Death Valley National Monument, which extends into Nevada, is in eastern California about 150 miles east of Fresno and 80 miles west of Las Vegas, Nevada. A desert surrounded by mountains, the monument encompasses 2,067,627 acres, which is more than 3,000 square miles. The desert scenery is colored with greens, reds, blues, and blacks for as far as the eye can see. Temperatures of the valley are forbiddingly high in summer; but in fall, winter, and spring the average is 79°F. Within the monument is Badwater Basin, at 282 feet below sea level the lowest point in the Western Hemisphere. The desert contains 200 square miles of salt flats, and in some areas there are tens of square miles of dunes. The valley is surrounded by pine-covered mountains that rise as high as 11,000 feet and are snow-capped in winter.

Barren as the valley seems, it supports at least twenty-two species of flowering plants, which during a rainy spring (more than 2 inches of precipitation) burst into bloom. Monument wildlife includes herds of desert bighorn that live in the foothills of the mountains, five or six saltwater-fish species that live nowhere else on earth, and countless birds during migrations. The monument has a marsh area, for instance, that attracts migrating geese and ducks, herons, egrets, ibises, and other waterfowl. Hiking, bicycling, camping, and motor touring are popular, but visitors are reminded to bear in mind the terrain's general lack of water and its frequently high summer temperatures. *Monument mailing address:* Death Valley, CA 92328. *Monument phone:* (619) 786-2331.

Furnace Creek Inn

The Furnace Creek Inn was originally fourteen rooms constructed of adobe by the Panamint Indians for use by the management of the U.S. Borax Corporation for rest and relaxation. Opened to the public in the 1930s and since added to, the inn is a Spanish-Colonial–style building at the mouth of Furnace Creek, on a knoll overlooking the valley floor. It is surrounded by an oasis of lawns with gardens, fruit trees, ponds with goldfish, and twelve species of palm trees. The grounds include a spring-fed swimming pool, lighted tennis courts, and badminton and shuffleboard facilities. The inn has bicycles for rent nearby, a gift shop, a Jacuzzi, a sauna, and two dining rooms. The main dining room is formal, and gentlemen are required to wear jackets. The Oasis room is more casual.

The luxury-style guest rooms have king-size, double, or twin beds (with roll aways available for children), wall-to-wall carpeting, and air-conditioning. Most have patios or balconies overlooking the garden; several have nonworking fireplaces. There are also two living room–bedroom suites, one with a wet bar. Guests at the inn may use the eighteen-hole golf course, stables, and volleyball courts at the nearby Furnace Creek Ranch (see below). The inn operates on the modified American plan only and includes breakfast and dinner.

Accommodations: 68 rooms (including two 1-bedroom suites) with private bath. *Pets:* Not permitted. *Open:* Mid-October through Mother's Day (mid-May). *Mailing address:* Fred Harvey, Inc., Box 1, Death Valley, CA 92328. *Phone:* (619) 786-2361. For reservations, call the Furnace Creek Ranch (below) at (619) 786-2345. *Driving instructions:* Furnace Creek Inn is off Route 190 at Furnace Creek.

Furnace Creek Ranch

Owned and operated by the same concession that runs the Furnace Creek Inn, the Furnace Creek Ranch is just down a slope from the inn. Remodeled in 1981, it has 225 guest rooms, with about 200 deluxe rooms in four two-story buildings and one single-story building, along with 25 "rustic" cabins. Most of the deluxe rooms have king-size or double beds, carpeting, private bath, air-conditioning, and a telephone; and some have views of the golf course, the mountains, or the pool area. The rustic cabins all have two double beds accommodating four, a private bath, and air-conditioning and are set along the road near the ranch complex.

The complex includes a steak house, a coffee shop, a bar-lounge, a cafeteria, and a general store that sells groceries, sundries, and gifts. The grounds include a 10-acre area with trees, playgrounds, basketball and volleyball courts, a swimming pool, and an eighteen-hole golf course. The stables offer two 2½-hour guided horseback trips daily. The complex is open the year round, although the cabins and coffee shop are closed in summer. (High season is the reverse of most other resorts, and the reduced-rate period is from June 1 to mid-October.) For guests arriving by air, there's a landing strip that accommodates private planes and small jets.

Accommodations: 200 deluxe lodge rooms and 25 rustic cabins, all with private bath. *Towels and linens:* Provided. *Cook-*

ing and eating utensils: Not provided. *Stove and refrigerator:* Not provided. *Pets:* Not permitted. *Open:* All year, except cabins and coffee shop, which are closed in summer. *Mailing address:* Fred Harvey, Inc., Box 1, Death Valley, CA 92328. *Phone:* (619) 786-2345. *Driving instructions:* Furnace Creek Ranch is on Route 190 at Furnace Creek.

Stove Pipe Wells Village

Situated almost exactly at sea level about 26 miles northwest of Furnace Creek Ranch, Stove Pipe Wells Village is a complex of modern motel-type buildings with seventy-nine guest rooms, a saloon, a dining room, a general store, a service station, and a landing strip. The main building has a large lobby and a gift shop, and the facilities include a swimming pool heated by a mineral spring. The decor of the buildings' exteriors is Western, and the saloon and dining room have wood-paneled walls and Western paintings and appointments. The dining room has a stone fireplace.

The guest rooms vary in size and appointments. A typical room has two double beds, wall-to-wall carpeting, air-conditioning, a private bath, and a view of the mountains.

Accommodations: 79 rooms with private bath. *Pets:* Not permitted. *Open:* All year. *Mailing address:* Death Valley, CA 92328. *Phone:* Call 619 operator and ask for Stovepipe Wells number 1. *Driving instructions:* Stove Pipe Wells Village is on Route 190.

Nine hundred thousand years ago, give or take a few, a huge lava flow cracked vertically as it cooled and formed the Devil's Postpile, which looks more like stacked and fallen columns than a pile of posts. The standing columns, which one observer likened to a giant pipe organ, range in height from 40 to 60 feet. The monument, in eastern California, consists of 798 acres surrounded by vast tracts of national land: Yosemite National Forest to the northwest, Inyo National Forest to the northeast, and the Sierra National Forest to the west and south. The John Muir Trail, which runs between Yosemite and Kings Canyon national parks, passes through the monument, as does the San Joaquin River.

The monument contains the Rainbow Fall (over which the San Joaquin River falls almost 150 feet), so named because most afternoons, when the sun's just right, rainbows form in the mists from the falling water. The terrain is ruggedly mountainous, and the monument has a large population of bears—so many that federal law sets standards for proper food storage in and around all camp areas. Visitors should stay on the designated trails, exercise care when exploring cliffs and gorges, and be prepared for sudden summer thundershowers. *Monument mailing address:* PO Box 501, Mammoth Lakes, CA 93546. *Monument phone:* (209) 565-3341.

Red's Meadow Resort and Cabins

Two miles from the Devil's Postpile and a mile from the Rainbow Fall, at an elevation of 7,500 feet, is Red's Meadow Resort, which consists of a general store; a pack station that outfits hikers and horseback riders and does work for the National Forest Service; the Mule House Café, which serves breakfast and lunch; and three forty-year-old A-frame pine cabins situated amid pines and firs beside a small stream.

Each cabin has one double and three single beds, a private bath, a complete kitchen with cooking and eating utensils, tiled floors because of all the pumice hereabouts, a couch, and paneled walls. Two of the cabins overlook the creek; the other, a wooded area. The resort also has two motel rooms with bath and kitchen.

Red's Meadow Resort conducts a number of pack trips, which range from one to twelve days, including some for which the staff takes care of all preparations, including cooking.

Accommodations: 2 motel rooms and 3 cabins, all with private bath. *Towels and linens:* Provided. *Cooking and eating utensils:* Provided. *Stove and refrigerator:* Provided. *Pets:* Not permitted. *Open:* Mid-June through hunting season (mid-October). *Mailing address:* PO Box 395, Mammoth Lakes, CA 93546. *Phone:* (619) 934-2345. *Driving instructions:* From Bishop take U.S. 395 north 40 miles to Route 203, then take Route 203 west for 7 miles.

Inyo National Forest is in eastern California. The 150-mile-long forest is in the Sierra Nevada mountains on the eastern borders of Yosemite, Kings Canyon, and Sequoia national parks. It contains some 900 lakes, and three forest fish hatcheries stock its numerous streams with rainbow and golden trout. (Brown trout are native to these streams.) The mountains are high and rugged, with many peaks exceeding 10,000 feet in elevation. The forest contains Devil's Postpile National Monument and Mammoth Mountain Ski Area, the most heavily used downhill ski area in the country. (The facilities at Mammoth Mountain can accommodate 18,000 skiers at a time.)

The forest is wooded primarily with conifers, the most common species being Geoffrey and lodgepole pine and red fir. Small stands of ponderosa pine are scattered throughout, and cottonwood is common along the banks of the streams. Bird and animal life is abundant, including bald and golden eagles. *Forest mailing address:* Mammoth Lakes, CA 93546. *Forest phone:* (619) 934-2505.

Tamarack Lodge Resort and Cabins

Twenty miles southeast of Yosemite National Park and about 12 miles east of Devil's Postpile National Monument, Tamarack Lodge, at an elevation of 8,600 feet, consists of a 1924 wood-frame lodge with twelve guest rooms and a restaurant, plus twenty-five wood-frame cabins. The carpeted dining room, which has lake views, serves meals both to the public and guests. The main lodge also has a large lobby with a stone fireplace.

The lodge bedrooms are rustic but comfortable, and all but four have views of the lake. Eight of the rooms share baths, and four have private baths. The twenty-five wood-frame cabins in a grove of pines behind the main lodge have views of Twin Lakes. The cabins vary in size from one to four bedrooms and can accommodate a maximum of two to twelve people. Each has a fully equipped kitchenette, wood paneling, and a private bath.

Accommodations: 12 lodge rooms, 4 with private bath, and 25 cabins with private bath. *Towels and linens:* Provided. *Cooking and eating utensils:* In cabins. *Stove and refrigerator:* In cabins. *Pets:* Permitted in cabins only. *Open:* All year. *Mailing address:* Box 69, Mammoth Lakes, CA 93546. *Phone:* (619) 934-2442. *Driving instructions:* Take Route 395 to Route 203 north of Bishop, proceed for about 2½ miles through Mammoth Village. Route 203 becomes Lake Mary Road, which forks. The right fork is Tamarack Lodge Road and runs to the lodge.

In northern California, at the southern tip of the Cascade Mountain Range, Lassen Volcanic National Park encompasses 106,372 acres. The Cascades' many volcanoes include Mount St. Helens and Mount Rainier to the north and are a part of the Pacific "Ring of Fire." The area, originally designated Lassen Peak and Cinder Cone National Monument, was given park status in 1914 after violent eruptions brought the volcanoes to national attention. The varied terrain's active vulcanism generates hot springs, steaming fumaroles, mud pots, and sulfurous vents, while picturesque lakes dot the landscape, surrounded by stands of mature conifers.

Activities include horseback riding, bicycling, fishing, boating, and, in winter, downhill skiing. Hiking opportunities include a walk to the summit of Lassen Peak (elevation 10,457 feet) or along a trail leading to Bumpass Hell, an area of hot springs and mud pots. Many small, scenic mountain lakes are easily accessible on foot or horseback; at the "Devastation Area," where all plant life was wiped out after the eruption, young pines are taking hold. *Park mailing address:* PO Box 100, Mineral, CA 96063. *Park phone:* (916) 595-4444.

Drakesbad Guest Ranch

Originally an 1860s homestead, Drakesbad Guest Ranch is a group of buildings beside a creek among pines, firs, and cedars. Accommodations consist of six rooms with half bath above the main lodge, four small cabins with half bath, and six bungalows with private bath. In a separate lodge building is a restaurant where all meals are served and a lounge with a fireplace. The lodge rooms and most of the other accommodations have no electricity and are lighted by kerosene lamps to maintain a rustic atmosphere.

All accommodations are rustic and simply furnished. Some have a private bath; but most are without bath, and guests use a central shower facility. Kerosene lamps provide light, and propane heaters provide warmth. An entire side of each bungalow can be opened up, and a few of these duplex units can be rented as suites of two adjoining rooms with connecting bath.

Ranch facilities include riding stables, hot tubs, and a naturally heated swimming pool open to guests twenty-four hours a day. Guests can arrange for the restaurant to prepare pack lunches, and the ranch offers many horseback trips. Drakesbad operates on the American plan—all meals are included in the rates.

Accommodations: 19 rooms, most with shared bath. *Pets:* Not permitted. *Open:* Mid-June through mid-September. *Mailing address:* Drakesbad Guest Ranch, Chester, CA 96060. *Phone:* (916) Drakesbad 2 (via Susanville operator); off season: California Guest Services, 2150 Main Street, Suite 7, Red Bluff, CA 96080. (916) 529-1512. *Driving instructions:* From Red Bluff take Route 36 east to Route 89, then go north on Route 89 to the park.

Pfeiffer Big Sur State Park is in the Big Sur River Valley in central California, about 26 miles south of Carmel and 3 miles inland from the Pacific Ocean. It's 820 acres, in a wooded, rugged canyon with sections of dry chaparral, constitute the southernmost redwood park. Usually redwoods wouldn't grow in such a dry area, but they are found in this park along the river and in some of the sheltered canyons. Other common trees include black walnuts, sycamores, black cottonwoods, alders, willows, and big-leaf maples. The park's average elevation is 800 feet, surrounded by much higher mountains. Wildlife includes black-tailed deer, foxes, an occasional mountain lion or coyote, and wild boars, which were introduced into the area by a wealthy rancher. These animals can weigh up to three hundred pounds, and, with their extremely sharp tusks, can be dangerous when cornered or surprised. Among the bird life are juncos, Steller's jays, turkey vultures, owls, and red-tailed hawks, as well as a large population of belted kingfishers, often seen hovering above the river against a backdrop of redwoods and black cottonwoods.

The park has 10 miles of hiking trails—including a mile-long self-guiding trail and another leading to a rocky gorge at the park's northern end where there's a small, scenic waterfall. The river is too shallow for swimming, but visitors like to wade. *Park phone:* (408) 667-2315.

Big Sur Lodge

The Big Sur Lodge complex is beside the Big Sur River and includes a restaurant with a patio overlooking the river, a coffee shop, two grocery stores, a Laundromat, a swimming pool, and a recreation building with pool and Ping-Pong tables and saunas.

The complex also has sixty-one redwood cabins overlooking the mountains, each with wall-to-wall carpeting, wood-paneling, contemporary furnishings, and a private bath. Many cabins have vaulted ceilings, fifteen have a kitchenette, twenty four have a fireplace, and thirty eight are two-room suites.

Accommodations: 61 cabins with private bath. *Towels and linens:* Provided. *Cooking and eating utensils:* Not provided. *Stove and refrigerator:* In 15 cabins. *Pets:* Not permitted. *Open:* All year. *Mailing address:* Pfeiffer State Park, PO Drawer B, Big Sur, CA 93920. *Phone:* (408) 667-2171. *Driving instructions:* Big Sur Lodge is off Route 1, about 26 miles south of Carmel.

Jointly administered, Sequoia National Park to the south and Kings Canyon National Park to the north form a single unit of 846,989 acres in eastern California, about 60 miles east of Fresno in the Sierra Nevada mountains. This ruggedly beautiful range has seventy-five summits that are higher than 11,000 feet. Twenty are higher than 12,000 feet, and seven reach above 14,000 feet. At the parks' eastern boundary is Mount Whitney, at 14,494 feet the tallest in the contiguous United States. The parks are bordered to the east, north, and southeast by Inyo National Forest; to the west by Sierra National Forest; and to the south by the Sequoia National Forest.

Among the many natural wonders in the parklands, most of which are inaccessible to automobiles, are precipitous canyons and hundreds of lakes and streams, alpine meadows, and miles of trails. Wildlife includes golden eagles, black bears, mule deer, and cougars. The giant sequoia trees, which occur in groves, are the largest living things, and the General Sherman Tree, with a diameter at its base of 32 feet and rising 275 feet, is the biggest and oldest of them—estimates place its age at from 2,000 to 2,500 years. Among other scenic highlights of these impressive parks are the Giant Forest area, Moro Rock, Crystal Cave, Crescent Meadow, Grant Grove, Cedar Grove, Roaring River Falls, Zumwalt Meadow, North Dome, and Grand Sentinel. Popular activities include hiking, horseback riding, fishing, skiing, and guided walks and other interpretive programs. *Parks' mailing address:* Three Rivers, CA 93271. *Parks' phone:* (209) 565-3341.

A concession, Guest Services Inc., administers lodges and accommodations in Sequoia and Kings Canyon National Parks, handling reservations and inquiries for those listed below. *Mailing address:* Sequoia National Park, CA 93262. *Phone:* (209) 565-3373. *Driving instructions:* Call Guest Services, Inc., for directions.

Giant Forest Lodge and Cabins

Surrounded by the huge trees, Giant Forest Lodge is in Sequoia National Park at an elevation of 6,400 feet. Its rustic wood-frame buildings contain three types of accommodations, as well as a cafeteria, a service station, a grocery store, and a gift shop that are open all year. The lodge's buffet dining room is open in summer only.

Guest accommodations include: 83 motel rooms with private bath; 67 wood-frame cabins with private bath; and 107 rustic, wood-frame cabins with shared bath. Five of the motel rooms are specially equipped for the handicapped. Some rustic cabins have porches, some are without electricity, and all share a central lavatory and shower facility. Most have a wood or oil stove for heat, as well as a patio with a wood stove for cooking.

Accommodations: 83 motel rooms with private bath and 174 cabins, 67 with private bath. *Towels and linens:* Provided. *Cooking and eating utensils:* In some units. *Stove and refrigerator:* In some units. *Pets:* Not permitted. *Open:* All year, except for rustic cabins, which close in winter. *Mailing address, phone, and driving instructions:* See above.

Bearpaw Meadow Camp

On a ridge 7,800 feet up in Sequoia National Park, Bearpaw Meadow camp is accessible only via an 11-mile hike. Views are splendid, and the camp accommodations—six tent cabins with wooden floors, canvas sides, and canvas tops—are rustic but comfortable. They have no cooking facilities or electricity, but bath facilities are set centrally in the complex, which also has a dining tent that serves three meals a day and snacks. Camp rates include lodging and meals.

Accommodations: 6 tent cabins with shared bath. *Towels and linens:* Provided. *Cooking and eating facilities:* All meals provided. *Stove and refrigerator:* Not provided. *Pets:* Not permitted. *Open:* Late June through early September. *Mailing address, phone, and driving instructions:* See above.

Stony Creek Lodge

Between Sequoia and Kings Canyon national parks, in Sequoia National Forest at an elevation of 6,720 feet, Stony Creek Lodge has eleven carpeted motel rooms with private bath, as well as a restaurant, a gift shop, and a store selling groceries and sundries. Each of the motel rooms, which occupy the second floor of a rustic wooden building, has a private bath and can accommodate up to five people.

Accommodations: 11 rooms with private bath. *Pets:* Not permitted. *Open:* Mid-May through mid-October. *Mailing address, phone, and driving instructions:* See above.

Grant Grove

Grant Grove, site of the General Grant Tree, the second-largest living thing, is in what was was once General Grant National Park but was later incorporated into Kings Canyon National Park. Separated from the main section of the park, this was the first area here to be designated a park, to stop logging activities that would have ruined the forest. Reminders of this early effort at lumbering can still be seen.

Accommodations are in forty-nine wood-frame cabins, nine with carpeting and private baths. The others, classified as "rustic," with neither bath nor electricity, have wood stoves for heat and share a central bath and shower. The complex also includes a restaurant, a store selling groceries and sundries, a service station, and a gift shop.

Accommodations: 49 cabins, 9 with private bath. *Towels and linens:* Provided. *Cooking and eating utensils:* In some rustic units. *Stove:* Wood stove in some rustic units. *Refrigerator:* Not provided. *Pets:* Not permitted. *Open:* All year (only 9 modern and 15 rustic cabins in winter). *Mailing address, phone, and driving instructions:* See above.

Cedar Grove Lodge

Cedar Grove Lodge is at the bottom of Kings Canyon on Kings River at an elevation of 4,800 feet. On its top floor, the rustic wood-frame lodge has eighteen motel-type motel units that are carpeted and can each accommodate up to four. The building also has a balcony with easy chairs at one end of the second floor, as well as a snack bar, a gift shop, and a store selling groceries and sundries.

Accommodations: 18 rooms with private bath. *Pets:* Not permitted. *Open:* Mid-May through October. *Mailing address, phone, and driving instructions:* See above.

Bordered on the north by Plumas National Forest and on the south by Eldorado National Forest, Tahoe National Forest is in northern California about 150 miles northeast of San Francisco. Its 1.2 million acres along the Sierra Nevada vary in elevation from about 2,500 to 9,000 feet. The heavily wooded terrain has a wide variety of wildflowers and trees, predominantly Douglas firs but also red and white firs, western white pines, sugar pines, Ponderosa pines and cedars, hemlocks, and oaks. The forest includes many small lakes and streams, and one of its several rivers is the fast-flowing north fork of the Yuba. Mammals commonly found here are mule deer, black bears, foxes and raccoons; and the rich bird life includes bald and golden eagles, turkey vultures, red-tailed hawks, and many passerines.

Hundreds of miles of trails include a section of the Pacific Crest Trail, which runs from Canada to Mexico. Forest activities include fishing for trout and bass, mountain climbing, camping, snowmobiling, cross-country skiing, and downhill skiing at three facilities. *Forest mailing address:* Highway 49 and Coyote Street Nevada City, CA 95959. *Forest phone:* (916) 265-4531.

Sierra Shangri-La

Along the banks of the Yuba River at an elevation of 3,100 feet, Sierra Shangri-La has a stone-and-wood lodge and eight cabins, all with a river view. A 12-foot-high flood wall, constructed of 20,000 tons of stone, separates the buildings from the river. Although the main lodge serves principally as the owners' residence, it has a two-bedroom efficiency apartment with a fully equipped kitchenette and a private bath.

The eight wood-frame cabins vary in size, accommodating from three to eight people. Each has a fully equipped kitchenette, a private bath, wood-paneling in some rooms, and either a fireplace or a potbellied stove. Three cabins are on top of the stone wall directly overlooking the river.

Accommodations: 1 lodge apartment, 3 bed-and-breakfast rooms, and 8 cabins, all with private bath. *Towels and linens:* Provided. *Cooking and eating utensils:* Provided. *Stove and refrigerator:* Provided. *Pets:* Not permitted. *Open:* All year. *Mailing address:* Sierra Shangri-La, Route 49, PO Box 285, Downieville, CA 95936. *Phone:* (916) 289-3455. *Driving instructions:* Sierra Shangri-La is on Route 49 about 3 miles east of Downieville.

Yosemite National Park is in the Sierra Nevada mountains in central California, about 180 miles east of San Francisco. Its 760,917 acres, with an enormous range of habitats and scenery, vary in elevation by about 11,000 feet, having Mount Lyell at 13,114 feet, its highest summit. The park also contains the three largest exposed granite monoliths in the world, as well as the highest waterfall in North America, Yosemite Falls, which drops 1,750 feet over two precipices; Ribbon Falls, which drops 1,612 feet; and Bridal Veil and Nevada Falls, both dropping a mere 600 feet.

Yosemite Valley and the surrounding mountain ranges were (and are) subject to the same geological forces as the entire Sierra Nevada range, created as the Pacific plate collided with and slid under the North American plate, forcing an uplifting of the North American plate. The western edge of the Sierra Nevada rises gradually, but the eastern slopes are much more precipitous due to the gradual subsidence and erosion of the North American plate to the east of the mountain ranges.

The area around Yosemite Valley was formed when a huge block of granite covering roughly 3,200 square miles was uplifted along a series of geologic faults. Water runoff eroded the block of granite, which was followed by four separate glaciers in the Yosemite Valley that flowed down from the summits of the Sierra Nevadas. This is still a very active geological area—the next most active after Mount St. Helens in Washington—with a high level of thermal and earthquake activity. Geologists anticipate some kind of major activity, perhaps an eruption, especially in the Mammoth Mountain area, forty miles to the south of Yosemite Park.

Yosemite Valley is at an elevation of about 4,000 feet and surrounded by such peaks as Half Dome and El Capitan, which rise to 8,842 and 7,569 feet, respectively. The park's largest stand of giant sequoias is Mariposa Grove; and Tuolumne Meadows, at 8,600 feet, is the largest subalpine meadow in the Sierra Nevada.

With more than 1,300 species of flowering plants, including patches of dogwood among the conifers and oaks, Yosemite Park is a visual delight all year. Sections generously sprinkled with hardwoods exhibit stunning fall foliage, and spring brings a profusion of wildflowers and the dramatic effects of melting snow—

fast-flowing streams and thunderous waterfalls.

Popular activities include hiking, mountain climbing, horseback riding, bicycling, and downhill and cross-country skiing. The park has hundreds of miles of hiking trails, 90 miles of marked cross-country ski trails, a mountaineering school, and many sightseeing tours, interpretative talks, and nature programs.

Amtrak trains stop at Merced, 60 miles away. Call (209) 383-1563 to make advance reservations for the bus from there to the park. *Park address:* Box 577, Yosemite National Park, CA 95389. *Park phone:* (209) 372-4461.

Note: All accommodations listed below are operated by the Yosemite Park and Curry Company, founded in the last century by the Curry family, which built and operated several of the hotels. Acquired by MCA in 1962, the company has installed a computerized reservation system; should you have any difficulty reaching it, call again. For information and reservations, contact Yosemite Park and Curry Company, 5410 East Holme, Fresno, CA 93727. *Phone:* (209) 252-4848.

Ahwahnee Hotel

At the base of a sheer granite cliff, the Ahwahnee Hotel, listed in the National Register of Historic Places, is the most luxurious of all the accommodations at Yosemite. It is a large castle-like building constructed of stone and cedar. When the hotel was erected in 1927, no expense was spared: It has four parlors, including the 80-foot-long Great Lounge, with its high walk-in fireplace; ninety-nine guest rooms in the main hotel; a pool; tennis courts; a gift shop; and trails that wander through the pine forest at its borders. Granite columns support the dining room's 130-foot-long and 34-foot-high ceiling. Wrought-iron chandeliers hang from the exposed-pine beams. The hotel is decorated with Indian motifs; and the lounges have couches, floor-to-ceiling windows, and the original antique furnishings from 1927.

The guest rooms were refurbished over a three-year period. Each has a private bath (some with showers, some with tubs), a telephone, framed tapestries of rugs formerly used in the hotel, room service, and wall-to-wall carpeting. A few have a balcony or a fireplace.

The complex also includes twenty-four bungalow cottages, each with one room accommodating two to four, one double

81

bed (some have an additional sofa bed), carpeting, a telephone, a private bath, a small patio, and room service. Set by the river, most have views of Half Dome, Glacier Point, or Yosemite Falls.

The dining room at the Ahwahnee is somewhat formal, and men are expected to wear jackets at dinner. Complimentary afternoon tea and cookies are served at 5 P.M. by the fireplace in the Great Lounge; a complimentary demitasse is available at 7 P.M. The cocktail lounge has wide-screen television, and a game room has another television set for children. Baby-sitting is available.

Accommodations: 99 rooms and 24 cottages, all with private bath. *Towels and linens:* Provided. *Pets:* Not permitted. *Open:* All year. *Mailing address and phone:* See above. *Driving instructions:* Take Route 120, 140, or 41 to Yosemite National Park, then follow the signs to Yosemite Valley; at Yosemite Village, follow the signs to the hotel.

Hotel Wawona

The Hotel Wawona, a group of Victorian-style buildings constructed between 1870 and 1915, is the only hotel operated by the Curry Company that lies outside Yosemite Valley, 6 miles from the park's south entrance. The main hotal building, completed in 1879, is listed in the National Register of Historic Places. The complex has a large lawn sprinkled with chairs and shaded by incense cedars, as well as a swimming pool, tennis courts, a nine-hole golf course, stables and horseback riding, a pioneer-history center with a self-guided trail past frontier cabins, and nature trails. The sun parlor has a fireplace, couches, rattan furnishings, and inlaid wood paneling. All public rooms are furnished entirely with antiques.

Each of the sixty-three guest rooms opens onto a veranda and is furnished with antiques; about half have either a brass or a wooden bedstead. Suites with two bedrooms connected by a bath are available.

The hotel has a full-service dining room where men are requested to wear jackets for dinner.

Accommodations: 63 rooms, 44 with private bath. *Pets:* Not permitted. *Open:* Easter through Thanksgiving. *Mailing address and phone:* See above. *Driving Instructions:* Hotel Wawona is 6 miles from the south entrance to Yosemite National Park.

Yosemite Lodge (and Cabins)

Near the Merced River, Yosemite Lodge is a group of cabins and long wood-frame buildings from which you can see the up-

per and lower Yosemite Falls, Glacier Point, and Half Dome. Covered walkways connect the main complex of buildings, which include two restaurants, a cafeteria, a lounge with a fireplace, a bar, a gift shop, a bicycle-rental stand, a post office, and a swimming pool.

Accommodations include 226 deluxe lodge rooms, each with carpeting, a private bath, and a private patio or its own balcony overlooking the woods. In addition, there are fifty one-room cabins, recently refurbished, each with a private bath (some with a shower, and some with both a shower and a tub). An additional eighty-nine cabins have one room with beds, a dresser, and linens. Some have a private bath; others share a central shower facility.

The complex has an outdoor amphitheater where park rangers and naturalists give evening interpretive talks and slide shows during the summer months. Guests can make sightseeing reservations in the lodge lobby.

Accommodations: 226 rooms with private bath and 139 cabins, most with private bath. *Towels and linens:* Provided. *Cooking and eating utensils:* Not provided. *Stove and refrigerator:* Not provided. *Pets:* Not permitted. *Open:* All year. *Mailing address and phone:* See above. *Driving instructions:* Request detailed information when making reservations.

Curry Village

Curry Village, near Glacier Point, is a complex of rustic wooden buildings, as well as cabins and tent cabins. The complex includes a cafeteria, a hamburger stand, a swimming pool, a gift shop, a sporting-goods shop (where fishing licenses can be obtained), a cocktail patio, a bicycle-rental stand, an ice-skating rink (open November through February), and an outdoor amphitheater used in summer for talks and slide shows.

The eighteen lodge rooms are somewhat small, but each has wall-to-wall carpeting, a telephone, and a private bath. There are also 173 one-room cabins, accommodating two to four persons, which come with beds, linens, a dresser, and maid service. Ninety-six have a private bath; the balance share a central bath and shower facility. From spring through fall, when the weather is warm, 408 tent cabins are available, used mostly by families, each with a wooden floor, canvas sides and top, and electricity but no heat or running water.

Accommodations: 18 lodge rooms with private bath; 173 cabins, 96 with private bath; and 408 tent cabins with shared bath. *Towels and linens:* In lodge and cabins. *Cooking and eating utensils:* Not provided. *Stove and refrigerator:* Not provided. *Pets:* Not permitted. *Open:* Lodge and cabins, all year. *Mailing address and phone:* See above. *Driving instructions:* Request detailed information when making reservations.

Housekeeping Camp

Housekeeping Camp, along the Merced River a half mile south of Yosemite Village, has three hundred concrete-and-canvas cabins, a grocery store, a coin laundry, a central bath-and-shower complex, and a swimming pool. The cabins have three walls, a concrete floor, a canvas roof, and a sliding canvas door opening onto a patio with a canvas roof, encircled by a fence of saplings. Each patio has a table and chairs, an electrical outlet, and a wood stove. Guests may prepare meals on the wood stove and can rent cooking and eating utensils.

Accommodations: 300 cabins with shared bath facilities. *Towels and linens:* Can be rented. *Cooking and eating utensils:* Can be rented. *Stove and refrigerator:* Not provided. *Pets:* Not permitted. *Open:* Memorial Day through Labor Day. *Driving instructions:* Housekeeping Camp is ½ mile south of Yosemite Village.

Colorado

State map and tourist information: Board of Tourism, 5500 S. Syracuse, #267, Englewood, CO 80111; 303-779-1067. **State parks:** *Information:* Division of Parks, 1313 Sherman St., Rm. 618, Denver, CO 80203; 303-866-3437. **National parks:** Contact parks directly.

Black Canyon of the Gunnison National Monument is in western Colorado about 10 miles east of Montrose. They call it Black Canyon because it's (well, almost) black, except perhaps around noon, when sunlight manages to illuminate for a while its otherwise shadowed floor and flicker on the Gunnison River. Sheer walls of dark schist, weathered and streaked with granite, drop precipitously, sometimes as far as 2,700 feet, to the river that formed this deep, narrow canyon by erosion. The river was named after a Captain Gunnison of the U.S. Army Corps of Engineers, who was killed by Indians while exploring this area in 1853.

The national monument consists of 13,627 acres, 11,180 of them designated wilderness area, and contains the largest lake in Colorado, Blue Mesa Reservoir, which has 111 miles of shoreline. Boating, fishing, wind-surfing, and swimming are all regular activities. The forests are thick with Douglas firs and quaking aspens, the latter of which look spectacular when they turn yellowish gold in the fall and quiver in the slightest breeze. *Monument mailing address:* Box 1648, Montrose, CO 81402. *Monument phone:* (303) 240-6522.

Star Valley Ranch

At an elevation of 8,600 feet, you can stay in a log cabin overlooking the Cement River, which the state stocks weekly with trout. The eighteen cabins are spread about on 6 acres studded with wildflowers. (One guest identified a hundred different species around her cabin.)

Two types of log cabins are available—small and large. The small cabins, built in 1930s, have private baths with towels, propane heat, kitchens stocked with cooking and eating utensils, beds covered with fresh linens and down comforters, and handmade pine furniture. They are decorated with photographs by Doug Martin, a Colorado wildlife photographer. The larger cabins, built in the 1970s, have completely equipped kitchens and private bathrooms, chinked log walls, fireplaces, and large lofts overlooking their living rooms. Photographs decorate their walls too.

The most popular pastimes around here are skiing and hunting. The Crested Butte Ski Resort is 9 miles away, and Aspen is just as close but requires an eight-hour ride when there's snow.

Sports Illustrated rated this valley one of the best in the country for deer and elk hunting.

Accommodations: 18 cabins with private bath. *Towels and linens:* Provided. *Cooking and eating utensils:* Provided. *Stove and refrigerator:* Provided. *Pets:* Not permitted. *Open:* All year. *Mailing address:* Crested Butte, CO 81224. *Phone:* (303) 349-5517. *Driving instructions:* From Crested Butte take Route 135 south 8 miles. Look for the Star Valley Ranch sign on the right.

Mesa Verde National Park covers 52,036 acres in southwestern Colorado, about 38 miles west of Durango and 48 miles northeast of Four Corners, the only point in the United States that's on the borders of four states—Colorado, Utah, Arizona, and New Mexico. *Mesa verde* means "green mesa." This is the only park in the national system set aside to preserve an area of historical significance. The mesa was inhabited by an advanced agrarian people, who abandoned the area in the last years of the thirteenth century, possibly due to changing environmental influences such as drought and the depletion of timber, soil, and animal resources. They left behind hundreds of ruins, which range from pit houses dug into the ground to cave dwellings in alcoves. Many of the ruins here can be inspected freely by visitors, but many others cannot be entered unless a park ranger is present. The Cliff Palace is one cliff dwelling with 127 rooms.

The pre-Columbian Mesa Verde civilization left no written records; so the principal means of dating their occupation of the area is dendrochronology, a sophisticated technique of comparing the rings in trees cut recently with those in trees cut when the ancient structures were built. Elevations on the mesa range

from 7,000 to 8,500 feet, and sightseeing is the main activity. The visitors' center operates several interpretative programs about the Mesa Verde civilization; there's also a museum, as well as two self-guided auto tours of the area. *Park mailing address:* Superintendent, Mesa Verde National Park, CO 81330. *Park phone:* (303) 529-4465.

Far View Motor Lodge

Far View Motor Lodge, at an altitude of 8,050 feet, is a group of modern buildings with 150 guest rooms, a restaurant, a bar, and a gift shop. The main lodge contains a large restaurant with exposed-beam ceilings and Indian-motif decorations such as Navaho rugs hanging on the walls. The view from the restaurant encompasses parts of four states; and fish, turkey, and lamb are the most common entrées.

Each guest room has wall-to-wall carpeting, a private bath, and a private balcony. The views from the rooms are as expansive as those from the restaurant, and you can see all four states from almost any guest room.

Accommodations: 150 rooms with private bath. *Pets:* Not permitted. *Open:* May through mid-October. *Mailing address:* Mesa Verde Company, Box 277, Mancos, CO 81328. *Phone:* (303) 529-4421. *Driving instructions:* Far View Motor Lodge is off U.S. 160 about 10 miles east of Cortez and 38 miles west of Durango.

Florida

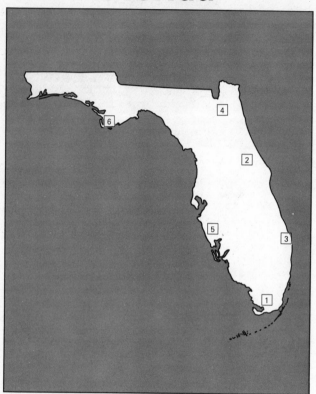

State map and tourist information: Dept. of Commerce, Div. of Tourism, 410 Collins Bldg., Tallahassee, FL 32301; 904-487-1462. **State parks:** *Information:* Dept. of Natural Resources, Bureau of Education & Information, Marjory Stoneman Douglas Bldg., 3900 Commonwealth Blvd., Tallahassee, FL 32303; 904-488-7326. *Entrance fees:* Nominal; waived for lodgers. *Reservations:* Contact individual parks. No deposit currently required for most parks. Make reservations well in advance. Most parks accept reservations no more than 4 months in advance; Hontoon, no more than 60 day in advance. *Restrictions:* No hunting. No alcohol. Dogs must be leashed (not allowed in lodgings). *Facilities:* Available all year.

Everglades National Park is in southwestern Florida, about 40 miles west of Miami. Its 1,400,533-acres cover the better part of the southwestern tip of the Florida peninsula and include just about all of Florida Bay, formed by the Florida Keys. The Everglades is a delicate, threatened environment. As a habitat, it supports a wide range of life forms, and visitors seldom forget the experience of coming upon a marsh area and seeing thousands of great white herons, anhingas cruising or fishing, bald eagles soaring overhead or watching from treetops, or the many other varieties of birds, including yellow- and black-crowned night herons, storks, roseate spoonbills, ospreys, and flamingos. To a birder, the Everglades can be thrilling.

Other wildlife includes manatees, alligators and crocodiles, black bears, and panthers. The subtropical plant life is lush— the Seminole Indians had a term for the area that is roughly translated as "river of grass," an apt description. The Everglades is an intricate system of waterways, islands, channels, ponds, streams and marshes (both freshwater and saltwater). Streams may be lined with mangroves or stands of mahogany and patches of cypress and palm.

Activities include birding, boating, and fishing. The park's naturalist service offers numerous interpretative programs, and visitors can choose from many guided boat, bus, and fishing trips. Marina facilities accommodate private boats, and concessionaires rent out canoes, powerboats, and houseboats. Biking is also popular, as are the self-guided hiking trails. *Park mailing address:* PO Box 279, Homestead, FL 33030. *Park phone:* (305) 247-6211.

Flamingo Lodge, Marina & Outpost

Flamingo Inn, a series of motel-style lodge buildings along Florida Bay, has 103 lodge rooms in several buildings, as well as twelve cottages, a marina, and a restaurant. The restaurant building also has a gift shop, a bar, and an area staffed with park naturalists. Lodge guest rooms, classified "first class" and "standard," differ primarily in such appointments as carpeting, bedspreads, and draperies. ("First class" rooms, for instance, have plusher carpeting and coordinated bedspreads and drapes.) All the lodge rooms have views of the bay, and all have air-

93

conditioning, television, a telephone, and a private bath.

Each of the cottages, some of which are carpeted, is in a wooded area and has a fully equipped kitchenette, air-conditioning, and a private bath.

Accommodations: 103 lodge rooms and 12 cottages, all with private bath. *Towels and linens:* Provided. *Cooking and eating utensils:* In cottages. *Stove and refrigerator:* In cottages. *Pets:* Permitted if leashed, and with advance notice. *Open:* All year. *Mailing address:* Flamingo, FL 33030. *Phone:* (813) 695-3101. *Driving instructions:* From Homestead take Route 27 west to park entrance, then follow the park road to Flamingo, about 38 miles.

Hontoon Island State Park, in central Florida, is about 35 miles north of Orlando and a few miles south of Ocala National Forest. The 1,650-acre park occupies all of Hontoon Island, surrounded by the St. Johns and Hontoon Dead rivers and Snake Creek. Park docking facilities serve those who arrive by boat, and a free service from the mainland parking lot ferries those arriving by automobile. The terrain is flat and wooded in places with oaks and cabbage palms; one section is a pine flatwoods with generous stands of slash and pond pines. The habitats attract a large variety of bird life, and visitors will almost certainly see little and great blue herons, ospreys, great egrets, and red-shouldered hawks. A herd of white-tailed deer, most easily spotted in the morning, inhabits the island, as do alligators and bob-cats. One rather large alligator, popular with visitors, has taken to sunning in the grass beside the boat dock.

Picnicking, camping, and fishing, especially for bass and bream, are the standard activities. There are no swimming facilities.

Hontoon Island State Park has available six primitive wood-frame cabins, in a grove of oaks and cabbage palms, that have bunk beds and can accommodate four or six. Each cabin has a screened front porch with lawn furniture and a charcoal grill and a picnic table immediately outside, but there are no bathrooms and no kitchens. Showers and toilets are in a central facility. Guests are expected to purchase supplies (food, etc.) on the mainland before arriving and to bring along any needed equipment such as gas camping stove.

Accommodations: 6 cabins with shared bath. *Towels and linens:* Not provided. *Cooking and eating utensils:* Not provid-ed. *Stove:* Outside charcoal grill. *Refrigerator:* Not provided. *Pets:* Not permitted. *Open:* All year. *Mailing address:* 2100 W. French Ave., Orange City, FL 32763. *Phone:* (904) 734-7158. *Driving instructions:* From De Land take Route 44 southwest to Hon-toon Road, turn left and proceed to Old New York Road; turn left again and follow Old New York Road to the Hontoon Island parking lot.

Jonathan Dickinson State Park, 10,000 acres of land and river in southeastern Florida, is about 25 miles north of West Palm Beach and 2 ½ miles inland from the Atlantic Ocean. The relatively flat terrain is occasionally brackish and is wooded in parts with scrub oaks and longleaf pines. The park, noted for its seven hundred plant varieties, has abundant wildlife including bobcats, Florida panthers, foxes, wild hogs, and deer. Many birds sojourn here—bald eagles, ospreys, ibises, egrets, herons, jays.

Activities include bicycling and hiking. Rowboats and canoes can be rented, and there are playground areas and an area for field sports.

The park has seven modern wood-frame cabins along the Loxahatchee River. Each has kitchen facilities, a living and dining area, a bedroom, and a private bath. Cabins are air-conditioned and accommodate up to four.

Accommodations: 7 cabins with private bath. *Towels, linens, and pillows:* Not provided. *Cooking and eating utensils:* Provided. *Stove and refrigerator:* Provided. *Pets:* Not permitted. *Open:* All year. *Mailing address:* 16450 SE Federal Highway, Hobe Sound, FL 33455. *Phone:* (305) 746-5804. *Driving instructions:* Jonathan Dickinson State Park is off U.S. 1 about 13 miles south of Stuart.

Mike Roess Gold Head Branch State Park is in northeastern Florida, about 40 miles southwest of Jacksonville and 20 miles west of the St. Johns River. The 1,561-acre park, like most of Florida's state parks, is preserved mainly in its natural state: Three of its five lakes are spring-fed, and the terrain is primarily a sand-hill community, with turkey oaks, longleaf pines, grasses, and wildflowers. A spring-fed stream and its ravine wind through the area, a habitat for many species of bird life. In winter, eagles and osprey abound; red-tailed and marsh hawks are also common. Great and snowy egrets and great blue, black-crowned, and green herons stalk the waters.

Hiking, fishing (there's a large population of bass), and swimming are the most popular activites. The park has a beach and a bathhouse.

Mike Roess Park has fourteen cabins, accommodating six each, that overlook Little Lake Johnson. Five of the cabins are built of concrete block, while nine wood-frame cabins, built in the 1930s by the Civilian Conservation Corps, have fireplaces of native stone. Each cabin has a kitchen, a private bath, a living room with a sofa bed, a dining area, and the five block cabins have a separate bedroom.

Accommodations: 14 cabins with private bath. *Towels, linens, and pillows:* Pillows only provided. *Cooking and eating utensils:* Basic pots & pans only. *Stove and refrigerator:* Provided. *Pets:* Not permitted. *Open:* All year. *Mailing address:* Route 1, Box 545, Keystone Heights, FL 32656. *Phone:* (904) 473-4701. *Driving instructions:* Mike Roess Gold Head Branch State Park is off Route 21, about 6 miles northeast of Keystone Heights.

Myakka River State Park is in southwestern Florida, about 17 miles southeast of Sarasota and roughly that distance from the Gulf of Mexico. The park's 29,000 acres encompass two lakes (one is roughly 800 acres; the other, about 300), and fishing is the number-one activity. Anglers go after panfish and bass, which average about five pounds, with larger ones occasionally approaching ten. A concessionaire rents out canoes. Most of the area is in its natural state, and the park naturalists offer campfire programs, guided walks, and a Sunday-morning program for beginning birders.

A wide array of bird life includes ospreys, peregrine falcons, swallow-tailed kites, roseate spoonbills, egrets, herons, sandhill cranes, and golden and bald eagles. There are 1,800 species of plants, and wildflowers bloom almost all year long.

Myakka River State Park has five cabins accommodating six in each. Built of palm logs in the 1930s by the Civilian Conservation Corps, they overlook a freshwater marsh. Each has a native-stone fireplace, one large living and sleeping area, and a separate kitchen.

Accommodations: 5 cabins with private bath. *Towels, linens, and pillows:* Not provided. *Cooking and eating utensils:* Not provided. *Stove and refrigerator:* Provided. *Pets:* Not permitted. *Open:* All year. *Mailing address:* Route 1, Box 72, Sarasota, FL 33583. *Phone:* (813) 924-1027. *Driving instructions:* Myakka River State Park is off Route 72 about 17 miles east of Sarasota.

T. H. Stone Memorial—St. Joseph Peninsula State Park, 2,516 acres with 10 miles of sandy beach, is in Florida's northwestern panhandle, about 40 miles southeast of Panama City. The peninsula it occupies is immediately west of St. Vincent Island and encloses St. Joseph Bay. Most of the park is in its natural state, especially the 1,650-acre wilderness-preserve area. The terrain, mainly dunes partially covered by dune grass and a few stands of slash and sand pine, is the habitat of a large variety of shore birds, among them egrets, herons, ospreys, and bald eagles.

Popular activities include swimming, hiking, and fishing. There are miles of unspoiled beaches, and visitors frequently go scalloping.

The park has 8 cabins, each of which has a boardwalk to the bay, a fireplace (firewood can be purchased at the park), a screened porch, and central heat and air-conditioning. The cabins are furnished with two double beds, a sofa bed, and a day bed; they have kitchenettes that include basic cooking pots and utensils, but no dishes or flatware.

Accommodations: 2 cabins with private bath. *Towels, linens, and pillows:* Not provided. *Cooking and eating utensils:* Provided. *Stove and refrigerator:* Provided. *Pets:* Not permitted. *Open:* All year. *Mailing address:* Star Route 1, Box 200, Port St. Joe, FL 32456. *Phone:* (904) 227-1327. *Driving instructions:* From Port St. Joe take U.S. 98 east, then take Route 30 to T. H. Stone Memorial—St. Joseph Peninsula State Park.

Georgia

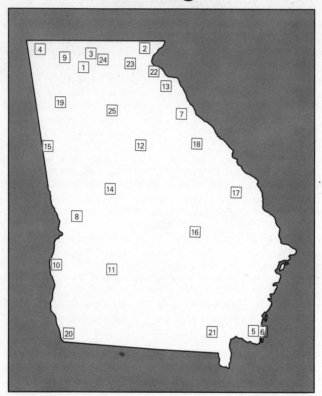

State map and parks information: Parks & Historic Sites Div., 270 Washington St., Rm. 707, Atlanta, GA 30334; 404-656-2770. *State tourist information:* Dept. of Industry & Trade, PO Box 1776, Atlanta, GA 30301; 404-656-3545. **State parks:** *Entrance fees:* None. *Reservations:* Contact individual park and send deposit for first night's lodging or use credit card. Reservations recommended 30 days in advance. Minimum stay, 7 days between early June and Labor Day. Not accepted more than 11 months in advance. *Restrictions:* No hunting. No alcohol in public; permitted in private rooms. Dogs must be leashed (not allowed in lodgings). *Facilities:* Swimming, June—Labor Day. Golf, hiking trails, and interpretative programs, open all year.
100

Amicalola Falls State Park is in northern Georgia, at the southern edge of the Chattahoochee National Forest, roughly 60 miles north of Atlanta. The 700-acre park, in the Blue Ridge Mountains and ranging in elevation from 1,800 to 2,544 feet, is named after Amicalola Falls, which drop 729 feet over seven cascades. The falls, generated by a stream running down Amicalola Ridge, are obscured in some places as it drops through dense forest. ("Amicalola" is a Cherokee word for "tumbling waters.") Heavily wooded with oaks, hickories, maples, and beeches, the terrain is ruggedly mountainous in parts and is especially scenic in spring, when the mountain laurels and dogwoods are in bloom along Amicalola Falls Gorge.

A regular activity is hiking, and in addition to 3 miles of trails, the park is also the southern approach to the Appalachian Trail, which begins at Springer Mountain and runs to Mount Katahdin in Maine. There are, as well, camping, picnicking, and playground facilities, and anglers try their luck in the stream and lake.

Amicalola Falls State Park has fifteen wood-frame cabins. Ten have porches and are situated on top of Amicalola Ridge; the other five are in lower terrain. Views are of mountaintop vistas or wooded areas and a stream. All cabins, which vary in size from one to three bedrooms, have a fully equipped kitchenette and a private bath. Ten have a fireplace.

Accommodations: 15 cabins with private bath. *Towels and linens:* Provided. *Cooking and eating utensils:* Provided. *Stove and refrigerator:* Provided. *Pets:* Not permitted. *Open:* All year. *Mailing address:* Star Route, Dawsonville, GA 30534. *Phone:* (404) 265-2885. *Driving instructions:* Amicalola Falls State Park is off Route 52, via Route 183, about 16 miles northwest of Dawsonville.

Black Rock Mountain State Park is 1,207 acres in northeastern Georgia, about 100 miles northeast of Atlanta and 10 miles south of the North Carolina border. Within the boundaries of the Chattahootchee National Forest, the park is named for Black Rock Mountain, which has an elevation of 3,600 feet. The very top of the mountain is a sheer rock escarpment composed of black granite, and the view from its summit encompasses some 80 miles. Although Black Rock's summit is bald, its sides are thickly wooded, mainly with oaks, hickories, tulip trees, honey locusts, and pines. Characteristic wildlife includes foxes, black bears, and wild turkeys, as well as an assortment of passerine birds.

The park's 17-acre lake is set aside for fishing only (no swimming or boating) and has camping and picnicking facilities. Hiking is the main activity, and there are 8 miles of trails, one of which runs for 5 miles and becomes quite rugged in some sections.

Black Rock Park has ten wood-frame cabins at the summit of the mountain. Five have views of the town of Clayton, and the others look out at woods. The cabins vary in size from two- to three-bedroom units that can accommodate from six to ten people. Each unit has a fully equipped kitchenette, an open porch, and a private bath and a half. Five cabins have fireplaces, and the other five have Franklin stoves.

Accommodations: 10 cabins with private bath. *Towels and linens:* Provided. *Cooking and eating utensils:* Provided. *Stove and refrigerator:* Provided. *Pets:* Not permitted. *Open:* All year. *Mailing address:* Mountain City, GA 30562. *Phone:* (404) 746-2141. *Driving instructions:* Black Rock Mountain State Park is off U.S. 441, about 3 miles north of Clayton.

Chattahoochee National Forest, in northern Georgia at the southern end of the Appalachian and Blue Ridge mountains, is bordered by Cherokee National Forest in Tennessee, Nantahala and Pisgah National Forests in North Carolina, and Sumter National Forest in South Carolina. Chattahoochee forest encompasses 855,922 acres and varies in elevation from around 1,000 feet to 4,784 feet at Brasstown Bald, the highest summit in Georgia. The terrain, which varies from gentle hills to rugged escarpments, is wooded primarily with oaks, hickories, pines, rhododendrons, mountain laurels, and wild azaleas. Among numerous lakes are Lake Conasauga, which is on top of a mountain, and Lake Winfield Scott, a famous trout lake. The Chattooga Wild and Scenic River is in the very northeast corner of the state and marks the boundary with South Carolina. The Chattooga—which was where the movie *Deliverance* was filmed—is an extremely popular white-water run; although no permit is required (school and commercial groups excepted) to raft on the river, forest rangers strongly suggest that all but the very experienced take one of the many guided raft trips rather than try it alone. Rangers also request that rafters register at one of the put-in points along the river.

Activities include camping, fishing, swimming, hunting, and hiking. A 70-mile section of the Appalachian Trail passes through the forest from Springer Mountain in Georgia to Bly Gap in North Carolina. Hunting is permitted in season, the major targets being deer, grouse, quail, wild turkeys, and black bears. The forest is close to several of Georgia's state parks and encompasses a downhill ski area and the Tallulah Gorge, which is 1,200 feet deep at one point and has a waterfall. *Mailing address:* Chattahoochee National Forest, 508 Oak Street, Gainesville, GA 30501 (attention: Rachel Schneider). *National Forest phone:* (404) 536-0541.

Lake Rabun Hotel

A rustic 1922 stone-and-wood lodge-type building, Lake Rabun Hotel is privately owned and sits at an elevation of 1,900 feet, across the road from Lake Rabun, which has 28 miles of shoreline. In a heavily wooded area, the hotel is surrounded by oaks, white pines, hemlocks, and dogwoods.

Of the sixteen guest rooms, six have semiprivate baths or half baths (toilet and sink), and the other ten share baths. The lobby has a large stone fireplace and handmade furniture fashioned from rhododendron and mountain laurel twigs. Guests are offered a complimentary Continental breakfast.

Accommodations: 16 rooms with shared bath. *Pets:* Not permitted. *Open:* April through October. *Mailing address:* Lake Rabun Hotel, Lakemont, GA 30552. *Phone:* (404) 782-4946. *Driving instructions:* From Clayton take U.S. 441 or 23 south for 6 miles, then turn right onto Lake Rabun Road; proceed for 150 feet and take a sharp left—follow this road for 3 miles, bearing right each time it forks. Look for the hotel on the right.

Cloudland Canyon State Park's 2,120 acres are in northwestern corner of Georgia, about 120 miles northwest of Atlanta, 10 miles east of the Alabama border, and 20 miles south of the Tennessee border. The park, on the western slopes of Lookout Mountain, ranges in elevation from 800 to 1,900 feet. A deep, scenic gorge formed by Sitton Gulch Creek runs through the park, with a scenic overlook perched above the abyss. Sitton Gulch Creek has several falls, one cascading 92 feet.

Activities include picnicking and hiking. The park has nature trails, a visitors' center, and a playground.

The park has sixteen cottages, five of which overlook the gorge, varying in size from two to three bedrooms and accommodating from six to ten people. Each cottage has a fireplace, a porch, carpeting, a kitchen, and a private bath with shower. The 11 cabins that don't overlook the gorge are secluded from one another and are located along a path.

Accommodations: 16 cottages with private bath. *Towels and linens:* Provided. *Cooking and eating utensils:* Provided. *Stove and refrigerator:* Provided. *Pets:* Not permitted. *Open:* All year. *Mailing address:* Route 2, Rising Fawn, GA 30738. *Phone:* (404) 657-4050. *Driving instructions:* Cloudlands Canyon State Park is off Route 136, about 21 miles northwest of La Fayette.

The 500-acre Crooked River State Park is in the southeastern corner of Georgia, about 5 miles due west of Cumberland Island and 7 miles north of the Florida border. In part an offshoot of the inland waterway, the Crooked River is certainly crooked, seeming to wind around and around itself. It's also brackish (mostly salt water) and surrounded by marsh areas filled with birds, especially during migration season, including little, green, black-crowned, and great blue herons; snowy and great egrets; ibises; a variety of ducks and geese; and ospreys and bald eagles. The terrain is wooded primarily with oaks, long leaf and slash pines, dogwoods, cedars, and palmettos. In the Crooked River, which extends inland about 80 miles, anglers go after *saltwater* fish—sea trout, whiting, and flounder. The river is also full of blue crabs and shrimp. The park has a swimming pool (seasonal), boat docks (no rentals), a miniature golf course (seasonal), hiking trails, and camping and picnicking facilities.

The park is 7 miles from the ocean, and visitors should consider a day trip to the Cumberland Island National Seashore, which is immediately off the Atlantic coast due east of the park.

The park has available eleven wood-frame cabins located next to the Crooked River. Two- and three-bedroom units, they can accommodate from eight to twelve people, and each has a fireplace and a screened porch, as well as a fully equipped kitchenette and a private bath.

Accommodations: 11 cabins with private bath. *Towels and linens:* Provided. *Cooking and eating utensils:* Provided. *Stove and refrigerator:* Provided. *Pets:* Not permitted. *Open:* All year. *Mailing address:* 3092 Spur 40, St. Marys, GA 31558. *Phone:* (912) 882-5256. *Driving instructions:* Go 12 miles east of Kingsland on Route 40, then 7 miles north on a spur of Route 40 to Crooked River State Park.

Cumberland Island National Seashore comprises some 36,544 acres, of which 26,153 are land—the rest being composed of salt marsh, river, and sound. Cumberland, the largest of Georgia's Golden Isles, is a mile or so off the Georgia coast, about 10 miles north of the Florida border, accessible only by boat.

The island seems enchanted, especially at its interior, which is filled with exotic flowers, palmettos, and live oaks draped with Spanish moss. Tree species include willow and laurel oak, longleaf and loblolly pine, and magnolia. The terrain is close to sea level, reaching a high elevation of about 40 feet, although the actual land mass varies with the tide. Bird life is spectacular, and in late summer and autumn the island is a haven for shore-birds—snowy and great egrets; great blue, little blue, Louisiana, and black-crowned night herons; glossy and white ibises; storks; pelicans; squadrons of sanderlings chasing the waves; hawks; black skimmers; and nearly 300 other species. Other wildlife in-cludes deer, raccoons, alligators, turtles, crabs, and oysters.

Cumberland Island is about 18 miles long, about 3 miles wide at its broadest, and arguably one of the most beautiful of the numerous barrier islands along the Atlantic, rivaling such places as Fire Island in New York and Assateague in Virginia. Access to the island is limited to two boatloads a day (140 people each). *Park mailing address:* Box 806, St. Marys, GA 31558. *Park phone:* (912) 882-4335.

Greyfield Inn

Privately owned by descendants of Thomas Carnegie (brother of the industrialist Andrew Carnegie), the Greyfield Inn is the last remaining structure of the original Carnegie estate, which at one time encompassed Cumberland Island in its entirety. Furnished with many antiques and family heirlooms, the inn has a good deal of dark-stained wood paneling, numerous Oriental rugs, subdued lighting, and a library filled with the classics.

The guest rooms vary considerably in size, from fairly small to quite large, and each is decorated differently. One accommoda-tion, the two-room "honeymoon suite," has its own sitting room and a large Victorian bed covered with an antique spread. All but one of the rooms share a bath.

The inn serves a light breakfast and a single-entrée dinner.

Accommodations: 9 rooms, 1 with private bath. *Pets:* Not permitted. *Open:* All year. *Mailing address:* Drawer B, Fernandina Beach, FL 32034. *Phone:* (904) 261-6408. *Driving instructions:* Cumberland Island is accessible either by the National Park Service boat from St. Mary's, Georgia, or by private boat from Fernandina Beach, Florida. Guests must make prior transportation arrangements with the inn.

Elijah Clark State Park is in northeastern Georgia, about 120 miles east of Atlanta on the shores of Clark Hill Lake, a 72,000-acre impoundment of the Savannah River. The work of the Army Corps of Engineers, this is the largest man-made lake east of the Mississippi. The 447-acre park takes its name from Elijah Clark, who moved to this area from North Carolina and is generally credited with keeping the Revolutionary War active in Georgia, preventing the British Army, which had already taken Savannah and numerous points north, from capturing the area. As a result the British burned his two log cabins to the ground. As part of its memorial to the hero, the park has reproductions of these log cabins, built according to historical specifications with eighteenth-century tools. They are furnished with antiques.

The slightly hilly terrain, wooded primarily with loblolly and jack pines, also includes such hardwoods as oaks, hickories, maples, sweet gums, some elms, and many dogwoods. Characteristic wildlife includes deer, foxes, raccoons, and an occasional black bear. Bird life is particularly rich—blue and green herons, mallards, pintails, mergansers, a variety of coots, green-winged teals, and red-tailed and -shouldered hawks. Bald and golden eagles are seen here frequently enough that park rangers suspect there are nesting pairs in the park.

There is a sand beach with a bathhouse, a nature trail, a miniature-golf course, boat-launching facilities (no rentals), picnicking and camping areas, and a lake full of fish. Anglers mainly go after largemouth bass, although hybrids—a cross of a white and a striped bass that results in an unusually large and fighting fish—may be the most sought-after fish in two to three years.

The park has twenty wood-frame cabins that are right on the water. Two-bedroom units, the cabins can accommodate as many as eight people, and each has a fully equipped kitchenette, a fireplace, a sundeck, and a screened porch. One cabin is set slightly back from the lake and has no view of the water.

Accommodations: 20 cabins with private bath. *Towels and linens:* Provided. *Stove and refrigerator:* Provided. *Pets:* Not permitted. *Open:* All year. *Mailing address:* Route 4, Box 293, Lincolnton, GA 30817. *Phone:* (404) 359-3458. *Driving instructions:* Elijah Clark State Park is off U.S. 378, 7 miles northeast of Lincolnton.

Franklin D. Roosevelt State Park comprises 4,980 acres in western Georgia, about 70 miles west of Macon and 20 miles east of the Alabama border, overlooking Pine Mountain Valley. The park was dedicated in honor of President Franklin Roosevelt, who spent much time at the "Little White House" in nearby Warm Springs where, in 1945, he died while posing for a portrait, which still hangs there in its unfinished state. A mixture of hard and soft woods in the park includes a large population of dogwoods, mountain laurels, and flame azaleas, and one area is rife with wild violets. Activities include swimming in the park's pool, horseback riding, picnicking, boating (there's a dock), and fishing. The 23-mile-long Pine Mountain Trail is well marked.

All but four of the park's twenty-one cabins are along the lake. Seventeen are constructed of logs and five are of wood-frame design. Each has either one or two bedrooms, a fireplace, a kitchen, and a private bath, and seventeen have a screened porch.

Accommodations: 21 cabins with private bath. *Towels and linens:* Provided. *Cooking and eating utensils:* Provided. *Stove and refrigerator:* Provided. *Pets:* Not permitted. *Open:* All year. *Mailing address:* PO Box 749, Pine Mountain, GA 31822. *Phone:* (404) 663-4858. *Driving instructions:* Franklin D. Roosevelt State Park is off Route 190, about 5 miles southeast of Pine Mountain.

Fort Mountain State Park, in northwestern Georgia about 80 miles north of Atlanta and 20 miles south of the Tennessee border, comprises 2,526 acres in an area generally considered the terminus of the Blue Ridge Mountains. The park is named for a stone wall encircling Fort Mountain (elevation 2,855 feet), which was possibly built by indigenous Indians in the twelfth century; other conjectures attribute the wall to the explorer Hernando De Soto's men or to British agents during the Revolutionary War. The wall is low—2 feet tall—and 1,855 feet long, with an average width of 12 feet. Periodically along its length, pits appear that may have been part of some sort of defensive mechanism. The mountain is thickly wooded with oaks, hickories, pines, rhododenrons, mountain laurels, dogwoods, wild azaleas, sourwood, and red maples; and slightly below its summit is a 17-acre lake. Its cold waters attract anglers, who come here after bass or trout. The park has a beach with a bathhouse, a few small waterfalls, and numerous scenic overlooks.

Fort Mountain State Park has available fifteen wood-frame cabins, which are in a wooded area. The cabins have either two or three bedrooms, a fully equipped kitchenette, a porch, a fireplace, and a private bath.

Accommodations: 15 cabins with private bath. *Towels and linens:* Provided. *Cooking and eating utensils:* Provided. *Stove and refrigerator:* Provided. *Pets:* Not permitted. *Open:* All year. *Mailing address:* Route 7, Box 1K, Chatsworth, GA 30705. *Phone:* (404) 695-2621. *Driving instructions:* Fort Mountain State Park is off U.S. 52, about 7 miles northeast of Chatsworth.

The 364-acre George T. Bagby State Park is in southwestern Georgia, about 70 miles south of Columbus, on the eastern shore of Walter F. George Reservoir, whose western shore is in Alabama. The reservoir, noted for its good fishing, is an impoundment of the Chattahoochee River, which runs through Georgia's level, wooded plains, through Florida, and into the Gulf of Mexico. The park is named for a Georgia politician and conservationist who spent thirteen years in the state's House of Representatives, directed the Georgia Bureau of Investigations and the Game and Fish Department, and who was deputy commissioner of the state's Department of Natural Resources.

Activities include fishing, boating, and waterskiing—there are launching facilities and no limitations on horsepower—and hiking on several trails that run through fertile wooded areas. There are numerous sites for picnicking, but the park has no swimming facilities.

Bagby State Park has five wood-frame cabins on the shore of the reservoir. They are two-bedroom units accommodating up to eight, and each has a porch and views of the lake and the surrounding woods, as well as a fully equipped kitchen and a living-dining area with a fireplace.

Accommodations: 5 cabins with private bath. *Towels and linens:* Provided. *Cooking and eating utensils:* Provided. *Stove and refrigerator:* Provided. *Pets:* Not permitted. *Open:* All year. *Mailing address:* Route 2, Box 116, Georgetown, GA 31754. *Phone:* (912) 768-2660. *Driving instructions:* George T. Bagby State Park is off Route 39, about 15 miles north of Fort Gaines.

Georgia Veterans Memorial State Park is in southwestern Georgia, about 30 miles northeast of Albany on the shores of Lake Blackshear, an 1,300-acre impoundment of the Flint River. The 1,307-acre park, dedicated in 1946, now honors all Georgia veterans who died for their country from the French and Indian War through World Wars I and II and Vietnam. An outdoor military display includes a B-29 bomber, an F-84 Thunderstreak, four tanks, and numerous pieces of field artillery, along with a small military museum. Fairly hilly with numerous open spaces, the terrain is wooded primarily with yellow, shortleaf, and loblolly pines, and red and cork oaks, including the largest cork oak in Georgia. At certain points along the shores of the lake, the trees are slightly underwater and draped with Spanish moss.

The park has a large population of deer, and in the swampy areas, which are difficult to reach except by boat, are alligators. Bird life includes quail, various species of geese and ducks, and many hawks. Park rangers think two bald eagles seen for some time in the area might be nesting residents. The park has a sand beach with a bathhouse, a swimming pool, two launching ramps (no rentals), and camping and picnicking facilities. Waterskiing and fishing are regular activities, with largemouth bass, crappies, bream, shellcrackers, and hybrids being the most sought-after fish.

The park has ten wood-frame cabins along the shore of Lake Blackshear. Two-bedroom units, they can accommodate eight, and each has a fireplace, a fully equipped kitchenette, and a private bath. Five have a screened porch, and the other five have a sun deck.

Accommodations: 10 cabins with private bath. *Towels and linens:* Provided. *Cooking and eating utensils:* Provided. *Stove and refrigerator:* Provided. *Pets:* Not permitted. *Open:* All year. *Mailing address:* Route 3, Cordele, GA 31015. *Phone:* (912) 273-2190. *Driving instructions:* The park is off U.S. 280, about 9 miles west of Cordele.

Hard Labor Creek comprises 5,805 acres in northern Georgia, about 55 miles east of Atlanta. There are two versions of how the creek got its name: One legend claims that the area, at one time part of a plantation, was extensively tilled by slaves who became exasperated with the rocky soil and dubbed the land and the creek that ran through it "hard labor." A second attributes the name to the difficulties encountered by Indians migrating through the area. They supposedly called the creek "hard labor" because it was so difficult to cross. Recently a group of boys crossing the creek came across an 18-foot alligator arduously laboring to get to its other side. They somehow managed to get it into the back of a pickup truck and take it to a veterinarian, who, performing a diagnosis from 20 feet, declared the alligator healthy as he rushed to the nearest phone.

The terrain, though for the most part flat and wooded with pines, has some hilly sections, particularly on the golf course, which Golf magazine categorized as one of the most beautiful and challenging public courses in the country. A 275-acre lake, which feeds the creek, has a beach with a bathhouse and boats for rent. Anglers fish the lake for bass, crappies, bream, and catfish, and other facilities include hiking, camping, picnicking, and playground areas and 30 horse stalls and 20 miles of riding trails.

The park has twenty wood-frame cabins in a wooded area. Several have views of the lake, fifteen have a screened porch, and another five have an open porch. All cabins, which are two-bedroom units accommodating eight, have a fireplace, a fully equipped kitchenette, and a private bath.

Accommodations: 20 cabins with private bath. *Towels and linens:* Provided. *Cooking and eating utensils:* Provided. *Stove and refrigerator:* Provided. *Pets:* Not permitted. *Open:* All year. *Mailing address:* PO Box 247, Rutledge, GA 30663. *Phone:* (404) 557-2863. *Driving instructions:* Hard Labor Creek is about 5 miles off I-20, near Rutledge.

Hart State Park's 147 acres are in northeastern Georgia, about 100 miles northeast of Atlanta on the shores of Hartwell Lake, an impoundment of the Savannah River that forms the border with South Carolina. The lake has 962 miles of shoreline and large populations of bass, crappies, pike, bream, and hybrids (a cross of a white and a striped bass). Boating is a leading activity, and facilities include two launching ramps. (The park has no boats for rent, but visitors can rent them at a nearby concession.) The lake also sees a good deal of waterskiing and sailing. The hilly terrain is wooded primarily with oaks, poplars, hickories, pines, wild azaleas, and mountain laurels, which provide color in spring and autumn. Wildlife includes large numbers of raccoons, rabbits, and squirrels, and deer are seen occasionally. Bluebirds, robins, jays, and hummingbirds are common, and in winter a flock of Canada geese settles on the lake.

The lake has a sandy beach with a bathhouse, and the inland areas offer picnicking and camping facilities. The Cricket Theater is the site of naturalist programs, including interpretative talks, slide shows, and hayrides.

The park has five mobile homes in a cove right beside the lake, each with a view. Two-bedroom units, the mobile homes can accommodate up to six, and each has a fully equipped kitchenette, a private bath, heat, and air-conditioning.

Accommodations: 5 mobile homes with private bath. *Towels and linens:* Provided. *Cooking and eating utensils:* Provided. *Stove and refrigerator:* Provided. *Pets:* Not permitted. *Open:* All year. *Mailing address:* 1515 Hart Park Road, Hartwell, GA 30643. *Phone:* (404) 376-8756. *Driving instructions:* Hart State Park is off U.S. 29, about 3 miles north of Hartwell.

Indian Springs State Park comprises 523 acres in central Georgia, roughly 50 miles southeast of Atlanta and 10 miles west of Oconee National Forest. The area was originally the province of the Creek Indians, who felt its sulfur spring benefited both body and spirit. In 1792 a government scout discovered the spring and confused its smell with that of gunpowder, and the area became known for some time as Gunpowder Springs. The State of Georgia acquired the land in a treaty with the Creeks, who later murdered their chief negotiator for betraying them to the white men.

The park, later developed by the Civilian Conservation Corps in the 1930s, has activities such as fishing, boating, hiking, picnicking, and miniature golf. There is a beach with a bathhouse, a boat dock with launching facilities and rentals, a playground, a self-guiding nature trail, and a museum with exhibits depicting the history of the Creek civilization.

The park's ten rustic wood-frame cabins are along a road that runs to the lake. Eight have a lake view, and each can accommodate eight people with two bedrooms, a screened porch, a kitchen, a fireplace, central heating and air-conditioning, and a private bath.

Accommodations: 10 cabins with private bath. *Towels and linens:* Provided. *Cooking and eating utensils:* Provided. *Stove and refrigerator:* Provided. *Pets:* Not permitted. *Open:* All year. *Mailing address:* Indian Springs, GA 30231. *Phone:* (404) 775-7241. *Driving instructions:* Indian Springs State Park is off Route 42, about 4 miles southeast of Jackson.

John Tanner State Park's 139 acres in northwestern Georgia, about 40 miles west of Atlanta and 10 miles east of the Alabama border, were developed in 1957 as a private recreation area by a local businessman, John Tanner, who in 1971 sold it to the state. A moderately hilly terrain is wooded mainly with oaks, hickories, tulip trees, pines, lots of dogwood, and a few redbuds. One of the park's two lakes has the largest sand beach in the Georgia park system. A bathhouse is near the beach area, and visitors can rent either paddleboats or canoes. The lakes feed several freshwater marshes that are heavily populated with mallards and wood ducks and that in spring are riotous with wildflowers. A permanent resident here is a solitary swan, whether bachelor or spinster nobody knows, and in winter a crane spends a few months. A nature trail half a mile long is at the head of one of the lakes, and there are enclosed picnic shelters, a one-mile exercise course that encircles the lake, a miniature-golf course, and camping and picnicking facilities.

Tanner Park Group Lodge and Apartments

The park has six one-bedroom efficiency apartments in a brick building overlooking the lake and the beach. The apartments can accommodate four, and each has a fully equipped kitchenette, a porch, and a private bath. A group lodge, which will accommodate forty people in six dormitory-type rooms, has a large kitchen, a dining-meeting room with a stone fireplace, a screened porch, and a private dock on a 12-acre lake.

Accommodations: 6 apartments with private bath and 1 group lodge with shared bath. *Towels and linens:* Not provided at the lodge. *Cooking and eating utensils:* Provided. *Stove and refrigerator:* Provided. *Pets:* Not permitted. *Open:* All year. *Mailing address:* 354 Tanner's Beach Road, Carrollton, GA 30117. *Phone:* (404) 832-7545. *Driving instructions:* John Tanner State Park is off Route 16, about 6 miles west of Carrollton.

Little Ocmulgee State Park's 1,397 acres are in southern Georgia, about 125 miles due west of Savannah. The park began during the Depression, when local citizens who wanted a recreational area started donating land along the Little Ocmulgee River. The Civilian Conservation Corps undertook most of the development, building a dam on the Little Ocmulgee, which created a 265-acre lake surrounded by sand hills wooded with Georgia pines and oaks and frequented by anglers, boaters, and water-skiers. Fishing boats and canoes are for rent, and there is a dock and launching facilities (there is no horsepower limitation on the lake). The park has a swimming pool, a few nature trails, and an eighteen-hole golf course with a clubhouse and club and cart rentals.

The park has ten wood-frame cabins along the shore of the lake, all with views of the water. They have either one or two bedrooms, and the larger cabins can accommodate as many as eight. Each has a fully equipped kitchen and a living-dining area and is heated and air-conditioned.

Accommodations: 10 cabins with private bath. *Towels and linens:* Provided. *Cooking and eating utensils:* Provided. *Stove and refrigerator:* Provided. *Pets:* Not permitted. *Open:* All year. *Mailing address:* PO Box 97, McRae, GA 31055. *Phone:* (912) 868-2832. *Driving instructions:* Little Ocmulgee State Park is off U.S. 319-441, roughly 2 miles north of McRae.

Magnolia Springs State Park, in eastern Georgia about 100 miles east of Macon and 20 miles west of the South Carolina border, is named for a cold-water spring that flows at a rate of about 9 million gallons a day, forming a small, crystal-clear pool. The 948-acre park is on the site of a Civil War prison that in 1864 was the largest prison in the world; many of its remains still stand, and a nature trail now winds around the old prison compound. The park, with a wide variety of passerine birds, is cruised occasionally by a hawk and wooded primarily with pines, oaks, magnolias, hickories, maples, and dogwoods. There are some sizable stands of wild azaleas here, and in spring the area is full of wildflowers. Among other wildlife are alligators who loll around in the lake, and turtles who probably avoid them.

There is a swimming pool, camping and picnicking facilities, and rowboat and paddleboat rentals. No swimming is allowed on the lake, which is probably fortunate considering its alligators, but the park has launching facilities, waterskiing, and fishing, especially for bass, bream, and catfishes. The park is next to the Millen National Fish Hatchery, which raises fish for stocking public and private waters and has a small aquarium housing fish and alligators.

The park has five wood-frame cabins in a wooded area overlooking the lake. They vary in size from two to three bedrooms and can accommodate either eight or twelve. Each has a fully equipped kitchenette, a screened porch, a fireplace, and a private bath.

Accommodations: 5 cabins with private bath. *Towels and linens:* Provided. *Cooking and eating utensils:* Provided. *Stove and refrigerator:* Provided. *Pets:* Not permitted. *Open:* All year. *Mailing address:* Route 5, Box 488, Millen, GA 30442. *Phone:* (912) 982-1660. *Driving instructions:* Magnolia Springs State Park is off U.S. 25, about 5 miles north of Millen.

Mistletoe State Park, named for a small town nearby, Mistletoe Corner, where the trees are heavily laden with mistletoe, comprises 1,920 acres in northeastern Georgia, about 110 miles east of Atlanta on the shores of Clark Hill Lake, a 78,000-acre impoundment of the Savannah River. The work of the Army Corps of Engineers, it is the largest man-made lake east of the Mississippi, with 1,200 miles of shoreline. The lake is rife with largemouth bass, crappies, and bream, and a population of hybrids—a cross of a white and a striped bass that results in an unusually large fighting fish—is growing rapidly. The park's terrain is relatively flat with a few hilly areas. Loblolly and jack pines are the predominant trees, and oaks and maples are also commonly found. There are many dogwoods (dogwood admirers should note that the trees begin to bloom here in late March). The park has a large herd of deer—the exact number unknown—and ten to fifteen at a time are often seen, especially at dawn, near the comfort stations.

The park has a sand beach with a bathhouse and a diving platform, three launching ramps, picnicking and camping facilities, a playground, and 6 miles of well-groomed and blazed nature trails that run through some of the more heavily wooded areas. A wildlife observation tower elevated about 15 feet overlooks a field in the middle of the woods. Dawn and dusk are the best times to watch.

The park has five wood-frame cabins directly on the lake. Each has a fully equipped kitchenette, two bedrooms and two baths, and a fireplace; each bedroom has its own porch.

Accommodations: 5 cabins with private bath. *Towels and linens:* Provided. *Cooking and eating utensils:* Provided. *Stove and refrigerator:* Provided. *Pets:* Not permitted. *Open:* All year. *Mailing address:* Route 1, Box 117F, Appling, GA 30802. *Phone:* (404) 541-0321. *Driving instructions:* Mistletoe State Park is 12 miles north of I-20 (exit 60).

Red Top Mountain State Park encompasses 1,950 acres in north-western Georgia, about 47 miles north of Atlanta along the shores of Lake Alltoona. Surveyors in the 1920s called the mountain "red top" because of the clay in the soil near its summit. A rather hilly terrain reaches elevations of 1,150 feet, and the predominant trees are loblolly pines, oaks, and dogwoods. Characteristic wildlife includes many deer, as well as raccoons, squirrels, and rabbits; the park supports numerous passerine birds, and during migrations, waterfowl stop by to rest on Lake Alltoona.

There is a sand beach with a bathhouse, picnicking and camping facilities, four launching ramps for boats—but no rentals—a miniature-golf course, and a playground. Many hikers use the trail system with a ¾-mile nature trail and a 7-mile hiking trail that skirts the lake's shore for a distance and then heads up toward the higher elevations, through thickly wooded areas. Anglers come to fish the lake for bass and crappies, and many boaters come to waterski.

The park has eighteen wood-frame cabins in a wooded area beside the lake. They are two-bedroom units accommodating up to eight, and each has a fully equipped kitchenette, a porch overlooking the water, a fireplace, and a private bath.

Accommodations: 18 cabins with private bath. *Towels and linens:* Provided. *Cooking and eating utensils:* Provided. *Stove and refrigerator:* Provided. *Pets:* Not permitted. *Open:* All year. *Mailing address:* Route 7, Cartersville, GA 30120. *Phone:* (404) 974-5183. *Driving instructions:* The park is 1 ½ miles east of the Red Top exit off I-75.

Seminole State Park, 343 acres in the southwestern corner of Georgia, is at once 10 miles north and east of the Florida border, on the shores of Lake Seminole, a 37,500-acre impoundment of the Chattahoochee and Flint rivers and Spring Creek. The terrain here is relatively flat and wooded with slash and longleaf pines, lots of dogwood, and several species of oak. Stands of red oaks are scattered throughout the park, and two of the cabins here are almost entirely surrounded by them. The park is named in honor of the Seminole Indians, who resided in the area long before white settlers came. Characteristic wildlife includes deer, foxes, and raccoons, and the area supports a large variety of passerine birds and a few hawks. The lake is rich with bass, perch, hybrids, and crappies, and visitors can rent either fishing or pontoon boats. There is also a sandy beach with a bathhouse, picnicking and camping facilities, a playground, and boat-launching facilities. Waterskiing is a regular park activity.

Seminole Park has ten wood-frame cabins, each accommodating six, in a wooded area beside the lake. Each has two bedrooms, a porch, a kitchenette, heat, and air-conditioning.

Accommodations: 10 cabins with private bath. *Towels and linens:* Provided. *Cooking and eating utensils:* Provided. *Stove and refrigerator:* Provided. *Pets:* Not permitted. *Open:* All year. *Mailing address:* Route 2, Donalsonville, GA 31745. *Phone:* (912) 861-3137. *Driving instructions:* Seminole State Park is off Route 39 about 16 miles south of Donalsonville.

Stephen C. Foster State Park, named after one of America's best-known songwriters, is in southeastern Georgia, roughly 230 miles southwest of Savannah and 100 miles northwest of Jacksonville, Florida. Its 80 acres are on Jones Island, in the midst of the 396,000-acre Okefenokee National Wildlife Refuge. Usually referred to as a swamp, the Okefenokee is actually an enormous peat-filled bog, wooded mainly with cypress and black gum but also including slash and loblolly pines, sweet gums, live oaks, and magnolias. The many Okefenokee waterways—one of which is the Suwannee River—are the color of tea from all the tannic acids discharged into their waters by the cypresses and other swamp plants. The wildlife is widely varied, with herons, egrets, ibises, sandhill cranes, anhingas, alligators, bobcats, and bears.

Visitors can rent canoes or motorboats to go fishing or boating, or they can launch their own craft at the park's launching site (motors must be electric or maximum 10 horsepower). The Trembling Earth Nature Trail, which begins near the boat basin, has a boardwalk running through various habitats.

The park has nine wood-frame cottages in a wooded area about 100 yards from the water. These two-bedroom units can accommodate as many as eight, and each has a screened porch, a kitchen, and a private bath with shower.

Accommodations: 9 cottages with private bath. *Towels and linens:* Provided. *Cooking and eating utensils:* Provided. *Stove and refrigerator:* Provided. *Pets:* Not permitted. *Open:* All year. *Mailing address:* Route 1, Fargo, GA 31631. *Phone:* (912) 637-5274. *Driving instructions:* From Fargo take U.S. 441 southeast for half a mile, then take Route 177 northeast for about 18 miles.

Tugaloo State Park's 393 acres are in northeastern Georgia, about 100 miles northeast of Atlanta, on a hilly, wooded peninsula jutting into the western shores of Hartwell Reservoir, which forms the border with South Carolina. The park was named after the Tugaloo River, which was impounded by Hartwell Dam and formed a 56,000-acre reservoir with 962 miles of shoreline. Boating, fishing, and swimming are among the activities, and facilities include a beach with a bathhouse, and launching and docking areas. Numerous trails wind through the park, including a self-guided nature trail, along with several picnicking areas, a playground, and a miniature-golf course. At the park's pavilion, bluegrass concerts are given frequently in summer.

Tugaloo Park's twenty wood-frame cabins are on the lake, have two bedrooms, and can accommodate up to eight. Each is heated and air-conditioned and comes with a fully equipped kitchen. Some cabins have screened porches, some have patios, and all have a fireplace and a private bath.

Accommodations: 20 cabins with private bath. *Towels and linens:* Provided. *Cooking and eating utensils:* Provided. *Stove and refrigerator:* Provided. *Pets:* Not permitted. *Open:* All year. *Mailing address:* Route 1, Box 300, Lavonia, GA 30553. *Phone:* (404) 356-4362. *Driving instructions:* Tugaloo State Park is off Route 328 about 6 miles north of Lavonia.

Unicoi State Park is in northeastern Georgia, in the Chattahoo-chee National Forest, about 100 miles northeast of Atlanta and 35 miles south of Brasstown Bald, the highest point (elevation 4,784 feet) in Georgia. The 1,023-acre mountainous terrain is wooded with pines and poplars, hemlocks and oaks, as well as a generous sprinkling of mountain laurels and rhododendrons, which decorate the mountains in spring. Visitors should travel just north of the park to Anna Ruby Falls on the slopes of Tray Mountain. Smith Creek, which flows into Unicoi Lake, is fed by two creeks that form a twin waterfall—Curtis Creek drops 153 feet, and York Creek, 50 feet.

Unicoi Lake has two beaches and a marina that rents rowboats and canoes during the summer. The Appalachian Trail runs near the park, making hiking one of the leading activities, along with bicycling, fishing, and tennis. There is a golf course adjacent to the park. A craft shop specializes in handmade Appalachian craft pieces, and the park sponsors craft demonstrations, Appalachian arts and crafts workshops, and programs in Appalachian culture.

Unicoi Lodge and Cabins

The park has two types of accommodations, including lodge rooms and cabins. Unicoi Lodge and Conference Center has 100 rooms arranged in four "lodging clusters," each with a common room and a fireplace. The clusters are arranged to make each one suitable for a conference, but conferences are only permitted in the common rooms if a single group occupies the entire cluster. The guest rooms and the common rooms are sleekly modern, nicely appointed, and paneled in cedar. Some guest rooms have lofts, and all have carpeting, individual climate controls, a telephone, and a private bath. The lodge complex houses a bright dining room with exposed-wood walls and chandeliers.

The park also has twenty-nine "teardrop," "barrel," and chalet-style cottages, 20 of which are in the woods near the lake. Architecturally interesting, built among the trees, and set on stilts, the cottages vary in size from one- to three-bedroom units. Twenty have a porch and a fireplace, are near the creek, and can accommodate from four to six people. Five are located on the road to Anna Ruby Falls.

Accommodations: 100 lodge rooms and 29 cottages, all with private bath. *Towels and linens:* Provided. *Cooking and eating utensils:* In cottages. *Stove and refrigerator:* In cottages. *Pets:* Not permitted. *Open:* All year. *Mailing address:* PO Box 256, Helen, GA 30545. *Phone:* (404) 878-2201. Reservations: (404) 878-2824. *Driving instructions:* Unicoi State Park is off Route 356, just north and east of Helen.

Vogel State Park is in northern Georgia, in the Chattahoochee National Forest about 75 miles north of Atlanta. In the Blue Ridge Mountains, the 221-acre park has an average elevation of about 2,450 feet and is thickly wooded with oaks, maples, beeches, mountain laurels, white pines, and cedars. It is named for the Vogel family, who donated the parkland to the state in 1928, having acquired 65,000 acres in the area, hoping it would be a good source for tanbark for their Milwaukee leather factory. Much to the benefit of the state, they discovered a better source of tanbark in South America. Among many scenic overlooks is Vogel Knob, from which Blairsville can be seen in the distance. A trail system includes a ½-mile nature trail, a 4½-mile hiking tail, and a 12-mile backpacking trail. The park is a stopover point for hikers on the Appalachian Trail, which is 3 miles away.

A 21-acre lake has a sand beach and a bathhouse, and visitors can rent paddleboats. At the beginning of trout season the Fish and Game Department stocks the lake with four hundred 8- to 10-inch rainbow trout. Among other facilities are baseball and badminton fields, picnicking and camping areas, and a miniature-golf course.

The park has thirty-six wood-frame cabins, some on a hill and some beside a stream. Several have lake views, each has a fireplace, and some have a porch. They range in size from one to three bedrooms and can accommodate up to ten people. Each cabin also has a fully equipped kitchenette and a private bath.

Accommodations: 36 cabins with private bath. *Towels and linens:* Provided. *Cooking and eating utensils:* Provided. *Stove and refrigerator:* Provided. *Pets:* Not permitted. *Open:* All year. *Mailing address:* Route 1, Box 1230, Blairsville, GA 30512. *Phone:* (404) 745-2628. *Driving instructions:* Vogel State Park is off U.S. 19-129, about 11 miles south of Blairsville.

Specifically designed for recreational activities for the handicapped, Will-A-Way Recreation Area is within Fort Yargo State Park, 1,814 acres in northern Georgia, about 40 miles northeast of Atlanta. Wooded mainly with pines and oaks, Will-A-Way has numerous facilities that are wheelchair accessible, including a paved nature trail that runs for a quarter of a mile through a section of hardwoods to a marshy area rife with waterfowl and wildflowers (especially in spring). Great blue herons and several species of egrets and ducks are frequently sighted here, and red-tailed hawks often cruise overhead. The recreation area has a beach and a pool that are wheelchair accessible, and visitors can rent pontoon boats that have been specially modified to accommodate those in wheelchairs.

Other facilities include picnicking areas and a fishing dock from which anglers can hook bass, crappies, bream, or catfishes.

Will-A-Way's special accommodations consist of three wood-frame cabins in a wooded area, with a partial view of the 261-acre lake, and a group camp. Of rustic design, the two-bedroom cabins will accommodate up to six. They are fully accessible, and each has a fully equipped kitchenette, a private bath, and a fireplace.

The group camp, also fully accessible, can accommodate up to 250 people in sixteen sleeping cottages arranged in four groups. The camp has a central dining hall with kitchen facilities.

Accommodations: 3 cabins with private bath and 1 group camp with shared bath. *Towels and linens:* Provided. *Cooking and eating utensils:* Provided. *Stove and refrigerator:* Provided. *Pets:* Not permitted. *Open:* All year. *Mailing address:* Winder, GA 30680. *Phone:* (404) 867-5313. *Driving instructions:* Will-A-Way Recreation Area is off Route 81 about a mile south of Winder.

Hawaii

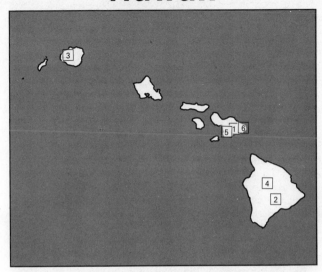

State map and tourist information: Hawaii Visitor's Bureau, 2270 Kalakaua Ave., Suite 804, Honolulu, HI 96815; 808-923-1811. **State parks:** *Information:* Div. of Parks, PO Box 621, Honolulu, HI 96809; 808-548-7455. *Entrance fees:* None. *Reservations:* Contact individual park. Deposits from $25 to 50% of full payment, check or credit card (certain parks only). Reservations recommended 6 months in advance for early June—early September; Mauna Kea 1 year in advance for early November—January. Maximum stay, 5 nights. *Restrictions:* No hunting, alcohol, pets, or camping vehicles. Children must be accompanied by an adult for camping. *Facilities:* Swimming and hiking trails, open all year.

Haleakala National Park is in southeastern Maui, the "Valley Isle." The island was formed by two volcanoes that millions of years ago emerged from the ocean floor and then became joined as an isthmus—in this case a valley—connected them. The 28,665-acre park is divided into three sections. Most of it consists of Haleakala Crater, a 7 ½-mile-long, 2 ½-mile-wide depression that drops some 3,000 feet from the highest summit along the rim, which reaches a height of 10,023 feet. Many multicolored cinder cones rise from the crater's floor and walls, some of them as high as 600 to 700 feet. Visitors may walk down into the crater on well-marked trails.

The park also includes a stretch along the ocean, as well as the Kipahulu Valley, which is marked by waterfalls and clear pools. The pools of the Oheo Gulch are frequented by swimmers used to cold water, although the swimming here can be dangerous when the water rushes in after a rainstorm. Another section of the park has an unusually lush rain forest, which receives some 250 inches of rain per year.

The National Park Service maintains three wood-frame cabins in Haleakala Crater, at elevations ranging from 6,300 to 7,200 feet. They are beside well-marked trails and can be reached only by hikes that range from five to eight hours. Each has twelve built-in bunks, cold running water (since water is scarce in the park, faucets may run dry), a kitchen with a wood stove, a dining table with benches, a potable water supply, and wood for the stove. Pit toilets are within 100 feet of the cabins. There is a maximum stay of two nights in the same cabin, and a limit of three nights a month in the crater. Reservations are a must; prospective visitors are advised to write the park at least three months in advance.

Accommodations: 3 cabins with shared privy. *Towels and linens:* Not provided. *Cooking and eating utensils:* Provided. *Stove:* Provided, with wood. *Refrigerator:* Not provided. *Pets:* Not permitted. *Open:* All year. *Mailing address:* PO Box 369, Makawao, Maui, HI 96768. *Phone:* (808) 572-9306. *Driving instructions:* The Haleakala visitors' center is 11 miles from the west entrance to the park, which is a one-hour drive from Kahului via Routes 37, 377, and 378.

Hawaii Volcanoes National Park encompasses 229,998 acres, more than 123,000 of which are designated wilderness. The park takes its name from its two volcanoes—Mauna Kea, at 13,796 feet the highest peak in the state, and Kilauea, elevation 4,077 feet. The first is extinct, but the second made the news when it erupted in 1983 and again in 1984, almost immediately after a major eruption by Mauna Loa, 25 miles away. The two volcanoes had not erupted together in more than a hundred years. The park operates a 24-hour-a-day information service ([808] 967-7977)—a "hot line," if you will—that informs callers of current or potential volcanic activity. During periods of activity, which are frequent, park officials put up temporary signs directing visitors to the best and safest vantage points.

The park encompasses everything from rain forests drenched by upward of 175 inches of precipitation a year to veritable deserts of lava dunes and to expansive, grass-carpeted meadows sprinkled with exotic trees such as tall lehuas. The many species of exotic flora include alpine silverswords, tree lobelias, shrubby violets, and twenty-two species of Hawaiian honeycreeper. There are 150 miles of trails, a bird sanctuary, an art center, interpretative programs, nature walks, and two extraordinarily scenic roads—Crater Rim Drive and Chain of Craters Road. *Park mailing address:* Superintendent, Hawaii Volcanoes National Park, HI 96718. *Park phone:* (808) 967-7311.

Volcano House—Namakani Paio Cabins

On the rim of Kilauea Crater, elevation 4,077 feet, is Volcano House, a two-story wooden lodge with thirty-seven guest rooms, a dining room, and a cocktail lounge and lobby, both with fireplaces in which fires have been burning continuously for more than a hundred years, even though the present Volcano House has been standing for only forty-two. When the previous building on this site burned down in 1940, park rangers snatched an ember from its fireplace and transferred it to a fireplace in a nearby building. Started by an original owner of Volcano House, the fire burns in tribute to the fire goddess Pele, daughter of the earth and the sky.

A rain forest of tree ferns surrounds Volcano House, whose dining-room windows overlook Kilauea Crater and, in the dis-

tance, Mauna Loa. Several guest rooms, the cocktail lounge, and a central porch also overlook the crater, which is rife with lehua flowers. At night you can occasionally see fire fountains and clouds lighted from below—the work of distant eruptions.

The rooms in Volcano House are smallish and accommodate a maximum of three. Each has carpeting and heaters, oversize furniture, and a private bath, but no television or radio.

Three miles (fifteen minutes) away, at Namakani Paio, are ten cabins administered by Volcano House. Each has a double and two single bunk beds and can accommodate a maximum of four persons. They have electric light but no outlets for appliances and no kitchen, although they share an outdoor grill. Cabins also share sanitation and shower facilities with nearby campsites.

Accommodations: 37 hotel rooms with private bath and 10 cabins with shared bath. *Towels and linens:* Provided (fee charged in cabins). *Cooking and eating utensils:* Not provided. *Stove:* Outdoor grills shared. *Refrigerator:* Not provided. *Pets:* Not permitted. *Open:* All year. *Mailing address:* Hawaii Volcanoes National Park, PO Box 53, HI 96718. *Phone:* (808) 967-7321. *Driving instructions:* Volcano House is 30 miles from Hilo, via Route 11, and 76 miles (or 2½ hours) from Kona, also on Route 11.

Kokee State Park, near the western coast of Kauai Island, is a 4,345-acre reserve at about 3,600 feet elevation adjacent to Waimea Canyon State Park, which preserves a large and deep multicolored gorge. Kokee State Park itself is above the Kalalau Valley, with its sheer rock cliffs, waterfalls, and lush vegetation. Kalalau Lookout, elevation 4,000 feet, overlooks the verdant valley and the Pacific Ocean at its mouth. There are about 45 miles of trails for hikers; some are easy strolls, but others require planning and a good deal of stamina. The Alakai Swamp Trail passes through a bog and ends at an overlook of the Hanalei beaches. Another trail passes through a rain forest in the valley.

Other activities include plum picking at the end of summer, trout fishing in any number of streams, and pig hunting in designated areas. *Park mailing address:* PO Box 1671, Lihue, HI 96766. *Park phone:* (808) 245-4444.

Kokee Lodge

At an elevation of 3,600 feet, Kokee Lodge has a lodge-restaurant and twelve housekeeping cabins. The lodge is right next to the Kokee Natural History Museum, which has interpretative displays of the area's flora, fauna, and geology, and sells books and maps. The restaurant serves breakfast and lunch every day but serves dinner only on Friday and Saturday nights.

The cabins range in size from one room to two-bedroom units accommodating from three to seven persons. Each has a kitchenette, a private bath with shower, a fireplace, and fireplace wood. The maximum stay here, however, is limited to five days.

Accommodations: 12 cabins with private bath. *Towels and linens:* Provided. *Cooking and eating utensils:* Provided. *Stove and refrigerator:* Provided. *Pets:* Not permitted. *Open:* All year. *Mailing address:* PO Box 819, Waimea, Kauai, HI 96796. *Phone:* (808) 335-6061. *Driving instructions:* From Lihue take Route 50 southwest to Waimea Canyon Road, then take Route 55 to the park. Total driving time is an hour and a half.

Mauna Kea State Park is on the island of Hawaii about 35 miles west of Hilo on the southern slope of Mauna Kea, at 13,796 feet the highest summit in Hawaii. Nearby Mauna Loa, 15 miles to the south, has recently erupted, producing a 30-foot-high, 100-yard-wide lava flow. Making its way over seven miles down the side of the volcano, it seems entirely likely that accumulations of lava around Mauna Loa's crater might increase its height. Before the eruption, Mauna Loa's elevation was 13,680 feet, or 116 feet lower than Mauna Kea. Visitors to Mauna Kea State Park will probably be able to see, in the distance, flashes of fire from Mauna Loa for some time.

Mauna Kea State Park, which comprises 700 acres, is on the slope of Mauna Kea at an elevation of 6,500 feet. The terrain is thinly wooded, with large sections of shrubland. Parts of the terrain are rugged, as is the access road, Saddle Road. (Visitors planning to come here should check the conditions of their car rental leases since several of the companies prohibit renters from taking cars along Saddle Road.) The park is surrounded by the Pohakuloa Game Area, with the result that wild pig, sheep, and bird hunting takes place immediately outside the park's perimeter. Hiking, picnicking, and birding are the only activities available. At certain times, the military carries on maneuvers in this area.

Mauna Kea State Park has seven wood-frame cabins in a thinly wooded area. Two-bedroom units, the cabins can accommodate up to six people. Each has a fully equipped kitchenette, a living room, and a private bath. Five of the cabins have fireplaces for which the park supplies one free load of firewood. The other two cabins are heated electrically. In addition, the park has two group lodges, each accommodating thirty-two people. These have central sanitary and shower facilities.

Accommodations: 7 cabins with private bath and 2 group units with shared bath. *Towels and linens:* Provided. *Cooking and eating utensils:* Provided. *Stove and refrigerator:* Provided. *Pets:* Not permitted. *Open:* All year. *Mailing address:* Mauna Kea State Park Cabins, c/o Department of Land and Natural Resources, Division of State Parks, PO Box 936, Hilo, HI 96721. *Phone:* (808) 961-7200. *Driving instructions:* Mauna Kea State Park is off Route 20 about 35 miles west of Hilo. Prospective guests should call or write for specific instructions.

In the Kula Forest Reserve on the island of Maui, Polipoli Springs State Recreation Area comprises 2 acres near the base of the western slope of Haleakala Crater. Formed by lava erupting upward through a crack in the Pacific Plate, Haleakala rises 10,023 feet above sea level, but the height of the volcano from its base below the ocean to its summit measures some 30,000 feet. Although the seismographic record suggests earthquake activity within the volcano, Haleakala hasn't erupted since 1790, when lava flowed down its southwest side and altered the coastline of Maui.

An extensive trail system winds through the Kula Forest Reserve and affords panoramic views. When the weather's clear, you can gaze over central and western Maui, Kahoolawe, Molokai, and Lanai. The wildlife here is as exotic as the vegetation, and birders will be especially interested in red 'i'iwis and Maui parrotbills. The park has pig- and bird-hunting seasons.

The recreation area has one cabin, which will accommodate up to ten people. The three-bedroom wooden building, at an elevation of 6,200 feet in the fog belt of Kula Forest, is fully furnished and comes with a rest room and a shower (the shower has cold water only, but the sink has hot water), linens but no towels, a gas stove, and cooking and eating utensils. There is no electricity, but a gas heater and four Coleman lanterns are supplied. The cabin can be reached only by four-wheel-drive vehicles.

Accommodations: 1 cabin with private bath. *Linens:* Provided. *Towels:* Not provided. *Cooking and eating utensils:* Provided. *Stove:* Provided. *Refrigerator:* Not provided. *Pets:* Not permitted. *Open:* All year. *Mailing address:* PO Box 1049, Wailuku, Maui, HI 96793. *Phone:* (808) 244-4354. *Driving instructions:* Polipoli Springs State Recreation Area is 9.7 miles upland from Kula on Waipoli Road, which is off Kekaulike Avenue (Route 377). A four-wheel-drive vehicle is necessary.

Waianapanapa State Park's 120 acres are at the eastern tip of Maui. Among its natural wonders are the legendary Waianapanapa cave and *heiau,* a place of ancient worship. A wildly rugged terrain includes a coastline of low volcanic cliffs, where adventurous types will want to try a hike on an ancient trail running along the coast. Other points of interest are a natural stone arch, blowholes, sea stacks, and a small black-sand beach frequented by fishermen and swimmers. Visitors should keep in mind, however, that the ocean is extremely rough and dangerous at times, especially when the wind comes up.

The park has twelve housekeeping cabins 300 yards from the beach. They are fully furnished, and each has an electric range, a refrigerator, towels and linens, cooking and eating utensils, and a rest room and shower.

Accommodations: 12 cabins with private bath. *Towels and linens:* Provided. *Cooking and eating utensils:* Provided. *Stove and refrigerator:* Provided. *Pets:* Not permitted. *Open:* All year. *Mailing address:* PO Box 1049, Wailuku, Maui, HI 96793. *Phone:* (808) 244-4354. *Driving instructions:* Waianapanapa State Park is off Hana Highway (Route 360), 52.8 miles east of Kahului Airport.

Idaho

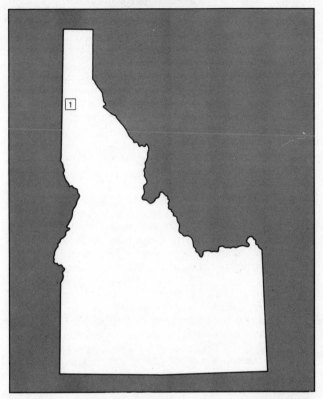

State map and tourist information: Dept. of Economic Development, Statehouse Mall, Boise, ID 83720; 208-234-2470. **State parks:** *Information:* Dept. of Parks, Statehouse Mall, Boise, ID 83720; 208-334-2154. *Entrance fees:* $1 per vehicle (certain parks only); waived for lodgers. *Reservations:* Contact individual lodgings. Reservations recommended 6 to 8 weeks in advance for early June—early September. Deposit (certain lodgings only) payable by check or credit cards. *Restrictions:* Hunting limited to certain parks only. Dogs must be leashed (not allowed in lodgings). *Facilities:* Swimming and boating, June—September. Cross-country skiing and snowmobiling, December—March.

Heyburn State Park is in northwestern Idaho, about 30 miles west of Kellogg and 40 miles southeast of Spokane, Washington. The park consists of 7,838 acres, 2,333 of them water, along the shores of Lake Coeur d'Alene, in a section of Idaho that has many lakes formed by retreating glaciers. The park's three interconnected lakes are the site of a curious phenomenon: If you happen to be out on the lakes, you can see a channel that looks like a strong ocean current, which is the St. Joe River actually flowing through two of them.

The lakes are surrounded by 3,000-foot-tall mountains, which are thickly wooded, primarily with conifers. Predominant are white and red firs, tamaracks, pond pines and, most of all, white pines. The largest stand of white pines in the entire country is in St. Joe National Forest, a 100-square-mile reserve about 10 miles south of Heyburn State Park.

Park activities include fishing, boating, camping, hiking, swimming, sledding, cross-country skiing, snowmobiling, ice-skating, and ice fishing. The wide variety of wildlife includes deer, elks, and bears. Bird life is especially rich, with trumpeter swans, little and great blue herons, bald eagles, and one of the largest concentrations of ospreys in the country. *Park phone:* (208) 686-1308.

Rocky Point Lodge

Rocky Point Lodge, 100 yards from the shore of Lake Coeur d'Alene and overlooking it, comprises a rustic log building built in the 1930s by the Civilian Conservation Corps, a small motel unit, a restaurant, a cocktail lounge, and a marina. The main lodge has six guest rooms on its top floor and a restaurant, a cocktail lounge with a stone fireplace, and a game room on its ground floor.

Guest rooms in the main lodge are simply furnished, have hardwood floors, and share two baths at the end of the hall. The motel unit has eight guest rooms, each with wall-to-wall carpeting and a kitchenette. Most rooms, in both the lodge and motel, have views of the lake.

The marina offers launching facilities, gasoline, and rentals of fishing boats with small motors. The complex also includes a store that sells groceries and sundries.

Accommodations: 14 rooms, 8 with private bath. *Towels and linens:* Provided. *Cooking and eating utensils:* Not provided. *Stove and refrigerator:* In motel units. *Pets:* Check in advance. *Open:* June through September. *Mailing address:* Heyburn State Park, Route 1, Box 218, Plummer, ID 83851. *Phone:* (208) 686-1380 in summer; (208) 686-9967 off season. *Driving instructions:* Heyburn State Park is on Route 5 about 6 miles east of Plummer.

Benewah Resort Lodge and Cabins

On the shore of Lake Coeur d'Alene, Benewah Resort consists of five wood-frame cabins, a marina, and a large cedar-frame lodge that has two dining rooms on two levels overlooking the lake, a cocktail lounge, and a game room with billiard and card tables.

The cabins, each with a kitchenette, can accommodate from two to four people. The cabins have no running water, but sanitary and shower facilities are in a central location. Campgrounds and a trailer court are adjacent to the complex, which also includes a store selling groceries and sundries. The marina has rowboats for rent.

Accommodations: 5 cabins with shared bath. *Towels:* Not provided. *Linens:* Provided. *Cooking and eating utensils:* Not provided. *Stove and refrigerator:* Provided. *Pets:* Permitted with advance notice. *Open:* Mid-April through October. *Mailing address:* St. Maries, ID 83861. *Phone:* (208) 245-3288. *Driving instructions:* Heyburn State Park is on Route 5 about 6 miles east of Plummer.

Illinois

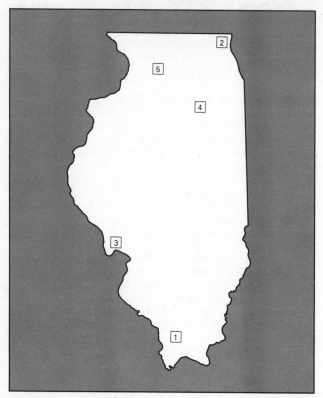

State map and tourist information: Dept. of Commerce, Office of Tourism, 620 E. Adam St., Springfield, IL 62701; 217-782-7139. **State parks:** *Information:* Dept. of Conservation, Bureau of Lands & Historical Sites, 405 E. Washington St., Springfield, IL 62706; 217-782-6752. *Entrance fees:* None. *Reservations:* Contact individual park; deposit and reservation procedures vary. Reservations recommended at least 6 weeks in advance for mid-April—early October. *Restrictions:* Hunting limited to certain parks only. Children under 17 must be accompanied by an adult at all times. Dogs must be leashed (not allowed in lodgings). *Facilities:* Swimming, boating, and canoeing, Memorial Day—Labor Day. Golf, tennis, hiking, bicycling, and horseback riding, April—October.

Giant City State Park was named for a group of huge blocks of sandstone that resemble, except for the absence of taxicabs and other hallmarks of civilization, city streets. The blocks, at one time part of a larger formation, which split into sections as softer rock beneath it eroded, apparently slid down a slippery shale slope to their current positions.

The park is in southwestern Illinois, about 12 miles south of Carbondale, and consists of 3,694 acres. It is bordered on the east and west by the Shawnee National Forest, which takes up almost the entire southern tip of Illinois.

The park's attractions include the Devil's Stand-Table, a tall sandstone formation with a natural platform on top, and the Stone Fort, a primitive structure of loose stones enclosing several acres on top of an 80-foot sandstone cliff. (The structure was apparently used to trap buffalo.) The park terrain is wooded with tulip trees, sweet gums, winged elms, red maples, and 71 other species, including Hercules'-club, whose bark is an old-time remedy for toothache. (Chewing the bark or leaves numbs the mouth.) Indigenous flowers include trillium, spring beauty, jack-in-the-pulpit, shooting star, and 166 other species.

The park has a reconstructed cabin representative of life in the 1880s, as well as a strange-looking water tank with an observation tower, which won the 1972 "Steel Tank of the Year Award" for "daring artistic design." There are miles of interpretative trails plus fishing and boating facilities on Little Grassy Lake, the shore of which the park leases from the U.S. Fish and Wildlife Service. *Park phone:* (618) 457-4836.

Giant City State Park Lodge and Cabins

In the southern part of the park is the stone-and-log Giant City State Park Lodge. The main edifice and the chimney were built with multicolored stone, and the balconies were built with logs. The building has a large lounge and dining room, a snack bar, and a banquet hall.

The lodge also has twelve modern cabins with heat, air-conditioning, wall-to-wall carpeting, television, and private baths.

Accommodations: 12 cabins with private bath. *Towels and linens:* Provided. *Cooking and eating utensils:* Not provided. *Stove and refrigerator:* Not provided. *Pets:* Permitted on leashes only. *Open:* March 1 through November 20. *Mailing address:* Giant City State Park, PO Box 57, Makanda, IL 62958. *Phone:* (618) 457-4921. *Driving instructions:* Giant City State Park is roughly 12 miles south of Carbondale off U.S. 51.

Reminder: Rates and credit-card information are listed in the index.

Illinois Beach State Park, north of Chicago, consists of 5,000 acres that follow the shore of Lake Michigan for 7½ miles. The park, famous for its dunes and beach, is divided into three sections—a recreation section, a nature-study area, and a wildlife refuge. The Dead River, which drains the dunes and the uplands into Lake Michigan, flows through and got its name because it turns into a pond when its mouth gets blocked by sand dunes created by storms on the lake. When sufficient water accumulates, however, it erodes channels through the sandbars and becomes a river again.

Another feature of the park is its man-made pine forest, which was planted by a late-nineteenth-century nurseryman who scattered seeds along the ridges south of the Dead River. The area is wooded primarily with Austrian and Scotch pines, although a few eastern white and pitch pines took hold as well.

The park has stands of scrub oak (black oak primarily) on some of its sandy ridges and supports more than five hundred species of plants—sea rocket, creeping juniper, dune willow, lupine, and bearberry, to name a few. Bird life is abundant, especially during migration: Bald eagles, ospreys, and peregrine falcons occasionally pass over; and all manner of geese, herons, and diving ducks stop by on their way north or south.

The park, open all year, has many hiking trails and 7½ miles of beach complete with three bathhouses with hot showers, dressing rooms, and toilets. *Park phone:* (312) 662-4811 or 662-4828.

Illinois Beach Holiday Inn Resort

Illinois Beach Holiday Inn Resort is a 96-room stone and glass building. The guest rooms feature air-conditioning and color television; and the lodge has a year-round indoor pool, dining facilities, a snack bar, a game room, a health club, saunas, a souvenir and gift shop, and a cocktail lounge. The facilities also include tennis and shuffleboard courts, and a golf course and riding stables are close by.

Accommodations: 96 rooms with private bath. *Pets:* Permitted on leashes only. *Open:* All year. *Mailing address:* Lakefront, Zion, IL 60099. *Phone:* (312) 249-2100. *Driving instructions:* Illinois Beach State Park is off Route 32, roughly 2 miles south of Zion and fewer than 10 miles north of North Chicago.

Immediately north of the confluence of the Illinois and Mississippi rivers, Pere Marquette State Park is a 7,245-acre reserve primarily perched on bluffs overlooking the Illinois River. The park, in southwestern Illinois, was named for Père (Father) Jacques Marquette, who arrived here in 1673 with the explorer Louis Jolliet.

The park contains eighteen sites indicating the presence of prehistoric peoples. One of these sites was a village located where the park lodge currently stands. The park's terrain is higher than that around it, and from several points along the bluffs, expansive vistas of the Illinois River and its backwaters can be seen.

Activities include fishing, boating, and horseback riding. A concession in the park arranges for scenic motorboat rides, and horses are available at the park stables. The park has more than 15 miles of hiking trails and a visitors' center with visual displays on the history of the park and the area. *Park mailing address:* Box 158, Grafton, IL 62037. *Park phone:* (618) 786-3323.

Pere Marquette Lodge and Guest Houses

Constructed in the 1930s by the Civilian Conservation Corps, Pere Marquette Lodge is an 18-bedroom stone-and-wood building in the southwestern corner of the park. It has a dining room, a large rustic lounge with a 700-ton stone fireplace, and one of the world's largest chess sets, a 12-foot-square board with figures 3½ feet tall.

The lodge also offers six four-room guest houses and a five-room guest house. The lodge rooms, as well as those in the guest houses, have heat, air-conditioning, televison, and private baths. Although there are no housekeeping facilities in the guest houses, the lodge has a swimming pool and a five-hole, par-three golf course.

The lodge and quest cottages are undergoing renovations during 1986 and 1987—visitors should make certain that their reservations for a stay don't conflict with construction work.

Accommodations: 17 lodge rooms and 29 guest-house rooms, all with private bath. *Pets:* Permitted if leashed. *Open:* All year. *Mailing address:* Pere Marquette State Park, PO Box 75, Grafton, IL 62037. *Phone:* (618) 786-3351. *Driving instructions:* Pere Marquette State Park is off Route 100, 5 miles west of Grafton.

Starved Rock State Park, in north-central Illinois, roughly 80 miles southwest of Chicago and 60 miles northeast of Peoria, is 2,524 acres bordered to the north by the Illinois River, about 5 miles of whose shoreline is parkland, and to the west by a 500-acre nature preserve. It got its name from an old Indian legend of how the Potawatomi Indians avenged the death of Pontiac, chief of their allies the Ottowa. Pontiac, the legend has it, was murdered by an Illiniwek Indian during a tribal council, infuriating the Potawatomi so intensely that they attacked the Illiniwek, who fled to the top of a 125-foot sandstone butte to take refuge. The Potawatomi surrounded the rock, and the besieged Illiniwek starved.

Although surrounded by flatland, the terrain next to the Illinois River is rocky and forested. The park has eighteen canyons formed of Saint Peter's sandstone eroded by streams. At the head of each stream, you can see waterfalls during the spring thaw and periods of heavy rain. (Regardless of weather or season, there's always a waterfall at the head of St. Louis Canyon.) The park contains several different habitats, and a wide variety of trees are in evidence: Black, white, and red oaks; basswoods; sugar maples; red and white cedars; cottonwoods; black willows; and ashes, to name a few.

The park's plant life includes witch hazels, wild hydrangeas, trilliums, harebell, spiderworts, wild irises, and skunk cabbages. (Skunk cabbages appear in the spring and generate so much metabolic heat that they melt the snow around them.) The park, open all year, is particularly rich in bird life: Cedar waxwings, cliff swallows, wood ducks, indigo buntings, and red-tailed hawks are all common. White-tailed deer and flying squirrels are also abundant. *Park mailing address:* Box 116, Utica, IL 61373. *Park phone:* (815) 667-4726.

Starved Rock Lodge and Cabins

Perched on a high bluff immediately southwest of Starved Rock, Starved Rock Lodge is a 45-bedroom stone-and-log building, most of which was constructed in the 1930s by the Civilian Conservation Corps. All the rooms in the lodge are air-conditioned, and the building has a pine-paneled dining room and a lounge with a double fireplace. The lodge also has 24 cabins, each of which has heat, air-conditioning, and a complete bath.

Accommodations: 45 lodge rooms and 24 cabins, all with private bath. *Open:* All year. *Mailing address:* PO Box 471, Utica, IL 61373. *Phone:* (815) 667-4211. *Driving instructions:* Starved Rock State Park is about 4 miles east of Oglesby, at the intersection of Routes 178 and 71, 4 miles south of I-80.

Reminder: Rates and credit-card information are listed in the index.

White Pines Forest State Park, a 385-acre tract in northwestern Illinois about 40 miles west of De Kalb, takes its name from the extensive virgin stand of eastern white pines it was mandated to preserve. Eastern white pines are among the largest and most beautiful of the northeastern conifers. Extensively harvested ever since the Pilgrims arrived at Plymouth Rock, their size and abundance gave the impression that they were an inexhaustible source of lumber. The stand of eastern white pines in White Pines Forest State Park is the last such stand in Illinois, which acquired it for preservation in 1927.

The Indians who occupied this area until the 1830s considered the eastern white pine a valuable medicinal resource and apparently used its inner bark as a cure for a variety of lung diseases. They took "saunas" in tepees suffused with smoke from its burning needles. Black Hawk, a Sac Indian warrior chief who refused to give up land to the white men, fought some of his final battles in this area.

In addition to the eastern white pines, the park contains an abundance of hardwoods, including oaks, elms, ashes, maples, and hickories, as well as many flowering plants such as spring beauties, trout lilies, bloodroots, and Solomon's seals. The park has miles of hiking trails and, in summer, interpretative programs.

White Pines Park Lodge and Cabins

In the northeastern section of the park, where Whispering Pine Trail meets Look Out Trail, are the White Pines Park Lodge and its associated cabins. The lodge, which is L-shaped, has a lounge decorated with Indian motifs and a dining room. Most of the cabins, which are arranged in two rows just north of the lodge, have one room, although a few have two or four bedrooms (those with four have two baths). The dining room serves breakfast, lunch, and dinner and is open from 8 A.M. to 6 P.M.

Accommodations: 16 cabins with private bath. *Towels and linens:* Provided. *Cooking and eating utensils:* Not provided. *Stove and refrigerator:* Not provided. *Pets:* Permitted if on leashes. *Mailing address:* 6712 W. Pines Road, Mount Morris, IL 61054. *Phone:* (815) 946-3817. *Driving instructions:* White Pines Forest State Park is off U.S. 52, 12 miles north of Dixon, Illinois.

Indiana

State map and tourist information: Dept. of Commerce, Tourism Div., 1 N. Capitol Ave., Indianapolis, IN 46204; 800-858-8073 (out-of-state), 800-622-4464 (in-state). **State parks:** *Information:* Dept. of Natural Resources, Div. of State Parks, 616 State House Bldg., Indianapolis, IN 46204; 317-232-4124 (out-of-state), 800-622-4931 (in-state). *Entrance fees:* $1.50 per vehicle; waived after first admittance for lodgers. *Reservations:* Contact individual lodgings. Deposit for first night's lodgings, payable by check, required 10 days in advance. Reservations recommended two to three months in advance for early May—early September and early November—January. Accepted up to a year in advance. *Restrictions:* No hunting. Children under 18 must be accompanied by an adult (when camping). Dogs must be leashed (not allowed in lodgings). *Facilities:* Swimming and interpretative programs, Mem. Day—Labor Day. Boating and tennis, April—October.

Brown County State Park is 15,543 acres in south-central Indiana immediately north of Hoosier National Forest and roughly mid-way betwen Bloomington and Columbus, Indiana. The area is one of wooded hills, with extensive stands of hardwoods setting the tone, especially in autumn, when the turning leaves color the hills with yellows, reds, and oranges.

The park's facilities include an Olympic-size swimming pool, an archery range, bridle trails (there's a separate camping area for people who bring horses), picnic areas, playgrounds, a nature center, and miles of hiking trails. *Park mailing address:* Box 116, Nashville, IN 47448. *Park phone:* (812) 988-6406.

Abe Martin Lodge and Cabins

Built in 1932, Abe Martin Lodge is a sixteen-room, single-story brick building with twenty-three wooden cabins scattered around it. The lodge has a large lobby with two fireplaces. Its rustic dining room with brick walls and an exposed-beam ceiling serves three meals a day.

The guest rooms here are clean, comfortable, and modern, and many offer fine views. On Skunk Ridge are an additional twenty modern housekeeping cabins, each of which has two bedrooms, a kitchen, a bathroom, a living room, and a deck overlooking woods. These cabins are two stories high, and can accommodate as many as eight people. Each has a wood stove.

Accommodations: 16 lodge rooms and 43 cabins, all with private bath. *Towels and linens:* Provided. *Cooking and eating utensils:* In housekeeping cabins. *Stove and refrigerator:* In housekeeping cabins. *Pets:* Not permitted. *Open:* All year. *Mailing address:* Brown County State Park, PO Box 25, Nashville, IN 47448. *Phone:* (812) 988-4418. *Driving instructions:* The park is 3 miles south of the Nashville, Indiana, business district on Route 135.

Chain O' Lakes State Park's 2,678 acres are in northeastern Indiana, about 30 miles northwest of Fort Wayne. This general area is Indiana's Lake Country; and indeed, Chain O' Lakes State Park has eleven lakes formed by glaciers, nine connected by channels. The terrain is hilly and wooded primarily with oaks and maples and several varieties of conifers. Visitors can rent either rowboats or canoes, but motorboats are allowed only if equipped with electric trolling motors. In addition to boating, fishing is popular; anglers come home primarily with panfish and trout.

Other activities include swimming (there's a beach with a bathhouse), bicycling (rentals available), and hiking. In winter ice-skating and ice-fishing are popular, and the park has several cross-country ski trails including one three-quarters of a mile long and another a little less than 3 miles long.

Chain O' Lakes State Park has eighteen rustic wooden cabins of a split A-frame design with skylight windows and screened porches, each with a swing and a picnic table. Each cabin has two bedrooms, a private bath with a shower, and a living room that includes two couches, two easy chairs, and a wood stove. The cabins are on a heavily wooded hillside that overlooks Long Lake.

Accommodations: 18 cabins with private bath. *Towels and linens:* Not provided. *Cooking and eating utensils:* Not provided. *Stove and refrigerator:* Provided. *Pets:* Not permitted. *Open:* April through October. *Mailing address:* Route 2, Box 54, Albion, IN 46701. *Phone:* (219) 636-2654. *Driving instructions:* Chain O' Lakes State Park is on Route 9 about 5 miles southeast of Albion.

Clifty Inn

Chain O' Lakes State Park

Clifty Falls State Park has 1,360 acres across the Ohio River from Milton, Kentucky. The park takes its name from various waterfalls, the largest being Big Clifty Falls, which plummets more than 70 feet over a sheer rock ledge to the canyon floor. Trails meander through the park and skirt its precipitous cliffs and canyons. Littered with boulders, the bottoms of some parts of Little Creek Canyon are illuminated by sunlight only briefly before and after noon, a phenomenon that recalls Black Canyon in Colorado.

The park has a well-staffed nature center with exhibits on the natural history of the area, as well as an Olympic-size swimming pool with a 65-foot waterslide, tennis courts, a cultural program with performances during the summer, and picnic and playground areas. *Park mailing address:* 1501 Green Road, Madison, IN 47250. *Park phone:* (812) 273-5495.

Clifty Inn

Overlooking the Ohio River, the Clifty Inn is a group of sleek, modern wooden structures, starkly but attractively rectilinear. The inn's dining room seats 250 and has random-width pine flooring, wood-paneled walls, and a view of the Ohio River. The inn's lounge has wood paneling and wooden floors, as well as casual lounging furniture and a fireplace. The facilities include both a large banquet or conference hall that overlooks the town of Madison and a smaller dining room that can accommodate as many as fifty people. The guest rooms are modern, and each comes with color television and a telephone.

Accommodations: 72 rooms with private bath. *Pets:* Not permitted. *Open:* All year. *Mailing address:* Box 387, Madison, IN 47250. *Phone:* (812) 265-4135. *Driving instructions:* Clifty Falls State Park is off Route 62, about a mile northeast of Hanover.

In southwestern Indiana's Spencer County, Lincoln State Park is a 1,747-acre reserve across the road from the Lincoln Boyhood National Memorial. Operated by the National Park Service, the memorial preserves such things as the Lincoln cabin site and the Historic Trail of Stones and has a building with exhibits on Abraham Lincoln's life.

Lincoln State Park itself is an example of the wooded, rolling hills of southwestern Indiana. The area is thick with oaks, maples, poplars, and a variety of pines, along with many dogwoods and redbuds, which flower in early spring.

The park has an 85-acre lake with a beach and a bathhouse. Visitors can rent both canoes and rowboats, and motorboating is permitted but only with electric trolling motors. Four well-marked hiking trails, ranging in difficulty from easy to moderate, wind through the park.

A hundred or so yards from the lake, in a grove of pines, are ten two-bedroom cabins constructed of western cedar. Of the two bedrooms, one has a double bed, and the other has two bunk beds. The cabins come equipped with stove and refrigerator and have a private bath with a shower. They're paneled with cedar and have a combination kitchen, dining room, and sitting area. Each cabin has a screened porch.

Accommodations: 10 cabins with private bath. *Towels and linens:* Not provided. *Pillows:* Provided. *Cooking and eating utensils:* Cooking utensils only. *Stove and refrigerator:* Provided. *Pets:* Not permitted. *Open:* April 1 through the Sunday after Thanksgiving. *Mailing address:* Box 216, Lincoln City, IN 47552. *Phone:* (812) 937-4710. *Driving instructions:* The cabins are 4 miles south of Dale on Route 231.

An 1,833-acre reserve in southwestern Indiana, roughly 15 miles northwest of Bloomington, McCormick's Creek State Park, named after an early settler, was the first state park in Indiana. It was dedicated as part of Indiana's centennial celebration in 1916.

The terrain is heavily wooded, and its most notable feature is a limestone canyon more than 95 feet deep. The canyon was formed by McCormick's Creek, at one time an underground stream which eroded a tunnel through the limestone bedrock, the roof of which finally caved in to form the canyon. At one place in the canyon there's a delicate waterfall, overhung by trees and surrounded by limestone cliffs.

Activities include horseback riding, hiking, swimming, tennis, and fishing, and the park has a visitors' center and naturalist service.

In a wooded area in the southwestern section of the park are fourteen wood-frame cabins. They can each accommodate as many as six people and are simply furnished (table and chairs, two bunk beds, twin beds). They have gas stoves for heat, screened porches, and bathrooms with hot and cold running water.

Accommodations: 14 cabins with private bath. *Towels and linens:* Not provided. *Cooking and eating utensils:* Not provided. *Stove and refrigerator:* Provided. *Pets:* Not permitted. *Open:* April through November. *Mailing address:* Route 1, Box 72, Spencer, IN 47460. *Phone:* (812) 829-2235.

Canyon Inn

Built in something of a Georgian style, Canyon Inn has been modernized and added to over the years. Originally a farmhouse, it was for a time owned by a physician who operated it as a sanatorium and orphanage. It has two-story-high fluted columns before its entrance, the facade on either side faced with brick.

The inn has a column-supported dining room that holds 175 people, a large banquet and meeting hall with a cathedral ceiling and wrought-iron chandeliers, a rustic lounge with a brick fireplace and molded ceilings, an outdoor swimming pool, and a recreation center with facilities for handball, basketball, shuffleboard, volleyball, billiards, and table tennis. The guest rooms

come with color television and telephones.

Accommodations: 78 rooms with private bath. *Open:* All year. *Mailing address:* McCormick's Creek State Park, PO Box 71, Spencer, IN 47460. *Phone:* (812) 829-4881. *Driving instructions:* McCormick's Creek State Park is off Route 46 about 15 miles northwest of Bloomington.

In the northeastern corner of Indiana, about 5 miles south of Michigan, is Pokagon State Park, encompassing 1,203 acres. The park is bordered by two connected lakes—Lake James, the third-largest natural lake in the state, and Lake Lonidaw. There are two sandy beaches for lake swimming; and for those who prefer boating, rowboats and paddleboats are available for rent. Motorboats are permitted but must be launched from outside the park. Other summer activities include basketball, volleyball, shuffleboard, horseback riding, and tennis. Many trails wind through the park, which has a 300-acre nature preserve with a nature center offering guided walks and lectures.

The park is also set up for winter activities, the most popular of which are sledding, ice-skating, cross-country skiing, and tobogganing. (The park has Indiana's only refrigerated toboggan run.) *Park mailing address:* RR 2, Box 129, Angola, IN 46703. *Park phone:* (219) 833-2012.

Potawatomi Inn and Cabins

A rambling Tudor-style structure, the Potawatomi Inn is on the shore of Lake James. In addition to the main building there are also sixteen wooden cabins set in a wooded area.

The inn's pillar-supported dining room, which seats 250, overlooks the lake and serves three meals a day. The large lounge has brick walls, a patterned brick-and-concrete floor, a large brick fireplace, a card table, and an adjoining porch that overlooks the lake.

The guest rooms are clean, comfortable, and modern, each with television (except in the cabins) and a telephone. The cabin rooms resemble the inn rooms and are so situated that one can see the lake from them only in winter, when the trees (including elms, oaks, dogwoods, and maples) have lost their leaves. The inn has an indoor swimming pool with sauna and Jacuzzi, a 500-seat conference room, and two meeting rooms.

Accommodations: 80 rooms and 16 cabin rooms, all with private bath. The cabins have no kitchen facilities. *Pets:* Not permitted. *Open:* All year. *Mailing address:* Pokagon State Park, PO Box 37A, Route 2, Angola, IN 46703. *Phone* (219) 833-1077. *Driving instructions:* Pokagon State Park is on Route 727 1½ miles south of the junction of I-80/90 and I-69.

Driving instructions: Pokagon State Park is on Route 727 1½ miles south of the junction of I-80/90 and I-69.

With 3,840 acres, Potato Creek State Park is in northwestern Indiana about 10 miles south of South Bend. The recreation area used to be farmland, and its terrain is relatively flat, a mixture of fields and patches of maple woods. The swamp rose, which blooms from June through August, is prevalent in a section of the recreation area set aside as a nature preserve, and the 300-acre Worster Lake is rife with bass, bluegills, and crappies.

The lake has a 1,100-foot sandy beach with a bathhouse, and visitors can rent rowboats and canoes. The recreation area has a boat launch, and electric motors are permitted. Other activities include bicycling (rentals available), cross-country skiing (rentals available), and hiking. The area has a visitors' center and naturalist service.

The recreation area has nine wood-frame cabins, built in 1982. Each can accommodate eight and has vaulted ceilings, two bedrooms, a living area, and a bath with shower.

Each living room has two sofa beds, three occasional chairs, and two rocking chairs; and there's a kitchenette off the living area. One of the bedrooms has a double bed, and the other has twins. Between the two bedrooms is a dressing area.

Accommodations: 9 cabins with private bath. *Towels and linens:* Not provided. *Cooking utensils:* Provided. *Eating utensils:* Not provided. *Stove and refrigerator:* Provided. *Pets:* Not permitted. *Open:* All year. *Mailing address:* 25601 State Road 4, North Liberty, IN 46554. *Phone:* (219) 656-8186. *Driving instructions:* Potato Creek State Park is on Route 4 about 3 miles east of North Liberty.

In southwestern Indiana, about 25 miles south of Terre Haute, Shakamak State Park is 1,766 acres developed in the 1930s by the Civilian Conservation Corps (CCC), which did extensive erosion-control work, planted trees, and built many structures. The park's group building, for example, originally served as the CCC camp. The area used to be farmland, but today it's moderately wooded with, among other species, black locust, maple, white oak, wild cherry, dogwood, sassafras, ash, and yellow poplar.

The park has three man-made lakes, which the state periodically stocks. Anglers fish for bass, crappies, bluegills, or channel cat. Visitors can rent rowboats or paddleboats, and the park has a launch ramp, although electric motors only are permitted. One of the lakes has a beach for swimming, and all three usually have waterfowl, such as Canada geese, wood ducks, and a few pairs of loons. Other wildlife includes deer, raccoons, foxes, and of late, a coyote or two. Bicycling and horseback riding are also popular.

The park has twenty-nine split-log wood-frame cabins, twenty-six of which are in a wooded area beside the lake. The cabins vary in size and can accommodate from four to six people. Eight have cold water only and no bath. (Lavatory and shower facilities are in a central location.) Most have bathrooms with a shower and hot and cold running water, a screened porch, a living area, two bedrooms, and a wood stove.

Accommodations: 29 cabins, 21 with private bath. *Towels and linens:* Not provided. *Cooking and eating utensils:* Not provided. *Stove:* Provided. *Refrigerator:* Provided. *Pets:* Not permitted. *Open:* April through October. *Mailing address*: Route 2, Box 120, Jasonville, IN 47438. *Phone:* (812) 665-2158. *Driving instructions:* Shakamak State Park is about 25 miles south of Terre Haute, just east of the intersection of Routes 159 and 48.

Spring Mill State Park is in south-central Indiana, south and east of Hoosier National Forest, about 35 miles southeast of Bloomington. The park, 1,319 acres in size, is of both naturalistic and historical significance.

The natural attractions include Donaldson Woods Nature Preserve, a 67-acre virgin hardwood forest, through which a hiking trail lined with dogwoods meanders. The most scenic seasons are spring, when the dogwoods are flowering, and fall, when the hardwoods—tulip trees, white oaks, and maples for the most part—are changing color. Another natural feature of the park is its system of underground caves—Twin, Donaldson, and Bronson. Visitors can take a boat tour of Twin Cave or, when accompanied by the park naturalist, hike through Bronson or Donaldson.

The park has an elaborate historical restoration: Pioneer Village, which consists of numerous historical buildings, including an 1816 limestone gristmill that still grinds corn by means of a water wheel that turns a huge stone. Also reconstructed here are several pioneer houses, a mill office, a barn, a meeting house, a distillery, and a tavern. The park also has a memorial to Virgil Grissom, the second American in space, that includes the astronaut's space suit, a montage of photographs depicting his life, and *Molly Brown,* a Gemini space capsule. *Park mailing address:* RR 2, Box 376, Mitchell, IN 47446. *Park phone:* (812) 849-4129.

Spring Mill Inn

Built in 1939 and remodeled in 1976, the Spring Mill Inn is a three-story limestone building with wings on either side. Accommodations include use of indoor and outdoor swimming pools connected by a moat that runs under a glass wall, plus a lounge with a limestone fireplace, red wall-to-wall carpeting, and wood-paneled pillars. There's a game room next to the pool, and the grounds have tennis courts and riding stables (seasonal). Each guest room has wall-to-wall carpeting, color television, a telephone, and reproduction Colonial-style furnishings.

The inn has a large dining room that serves three meals a day to the public as well as guests. Another large room is the conference room, which has wood-paneled walls, an exposed-

161

beam ceiling, and an angled wall of glass that faces the treetops.

Accommodations: 75 rooms with private bath. *Pets:* Not permitted. *Open:* All year. *Mailing address:* PO Box 68, Mitchell, IN 47446. *Phone:* (812) 849-4081. *Driving instructions:* Spring Mill State Park is off Route 60 about 5 miles east of Mitchell.

In west-central Indiana, roughly 15 miles southwest of Craw-fordsville, Turkey Run State Park encompasses 2,382 acres and takes its name from a phenomenon early residents of the area witnessed with some frequency: Huge flocks of wild turkeys used to gather together under some of the area's overhanging cliffs, perhaps, some think, for protection.

The park has many gorges and canyons, the most striking of which is Rocky Hollow, a sandstone precipice. The terrain is wooded with hemlock, tulip, oak, walnut, and sycamore trees and has a few noteworthy man-made structures such as a covered bridge and an old log church. Activities include bicycling, horseback riding, fishing, swimming and tennis. *Park mailing address:* RR 1, Marshall, IN 47859. *Park phone:* (317) 597-2635.

Turkey Run Inn and Cabins

A colonial-style structure built in 1917, the Turkey Run Inn, (at that time called the Turkey Run Hotel) almost immediately became a popular resort. The inn has been modified over time and currently has fifty-one rooms and, right next to it, twenty-one wooden cabins with no housekeeping facilities.

Facilities at the inn include a dining room with wood floor-ing and brick columns, a 400-seat banquet hall, an outdoor pool, and tennis courts. The guest rooms are modern and comfort-able. Most have television, and each has a telephone.

Accommodations: 51 inn rooms and 21 cabins all with private bath. *Pets:* Not permitted. *Open:* All year. *Mailing address:* Box 444, Marshall, IN 47859. *Phone:* (317) 597-2211. *Driving in-structions:* Turkey Run State Park is on Route 47 about 2 miles east of its junction with U.S. 41.

In southeastern Indiana, 14 miles south of Richmond and about 8 miles west of the Ohio border, Whitewater Memorial State Park has of 1,710 acres. Dedicated in 1949 as a memorial to World War II veterans, the park is at the northern tip of Brookville Lake, which is 17 miles long and 1 mile wide. The park also contains a 195-acre lake inhabited by bluegills, crappies, and bass and patrolled by Canada geese, wood ducks, and mallards.

Whitewater Lake has a beach for swimming, and rowboats and paddleboats are available for rent. Visitors can launch their own motorboats in the park, although only electric motors are permitted. Horseback riding is popular, and the park maintains a horsemen's camp and a saddle barn, as well as bridle trails (horses can also be rented). The park is a stopover point on the Whitewater Valley Bicycle Route, a 66-mile scenic course that runs from Richmond to Batesville and then connects with the Hoosier Hills Bicycle Route, a 27-mile run that ends in Versailles State Park.

Another noteworthy feature is the Hornbeam Nature Preserve, which has large stands of hornbeams (ironwood and blue beech). The visitors' center, which uses solar energy as its main heat source, was the first such structure erected by the State of Indiana.

In a lightly wooded area in the southwestern section of the park are four recently built wooden cabins, which overlook Brookville Lake and have cathedral ceilings with skylight windows, two bedrooms, a bath with a shower and tub, a living room with a sleeper sofa and occasional chairs, and a screened porch. The cabins are heated by a combination of an electric furnace and a wood stove. They are equipped with kitchenettes, and each accommodates up to eight people.

Accommodations: 4 cabins with private bath. *Towels and linens:* Not provided. *Cooking utensils:* Provided. *Eating utensils:* Not provided. *Stove and refrigerator:* Provided. *Pets:* Not permitted. *Open:* All year. *Mailing address:* Whitewater Memorial State Park, RR 2, Liberty, IN 47353. *Phone:* (317) 458-5565. *Driving instructions:* Whitewater Memorial State Park is off Route 101, roughly a mile south of Liberty.

Iowa

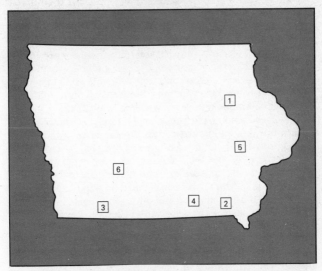

State map and tourist information: Development Commission, 600 E. Court Ave., Suite A, Des Moines, IA 50309; 515-281-3679. **State parks:** *Information:* Conservation Commission, Wallace State Bldg., Des Moines IA 50319; 515-281-5145. *Entrance fees:* None. *Reservations:* Contact individual parks. Recommended 4 to 5 months in advance for Mem. Day—Labor Day; summer months accepted at the beginning of the year; minimum stay, one week. $25 deposit, payable by check only, within 5 days. *Restrictions:* No hunting. Boating, registration required (obtained at county recorders). Dogs must be leashed (not allowed in lodgings). *Facilities:* Swimming and boating, Mem. Day—Labor Day.

Backbone State Park, 1,780 acres in northeastern Iowa about 45 miles north of Cedar Rapids, takes its name from a quarter-mile rock ridge running through its center that looks like a giant backbone. The formation used to be called "Devil's Backbone," and its rugged terrain—terraced escarpments, sheer precipices, grottoes, and caverns—has given rise over the years to tall tales of Indian massacres, shoot-outs between outlaws and lawmen, and similiar romantic adventures. Bordered on both south and north by the Maquoketa River, which virtually makes a U-turn as it changes direction, the formation is the highest point in north-eastern Iowa and a marked contrast to the surrounding farm-land. Windswept pines bend over some of its cliffs, and moun-tain climbers practice their skill on the steeper precipices.

In addition to the river and Lamont Creek, there is a 100-acre man-made lake with a sand beach and a bathhouse. Numerous trails, many of them marked, run through the park, immediate-ly outside of which lies a Conservation Commission pine forest. The Backbone Golf and Country Club, adjacent to the park's northern boundary, is open to the public. There is a boat-launching ramp (electric motors only, 10-horsepower maximum) and, in winter, facilities for snowmobiling.

On a cliff wooded with oaks, hickories, and some pines are eighteen modern housekeeping cabins. They overlook the lake about 50 yards away, but the water view is obscured by oak leaves except in winter.

The cabins were designed for four—but the park will rent cots in case you show up with six—and each has a bedroom with a double bed, a living area with a sofa bed, a kitchenette, and a private bath with shower.

Accommodations: 18 cabins with private bath. *Towels and linens:* Not provided. *Cooking and eating utensils:* Provided. *Stove and refrigerator:* Provided. *Pets:* Permitted if leashed. *Open:* Mid-May through mid-September. *Mailing address:* Dundee, IA 52038. *Phone:* (319) 924-2527. *Driving instructions:* Backbone State Park is off Route W69, half a mile north of Dundee and 5 miles south of Strawberry Point.

The 1,653-acre Lacey-Keosauqua State Park is in southeastern Iowa, just south of Keosauqua and about 10 miles north of the Missouri border. A horseshoe bend in the Des Moines River forms the northern boundary of the park, which has a terrain that varies from floodplain to cliffs, limestone gorges, meadows, and wooded hills. The area is wooded primarily with oaks, maples, elms, hickories, ashes, basswood, cedars, and spruces. Many of the trees are both large and old—some nearly two hundred years. At one time sections of the park were inhabited by woodsmen who harvested trees on the park's southern ridge, where hikers can follow a trail that runs by the ruins of their cabins. The Mormon Trail crosses the Des Moines River at Ely's Ford.

A wide variety of wildlife, including deer, red foxes, raccoons, and opossums inhabit the area, and waterfowl congregate on the Des Moines River as well as on the park's 30-acre lake.

The lake has a sand beach with a bathhouse, and visitors can rent rowboats or paddleboats. Other activities include camping, picnicking, and fishing. (The Des Moines River has an abundance of catfishes).

Lacey-Keosauqua State Park has six one-bedroom, wood-frame cabins in a wooded area that can accommodate up to four people. Each has a fully equipped kitchenette and a private bath.

Accommodations: 6 cabins with private bath. *Towels and linens:* Not provided. *Cooking and eating utensils:* Provided. *Stove and refrigerator:* Provided. *Pets:* Not permitted. *Open:* Mid-May through mid-October. *Mailing address:* Box 398, Keosauqua, Iowa 52565. *Phone:* (319) 293-3502. *Driving instructions:* The park is off Route 1 half a mile south of Keosauqua.

The major Indian tribes inhabiting the Iowa plains held powwows and festivals in prime hunting areas, including the 700 acres of what is now Lake of Three Fires State Park, in southwestern Iowa about 80 miles southeast of Council Bluffs and 10 miles north of the Missouri border. When representatives from various Indian nations arrived for the powwow, they looked for the smoke of three fires, usually emanating from a high point in the terrain and indicating precisely where the powwow was to be held.

Heavily wooded with oaks, hickories, and ashes, the park has a 97-acre man-made lake with a bathhouse and a sand beach. Activities include swimming, boating, fishing, and hiking, with boats and motors for rent at a concession near the beach. Anglers can also rent fishing equipment to go after bass, catfishes, bullheads, bluegills, and tiger muskellunge. Of several trails in the park, one encircles the lake for 13 miles. There are also bridle trails—but no horses for hire—and the park administration is currently developing a system of snowmobile trails.

The park's six cabins—arranged in a semicircle at a point beside the lake and set in an area wooded with oaks, hickories, and ashes—were built in the 1930s by the Civilian Conservation Corps. One is immediately on the lake, and another sits on a high bank overlooking it; four cabins in all have lake views.

The cabins have knotty-pine paneling and a kitchenette. Although they have hot and cold running water, they lack shower facilities, which are in a central building near the camping area.

Accommodations: 6 cabins with shared bath. *Towels and linens:* Not provided. *Cooking and eating utensils:* Provided. *Stove and refrigerator:* Provided. *Pets:* Permitted if leashed. *Open:* May through September. *Mailing address:* Route 4, Bedford, IA 50833. *Phone:* (712) 523-2700. *Driving instructions:* Lake of Three Fires State Park is off Route 49, 3 miles north of Bedford.

Lake Wapello State Park is in a somewhat remote area with gently rolling hills in southeastern Iowa, 20 miles north of the Missouri border and immediately southeast of Stephens State Forest near the tiny towns of Drakesville (population 260) and Unionville (population 271). The park has some 1,168 acres, 289 of which are covered with water, and is wooded primarily with white oaks, some red oaks, and honey locusts. There are even a few elms trying to stage a comeback.

Wildlife includes snowy owls—who come especially during years when the population of Arctic lemmings is low—deer, pheasant, quail, an occasional bald eagle, and wild turkeys, which Iowa has been successfully reintroducing. The man-made Lake Wapello is stocked with bluegills, tiger muskellunge, white and yellow bass, perch, and other fish. Rowboats and canoes are available for rent, and electric trolling motors are allowed on the lake, but you have to bring your own.

Seven miles of hiking trails encircle the lake, which has a 600-foot-long sand beach and a 200-foot-long limestone boathouse built by the Civilian Conservation Corps. Another CCC structure, a stone shelter at one of the picnic grounds, is on a knoll overlooking the lake.

In the northwestern part of the park, on a gentle slope overlooking the lake, are thirteen wood-frame cabins, about half of which were built by the CCC. Although designed to accommodate four, the cabins can generally handle six. Each has a lake view, a fireplace, wall-to-wall carpeting, a kitchenette, a porch, and a bath with a shower. Visitors who bring their own boats to the park, or even rent one while here, can pull it onto the shore in front of the cabin.

Accommodations: 13 cabins with private bath. *Towels and linens:* Not provided. *Cooking and eating utensils:* Provided. *Stove and refrigerator:* Provided. *Pets:* Not permitted. *Open:* Early May through mid-October. *Mailing address:* RR1, Drakesville, IA 52552. *Phone:* (515) 722-3371. *Driving instructions:* Lake Wapello State Park is off Route 273, about 6 miles west of Drakesville.

The 840-acre Palisades-Kepler State Park is in eastern Iowa, about 12 miles southeast of Cedar Rapids, along both the east and west banks of the Cedar River, which is bordered in parts by palisades—sheer rock escarpments that rise as high as 70 feet. The terrain here varies from floodplain to vertical cliffs, deep ravines, and upland hardwood forests, wooded primarily with oaks, maples, elms, ashes, box elders, poplars, and basswood. The park is the site of numerous archaelogical finds, including a mammoth's molar, rock-embedded fossils, and Indian artifacts and burial mounds. There are 7 miles of hiking trails, including a path that runs along the top of the palisades and two half-mile interpretative trails.

Activities here include camping, picnicking, fishing, and swimming. There are no supervised swimming areas in the park, but guests may use sandbars in the Cedar River as beaches, although they swim at their own risk. Fishing includes catches of northern walleyes and channel and flathead catfishes. Rowboats and paddleboats are available for rent.

Palisades-Kepler State Park has four wood-frame cabins in a wooded area near the campground. Each has a fully equipped kitchenette, a private bath, a sofa bed in the main room, and a patio. Each can accommodate four people.

Accommodations: 4 cabins with private bath. *Towels and linens:* Not provided. *Cooking and eating utensils:* Provided. *Stove and refrigerator:* Provided. *Pets:* Not permitted. *Open:* The week prior to Memorial Day through mid-September. *Mailing address:* 700 Kepler Drive, Mt. Vernon, Iowa 52314. *Phone:* (319) 895-6039. *Driving instructions:* Palisades-Kepler State Park is off U.S. 30 about 4 miles west of Mt. Vernon.

Within the rolling hills of the Raccoon River valley and surrounded by farmland, Springbrook State Park is a 794-acre reserve in southwestern Iowa about 50 miles northwest of Des Moines. It is thickly wooded with oaks, hickories, and maples, and has an unusual characteristic: Sections of prairie, resembling large patches of farmland, open up right in the middle of timberland. A large herd of deer, numbering about 300 to 400 in winter, dines off whatever saplings manage to take hold in the prairie areas. Walnuts, basswood, and cottonwoods line the river.

A 27-acre man-made lake, with a large sand beach and a bathhouse, is fed by Springbrook Creek. Usually quite clear, you can see your toes in water 5 feet deep. Catfish, bluegill, largemouth bass, and crappies inhabit the lake, and boats are available for rent. The lake is also a popular spot for ice-fishing. Other facilities include 200 modern and 20 rustic campsites, the latter reachable only by hiking across a foot bridge.

Overlooking the lake on the west are six single-room clapboard cabins built in the 1930s by the Civilian Conservation Corps. Each has a vaulted ceiling, pine paneling, a double bed and a studio couch, a refrigerator and a stove, and a toilet but no shower or hot water. Guests have use of the showers in a central facility near the camping area.

Also available is a group lodge that includes a central building with a kitchen, a dining hall, and showers and toilets, flanked by nine sleeping cabins that can accommodate up to fourteen each. The lodge and cabins were built by the CCC as their original camp, then remodeled into an education center, and later put back into use as a group camp.

Accommodations: 1 group lodge with nine sleeping cabins and 6 cabins, all with shared bath. *Towels and linens:* Not provided. *Cooking and eating utensils:* Provided. *Stove and refrigerator:* Provided. *Pets:* Not permitted. *Open:* Memorial Day through September. *Mailing address:* Route 1, Box 49, Guthrie Center, IA 50115. *Phone:* (515) 747-3591. *Driving instructions:* Springbrook State Park is on Route 384, which is off Route 25, about 7 miles north of Guthrie Center.

Kentucky

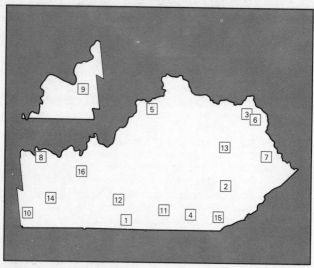

State map and tourist information: Dept. of Travel Development, 22nd Flr., Capitol Plaza Tower, Frankfort, KY 40601; 800-225-TRIP or 502-564-4930 (in western U.S.). **State parks:** *Information:* Dept. of Parks, Capitol Plaza Tower, 10th Flr., Frankfort, KY 40601; 502-564-2172. *Entrance fees:* None. *Reservations:* Call 800-255-PARK or 502-564-8799 (in western U.S.). Send deposit for first night's lodging; use phone and credit card if check-in date is within 10 days of making reservation. Reservations accepted (and recommended) up to 1 year in advance, particularly for Mem. Day—Labor Day. Maximum stay, 14 days. *Restrictions:* No hunting. Dogs must be leashed (not allowed in lodgings). *Facilities:* Swimming, Mem. Day—Labor Day. Interpretative programs and horseback riding, April—October. Golf and tennis, open all year.

Barren River Lake State Resort Park is in southern Kentucky, 106 miles south of Louisville and 15 miles north of the Tennessee border. The 1,799-acre park is along the shore of the 10,000-acre Barren River Lake, which has a sand beach with a bathhouse, as well as a marina with fishing and pontoon boats for rent. Fishermen go after walleyes, bluegills, muskellunge, and large-mouth and smallmouth bass. Other activities include bicycling, horseback riding, hiking, basketball, shuffleboard, tennis, and golf on the park's nine-hole golf course.

Barren River Lake Lodge and Cottages

Barren River Lake Lodge, on a peninsula that juts into the lake, is a group of rustic wooden buildings of modern design. The lodge has a restaurant, a gift shop, and fifty-one guest rooms, each with wall-to-wall carpeting, color television, a telephone, 2 queen- or 1 king-size bed, air-conditioning, and a private bath.

The lodge also administers twelve two-bedroom "executive" cottages, each with a living room, a dining area, a fully equipped kitchen, a private bath, two bedrooms, color television, a telephone, and central air-conditioning. A swimming pool is near-by for use by both lodge and cottage guests.

Accommodations: 51 lodge rooms and 12 cottages, all with private bath. *Towels and linens:* Provided. *Cooking and eating utensils:* In cottages. *Stove and refrigerator:* In cottages. *Pets:* Not permitted. *Open:* All year. *Mailing address:* Barren River Lake State Resort Park, Lucas, KY 42156. *Phone:* (502) 646-2151. Toll Free: 1-800-862-0261 (in Kentucky); 1-800-325-0057 (out of state). *Driving instructions:* Barren River Lake State Resort Park is on U.S. 31E, about 14 miles southwest of Glasgow.

Barren River Lake State Resort Park

Buckhorn Lake State Park

The 856-acre Buckhorn Lake State Park is in southeastern Kentucky, about 60 miles north of the Kentucky-Virginia-Tennessee border, near the northern tip of the Daniel Boone National Forest. Situated among mountains, the 1,250-acre Buckhorn Lake, an impoundment of the Kentucky River, has a sand beach with a bathhouse, as well as a marina that rents fishing boats, pontoon boats, and rowboats. Smallmouth and largemouth bass, crappies, bluegills, and channel catfish are the most commonly caught species of fish. Two hiking trails wind through the terrain, one of which passes a series of nature stations. The park also has tennis courts.

Buckhorn Lodge

Buckhorn Lodge is a modern, stone-and-wood modified A-frame on a rise overlooking the lake, with a restaurant, a gift shop, and meeting and banquet facilities. Each of the thirty-six guest rooms has wall-to-wall carpeting, color television, a telephone, two double beds, air-conditioning, and a private bath. Some of the rooms have balconies and views of the lake. A swimming pool is reserved for lodge guests.

Accommodations: 36 rooms with private bath. *Towels and linens:* Provided. *Pets:* Not permitted. *Open:* March 1 to December 22. *Mailing address:* Buckhorn Lake State Park, HC-36, Box 1000, Buckhorn, KY 41721. *Phone:* (606) 398-7510. Toll free: 1-800-633-9945 (in Kentucky); 1-800-325-0058 (out of state). *Driving instructions:* Buckhorn Lake State Park is off Route 28, about 25 miles west of Hazard.

Carter Caves State Park is in northeastern Kentucky, about 40 miles west of where Kentucky meets Ohio and West Virginia at the Ohio River. The 1,239-acre park contains a series of caves, where lighted and unlighted cave tours are available. Miles of hiking trails wind through the park, including some that cross over natural bridges. Other activities include canoeing on Tygart Creek and fishing the park's 45-acre lake for muskellunge, crappies, bream, or bass. The park has two swimming pools, a nine-hole golf course, a miniature-golf course, a riding stable, and a nature center with interpretative exhibits, including a diorama of the caves.

Caveland Lodge and Cottages

Accommodations are available in the Caveland Lodge's twenty-eight guest rooms and in fifteen cottages. The lodge has a restaurant, a gift shop, and meeting and banquet facilities. Each guest room has wall-to-wall carpeting, color television, a telephone, air-conditioning, and a private bath.

The cottages vary in size from one to three rooms, each with a kitchen or kitchenette, color television, a telephone, air-conditioning, and a private bath. The one- and two-room cottages are designed to accommodate two people; the three-room units to accommodate four.

Accommodations: 28 lodge rooms and 15 cottages, all with private bath. *Towels and linens:* Provided. *Cooking and eating utensils:* In cottages. *Stove and refrigerator:* In cottages. *Pets:* Not permitted. *Open:* All year. *Mailing address:* Carter Caves State Park, Olive Hill, KY 41164. *Phone:* (606) 286-4411. Toll free: 1-800-432-1210 (in Kentucky); 1-800-325-0059 (out of state). *Driving instructions:* Carter Caves State Park is off Route 182, roughly 8 miles north of Olive Hill.

Cumberland Falls Park takes its name from Cumberland Falls, a 125-foot-wide precipice over which the Cumberland River drops 68 feet, making a sound like thunder and sending mist in every direction. The mist, as well as other phenomena geologists have yet to explain, creates an almost unique set of conditions: During a full moon the falls generate the only "moonbow" visible in the Western Hemisphere. Colorful though pale, the moonbow rises from the base of the falls and is most clearly visible during the winter months. Weather permitting, the moonbow can be seen on the three nights when the moon is fullest. (The only other place in the world to see a moonbow is Victoria Falls in Africa.)

The 1,794-acre park is in southeastern Kentucky, about 90 miles south of Lexington and 15 miles north of the Tennessee border. Within the boundaries of Daniel Boone National Forest, the park is popular among hikers and has 26 miles of trails. Other activities include horseback riding, fishing in the Cumberland River, tennis, and swimming in the park's Olympic-size pool. A concessionaire conducts white-water rafting trips on the Cumberland River below the falls. (Call (606) 523-0629.) The park also sponsors many special events such as Laurel and Hardy film festivals and nature-photography workshops. Square dancing is a summertime tradition in the park.

Cumberland Falls Lodge and Cabins

The lodge at Cumberland Falls is a log building with fifty-four guest rooms, a dining room, a gift shop, a coffee shop, a grocery store, and banquet and meeting facilities. One wall of the restaurant has picture windows that overlook the river. Each guest room has wall-to-wall carpeting, a private bath, color television, a telephone, and air-conditioning. Most overlook trees, although there are two "honeymoon suites" that have views of the river. (Each honeymoon suite has a queen-size bed, instead of the usual two double beds, and a love seat.)

The lodge also administers twenty "woodland duplexes, " which can either be shared or rented in their entirety. These side-by-side pairs have wall-to-wall carpeting, color television, telephones, air-conditioning, and baths but no kitchen facilities.

Also available are twenty-five efficiency cottages, which vary

in size from one to three rooms and are decorated and appointed in the same fashion as the lodge rooms and woodland duplexes. However, the efficiencies have completely equipped kitchens.

Accommodations: 54 lodge rooms, 20 woodland duplexes, and 25 cottages, all with private bath. *Towels and linens:* Provided. *Cooking and eating utensils:* In cottages only. *Stove and refrigerator:* In cottages only. *Pets:* Not permitted. *Open:* All year, except two weeks at Christmas. *Mailing address:* Corbin, KY 40701. *Phone:* (606) 528-4121. *Driving instructions:* Cumberland Falls State Resort Park is on Route 90, about 20 miles southwest of Corbin.

General Butler State Resort Park is in the Ohio River Valley in northern Kentucky, about 70 miles northwest of Lexington and 50 miles southwest of Cincinnati, Ohio. The park takes its name from a local hero in the War of 1812. The 809-acre park has a 30-acre lake with a sand beach, a bathhouse, rowboats and paddleboats for rent, as well as a nine-hole golf course and numerous hiking trails. For winter activities, the park has 17 acres of ski slopes with a 300-foot vertical drop, a snow-making system, illumination for night skiing, three double chair lifts, and equipment rentals.

Butler Lodge and Cottages

Built of stone and glass, Butler Lodge has fifty-seven guest rooms, a large restaurant, a gift shop, and meeting and banquet facilities. It also has a large lobby with exposed-beam ceilings, hardwood floors, and a stone fireplace. Each guest room has wall-to-wall carpeting, color television, a telephone, two double beds, air-conditioning, and a private bath.

The lodge also administers twenty-two cottages with one, two, or three bedrooms, each with color television, a telephone, a kitchen, air-conditioning, and a private bath. There is a swimming pool reserved for use by lodge and cottage guests.

Accommodations: 57 lodge rooms and 22 cottages, all with private bath. *Towels and linens:* Provided. *Cooking and eating utensils:* In cottages. *Stove and refrigerator:* In cottages. *Pets:* Not permitted. *Open:* All year. *Mailing address:* General Butler State Resort Park, PO Box 325, Carrollton, KY 41008. *Phone:* (502) 732-4384. *Driving instructions:* General Butler State Resort Park is off Route 227 about 2 miles south of Carrollton.

Greenbo Lake State Resort Park is in northeastern Kentucky, about 20 miles west of where Kentucky meets Ohio and West Virginia at the Ohio River. The 3,330-acre park includes the 225-acre Greenbo Lake, which has a sand beach with a bathhouse and a marina that has a launch ramp (7½-horsepower limit) along with rowboat, paddleboat, motorboat, pontoon boat, and canoe rentals. Anglers go after catfishes, bluegills, and black bass, among others.

The park has miles of hiking trails, including the 25-mile Michael Tygart trail within the park, which joins the 125-mile Jenny Wiley trail that runs from South Shore (across from Portsmouth, Ohio) up to Jenny Wiley State Park in Crestonsburg. Activities include tennis, miniature golf, and shuffleboard. A concession adjacent to the park has horses for riding.

Jesse Stuart Lodge

Jesse Stuart Lodge is a strikingly modern, three story building with thirty-six guest rooms, a gift shop, a swimming pool, and a restaurant, as well as meeting and banquet facilities. All of its furnishings, from draperies to end tables and lamps, were made in Kentucky. Each guest room has wall-to-wall carpeting, color television, a telephone, two double beds, a private bath, and a private patio (ground-floor rooms) or a balcony overlooking the lake.

Accommodations: 36 rooms with private bath. *Pets:* Not permitted. *Open:* All year. *Mailing address:* Greenbo Lake State Resort Park, HC 60, Box 562, Greenup, KY 41144. *Phone:* (606) 473-7324. *Driving instructions:* Greenbo Lake State Resort Park is off Route 1 about 8 miles southwest of Greenup.

Jenny Wiley State Park is in eastern Kentucky about 25 miles northwest of Pikeville and 30 miles west of the West Virginia border. The park takes its name from a pioneer woman who was held captive by Cherokee Indians for eleven months. The 1,700-acre park, bordered by Dewey Lake, is in heavily wooded, mountainous Appalachian terrain. A scenic "skylift" (chairlift) runs from a point 2 miles from the lodge to the summit of Sugar Camp Mountain (elevation, 1473 feet).

The park has a summer music theater, sponsored by the semiprofessional Jenny Wiley Drama Association, that puts on musicals from mid-June through August. A full-time recreational director plans dances and other social events. Activities include pool swimming, horseback riding, boating (rentals available), fishing, hiking, and golf on a nine-hole golf course, and miniature golf.

Jenny Wiley Lodge and Cabins

The park includes a modern lodge and sixteen cottages. The lodge has a restaurant, a gift shop, meeting and banquet facilities and forty-eight guest rooms, each with wall-to-wall carpeting, color television, a telephone, air-conditioning, and a private bath. There is also one suite with a living room, a wet bar, a bedroom with a queen-size bed, and furnishings and appointments similar to those in the other guest rooms.

The cottages have either one or two bedrooms and are equipped with a complete kitchen, air-conditioning, color television, a telephone, a living room, and a private bath.

Accommodations: 48 lodge rooms and 16 cottages, all with private bath. *Towels and linens:* Provided. *Cooking and eating utensils:* In cottages. *Stove and refrigerator:* In cottages. *Pets:* Not permitted. *Open:* All year. *Mailing address:* NC 66, Box 200, Prestonburg, KY 41653. *Phone:* (606) 886-2711. *Driving instructions:* Jenny Wiley State Park is 5 miles east of the intersection of Route 23/460, and Route 80/3, on Route 3.

John James Audubon State Park comprises 692 acres in northwestern Kentucky, about 110 miles west of Louisville and a few miles south of the Ohio River and Indiana. The park takes its name from the great naturalist and artist, and one of its treasures is the John James Audubon Memorial Museum, a Tudoresque, castle-like stone building where 126 prints from *The Birds of America* are on display. The museum is open daily from April through October and on weekends during the rest of the year except for January, when it is closed.

The park has two lakes—a 28-acre lake with a sandy beach and bathhouse, paddleboat rentals, and a 12-acre nature-preserve lake. Fishing is permitted on both lakes, and other recreational facilities include a nine-hole golf course and tennis courts. Three-hundred-twenty-five acres of the park have been set aside as a wildlife preserve where hiking trails wind through. The park has a gift shop specializing in wildlife prints and bird-related products.

The park has five one-bedroom cottages, each with a living room, a kitchen, color television, air-conditioning, a fireplace, and a private bath. Unlike cottages in other Kentucky parks, they do not have telephones, although pay phones are nearby.

Accommodations: 5 cottages with private bath. *Towels and linens:* Provided. *Cooking and eating utensils:* Provided. *Stove and refrigerator:* Provided. *Pets:* Not permitted. *Open:* All year. *Mailing address:* Henderson, KY 42420. *Phone:* (502) 826-2247. *Driving instructions:* John James Audubon State Park is off U.S. 41 near the northern tip of Henderson County.

9 *Kentucky Dam Village State Resort Park* **KENTUCKY**

The 1,200-acre Kentucky Dam Village State Resort Park is in southwestern Kentucky, at the northern tip of Kentucky Lake, across the water from Land Between the Lakes peninsula. The 160,000-acre man-made lake, formed by damming the Tennessee River during the 1940s, boasts the largest docking facility in the Kentucky park system, where visitors can rent fishing boats, rowboats, pedal boats, or houseboats. It has a sand beach with

185

a bathhouse. Ashore, activities include hiking, horseback riding, tennis, and golf on an eighteen-hole course.

The park has a 4,000-foot lighted and paved airstrip with fueling facilities for jet and conventional aircraft. Also available are courtesy cars for lodge and cottage guests. *Park phone:* 1-800-325-0146; in Kentucky: 1-800-633-4223.

Kentucky Dam Village Lodges, Cottages, and Marinas

Kentucky Dam Village has a variety of accommodations including two lodges, eighty-six cottages of six types, and houseboats of two sizes.

Henry Ward Lodge is a modern brick-and-wood building with sixty-two guest rooms, a large dining room, a lobby, and a lounging area. Village Green lodge, of similar design with thirteen guest rooms, is across the highway about ¼ mile away on a peninsula that juts out into the lake. Each of the guest rooms in the lodges has wall-to-wall carpeting, two double beds, color television, a telephone, a private bath, and sliding glass doors that lead onto private balconies that overlook either Kentucky Lake or wooded hills.

The eighty-six cottages vary in size from one-bedroom two-person cottages to three-bedroom "executive" cottages. Each has a private bath, color television, a telephone, a kitchen, and air-conditioning. The executive cottages have two baths and a large kitchen. The park also offers 50- and 58-foot houseboats, each of which can accommodate up to eight people and is equipped with linens, cooking utensils, a kitchenette, a bath, and water-safety devices.

There is a swimming pool reserved for lodge and cottage guests.

Accommodations: 75 lodge rooms, a varying number of houseboats, and 86 cottages, all with private bath. *Towels and linens:* Provided. *Cooking and eating utensils:* In cottages and houseboats. *Stove and refrigerator:* In cottages and houseboats. *Pets:* Not permitted. *Open:* All year. *Mailing address:* PO Box 69, Gilbertsville, KY 42044. *Phone:* (502) 362-4271 for lodge and cottage reservations. Houseboat reservations are made with the marina. Call (502) 362-8500. *Driving instructions:* Kentucky Dam Village State Resort Park is at the junction of U.S. 62 and U.S. 641, off I-24, roughly 20 miles east of Paducah.

Lake Barkley State Resort Park is in southwestern Kentucky, across the water from the Land Between the Lakes peninsula and on the eastern shore of the 57,920-acre Lake Barkley, about 15 miles north of the Tennessee border. The park consists of 3,600 acres of shoreline and hilly terrain wooded with oaks, maples, hemlocks, hickories, spruces, beeches, and tulip trees. A bay of Lake Barkley has a sandy beach with a bathhouse.

The park has 9 miles of hiking trails, four lighted tennis courts, a trapshooting range, horseback riding, waterskiing, and a full-service marina with launching facilities and fishing boats, motorboats, and paddleboats for rent. Other facilities include a fitness center with Nautilus equipment and hand-ball courts. The park has a 4,800-foot lighted and paved airstrip.

Barkley Lodge and Cottages

On the east side of Lake Barkley, Barkley Lodge is a heavily timbered stone-and-glass building. Designed by Edward Durell
187

Stone, it fans out in a semicircle and has 120 guest rooms overlooking the lake. The main section of the lodge has a restaurant, a coffee shop, and meeting and banquet facilities. Each accommodation has wall-to-wall carpeting, color television, a telephone, air-conditioning, and a balcony overlooking the lake. Four suites are available with a living room, two bedrooms, a wet bar, two baths, and a balcony.

The lodge also administers nine wood-frame "executive" cottages, each with a living room, a dining area, a fully equipped kitchen, color television, a telephone, and air-conditioning. The cottages are about a mile from the lodge, and some have views of the lake. There is a swimming pool reserved for lodge and cottage guests, who are also entitled to free tennis and trapshooting lessons in the park, as well as courtesy car service from the park's airstrip.

Accommodations: 120 rooms and 9 cottages, all with private bath. *Towels and linens:* Provided. *Cooking and eating utensils:* In cottages. *Stove and refrigerator:* In cottages. *Pets:* Not permitted. *Open:* All year. *Mailing address:* Lake Barkley State Resort Park, PO Box 790, Cadiz, KY 42211. *Phone:* (502) 924-1171. *Driving instructions:* Lake Barkley State Resort Park is on U.S. 68, about 7 miles southwest of Cadiz and 60 miles south of Paducah, Kentucky.

On 3,400 acres, Lake Cumberland State Resort Park is in southern Kentucky, about 100 miles south of Lexington and 20 miles north of the Tennessee border. The park, situated along the 50,250-acre, 101-mile-long Lake Cumberland, has a marina with launching facilities, open and closed slips, and boats for rent—rowboats, fishing boats, pontoon boats, and houseboats. The fish most frequently caught are largemouth and smallmouth bass, bluegills, crappies, walleyes, and rainbow trout.

The park has two swimming pools, lighted tennis courts, shuffleboard courts, bicycle rentals, hiking and horseback-riding trails, a nine-hole golf course, and a miniature-golf course.

Lake Cumberland Lodges, Cottages, and Marina

Lake Cumberland resort has three types of accommodations—lodges, cottages, and houseboats (operated by an independent concessionaire). Lure Lodge has a restaurant, a gift shop, meeting and banquet facilities, and forty-eight guest rooms, each with wall-to-wall carpeting, color television, a telephone, air-conditioning, a private bath, and a balcony overlooking the lake. Pumpkin Creek Lodge, about ¼ mile away, has a meeting room and thirteen guest rooms. Six rooms have double beds, three have queen-size beds, and three one-bedroom suites have a wet bar and a private balcony overlooking the lake. The suites connect and can be combined to make two-bedroom accommodations.

The thirty cottages—one-bedroom, two-bedroom, and two-bedroom "Wildwood" cottages—each have a kitchen, color television, a telephone, air-conditioning, and a private bath. The Wildwood cottages are like the others, except that each has a fireplace and a deck. The two-bedroom cottages have screened porches.

Visitors can also rent houseboats, each of which can accommodate up to eight people and comes equipped with a kitchen, linens, cooking implements, and life jackets. (Inexperienced boaters will be shown how to operate the boats.)

One of the park's swimming pools is reserved for use by guests at the lodges and cottages.

Accommodations: 61 rooms in two lodges, plus 50 houseboats and 30 cottages, all with private bath. *Towels and linens:* Pro-

vided. *Cooking and eating utensils:* In cottages and houseboats. *Stove and refrigerator:* In cottages and houseboats. *Pets:* Not permitted. *Open:* All year, except one week at Christmas. *Mailing address:* Jamestown, KY 42629. *Phone:* (502) 343-3211 for lodge and cottage reservations. Houseboat reservations should be made with the marina, (502) 343-3236. *Driving instructions:* Lake Cumberland State Resort Park is off U.S. 127 and Route 92, about 15 miles south of Jamestown.

The 51, 354-acre Mammoth Cave National Park, in south-central Kentucky about 25 miles northeast of Bowling Green, was established to preserve Mammoth Cave, the longest recorded cave system in the world. Spelunkers have explored and mapped 315 miles of the cave, which is on five levels, or tiers, that reflect the five different levels of the Echo River. A tributary of the Green River, the Echo River flows through the lowest level of the cave, some 360 feet underground, and continues to cut caverns into the limestone deposited by an ancient sea. Other underground streams also continue to shape the cave, which has deep pits, vast "amphitheaters, " stalagmites, stalactites, delicate crystalline formations, and flowstone formations. One of the largest flowstone formations is called Frozen Niagara because it looks like a huge frozen waterfall. The formation is composed of travertine, or cave onyx, deposited drop by drop over millions of years.

The park has a well-staffed visitors' center, and tours of the cave are conducted daily except Christmas. The tours vary in length and difficulty, ranging from half-mile, hour-and-a-half tours designed for people confined to wheelchairs to 5-mile, six-hour treks that require hard hats with headlamps. Getting down on all fours to pass through low, narrow crawlways is common.

Above ground, the terrain consists of forested hills and valleys, and 25 miles of the Green River are within the park boundaries. A cruise ship, *Miss Green River,* makes hour-long journeys up and down the river several times each day. Hiking, camping, and tennis are also regular park activities. *Park mailing address:* Mammoth Cave, KY 42259. *Park phone:* (502) 758-2251.

Mammoth Cave Hotel and Cottages

The Mammoth Cave Hotel has several buildings with four types of accommodations. The main hotel is a 1965 brick-and-glass building with a restaurant, a gift shop, and thirty-eight guest rooms, each with wall-to-wall carpeting, color television, a private bath, and sliding glass doors leading to a balcony or patio. The hotel is on a ridge that overlooks a wooded ravine, which about half of the guest rooms face.

A short walk from the hotel, at the edge of a wooded area, is the Sunset Point Motor Lodge, a single-story motel with twenty guest rooms, each of which has color television, air-conditioning, and a private bath. All rooms face the woods on one side.

Also available are wood-frame "hotel" cottages, with appointments like those in the motor lodge, and "woodland" cottages—rustic units without air-conditioning or television. The woodland cottages are two-room units scattered in a wooded area.

Accommodations: 38 hotel rooms, 20 motel rooms, and 48 cottages, all with private bath. *Towels and linens:* Provided. *Cooking and eating utensils:* Not provided. *Stove and refrigerator:* Not provided. *Pets:* Permitted in the kennnel. *Open:* All year. *Mailing address:* National Park Concessions, Inc., General Offices, Mammoth Cave, KY 42259. *Phone:* (502) 758-2225. *Driving instructions:* From Bowling Green take I-65 north to Route 70; then go west on Route 70 to the park entrance.

The 1,934-acre Natural Bridge State Park is in eastern Kentucky, about 50 miles southeast of Lexington, within the boundaries of Daniel Boone National Forest. The park is named for its main attraction, the 65-foot high natural sandstone bridge. A "skylift" runs up to the bridge, providing passengers with panoramic mountain views of eastern Kentucky. Another scenic attraction is the Red River Gorge Geologic Area at the park's edge, where hiking trails run along its rim. Although best known for Natural Bridge, mentioned above, the park and geologic area—administered by the U.S. Forest Service—contain over 150 other arches within a five mile radius of Natural Bridge. The other arches range in size from 4 feet to 90 feet in diameter.

Two differing forests are within the park: At lower levels are mixed deciduous trees, hemlock and beech; up on the ridges, oak and pine are predominant. The 54-acre Mill Creek Lake has boat rentals in summer and is stocked with rainbow trout; anglers also go after bass and crappies. Park activities include hiking, backpacking, horseback riding, and tennis, and the park has a swimming pool.

Natural Bridge Park Lodge and Cottages

The park lodge is a modern stone-and-wood building on a rise overlooking a tributary of the Red River. The lodge has a restaurant, a gift shop, meeting and banquet facilities, and thirty-five guest rooms, each with wall-to-wall carpeting, color television, a telephone, a private bath, and a balcony overlooking either the creek or the woods.

The lodge also administers ten rustic cottages a half mile away. A combination of frame and log construction, each has a kitchen, color television, a telephone, carpeting, and a screened porch. Two of the cottages have fireplaces.

Accommodations: 35 lodge rooms and 10 cottages, all with private bath. *Towels and linens:* Provided. *Cooking and eating utensils:* In cottages. *Stove and refrigerator:* In cottages. *Pets:* Dogs permitted (damage deposit required). *Open:* Lodge all year, except for two weeks at Christmas and New Years; cottages, April through October. *Mailing address:* Slade, KY 40376. *Phone:* (606) 663-2214. *Driving instructions:* From the Bert T. Combs Mountain Parkway, exit at Slade and take Route 11 south about 2 miles.

Pennyrile Forest State Park is in western Kentucky, about 75 miles west of Bowling Green. The 15,000-acre state forest borders the Tradewater River and Lake Beshear. The state-park portion of the forest consists of 435 acres, including a 55-acre lake with a sand beach and a bathhouse. Facilities include boats for rent and a nine-hole golf course, tennis courts, miniature golf, shuffleboard, numerous hiking trails, and horses (from Memorial Day to Labor Day only).

Pennyrile Forest Lodge and Cabins

The park has a rustic stone-and-wood lodge with a restaurant, a gift shop, meeting and banquet facilities, and twenty-four guest rooms, each with wall-to-wall carpeting, color television, a telephone, two double beds, air-conditioning, and a private bath.

The lodge also administers three types of cottages—one-room efficiencies, one-bedroom cottages, and two-bedroom cottages. The cottages can accommodate from two to six people, and each has color television, a telephone, a kitchenette, air-conditioning, and a private bath. A swimming pool is reserved for lodge and cottage guests.

Accommodations: 24 lodge rooms and 19 cottages, all with private bath. *Towels and linens:* Provided. *Cooking and eating utensils:* In cottages. *Stove and refrigerator:* In cottages. *Pets:* Not permitted. *Open:* All year, except for two weeks at the end of December and the beginning of January. *Mailing address:* Route 4, Box 137, Dawson Springs, KY 42408. *Phone:* (502) 797-3421. *Driving instructions:* Pennyrile Forest State Park is off Route 109, about 5 miles southeast of Dawson Springs.

15 *Pine Mountain State Park*   **KENTUCKY**

The 2,500-acre Pine Mountain State Park is in southeastern Kentucky, about 100 miles southeast of Lexington near Cumberland Gap and the point where the Kentucky, Tennessee, and Virginia borders meet. Adjacent to Kentucky Ridge State Forest, the park is hilly and wooded, primarily with oaks, maples, hemlocks, spruces, beeches, and tulip trees. There are five hiking trails, one leading to Chained Rock, which rises about 1,200 feet above the surrounding terrain, offering a bird's-eye view of the town of Pineville. Each May the park holds a mountain-laurel festival.

Activities include golf on the nine-hole course, miniature golf, shuffleboard, basketball, and volleyball.

Pine Mountain Lodge and Cabins

Pine Mountain is a thirty-bedroom rustic stone-and-wood lodge of modern design that includes a restaurant, a gift shop, an upper and a lower lounge with fireplaces, and meeting and

195

banquet facilities. Each guest room has wall-to-wall carpeting, color television, a telephone, a private bath, and sliding glass doors that lead to private balconies that overlook Kentucky Ridge State Forest.

The lodge also administers twenty cottages, half of which have one bedroom and the other half two. The one-bedroom cottages, built of logs, are on a steep hill. The two-bedroom cottages are of frame construction. All have color television, telephones, kitchens, air-conditioning, and private baths. There is a swimming pool reserved for use by lodge, camping, and cottage guests only.

Accommodations: 30 lodge rooms and 20 cottages, all with private bath. *Towels and linens:* Provided. *Cooking and eating utensils:* In cottages. *Stove and refrigerator:* In cottages. *Pets:* Discouraged (a damage deposit may be required). *Open:* All year, except for the one-bedroom cottages which are closed from December through March. *Mailing address:* PO Box 610, Pine Mountain State Park, Pineville, KY 40977. *Phone:* (606) 337-3066. *Driving instructions:* Pine Mountain State Park is off U.S. 25E on Route 190, a little more than a mile southeast of Pineville.

The 377-acre Rough River Dam State Resort Park is in north-western Kentucky, roughly 70 miles southwest of Louisville, bordering Rough River Lake, a 4,860-acre impoundment of the Rough River. Sixty different species of fish inhabit the lake, which has a beach and bathhouse, a marina with launching facilities, open and closed slips, and fishing boats, rowboats, and pontoon boats for rent. *Lady of the Lake,* a cruise boat, makes excursions around the lake from Memorial Day to Labor Day.

Activities include hiking, volleyball, tennis, shuffleboard, archery, miniature golf, and golf on the park's nine-hole, par-3 course.

Rough River Lodge and Cottages

Rough River Lodge is a modern stone-and-glass building with a restaurant, a gift shop, and banquet and meeting facilities and forty guest rooms, each with wall-to-wall carpeting, color television, a telephone, a private bath, and a balcony. The accommodations also include fifteen two-bedroom cottages, each with a living room, a kitchen, color television, a telephone, air-conditioning, and a private bath. There is a swimming pool reserved for lodge and cottage guests.

Accommodations: 40 lodge rooms and 15 cottages, all with private bath. *Towels and linens:* Provided. *Cooking and eating utensils:* In cottages. *Stove and refrigerator:* In cottages. *Pets:* Not permitted. *Open:* All year except two weeks at the end of December and beginning of January. *Mailing address:* Rough River Dam State Resort Park, Falls of Rough, KY 40119. *Phone:* (502) 257-2311. *Driving instructions:* Rough River Dam State Resort Park is off Route 79, about 15 miles south of Hardinsburg.

Louisiana

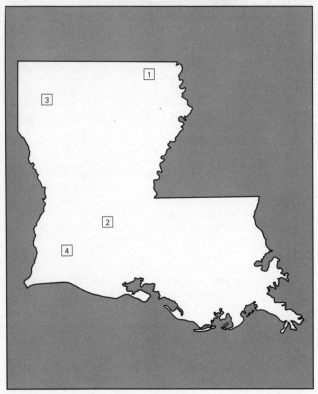

State map and tourist information: Office of Tourism, PO Box 44291, Baton Rouge, LA 70804; 505-925-3860. **State parks:** *Information:* Office of State Parks, PO Drawer 1111, Baton Rouge, LA 70821; 504-925-3830. *Entrance fees:* $1 per vehicle, up to 4 people; waived for lodgers. *Reservations:* Contact individual park. Deposit for first night's lodgings must be received within 7 days. Reservations for January 1—May 31 accepted October 1 annually, by telephone only (after October 10, by telephone and in writing); June 1—December 31, accepted January 1 annually, by telephone only, (after January 10, by telephone and in writing). Recommend that reservations be made in the first week of January and October. Maximum stay, 14 days. *Restrictions:* No hunting. Children under 18 must be accompanied by an adult. Dogs must be leashed (not allowed in lodgings). *Facilities:* Open all year.

The 522-acre Chemin-A-Haut State Park is in northeastern Louisiana, roughly 10 miles north of Bastrop and 5 miles south of the Arkansas border. "Chemin-A-Haut" comes from the French that means, literally, "high road." The term applies to an Indian Trail used many years ago as a migration route. The reason a high road was necessary for traveling through this part of Louisiana has to do with bayous, two of which—Bayou Chemin-A-Haut and Bayou Bartholemew—intersect here. The park's terrain consists of cypress-lined and wildflower-studded bayous and, on somewhat higher ground, thick stands of mature virgin pines.

The park contains an artificial lake, which is stocked with varieties of freshwater fish, and has a boat-rental concession. The swimming pool here is open from June through September, and a trail meanders through wooded sections of the park.

The park has three wood-frame cabins and a group lodge. The cabins are in a grove of oaks and pines about 300 yards from the lake. These cabins, which can accommodate as many as eight, are one room with brick fireplaces, fully equipped kitchen facilities, screened porches, and private baths.

The group lodge, which is near the cabins, was designed to accommodate a party of up to twenty-six. It consists of a dormitory and a main lodge with a fireplace, rest rooms, a large kitchen, and a large meeting or dining area.

Accommodations: 3 cabins with private bath and a group lodge with shared baths. *Towels:* Not provided. *Linens:* Provided. *Cooking and eating utensils:* Provided. *Stove and refrigerator:* Provided. *Pets:* Permitted if on leashes, but not in public buildings. *Open:* All year. *Mailing address:* Route 5, Box 617, Bastrop, LA 71220. *Phone:* (318) 281-5805. *Driving instructions:* Chemin-A-Haut State Park is off Route 139 about 10 miles north of Bastrop.

Chicot State Park, in southern Louisiana about 70 miles northwest of Baton Rouge, comprises 6,480 acres and encircles a 2,000-acre reservoir stocked with breams, bass, crappies, and other freshwater fish. The park is adjacent to the Louisiana State Arboretum, a 300-acre area displaying more than 150 species of native Louisiana plant life. Boating and fishing are perhaps the most popular park activities, and there are three launching sites, a boat house, and boat-rental facilities, as well as a fishing dock for youngsters.

The park has an Olympic-size swimming pool overlooking the lake, which is open from Memorial Day through Labor Day, and a hiking and backpacking trail, complete with primitive campsites along the way, that runs around the perimeter of the lake. The park itself is open all year.

Chicot State Park Lodge and Cabins

The park has twenty-seven wood-frame cabins available about 200 feet from the lake in an area wooded primarily with hickories, pines, and oaks. Twelve of the cabins have two rooms, each of which has a screened porch and sleeps four. Fifteen cabins have two bedrooms that sleep six, a living and dining area, and heat and air-conditioning. All have full kitchen facilities.

The Conservation Lodge at the northern end of the lake has its own boathouse for use by visitors and sleeps twelve on two double and four bunk beds. The great room has a fireplace, a game table, and a ceiling fan. The lodge has a full kitchen and bath, as well as central heat and air-conditioning.

Chicot Park also has two Group Camps. Group Camp I, on the south shore of the lake, accommodates up to 160 persons, with a dormatory that sleeps 100 and five cabins that sleep twelve people each, built over the lake and connected by boardwalk. This lodge has a kitchen, a dining room and a swimming pool and is accessible to the handicapped.

Accommodations: 27 cabins and 1 group lodge, all with private bath, and 2 group camps. *Towels:* Not provided. *Linens:* Provided. *Cooking and eating utensils:* Provided. *Stove and refrigerator:* Provided. *Pets:* Permitted if on leashes, but not in public buildings. *Open:* All year. *Mailing address:* Route 3, Box 494, Ville Platte, LA 70586. *Phone:* (318) 363-2403. *Driving instructions:* Chicot State Park is off Route 3042 about 6 miles north of Ville Platte.

Lake Bistineau, in northwestern Louisiana about 30 miles east of Shreveport, has a curious history. It was formed in 1800, when a logjam in the Red River flooded thousands of acres of land. The lake was eventually drained by dredging in the late nineteenth century, but it appeared again when a permanent dam was erected on Loggy Bayou. Today the lake has a surface area of about 27 square miles and an average depth of 7 feet, getting as deep as 25 feet in places.

Lake Bistineau State Park, which occupies 750 acres on the western shore of the lake, is popular among boaters, fishermen, swimmers, and birders. Visitors can rent boats or launch their own, and anglers can hook black crappies, yellow and largemouth bass, redear sunfish, bluehead chubs, and bluegills. The park has a beach, a swimming pool, and hiking trails. American kestrels and red-tailed hawks are common, and a naturalist who maintains the park's bird-feeding station reports having seen fifty ruby-throated hummingbirds hovering about the nectar.

The park has thirteen wood-frame cabins in a grove of oaks and pines along the shore of Lake Bistineau, each with a lake view and two bedrooms, a fully equipped kitchen, air-conditioning, and a screened porch. About half of the cabins have fireplaces.

Accommodations: 13 cabins with private bath. *Towels:* Not provided. *Linens:* Provided. *Cooking and eating utensils:* Provided. *Stove and refrigerator:* Provided. *Pets:* Permitted on leashes, but not in cabins. *Open:* All year. *Mailing address:* PO Box 7, Doyline, LA 71023. *Phone:* (318) 745-3503. *Driving instructions:* Lake Bistineau State Park is east of Route 163 about 7 miles south of Doyline.

Comprising 1,068 acres of land and water, Sam Houston Jones State Park is in southwestern Louisiana, just west of the Calcasieu River and a few miles north of Calcasieu Lake. The park is at the confluence of the Calcasieu and Houston rivers and Indian Bayou, and large parts of its terrain are lagoons. Many hiking trails wind through these lagoons and through wooded areas, including a trail once used by stagecoaches that passes by several of the Calcasieu River tributaries. Another trail passes over a wooden bridge that spans a lagoon and is flanked on either side by heavy woods.

The park has boat-rental and launch facilities and two docks. In addition to boating and fishing, birding is popular: Being close to the Gulf of Mexico, this part of Louisiana is a natural stopping place for all manner of migrating birds. More than 200 species have been identified in the park and its environs.

Sam Houston Jones State Park has twelve wood-frame cabins situated among oaks and magnolias beside Indian Bayou. Each cabin, some of which can accommodate as many as eight, has either one or two bedrooms, a fully equipped kitchen, a private bath, and air-conditioning. Some have a screened porch.

Accommodations: 12 cabins with private bath. *Towels:* Not provided. *Linens:* Provided. *Cooking and eating utensils:* Provided. *Stove and refrigerator:* Provided. *Pets:* Not Permitted. *Open:* All year. *Mailing address:* Route 4, Box 290, Lake Charles, LA 70611. *Phone:* (318) 855-7371. *Driving instructions:* Sam Houston Jones State Park is off Route 378 about 12 miles north of the city of Lake Charles.

Maine

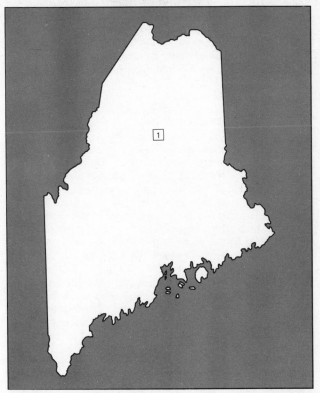

State map and tourist information: Maine Publicity Bureau, 97 Winthrop Street, Hallowell, ME 04347; 207-289-2423. **State parks:** *Information:* Dept. of Conservation, Bureau of Parks, State House Station 22, Augusta ME 04333; 207-289-3821. (For Baxter State Park information, contact park.) *Entrance fees:* $5 per vehicle (at Baxter State Park only for out-of-staters). *Reservations:* Contact park; Send payment for entire stay in advance. Reservations recommended 4 months in advance for mid May—October. *Restrictions:* Hunting limited to selected areas. No pets and no vehicles more than 9 feet high, 7 wide, 22 long. *Facilities:* Swimming and canoeing, mid June—September; hiking trails, May—October.

Baxter State Park, in north-central Maine at the southern terminus of the Allagash Wilderness Waterway, was a 200,000-acre gift from former Governor Percival P. Baxter to the State of Maine. His first bequest was made in 1931, when he donated 5,960 acres that included Mount Katahdin, at 5,268 feet the highest point in Maine. He donated other parcels of land over the years, with a final gift of 7,764 acres in 1962.

The park has 46 mountain peaks and ridges, 18 of which rise higher than 3,000 feet, and a terrain that varies from hilly to rugged. The Appalachian Trail—which begins in Georgia and extends for 2,050 miles—ends here at Mount Katahdin. Trees vary with the elevation, but the forest consists mainly of ashes, maples, birches, spruces, firs, and pines. The park supports a wide variety of wildflowers, ranging from high-elevation alpine species to stands of wild lupine and several types of wild orchids. Wildlife includes moose, deer, black bears, coyotes, foxes, bobcats, otters, and beavers. All manner of warblers, three-toed northern woodpeckers, migrating ducks and geese, red-tailed and broad-winged hawks, and nesting bald eagles are a few of the park's avian residents. The park has a few waterfalls.

Hiking, fishing, mountain climbing, camping, and backpacking are the principal park activities, and although most of the area is a wildlife preserve, there are sections where hunting is permitted. Facilities are primitive, and visitors should be prepared to purify any water they drink or cook with. There is no electricity.

The park has eleven log cabins in a wooded area along the shores of Daicey Pond. The cabins, varying in size and accommodating from two to four persons, have no water and no electricity and are lighted by propane lanterns. There are no showers, and sanitary facilities consist of outside pit toilets. The cabins have exposed-log interiors and minimal furnishings.

Accommodations: 11 cabins with privy. *Towels and linens:* Not provided. *Cooking and eating utensils:* Not provided. *Refrigerator:* Not provided. *Stove:* Wood stove for heat only. *Pets:* Not permitted. *Open:* One cabin is winterized and open all year; the others are open from May through October. *Mailing address:* 64 Balsam Drive, Millnocket, ME 04462. *Phone:* (207) 723-5140. *Driving instructions:* Take I-95 to the Medway exit; then take Route 157 northwest 28 miles.

Maryland

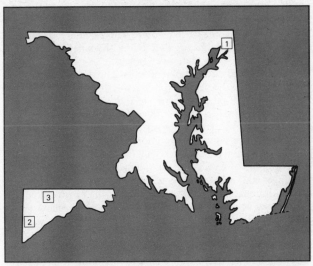

State map and tourist information: Dept. of Economic & Community Dev., 45 Calvert St., Annapolis, MD 21401; 301-269-2686. **State parks:** *Information:* Forest, Parks & Wildlife Service, Dept. of Natural Resources, Tawes State Office bldg., Annapolis, MD 21401; 301-269-3776. *Entrance fees:* $3 per vehicle (state residents) and $4 per vehicle (out-of-stater); waived for lodgers. *Reservations:* Applications for one weeks rentals accepted beginning Dec. 1 for June 1—Labor Day. Must be received by the Forest, Park & Wildlife Service by the 2nd Monday in January; Lottery held on the 3rd Monday in January and notification sent early February. $50 deposit required by the end of February. Reservations are accepted on a first-come, first-served basis for the off season. *Restrictions:* Hunting limited to certain parks only. No pets. Children under 18 must be accompanied by an adult. *Facilities:* Swimming, Mem. Day—Labor Day.

Elk Neck State Park is in northeastern Maryland, at the top of Chesapeake Bay, on a peninsula formed by the Northeast and Elk rivers about 30 miles northeast of Baltimore and near the 3,165-acre Elk Neck State Forest. The 2,400-acre park supports an unusually large population of white-tailed deer and encompasses diverse habitats—sandy beaches on the Northeast River, marshlands, and thickly wooded bluffs that rise as high as 250 feet above the river. The area is wooded mainly with oaks, maples, poplars, mountain laurels, and white pines; there are willows and bullrushes and wildflowers in the marshlands, where great blue herons and a wide variety of waterfowl frequently appear, especially during migrations.

The park has five well-marked hiking trails, which range from three-quarters of a mile to 2 miles long. (Maps are available at the ranger station.) A designated beach on the Northeast River has a bathhouse, and visitors may swim at their own risk at the park's other beaches. Fishermen go after white and yellow perch, rockfish, and catfish, and aluminum rowboats, with or without motors, are available for rent. Other facilities include picnic areas, three playgrounds, and interpretative programs.

The park has nine wood-frame cabins on a wooded bluff overlooking the Elk River. Two-bedroom units, they can accommodate from four to six people, and each has a kitchenette, a living area, and a screened porch. The cabins have cold running water in the kitchen but no shower or sanitary facilities, which are available in a central bathhouse.

Accommodations: 9 cabins with central shared bath. *Towels:* Not provided. *Linens:* Provided. *Cooking and eating utensils:* Not provided. *Stove and refrigerator:* Provided. *Pets:* Not permitted. *Open:* Mid-May through the second weekend in October. *Mailing address:* 4395 Turkey Point Road, North East, MD 21901. *Phone:* (301) 287-5333. *Driving instructions:* Elk Neck State Park is off Route 272, about 10 miles south of North East.

Herrington Manor State Park is in far-western Maryland about a mile from the West Virginia border. The 300-acre park is within the boundaries of the 6,825-acre Garrett State Forest, where Maryland's scientific forestry program began in 1906. The terrain is hilly and wooded primarily with oaks, hickories, maples, beeches, hemlocks, and pines. Twenty miles south of Mount Davis, the highest point in Pennsylvania, and 10 miles north of Backbone Mountain (3,360 feet), the highest point in Maryland, the park is in the Appalachian Mountains at an average elevation of about 2,500 feet. There is a 53-acre lake, an impoundment of Herrington Creek, that has a beach with a bathhouse and boats for rent—canoes and rowboats. Anglers fish the lake for trout and bass, and those who enjoy walking set out on the park's hiking trails, most of which connect with longer trails that go into Garrett State Forest.

Activities include bicycling (rentals available), picnicking, and cross-country skiing, as well as guided walks, campfire programs, and use of a nature center. A nearby attraction is Swallow Falls State Park, about 4 miles distant, with its scenic gorges and three waterfalls, one of which, Muddy Creek Falls, has a vertical drop of 63 feet, the largest in Maryland.

Herrington Manor State Park has twenty log cabins in a wooded area about a hundred yards from the lake. The cabins vary in size and can accommodate from two to six persons. Each has a kitchenette, a wood stove or a stone fireplace, a private bath, and an open porch.

Accommodations: 20 cabins with private bath. *Towels:* Not provided. *Linens:* Provided. *Cooking and eating utensils:* Provided. *Stove and refrigerator:* Provided. *Pets:* Not permitted. *Open:* 20 cabins are open mid-May to mid-September; 10 are open all year. *Mailing address:* RFD 5, Box 122, Oakland, MD 21550. *Phone:* (301) 334-9180. *Driving instructions:* Herrington Manor State Park is off county Route 20 about 5 miles northwest of Oakland.

New Germany State Park is in northwestern Maryland, about 7 miles south of the Pennsylvania border and 14 miles north of West Virginia. Its 300 acres are within the boundaries of the 53,000-acre Savage River Forest, which protects the watershed of the Savage River area and its impoundment, Westernport Reservoir. Hilly, rocky, and rugged, the terrain, at an average elevation of about 2,600 feet, is thickly wooded with red and white oaks, hickories, tulip trees, sugar and red maples, black and yellow birches, beeches, basswood, wild cherries, dogwoods, hemlocks, spruces, and eastern white pines. Deer, foxes, beavers, and raccoons are commonly found, and now and again a black bear passes through. The park and surrounding forest support a wide variety of birds, from wood ducks and belted kingfishers to scarlet tanagers, red-tailed hawks, and great horned owls.

A small dam impounding Poplar Lick forms a 13-acre lake that has two beaches and a bathhouse, as well as rowboat and paddleboat rentals. The lake is stocked with trout, and anglers also go after bass and catfishes. Among other facilities are hiking trails connecting with longer trails in the state forest, picnicking areas, a playground, and interpretative activities that include guided walks and campfire programs. In winter the park and forest hiking trails turn into cross-country ski trails, and snowmobilers use many of the forest's old logging roads.

New Germany State Park has eleven log cabins on a hillside thick with pines. Each has a kitchen-living area, knotty-pine paneling, a stone fireplace, an open porch, and a private bath. Cabins vary in size and can accommodate from two to six people; some have sleeping lofts.

Accommodations: 11 cabins with private bath. *Towels:* Not provided. *Linens:* Provided. *Cooking and eating utensils:* Provided. *Stove and refrigerator:* Provided. *Pets:* Not permitted. *Open:* Third Friday of May through the second Saturday of October; four cabins are open all year. *Mailing address:* Route 2, Grantsville, MD 21536. *Phone:* (301) 895-5453. *Driving instructions:* Take U.S. 48 to Grantsville, then pick up Lower New Germany Road and follow it south for 5 miles.

Massachusetts

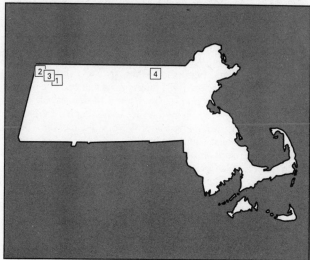

State map and tourist information: Dept. of Commerce, Tourist Office, 100 Cambridge St., 13th Floor, Boston, MA 02202; 617-727-3201. **State parks:** *Information:* Div. of Forest & Parks, 100 Cambridge St., Boston, MA 02202; 617-727-3180. *Entrance fees:* $3 per vehicle daily; waived for lodgers and senior citizens. *Reservations:* Contact individual parks. Reservations accepted January 1 (and recommended by mid-April) for June 1—Labor Day. Reservations recommended 2 weeks in advance during off season. $20.00 deposit must be received within 10 days. Minimum stay, 1 week; maximum stay, 2 weeks from June 1—Labor Day; 2-night minimum during rest of the year. *Restrictions:* Dogs must be leashed. Children under 18 must be accompanied by an adult (camping only). *Facilities:* Swimming, boating, and interpretative programs, Mem. Day—Labor Day. Cross-country skiing and snowmobiling, December—March.

Mohawk Trail State Forest, about 7,000 acres in northwestern Massachusetts roughly 11 miles southeast of North Adams and 8 miles south of the Vermont border, is named for an Indian trail that ran from North Adams to just outside Boston; sections of it are still in use. The mountainous terrain—elevations range from 1,200 to 1,961 feet—is wooded primarily with oaks, maples, white pines, hemlocks, ashes, spruces, and mountain laurels, with a plantation of red pines in one section. The forest's southern boundary is marked by Hawks Mountain, elevation 1,880 feet, which as its name implies is frequented by hawks, especially during the fall migration. Wildlife includes deer, black bears, foxes, bobcats, and coyotes.

Cold River runs through the forest, as does Indian Spring, which flows from a fissure in the rocks, forms a very small stream, then empties into the river. A swimming area has been formed by diverting the Cold River, and of 13 miles of hiking trails, almost 11 are used as snowmobile trails in winter. Activities also include cross-country skiing, snowshoeing, hunting, picnicking, and fishing (the Cold River is stocked with trout). The forest is within 5 miles of a downhill-ski area.

The forest's five log cabins are in a thickly wooded area at the base of Todd Mountain. Two have three rooms and can accommodate five people. These units have cold running water in summer. The other two cabins have one room and can accommodate three, with water available at an outside spigot. All have exposed-log interiors, porches, a stone fireplace with wood-stove insert, as well as outside fireplaces and bunk beds made of logs. There are no showers, and sanitary facilities consist of outside pit toilets. The cabins are inaccessible by auto during the winter months (¼ mile hike required).

Accommodations: 5 cabins with privy. *Towels and linens:* Not provided. *Cooking and eating utensils:* Not provided. *Stove and refrigerator:* Wood stove and outside fireplace only. *Pets:* Permitted if leashed. *Open:* All year. *Mailing address:* PO Box 7, Charlemont, MA 01339. *Phone:* (413) 339-5504. *Driving instructions:* Mohawk Trail State Forest is on Route 2, 23 miles west of the I-91 rotary at Greenfield, Massachusetts.

Mount Greylock State Reservation is a 10,500-acre forest in north-western Massachusetts, about 8 miles south of the Vermont border and about the same distance east of the New York border. In the Berkshire Mountains, the reservation ranges in elevation from 1,200 to 3,941 feet and encompasses Mount Greylock, the highest point in Massachusetts. From its summit the panoramic view extends to five states—Connecticut, Massachusetts, New Hampshire, New York, and Vermont. The mountainous terrain is wooded primarily with beeches, birches, maples, and mountain laurels. Some 35 miles of hiking trails include a 14-mile section of the Appalachian Trail, which passes over the summit of Greylock. The reservation includes several small streams, a few small ponds, and a steep-walled glacial cirque, or funnel-like area, lined with 100-year-old red spruces. Characteristic wildlife includes deer, raccoons, foxes, wild turkeys, and black bears. The reservation has an unusually large population of American kestrels (sparrow hawks), and Mount Greylock is an excellent vantage point for hawk watchers, especially during the fall migration.

Activities include bicycling, hiking, camping, picnicking, hunting, horseback riding, cross-country skiing, and snowmobiling. Interpretative programs are offered in the summer months, and the visitors' center's displays (open all year) include one covering the Civilian Conservation Corps' history in the area. *Park phone:* (413) 499-4262.

Bascom Lodge

On the southern slope of Mount Greylock about 100 feet below its summit is the rustic stone-and-log Bascom Lodge, owned by the Massachusetts Department of Environmental Management and operated by the Appalachian Mountain Club. It has a dining room that overlooks the Berkshires' rolling hills, a large lobby with a stone fireplace, and an enclosed sunporch that also offers panoramic views.

The six guest rooms have hardwood floors partially covered by area rugs, wooden dressers, and iron beds. The rooms on the west side of the lodge have mountain views, and those on the east side are flooded with sunlight in the morning. Varying in size and accommodating from four to ten, the rooms all share baths.

Accommodations: 6 rooms with shared bath. *Pets:* Not permitted. *Open:* May through October. *Mailing address:* Mount Greylock State Reservation, Rockwell Road, Lanesboro, MA 01237. *Phone:* (413) 743-1591. *Driving instructions:* Mount Greylock State Reservation is off Route 7, about 3 miles north of Lanesboro.

Savoy Mountain State Forest, 10 miles long and 5 miles wide, is in northwestern Massachusetts, about 6 miles southeast of North Adams and about the same distance south of the Vermont border. Its 11,500 acres in the Berkshire Mountains, are hilly, have an average elevation of close to 2,000 feet, and are thickly wooded, primarily with hemlocks, beeches, red and sugar maples, and white ashes, as well as with quite a bit of mountain laurel, especially around the forest's five ponds. Several streams run through the forest including Ross Brook, which feeds Tannery Falls with its vertical 75-foot drop. Parker Brook, which feeds Tannery Pond, merges with Ross Brook at the bottom of the falls. Other scenic features include several balanced rocks and freshwater swamps. Dressed up with lady's slippers and purple trilliums, the swamps attract great blue herons, egrets, and other waterfowl.

The forest is an excellent place for hawk watchers, primarily during the fall migration, when red-tailed, broad-winged, and sharp-shinned hawks and goshawks soar above. Characteristic wildlife includes deer, red foxes, and quite a few black bears.

Activities include hiking on 30 miles of trails, bicycling on Town Road, swimming at two of the ponds (one with lifeguards in summer), horseback riding (no rentals), camping, picnicking, fishing, snowmobiling, hunting, cross-country skiing, and off-road-vehicle use.

The forest has three rustic 1930s log cabins constructed of red spruce by the Civilian Conservation Corps in a wooded area overlooking South Pond. Each is furnished with bunk beds, a picnic table, and benches, as well as a wood stove for heat and outdoor fireplaces for cooking. The cabins have no running water, and sanitary facilities consist of outdoor pit toilets. Showers are available at a central facility in summer only.

Accommodations: 3 cabins with privy and central showers. *Towels and linens:* Not provided. *Cooking and eating utensils:* Not provided. *Stove:* Wood stove and outside fireplace. *Refrigerator:* Not provided. *Pets:* Not permitted. *Open:* All year. *Mailing address:* RFD 2, North Adams, MA 01247. *Phone:* (413) 663-8469. *Driving instructions:* Savoy Mountain State Forest is on Central Shaft Road about 3 miles south of Route 2 and Florida, Massachusetts.

Willard Brook State Forest is in north central Massachusetts, about 6 miles north of Fitchburg and 4 miles south of the New Hampshire border. Its 5,000 acres are in a thickly wooded valley, the predominant trees being oaks, maples, birches, poplars, and spruces. Stocked with trout, Willard Brook winds through the valley, as do some dozen hiking trails that vary in length from 1 to 5 miles. One trail follows the brook for 3 miles and then runs up into the hills. Damon Pond has a sand beach with a bathhouse, and other facilities include campsites, picnicking areas, snowmobile and cross-country ski trails, bridle paths, and fishing areas. Characteristic wildlife include deer, foxes, and raccoons, while the forest supports a variety of birds, including passerines, pheasant, and hawks.

The forest's four rustic log cabins, built in the 1930s by the Civilian Conservation Corps, are in a wooded area and vary in size from one to three rooms accommodating up to five people. Each has a refrigerator and a stone fireplace, where guests can cook (or bring their own stove). The cabins come with running water but have no showers. Sanitary facilities consist of outside pit toilets.

Accommodations: 4 cabins with running water and privy. *Towels and linens:* Not provided. *Cooking and eating utensils:* Not provided. *Stove:* Fireplace provided. *Refrigerator:* Not provided. *Pets:* Not permitted. *Open:* May through October. *Mailing address:* RFD, Route 119, West Townsend, MA 01474. *Phone:* (617) 597-8802. *Driving instructions:* Willard Brook State Forest is off Route 119, approximately 15 miles west of Groton.

Michigan

State map and tourist information: Dept. of Commerce, Travel Bureau, 333 S. Capitol Ave., Box 30226, Lansing MI 48909; 517-373-1195. **State parks:** *Information:* Dept. of Natural Resources, Parks Div., PO Box 30028, Lansing, MI 48909; 517-373-1270. *Entrance fees:* $2 per vehicle daily; $10, annually. *Reservations:* Contact individual park. Full payment required within 2 weeks. Some parks accept reservations in early January; others, up to 1 year in advance. *Restrictions:* Dogs must be leashed in camping and picnic areas (not allowed in lodgings). *Facilities:* Swimming, boating, and interpretative programs, Mem. Day—Labor Day. Cross-country skiing and snowmobiling, November—March. Horseback riding, April—October.

215

Fort Custer State Recreation Area is in southwestern Michigan about 15 miles northeast of Kalamazoo. The 3,033-acre recreation area, bordered for 4 miles by the Kalamazoo River, varies in terrain from a level floodplain near the river to a succession of gently rolling hills wooded primarily with oaks, hickories, maples, black locusts, and pines. The area's three lakes range in size from 50 to 200 acres. The largest, Eagle Lake, has a 1,000-foot sand beach with a bathhouse and a snack bar concession. Characteristic wildlife includes deer, mink, squirrels, wild turkeys, red-tailed hawks, Cooper's hawks, and an occasional bald eagle. The park has the largest concentration of bluebirds in the state, and birders often travel here from hundreds of miles away.

Activities include swimming, hiking, cross-country skiing, and picnicking. The area was formerly used by the military, and cross-country skiers and hikers benefit from an elaborate series of unmarked roads and trails.

Fort Custer Recreation Area has one rustic, wood-frame group cabin in a wooded area near Jackson Lake that can accommodate twenty people in bunk beds. It has no plumbing—sanitary facilities consist of a pit toilet outside—and occupants must draw water from a nearby pump. The cabin has no electricity, but it is heated by a wood stove.

Accommodations: 1 group cabin with privy. *Towels and linens:* Not provided. *Cooking and eating utensils:* Not provided. *Stove and refrigerator:* Not provided. *Pets:* Permitted if leashed. *Open:* All year. *Mailing address:* 5163 West Fort Custer Drive, Augusta, MI 49012. *Phone:* (616) 731-4200. *Driving instructions:* Fort Custer Recreation Area is off Route 96, about half a mile west of Augusta.

Island Lake Recreation Area is in southeastern Michigan, roughly 20 miles north of Ann Arbor. Its 3,466 acres are hilly and wooded with oaks, hickories, maples, and several species of pines. Of particular note is a 7-mile stretch of the Huron River, a protected scenic river almost entirely undeveloped. The river winds through bluffs and woods, with an old canoe camp the only sign of civilization. Deer and foxes frequent the recreation area, as do orioles, bluebirds, ducks, and red-tailed hawks. Activities include fishing, hiking, hunting, and swimming. Two of the park's three beaches have bathhouses; the other has pit toilets.

Island Lake has one wood-frame group cabin that can accommodate twenty people in bunk beds. The cabin, in a wooded area between Island Lake and the Huron River, has a wood stove for heat and for warming food and beverages (firewood is supplied). There is neither electricity nor plumbing, and occupants must draw water from a pump outside the cabin. Sanitary facilities consist of a pit toilet outside.

Accommodations: 1 group cabin with privy. *Towels and linens:* Not provided. *Cooking and eating utensils:* Not provided. *Stove and refrigerator:* Not provided. *Pets:* Not permitted. *Open:* All year. *Mailing address:* 12950 East Grand River, Brighton, MI 48116. *Phone:* (313) 229-7067. *Driving instructions:* Island Lake Recreation Area is off I-96 (exit 151) about 3 miles east of Brighton.

Isle Royale National Park is an island in Lake Superior about 70 miles north of the northwestern Michigan mainland. The 571,796-acre park, 45 miles long and 9 wide, is the largest island in Lake Superior and is, in fact, closer to the mainland of Canada than to that of the United States. (Ontario is only 15 miles away.) Although there are 166 miles of hiking trails, there are no roads and no vehicles; the only way to get here is by boat or sea-plane. The wild terrain consists of volcanic rock that was at one time submerged under Lake Superior and, before that, under a mile-thick glacier which carved out scores of basins that are now lakes. Elevations vary from 602 feet (Lake Superior's height above sea level) to 1394 feet, and the area is wooded with tamaracks, cedars, balsams, spruces, maples, and alders.

The island was once extensively mined for copper (the remains of pre-Columbian copper mines are visible) and heavily trapped for fur. The mammal population was almost eradicated, but these days beavers, mink, muskrats, and black bears thrive. There was once an overpopulation of moose on the island, but timber wolves appeared in time to provide a natural check to the overabundance.

The concessionaire offers charter fishing and runs a sightseeing boat, and the park's naturalist service has interpretative programs and guided walks.

Park Mailing address: 87 North Ripley Street, Houghton, MI 49931. *Phone:* (906) 482-0984.

Rock Harbor Lodge and Cabins

Rock Harbor Lodge is a group of four two-storied motel-style buildings and ten duplex cabins. Facilities include a gift shop, a dining room, and coffee shop that overlook Rock Harbor Cove, a marina with a store, boat rentals, charter fishing craft, and dock space. The motel rooms, on two levels, overlook the lake. Each room has wall-to-wall carpeting and a private bath, and each lower-level room has a balcony. Overlooking Tobin Harbor, the housekeeping cabins are a quarter of a mile from the main lodge buildings. Each has a fully equipped kitchenette, a private bath, and maid service.

Accommodations: 60 motel rooms and 20 housekeeping

cabins, all with private bath. *Towels and linens:* Provided. *Cooking and eating utensils:* In cabins. *Stove and refrigerator:* In cabins. *Pets:* Not permitted. *Open:* May through September. *Mailing address:* National Park Concessions Inc., PO Box 405, Houghton, MI 49931. *Phone:* (906) 337-4993; (502) 773-2191 in winter. *Driving instructions:* Isle Royale National Park is accessible only by boat or seaplane; ask for travel instructions when making reservations. Ferries leave from Houghton and Copper Harbor, Michigan, and Grand Portage, Minnesota; and daily seaplane is available.

J. W. Wells State Park is in northwestern Michigan on the shores of Green Bay about 23 miles north of Menominee. Its 974 acres include 3 miles of Green Bay shoreline and a primarily softwood forest—hemlocks, white cedars, white pines—although there are scattered stands of oak and maple. A wide variety of wildlife includes deer, wild turkeys, foxes, grouse, pheasants, gray and fox squirrels, and snowshoe hares. Green Bay is rife with waterfowl, especially during migrations, and visitors will see mergansers, canvasbacks, Canada geese, scaup, black ducks, and mallards. Red-tailed hawks are common; bald eagles and snowy owls are occasionally sighted; and although you may not see them, you will frequently hear pileated woodpeckers.

Hiking, camping, swimming, picnicking, and cross-country skiing are the most popular activities at the park, which has 7 miles of well-marked and well-groomed cross-country ski trails that also serve as hiking trails. For swimming there's a sand beach with a modern bathhouse. State lands near the park offer hunting and fishing—Menominee County is famous for its large deer herd; and Big Cedar River, for its trout and smallmouth bass.

J. W. Wells State Park has six rustic stone-and-log group cabins built by the Civilian Conservation Corps in the 1930s that are in the northern section of the park. Overlooking Green Bay, each can accommodate from one to eight people in bunk beds, and each has a barrel stove for heat and simple cooking and an electric light or gas lantern (but no outlets and no plumbing facilities). Water must be carried from a pump about 100 yards away, and sanitary facilities consist of pit toilets outside. The park provides bulk wood for the stoves and saws for cutting it up.

Accommodations: 6 cabins with privy. *Towels and linens:* Not provided. *Cooking and eating utensils:* Not provided. *Stove:* Wood stove only. *Refrigerator:* Not provided. *Pets:* Permitted if leashed. *Open:* All year. *Mailing address:* M-35, Cedar River, MI 49813. *Phone:* (906) 863-9747. *Driving instructions:* J. W. Wells State Park is off Route 35 about 23 miles north of Menominee.

Ortonville State Recreation Area, 4,500 acres in southeastern Michigan about 20 miles southeast of Flint, has seventeen lakes and is moderately wooded with oaks, hickories, maples, and red and eastern white pines. The hilly terrain is characteristic of a glacial moraine: When the glaciers melted and receded, they left huge deposits throughout the area, creating alternating valleys and hills, which rise as high as 1,200 feet and afford panoramic views. Three lakes are stocked with brown trout and have large populations of bass and other panfish. The recreation area has a beach, 2 miles of cross-country skiing and hiking trails, a riding stable, and a rifle range, and is within 10 miles of the Mount Holly and Pine Knob ski areas.

Ortonville State Recreation Area has one rustic wood-frame group cabin set in the middle of the woods and accommodating up to twenty people in bunk beds. There is a wood stove for heat, and the recreation area supplies wood in bulk, but cabin users must bring their own tools for cutting it to size. The cabin has no plumbing or electricity, and sanitary facilities consist of a pit toilet outside. Water must be carried from a pump about 200 yards away.

Accommodations: 1 group cabin with privy. *Towels and linens:* Not provided. *Cooking and eating utensils:* Not provided. *Stove and refrigerator:* Not provided. *Pets:* Permitted if leashed. *Open:* All year. *Mailing address:* 5779 Hadley Road, Ortonville, MI 48462. *Phone:* (313) 627-3828. *Driving instructions:* Ortonville State Recreation Area is off Route 15, about 1 ½ miles north of Ortonville.

Porcupine Mountains Wilderness State Park is in northwestern Michigan about 17 miles west of Ontonogan. Its 58,000 acres encompass about 20 miles of Lake Superior shoreline and are in a rugged, hilly area. Some of its hills and cliffs rise as high as 1,958 feet—only 22 feet lower than the highest point in the state—and the terrain is thickly wooded almost entirely with virgin hemlocks punctuated with scattered stands of maples and yellow birches. Fifty percent of the park's trees are first growth. Wildlife is abundant and includes bears, deer, and coyotes. Bald eagles nest here, and during migrations the park's three lakes and its Lake Superior coast attract many waterfowl.

Hiking and backpacking are the regular activities along the 80 miles of well-marked trails. Facilities include the Porcupine Mountain Ski Area, which has T-bar lifts, chairlifts, and tow ropes.

The park's thirteen wood-frame trailside cabins, which are much in demand during the trout and deer seasons, can be reached only on foot or, in some cases, by boat. Walking distances to the cabins from the parking area range from 1 to 4 ½ miles.

Cabins vary in size, accommodating from two to eight people. (Most accommodate four.) They are equipped with a wood stove (not suitable for cooking), basic cooking and eating utensils, a saw and an ax (wood is available nearby), and simple tables, chairs, and bunks. Those at Lake of the Clouds, Mirror Lake, and Lily Pond are equipped with rowboats and flotation devices. The cabins have no electricity or running water, and visitors are advised to bring a light source. Water is nearby, and each cabin has a pit toilet outside.

Accommodations: 13 cabins with privy. *Towels and linens:* Not provided. *Cooking and eating utensils:* Provided. *Stove and refrigerator:* Not provided. *Pets:* Permitted. *Open:* All year. *Mailing address:* 599 M-107, Ontonagon, MI 49953. *Phone:* (906) 885-5798. *Driving instructions:* The park is on Route 107 about 3 miles west of Silver City.

Van Riper State Park is a 10,000-acre reserve in northwestern Michigan about 30 miles west of Marquette in the Upper Peninsula that separates Lake Michigan and Lake Superior. The park is in the Huron Mountains 10 miles south of Mount Curwood, at 1,980 feet the highest point in Michigan. The hilly and rocky terrain is wooded primarily with birches, maples, scattered stands of eastern white pines, Norway spruces, and cedars. Deer, grouse, and hawks are common, and black bears occasionally amble by. There are three small lakes—sections of which are surrounded by rock bluffs—but no motors of any kind are permitted. Although fishing is a regular activity, no organic bait is permitted, bass smaller than 18 inches have to be thrown back in, and muskellunge fishing is permitted on a catch-and-release basis only. There are no designated swimming areas, but visitors are free to swim at their own risk. Hikers have a choice of several trails that run through wooded areas and skirt the lakes. Deer hunting and backpack camping are also popular.

Van Riper park has two rustic wood-frame cabins at the northwestern end of Craig Lake. The larger cabin, which has sleeping accommodations for fourteen people, has a combination recreation-dining room with a stone fireplace, three bedrooms, and a kitchen with a liquid propane stove and a gas refrigerator. The fireplace is the only heat source. The smaller cabin, accommodating six people in two bedrooms, has a main room with a wood stove for heat, as well as a liquid-propane refrigerator and stove. The cabins have no electricity and no plumbing. Water must be carried from an outside pump, and sanitary facilities consist of vault toilets outside the cabins.

Accommodations: 2 cabins with vault toilet. *Towels and linens:* Not provided. *Cooking and eating utensils:* Not provided. *Stove and refrigerator:* Provided. *Pets:* Not permitted. *Open:* May through October. *Mailing address:* PO Box 66, Champion, MI 49814. *Phone:* (906) 339-4461. *Driving instructions:* Van Riper State Park is off U.S. 41 near Champion—call for specific directions.

Waterloo State Recreation Area's 20,000 acres are in southeastern Michigan about 20 miles west of Ann Arbor. The terrain varies from low swampy areas to heavily wooded hills with elevations of about 900 feet, forested with hickories, oaks, maples, poplars, cedars, and spruces. There are 21 lakes, numerous streams, and a unique feature—bogs. A black spruce bog in the park is the southernmost one in the Western Hemisphere. Characteristic wildlife includes deer, foxes, and raccoons. Of particular note is the concentration of sandhill cranes, seen especially at dawn and dusk during spring and fall. Unusually graceful, sandhill cranes are about the size of great blue herons, with wingspans of up to 7 feet. They have gray bodies and brilliant red crowns.

Park activities include hiking on miles of trails, swimming, fishing, hunting, horseback riding, cross-country skiing, and ice fishing. Groups of student naturalists come frequently to study the unique assortment of habitats, and the nature center offers numerous interpretative activities. Although there are no supervised swimming areas, you can swim at your own risk on many lakes, and Portage Lake has a large sand beach. Adjacent to the recreation area is a riding stable offering guided horse trips.

The recreation area has two rustic cabins and two group cabins. The rustic cabins, in a wooded area and accommodating twenty people each, have no electricity and no running water. Light is provided by two kerosene lanterns, water must be carried from a pump 100 yards away (water buckets are not provided), and sanitary facilities consist of outside vault toilets. Each cabin has twenty built-in bunks stacked three high, a wood stove for heat and light cooking, and an outside campfire circle.

Two group camps, one at Cedar Lake and one at Mill Lake, will accommodate 120 and 140 people respectively. These accommodations consist of sleeping cabins, a central bath-shower facility, and kitchen and dining facilities. Each group camp, fairly modern and with electricity, has an infirmary. Cedar Lake has seven sleeping cabins; Mill Lake, eight.

Accommodations: 2 rustic cabins with privy and 2 group camps with shared bath. *Towels and linens:* Not provided. *Cooking and eating utensils:* At group camps. *Stove and refrigerator:* At group camps. *Pets:* Not permitted. *Open:* January through November. *Mailing address:* 16345 McClure Road, Chelsea, MI 48118. *Phone:* (313) 475-8307. *Driving instructions:* Waterloo State Recreation Area is off I-94 (exit 156).

The 7,514-acre Wilderness State Park is in northern Michigan about 25 miles northwest of Cheboygan, on the tip of Michigan's Lower Peninsula. It is on a smaller peninsula that forms Sturgeon Bay. Encroaching on the land here, the bay's many inlets have formed a series of brackish marshes on the west side of the park, which attract a wide variety of waterfowl, including ducks, geese, herons, egrets, bald eagles, and ospreys. Eastward in the park the marshes give way to ridges wooded primarily with spruce, balsam fir, tamarack, oak, maple, and birch trees. The park also hosts various species of wild orchids, including showy orchids, calypsos, and lady's slippers.

Activities include swimming from miles of unsupervised beach, hunting, snowshoeing, snowmobiling, and hiking on 12 ½ miles of trails.

Wilderness State Park has rustic wood-frame trailside cabins and rustic frontier cabins. The trailside cabins are in remote wooded areas of the park, but all are accessible by car except for one which can be reached only by a 2-mile hike or by boat. (In summer this cabin is accessible only on foot, passing through 100 feet of 18-inch-deep water.) These trailside cabins have stone fireplaces and small wood stoves for heating and light cooking, along with basic cooking and eating utensils. Visitors are advised to bring a light source and an ax for splitting wood, which is available nearby. All trailside cabins lack electricity and running water but are equipped with pit toilets. Water is available at pumps.

The three frontier cabins, also in a remote, wooded section of the park, can accommodate up to twenty-four people each and have minimal electricity, pit toilets, and hand pumps for water. They are heated by either a wood stove or a fireplace but have no cooking or eating utensils.

Accommodations: 8 cabins with privy. *Towels and linens:* Not provided. *Cooking and eating utensils:* In trailside cabins. *Stove:* Wood stove for light cooking in some units. *Refrigerator:* Not provided. *Pets:* Not permitted. *Open:* All year. *Mailing address:* Carp Lake, MI 49718. *Phone:* (616) 436-5381. *Driving instructions:* Wilderness State Park is off Route C81, 10 miles west of Carp Lake.

Yankee Springs Recreation Area is on 5,000 acres in southwestern Michigan, roughly halfway between Grand Rapids and Kalamazoo and adjacent to the 15,000-acre Barry Game Area. Moderately hilly, the recreation area has nine lakes, including Gun Lake, which feeds Gun River, a tributary of the Kalamazoo. Several lakes are stocked with brown and rainbow trout and walleye, and Gun Lake has a sand beach with a bathhouse and a picnic area. Thickly wooded—primarily with oaks, maples, hickories, dogwoods, sumacs, white pines, and white cedars— the area is particularly scenic in spring, when the dogwoods bloom, and in autumn, when the hardwoods turn color. Abundant wildlife here and in the adjoining game area includes deer, grouse, pheasants, Canada geese, red-tailed hawks, and bluebirds. Pileated woodpeckers have been giving the rangers trouble: For some reason these birds have developed a weakness for wooden signs.

Hiking, swimming, camping, fishing, and cross-country skiing are the most popular activities. The well-groomed 10-mile-long double-loop, cross-country ski trail is also used for hiking.

Yankee Springs has seventeen wood-frame cabins designed for groups in a wooded area along Chief Noonday and Long lakes. The cabins are arranged in "outdoor centers" consisting of a group of cabins (one has seven; the other, eight), a central kitchen–dining hall, and a shower house. Kitchen and shower facilities are available only to groups renting an entire outdoor center, each of which accommodates 120 people.

Cabins are also available individually, and they vary in size from units accommodating ten persons to units sleeping twenty-four. Some have fireplaces that may be used for cooking, and all are heated by gas heaters. The cabins are rustic, with no running water or toilet facilities. Water must be carried from about 2 miles away, and sanitary facilities consist of pit toilets outside.

Accommodations: 17 group cabins with privy. *Towels and linens:* Not provided. *Cooking and eating utensils:* Not provided. *Stove and refrigerator:* Not provided. *Pets:* Not permitted. *Open:* All year. *Mailing address:* 2104 Gun Lake Road, Middleville, MI 49333. *Phone:* (616) 795-9081. *Driving instructions:* Take U.S. 131 to exit 61, then take Route A-42 east 8 miles and look for signs for Yankee Springs Recreation Area.

Minnesota

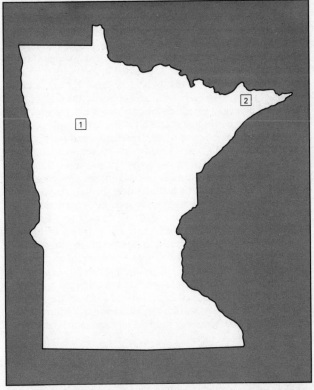

State map and tourist information: Tourist Information Center, 240 Bremer Bldg., 419 N. Roberts St., St. Paul, MN 55101; 800-328-1461 (out-of-state), 800-652-9747 (in-state). **State parks:** *Information:* Recreation Information, Space Center Bldg., 2nd Flr., 444 Lafayette St., St. Paul, MN 55101; 612-296-4776. *Entrance fees:* $4 per vehicle daily, $15, annually (Minnesota residents $3 daily, $10 annually; $5 annually for senior citizens). *Reservations:* Contact individual park. $20 deposit required within 10 days. Accepted beginning April 1 for early June—early September. If booking a Friday night, must stay Saturday night. *Restrictions:* No hunting or alcohol. Dogs must be leashed (not allowed in lodgings). Children must be accompanied by an adult for camping. Some parks do not permit vehicles longer than 22 feet. *Facilities:* Swimming, May 15—early September. Boating, April—October. Cross-country skiing and snowmobiling, December—March.

Itasca State Park's 32,000 acres are in northwestern Minnesota about 80 miles west of Grand Rapids and about 100 miles southeast of Grand Forks. The park's name comes from a term coined by the early-nineteenth-century explorer H. R. Schoolcraft, who first described Lake Itasca as the source of the Mississippi. "Itasca" comes from the Latin *verITAS CAput,* which is translated roughly as "true head." The park is littered with more than 100 lakes (the largest is the 1,000-acre Lake Itasca), and the Mississippi River begins its 2,552 mile course to the Gulf of Mexico here. The terrain, with elevations between 1,475 and 1,700 feet, is wooded with sugar maples, birches, aspens, elms, ashes, basswoods, pines, black spruces, tamaracks, and white cedars. Among these are a 120-foot-tall red pine—10 feet in circumference and the second largest of its species on record—and Minnesota's record white pine, which measures 173 inches around and 112 feet tall. Common wildlife includes deer, beavers, coyotes, and black bears; and among frequently seen birds are bald eagles, ospreys, and great blue herons, all of whom nest here. Frequently observed as well is the park's large population of loons.

The park is particularly rich in interpretative programs and trails, including a wilderness drive and a trail leading to the record white pine. The park has an observation tower, 500-year-old Indian burial mounds, a University of Minnesota Forestry and Biological Station, boat-launching and -rental facilities, a restaurant, a souvenir shop, a natural-history museum, a wilderness area comprising 2,000 acres of virgin forest, and numerous scenic overlooks.

Douglas Lodge and Cabins

Douglas Lodge and Cabins is a complex of buildings that range from a main lodge built in 1905 of exposed logs to a two-story motel unit, a group lodge, sleeping cabins, and housekeeping cabins.

The main lodge has a dining room, a lobby, a stone fireplace, an office, a coffee shop, 3 meeting rooms, and guest rooms on the second floor, which consist of three 2-bedroom suites with private bath and four rooms that share a central bath. The fifteen cabins, some built of logs (some from 1905, some from the 1930s), vary in having from one to three bedrooms. Six of these have fireplaces, and each has a private bath. A fourplex log cabin (1930s) has four separate units, each of which has a screened porch, a private bath, and a fireplace.

Nicollet Court, the two-story motel unit, has eighteen guest rooms and a lounge–conference room. Ten of the motel rooms have double beds, eight have twin beds, and all have a private bath. The Club House (1913), another log building with ten sleeping rooms and a main lobby, is used mainly by families or groups. Six of its rooms have shared baths and four have private baths.

The park's six housekeeping cabins, built in 1935, are in the campground area. Each has a fully equipped kitchenette, sleeping accommodations for four, and a half bath (toilet and lavatory), with occupants sharing the campground's central shower facility.

A two-bedroom housekeeping cabin, located on Squaw Lake, has an outdoor pit toilet and water source, comes with a boat, and requires that guests bring their own towels and linens.

Accommodations: 10 lodge rooms, 18 motel rooms, 1 group lodge, 15 cabins, 1 fourplex cabin, and 7 housekeeping cabins, most with private bath. *Towels and linens:* Provided, except at Squaw Lake cabin. *Cooking and eating utensils:* In housekeeping cabins. *Stove and refrigerator:* In housekeeping cabins. *Pets:* Permitted, with restrictions—check in advance. *Open:* Memorial Day weekend to first weekend in October—check in advance. *Mailing address:* Lake Itasca, MN 56460. *Phone:* (218) 266-3656. *Driving instructions:* Itasca State Park is 20 miles north of Park Rapids on Route 71.

Superior National Forest is in northeastern Minnesota, along the western shores of Lake Superior and the Canadian border. One of the most heavily used wilderness areas in the nation, the forest consists of some 3 million acres, about a third of which are essentially a canoeing wilderness. The forest has scores of lakes and streams, and canoers can paddle their way through hundreds of square miles. Long-distance canoe travel here requires much shorter portages than such journeys of similar distance almost anywhere else in the country. Predominant trees in the forest are white and black spruce, fir, aspen, and birch, and the elevations rise as high as 2,301 feet (at Eagle Mountain, the highest point in Minnesota).

Rugged in places and oftentimes rocky, Superior National Forest is also popular among kayakers, fishermen, and hunters. The forest has two downhill ski areas and miles of cross-country trails. Common mammals in the area include deer, moose, and black bears; and among frequently sighted birds are Canada and snow geese, mallards, canvasbacks, red-tailed hawks, whistling swans, bald eagles, and especially ravens. *Forest mailing address:* Gunflint Ranger Station, PO Box 308, Grand Marais, MN 55604. *District phone:* (218) 387-1750.

Gunflint Lodge

Owned by one family for fifty-five years, Gunflint Lodge overlooks Gunflint Lake and, in the distance, Canada. The lodge consists of a group of buildings including log cabins and motel-type structures with such facilities as a trading post, a tennis court, a marina, and a sauna. Most guests come here on a package basis, and staff members organize activities as diverse as day trips to observe beaver colonies and fishing excursions after walleye and trout. This is a center for cross-country skiing in winter.

The main lodge has a fifty-seat restaurant with handmade birch tables and chairs and a picture window overlooking the lake (the food is included in the price of lodging). Also in the main lodge is a lounge with exposed-beam ceilings, a fireplace, and a large window overlooking the lake.

Accommodations consist of four suites in a motel-type building and nineteen wood-frame cabins. The suites have a living room with a fireplace, two bedrooms, and a private bath.

The cabins, paneled in pine, birch, or oak, have wall-to-wall carpeting, a living room, a fireplace, and a private bath. Most guest rooms and cabins overlook the lake.

Accommodations: 4 suites and 19 cabins with private bath. *Towels and linens:* Provided. *Cooking and eating utensils:* Not provided. *Stove and refrigerator:* Not provided. *Pets:* Permitted. *Open:* Mid-May through mid-October and late December through March. *Mailing address:* Gunflint Lodge, Gunflint Trail, PO Box 100, Grand Marais, MN 55604. *Toll-free phone:* (800) 328-3362 in Minnesota, (800) 328-3325 elsewhere. *Driving instructions:* From Grand Marais take Route 12 (Gunflint Trail) north and west for 44 miles to the lodge.

Bearskin Lodge

Along the shores of East Bearskin Lake, Bearskin Lodge has a main lodge complex and eight log cabins. The lodge complex consists of twenty wood-frame buildings fashioned of pine or aspen. The main lodge building has a wing with four three-bedroom apartments, each with a kitchen, a living room, either a patio or a balcony, and a lake view. Several units have two baths. The main lodge also has a lounge—furnished with couches and chairs and a granite fireplace—that is two stories high and overlooked by the dining room, which in turn overlooks the lake and has a screened dining area. There's a gift

shop, a sauna, and a recently completed hot-tub house.

The cabins are paneled in knotty pine, and each has a fully equipped kitchenette, a living room, a private bath, and either hardwood or tile flooring. One unit has a fireplace, one has a wood stove, two have screened porches, and one has a large open deck. Each of the cabins has a lake view and a private dock.

The lodge rents boats, motors, and canoes and has 35 miles of cross-country ski trails. It is part of the ski lodge-to-lodge program, whereby cross-country skiers can make their way from one lodge to another.

Accommodations: 8 cabins and 4 apartments, all with private bath. *Towels and linens:* Provided. *Cooking and eating utensils:* Provided. *Stove and refrigerator:* Provided. *Pets:* Not permitted. *Open:* All year. *Mailing address:* Gunflint Trail #10, Grand Marais, MN 55604. *Phone:* (218) 388-2292; toll-free in Minnesota: (800) 622-3583; toll-free elsewhere: (800) 328-3325. *Driving instructions:* From Grand Marais take Gunflint Trail (Route 12) for 27 miles, then take Bearskin Road east for one mile.

Borderland Lodge

On a peninsula formed from a granite outcropping that juts into Gunflint Lake, Borderland Lodge has a main lodge and eleven cabins. Built in the 1970s around a 1921 native-stone fireplace, the main lodge has a lounge—with couches, easy chairs, television, and a piano—as well as a grocery store, a gift shop, a dining room that overlooks the lake, and a sun deck, which also overlooks the lake. The building also houses two villas that are two-bedroom apartments, each accommodating from four to six persons. Each villa has a kitchenette, a living room, wall-to-wall carpeting, a private bath, and a deck with lake views.

The cabins vary in size. Each can accommodate from two to ten people and has a kitchenette, a private bath, a living room or living area with couches and easy chairs, and a deck or a porch overlooking the lake. (One cabin has no lake view.) All have wood paneling, and all but one have carpeting. Four have fireplaces.

The lodge participates in a ski-lodge-to-lodge program and rents out boats, motors, and canoes, as well as offering a guide service.

Accommodations: 2 villas and 11 cabins, all with private bath. *Towels and linens:* Provided. *Cooking and eating utensils:* Provided. *Stove and refrigerator:* Provided. *Pets:* Check in advance. *Open:* All year. *Mailing address:* GT Box 102, Grand Marais, MN 55604. *Phone:* (218) 388-2233. *Driving instructions:* From Grand Marais take Gunflint Trail (Route 12) 47 miles to Route 46 and look for the lodge's sign.

Cascade Lodge

Surrounded by pines, birches, and aspens, Cascade Lodge complex has a main lodge building with thirteen guest rooms, a restaurant, a motel-type building, and eight cabins overlooking Lake Superior, from which it is separated by Route 61. The main lodge has a lounge (the Fireplace Room) with an exposed-beam ceiling, a fireplace, and a picture window overlooking the lake, and a parlor with television, a game table, a grand piano, and hunting trophies.

The thirteen lodge rooms have wall-to-wall carpeting and a private bath; eight have a lake view, and the other five have views of the forest. The four rooms in the motel unit have wood-paneled walls, wall-to-wall carpeting, a private bath, and views

233

of either the lake or a wooded area and a stream.

The cabins vary in size and construction and can accommodate from two to six adults. Four cabins are built of logs and have exposed-log interiors, carpeting, and a private bath. The other four are of wood-frame construction; each of these has carpeting and a private bath, and a few have wood paneling.

Accommodations: 13 lodge rooms, 4 motel rooms, and 8 cabins, all with private bath. *Towels and linens:* Provided. *Cooking and eating utensils:* In some units. *Stove and refrigerator:* In some units. *Pets:* Permitted in cabins only. *Open:* All year. *Mailing address:* Cascade Lodge, PO Box 693, Grand Marais, MN 55604. *Phone:* (218) 387-1112. *Driving instructions:* Cascade Lodge is on U.S. 61, about 9 miles southwest of Grand Marais.

Nor' Wester Lodge

On the shore of Poplar Lake, which is lined with red and white pines, Nor' Wester Lodge comprises a main lodge, four villas, and six cabins. The main lodge—constructed in the 1930s of pine and spruce logs and added to over the years—has a solar-passive dining room that overlooks the lake; a lounge with a stone fireplace, couches, and chairs; a sitting and television room; and a gift counter. The four villa units are wood-frame buildings, each with knotty-pine paneling, four bedrooms, and two baths. They can accommodate from two to fourteen, and each has a living room with sliding glass doors, a porch overlooking the lake, and a fully equipped kitchen.

The six cabins vary in size from one to three bedrooms and can accommodate from four to ten people. Each has a fully equipped kitchenette, a living room, a private bath, and either hardwood flooring or carpeting. Two of the cabins have Franklin stoves, and one is on a peninsula wooded with a stand of red pines.

The lodge has boats for rent and participates in a ski-lodge-to-lodge program.

Accommodations: 4 villas and 6 cabins, all with private bath. *Towels and linens:* Provided. *Cooking and eating utensils:* Provided. *Stove and refrigerator:* Provided. *Pets:* Check in advance. *Open:* All year. *Mailing address:* Gunflint Trail, Grand Marais, MN 55604. *Phone:* (218) 388-2252. *Driving instructions:* Nor' Wester Lodge is on Gunflint Trail (Route 12), 30 miles north of Grand Marais.

Trout Lake Resort

On the shore of Trout Lake, Trout Lake Resort includes eight cabins spread about on 40 acres wooded with birches, aspens, spruces, balsam firs, and numerous species of pine. Constructed either of jack or white pine, the cabins vary in size and can accommodate from 2 to 12 people. Each has a knotty pine interior, a private bath, and a fully equipped kitchen. Four cabins are directly on the lake, and the other four are on a hill overlooking the lake.

In addition to the cabins, the complex also has a store that sells basic groceries (staples, frozen foods, ice cream, beer, bread and butter, etc), a screened area for lounging, a picnic area overlooking the lake, a swing set for children, and a cement-block fireplace for guests.

Accommodations: 8 cabins with private bath. *Towels and linens:* Provided. *Cooking and eating utensils:* Provided. *Stove and refrigerator:* Provided. *Pets:* Check in advance. *Open:* Mid-May through mid-October. *Mailing address:* Trout Lake Resort, East Star Route 1, Box 660, Grand Marais, MN 55604. *Telephone:* (218) 387-1330. *Driving instructions:* From Grand Marais, take Gunflint Trail 10 miles north; look for the Trout Lake Resort sign.

Mississippi

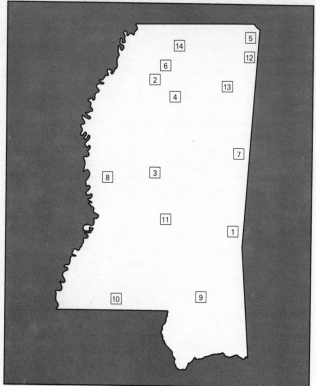

State map and tourist information: Div. of Tourism, PO Box 849, Jackson, MS 39205; 601-359-3414. **State parks:** *Information:* Parks Bureau PO Box 10600, Jackson MS 39209; 601-961-5006. *Entrance fees:* None. *Reservations:* Contact individual park; Accepted beginning January 2 of each year for the summer season, May—mid Sept. Deposit for first night's lodgings required for 2—7 day stay; deposit for two nights for 8-14 day stay; check or credit card. Maximum stay, 14 days. Minimum, 3 nights during summer and on holiday weekends; and 2 nights rest of the year. *Restrictions:* Hunting available in Leroy Percy S.P. only. Dogs must be leashed (not allowed in lodgings). No alcoholic in dry counties; no speedboats. *Facilities:* Swimming, late May—early September. Interpretative programs, by request. Boating, April—October.

Clarkco State Park, 815 acres in southeastern Mississippi about 20 miles south of Meridian and 5 miles north of Quitman, is at an elevation of about 400 feet on terrain covered by oaks, maples, hickories, pines, and dogwoods. A 65-acre lake has a small beach for swimming, and visitors can also rent paddleboats, canoes, or fishing boats. A day-use lodge overlooking the lake has a bathhouse, a snack bar, a camp store, and a meeting room. Most of the acreage is undeveloped, although there are 3 ½ miles of well-marked nature trails. Other activities include tennis on lighted courts and picnicking.

Clarkco State Park has twelve wood-frame cabins along the lakeshore. Each has a private pier, a porch, a fully equipped kitchenette, and a private bath. Cabins vary in size from one room to three-bedroom units and can accommodate from two to eight people. Two cabins have fireplaces.

Accommodations: 12 cabins with private bath. *Towels and linens:* Provided. *Cooking and eating utensils:* Provided. *Stove and refrigerator:* Provided. *Pets:* Permitted. *Open:* All year. *Mailing address:* Route 1, Box 186, Quitman, MS 39355. *Phone:* (601) 776-6651. *Driving instructions:* Clarkco State Park is off U.S. 45 about 20 miles south of Meridian.

George Payne Cossar State Park is in northern Mississippi about 40 miles southwest of Oxford. Its 810 acres are on a peninsula that juts into Enid Lake, an impoundment of the Yocona River covering 25,000 to 45,000 acres, depending on the water level. The peninsula, varying in width from a mile where it meets the land to perhaps 200 yards at its tip, is moderately wooded with oaks, hickories, and a few pines. On a well-marked double-loop hiking trail, hikers can choose a 1 ½-mile or a 3 ½-mile walk, or both. The trail runs through wooded sections dotted with small meadows filled with wildflowers.

The park rents out small aluminum rowboats that can take an electric trolling motor and that may be used to go after the lake's large population of crappies, white perch, and catfishes. There is also a swimming pool with a bathhouse, as well as a restaurant overlooking the lake.

The park has eight wood-frame cabins in side-by-side pairs. Each cabin has a fully equipped kitchenette, a screened porch, a brick fireplace, and a private bath. The accommodations are in a wooded area near the lake, and four cabins have lake views.

Accommodations: 8 cabins with private bath. *Towels and linens:* Provided. *Cooking and eating utensils:* Provided. *Stove and refrigerator:* Provided. *Pets:* Not permitted. *Open:* All year. *Mailing address:* Route 1, Oakland, MS 38948. *Phone:* (601) 623-7356. *Driving instructions:* George Payne Cossar State Park is off Route 32 about 8 miles east of Oakland.

Holmes County State Park is in central Mississippi about 50 miles north of Jackson and a quarter mile east of I-55. Its 463 acres are relatively flat, with a few gentle hills and ridges, and are wooded with oaks, hickories, pines, sweet gums, and dogwoods. The smaller of two lakes covers 12 acres and has a beach for swimming, as well as paddleboat rentals. The larger lake is used mostly for fishing, and anglers can rent aluminum rowboats that will take an electric trolling motor and go after bream and bass. A 4-mile nature trail goes by both lakes and through woods where visitors may encounter deer, raccoons, beavers, and opossums. Wildlife also includes a large population of bluejays, cardinals, and red-winged blackbirds.

Other popular activities are camping, picnicking, and roller skating, for which the activity building is reserved on certain days. Visitors keen on the sport should call ahead for a schedule of skating sessions.

The park has twelve wood-frame cabins in a wooded area beside the lake that can accommodate from four to six people. Each has a fully equipped kitchenette, a private bath, and six have a lake view. Some have porches, and all but one have fireplaces.

The park also has a large dormitory-style group camp that can sleep a hundred people, as well as a separate dining building with kitchen facilities, a meeting room, and an amphitheater.

Accommodations: 12 cabins with private bath and a group lodge with shared bath. *Towels and linens:* Provided in cabins only. *Cooking and eating utensils:* Provided in cabins only. *Stove and refrigerator:* Provided in cabins only. *Pets:* Not permitted. *Open:* All year. *Mailing address:* Route 1, Box 153, Durant, MS 39063. *Phone:* (601) 653-3351. *Driving instructions:* Holmes County State Park is a quarter of a mile east of I-55's exit 150.

Hugh White State Park, 1,170 acres in northern Mississippi about 40 miles south of Oxford, is named after a former governor of Mississippi and is along the shores of Grenada Lake, a 64,600-acre impoundment of the Tallahatchie River. Its gentle hills are wooded primarily with oaks, hickories, pines, dogwoods, and redbuds. Most activities center around the lake, with its population of crappies, black and striped bass, perch, and catfishes. There is a bait and tackle shop, as well as launching facilities for those bringing their own powerboats. Visitors can also rent small rowboats that take electric trolling motors. Other water activities include water-skiing and swimming, and there's a sand beach with a bathhouse, picnic and playground areas, and six tennis courts.

The park has twenty brick cabins arranged in ten side-by-side duplexes. Each cabin has a fully equipped kitchenette, a private bath, and a screened porch. Most cabins are on a bluff overlooking Grenada Lake; a few are in a wooded area immediately across the park road.

A group lodge facility, accommodating thirty-five people in four brick buildings with shared baths and kitchen facilities, may be rented separately; but preference is given to groups. Overlooking Grenada Lake and the dam is a motel unit with ten rooms, each of which has carpeting, a bedroom, and a sitting area. The motel-unit rooms have no cooking facilities but the park has a restaurant.

Accommodations: 10 motel rooms and 20 cabins, all with private bath, plus 4 group lodges with shared bath. *Towels and linens:* In cabins and motel. *Cooking and eating utensils:* In cabins and group lodges. *Stove and refrigerator:* In cabins. *Pets:* Not permitted. *Open:* All year except Christmas. *Mailing address:* PO Box 725, Grenada, MS 38901. *Phone:* (601) 226-4934. *Driving instructions:* Hugh White State Park is off Route 8 about 5 miles east of Grenada.

J. P. Coleman State Park, on 1,468 acres about 13 miles north of Iuka, is at the northeastern tip of Mississippi by Pickwick Lake, an impoundment of the Tennessee River. Its hilly terrain is thickly wooded with oaks, tulip trees, sweet gums, hickories, pines, cedars, cypresses, and dogwoods. Activities center on the lake and its full-service marina, including rowboat rentals. Fishing is for bass, crappies and bream. There is a swimming pool with a bathhouse, plus picnic and playground areas and a nature trail that runs through hilly woods. A restaurant, open to visitors from Memorial Day through Labor Day, also operates the year round for catering, using a banquet room that accommodates moderate-sized groups.

The park has twenty brick cabins on a wooded bluff overlooking the lake. Each has a fully equipped kitchenette, a private bath, and either a screened porch or a porch that's been converted to a den. Four cabins have fireplaces.

Five motel units are also available on the second floor of the building that houses the restaurant, each with a deck overlooking the lake. One unit is a suite with two bedrooms and two baths.

Accommodations: 5 motel units and 20 cabins, all with private bath. *Towels and linens:* Provided. *Cooking and eating utensils:* In cabins. *Stove and refrigerator:* In cabins. *Pets:* Not permitted. *Open:* All year. *Mailing address:* Route 5, Box 504, Iuka, MS 38852. *Phone:* (601) 423-6515. *Driving instructions:* J. P. Coleman State Park is off Route 25 about 13 miles north of Iuka.

Named for a former Mississippi state legislator, John W. Kyle State Park comprises 784 acres in northwestern Mississippi about 20 miles northwest of Oxford along the shores of Sardis Lake, an impoundment of the Tallahatchie River. The hilly terrain is moderately wooded, mostly with oaks, hickories, poplars, pines, and dogwoods. It is a popular spot for boating, swimming, and fishing, with crappies the main targets of anglers, who can rent small fishing boats here. Among the facilities are a pool with bathhouse, four lighted tennis courts, a football field, and a recreation building with a basketball court that converts into a roller-skating rink. (Interested visitors should check in advance for the schedule of skating sessions.)

A wide range of wildlife includes deer, foxes, opossums, and raccoons, as well as a variety of bird life—quail, ducks, geese, herons, egrets, red-tailed and broad-winged hawks, and golden eagles.

The park has twenty brick cabins in side-by-side pairs, all of which are available throughout the year. Cabins vary in size, accommodating four to eight people, and each has a fully equipped kitchenette and a private bath. Some are right by the lake, while others are set back in the woods. Ten have fireplaces; the others, screened porches.

The park also has a group lodge comprising two dormitory-style buildings, which can accommodate sixty-four people each, and a central dining-kitchen-meeting building, both of wood-frame construction.

Accommodations: 20 cabins with private bath and a group lodge with shared bath. *Towels and linens:* In cabins. *Cooking and eating utensils:* In cabins and group dinning hall. *Stove and refrigerator:* In cabins. *Pets:* Permitted. *Open:* All year. *Mailing address:* Route 1, Box 115, Sardis, MS 38666. *Phone:* (601) 487-1345. *Driving instructions:* John W. Kyle State Park is off Route 315 about 9 miles east of Sardis.

Lake Lowndes State Park, 750 acres in eastern Mississippi, about 10 miles southeast of Columbus and 2 miles west of the Alabama border, has a mixed terrain, mostly flat with some hilly sections. It is wooded with oaks, hickories, maples, dogwoods, redbuds, and pines; and in spring certain areas of the park are colored by wildflowers. This is a recreation-oriented park with three much used softball fields, a football and soccer field, six tennis courts, and indoor facilities for basketball, volleyball, badminton and tennis. Other facilities include a beach for swimming, playgrounds, picnic areas, a nature trail, a snack bar, and a fast-food restaurant. Paddleboats and fishing boats are for rent at the 150-acre lake, where anglers go after bream, bass, crappies, and catfishes.

The park has four wood-frame cabins in a wooded section beside the lake, each accommodating six people and having two bedrooms, a fully equipped kitchenette, a private bath, a fireplace, and a rear deck overlooking the lake.

Accommodations: 4 cabins with private bath. *Towels and linens:* Provided. *Cooking and eating utensils:* Provided. *Stove and refrigerator:* Provided. *Pets:* Not permitted. *Open:* All year. *Mailing address:* Route 4, Box 277 D, Columbus, MS 39702. *Phone:* (601) 328-2110. *Driving instructions:* Lake Lowndes State Park is off Route 69 about 8 miles southeast of Columbus.

Leroy Percy State Park is in western Mississippi, about 20 miles south of Greenville and 60 miles north of Vicksburg, in the delta lowlands of the Mississippi River. Its 2,442 relatively flat and low acres contain bottomland hardwoods—oaks, poplars, beeches—and cypresses. Much of the park, the oldest in the Mississippi state-park system, is operated as a wildlife-management area. One attraction is four hot artesian wells that feed a pond inhabited by alligators. The habitat is fenced in, and visitors can get a good look at the alligators from a board-walk that runs over the pond and can even feed them one of their favorite treats, a bag of marshmallows, available at the park store. The park naturalists engage in wildlife-rehabilitation projects such as nursing a young fawn with a broken leg back to health.

The park has paddleboats and fishing boats for rent, while anglers go after crappies, bass, bream, and catfishes in the bayou-like lake. Ducks, geese, egrets, herons, and eagles, among other birds, come here to winter. Park facilities include a swimming pool, a snack bar and restaurant, and a nature center.

The park has five wood-frame cottages in a wooded area. The cottages, each of which has a fully equipped kitchenette, a porch, and a fireplace, have either one or two bedrooms and accommodate from four to eight people.

Accommodations: 5 cabins with private bath. *Towels and linens:* Provided. *Cooking and eating utensils:* Provided. *Stove and refrigerator:* Provided. *Pets:* Permitted. *Open:* All year. *Mailing address:* PO Box 176, Hollandale, MS 38748. *Phone:* (601) 827-5436. *Driving instructions:* Leroy Percy State Park is off Route 12W, about 5 miles west of Hollandale.

Named for a former governor of Mississippi, the 805-acre Paul B. Johnson State Park, in southeastern Mississippi about 5 miles south of Hattiesburg, is on the western edge of De Soto National Forest. Its piney-woods terrain is relatively flat, with sandy soil. Some oaks grow among the pines, and in spring and fall there are many wildflowers, especially in the marshy areas. The park has a spring-fed lake with a swimming area and bathhouse, canoes, fishing boats, or paddleboats for rent, and launching facilities for those who bring their own boats. Activities also include waterskiing, field sports, and fishing. A self-guided nature trail winds through the woods and over several wooden foot-bridges that traverse marshy areas rife with purple martins, blackbirds, herons, and egrets.

The park has sixteen cabins, which are among pines and have lake views. Cabins with private piers are suited to visitors who bring their own boats. Twelve are of brick, and the other four are in two side-by-side wood-frame duplex units. Each cabin has a patio area with a picnic table and grill. Those in the duplex units have fireplaces and porches.

The park also has a group lodge accommodating 110 people and a 150-seat cafeteria. The park restaurant also often caters to large groups staying at the lodge.

Accommodations: 16 cabins with private bath and a group lodge with shared bath. *Towels and linens:* In cabins. *Cooking and eating utensils:* In cabins. *Stove and refrigerator:* In cabins. *Pets:* Permitted if leashed. *Open:* All year. *Mailing address:* Route 3, Box 408, Hattiesburg, MS 39401. *Phone:* (601) 582-7721. *Driving instructions:* Paul B. Johnson State Park is off U.S. 49, about 15 miles south of Hattiesburg.

Percy Quin State Park is in southwestern Mississippi, about 10 miles north of the Louisiana border and 6 miles south of McComb. Its 1,700 acres are a mixture of level and hilly areas wooded primarily with loblolly, longleaf, and shortleaf pine, as well as oaks, maples, hickories, dogwoods, and redbuds. The 652-acre lake has a sand beach. Visitors can launch their own craft or rent paddleboats, canoes, and small aluminum rowboats that can take electric trolling motors. Fishing is for crappies, bream, and bass. A nature trail runs through woods and over a swinging bridge that traverses a narrow part of the lake, which is frequented by ducks, geese, hawks, and occasionally eagles.

A popular attraction is the Liberty White Railroad Museum, housed in an old caboose. Activities also include picnicking and camping, and the park has a miniature-golf course, a basketball court, a camp store, and a playground.

Percy Quin has twenty-two brick cabins, some with fireplaces, overlooking the lake. Each of the cabins, which vary in size from one to three bedrooms and can accommodate from two to twelve people, has a fully equipped kitchenette, a private bath, and either a screened or an unscreened porch. The park also has a group lodge facility that accommodates up to two hundred.

Accommodations: 22 cabins with private bath and a group lodge with shared bath. *Towels and linens:* In cabins. *Cooking and eating utensils:* In cabins. *Stove and refrigerator:* In cabins. *Pets:* Permitted. *Open:* All year. *Mailing address:* Route 3, McComb, MS 39648. *Phone:* (601) 684-3938. *Driving instructions:* Percy Quin State Park is off I-55 (exit 5), about 6 miles south of McComb.

Roosevelt State Park's 862 acres are in central Mississippi, about 25 miles east of Jackson and 2 miles west of Bienville National Forest. The slightly hilly terrain is wooded mostly with oaks, hickories, sweet gums, elms, cedars, dogwoods, redbuds, and longleaf and loblolly pines. The local beaver population keeps trying to dam up a 160-acre lake, which has a beach for swimming and a new bathhouse. Visitors can rent paddleboats, canoes, and small aluminum rowboats that will take an electric trolling motor, to go after bream and crappies.

The park's five nature trails, each about 2 miles long, are popular, as are softball, picnicking, volleyball, miniature golf, and tennis on two lighted courts. The park lodge, Alfreda, a modern-looking, shingle-sided building with a stone patio, has convention facilities for up to 200 people that include one large meeting and banquet room along with two smaller ones, a kitchen, and a snack bar open only in the summer.

Roosevelt State Park has twelve wood-frame cabins in woods beside the lake. The cabins have one to three bedrooms, and can accommodate from four to twelve people. Each has a fully equipped kitchenette, a private bath, and a screened porch. Five have fireplaces.

The park also has eight rustic wooden group lodges that accommodate thirteen each, dormitory-style in bunk beds, with a separate room for a counselor. Each lodge has electric hot-air heating and air-conditioning and shared shower and toilet facilities. Rental of these cabins, used frequently by church groups, includes use of the nearby pavilion and its barbecue pit. The outdoor stone patio also has a fireplace. No kitchen facilities are available, but the park catering service generally supplies meals for an additional fee.

Accommodations: 12 cabins with private bath and 8 group lodges with shared baths. *Towels and linens:* In cabins only. *Cooking and eating utensils:* In cabins only. *Stove and refrigerator:* In cabins only. *Pets:* Permitted with advance notice. *Open:* All year. *Mailing address:* Morton, MS 39117. *Phone:* (601) 732-6316. *Driving instructions:* Roosevelt State Park is off I-20 (exit 25), about 2 miles south of Morton.

Tishomingo State Park is in the northeastern corner of Mississippi, roughly 20 miles east of Booneville and 3 miles west of the Alabama border. Its 1,500 acres lie in the foothills of the Tennessee Mountains, about 10 miles south of the 806-foot Woodall Mountain, the highest in Mississippi. The hilly terrain, with many outcroppings of rock, is at an elevation of 700 feet and contains many rare ferns and wildflowers, including wild japonicas and violets. Wooded primarily with white oaks, pines, tulip trees, cedars, and cypresses, the park is divided by Bear Creek, a north-flowing tributary of the Tennessee River that is popular among canoers. Visitors can sign up for an 8-mile, 2½ hour canoe float down the creek.

A 13-mile nature-trail system runs through an area thick with wildflowers, along ridges and outcroppings, and over a swinging bridge across Bear Creek. The Natchez Trace, an 8,000-year-old trail, passes through the park. Canoes, paddleboats, or fishing boats may be rented, and there is a swimming pool, a playing field, a restored 1830s frontier cabin, and a wildlife interpretation museum.

Tishomingo State Park has six one-bedroom stone cabins that can each accommodate up to six. All are on a ridge above Bear Creek, which can be seen from the cabins in fall after the trees have lost their foliage. Each has a fully equipped kitchenette and a private bath. Three have two fireplaces each—one in the living room and one in the bedroom—and the other three each have one fireplace. Five cabins have porches, and one has a patio.

Accommodations: 6 cabins with private bath. *Towels and linens:* Provided. *Cooking and eating utensils:* Provided. *Stove and refrigerator:* Provided. *Pets:* Permitted. *Open:* All year. *Mailing address:* Route 1, Box 310, Dennis, MS 38838. *Phone:* (601) 438-6914. *Driving instructions:* Tishomingo State Park is off Route 25, about 3 miles north of Dennis.

The 822-acre Tombigbee State Park, in northeastern Mississippi about 6 miles southeast of Tupelo and 25 miles west of the Alabama border, is wooded primarily with oaks and hickories, which follow the terrain's rolling hills and ridges. A nature trail with two loops and twenty-seven interpretative stations winds through the park, which also has a 100-acre spring-fed man-made lake. The area's wide range of wildlife includes deer, raccoons, coyotes, foxes, bobcats, beavers, muskrats, mink, and opposums, plus many birds. Fishing and boating are popular, and visitors can rent canoes, paddleboats, and fishing boats to go after the generous population of bream, bass, crappies, and catfishes. Swimming facilities consist of a grassy beach with a bathhouse.

The park has six wood-frame cabins built in the 1930s by the Civilian Conservation Corps, which vary in size and can accommodate from two to six people. Four cabins are right on the lake, and two are just across the park road. Some cabins have porches, some have decks, and some have both; each has a fireplace, a fully equipped kitchenette, and a private bath.

The park also has a group camp facility consisting of two dormitory buildings, which sleep up to 100 people each, and a central building with kitchen and dining facilities. The dormitories, as well as the main building, have toilet and bath facilities.

Accommodations: 6 cabins with private bath, and a group camp with shared bath. *Towels and linens:* In cabins. *Cooking and eating utensils:* Provided. *Stove and refrigerator:* In cabins. *Pets:* Permitted. *Open:* All year. *Mailing address:* Route 2, Box 336E, Tupelo, MS 38801. *Phone:* (601) 842-7669. *Driving instructions:* Tombigbee State Park is off Route 6 about 6 miles south of Tupelo.

Wall Doxey State Park, on 855 acres in northern Mississippi, is about 20 miles north of Oxford and a mile west of Holly Springs National Forest. The slightly hilly terrain is wooded primarily with oaks, hickories, maples, dogwoods, redbuds, and pines. The park's 45-acre spring-fed lake has a beach for swimming and a three-level diving pier. Fishing for bass, bream, and catfishes is popular and visitors can rent canoes, paddleboats, and small aluminum rowboats that will take an electric trolling motor. Other activities include picnicking, field sports, and hiking on a 2 ½-mile nature trail that runs around the shore of the lake.

Wall Doxey State Park has nine wood-frame "vacation" cabins in a wooded area near the lake, most with lake views. They have one or two bedrooms and can accommodate from four to seven people. Each has a fully equipped kitchenette, a private bath, and a fireplace; most have screened porches.

The park also has eight dormitory-style group "camp" cabins used for family reunions, business meetings, and church outings. Each cabin accommodates up to twelve each in bunk beds with one private room for a counselor or group leader. Along with shared shower and toilet facilities, each cabin has electric hot-air heating and air-conditioning. Meals are generally served in the group-camp dining hall and are prepared by the park staff.

Accommodations: 9 cabins with private bath and eight group-camp cabins with shared bath. *Towels and linens:* Provided in vacation cabins only. *Cooking and eating utensils:* Provided in vacation cabins and in the group camp dining hall. *Stove and refrigerator:* Provided in vacation cabins only. *Pets:* Permitted. *Open:* All year. *Mailing address:* Holly Springs, MS 38635. *Phone:* (601) 252-4231. *Driving instructions:* Wall Doxey State Park is off Route 7, about 7 miles south of Holly Springs.

Missouri

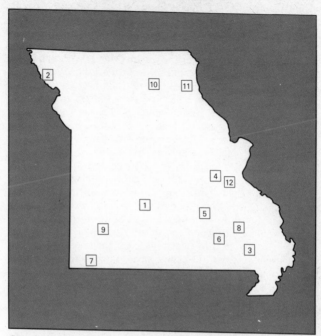

State map and tourist information: Div. of Tourism, PO Box 1055, Jefferson City, MO 65102; 314-751-4133. **State Parks:** *Information:* Div. of Parks, PO Box 176, Jefferson City, MO 65102; 314-751-2479. *Entrance fees:* None. *Reservations:* Contact individual lodgings. Deposit of first night's lodgings payable within 7 to 10 days. Reservations accepted and recommended (for Montauk, Roaring Brook, and Bennett Parks due to trout fishing) beginning December 31; recommended by early March for all other parks. Minimum stay, 2 nights. *Restrictions:* No hunting. Dogs must be leashed (not allowed in lodgings). *Facilities:* Swimming, Mem. Day—Labor Day. Trout fishing, March 1—October 31.

The 1,221-acre Bennett Spring State Park, in southern Missouri about 50 miles northeast of Springfield, takes its name from a spring-fed stream that runs for 1½ miles through the park at the rate of 96,000 gallons per day. The stream is favored by trout fishermen, and daily during the season (March 1 through October 31), it is stocked with rainbow trout. Park facilities include a store that sells groceries, tackle, and trout licenses (including a one-day license). Deer, wild turkeys, red foxes, and squirrels are frequently sighted, and in winter bald eagles come to fish. The park has no canoes for rent, but it is often both a starting and finishing point for trips on the Niangua River.

Additional facilities include a swimming pool with a bathhouse, a dining lodge, two playgrounds, and an interpretative center that offers nature walks and other organized activities.

The park's eighty-two cabins, arranged in single, duplex, and quadriplex units, vary in size as well as construction, ranging in from one to three bedrooms and from wood-frame to stone to a combination of wood and stone. The cabins are in several areas—near the head of the spring, near the river, or near the pool. Seventy-three of the cabins have a kitchenette, some have a porch or a patio, and some are carpeted. All have heat, air-conditioning, and a private bath.

Accommodations: 82 cabins with private bath. *Towels and linens:* Provided. *Cooking and eating utensils:* In some units. *Stove and refrigerator:* In some units. *Pets:* Not permitted. *Open:* March through October. *Mailing address:* Route 16, Box 750, Lebanon, MO 65536. *Phone:* (417) 532-4338 (park superintendent) or (417) 532-4307 (cabin reservations). *Driving instructions:* Bennett Spring State Park is on Route 64, about 12 miles west of Lebanon.

Big Lake State Park in northwestern Missouri, about a mile north of the intersection of the Kansas, Nebraska, and Missouri borders at the Iowa Sac and Fox Indian Reservation. The 111-acre park is along the shore of Big Lake, which at one time was a part of the Missouri River. When the Missouri changed its course slightly, moving miles west and abandoning one of its branches, the former river course became a 625-acre lake. The adjacent terrain is relatively flat and wooded primarily with cottonwoods and sycamores. The park was once farmland and now is in the process of being reforested—in 1984 park personnel planted three hundred 5-foot tall redbud saplings as well as a stand of young sycamores. Six miles from the Squaw Creek National Wildlife Refuge, the park supports a population of small mammals—raccoons, rabbits, opossums, squirrels—and is the nesting grounds for several pairs of bald eagles, who show up in late winter and raise their young through early spring. The eagles like fishing in the lake as do fishermen, who go after carp, catfishes, and crappies.

Although the park has no designated beach, it has a swimming pool with a bathhouse, picnicking and camping areas, a playground, a boat dock with launching facilities, and a restaurant.

In the park are eight wood-frame cabins and twenty-two motel rooms, all overlooking Big Lake. Each motel room has wall-to-wall carpeting, a color television, a private bath, and either a balcony or a porch that overlooks the lake. There is a dining room adjacent to the motel building.

A short walk north of the motel units are the eight cabins, which are one-bedroom units accommodating 4 people. Each has a fully equipped kitchenette, wood-paneled walls, a screened porch, a private bath, and an outdoor barbecue pit and a picnic table.

Accommodations: 22 motel rooms and 8 cabins, all with private bath. *Towels and linens:* Provided. *Cooking and eating utensils:* In cabins. *Stove and refrigerator:* In cabins. *Pets:* Not permitted. *Open:* Mid-April through November. *Mailing address:* Bigelow, MO 64225. *Phone:* (816) 442-3770 or 442-5683. *Driving instructions:* Big Lake State Park is off Route 111 about 11 miles southwest of Mound City.

Lake Wappapello State Park is a 1,854-acre reserve in south-eastern Missouri, about 20 miles north of Poplar Bluff in the Mark Twain National Forest along the shores of the 8,600-acre Lake Wappapello. The hilly terrain is rugged in places, wooded mainly with oaks, hickories, and southern pines. Elevations vary from about 300 to 600 feet, where there are scenic panoramas. The best way to see the park is from its network of trails, which total about 22 miles, 15 of which comprise a popular backpacking trail. Lake Wappapello is frequented by fishermen, who go after catfishes, bluegills, crappies, and bass. A concessionaire rents fishing boats with 7 ½-horsepower motors, as well as paddleboats and pontoon boats; the marina has launching facilities, slips, and a store that sells bait and tackle. The park has a sand beach.

Deer, wild turkeys, raccoons, foxes, possums, great blue herons, ducks, and geese are frequently sighted in the park, and bald eagles spend the winter at the lake.

The park has eight wood-frame cabins on a wooded hillside above the lake, though without a lake view. Seven of the cabins can accommodate six people, and the eighth can accommodate ten. Each has carpeting, a fully equipped kitchenette, heat, air-conditioning, a private bath, and an outdoor picnic table and grill.

Accommodations: 8 cabins with private bath. *Towels and linens:* Provided. *Cooking and eating utensils:* Provided. *Stove and refrigerator:* Provided. *Pets:* Not permitted. *Open:* Last weekend in March through October. *Mailing address:* Williamsville, MO 63967. *Phone:* (314) 297-3247. *Driving instructions:* From Poplar Bluff take U.S. 67 north for 12 miles, then take Route 172 east for 9 miles.

Meramec State Park is in eastern Missouri, in the Meramec River valley about 55 miles southwest of St. Louis. Its 7,155 acres are hilly and thickly wooded with oaks, hickories, maples, walnuts, dogwoods, redbuds, and small, scattered stands of pines. One section has a cave, almost a mile long, with stalactite and stalagmite formations. The park's naturalist service offers an interpretative tour of the cave and its geological features.

The Meramec River is quite popular among canoeists, who frequently arrange with a concessionaire to drive them upriver, then meet them downstream after a trip of about two hours. The river also attracts fishermen, who go after bass and perch. Several hiking trails vary in length from a mile to 6 miles. Characteristic wildlife includes deer, wild turkeys, and foxes, and a varied bird life includes cardinals, bluebirds, red-tailed hawks, and bald eagles, who winter in the Meramec valley.

The park has nineteen rustic wood-frame cabins, some with views of the river. The cabins vary in size—accommodating from two to fourteen people—and in appointments—some with a porch or a deck. Each has a fully equipped kitchenette, a stone fireplace, and an outside picnic table and barbecue pit.

Accommodations: 19 cabins with private bath. *Towels and linens:* Provided. *Cooking and eating utensils:* Provided. *Stove and refrigerator:* Provided. *Pets:* Not permitted. *Open:* April through October. *Mailing address:* PO Box 57, Sullivan, MO 63080. *Phone:* (314) 468-6072 (park information) or 468-6519 (accommodations). *Driving instructions:* Meramec State Park is off Route 185 South, 4 miles east of Sullivan.

Montauk State Park's 1,358 acres are in southeastern Missouri, between the two northernmost sections of the Mark Twain National Forest, about 90 miles south of Jefferson City. The hilly and wooded terrain is forested mainly with oaks, maples, hickories, sycamores, pines, dogwoods, and redbuds. Trout fishing is by far the most important activity, and in season the Current River is stocked daily with rainbow trout. The Current River flows swiftly, making this also a popular spot for canoeing and inner tube rafting. The river's headwaters begin in the park, which has seven springs bubbling up 42 million gallons of cold, clear water a day. The developed areas are near the springs and an old gristmill that was active in the early twentieth century.

Accommodations include sixteen motel rooms and twenty-six rustic wood-frame cabins. The motel rooms, each with private bath, are in two wings flanking the rustic-looking A-frame dining room. The cabins, all with private bath, vary in size and appointments and are scattered throughout the park. Some are on the river, some have wall-to-wall carpeting, one has a fireplace, and eighteen have a fully equipped kitchenette. Eight "sleeper cabins" have no kitchen.

Accommodations: 16 motel rooms and 26 cabins, all with private bath. *Towels and linens:* Provided. *Cooking and eating utensils:* In 18 cabins. *Stove and refrigerator:* In 18 cabins. *Pets:* Not permitted. *Open:* March through October. *Mailing address:* Route 5, Salem, MO 65560. *Phone:* (314) 548-2525. *Driving instructions:* Montauk State Park is off Route 119 about 21 miles south of Salem.

The Ozark National Scenic Riverways, with elevations ranging from 800 to 1,400 feet, are in southeastern Missouri, between the two largest sections of the Mark Twain National Forest. Long, narrow, and unspoiled (no dams, no marinas, no hydroelectric plants), the riverways encompass 65,000 acres along a 134-mile stretch of the Current and Jacks Fork rivers, which flow through limestone bluffs and dense forests of oaks and hickories colored in spring with flowering dogwoods and redbuds. The entire area was at one time beneath a large sea that deposited layers of dolomite, which the rivers and the springs have been eroding ever since. Along the bluffs are found some two hundred caves formed by numerous springs, which vary from some with a slow trickle to one with a daily flow of 286 million gallons, aptly named Big Spring. The waterways are populated with kingfishers, wood ducks, sandpipers, green and great blue herons, teals, bald eagles, and ospreys. Characteristic wildlife includes deer, foxes, coyotes, occasional black bears, raccoons, and squirrels. Popular activities include hiking, canoeing, and fishing for smallmouth bass and sunfishes.

Big Springs Cabins

The Big Springs Cabin complex comprises a large stone lodge-building with a dining room overlooking Big Spring, a crafts shop, and fourteen cabins—some wood-frame, some stone and beam—built in the 1930s by the Civilian Conservation Corps. (Every building in the complex is listed in the National Register of Historic Places.) The cabins are on a wooded bluff and vary in size, accommodating from two to six people. Each has a private bath, a stone fireplace, a screened porch, hardwood floors, a kitchenette, and an outdoor barbecue pit and a picnic table.

Accommodations: 14 cabins with private bath. *Towels and linens:* Provided. *Cooking and eating utensils:* Not provided. *Stove and refrigerator:* Provided. *Pets:* Not permitted. *Open:* April through October. *Mailing address:* PO Box 602, Van Buren, MO 63965. *Phone:* (314) 323-4423. *Driving instructions:* Big Springs Cabins are off Route 103 about 4 miles south of Van Buren.

Roaring River State Park is in southwestern Missouri, about 50 miles south of Springfield and 10 miles north of the Arkansas border, at the western edge of the southernmost section of the Mark Twain National Forest. They call it Roaring River because it roars while rushing through the 3,400-acre valley that forms the park, most of which was donated to the state by a wealthy St. Louis soap manufacturer. In springtime a waterfall intensifies the work of a spring that gushes 20 million gallons a day at the headwaters of Roaring River.

The terrain, at an average elevation of about 1,200 feet, is wooded with oaks, hickories, walnuts, dogwoods, redbuds, cedars, and pines. Although three thousand acres of the park have been left in a wild state, hiking trails run through this otherwise undeveloped area. A park ranger says he sees ospreys fishing in the river, along whose shores bald eagles winter. (A trout-fishing derby is held here each October.)

The park has a swimming pool, a restaurant, and a retail outlet selling souvenirs and fishing equipment.

Visitors to the park can stay either in cabins or in a motel overlooking the river. Twenty-three are wood-frame cabins and another three, behind a fish hatchery, are built of stone. Some cabins are side-by-side duplexes—in a wooded area—and some are quadriplexes—alongside the highway. Each has a kitchenette, a living room with sofa bed, and a private bath. Some cabins have an open or a screened porch.

The motel, next to the restaurant, has twenty-two rooms, each with wall-to-wall carpeting, color television, a private bath, and a view of the river.

Accommodations: 22 motel rooms and 26 cabins, all with private bath. *Towels and linens:* Provided. *Cooking and eating utensils:* Not provided. *Stove and refrigerator:* In cabins. *Pets:* Not permitted. *Open:* March through Halloween. *Mailing address:* PO Box D, Cassville, MO 65625. *Phone:* (417) 847-2539 (park) or 847-2330 (cabins). *Driving instructions:* Roaring River State Park is off Route 112, about 7 miles southeast of Cassville.

Sam A. Baker State Park is in southeastern Missouri, about 40 miles north of Poplar Bluff and midway between the two eastern sections of the Mark Twain National Forest. Its 5,148 acres are in the St. Francois Mountains and are bordered by Big Creek and the St. Francis River. The hilly terrain is wooded primarily with oaks, butternuts, cedars, dogwoods, and redbuds; 12-mile hiking trail winds through the park and over the summit of Mudlick Mountain, which affords an extended view from 1,223 feet up. In spring the park is rife with wildflowers as well as blossoming dogwoods and redbuds; in autumn the foliage is quite scenic.

The park has a swimming area with a bathhouse on the bank of Big Creek, canoe rentals, a volleyball court, a Family Bluegrass Weekend in summer, an interpretative center with exhibits explaining the area's natural history, as well as a restaurant (open Memorial Day through Labor Day) overlooking Big Creek.

The park has seventeen cabins of either wood-frame or stone construction, in a wooded area a short walk from the restaurant. Some cabins have open porches, some have stone fireplaces, and one is merely a sleeping cabin with no kitchen facilities. All but the sleeping cabin have fully equipped kitchenettes and can accommodate from two to fourteen people. The cabin that sleeps fourteen has five bedrooms and a living room with two sofa beds. All cabins have a private bath.

Accommodations: 17 cabins with private bath. *Towels and linens:* Provided. *Cooking and eating utensils:* In 16 cabins. *Stove and refrigerator:* In 16 cabins. *Pets:* Not permitted. *Open:* First weekend in April through the last weekend in October. *Mailing address:* RFD 1, Patterson, MO 63956. *Phone:* (314) 856-4411. *Driving instructions:* Sam A. Baker State Park is off Route 143, roughly 3 miles north of Patterson.

Stockton State Park is in southwestern Missouri about 30 miles northwest of Springfield. Its 2,017 acres are on Missouri's Ozark Plateau—with an average elevation of about 1,300 feet—overlooking the 21,000-acre Stockton Reservoir. Of the trees here, 95 percent are hardwoods, and the terrain's forested areas are essentially an oak and hickory climax forest. A wide variety of wildlife includes deer, foxes, coyotes, and wild turkeys, and migrating waterfowl find Stockton Reservoir a good place to sojourn.

Almost all activities center on the reservoir, which has a sand beach with a bathhouse and rental facilities for paddleboats, pontoon boats, powerboats, fishing boats, and jet skis. The most sought-after fish are walleyes, bass, crappies, catfishes, and bluegills. The park offers camping and picnicking facilities and has a full-service marina with launching facilities, as well as a restaurant.

The park has eleven rooms, ten in a single-story motel beside the reservoir, and one room in the restaurant building. Each has carpeting, color television, and a private bath, as well as a view of the reservoir. The park restaurant, which serves meals to both guests and the public (March through November) also overlooks the water.

Accommodations: 11 rooms with private bath. *Pets:* Not permitted. *Open:* March through November. *Mailing address:* Route 3, Dadeville, MO 65635. *Phone:* (417) 276-5422. *Driving instructions:* Stockton State Park is off Route 6 about 8 miles south of Stockton.

Thousand Hills State Park is in northeastern Missouri about 4 miles west of Kirksville and 30 miles south of the Iowa border. Its 3,192 acres, in a hilly area with elevations averaging just under 1,000 feet, are wooded with oaks and hickories broken up by a few stands of aspens. The man-made 702-acre Forest Lake, which has a beach with a bathhouse, is a favorite spot for boating and fishing, with anglers going mainly after bass and crappies. There are launching facilities (with a 90-horsepower limit on the lake), and a concessionaire rents speedboats, pontoon boats, canoes, and paddleboats and runs the general store, selling groceries and sundries, bait, tackle, and other fishing supplies.

The park service offers nature walks in summer on several short, easy-to-follow trails, and hikers are likely to spot deer, wild turkeys, raccoons, woodpeckers, nuthatches, and during fall and spring, migrating eagles. Other activities include camping and picnicking.

The park has ten cabins arranged in five side-by-side duplex units constructed of brick. Each cabin has two bedrooms accommodating four, as well as wall-to-wall carpeting, color television, a private bath, and a patio with picnic table and grill. Between each unit is a kitchen that can only be rented by the occupants of one of the duplex cabins. The cabin units are beside the lake and have views of it, as does the nearby restaurant, which operates from April through mid-December.

Accommodations: 10 cabins with private bath. *Towels and linens:* Provided. *Cooking and eating utensils:* Provided. *Stove and refrigerator:* Available to half the cabins when rented singly. *Pets:* Not permitted. *Open:* April through October. *Mailing address:* Kirksville, MO 63501. *Phone:* (816) 665-7119. *Driving instructions:* Thousand Hills State Park is on Route 157, off Route 6.

The 273-acre Wakonda State Park, in northeastern Missouri about 60 miles southeast of Kirksville and a mile west of the Mississippi River, is on reclaimed land that was at one time river bottomland, later a sand-and-gravel mining area. The relatively flat terrain is sparsely wooded with cottonwoods. A 75-acre lake, which boasts the largest and purest sand beach in the Missouri park system, has a modern bathhouse. Visitors can rent canoes and fishing boats or paddleboats.

The wildlife population includes some deer as well as raccoons, opossums, and rabbits, and migrating waterfowl rest on the lake and the nearby shores of the Mississippi. The park also has picnicking and camping facilities and a snack bar. The snack bar is open from Memorial Day through Labor Day.

The park has fourteen cabins beside the lake in seven side-by-side wooden duplex units. Each cabin, which will accommodate four, has carpeting, a living room with a sofa bed, and a private bath. Between each two cabins is a kitchen that can be rented by the occupants of only one of the cabins in a duplex unit. Each duplex unit may also be rented as a single, and one comes without a kitchen between its two cabins. The park's security gate at the entrance closes from 11 P.M. to 7:30 A.M. during the open season.

Accommodations: 14 cabins with private bath. *Towels and linens:* Provided. *Cooking and eating utensils:* Provided. *Stove and refrigerator:* Available in half the cabins when rented singly. *Pets:* Not permitted. *Open:* Mid-April through October. *Mailing address:* LaGrange, MO 63448. *Phone:* (314) 655-2280. *Driving instructions:* Wakonda State Park is on U.S 61, about 2.5 miles south of LaGrange.

Washington State Park is in southeastern Missouri, about 30 miles southwest of St. Louis. Its 1,415-acre terrain is hilly, with elevations ranging from 1,000 to 1,300 feet, and wooded mainly with hickories, post oaks, eastern red cedars, dogwoods, and redbuds. The Big River borders the park and attracts both fishermen and canoeists. Along its shores are several prehistoric Indian petroglyphs, or rock carvings, considered to be the work of the Mississippian Indian and estimated to be between six hundred and a thousand years old. They are all close to each other, and it seems likely that their location, in an area of rock outcroppings, was once a sacred site. Among characteristic wildlife are deer, wild turkeys, red and gray squirrels, red and gray foxes, raccoons, and coyotes.

Activities include picnicking, camping, hiking, backpacking, and swimming at both a beach on Big River and a swimming pool. Other facilities include a restaurant and 12 miles of hiking trails.

The park has eight wood-frame cabins in a wooded area, each accommodating six people and varying slightly in appointments—four have wood paneling, and the other four have carpeting. Each has a fully equipped kitchenette, air-conditioning, a porch, a private bath, and an outdoor picnic table and barbecue pit.

Accommodations: 8 cabins with private bath. *Towels and linens:* Provided. *Cooking and eating utensils:* Provided. *Stove and refrigerator:* Provided. *Pets:* Not permitted. *Open:* April through October. *Mailing address:* Route 2, De Soto, MO 63020. *Phone:* (314) 586-2995 (park information); 438-4106 (accommodations off season); or 586-6696 (accommodations in season). *Driving instructions:* Washington State Park is off Route 21, 14 miles north of Potosi.

Montana

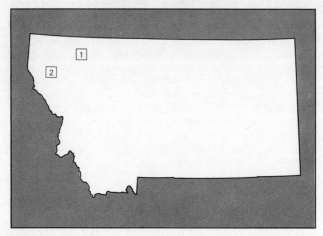

State map and tourist information: Dept. of Commerce, Tourist Bureau, 1424 Ninth Ave., Helena, MT 59601; 406-444-2654 or 406-3760. **State parks:** *Information:* Parks Div., 1420 E. Sixth Ave., Helena, MT 59601; 406-444-3750. **National parks:** Contact parks directly.

In northwestern Montana, Glacier National Park encompasses 1,013,594 acres contiguous with the approximately 390,000 acres of Canada's Waterton Lakes National Park. On June 30, 1932, Glacier National Park was proclaimed a part of a U.S.-Canadian joint venture: Waterton–Glacier International Peace Park, more than 1.4 million acres intended to symbolize peace and brotherhood in the international community.

The park is a majestic combination of precipitous mountain peaks, many higher than 10,000 feet; streams; alpine meadows studded with pink harebells, yellow columbines, and bear grass; and crystal-clear lakes. Bears, deer, mountain goats, and eagles frequent the area; and what seem to be moving patches of snow turn out to be bighorn sheep. The park takes its name from its more than fifty glaciers, and its terrain is riddled with valleys carved millennia ago by receding glaciers that left behind more than two hundred lakes. Towering stands of spruce and pine line the lakes and streams and cover the foothills up to the timberline.

Glacier National Park has more than 700 miles of bridle path and hiking trails and an automobile road that is one of the most scenic in the country. Going-to-the-Sun-Road bisects the park, running from Saint Mary on the east to Apgar on the west, skirts the shores of both Saint Mary Lake and Lake McDonald, follows the timberline across the Continental Divide at Logan Pass, and demands frequent stops to admire the spectacle. *Park mailing address:* West Glacier, MT 59936. *Park phone:* (406) 888-5441.

Note: All the accommodations below, except for the Granite Park and Sperry Chalets, are operated by Glacier Park Inc. For reservations and information, write: Glacier Park, Inc., Greyhound Tower, Station 5185, Phoenix, AZ 85077. *Phone:* (406) 226-5551 (mid-May to mid-September) or (602) 248-2600 (mid-September to mid-May).

Glacier Park Lodge

When the Glacier Park Lodge was completed, it was referred to by local Indians as Om-Coo-La-Mush-Taw, the big-tree lodge, owing, no doubt, to the huge logs that serve as pillars in the lobby. These supports, sixty 40-foot-tall, 40-inch-diameter Douglas fir trunks, were about eight hundred years old when

they were cut and still have their original bark. More modest timbers of white cedar support the building's verandas.

The lodge, built by the Great Northern Railway between 1912 and 1914, is on the east side of the park immediately outside its boundary. Half of its 155 rooms have views of the mountains; the other half overlook the grounds—manicured lawns and flower gardens. Most rooms, except for those on the third floor, have balconies; and all have hardwood floors partially covered with throw rugs. On the grounds is a heated swimming pool with mountain view, as well as a nine-hole golf course. Meals are served in the lodge dining room.

Accommodations: 155 rooms with private bath. *Pets:* Permitted. *Open:* Early June to early September. *Mailing address and phone:* See above. *Driving instructions:* Glacier Park Lodge is near the east entrance to the park, quite close to East Glacier, which is accessible via U.S. 2 or Route 49.

Lake McDonald Lodge and Cabins

The "original" Lake McDonald Lodge was built in 1914 by George Snyder, a wealthy man who used the place as a retreat for himself and his friends before the area was designated a national park. In the present building the paneled lobby, three stories high and supported by cedar beams, bark and all, has a huge stone fireplace with pictograph carvings—attributed to Charles Russell, the noted painter of Old West subjects—of bighorn sheep, moose, elk, deer, and bald eagles.

A clapboard building with the air of a Swiss chalet, the lodge is in the park's western section, on the shore of Lake McDonald. The building's extensive system of balconies has flower boxes filled with snapdragons, nasturtiums, and petunias, as well as rocking chairs and views of mountains that tower 5,000 feet over the lake. The back balconies afford views of the lake and mountains.

In addition to its 101 guest rooms, the full-service lodge offers various types of cabins for rent, as well as a varied dining-room menu.

Accommodations: 101 rooms with private bath. *Pets:* Permitted. *Open:* Early June through early September. *Mailing address and phone:* See above. *Driving instructions:* Follow U.S. 2 to West Glacier, then take Going-to-the-Sun Road directly to the head of Lake McDonald and the lodge.

Many Glacier Hotel

On the shore of Swiftcurrent Lake, against a backdrop of mountains, the imposing Many Glacier Hotel is in the Swiss style, inside and out. The busboys, luggage handlers, maids, and waitresses wear either lederhosen or dirndl dresses, and plaques representing the Swiss cantons hang in the dining room. This room has a three-story-high cathedral ceiling, supported by a dozen logs at its perimeter, and a free-standing fireplace, surrounded by seats at its center. The lobby wall facing Swiftcurrent Lake is largely of glass.

The rooms, many of which have private balconies, vary but most have beamed ceilings.

During the summer the hotel continues a tradition from the 1960s, when students from college drama and music departments began staging a variety of entertainments—musicals, concerts, songfests, and serenades.

Accommodations: 207 rooms with private bath. *Pets:* Permitted. Open: Early June to early September. *Mailing address and phone:* See above. *Driving instructions:* From Browning take U.S. 89 north to Babb, then take the paved road that runs west directly to the hotel.

Swiftcurrent Motor Inn and Cabins

Situated in Many Glacier Valley, about a mile from Swift-current Lake, the motel-style Swiftcurrent Motor Inn has sixty-two guest rooms and twenty-six wood-frame cabins. The motel has two wings with rooms, each of which has wall-to-wall carpeting and a private bath. The rooms overlook trees, and when you step outside you see mountains. The cabins are rustic and have electricity, a sink with cold running water, and a table with benches and can accommodate from four to six people. The motor inn is near a popular campground area and is frequently used to accommodate the overflow of guests at the Many Glacier Hotel. The complex includes a camp store and a coffee shop.

Accommodations: 62 motel rooms with private bath, 26 cabins with central shared baths. *Towels and linens:* Provided. *Cooking and eating utensils:* Not provided. *Stove and refrigerator:* Not provided. *Pets:* Permitted. *Open:* Late June through early September. *Mailing address and phone:* See above. *Driving instructions:* Swiftcurrent Motor Inn is 12 miles west of Babb, Montana, on the park road.

Rising Sun Motor Inn and Cabins

Overlooking picturesque Saint Mary's Lake, the Rising Sun Motor Inn has a motel-style building with thirty-six rooms along with thirty-five cabins. The motel rooms and the cabins both have wall-to-wall carpeting and private baths, and all overlook trees. The complex also includes a restaurant overlooking Saint Mary's Lake and a camp store, with a large campground nearby.

Accommodations: 36 rooms and 35 cabins with private bath. *Towels and linens:* Provided. *Cooking and eating utensils:* Not provided. *Stove and refrigerator:* Not provided. *Pets:* Permitted. *Open:* Late June through early September. *Mailing address and phone:* See above. *Driving instructions:* The Rising Sun Motor Inn is on Going-to-the-Sun-Highway, 6 miles west of Saint Mary.

Village Inn

Built along the shore of Lake McDonald just inside the west entrance to the park at Apgar, the Village Inn is a two-story motel-style building with thirty-six guest rooms. The rooms vary quite a bit and include twelve efficiency units with fully equipped kitchenettes and one- and two-bedroom units with or without kitchenettes. There are also two-bedroom units that have a living room but no kitchenette. All the rooms have wall-to-wall carpeting and a private bath. Each has a view of Lake McDonald.

The Village Inn has no restaurant, but guests can dine at Lake McDonald Lodge, a short drive away.

Accommodations: 36 rooms with private bath. *Towels and linens:* Provided. *Cooking and eating utensils:* Provided in efficiency units. *Stove and refrigerator:* Provided. *Pets:* Permitted. *Open:* Late May through mid-September. *Mailing address and phone:* See above. *Driving instructions:* The Village Inn is 2 miles inside the west entrance, at Apgar.

Prince of Wales Hotel

On the Canadian side of the park, at the northern end of Waterton Lake, Prince of Wales Hotel is a large, rambling, peak-roofed and gabled Bavarian-looking building built in 1927 by the Great Northern Railway. The hotel has eighty-two guest rooms, a four-story-high lobby with a huge chandelier and large windows, a gift shop, a lounge-bar, and a restaurant with a sweeping view of Waterton Lake. The guest rooms are simply but comfortably furnished, and each has a private bath. The rooms are on five floors, although the top-floor rooms aren't accessible by elevator and require walking a flight of steps. The rooms on the first four floors have tubs in the bathrooms, and those on the top floor have showers. The hotel, which is on a bluff overlooking the seven-mile-long lake, is billed as having a view of the longest unguarded international frontier in the world.

Accommodations: 82 rooms with private bath. *Pets:* Not permitted. *Open:* Early June through mid-September. *Mailing address and phone:* See above. *Driving instructions:* Prince of Wales Hotel is off Canada Highway 5, at the head of Waterton Lake, about 30 miles west of Cardston, Alberta.

Granite Park and Sperry Chalets

Constructed in 1914, Granite Park and Sperry Chalets are rustic, peaked-roof buildings built of native stone. Both chalets are located in remote, beautiful sections of the park that are accessible only by trails. Visitors here can either hike to the chalets, which takes about four hours, or arrange to rent horses. Both chalets operate on the American plan (three meals included).

Sperry Chalet is at an elevation of 6,500 feet on the western face of Gunsight Mountain, on an Alpine ledge overlooking Lake McDonald. The chalet has seventeen guest rooms, each of which has a sink with cold running water and kerosene lamps for light. Shower and sanitary facilities are in a detached building close to the chalet.

Granite Park Chalet is on a lava outcropping at the northern end of the Garden Wall formation. It has twelve guest rooms lit by candle light that share sinks with cold running water out on the balcony. Shower and sanitary facilities are in a detached building.

275

Both chalets have dining and lounge rooms that are illuminated by mantled lanterns.

Accommodations: 29 rooms in 2 chalets, all with shared bath. *Towels and linens:* Provided. *Pets:* Horses permitted (no grazing is allowed, and those who bring their own horses must also pack feed). *Open:* July through Labor Day. *Mailing address:* Belton Chalets, Inc., Box 188, West Glacier, MT 59936. *Phone:* (406) 888-5511. *Driving instructions:* Call or write for specific driving and hiking instructions.

In the northwestern corner of Montana, contiguous with the Kaniksu National Forest in the Idaho panhandle and with the Canadian border, Kootenai National Forest encompasses 2½ million rugged acres varying in elevation from about 2,000 feet to 9,700 feet at the summit of Snowshoe Peak. At lower elevations, the forest is wooded primarily with ponderosa pines and Douglas firs, which give way to alpine firs, grand firs, cedars and hemlocks, and finally at the highest points, only gnarled Englemann spruces. Grizzly bears, virtually extinct in the contiguous United States, inhabit a few small pockets near the Canadian border, such as the 90,000-acre Cabinet Wilderness Area, which also supports a healthy population of black bears, white-tailed and mule deer, bighorn sheep, moose, and elk. Bald eagles are frequently observed along the Kootenai River, and ospreys and northern goshawks are common. The Cabinet Wilderness is an area of high, rugged peaks riddled with some 70 small lakes. Trails wind through forest, past lakes and alpine meadows.

At the summit of Big Creek Baldy at an elevation of 5,700 feet, the forest maintains a 225-square-foot, wood-frame fire tower that stands on 41-foot-tall legs and is surrounded by wind-twisted lodgepole pines. The tower is a single room completely enclosed by glass, and in the center there's a map board, or "fire finder," with a sighting device. The tower doesn't operate as a fire tower anymore, having been superceded by aerial surveys and other modern fire-finding methods, but it is now available as an overnight accommodation.

Reached by way of some 50 stairs, the tower is equipped with a wood stove, and propane lights, stove, and heater, and two double beds. The tower has no plumbing, and sanitary facilities consist of an outhouse about 100 yards from the base of the tower. Guests are advised to bring their own provisions, although forest rangers supply the tower with four 5-gallon bottles of water.

Accommodations: 1 tower with outside privy. *Towels and linens:* Not provided. *Stove and refrigerator:* Propane stove only. *Open:* All year. *Mailing address:* Kootenai National Forest, Star Route 1, Box 275, Libby, MT 59923. *Phone:* (406) 293-7741. *Driving instructions:* The Libby Ranger Station is 1 mile east of Libby on Highway 37.

Nebraska

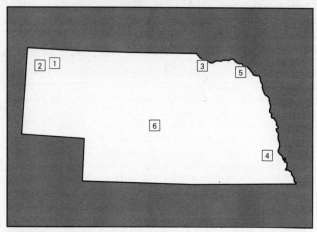

State map and tourist information: Dept. of Tourism, PO Box 94666, 301 Centennial Mall South, Lincoln, NE 68509; 402-471-3796. **State parks:** *Information:* Parks Div., 2200 North 33rd St., Lincoln, NE 68503; 402-464-0641. *Entrance fees:* $2 per vehicle daily; $10 annually. *Reservations:* Contact individual parks. 2-night deposit (cabins), 1-night deposit (lodges); by check or credit card within 10 days. Accepted beginning the first working day in January. Recommended in the first week in January for Mem. Day—Labor Day; maximum stay, 2 weeks. *Restrictions:* Hunting limited to selected parks. Dogs must be leashed (not allowed in lodgings). No alcohol. *Facilities:* Boating, swimming, and interpretative programs, Mem. Day—Labor Day.

Chadron State Park is in northwestern Nebraska, about 100 miles northeast of Scottsbluff in the 50,853-acre Pine Ridge section of the Nebraska National Forest. The Pine Ridge, a 20-mile-wide, 100-mile-long escarpment at the northern tip of Nebraska's High Plains, has elevations ranging from 2,500 to 4,000 feet and a rugged and wooded terrain of steep, jagged ridges, buttes, and streams. The characteristic tree here is the ponderosa pine, but others commonly found include ashes, cottonwoods, elms, and junipers. The plentiful bird life includes red-tailed and marsh hawks, golden eagles, wild turkeys, orioles, turkey vultures, and mountain bluebirds.

The 801-acre park was named after a nineteenth-century fur trader; and the Trading Post center has exhibits and demonstrations explaining the early history of fur trading and trapping. Other activities include hiking on a series of trails ranging in length from 1 to 8 miles, guided horseback trail rides, swimming in the park's pool, boating (rentals available) in the lagoon, and fishing in Chadron Creek, which is stocked with rainbow and brown trout. The park also sponsors campfire film programs.

The park has twenty-two cabins, sixteen of which have two bedrooms and a fully equipped kitchenette. Six cabins are in a "multi-use facility," a complex of three motel-type units that can be rented as a group camp and that has kitchen facilities for sixty and a meeting room.

Accommodations: 22 cabins with private bath. *Towels and linens:* Provided. *Cooking and eating utensils:* Provided. *Stove and refrigerator:* Provided. *Pets:* Permitted. *Open:* Memorial Day through Labor Day. *Mailing address:* Chadron, NE 69337. *Phone:* (308) 432-2036. *Driving instructions:* Chadron State Park is off U.S. 385, about 10 miles south of Chadron.

Fort Robinson State Park, 22,000 acres in all, is in northwestern Nebraska, about 5 miles south of Oglala National Grassland along the 20-mile-wide, 100-mile-long Pine Ridge escarpment at the northern edge of the state's High Plains. The rugged area, characterized by precipitous ridges, buttes, and streams, is at an average elevation of roughly 4,000 feet. The terrain is heavily wooded with ponderosa pines, cottonwoods, elms, ashes, and a variety of grasses and shrubs. Turkey vultures, red-tailed hawks, and northern harriers are common, and a golden eagle is occasionally sighted.

The park is named for Fort Robinson, built in 1874 as a protective measure against hostile Indians, one of whom, Crazy Horse, was killed here during an escape attempt. The fort—formerly the site of the famous Cheyenne Outbreak, a U.S. Department of Agriculture research center, and a World War II prisoner-of-war camp—is now Nebraska's largest state park.

Many of the fort's buildings are still intact and have been incorporated into the park accommodations. One park museum commemorates the fort's early days, another deals with the area's natural features; there is also a playhouse, a swimming pool, and a stagecoach. Among many special activities organized by the park are horseback and jeep rides, wildlife tours, cookouts, rodeo events, and film programs.

Fort Robinson Lodge and Cabins

Fort Robinson Lodge and its associated cabins offer several types of accommodations. The lodge itself, a 1909 building that originally served as an enlisted men's barracks, has twenty-three rooms with private bath, a restaurant, and a large room suitable for meetings.

Of twenty-four adobe cabins, several of which served in 1887 as officers' quarters, ten have two bedrooms; seven have three bedrooms; and ten have four bedrooms. Each unit can accommodate from four to eight people and comes equipped with a private bath, a kitchen, and towels, linens, and utensils.

Four multiple-bedroom units, constructed of brick, served in 1909 as officers' quarters. These units, with shared bath, are equipped for housekeeping and, depending on the particular unit, can accommodate from twelve to thirty people.

Commanche Hall, the 1909 bachelor officers' quarters, is a group facility with shared bath and kitchen and dining facilities. It will accommodate sixty.

Accommodations: 23 lodge rooms and 24 cabins, all with private bath; 4 multiple-bedroom units and 1 group facility, all with shared bath. *Towels and linens:* Provided. *Cooking and eating utensils:* Provided. *Stove and refrigerator:* In cabins. *Pets:* Not permitted. *Open:* Memorial Day through Labor Day and on a limited basis until mid-November. *Mailing address:* Box 392, Crawford, NE 69339. *Phone:* (308) 665-2660. *Driving instructions:* Fort Robinson State Park is on U.S. 20, about 3 miles west of Crawford.

Niobrara State Park is located in northeastern Nebraska, about three quarters of a mile south of the South Dakota border, along the Niobrara River 5 miles west of the Santee Indian Reservation. The terrain, in the Missouri River valley, is relatively flat and wooded primarily with cottonwoods, elms, oaks, and cedars. Of 408 acres, 200 have been left undeveloped, and although there are no designated hiking trails, visitors can wander through thickly wooded areas with a dense understory of tall grass. Characteristic wildlife includes deer, wild turkeys, pheasants, and coyotes. Wood ducks, herons, and egrets are commonly sighted on the park's lagoon, and bald eagles are seen frequently. One of the best ways to see the park is by horseback, and the facilities here include riding stables that offer guided tours hourly.

Activities include pool swimming, camping, paddleboating in the lagoon, and fishing for crappies, bluegills, catfishes, and bass.

Niobrara State Park has fifteen wood-frame cabins in a wooded area near the lake, with about half right on the water. These one- and two-bedroom units can accommodate from five to seven, and each has a fully equipped kitchenette, air-conditioning, a private bath, and a screened porch. The park also has a dining hall seating ninety, which it rents on a daily basis to groups.

Accommodations: 15 cabins with private bath. *Towels and linens:* Provided. *Cooking and eating utensils:* Provided. *Stove and refrigerator:* Provided. *Pets:* Permitted if leashed. *Open:* Memorial Day through Labor Day. *Mailing address:* Box 226, Niobrara, NE 68760. *Phone:* (402) 857-3373. *Driving instructions:* The park is off Route 12, half a mile west of Niobrara.

Platte River State Park is in eastern Nebraska about 25 miles southwest of Omaha. Opened in 1982, it is the newest addition to the Nebraska park system and reflects, in terms of facilities, some innovative thinking. The 404-acre park is along the bluffs overlooking the Platte River and is thickly wooded, primarily with oaks, maples, elms, poplars, and cottonwoods, which, by its predominance of hardwoods, produces a scenic autumn foliage. The park has some 20 miles of hiking trails, which wind through very hilly terrain overlooking the Platte River, as well as equestrian trails, where visitors can go on horseback rides through the bluffs. Other recreational facilities include a lake with a beach for swimming, a swimming pool, paddleboat rentals, tennis courts, and a small fishing pond. The park's craft center offers workshops in ceramics, leather crafts, and tepee making (one of the types of accommodations here is a tepee village). Also in the park is a conference center and a cafeteria-style restaurant overlooking the river.

Platte River Park has forty wood-frame cabins, a group lodge, a tent village, and a tepee village. Thirty of the cabins are "camper cabins," accommodating from four to six people, arranged in "pods" —groups of four to five cabins that share a central shower and sanitary facility. Although these units have no running water (water is available at outside hydrants), they do have electricity, fire grates, and kitchen tables and chairs.

The ten housekeeping, or "modern" cabins, each with wall-to-wall carpeting, a kitchenette, and a private bath, are scattered throughout the park. These vary in size from one to four bedrooms. Some have screened porches, and some have fireplaces. Each has an outside fire grate and a picnic table.

The Red Barn, a group lodge accommodating twenty in a dormitory—formerly the haymow—is in fact a converted red barn. The lodge is *not* equipped to house coed groups, but it does have complete cooking and dining facilities (exept for utensils), outside picnic tables, fire grates, and a common dining room as well as shower and sanitary facilities.

The tent and tepee villages consist, respectively, of four tents and four tepees equipped with wooden floors, outside picnic tables and fire grates, and outside vault toilets.

Accommodations: 40 cabins, 10 with private bath; 1 group

lodge with shared bath; 8 tepees and tents with vault toilets. *Towels and linens:* Not provided. *Cooking and eating utensils:* Not provided. *Stove and refrigerator:* In ten cabins and group lodge. *Pets:* Not permitted. *Open:* Memorial Day through November. *Mailing address:* RR 161A, Louisville, NE 68037. *Phone:* (402) 234-2217. *Driving instructions:* From Louisville take Route 50 a mile south to Spur 13E, then take Spur 13E west 2 miles.

Ponca State Park is in northeastern Nebraska, 23 miles northwest of Sioux City, Iowa, on the shores of the Missouri River. Its 892 acres are hilly and rise at one point 225 feet above the river, which is flanked on either by side by bluffs. The area is thickly wooded, primarily with oaks, cottonwoods, ashes, pines, hackberries, and some dogwoods, while its wildlife includes deer, foxes, raccoons, and coyotes. The terrain supports a wide variety of bird life—many warblers, sparrows, and, soaring above, eagles, turkey vultures, and red-tailed hawks. Some 20 miles of hiking trails include several bridle paths. Guided horseback tours leave from the stables each hour, and the typical ride passes along a high bluff overlooking the Missouri River and three states—Nebraska, Iowa, and South Dakota.

Park activities include pool swimming, camping, picnicking, boating, and fishing for catfishes, carp, and bluegills, as well as boating and waterskiing on the river. Although the park has no rental boats it does have a boat ramp. Cross-country skiing is becoming increasingly popular.

The park has fourteen wood-frame cabins in a wooded area about a quarter of a mile from the river. Two-bedroom units that accommodate a maximum of eight people, each has a fully equipped kitchenette, a screened porch, air-conditioning, and a private bath.

Accommodations: 14 cabins with private bath. *Towels and linens:* Provided. *Cooking and eating utensils:* Provided. *Stove and refrigerator:* Provided. *Pets:* Not permitted. *Open:* Memorial Day through Labor Day. *Mailing address:* PO Box 486, Ponca, NE 68770. *Phone:* (402) 755-2284. *Driving instructions:* Ponca State Park is off Spur 26E of Route 12, about 2 miles north of Ponca.

Victoria Springs State Recreation Area comprises 70 acres in central Nebraska about 20 miles north of Broken Bow. The park is named for two artesian springs that at one time were highly acclaimed for their curative powers. A Custer County judge once bottled and sold the water; and his log cabin, as well as another—the first post office in the county—is still in the park. The terrain is generally flat and wooded with mostly younger trees—cottonwoods, oaks, elms, and willows—because of a 1980 tornado that roared through the area, uprooting a good deal of its mature-tree growth. The ranger here says that everyone camping in the park that day became good friends as they stared at trees and debris flying by—it was so dark they couldn't see anything until lightning flashed.

On a small lake, anglers go after catfishes and bluegills, and sightseers cruise on paddleboats. Victoria Creek, which is stocked with trout, runs through the area. Deer, wild turkeys, pheasants, and hawks are frequently sighted, and at night you can hear the coyotes. The park has facilities for camping and picnicking as well as a playground for children. Although there are no designated hiking trails, visitors are welcome to wander anywhere in the recreation area.

Victoria Springs has two wood-frame cabins in a thinly wooded area beside the lake. The two-bedroom units can accommodate six people, and each has a fully equipped kitchenette, a private bath with shower, and a screened porch.

Accommodations: 2 cabins with private bath. *Towels and linens:* Provided. *Cooking and eating utensils:* Provided. *Stove and refrigerator:* Provided. *Pets:* Not permitted. *Open:* Memorial Day through Labor Day. *Mailing address:* HC 69, Box 117, Anselmo, NE 68813. *Phone:* (308) 749-2235. *Driving instructions:* Victoria Springs State Recreation Area is off Route 2, about 6 miles east of Anselmo.

Nevada

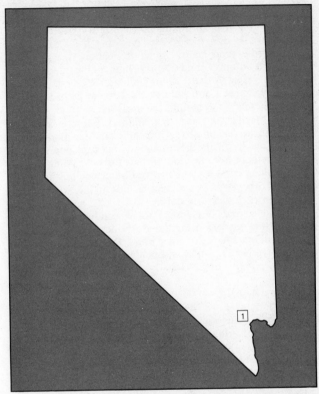

State map and tourist information: Commission on Tourism, 600 E. William St., Suite 207, Carson City, NV 89701; 702-885-4322. **State Parks:** *Information:* Division of State Parks, 201 S. Fall St., Rm. 119, Carson City, NV 89710; 702-885-4384. **National parks;** Contact park directly.

Lake Mead National Recreation Area, the first national recreation area established by an act of Congress, is in southeastern Nevada and a small section of northwestern Arizona, part of it only 20 miles from Las Vegas. Consisting of 1,496,600 acres, it was called Boulder Dam National Recreation Area until 1947. The reserve adjoins Grand Canyon National Park and includes two lakes created by dams on the Colorado River—Lake Mead, formed by Hoover Dam, and Lake Mohave, by Davis Dam. Several scenic roads run around the area.

Lake Mead is 105 miles long, and Lake Mohave is 67 miles long. Both are surrounded by high hills, forested plateaus, and desert. Concessions in the recreation area can supply visitors with everything from fast motorboats for waterskiing to patio boats, fishing boats, or houseboats. Fishing equipment is available, and other popular activities include hiking, which should be attempted judiciously during heat spells, and touring the dams. Guided tours of Hoover Dam are conducted almost every day, the slow seasons being the exception, and Davis Dam is open at all times for self-guided tours. *Recreation area mailing address:* 601 Nevada Highway, Boulder City, NV 89005. *Recreation area phone:* (702) 293-4041.

Echo Bay Resort

Overlooking Lake Mead, Echo Bay Resort consists of a hotel-style building with fifty-two guest rooms and a restaurant, a full-service marina with slips and rentals, a swimming pool, and a store that carries groceries, fishing gear, and sundries.

Each guest room has wall-to-wall carpeting, color television, a telephone, a private bath, and a balcony or patio. About three-quarters of the rooms have lake views.

There are also facilities for boat rentals—waterskiing boats, fishing boats, and houseboats. The houseboats are fully equipped with kitchens and cooking and eating utensils, as well as towels and linens; they range in size from 42 to 47 feet and can accomodate from six to ten people each.

Accommodations: 52 rooms and a varying number of houseboats, all with private bath. *Towels and linens:* Provided. *Cooking and eating utensils:* In houseboats. *Stove and refrigerator:* In houseboats. *Pets:* Permitted. *Open:* All year.

Mailing address: Overton, NV 89040. *Phone:* (702) 394-4000.
Driving instructions: From Las Vegas take U.S. 95 south 8 miles
past Henderson and look for signs to Echo Bay. Turn left on
North Shore Road and proceed 36 miles.

Lake Mead Resort

Lake Mead Resort is a group of single-story motel-style
buildings. The complex includes a marina, a swimming pool,
a restaurant, a bar, and a store that retails groceries, fishing
gear, and sundries.

Each guest room, most of which overlook the lake, has wall-
to-wall carpeting, color television, and a private bath. The
restaurant is about three-quarters of a mile from the rooms.
It floats on pontoons and, of course, has lake views. The restaurant area also has a coffee shop and a bar.

Accommodations: 44 rooms with private bath. *Pets:* Not
permitted. *Open:* All year. *Mailing address:* 322 Lakeshore
Road, Boulder City, NV 89005. *Phone:* (702) 293-2074. *Driving instructions:* From Las Vegas take U.S. 95 about 8 miles
past Boulder City. Look for a sign saying "Lake Mead
Marina."

Temple Bar Marina

A complex of buildings on the Arizona side of Lake Mead,
Temple Bar Marina has twenty-two guest rooms, a restaurant,
a full-service marina and a store selling groceries, fishing gear,
and sundries. Twelve of the guest rooms have wall-to-wall
carpeting, color television, and a patio with outdoor chairs. Half
of the rooms have views of the lake; half, of the desert. A shingled, frame building houses other guest rooms, which have carpeting and small patio areas. These rooms have limited water
views, and four of them have kitchenettes. There are also four
fishing cabins with rustic furnishings, refrigerators, and stoves;
but cooking and eating utensils and towels and linens are not
supplied. The fishing cabins have no baths; there's a central
lavatory and shower facility. The marina's restaurant and cocktail lounge are in a wood-frame building that overlooks the lake.

Accommodations: 22 rooms, 18 with private bath. *Towels
and linens:* Provided, except in fishing cabins. *Cooking and
eating utensils:* In housekeeping units but not in fishing cabins.
Stove and refrigerator: In housekeeping units and fishing cabins.

Pets: Not permitted. *Open:* All year. *Mailing address:* Temple Bar, AZ 86443. *Phone:* (602) 767-3400. *Driving instructions:* From Kingman, Arizona, take U.S. 93 north toward Hoover Dam; at the 19-mile marker look for a sign for the marina; turn left and proceed 28 miles.

Cottonwood Cove Resort and Marina

Cottonwood Cove Resort and Marina is a group of adobe-style brick motel buildings. The complex includes twenty-four guest rooms, a restaurant, a full-service marina, a bar, and a store selling groceries, fishing gear, and sundries.

All guest rooms overlook Lake Mohave, and each has wall-to-wall carpeting, color television, a telephone, and a private bath. Each room has sliding glass doors that open onto a patio, and six rooms have kitchenettes. The patios have barbecue units. The restaurant, half a block from the guest rooms, seats sixty people.

The marina also has houseboats available, fully equipped with kitchens, all utensils, towels and linens, and showers. Fishing, waterskiing, and patio boats are also for rent.

Accommodations: 24 rooms with private bath and a varying number of houseboats. *Towels and linens:* Provided. *Cooking and eating utensils:* In rooms with kitchenettes and on houseboats. *Stove and refrigerator:* In rooms with kitchenettes and on houseboats. *Pets:* Not permitted. *Open:* All year. *Mailing address:* PO Box 1000, Cottonwood Cove, NV 89046. *Phone:* (702) 297-1464. *Driving instructions:* From Las Vegas take U.S. 95 south to the town of Searchlight, look for the sign to the marina, and go east for 14 miles on Route 164.

Lake Mohave Resort

Lake Mohave Resort has fifty-one guest rooms, a restaurant, a full-service marina, and a store selling groceries, fishing gear, and sundries. The guest rooms, which are in three motel-style buildings, have wall-to-wall carpeting, color television, telephones, private baths, and kitchenettes. All of the rooms have views of the lake, and a few have private patios or balconies. The restaurant, in a nautical-looking building, overlooks the lake.

The resort also rents out houseboats, which are equipped with kitchens, showers, and towels and linens. Fishing, water-skiing, and patio boats are also available for rent.

Accommodations: 51 rooms with private bath and a varying number of houseboats. *Towels and linens:* Provided. *Cooking and eating utensils:* Provided. *Stove and refrigerator:* Provided. *Pets:* Not permitted. *Open:* All year. *Mailing address:* Bullhead City, AZ 86430. *Phone:* (602) 754-3245. *Driving instructions:* From Las Vegas take U.S. 95 south and Route 163 to Davis Dam, then turn right at Catherine 3 and watch for signs.

New Hampshire

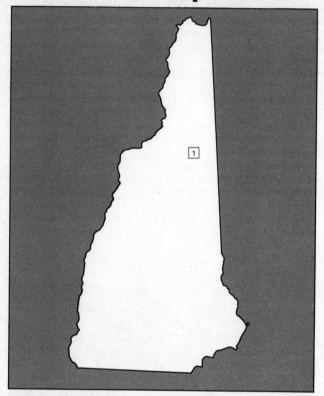

State map and tourist information: Vacation Travel, 105 Loudon Rd., PO Box 856, Concord, NH 03301; 603-271-2666. **State parks:** *Information:* Division of Parks, 105 Loudon Rd., PO Box 856, Concord, NH 03301; 603-271-3556. **National parks:** Contact park directly.

White Mountain National Forest is in northern New Hampshire, though a small section of it crosses the border into Maine. Its 750,000 acres vary in elevation from about 400 feet to 6,288 feet at the summit of Mount Washington, the highest point in the entire Northeast. The terrain is rugged and mountainous and wooded with a wide variety of trees including maples, oaks, wind-dwarfed spruces, and balsam firs. The forest encompasses both the Presidential and the Carter-Wildcat mountain ranges, with numerous summits above 4,000 feet. Rivers include the Wild Ammonoosuc, the Pemigewasset, the Mad, the Swift, and the Ellis. Mount Washington, perhaps the centerpiece of the forest, is renowned for some of the worst, most fickle weather in the world. The highest wind velocities recorded anywhere (231 miles per hour) were on its summit, and the trails to the top of the mountain have ominous signs warning climbers to turn back if the weather turns bad.

A boulder field around the top of the mountain gradually gives way to patches of grass and alpine meadows, and then to a section of wind-dwarfed spruces and firs bent almost entirely to the horizontal, with needles on their lee side only. Halfway down are thick woods filled with spruces, birches, and sugar maples. On a clear day you can see the Atlantic Ocean, 90 miles away, from the summit; on a cloudy day you can't see your feet; and on a windy day you can hardly stand up straight.

Tuckerman's ravine, with accumulations of snow of up to 100 feet, has the last skiing of the season in the Northeast. It attracts only the hardiest of skiers, however, since there are no lifts and it requires a several-mile hike part way up the mountain with skis, boots, and poles on one's back.

Wildlife includes moose, deer, black bears, bobcats, foxes, mink, and otters; a variety of bird life includes ducks, loons, scarlet tanagers, golden eagles, and peregrine falcons. Major activities include cross-country and downhill skiing, snowmobiling, snowshoeing, mountain climbing, canoeing and kayacking, scenic driving, fishing, swimming, hiking, backpacking, and nature study. *National Forest mailing address:* Box 638, Laconia, NH 03247. *National Forest phone:* (603) 524-6450.

Pinkham Notch Camp

Operated by the Appalachian Mountain Club, Pinkham Notch Camp is a complex of rustic-looking wooden buildings at the base of Mount Washington's eastern slope. A main lodge can accommodate 107 people in two- , three- , and four-bedded bunk rooms that are simply furnished with dressers and desks and have wood-paneled walls and hardwood floors. Bath facilities in the lodge are shared: Each floor has both men's and women's bathrooms. Lodge guests must have breakfast or dinner, or both, in the camp's dining room, and prices vary depending on which meal, or meals, are selected. The dining room, which has wood paneling and a large stone fireplace, operates on an all-you-can-eat philosophy and will prepare pack lunches at an additional charge.

An activities center, the Trading Post, includes, in addition to the dining room, an information center with hiking and skiing articles and guide books for sale, a snack bar, and a meeting room. Hikers and skiers congregate here to learn of trail conditions.

Accommodations: 34 bunk rooms with shared bath. *Towels and linens:* Provided. *Pets:* Not permitted. *Open:* All year. *Mailing address:* AMC Box 298, Gorham, NH 03581. *Phone:* (603) 466-2727. *Driving instructions:* Pinkham Notch Camp is on Route 16, 17 miles north of North Conway.

New Jersey

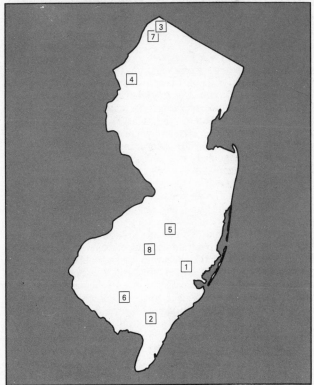

State map and tourist information: Tourist Information Bureau, 1 W. State St., Rm. 600, Trenton, NJ 08625; 609-292-5220. **State parks:** *Information:* Div. of Parks, CN 404, Trenton, NJ 08625; 609-292-1797. *Entrance fees:* $1—$4 per vehicle daily; waived for lodgers and senior citizens. *Reservations:* Lotteries for reservations are held the first working day after January 15th. Send application and payment for full stay plus $3.00 reservation fee to individual park. Winners are contacted at the end of January; payments refunded to others. Reservations for all dates throughout the year should be sent by early January. Cabins available on weekends only in fall and spring. From Mem. Day—Labor Day reservations are for a 7-day or 14-day period. *Restrictions:* Hunting and fishing, license needed (purchased at local sporting goods stores). Dogs must be leashed (not allowed in lodgings). No alcohol. *Facilities:* Swimming, Mem. Day—Labor Day.

Set aside by the state for recreation, timber production, and wildlife and water conservation, Bass River State Forest is on 13,645 acres about 25 miles north of Atlantic City. It is part of the Pine Barrens, a virtually undeveloped section of New Jersey comprising about a fifth of the state. The area is noted for its extensive pine and oak forests, several parts of which consist of dwarf trees—mature pines and oaks no taller than 6 feet—and for its water, which is the color of dark tea and unusually sweet. (The color comes from tannin, a component of the bark of white cedar, which seeps into the water.)

Bass River State Forest also has large tracts of pine and oak woods, miles of sand roads, and white cedar bogs (which were a leading source of the white cedar shingles used on the exterior of houses). A self-guided nature trail winds through the Absegami Natural Area, where the 67-acre Lake Absegami is bordered by a beach, a bathhouse, a snack bar, a small boat launch area, and a concession that rents boats during the summer months. Deer hunting is permitted, and anglers go after catfishes and pickerel.

Each of the six cabins on the north shore of Lake Absegami has a living room, two adjoining bunk rooms with double-deck bunks, a fireplace, a full kitchen with hot and cold running water, a bathroom with toilet and shower, and a screened porch.

The park also has six enclosed "camp shelters" in an area next to the cabins along Lake Absegami. Each cabin has two small bunk rooms accommodating four, a living room with a Franklin stove, a picnic table, and a fire grill for cooking. Although there is neither water nor electricity in the shelters, running water is close by (50 feet) from a pressurized hydrant, and the cabins share a flush toilet directly behind the units.

Six primitive closed lean-tos are also available on the opposite (south) side of the lake. Each is about 9 feet by 12 feet, cedar sided, and has a small wood stove for heat as well as an outside grill for cooking and a picnic table. Visitors must bring their own sleeping bags and mattresses.

Accommodations: 6 cabins with private bath. *Towels and linens:* Not provided. *Cooking and eating utensils:* Not provided. *Stove and refrigerator:* Provided. *Open:* Cabins and shelters: April through October; lean-tos: All year. *Mailing address:* PO Box 118, New Gretna, NJ 08224. *Phone:* (609) 296-1115. *Driving instructions:* Take the Garden State Parkway south to exit 52.

Wooded primarily with young pines, oaks, and white cedars, Belleplain State Forest is in New Jersey's coastal plain, 25 miles north of Cape May. The 11,679-acre forest contains a large pond and a lake named after Nummy, the last chief of the Lenape Indians—which has a beach with a bathhouse, a playground, and a snack bar, as well as a nature trail at its eastern end. Trails and roads, bordered here and there by holly and laurel, wind through the park, and a 6-mile hiking trail runs between Lake Nummy and East Creek Lodge, on the south shore of East Creek Pond.

East Creek Lodge and Lean-tos

A two-story concrete-block building, East Creek Lodge is set up to accommodate groups of up to twenty-four with a large living room, a kitchen with a six-burner gas stove, a 30-inch grill, two refrigerators, cooking and eating utensils, and hot and cold running water, as well as a bathroom with a shower and two dormitory rooms that sleep ten each plus two rooms that sleep two each. A screened porch adjoins the living room and overlooks the lake, where there's a boat dock and a swim-at-your-own-risk unimproved beach, out front on East Creek Lake.

Over on Lake Nummy are eleven primitive, closed lean-tos, each with a potbelly stove for heat. The lean-tos are wood-sided on three sides and have a Plexiglas front in winter which can be removed and replaced with screens during the summer months. Visitors must bring their own sleeping bags and mattresses. Outside is a picnic table, a fire ring and a barbeque grill for cooking. Flush toilets and showers are shared with the campsites.

Accommodations: Group lodge for up to 24 with shared bath; 11 lean-tos with shared bath. *Towels and linens:* Not provided. *Cooking and eating utensils:* In lodge. *Stove and refrigerator:* In lodge. *Open:* All year. *Mailing address:* Box 450, Woodbine, NJ 08270. *Phone:* (609) 861-2404. *Driving instructions:* Take the Garden State Parkway to exit 17, then take Route 550 west for 10 miles.

In the northwest corner of the state near the Delaware Water Gap National Recreation Area, High Point State Park comprises 14,002 acres donated to the state by the late Colonel and Mrs. Anthony R. Kuser. The park runs along the crest of the Kittatinny Mountains, which include High Point, the highest peak in New Jersey. There, at an elevation of 1,803 feet, is a 220-foot-high monument of New Hampshire granite from which you can see three states—New Jersey, New York, and Pennsylvania. From the top of the monument, which is dedicated to New Jersey's veterans, you can look west across the Delaware Valley at the Pocono Mountains, turn to the northeast and see the Catskills, and then turn again to the southeast to take in the farmlands of the Wallkill River Valley.

The park includes New Jersey's first designated natural area, the Dryden Kuser Natural Area, which consists primarily of Cedar Swamp, a 200-acre stand of virgin woodland rife with conifers—large hemlocks (a favorite habitat of owls), eastern white pines, black spruces, and an extensive stand of mature white cedars. The area extends from the New York State border toward High Point for about a mile; a trail that runs along a ridge affords hikers an excellent view of the swamp. The crystal-clear 20-acre Lake Marcia, within the park, has a beach for swimming.

The park also encompasses Steenykill Lake, where the state maintains two cabins along the eastern shore. Each cabin has a furnished 16- by 24-foot living room with a fireplace (firewood provided); three bedrooms; a kitchen with a sink, an electric range with an oven, and a refrigerator; and a bath with sink, toilet, and tub.

Accommodations: 2 cabins with private bath. *Towels and linens:* Not provided. *Cooking and eating utensils:* Not provided. *Stove and refrigerator:* Provided. *Open:* Mid-May through mid-October. *Mailing address:* RR 4, Box 287, Sussex, NJ 07461. *Phone:* (201) 875-4800. *Driving instructions:* From Sussex, New Jersey, take Route 23 northwest 8 miles.

Jenny Jump State Forest is in northwestern New Jersey along the Jenny Jump Mountains, just south of Interstate 80 near the village of Hope. The 1,118-acre forest consists of several separate parcels that follow the Jenny Jump ridge for a little more than 8 miles. The forest varies in elevation from 400 to 1,100 feet, and several trails pass over its higher points and afford hikers some spectacular views of the Delaware Water Gap, Kittatinny Mountain and its valley, and High Point, at 1,803 feet the highest peak in New Jersey.

The forest is heavily wooded with a wide variety of trees, including yellow poplars, walnuts, oaks, maples, hemlocks, beeches, wild cherries, and gray birches.

The forest has two rustic camp shelters located close to the ranger's headquarters near the summit of Jenny Jump Mountain. Each shelter accommodates up to 4 in double-decker bunks and has a living room with a wood stove for heat and a table with benches, an outdoor pit toilet (no shower), and an outdoor fireplace for cooking. Guests can purchase firewood from the forest ranger.

Accommodations: 2 camp shelters with outdoor privy. *Towels and linens:* Not provided. *Cooking and eating utensils:* Not provided. *Stove and refrigerator:* Not provided. *Pets:* Not permitted. *Open:* April through October. *Mailing address:* Box 150, Hope, NJ 07844. *Phone:* (201) 459-4366. *Driving instructions:* From Hope take Route 519 north 4 miles, make the third right, and look for signs.

Lebanon State Forest is in south-central New Jersey, about 40 miles east of Philadelphia. Its 31,217 acres are part of New Jersey's Pine Barrens. One of the premier attractions of the forest is the Batona Trail, which runs for 40.6 miles, primarily through Wharton and Lebanon state forests. The trail—developed by a Philadelphia hiking club whose name, "Batona," is an acronym for "BAck TO NAture"—runs along the Batsto River and passes by Pakim Pond in Lebanon State Forest. Pakim Pond has a sand beach with a bathhouse and is a popular spot both for hikers on the trail and forest visitors.

The forest takes its name from the Lebanon Glass Works, which used to operate here during the 1850s and 1860s because of the generous amounts of silica yielded by the area's sandy soil. One of the natural phenomena the Pine Barrens is noted for is its cedar swamps, which have a primeval beauty; some of the best of these are found along the streams in the northern sections of Lebanon State Forest. The forest's numerous streams are popular among canoeists, and fishing is permitted although the fish population isn't terribly large. The forest also has a playground and picnic facilities.

Three wood-frame cabins overlook Pakim Pond. The cabins are one-room units with separate kitchens and half baths (no shower). Each kitchen has an electric range with an oven, as well as a refrigerator, a storage area, a storage closet, and a fireplace.

Accommodations: 3 cabins with half bath (showers in central facility). *Towels and linens:* Not provided. *Cooking and eating utensils:* Not provided. *Stove and refrigerator:* Provided. *Pets:* Not permitted. *Open:* April through October. *Mailing address:* PO Box 215, New Lisbon, NJ 08064. *Phone:* (609) 726-1191. *Driving instructions:* Lebanon State Forest is on Route 72, about 29 miles northwest of exit 63 from the Garden State Parkway.

Parvin State Park is in southwestern New Jersey, about 15 miles west of Vineland. Its 1,125 acres are about midway between the Pine Barrens and Delaware Bay, in a relatively flat section of the state, wooded predominantly with pines, oaks, and cedars. The park contains two small lakes; Parvin Lake, the larger of the two, roughly a mile long and a quarter of a mile wide, has a sand beach with a bathhouse. Visitors can rent canoes or rowboats from a concession, and there are launching facilities along its shore for those who bring their own. Although no gasoline motors are permitted on the lake, electric motors are allowed.

The park has 15 miles of hiking trails, a playground, and several picnic areas and supports a wide variety of birdlife, including great blue herons, rufous-sided towhees, sharp-shinned hawks, merlins, and summer tanagers, which are particularly common.

The park has fifteen wood-frame cabins along the northwest shore of Thundergust Lake, the smaller of the park's two lakes. Seven of the cabins have fireplaces, and the other eight have wood stoves. Each cabin has a terrace, as well as a living room whose entire side can be opened while protected by screens, a kitchenette, and a bath with a shower. Each cabin has a maximum capacity of six people.

Accommodations: 15 cabins with private bath. *Towels and linens:* Not provided. *Cooking and eating utensils:* Not provided. *Stove and refrigerator:* Provided. *Pets:* Not permitted. *Open:* April through October. *Mailing address:* RD 1, Box 374, Elmer, NJ 08318. *Phone:* (609) 692-7039. *Driving instructions:* Parvin State Park is on Route 540, about 6 miles west of Vineland.

Stokes State Forest is in northern New Jersey, just east of the Delaware Water Gap National Recreation Area. The 15,319-acre forest is bordered on the north by High Point State Park and on the west by the 2,234-acre Flatbrook-Roy Wildlife Management Area. The forest is heavily wooded with oaks, maples, hickories, birches, hemlocks, and cedars and has abundant stands of rhododendrons and mountain laurels. Situated along the Kittatinny Ridge, which extends far into Pennsylvania and into New York where it becomes the Shawangunk Mountains, the forest has several streams and lakes, including Tillman Brook, a stream noted for its mature hemlocks and rhododendrons.

Numerous trails run through the forest—including a 9-mile segment of the Appalachian Trail—providing frequent scenic panoramas, such as one at Sunrise Mountain where there's a stone rain shelter and views in all directions. Stony Lake has a sand beach with a bathhouse, and fishing for largemouth and smallmouth bass, trout, and perch is popular in that lake as well as in Lake Ocquittunk and several of the forest's streams.

The forest has twelve cabins available, ten of which accommodate a maximum of six each and are in a wooded area beside Lake Ocquittunk. Each of these cabins has a fireplace, a kitchen with cold running water, a refrigerator, a stove, and an attached pit toilet with an outside entrance.

A group cabin can accommodate twelve and is located three-quarters of a mile from the lake. The cabin has two stories: The main floor has a living room with a fireplace, a bunk room, a kitchen, and a screened porch; the second floor has two bunk rooms. Bathroom facilities consist of an outside pit toilet.

Another group cabin, located off Flatbrook Road about half a mile from the lake, accommodates up to eight in bunk beds. It has a fireplace, a refrigerator, a stove, cold running water, and an outside pit toilet. There are no shower facilities in the forest.

Accommodations: 10 cabins and 2 group cabins, all with outside pit toilets. *Towels and linens:* Not provided. *Cooking and eating utensils:* Not provided. *Stove and refrigerator:* Provided. *Pets:* Not permitted. *Open:* April through mid-December. *Mailing address:* RR 2, Box 260, Branchville, NJ 07826. *Phone:* (201) 948-3820. *Driving instructions:* U.S. 206 runs through Stokes State Forest about 5 miles northwest of Branchville.

In the late nineteenth century, Financier Joseph Wharton acquired large tracts of New Jersey's Pine Barrens, intending eventually to transport the vast amounts of water beneath its soil to Philadelphia. For reasons political and practical, his scheme never worked out, and New Jersey bought his holdings—about 108,000 acres—and created Wharton State Forest about 15 miles northwest of Atlantic City.

Its terrain consists of miles of pine and oak forest, numerous streams, many ponds, and several cedar swamps and cranberry bogs. Numerous roads and hiking trails wind through the pines, which host a varied array of flora and fauna. White-tailed deer, beavers, sharp-shinned hawks, turtles, and frogs are particularly common. There is a sand beach at Atsion Lake, along with picnic tables and a playground. *Visitors' center phone:* (609) 561-3262.

Nine wood cabins, along the shore of Atsion Lake, come in two sizes and can accommodate a maximum of from six to ten persons. The cabins have screened porches and fireplaces, for which park personnel supply a limited amount of wood. Each cabin is equipped with a stove and refrigerator, a kitchen sink, a private bath, and a shower.

Accommodations: 9 cabins with private bath. *Towels and linens:* Not provided. *Cooking and eating utensils:* Not provided. *Stove and refrigerator:* Provided. *Open:* April through October. *Mailing address:* RD 4, Batsto, Hammonton, NJ 08037. *Phone:* (609) 561-0024. *Driving instructions:* The Wharton State Park cabins are on Atsion Lake, off U.S. 206, about 7 miles north of Hammonton.

New Mexico

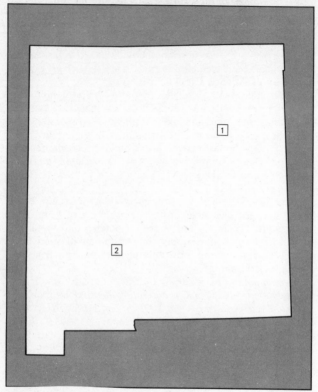

State map and tourist information: Office of Tourism, Bataan Memorial Bldg., Santa Fe, NM 87503; 800-545-2040 (out-of-state) and 505-827-6230 (in-state). **State parks:** *Information:* Div. of State Parks, PO Box 1147, Santa Fe, NM 87504-1147; 505-827-7465. *Entrance fees:* $1 per vehicle (some parks); waived for lodgers. *Reservations:* Contact individual lodgings. Reservations recommended 4 weeks in advance for late May—early September (more for holiday weekends). Deposit required at most lodgings; check or credit card. *Restrictions:* Hunting limited to certain parks only. Dogs must be leashed (not allowed in lodgings). *Facilities:* Swimming and boating, June—September.

Conchas Lake State Park in northeastern New Mexico is roughly 35 miles northwest of Tucumcari. The 742-acre park, at an elevation of about 4,200 feet, is along the shores of Conchas Lake, an impoundment of the Canadian and Conchas rivers. The terrain is mostly grass-covered prairie, lightly wooded with Chinese elms and junipers. Interestingly, although this area touches on the Southwest's piñon-juniper forest, there are no piñons. Mesas and buttes surround the park, as do some of the state's largest ranches, including the historic Bell Ranch, where cattle grazing along the banks of the lake are a common sight.

Boating, fishing, and waterskiing are the most popular activities, and concessionaires run marinas with slips, launching facilities, and boat rentals. At certain points along the lake, boaters can see ancient petroglyphs carved into rocks, believed to be the work of Comanche and Apache. Fishing here is good, and anglers go after walleyes, catfishes, bluegills, and largemouth bass. There are no designated swimming areas, but swimming is permitted on an at-your-own-risk basis. *Park mailing address:* PO Box 976, Conchas Dam, 88416. *Park phone:* (505) 868-2270.

Conchas Lodge and Marina

Conchas Lodge and Marina consists of two wings connected by a breezeway, as well as a marina and a grocery store. The lodge's main buildings house twenty-eight guest rooms, most of which overlook the lake, as do a restaurant and lounge. Each guest room has wall-to-wall carpeting, air-conditioning, and a private bath.

Small fishing boats are for rent at the marina, where a store sells fishing supplies and licenses.

Accommodations: 28 rooms with private bath. *Towels and linens:* Provided. *Stove and refrigerator:* Not provided. *Pets:* Discouraged—check in advance. *Open:* All year. *Mailing address:* Conchas Lodge and Marina, Box 1045, Conchas Dam, NM 88416. *Phone:* (505) 868-2988. *Driving instructions:* Conchas Lodge and Marina is off Route 104 about 35 miles northwest of Tucumcari.

Conchas North Dock

Conchas North Dock has ten rustic cabins, five mobile homes, two duplex cabins, a restaurant, a grocery store, and a marina. The cabins have no kitchenettes but come equipped with hot plates and refrigerators. They accommodate as many as eight and share a central toilet-and-shower facility. Each duplex unit—one accommodating four and the other, eight—has a fully equipped kitchenette, a fireplace, and a private bath. Each mobile home has a fully equipped kitchenette and a private bath, and can accommodate up to eight. All accommodations are back about a quarter of a mile from the lake, but the restaurant is at waterside.

Accommodations: 10 cabins with shared bath; 2 duplexes and 5 mobile homes with private bath. *Towels and linens:* Provided. *Cooking and eating utensils:* In duplexes and mobile homes. *Stove and refrigerator:* In duplexes and mobile homes (hot plate and refrigerator in cabins). *Pets:* Not permitted. *Open:* All year. *Mailing address:* Conchas North Dock Corporation, PO Box 1048, Conchas Dam, NM 88416. *Phone:* (505) 868-2251. *Driving instructions:* Conchas North Dock is on Route 104, roughly 40 miles northwest of Tucumcari.

Elephant Butte Lake State Park's 20,512 acres are along the shores of Elephant Butte Reservoir, an impoundment of the Rio Grande River in southwestern New Mexico. The park is about 5 miles east of Truth or Consequences and 30 miles east of Gila National Forest. The reservoir, which changes in size during the year, ranging from 25,000 to 36,000 acres (depending on water level) is 45 miles long and has 250 miles of shoreline, about 100 miles of which are accessible by road. Reddish-brown, Elephant Butte itself rises some 100 feet out of the reservoir. The park's terrain is at an average elevation of about 4,400 feet and consists mostly of desert areas broken up by buttes. Wooded areas are populated primarily by junipers, mesquites, yuccas, and cottonwoods. The land supports a good deal of wildlife, including foxes, mule deer, beavers, skunks, rabbits, and raccoons. Bird life is abundant, with many varieties of waterfowl—snow geese, blue geese, canvasbacks, teals—and several species of raptors, including northern harriers, red-tailed hawks, and golden eagles.

Popular activities include boating, fishing, swimming, and hiking. Several of the park's numerous trails are self-guided. One leads to the Black Bluffs, a series of lava cliffs rising 500 to 600 feet. *Park mailing address:* PO Box 13, Elephant Butte, NM 87935. *Park phone:* (505) 744-5421.

Damsite Recreation Area

A group of stone-and-adobe buildings with stuccoed exteriors, Damsite Recreation Area comprises fifteen cottages, a restaurant, a bar, and a marina with a retail store selling groceries, beer, and liquor, as well as fishing and boating supplies. It also rents out small boats with 9-horsepower motors.

The cottages, on a rise overlooking the lake along a road lined with cottonwoods and elms, vary in size and accommodate from two to four people. Like the restaurant building, they were built of stone in the 1940s. Most have small refrigerators, and seven have kitchenettes.

The restaurant-and-bar building, also overlooking the lake, is a long, low adobe structure with two fireplaces and exposed-beam ceilings. In season, dinner is served on the restaurant's lakeside patio, where dances are held on summer nights.

Accommodations: 15 cottages with private bath. *Towels and*

307

linens: Provided. *Cooking and eating utensils:* Not provided but may be rented. *Stove and refrigerator:* In seven cottages. *Pets:* Not permitted. *Open:* All year except in very cold weather. *Mailing address:* Box 77B, Engle Star Route, Truth or Consequences, NM 87901. *Phone:* (505) 894-2073. *Driving instructions:* Damsite Recreation Area is off Route 52, about 5 miles west of Engle.

Elephant Butte Resort Marina and Dry Dock

Elephant Butte Resort Marina and Dry Dock, a full-service marina, rents out small fishing boats, high-powered waterskiing boats, and houseboats. The three houseboats available are each 38 feet long and can accommodate up to ten people. Each has a barbecue grill, a bathroom with shower, an eight-track cassette deck, a patio table, folding chairs, and a kitchenette with a butane stove and oven, an icebox, and a sink. The houseboats also carry water-safety equipment and are easy to drive; marina staff will teach novices how to handle them by means of a brief shakedown cruise. A retail store at the marina sells groceries, beer and liquor, and fishing and boating supplies.

Accommodations: 3 houseboats with private bath. *Towels and linens:* Not provided. *Cooking and eating utensils:* Provided. *Stove:* Provided. *Refrigerator:* Icebox provided. *Pets:* Not permitted. *Open:* All year. *Mailing address:* PO Box X, Elephant Butte, NM 87935. *Phone:* (505) 744-5486. *Driving instructions:* Elephant Butte Resort Marina and Dry Dock is on Route 52 about 5½ miles north of Truth or Consequences.

Elephant Butte Inn

Half a mile from the park boundary, Elephant Butte Inn consists of forty-eight lodge rooms, a restaurant, a bar, tennis courts, a golf course, a heated pool, and meeting and banquet facilities. About half the guest rooms have lake views; and each has wall-to-wall carpeting, color television, a telephone, and a private bath. A few suites are also available.

Accommodations: 48 rooms with private bath. *Pets:* Not permitted. *Open:* All year. *Mailing address:* Route 52, PO Box E, Elephant Butte, NM 87935. *Phone:* (505) 744-5431. *Driving instructions:* Elephant Butte Inn is on Route 52, about 5½ miles north of Truth or Consequences.

New York

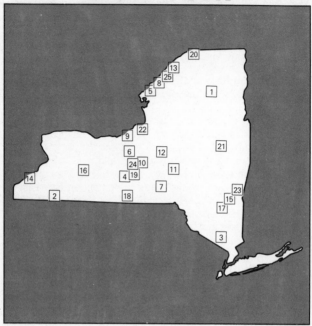

State map and tourist information: State Commerce Dept., Office of Tourism, 1 Commerce Plaza, Albany, NY 12245; 518-474-4116. **State parks:** *Information:* NYS Office of Parks, Recreation, and Historic Preservation, Albany, NY 12238; 518-474-0456. *Entrance fees:* $2.50–$3 per vehicle daily; waived for lodgers. *Reservations: For cabins,* write to the NYS Office of Parks for information and forms. Payment in full required with application. Summer reservations must be postmarked no earlier than January 2nd and no later than January 15th for lottery held on January 20th. Summer reservations postmarked after January 16th and before March 14th are processed by a daily lottery after all other requests from the original lottery have been processed. After March 14th summer reservations are on a first-come, first-served basis. Winter reservations (only three parks open) must be postmarked no earlier than October 1st and no later than October 15th for October 20th lottery. *For lodges,* contact individual parks. Deposit for first night's lodgings generally required. *Facilities:* Swimming & boating, Mem.— Labor Day. Golf & tennis, April—Labor Day. Cross-country skiing & snow-mobiling, November—March. *Restrictions:* Hunting limited to certain parks. Permits for alcohol available from the park manager. Dogs must be leashed and have proof of current innoculation. (Dogs not allowed in certain parks.)

The Adirondack region was once inhabited by the Iroquois Indians, who defended their prime hunting grounds against their rivals, the Canadian Algonquians, whom they referred to as *atirontaks*, an unflattering term meaning "bark eaters." This implied that the Algonquians, who couldn't compete with the Iroquois for the hunting grounds, were forced to eat bark to survive.

Adirondack State Park, in northeastern New York, is the largest designated wilderness in the eastern United States and the largest state park outside of Alaska, the whole park being about the size of Vermont and encompassing some 6 million acres, or about 9,000 square miles. Approximately 2.5 million acres are state owned and another 3.5 million acres are privately owned. The development and use of the land are currently supervised by the Adirondack Park Agency, formed in 1971, although the original protection derives from the New York State constitution of 1885, which mandated that the state-owned park remain "forever wild." A 1972 bond act authorized $1 billion for the acquisition of additional privately owned lands.

One of the most majestic sections of the park is commonly referred to as the "high peak" region, a wilderness area (no motor vehicles, no roads, no airplanes, and very few trails) encompassing the Seward, Santanoni, MacIntyre, and Great mountain ranges, with forty-two peaks higher than 4,000 feet and Mount Marcy, at 5,344 feet, the highest point in New York. Nine peaks have alpine summits above the timberline, with environments similar to northern Canadian tundra. These mountain ranges, having a resistance to erosion, are among the most ancient geologic formations in North America and are estimated to be 1.2 billion years old. They are a part of the Canadian Shield, a geologic structure that continues north into Quebec and Ontario. The mountains are composed chiefly of anorthosite, a rock uncommon everywhere except here and on the highlands of the moon.

The terrain, which varies enormously, includes 1,500 miles of rivers fed by 30,000 miles of brooks and streams and 2,759 lakes and ponds and is home to everything from great blue herons to balsam and spruce forests and alpine flowers. The state maintains hundreds of miles of hiking and snowmobile trails and stocks hundreds of streams. Licensed trappers run lines and go to market with beaver, otter, mink, fisher, eastern coyote, bobcat, and raccoon pelts. The hunting kill includes slightly fewer than 6,000 white-tailed deer and an average of 450 black bears annually.

Ten of the high peaks have marked trails maintained by the Adirondack Mountain Club, along with other local groups and the New York State Department of Environmental Conservation. The most popular canoe trips include the 55-mile section from Old Forge to Tupper Lake via the Raquette River chain; a 15-mile trip on the Oswegatchie River from High Falls to the five-ponds wilderness area; and the Hudson gorge from Newcomb to North River, which has white-water sections. Popular tourist attractions include Ausable Chasm, north of Au Sable Forks; the high-peaks region, which can be seen from Route 73 from Sacandaga Reservoir north to Malone; Lake Placid; Santa's Workshop at Whiteface Mountain; Fort Ticonderoga, beside Lake Champlain; Lake George village; the Adirondack Museum, at Blue Mountain Lake; and the Barton Garnet Mines, at North Creek.

Unfortunately, the most popular hiking trail, which leads up Mount Marcy, has been experiencing erosion, and hiking groups are limited to a maximum of ten. Equally unfortunate is the damage being caused by acid rain: About two hundred lakes above 2,000 feet are unable to support fish.

For trail maps and guidebooks, contact the Adirondack Mountain Club, 172 Ridge Street, Glens Falls, NY 12801 (518) 793-7737; for wildlife and forest information, contact the New York State Department of Enviromental Conservation, Ray Brook, NY 12977 (518) 891-1370; and for general information, contact the Adirondack Park Agency, Box 99, Ray Brook, NY 12977 (518) 891-4050.

Balsam House

On 20 acres that include a private 3½-mile-long lake, Balsam House is a towered, white clapboard structure with dark green trim. It was constructed in 1891, and its interior decor combines Victorian antiques with sleek modern pieces. The living room, where guests congergate, is painted in shades of purple, which are set off by forest green velvet drapes. The lounge, which features a stone fireplace, is painted with an enamel red.

The guest rooms include some antiques, such as oaken

bureaus, and come with chenille spreads and pastel color schemes. All have a private bath. The inn has a French Restaurant presided over by a Swiss chef. Rates include dinner and breakfast.

Accommodations: 20 rooms with private bath. *Pets:* Not permitted. *Open:* All year. *Mailing address:* Friends Lake Road, Chestertown, NY 12817. *Phone:* (518) 494-2828. *Driving instructions:* From Chestertown, take Route 8 west to Friends Lake Road and turn left. Then follow the signs to Balsam House.

The Point

In the northern part of Adirondack Park, about 15 miles east of Lake Placid, The Point is a 1930s Adirondack lodge constructed of peeled pine and cedar logs, one of the grand old private camps. Its several buildings, along the shore of Upper Saranac Lake, served at one time as the private retreat of the Rockefeller family.

The Point's luxurious Long House centers on the Great Hall,

an expansive room with large stone fireplaces at either end, overstuffed furniture, casement windows of leaded glass, trophy heads on the walls, and trophy skins on the hardwood floor. A terrace overlooks the lake, which is usually active with swimmers and boaters, skaters, or cross-country skiers. In the warmer months a barge leaving from The Point offers cocktail cruises.

The eight guest rooms come with stone fireplaces, cathedral ceilings, daily baskets of fruit and wine, and bouquets of fresh flowers. Each has its own special appointments.

The Point operates on the American Plan, with all meals included. Jackets and ties are required at dinner.

Accommodations: 8 rooms with private bath. *Children:* Not permitted. *Pets:* Not permitted. *Open:* May through March. *Mailing address:* Saranac Lake, NY 12983. *Phone:* (518) 891-5674. *Driving instructions:* Ask for precise instructions when making reservations.

314

Big Moose Inn

The rustic 1903 lodge-style Big Moose Inn is a little less than 15 miles north of Enchanted Forest on the shore of Big Moose Lake, one of the Fulton Chain Lakes, in a somewhat more remote area 60 miles north of Utica. Its sixteen rooms, with shared bath, are simple but comfortable. Some of the rooms overlook the lake, which has resident mallards and visiting Canada geese, loons, and brants, among others.

Meals at the inn are from a mainly traditional menu and in summer are often enjoyed on a deck fitted out with umbrellaed tables overlooking the lake.

Accommodations: 16 rooms with shared bath. *Pets:* Not permitted. *Open:* First weekend in May to mid-November and December 26 to end of snow in March. Closed Monday and Tuesday during Spring and Fall. *Mailing address:* Eagle Bay, NY 13331. *Phone:* (315) 357-2042. *Driving instructions:* Big Moose Inn is 5 miles west of Route 28 in Eagle Bay.

Garnet Hill Lodge

This authentic 1930s split-log lodge is in the southeastern portion of the Adirondack park, about 5 miles northeast of Bullhead Mountain and 15 miles west of Brant Lake. Its central room focuses on a garnet-stone fireplace surrounded by benches. Before and after dinner, which is served in this room, guests can play both regular and bumper pool.

Of the twenty-five guest rooms, four have a king-size and a double bed; the rest have a double bed and a set of bunk beds. The rooms usually contain desks and chairs, and most have exposed split-log walls, although some have pine paneling or wallpaper. Twenty rooms have private baths. Built originally to house miners who worked the nearby garnet mines, some rooms are in the original mine owner's house close by.

The lodge sells and rents skis, and offers instruction. Its more than 30 miles of ski trails, which are well-maintained, afford good hiking in the warmer months.

Accommodations: 25 rooms, 20 with private bath. *Pets:* Not permitted. *Open:* All year. *Mailing address:* North River, NY 12856. *Phone:* (518) 251-2821. *Driving instructions:* From the information center at the intersection of Routes 8 and 28, follow Route 28 north to 13th Lake Road, where there's a grocery store, then make a left and proceed for 5 miles to the lodge.

The Hedges on Blue Mountain Lake

Blue Mountain Lake is close to Blue Mountain, which peaks at 3,759 feet. The Hedges consists of two lodges, *circa* 1880 and 1922, and fourteen more modern cottages, on 12 acres of lakefront property. Each room is decorated differently, including some antique furnishings. Facilities include two large lounge-type rooms with fireplaces, a log cabin that's actually a game room, a library, and a dining room containing original oil and watercolor paintings of the Adirondacks. All guest rooms, two of which have fireplaces, are less than 100 feet from the dock.

Two eat-as-much-as-you-like meals are served each day at the Hedges, each accompanied by a salad bar and homemade breads. Although alcohol is permitted in the rooms, guests are asked not to bring any into the dining or lounge areas.

Originally built for a business tycoon, Hiram B. Duryea, a retired general who fought in the Civil War and who built an empire based on corn starch, the property was later acquired by the caretaker for the nearby Vanderbilt summer estate. Today the Hedges is considered by many to be one of the best small family resorts in the country.

Accommodations: 14 rooms and 14 cottages, all with private bath. *Towels and linens:* Provided. *Cooking and eating uten-*

sils: Not provided. *Stove and refrigerator:* Not provided. *Pets:* Permitted. *Open:* Mid-June through Columbus Day. *Mailing address:* Blue Mountain Lake, NY 12812. *Phone:* (518) 352-7325. *Driving instructions:* Take Route 28 or Route 30 to Blue Mountain Lake, which is about 110 miles northwest of Albany.

Hemlock Hall Lodge and Cottages

A rustic mountain lodge with a large porch, Hemlock Hall was built in 1898 along Blue Mountain Lake. The main lodge has eight guest rooms, all but three with private bath. There are also seven two-bedroom cottages, four one-bedroom cottages, and four motel rooms, all with private bath. Self-guiding nature trails are on the grounds, and other activities include canoeing, rowing, and sailing.

Meals are served family style and consist of a single entrée.

Accommodations: 8 lodge rooms, 5 with private bath; 11 cottages and 4 motel rooms, all with private bath. *Towels and linens:* Provided. *Cooking and eating utensils:* Provided. *Stove and refrigerator:* Provided. *Pets:* Not permitted. *Open:* May 15 to October 15. *Mailing address:* PO Box 114, Blue Mountain Lake, NY 12812. *Phone:* (518) 352-7706. *Driving instructions:* The village of Blue Mountain Lake is at the intersection of Routes 28, 28N, and 30. From there, take 28N for ¾ mile, watching for the lodge sign on the left. The lodge is a mile down a private road along the north shore of Blue Mountain Lake.

Adirondak Loj and Cabins

Operated by the Adirondack Mountain Club, Adirondak Loj is a rustic wood-frame lodge along the shores of Heart Lake with three wood-frame cabins. The main lodge has one coed dormitory, central bath and shower facilities, four smaller bunk rooms suitable for small groups or families, and four double rooms. The lodge also has a lounge area with a large stone fireplace, wood-paneled walls, and exposed-beam ceilings. Breakfast is included in the rates, and the dining room also prepares pack lunches and serves dinner. The complex includes a campground, lean-to sites, an information center with a small store that sells sundries and guidebooks, a shower and sanitary facility, and a public room for campers and the "general hiking public." The lodge is the starting point for cross-country skiing and snowshoeing, as well as for the trail up to Mount Marcy, at 5,344 feet the highest point in New York State.

Accommodations: 1 dormitory, 3 cabins, and 8 bunk rooms with shared bath. *Towels and linens:* Provided. *Cooking and eating utensils:* Not provided. *Stove and refrigerator:* Not provided. *Pets:* Check in advance. *Open:* All year. *Mailing address:* c/o Adirondack Mountain Club, Box 867, Lake Placid, NY 12946. *Phone:* (518) 523-3441. *Driving instructions:* Adirondac Loj is off Route 73 about 3 miles south of Lake Placid.

Johns Brook Lodges

Seven miles by trail from Adirondak Loj and at an elevation of 2,315 feet, Johns Brook Lodge is a rustic wood-frame building also operated by the Adirondack Mountain Club. The main lodge has a dormitory for both men and women and two smaller rooms that can accommodate four people each (the dormitories together accommodate 28), a central shower and sanitary facility, a dining room, and a lounge with wood-paneled walls, a stone fireplace, exposed-beam ceilings and a generous supply of reading materials. The dining room serves breakfast (included in the rates), packs lunches, and prepares dinner. The complex also includes two smaller lodges, one of which can accommodate six people and the other eight. These smaller lodges have stone fireplaces and are illuminated by propane lanterns, as is the entire complex.

Situated at scenic Johns Brook, the complex also has lean-tos with fireplaces.

Accommodations: 2 dormitories, 2 private rooms, and 2 small lodges, all with shared bath. *Towels and linens:* Not provided (visitors must bring their own sleeping bags). *Pets:* Not permitted. *Open:* The main lodge is open from late June through early September; the smaller lodges are open all year. *Mailing address:* Johns Brook Lodge, c/o Adirondack Mountain Club, Box 867, Lake Placid, NY 12946. *Phone:* (518) 523-3441. *Driving instructions:* The lodge is accessible by hiking trails, and prospective guests should write or call for specific driving and hiking instructions.

Allegany State Park, 65,000 acres in western New York, about 40 miles southeast of Lake Erie, is bordered on the south by the Allegheny National Forest in Pennsylvania, on the north by the Allegany Indian Reservation, and on the west by the Allegheny Reservoir. Its heavily wooded terrain includes American basswoods, bigtooth aspens, black ashes, pignut hickories, hemlocks, spruces, and pines. Birders spot bald eagles here.

There are miles of hiking trails, a 2-mile-long man-made lake with sandy beaches (no motorboats permitted), guided nature tours, organized games for children, and an amphitheater offering free movies (nature films, Walt Disney features, W. C. Fields movies, and so forth) three nights a week. The park also sponsors hootenannies, puppet shows, and other special events.

Quaker Area

The park has 230 cabins in its Quaker Area, all with a wood stove and an open porch. Five have a fireplace, a stove, and a refrigerator, and a few have four rooms. All cabins but one are without running water and have pit toilets; guests use a central shower facility. Constructed of wood, each contains four single beds with mattresses, tables, benches, and cupboards. Bulk firewood is available in spring and fall, and a small store sells bundles of wood as well as essential groceries and souvenirs.

Accommodations: 230 cabins with privy and shared central bath. *Towels and linens:* Not supplied. *Cooking and eating utensils:* Not provided. *Stove and refrigerator:* In some cabins. *Pets:* Permitted if in cages or on short leashes. *Open:* April to mid-December. *Mailing address:* Quaker Area, Salamanca, NY 14779. *Phone:* (716) 354-2182. *Driving instructions:* From Salamanca take Route 17 east to exit 18, then proceed for 5 miles to the park entrance.

Redhouse Area

The Redhouse Area of Allegany State Park has 140 wood-frame cabins varying in size and accommodating from four to six persons. One hundred of the cabins have kitchenettes with stoves and refrigerators, and the remaining forty have stoves only. None of the cabins has running water or bath and sanitary facilities, which are available in a central location. All the cabins have open porches, nine have fireplaces, and about a hundred have wood stoves for heat. Ninety-one are winterized and available all year.

Accommodations: 140 cabins with shared privy and bath. *Towels and linens:* Not provided. *Cooking and eating utensils:* Not provided. *Stove and refrigerator:* In most units. *Pets:* Not permitted. *Open:* All year. *Mailing address:* Allegany State Park, Redhouse Area, Salamanca, NY 14779. *Phone:* (716) 354-2545. *Driving instructions:* The Redhouse Area is off Route 17 (exit 19), about 7 miles southwest of Salamanca.

In the Hudson Highlands about 45 miles north of New York City, Bear Mountain and Harriman State Parks are jointly operated by the state and comprise some 55,000 acres. Their terrain varies from a brackish marsh on a 118-acre island in the Hudson to a chain of small mountains rising as high as 1,500 feet. The flora is varied: Hemlock forests merge with extensive hardwood stands; patches of rhododendron, laurel, and sumac are everywhere; and the swamps are thick with ferns and wildflowers. Hemlocks, cedars, oaks, tulip trees, beeches, maples, and tamaracks are especially common.

The park encompasses more than twenty-five lakes, most of them man-made. More than ninety species of birds nest here, and the woods are filled with white-tailed deer and raccoons, and wildcats are occasionally spotted. Numerous well-marked trails include a 17-mile stretch of the Appalachian Trail, which passes over nine summits on its way through the park. Activities include swimming at several beaches and a large pool, boating (with rentals) bicycling, and fishing, along with ice skating, cross-country skiing, snowmobiling, and sledding in winter.

Sebago Cabin Area

Next to Sebago Lake are forty-two rustic wood-frame cabins built in the 1930s by the Civilian Conservation Corps. They vary in size, with two, three, or four bedrooms. Each cabin is simply furnished with a table and four chairs, as well as four army-type steel-frame beds. Cabins come with a refrigerator, a propane stove, a picnic table, a fire pit, and a charcoal grill outside. Some cabins have a porch, and many have a view of the lake. Running water and sanitary and bath facilities are in a central location.

Accommodations: 42 cabins with central shared bath. *Towels and linens:* Not provided. *Cooking and eating utensils:* Not provided. *Stove and refrigerator:* Provided. *Pets:* Permitted if on short leash. *Open:* Late April through mid-October. *Mailing address:* Bear Mountain, NY 10911. *Phone:* (914) 351-2360. *Driving instructions:* The Harriman-Sebago Cabin Area is on Seven Lakes Drive, off Route 17, about 7 miles north of Sloatsburg.

Bear Mountain Inn and Cabins

Bear Mountain Inn comprises six buildings at various points

on the shore of Hessian Lake. The main building is a 75-year-old stone-and-wood lodge with thirteen guest rooms, a dining room seating five hundred, and a smaller Cub room. The guest rooms, all but one overlooking the lake, are furnished with contemporary pieces, and each has color television, a telephone, and a private bath.

The Overlook Lodge building has twenty-four guest rooms as well as conference facilities. Each guest room is spacious and has modern furnishings and color television. Twelve overlook the lake.

On the opposite side of Hessian Lake are four stone lodges, each with six guest rooms that are rented individually and share a central lobby with a fireplace. Each guest room has modern furnishings, color television, a telephone, and a private bath.

Accommodations: 61 lodge rooms and 4 small lodges with private bath. *Pets:* Not permitted. *Open:* All year. *Mailing address:* Bear Mountain State Park, Bear Mountain, NY 10911. *Phone:* (914) 786-2731. *Driving instructions:* Take the Palisades Interstate Parkway north past exit 15 and proceed to the traffic circle, which is the end of the parkway; take the traffic circle to the right onto Route 9W South—Bear Mountain Inn is a quarter of a mile south of the traffic circle, forty-five minutes from New York City.

Buttermilk Falls State Park is in central New York about 2 miles south of Ithaca and the southern end of Cayuga Lake. The park's 751 acres are in the scenic Finger Lakes region, and its centerpiece is Buttermilk Falls, a series of cascades and rapids. In all there are some ten waterfalls that drop within two heavily wooded glens. The area is thickly wooded, primarily with oaks, maples, poplars, birches, beeches, sassafras, hickories, and red and white pines. In addition to the park's many gorges and waterfalls there is the nearby Enfield Gorge (in Robert H. Treman State Park) and Taughannock Falls, which drops 215 feet straight down—both a short drive away.

Activities include swimming at a beach with a bathhouse, picnicking, and hiking. Various trails lead to particularly scenic points, as well as a Gorge Trail, which runs for about 5 miles. Snowmobiling and cross-country skiing are popular winter activities.

The park has seven cabins, each accommodating a maximum of four people. Each has a porch and a refrigerator but no stove. Running water is available outside the cabins, and each has an outside fireplace. Guests share a central shower and toilet facility.

Accommodations: 7 cabins with shared bath. *Towels and linens:* Not provided. *Cooking and eating utensils:* Not provided. *Stove:* Not provided. *Refrigerator:* Provided. *Pets:* Not permitted. *Open:* Mid-May to mid-October. *Mailing address:* RD 5, Ithaca, NY 14850. *Phone:* (607) 273-5761. *Driving instructions:* Buttermilk Falls State Park is off Route 13, about 2 miles from downtown Ithaca.

Canoe-Picnic Point State Park is in northern New York, about 25 miles west of Watertown on Grindstone Island in the St. Lawrence River, accessible only by boat. With elevations above the river reaching perhaps 50 feet, the 70-acre park is moderately wooded with oaks, walnuts, black locusts, birches, and a few maples. Characteristic wildlife includes occasional deer, foxes, raccoons, and black squirrels; and the park's position in the St. Lawrence attracts a large number of waterfowl, especially during migrations, when ducks, geese, eagles, and ospreys are seen either swimming offshore or soaring overhead.

The park has a playground and camping and picnicing areas. Boating and fishing are far and away the most popular activities, and the park has docking facilities. Anglers here go after pike, bass, perch, and bullheads. Many visitors boat over to Wellesley Island State Park or Grass Point, where there are recreational facilities and a marina available for use by guests of both parks.

The park has five wood-frame cabins on a wooded hillside. In the northeast section of the park, the cabins each accommodate four people and have no electricity except for the power supplied to the refrigerator. Showers are shared and are in a central location, and each cabin has a toilet and lavatory.

Accommodations: 5 cabins with shared bath. *Towels and linens:* Not provided. *Cooking and eating utensils:* Not provided. *Stove:* Not provided. *Refrigerator:* Provided. *Pets:* Not permitted. *Open:* Mid-May through mid-September. *Mailing address:* Canoe-Picnic Point State Park, c/o Cedar Point State Park, RD 2, Box 166, Clayton, NY 13624. *Phone:* (315) 654-2522. *Driving instructions:* The park is accessible only by boat, and prospective visitors should call in advance for specific instructions.

Cayuga Lake State Park comprises 197 acres in central New York, about 3 miles southeast of Seneca Falls and 40 miles southwest of Syracuse, at the northern end of Cayuga Lake. The largest of the Finger Lakes, Cayuga Lake is about 40 miles long and approximately 450 feet deep. It was formed, like the rest of the Finger Lakes, by glaciers, which over a period of a million years advanced and then retreated, in the process gouging the area's unique series of parallel lake valleys.

The park has a sandy beach with a bathhouse, a recreation and performing arts program, a playground, picnic areas, boat-launching facilities, and a marina. Activities include fishing and, in winter, cross-country skiing, sledding, and snowmobiling.

The park has fourteen cabins, thirteen of them accommodating four people and one accommodating six. Each smaller cabin has a kitchenette and a porch, while six cabins have inside toilets. The larger cabin has a stove and refrigerator, a fireplace, a porch, and a sink with running water. The cabins share a sanitary and shower facility in a central location.

Accommodations: 14 cabins, 6 with private toilet and all with shared central showers. *Towels and linens:* Not provided. *Cooking and eating utensils:* Not provided. *Stove and refrigerator:* Provided. *Pets:* Permitted if on short leash. *Open:* Mid-May through mid-October. *Mailing address:* 2664 Lower Lake Road, Seneca Falls, NY 13148. *Phone:* (315) 568-5163. *Driving instructions:* Cayuga Lake State Park is off Route 89, about 3 miles southeast of Seneca Falls.

Chenango Valley State Park, 10 miles northeast of Binghamton and about 65 miles south of Utica, encompasses both hilly and swampy areas in its 1,071-acre terrain. Softwoods predominate, with spruce and pine accounting for perhaps 75 percent of the forest, although oaks, birches, and maples produce their reds, yellows, and oranges during fall foliage. The park highlight is Chenango Lake, which is stocked with trout, bass, and pike and has a beach with a bathhouse and boat rentals. There are numerous biking, hiking, and nature trails, an eighteen-hole golf course, a playground, and a recreation and performing-arts program that offers frequent Dixieland and classical concerts in summer.

The park's twenty-four wood cabins are in two different areas—near the picnic area and near the golf course. Some have a porch (either screened or unscreened), some have a fireplace, and some have a wood stove. Each has a refrigerator, a stove, and a sink. All share a central sanitary and shower facility.

Accommodations: 24 cabins with central shared bath. *Towels and linens:* Not provided. *Cooking and eating utensils:* Not provided. *Stove and refrigerator:* Provided. *Pets:* Permitted if on short leash and upon presentation of a valid rabies vaccination certificate. *Open:* May to mid-October. *Mailing address:* RD 2, Box 593, Chenango Forks, NY 13746. *Phone:* (607) 648-5251. *Driving instructions:* From Binghamton take Route 7 north to I-88; get off onto Route 369 and the park.

De Wolf Point State Park comprises 13 acres on Wellesley Island in the St. Lawrence River about 30 miles north of Watertown. The island, 7 miles long and 5 miles wide, is one of the Thousand Islands that dot the St. Lawrence. The hilly and rocky terrain is wooded primarily with oaks and maples, and there are a few beeches and pines. Essentially small, quiet, and secluded, the park overlooks "Lake of the Isles." It has no beach, no hiking trails, and very few recreational facilities, although nearby Wellesley Island State Park has a beach, trails, and a nine-hole golf course, and the island itself offers many attractions and has several restaurants. The park does have docks, but visitors must have their own boats.

The area is at its most scenic during the fall foliage season, when the maple leaves turn orange and contrast with the dark blue of the St. Lawrence. Spring and fall migrations bring all sorts of waterfowl, as well as eagles and ospreys.

The park has fourteen rustic wood-frame cabins in a wooded area overlooking the St. Lawrence. Each can accommodate four people and has hardwood floors and a refrigerator but no running water. Shower and sanitary facilities are in a central location.

Accommodations: 14 cabins with central shared bath. *Towels and linens:* Not provided. *Cooking and eating utensils:* Not provided. *Stove and refrigerator:* Provided. *Pets:* Permitted if leashed. *Open:* Mid-May through mid-September. *Mailing address:* RD 1, Box W437, Alexandria Bay, NY 13607. *Phone:* (315) 482-2722. *Driving instructions:* De Wolf Point State Park is on Wellesley Island, off I-81 (3 miles after exit 51).

Fair Haven Beach State Park is in western New York, along the shores of Lake Ontario about 15 miles southwest of Oswego. At an average elevation of about 350 feet, the 865-acre park is thinly wooded with oaks, maples, ashes, beeches, and scattered stands of pines. The terrain varies from beaches on Lake Ontario and Fair Haven Bay to marshlands and rolling hills. The beach areas are noted for clay bluffs and chimneys that were formed by the erosion of glacial deposits and look like pinnacles, spires, or chimney-like peaks. Characteristic wildlife includes deer, raccoons, foxes, and squirrels. The lake and bay attract all types of waterfowl, especially during the migration seasons, and birders often sight bald eagles, ospreys, and red-tailed and other hawks. The marshlands also attract migratory birds such as herons, egrets, ducks, geese, and kingfishers.

Three miles of easy trails wind through the park's wooded areas. There is a beach with a bathhouse, boat rentals, launching facilities, a playground, and picnic sites with tables and shelters. Other activities include cross-country skiing (rentals available), snowmobiling, sledding, and recreation and performing-arts programs.

The park has thirty-one rustic wood-frame cabins in a wooded area. Some are along the shore of Sterling Pond; seven have a kitchenette; six have a fireplace; and each has an open porch. The cabins vary in size, accommodating from four to six persons. All are without plumbing, and guests obtain water from a central location. There are also central shower and sanitary facilities.

Accommodations: 30 cabins with shared bath. *Towels and linens:* Not provided. *Cooking and eating utensils:* Not provided. *Stove and refrigerator:* Provided. *Pets:* Permitted. *Open:* Mid-April through first weekend in November. *Mailing address:* Fair Haven, NY 13064. *Phone:* (315) 947-5205. *Driving instructions:* Fair Haven Beach State Park is off Route 104A, 1 ½ miles north of Fair Haven.

Fillmore Glen State Park is a 939-acre reserve in central New York, about 20 miles north of Ithaca in the scenic Finger Lakes. Heavily influenced by glacial activity, Fillmore Glen State Park has a beautiful limestone gorge with three waterfalls. Several bridges cross the creek in the upper falls area, and at one point a stone-arch bridge crosses the creek at the end of the gorge. The terrain is a mixture of level and slightly hilly, the predominant trees being oaks, maples, locusts, cottonwoods, and red and white pines. The stream running through the gorge forms a natural pool that has a small beach and bathhouse, and there are 6 miles of hiking trails. Characteristic wildlife includes deer and beavers, and now and then a wild turkey is sighted. The park supports a wide variety of passerine birds and has a small but occasionally visible population of pileated woodpeckers, which are large red-crested birds.

Activities include camping, picnicking, hiking, swimming, cross-country skiing, snowmobiling, and sledding; in season the naturalist service offers Saturday-night films on wildlife and other nature subjects.

The park has three rustic one-room wood-frame cabins in a thinly wooded area near a stream. Each accommodates four people, or six with extra cots, has a refrigerator and an open porch. Shower and sanitary facilities are in a central location.

Accommodations: 3 cabins with central shared bath. *Towels and linens:* Not provided. *Cooking and eating utensils:* Not provided. *Stove:* Not provided. *Refrigerator:* Provided. *Pets:* Permitted if properly vaccinated. *Open:* Mid-May to mid-October. *Mailing address:* RD 3, Moravia, NY 13118. *Phone:* (315) 497-0130. *Driving instructions:* Fillmore Glen State Park is on Route 38, about a mile south of Moravia.

Gilbert Lake State Park, 12 miles northwest of Oneonta, is at an elevation of 1,800 feet at its highest point, where there was once a fire tower, comprises 1,569 acres. Its terrain is one of rolling hills wooded mainly with maples, hemlocks, beeches, cedars, and ashes. Deer, beavers, rabbits, and woodchucks are commonplace here, as are wild turkeys and partridges. Those who are keen of eye can occasionally spot snowy owls, (pure white but for a few black markings) in the hemlocks.

Stocked with trout, bass, and bullheads, Gilbert Lake has a dam at one end and is used mainly for recreation. The park includes three small ponds, a beach with a bathhouse, a playground, a concession selling staples, hiking and biking trails, boat rentals, and a recreation and performing arts program.

The park has thirty-three rough-sided wood cabins, each with a fireplace, a screened porch, a stove and refrigerator, a toilet, and running water. Guests use a central shower facility.

Accommodations: 33 cabins with private bath and shared central showers. *Towels and linens:* Not provided. *Cooking and eating utensils:* Not provided. *Stove and refrigerator:* Provided. *Pets:* Permitted in cages or on short leash. *Open:* Mid-May to mid-October. *Mailing address:* Box 145, RD 1 Laurens, NY 13796. *Phone:* (607) 432-2114. *Driving instructions:* From Oneonta take Route 205 to Laurens, then take Route 12 north 4 miles to Gilbert Lake State Park.

Green Lakes State Park comprises 1,100 acres about 10 miles east of Syracuse in central New York. When the 3,000-foot-thick glacier that covered much of this area receded, torrential currents from its melting water carved out the basins of Round Lake (a national monument) and Green Lake. Both are deep (180 to 195 feet) and owe their uncanny greenness to their depth and clearness. The virtual absence of plant life and suspended materials in these lakes allows the shorter wavelengths (green and blue) of light to be reflected back to the surface. In addition, scientists have discovered a 3-foot layer of rosy pink water about 75 feet below the surface of both lakes, for which they have no explanation.

Round Lake is undeveloped and has been left wild, although an interpretative trail encircles it; and Green Lake, 2 miles in diameter, has a natural sand beach with a bathhouse along with swimming, fishing, and boating facilities. The terrain is a fine example of upland forest: Its habitats include swamps as well as extensive areas of forest wooded mainly with beeches, maples, oaks, spruces, pines, and tulip trees.

The park has seven cabins built of cedar in 1934 by the Civilian Conservation Corps on a hill overlooking Round Lake. Each has a kitchenette with a gas stove, a stone fireplace, a screened porch, and a toilet and running water. Guests use a central shower facility.

Accommodations: 7 cabins with shared shower. *Towels and linens:* Not provided. *Cooking and eating utensils:* Not provided. *Stove and refrigerator:* Provided. *Pets:* Permitted if on short leash. *Open:* End of May to mid-October. *Mailing address:* Fayetteville, NY 13066. *Phone:* (315) 637-6111. *Driving instructions:* From Syracuse, take Route 5 east about 10 miles to the park.

Kring Point State Park is in northern New York, along the shore of the St. Lawrence River about six miles northeast of Alexandria Bay. Wooded primarily with maples, oaks, beeches, willows, aspens, pines, and a few elms, the park is on a rock outcropping that juts into Goose Bay, a haven for waterfowl, especially during migrations, when thousands of ducks and geese congregate. Mallards, canvasbacks, black ducks, mergansers, grebes, coots, and teals are common, as are Canada geese and whistling swans. Eagles and ospreys also pass through. Whether it's migration season or not, gulls are everywhere you look—ring-bill and herring gulls are the most common, and greater black-backed, laughing, and Bonaparte's gulls are seen frequently.

The park is noted for its excellent fishing and has been the site several times of the Bass Anglers' Sportsmens Society Invitational Tournament, which carries a first prize of $50,000. The top bass fishermen in the country are invited to this event, and each is supplied with an identical boat and accompanied by a journalist to verify catches. Fishermen who aren't invited to this invitational tournament also come here, and in addition to bass they go after northern pike, perch, rock bass, muskies and sunfishes. Although the park itself has no boats for rent, it does have docking and launching facilities, and a concessionaire 500 yards away has fishing boats both with or without motors.

Other activities include swimming at the park's beach, which has a bathhouse, as well as camping, picnicking, and hiking. The park also has recreation and performing-arts programs.

Kring Point has eight wood-frame cabins in a thinly wooded area along the shore of Goose Bay. These two-room units can accommodate four persons. Half have refrigerators only, and the other half have stoves as well as refrigerators. Two have bathrooms with showers, and the others use a central bathhouse facility. Two cabins have wood stoves.

Accommodations: 8 cabins, 2 with private bath and 6 with shared bath. *Towels and linens:* Not provided. *Cooking and eating utensils:* Not provided. *Stove:* In 4 cabins. *Refrigerator:* Provided. *Pets:* Not permitted. *Open:* Mid-May through mid-October. *Mailing address:* RD 1, Redwood, NY 13679. *Phone:* (315) 482-2444. *Driving instructions:* Kring Point State Park is off Route 12, about 6 miles northeast of Alexandria Bay.

Lake Erie State Park is a 315-acre reserve on the shore of Lake Erie, in western New York. The shoreline here is bordered by medium to thick woods, with black locust the predominant tree. A variety of fish, including bass, catfishes, and salmon, inhabit the lake, and boat rentals are available nearby. The park has a beach with a bathhouse, limited performing-arts offerings, four playgrounds for all age groups, and cross-country skiing in winter.

Along 2 ½ miles of hiking and nature trails, colorful eastern bluebirds, indigo buntings, orioles, goldfinches, cedar waxwings, and cardinals stand out against a backdrop of black locust leaves.

The park has ten wooden cabins, each with wood floors and containing four bunks, a refrigerator, an electric stove, a sink, and an open porch. All cabins have outdoor grills. Sanitary and hot shower facilities are in a central location.

Accommodations: 10 cabins with central shared bath. *Towels and linens:* Not provided. *Cooking and eating utensils:* Not provided. *Stove and refrigerator:* Provided. *Pets:* Permitted if caged or on a short leash. *Open:* May 1 to mid-October. *Mailing address:* RD 1, Brocton, NY 14716. *Phone:* (716) 792-9214. *Driving instructions:* From I-90 take Route 60 North to Route 5, follow it west for 8 miles to Lake Erie State Park.

In southeastern New York, 30 miles north of Poughkeepsie and about 10 miles due west of the Massachusetts–Connecticut border, Lake Taghkanic State Park's 1,700 rocky acres are wooded with a mixture of hardwoods and softwoods, mainly ashes, oaks, birches, maples, spruces, and eastern white pines. The park, in an area generally referred to as the Taghkanic Hills, is frequented by campers, hikers, anglers, and birders.

Taghkanic Lake, which is filled with small- and largemouth bass, pickerel, and pike, has two beaches, as well as two bathhouses, rowboats for rent, and a boat-launching site (hand launch only), a playground, and nature and hiking trails.

There are cabins and cottages in two parts of the park. Two-, three-, and four-bedroom units, they all have kitchen facilities. The eighteen cottages on the lakeshore have a private bath with shower. Fifteen knotty-pine cabins, in the woods roughly a quarter of a mile from the lake, each have a stone fireplace and lavatory facilities but share a central shower house.

Accommodations: 33 cabins, 18 with private bath. *Towels and linens:* Not provided. *Cooking and eating utensils:* Not provided. *Stove and refrigerator:* Provided. *Pets:* Not permitted. *Open:* Mid-May through October. *Mailing address:* RD, Ancram, NY 12502. *Phone:* (518) 851-3631. *Driving instructions:* Taghkanic State Park has its own exit off the Taconic Parkway, 11 miles south of Hudson and 30 miles north of Poughkeepsie.

A 14,350-acre reserve, Letchworth State Park, about 40 miles south of Rochester and flanking the western edge of the Finger Lakes region, is often called the "Grand Canyon of the East." The Genessee River winds through here, at times between gorges of gray shale and sandstone 500 feet above water level. At one point in its course the river drops 272 feet in slightly less than 3 miles, cascading over three waterfalls, one of them 107 feet high.

The park was initiated by William Pryor Letchworth, a Quaker industrialist who donated more than 1,000 acres of land—and 17 miles of the Genessee River—to the state, which has since enlarged the acreage fourteenfold. There are miles of hiking, biking, and nature trails, two pools (one Olympic size), and a recreation and performing arts program.

The main park road passes along the western rims of all three waterfall gorges. The second of the three waterfalls, Middle Falls, is the highlight of the park and a spot that is among the most beautiful sights in the Northeast as rising mists form rainbows. Letchworth named this spot Glen Iris. ("Glen," is from the Welsh "glyn," meaning a small, narrow, and secluded valley; "iris," the daughter of Electra and Thaumas, was the Greek goddess of rainbows.) *Park phone:* (716) 493-2611.

The park has eighty-two cabins, fifteen of them winterized. The cabins vary in design and can accommodate from four to six people. The rustic winter cabins have a wood stove or a fireplace. All cabins have a stove for cooking and a refrigerator; forty-four of the summer cabins have interior flush toilets; and some have either a screened or an unscreened porch. A central sanitary and shower facility is in each of the areas where cabins are located.

Accommodations: 82 cabins with shared bath. *Towels and linens:* Not provided. *Cooking and eating utensils:* Not provided. *Stove and refrigerator:* Provided. *Pets:* Not permitted. *Open:* Easter through October. *Mailing address:* 1, Letchworth State Park, Castile, NY 14427. *Phone:* (716) 237-3303. *Driving instructions:* From Rochester take Route 390 to the Mount Morris exit; turn right at the exit and follow the signs to the park, about 2 miles away.

Glen Iris Inn and Lodge

Overlooking Middle Falls, Glen Iris Inn once served as William Pryor Letchworth's country estate. He acquired the building in about 1859, when it was a tavern, and enlarged it considerably, as indeed the owners had enlarged the original tavern built in 1820.

The full-service inn's several public rooms include a third-floor study with a vaulted-beam ceiling and a downstairs restaurant. A portico supported by pillars surrounds a good part of the inn, and a paneled stairway leads to its thirteen guest rooms; all are small but nicely appointed and sunny and have a private bathroom. A separate building, Pinewood Lodge, has seven connected ground-floor units, each with a kitchenette and a private bath.

Accommodations: 20 rooms with private bath. *Pets:* Not permitted. *Open:* Easter through October. *Mailing address:* 7, Letchworth State Park, Castile, NY 14427. *Phone:* (716) 493-2622. *Driving instructions:* Glen Iris Inn is in Letchworth State Park, 14 miles east of Warsaw via Routes 19 and 19A.

Mills-Norrie State Park is in southeastern New York, about 15 miles north of Poughkeepsie on a ridge overlooking the Hudson River and the Catskill Mountains. Its 1,100 acres are in the foothills of the Catskills, which are quite scenic and wooded mainly with red and white oaks, maples, walnuts, elms, butternuts, poplars, copper beeches, and dogwoods. The terrain is one of a river valley gradually giving way to rolling hills. The Hudson at this point has a U-shaped bottom that is below sea level. Though slow and old, it flows with a resigned majesty through a lush and hilly valley that is at its most spectacular in autumn, when the hardwoods turn color on the hills. Golden eagles occasionally appear, as do red-tailed hawks and migratory waterfowl. Deer, raccoons, and foxes are frequently sighted.

There are miles of hiking trails, an eighteen-hole golf course, camping and picnicking facilities, playground areas, a marina (no rentals), and cross-country and snowmobiling areas. Nearby attractions include Mills Mansion, the Vanderbilt and Roosevelt estates, and the historic town of Rhinebeck, which has a flying circus during the summer months.

The park has ten wood-frame cabins with slab siding and hardwood floors in a wooded area overlooking the Hudson River. They are two-bedroom units accommodating four people, each with a small living-dining room with table and chairs, a kitchenette, cold running water, and a screened porch. Shower and sanitary facilities are in a central location.

Accommodations: 10 cabins with central shared bath. *Towels and linens:* Not provided. *Cooking and eating utensils:* Not provided. *Stove and refrigerator:* Provided. *Pets:* Not permitted. *Open:* Mid-April through mid-October. *Mailing address:* Staatsburg, NY 12580. *Phone:* (914) 889-4646. *Driving instructions:* Mills-Norrie State Park is off Route 9, 3 miles north of Hyde Park and 4 miles south of Rhinebeck.

Newtown Battlefield State Park, 300 acres in the southern tier of New York about 5 miles south of Elmira and 5 miles north of the Pennsylvania border, was named for the only significant battlefield of the Sullivan-Clinton campaign to "pacify" northern New York, dominated until 1779 by the Iroquois Indians. New York City at the time was smaller than Philadelphia, and after the Revolutionary War, upper New York State was sparsely inhabited, the only permanent settlements being along the Hudson River. A Revolutionary War hero, General John Sullivan, joined forces with General James Clinton; following the war they swept through northern New York and succeeded in breaking the power of the Iroquois, burning Indian settlements, cornfields, and orchards in the process. The park was the site of a battle in which twelve Iroquois and three of Sullivan's men were killed.

The terrain, hilly and in places rugged, is at an average elevation of 1,500 feet and is heavily wooded, mainly with oaks, maples, and pines broken up with scattered stands of walnuts and spruces. Characteristic wildlife includes deer, foxes, raccoons, opossums, and squirrels. The park also supports a wide variety of woodland birds—cardinals, bluejays, grackles, woodpeckers, summer tanagers, bluebirds, wild turkeys, and red-tailed hawks. Facilities include 6 miles of hiking trails that range from easy to difficult; a playground area with a baseball field; and camping and picnicking areas. Winter activities include cross-country skiing, snowmobiling, and sledding.

Newtown Battlefield has five wood-frame cabins by a road and facing a wooded area. They are one-room units with concrete floors and can accommodate four people. Each has a kitchenette and a porch. Shower and toilet facilities are in a central location.

Accommodations: 5 cabins with shared bath. *Towels and linens:* Not provided. *Cooking and eating utensils:* Not provided. *Stove and refrigerator:* Provided. *Pets:* Dogs permitted. *Open:* Mid-April through mid-October. *Mailing address:* RD 2, Elmira, NY 14901. *Phone:* (607) 732-1096. *Driving instructions:* Newtown Battlefield State Park is off Route 17, about 4 miles southeast of Elmira.

Robert H. Treman State Park is in central New York, about 5 miles southwest of Ithaca and the southern tip of Cayuga Lake, the largest of the Finger Lakes. The 1,022-acre park is named after an Ithaca banker who acquired land around particularly scenic Finger Lakes areas, developed it, then donated it to the state. The first chairman of the Finger Lakes State Park Commission, Treman donated both this and Buttermilk Falls State Park. A heavily wooded terrain includes oaks, beeches, birches, hemlocks, and several species of pine. Enfield Gorge, a deep, 3-mile-long glacial gash, has twelve waterfalls. The uppermost of the gorge's three tiers is the most scenic and includes Lucifer Falls, which drops 115 feet over numerous precipices. A swimming hole formed by a dam at the end of the last gorge is surrounded by high bluffs and fed by the Lower Falls.

The park offers recreation programs, and its facilities include 8 miles of trails and numerous scenic overlooks, as well as picnicking areas, a bathhouse near the swimming area, and a playground. Among activities are fishing and, in winter, sledding and cross-country skiing.

The park has fourteen cabins; thirteen of them accommodate a maximum of four and have a refrigerator and a porch. The other cabin has a stove, a refrigerator, and a porch, and can accommodate six. There are no toilets or running water in the cabins, and guests use a central sanitary and shower facility.

Accommodations: 14 cabins with central shared bath. *Towels and linens:* Not provided. *Cooking and eating utensils:* Not provided. *Stove:* In 1 cabin. *Refrigerator:* Provided. *Pets:* Not permitted. *Open:* Mid-May through mid-October. *Mailing address:* RD 10, Ithaca, NY 14850. *Phone:* (607) 273-3440. *Driving instructions:* Robert H. Treman State Park is off Route 13, about 5 miles southwest of Ithaca.

Robert Moses State Park is in northern New York, on Barnhart Island in the St. Lawrence River, which forms the border between the United States and Canada. At one time a private estate, the 4,500-acre park occupies the better part of the island, relatively flat land with a few slightly hilly areas, patches of open meadows, and extensive stands of hardwoods including oaks, maples, beeches, elms, and hickories. Scattered stands of eastern white pines punctuate the hardwoods, and the understory is rife with wildflowers, including wild roses. There are lovely views of the river from numerous points in the park, which is at its most scenic during fall foliage when the reds and yellows of the maples stand out against the dark blue St. Lawrence. Characteristic wildlife includes deer, woodchucks, raccoons, and eastern coyotes, and the bird life is most abundant during the fall and spring migrations, when a wide variety of waterfowl stop by on their way north or south. Many species of ducks and geese pass through, while eagles and ospreys soar overhead.

Activities include hiking on 5 miles of trails, swimming at the large sand beach, which has a bathhouse, camping, picnicking, boating—there is a marina but no rentals—and fishing for bass, northern pike, and muskellunge. In winter the park draws cross-country skiers and snowmobilers. Nearby attractions include the Eisenhower Locks and the St. Lawrence Project visitors' center.

The park has fifteen wood-frame cabins in a thinly wooded area along the St. Lawrence River. Each has a kitchenette, wood-paneling, and a private bath with shower and hot and cold running water.

Accommodations: 15 cabins with private bath. *Towels and linens:* Not provided. *Cooking and eating utensils:* Not provided. *Stove and refrigerator:* Provided. *Pets:* Not permitted. *Open:* Mid-June through mid-October. *Mailing address:* Box 548, Massena, NY 13662. *Phone:* (315) 769-8663. *Driving instructions:* Robert Moses State Park is off Route 37, about 5 miles north of Massena.

Saratoga Spa State Park's 2,000 acres are in Saratoga Springs in eastern New York about 30 miles north of Albany. Except for the Vale of Springs, a small valley surrounding the mineral springs for which the area is famous, the terrain is relatively level and wooded primarily with eastern white pines, Norway and blue spruces, cedars, oaks, and mountain ashes. The Vale of Springs has numerous cold mineral springs as well as a spouting geyser, which is just about always active, spurting cold mineral water 10 feet into the air, in pulses. Characteristic wildlife includes deer, raccoons, an occasional black bear, and a plethora of chipmunks and squirrels. The pines are full of woodland songbirds, and hawks are frequently sighted, especially red-tails.

Perhaps the main attractions are the two mineral-spring bathhouses, one of which is open all year. One of the park's two golf courses is an eighteen-hole championship course with complete clubhouse facilities; and the other is a par-29 nine-hole course. Other facilities include three swimming pools accommodating five thousand bathers daily; 8 miles of bicycling and hiking trails; 28 miles of cross-country ski trails, with rentals; snowmobile trails; ice-skating rinks, among them a 400-meter outdoor rink used for championship meets; and two theaters. A performing-arts center has an indoor seating capacity of five thousand and lawn seating for another eight thousand; it is the site of some forty concerts each summer. The performing-arts programs include ballet and classical and rock music. The Philadelphia Orchestra, for example, performs each summer. The major attraction nearby is the Saratoga racetrack. *Park phone:* (518) 584-2000.

The Gideon Putnam Hotel and Convention Center

On the aptly named Avenue of Pines, Gideon Putnam Hotel and Convention Center is a 1934 five-story brick building with an attached convention center. The hotel has a lounge-bar, a restaurant, a gift shop, and 132 guest rooms. The guest rooms are tastefully appointed, with wall-to-wall carpeting, color television, a telephone, and a private bath. There are also executive suites and parlor suites consisting of a bedroom and an adjoining parlor with couches, chairs, and a table. The executive suites

are large rooms functioning as both bedroom and parlor—each has an alcove with a couch, easy chairs, and a table.

Accommodations: 132 rooms with private bath. *Pets:* Not permitted. *Open:* All year. *Mailing address:* PO Box 476, Saratoga Springs, NY 12866. *Phone:* (518) 584-3000. *Driving instructions:* From Albany take Route 9 north for 30 miles, then turn left on Avenue of the Pines—the hotel will be on your left. The park can also be reached via I-87 (Northway), exit 13N.

Selkirk Shores State Park, 1,000 acres in northern New York, on the shores of Lake Ontario about 20 miles northeast of Oswego, is bordered by three bodies of water—Lake Ontario, the Salmon River, and Rhinestone Creek. Its relatively flat terrain is wooded primarily with oaks, maples, beeches, and ashes. At the marshy areas near the river and the creek many migratory waterfowl congregate, especially herons, greater yellowlegs, sandpipers, diving and marsh ducks, and geese. The park itself supports a wide variety of birds and mammals, including deer, raccoons, foxes, grosbeaks, summer tanagers, red-tailed hawks, and occasionally eagles and ospreys.

There is a sandy beach with a bathhouse, camping and picnicking areas, a store selling groceries and sundries, a recreation and performing arts program, 6 miles of hiking trails, a nature trail, and a playground. Winter activities include cross-country skiing and snowmobiling.

Twenty-eight wood-frame cabins are in three different areas of the park; some, in a grove of pines; others, in thinly wooded areas. They vary in size and can accommodate from four to six. Each has a kitchenette, a fireplace, and a bathroom but no shower. The larger cabins have an open porch; the smaller ones have screened porches. Shower facilities for the cabins are in a central location.

Accommodations: 29 cabins with central shared bath. *Towels and linens:* Not provided. *Cooking and eating utensils:* Not provided. *Stove and refrigerator:* Provided. *Pets:* Not permitted. *Open:* Mid-April through mid-October. *Mailing address:* RD 3, Pulaski, NY 13142. *Phone:* (315) 298-5737. *Driving instructions:* Selkirk Shores State Park is off Route 3, about 5 miles south of Pulaski.

Taconic State Park (Copake Area) is in southeastern New York, about 35 miles northeast of Poughkeepsie. Long and narrow, the 5,000-acre reserve runs along New York's border at the point where Massachusetts and Connecticut meet. Mount Frissel, at 2,453 feet the highest point in Connecticut, is perhaps a quarter of a mile east of the park's center. A very hilly terrain ranges in elevation from about 700 feet to about 2,000 feet and is heavily wooded, mainly with oaks, maples, beeches, hemlocks, and eastern white pines.

The park includes one of New York's most scenic waterfalls, Bash Bish Falls, which happens to be in Massachusetts. The situation is rather unusual—Bash Bish Falls is actually within Massachusetts but is most accessible via a 1½-mile gorge trail in Taconic State Park. The falls is formed by Bashbish Brook, which drops 70 feet into a foaming pool surrounded by sheer rock escarpments. Just before the brook turns into a cascade, it is split into two streams by a huge boulder, with the result that there are actually two falls: one that goes "bash" and one that goes "bish."

The park has 35 miles of hiking trails, picnicking facilities, a beach with a bathhouse, interpretative programs, and sledding and snowmobiling areas.

Taconic State Park has seven cottages and five cabins along Bishbash Brook. Each cottage has an open porch, a fireplace, and a private bath with shower. Each cabin has a screened porch and cold water only. Cabins and cottages both have a kitchenette and inside toilets, while the cabins share a central shower facility.

Accommodations: 7 cottages with private bath and 5 cabins with central shared bath. *Towels and linens:* Not provided. *Cooking and eating utensils:* Not provided. *Stove and refrigerator:* Provided. *Pets:* Not permitted. *Open:* Mid-May through October. *Mailing address:* Copake Falls, NY 12517. *Phone:* (518) 329-3993. *Driving instructions:* Taconic State Park (Copake Area) is off Route 22, half a mile north of Copake.

In New York's Finger Lakes region, about 10 miles northwest of Ithaca, Taughannock Falls State Park takes its name from its spectacular 215-foot waterfall, the second highest east of the Rockies (*see* Fall Creek Falls State Park, Tennessee). "Taughannock," an Indian word meaning "great fall in the woods," aptly describes this natural attraction. A road skirting the canyon provides an excellent view of the falls, which can also be approached by a hike up the canyon. The Finger Lakes region is riddled with gorges, but the one here has escarpments as high as 400 feet and resembles—although officially it's not—a canyon.

Besides exploring the falls, activities include swimming at a beach with a bathhouse, boating (there is a launch site and a marina on Cayuga Lake), hiking, fishing, ice-skating, skiing, cross-country skiing, snowmobiling, and sledding.

In the northwestern section of the park are sixteen rustic wood-frame cabins with refrigerators but no stoves. The cabins have running water; sanitary and shower facilities are in a central location.

Accommodations: 16 cabins with central shared bath. *Towels*

and linens: Not provided. *Cooking and eating utensils:* Not provided. *Stove:* Not provided. *Refrigerator:* Provided. *Pets:* Permitted in cages or on a short leash. *Open:* Mid-May to mid-October. *Mailing address:* RD 3, Trumansburg, NY 14886. *Phone:* (607) 387-6739. *Driving instructions:* Taughannock Falls State Park is off Route 89 about 10 miles northwest of Ithaca.

Taughannock Farms Inn

An 1872 Victorian building, Taughannock Farms Inn is at the mouth of the Taughannock Gorge, with a view of Cayuga Lake, several parlors, a cocktail lounge, and four dining rooms. The inn has been a family operation for many years; The current innkeepers are the third generation to run it, and most of the waitresses have been working for the family from fifteen to twenty-five years.

The inn is furnished with many antiques, such as the inlaid, heavily carved and marble-topped tables in the cocktail lounge. There are several upstairs sitting rooms and three dining rooms, one of which overlooks the lake. All five guest rooms are furnished with antiques, and three have a private bath. There is also a large guest house containing two bedrooms, each with private bath.

Accommodations: 5 rooms, 3 with private bath. *Pets:* Not permitted. *Open:* Easter to Christmas. *Mailing address:* Route 89 at Taughannock Falls State Park, Trumansburg, NY 14886. *Phone:* (607) 387-7711. *Driving instructions:* Taughannock Farms Inn is on Route 89 about 8 miles northwest of Ithaca.

Wellesley Island State Park is on Wellesley Island in the St. Lawrence River about 30 miles north of Watertown. Its 2,636 acres are at an average elevation of about 262 feet and are wooded mainly with oaks, maples, beeches, and pines. Most of the terrain is wooded, rolling hills, and various overlooks afford views of the Canadian Channel in the St. Lawrence. Characteristic wildlife includes deer, raccoons, foxes, squirrels, and opossums; during migrations the river attracts a wide variety of waterfowl—ducks and geese pause here in their travels, and eagles and ospreys fish as they pass through. About 9 miles of hiking trails range in strenuousness from easy to moderately difficult, and the undeveloped areas include a 600-acre nature preserve.

The park also has a beach with a bathhouse, a marina with rental and launching facilities, a playground, a recreation and performing arts program, bicycle trails, picnicking and camping areas, and a nine-hole golf course. Its winter activities include cross-country skiing, snowmobiling, and sledding.

The park's ten rustic wood-frame cabins are in a wooded area overlooking the St. Lawrence and can accommodate four people. Each has a refrigerator but no stove except a wood stove for heat. The cabins have no plumbing; shower and sanitary facilities are in a central location.

Accommodations: 10 cabins with central shared bath. *Towels and linens:* Not provided. *Cooking and eating utensils:* Not provided. *Stove:* Not provided. *Refrigerator:* Provided. *Pets:* Permitted if leashed. *Open:* All year. *Mailing address:* RD 1, Box W437, Alexandria Bay, NY 13607. *Phone:* (315) 482-2722. *Driving instructions:* Take I-81 across the Thousand Islands Bridge; take the first right turn (exit 51) and follow the signs.

North Carolina

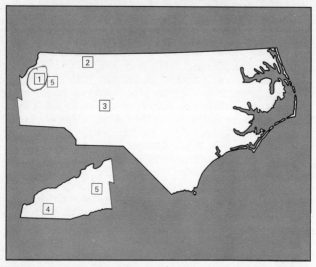

State map and tourist information: Travel & Tourism, 430 N. Salisbury St., Raleigh, NC 27611; 919-733-4171. **State parks:** *Information:* Div. of Parks, PO Box 27687, Raleigh, NC 27611; 919-733-4181. *Entrance fees:* None. *Reservations:* Request an application from individual park or the State Division of Parks; send full payment in advance, with application. Reservations accepted (and recommended) beginning early January. Rented only for one-week stays. *Facilities:* Swimming and interpretative programs, June 1—Labor Day. *Restrictions:* No hunting or alcohol. Dogs must be leashed (not allowed in lodgings).

The Blue Ridge Parkway is a 469-mile-long, 81,536-acre national park that follows, at the highest possible elevations, the crests of the southern Appalachian and Blue Ridge mountains. The parkway, which has no billboards and no commercial traffic, extends south from Shenandoah National Park in western Virginia to the Great Smoky Mountains National Park in western North Carolina, and has an average elevation of from 3,000 to 4,000 feet with sections above 5,000 feet. Many of its more than two hundred scenic overlooks have hiking trails leading into the forest, and there are a host of attractions along the way. Picnic areas, many with fireplaces, are scattered along the parkway, which is contiguous to a number of state parks—Crabtree Meadows, Craggy Gardens, Doughton Park, Julian Price Memorial Park, Linville Falls, Mount Pisgah State Park, E. B. Jeffress Park, and Cumberland Knob. It is possible to spend weeks leisurely driving up or down the parkway, stopping at parks and historical restorations, lodges, and museums. There is one basic rule to enjoying the parkway fully: Take your time.

Some major attractions are Richland Balsam Overlook, at 6,053 feet the highest point on the road; Humpback Rocks Visitor Center and Pioneer Farm; Mabry Mill, a reconstructed water-powered gristmill still in operation; the Museum of North Carolina Minerals; the Southern Highlands Folk Art Center; Mount Mitchell (elevation 6,684 feet), in a state park contiguous to the parkway; and the Craggy Gardens wild-rhododendron field.

Views from the parkway are spectacular at any time of year. In spring the rhododendrons and dogwoods bloom, and the autumn foliage is outstanding. *Parkway mailing address:* 700 Northwestern Bank Building, Asheville, NC 28801. *Parkway phone* (704) 259-0700.

Peaks of Otter Lodge (Virginia section)

Peaks of Otter Lodge comprises a rustic main lodge with exposed beams and a sun porch with a fireplace and three motel-type units with fifty-nine guest rooms. The main lodge has three guest suites, each with a living room, a bedroom, television, and a private bath. The lodge also has a dining room overlooking a lake and Sharp Top Mountain.

Each guest room has wall-to-wall carpeting, a private bath, and a view of the lake from either a terrace or a balcony.

Accommodations: 59 rooms and 3 suites, all with private bath. *Pets:* Not permitted. *Open:* All year. *Mailing address:* PO Box 489, Bedford, VA 24523. *Phone:* (703) 586-1081. *Driving instructions:* Peaks of Otter Lodge is on the Blue Ridge Parkway, at mile marker 86.6.

Rocky Knob Cabins (Virginia section)

Rocky Knob Cabins comprises seven wood-frame cabins. The complex is two miles from Mabry Mill, where there are a coffee shop, a gift shop, and an early-nineteenth-century mill that works via an elaborate system of channels and that was restored to its original condition and still grinds corn and grits.

The cabins, set up for housekeeping, have a maximum capacity of six. Each has a fully equipped kitchenette and a private bath.

Accommodations: 7 cabins with private bath. *Towels and linens:* Provided. *Cooking and eating utensils:* Provided. *Stove and refrigerator:* Provided. *Pets:* Not permitted. *Open:* May through October. *Mailing address:* Meadows of Dan, VA 24120. *Phone:* (703) 593-3503. *Driving instructions:* Rocky Knob Cabins are on the Blue Ridge Parkway at mile marker 174.

Bluffs Lodge (North Carolina section)

A motel-type building with twenty-four guest rooms, Bluffs Lodge is at an elevation of 3,600 feet in Doughton Park. A building near the lodge houses a restaurant, a coffee shop, a gift ship, and a service station.

Each guest room has wall-to-wall carpeting and a private bath. About half overlook the valley.

Accommodations: 24 rooms with private bath. *Pets:* Permitted. *Open:* May through October. *Mailing address:* Laurel Springs, NC 28644. *Phone:* (919) 372-4499. *Driving instructions:* Bluffs Lodge is on the Blue Ridge Parkway at mile marker 241.

Pisgah Inn (North Carolina section)

At the top of Mount Pisgah, elevation 5,000, Pisgah Inn is a rustic looking lodge built of cedar. Its dining room, which offers panoramic views from its windows, has exposed-beam ceilings, a parquet floor, and a deck. The facilities also include a snack bar, a gift shop, and a store that sells groceries and

351

camping supplies (the inn administers 140 camping sites.).

The fifty-one guest rooms in three separate buildings have wall-to-wall carpeting, color television, a porch or a balcony, contemporary furnishings, a private bath, and views of the valley.

Accommodations: 51 rooms with private bath. *Pets:* Not permitted. *Open:* Late April through October. *Mailing address:* PO Drawer 749, Waynesville, NC 28786. *Phone:* (704) 235-8228. *Driving instructions:* Pisgah Inn is on the Blue Ridge Parkway at Mile Marker 408.6.

This observation tower stands atop Moore's Knob   353

Hanging Rock State Park is in north-central North Carolina, about 30 miles north of Winston-Salem and 10 miles south of the Virginia border. The 6,000-acre park is in the Sauratown Mountains and ranges in elevation from about 1,000 to 2,900 feet. Moore's Knob, the highest point in the park, has an observation tower with a panoramic view of the mountains. The terrain is wooded primarily with white, red, and chestnut oaks, plus hickories, pines, sourwood, dogwoods, redbuds, mountain laurels, rhododendrons, azaleas, and scattered stands of hemlock. This scenic park has five waterfalls that cascade through three gorges. The Upper Cascades drop 100 feet in a series of seven short falls, while Lower Cascades drops 40 feet, making it the single highest falls in the park. A 30-foot deep cave, Tory's Den, is behind the Lower Cascades. Another waterfall, Window Falls, is surrounded by dense growths of mountain galax and rhododendron. All of the falls are accessible by trails that vary in length from one-fifth to three-quarters of a mile; the park's numerous other hiking trails varying in length from 1½ miles to more than 4 miles.

The park is named for Hanging Rock, a quartzite mass that rises 200 feet straight up. Characteristic wildlife includes gray foxes, raccoons, and some deer. Hanging Rock and Moore's Knob are fine places to watch hawks soaring, especially during the fall migration.

A 12-acre lake is frequented by fishermen and swimmers, and visitors can rent rowboats. Other facilities include a snack bar, a boat ramp, and camping and picnicking areas.

Hanging Rock State Park has six wood-frame cabins in a wooded area about a quarter of a mile from the lake. Each has four bedrooms, a fully equipped kitchenette, and a private bath, and can accommodate up to six.

Accommodations: 6 cabins with private bath. *Towels and linens:* Not provided. *Cooking and eating utensils:* Provided. *Stove and refrigerator:* Provided. *Pets:* Not permitted. *Open:* Early April through late October. *Mailing address:* PO Box 186, Danbury, NC 27016. *Phone:* (919) 593-8480. *Driving instructions:* Hanging Rock State Park is off Route 2015, about 2 miles north of Danbury.

Morrow Mountain State Park is in central North Carolina, 2 miles west of Uwharrie National Forest and about 50 miles south of Winston-Salem. The 4508-acre park is in the Uwharrie Mountains and ranges in elevation from 600 to 936 feet. The terrain varies from slightly hilly to steeply rugged and is wooded primarily with oaks, maples, poplars, willows, hickories, pines, dogwoods, mountain laurels, and rhododendrons. The park borders Lake Tillery, which forms the western end of Umharrie National Forest, and at one point sheer rock escarpments rise straight up out of the lake. The tallest of these, Big Rock, rises about 30 feet. Deer, raccoons, and foxes are common, as are rattlesnakes and copperheads. The park supports a wide variety of bird life, including several species of woodpeckers, swallows, cardinals, and red-tailed and red-shouldered hawks. Bald eagles frequently winter here, fishing in Lake Tillery.

Although there are no designated swimming areas, Lake Tillery has good fishing, the major catches being bass, bluegills, crappies, and catfishes. The lake has a fishing deck for the handicapped and rental rowboats. The park has numerous hiking trails, ranging from easy to difficult and from ½ mile to 4 miles. Other facilities include a swimming pool with a bathhouse; camping, picnicking and backpacking areas; a summer naturalist program that offers guided walks and interpretative activities; a natural-history museum with live-animal displays and exhibits of Indian artifacts; and the restored homestead of a doctor who once lived in the area.

Morrow Mountain has six wood-frame cabins in a wooded area near a stream. Two-bedroom units can accommodate as many as six, and each has a fully equipped kitchenette, tongue-and-groove paneling, a living room with a sofa bed, and a screened porch.

Accommodations: 6 cabins with private bath. *Towels and linens:* Not provided. *Cooking and eating utensils:* Provided. *Stove and refrigerator:* Provided. *Pets:* Not permitted. *Open:* April through November. *Mailing address:* Route 5, Box 430, Albemarle, NC 28001. *Phone:* (704) 982-4402. *Driving instructions:* Morrow Mountain State Park is off Routes 24, 27, and 73 about 5 miles east of Albemarle.

At the southwestern extremity of the North Carolina panhandle and contiguous with the Cherokee National Forest in Tennessee and Chattahoochee National Forest in Georgia, Nantahala National Forest includes some 516,000 acres. Within the forest several mountain chains—the Balsam, the Snowbird, the Nantahala, and others—rise above the plateau formed by the Appalachian ridges. Six-hundred and forty-five species of mammals have been observed here, as well as five distinct forest types—spruce and fir, white pine, yellow pine, cove hardwoods, and upland hardwoods. Larger mammal species include black bear, deer, and European wild boar, an introduced species that has been causing environmental problems in such places as the Great Smoky Mountain National Park, where they cannot be legally hunted. Bald eagles are sighted in winter, and the forest has been involved in a program to re-introduce golden eagles.

The forest encompasses several waterfalls, about 70 miles of the Appalachian Trail, frothy whitewater rivers, treeless mountain peaks, and dense tracts of forest. The Joyce Kilmer Memorial Forest, a 4,000-acre preserve beside Big and Little Santeetlah creeks and within Joyce Kilmer—Slick Rock Wilderness Area, is an extensive stand of virgin forest. Huge yellow poplars, oaks, hemlocks, beeches, and basswoods rise all around to heights of 125 feet. On sunny days at noon the forest is dappled with sunlight. At Whitewater Falls, the Whitewater River earns its name as it cascades 400 feet vertically across 500 feet.

"Nantahala" is a Cherokee word that means roughly "land of the noon-day sun," which apparently refers to the deeper parts of the Nantahala Gorge—the Indians, it seems, only saw the sun at noon when they were at the bottom. Whitewater canoeing, kayaking, and rafting are popular sports, and several organizations offer trips and instruction. *Forest address:* P.O. Box 2750, Asheville, NC 28802.

Nantahala Outdoor Center

Organized in 1972, Nantahala Outdoor Center specializes in outdoor adventure and instructions offering whitewater rafting, canoeing, and kayaking clinics; bicycle trips; backpacking; rock climbing clinics; and other instruction. The Center has several outposts in the southeast, but their main facilities are

just outside of Bryson City, North Carolina, and offer several types of accommodations.

On a ridge overlooking the Nantahala River and surrounded by oaks, maples, dogwoods, and conifers, are four wood-frame "vacation homes," which vary in size from two to ten bedrooms and can accommodate from four to thirteen people. Each has a private bath, a fully equipped kitchen complete with utensils, and a deck overlooking the forest. The Appalachian Trail passes beneath these structures, and when the trees are bare you can see the river about 100 yards distant. These units come with housekeeping service.

Also available are six rooms in a cinder block motel, each with a private bath and either two or three double beds. Two are completely equipped for the handicapped; one has a kitchenette; and one is a hostel room with six beds. The regular rooms

357

are supplied with towels and linens, but the hostel room is not.

The complex also has an outfitting store and a restaurant that serves family-style meals. The center is also an Appalachian Trail postal drop.

Accommodations: 4 houses and 6 motel rooms with private bath and hostel. *Towels and linens:* Provided in houses and motel rooms. *Stove and Refrigerator:* Provided in houses and 1 motel room. *Cooking and eating utensils:* Provided in houses and 1 motel room. *Pets:* Not permitted. *Open:* All year. *Mailing address:* U.S. 19W, Box 41, Bryson City, NC 28713. *Telephone:* (704) 488-9221 or 488-2175. *Driving instructions:* Nantahala Outdoor Center is on Route 19W, about 12 miles southwest of Bryson City.

Nantahala Village

On 200 acres beside Fontana Lake, Nantahala Village is a complex of buildings that includes 35 cabins, a lodge, a restaurant, a gift shop, riding stables, hiking paths, swimming pools, and tennis courts.

The cabins vary in construction—some are frame, some stone, and some log. Each has a private bath and kitchen with utensils; some units have fireplaces; and most come with a porch. Some cabins are set apart from each other in the woods, while others are in groups. Guests here can also stay in apartments, rooms in the lodge, or in one of several mobile homes.

The complex has meeting rooms, and the dining room, which has a stone fireplace, can accommodate 125 (banquets of that size can be arranged). The village is activity-oriented and can help with arrangements for everything from a day-hike, to a 7-day horseback trip, to a whitewater journey.

The village opens April 1 and closes October 31, although the dining room is open Thanksgiving and Christmas, and log cabins with fireplaces can be reserved by special arrangement.

Accommodations: 35 cabins, 14 lodge rooms, 4 mobile homes with private bath. *Towels and linens:* Provided. *Stove and refrigerator:* Provided in most units. *Cooking and eating utensils:* Provided in most units. *Pets:* Not permitted. *Open:* April through October (see above). *Mailing address:* Nantahala Village, P.O. Drawer J, Bryson City, NC 28713. *Telephone:* (704) 488-2826 or (800) 438-1507. *Driving instructions:* Nantahala Village is on US 19, 9 miles south of Bryson City.

The 478,000-acre Pisgah National Forest is in southern North Carolina, immediately northeast and southwest of Asheville. The forest, which divides at Asheville into two main sections that funnel outward in two directions, encompasses the major sections of the North Carolina Blue Ridge Mountains as well as the Black and Unaka ranges. The Black Mountains, a 15-mile range northeast of Asheville, has thirteen peaks higher than 6,000 feet, including Mount Mitchell (6,684 feet), the highest summit east of the Mississippi. The Blue Ridge Parkway, one of the nation's most scenic roads, runs through here and at Richland Balsam attains its highest elevation, 6,540 feet.

The forest is spectacular in autumn, when the hardwoods, mostly oaks, turn yellow, orange, and brown. Spring and early summer are also lovely, with dogwoods, azaleas, rhododendrons, wild irises, trilliums, and bluets seemingly everywhere you look.

The forest has many well-maintained trails and unforgettable sights. Looking Glass Rock is an enormous outcrop of granite that rises precipitously more than 370 feet from the surrounding terrain. Eternally wet from the water that seeps down its face, it got its name from the way it glistens in the sun. Looking Glass Falls is a 28-foot-wide, 72-foot-high cascade of water surrounded by sheer rock escarpments. Two unusual phenomena are visible in the forest: At certain times and under certain conditions, Mount Pisgah, when covered with snow, looks like a bride and groom gazing at each other; another summit, the Rat, resembles a rodent.

Pisgah National Forest apparently got its name from Mount Pisgah in ancient Palestine (now Jordan), from which Moses, according to Deuteronomy, viewed the Promised Land. *Forest mailing address:* PO Box 8, Pisgah Forest, NC 28768. *Forest phone:* (704) 877-3350.

High Hampton Inn

Privately owned, the big lodge-style High Hampton Inn is about 35 miles south of Waynesville. Built in 1933 and covered with chestnut bark shingles, it is on 2,600 acres of heavily wooded land complete with a man-made lake, tennis courts, stables, trapshooting and skeet facilities, and a golf course. The grounds are landscaped, and the property also includes many cottages, which are secluded and, like the main structure, sided with chestnut bark.

The twelve cottages, with accommodations ranging from one to fifteen guest rooms, are furnished with hand-carved wooden furniture and hooked rugs; some have a central sitting room and some have fireplaces. Guest rooms in the main building, also furnished with handmade wooden pieces, have rough pine paneling and, in many instances, a fireplace.

The inn's large lounge has a four-sided stone fireplace, overstuffed chairs, and game tables, and the restaurant, serving meals to both the public and guests, specializes in everything from home-smoked hams to pastries baked on the premises. Alcohol isn't served at the inn, although setups are available.

Accommodations: 133 rooms, including 35 lodge rooms with private bath and 98 cottage rooms in 12 cottages, mostly with private bath. *Pets:* Permitted if kept at the inn's kennels. *Open:* April through October. *Mailing address:* Box 338, Cashiers, NC 28717. *Phone:* (704) 743-2411. *Driving instructions:* High Hampton Inn is on Route 107 about 2 miles south of Cashiers.

Folkestone Lodge

Folkestone Lodge is in an area between Pisgah National Forest, Nantahala National Forest, and one-eighth mile from the Great Smoky Mountains National Park. Resembling a farmhouse and privately owned, Folkstone has stone walls and floors, pressed-tin ceilings, private baths with claw-footed tubs, and small stained-glass windows.

Guest rooms are furnished with many antiques, and each bed is covered with a crocheted spread. Oriental rugs are everywhere, and the guest rooms come complete with bowls of fresh fruit and vases of fresh flowers.

The dining room's floor-to-ceiling windows face the mountains, and meals are served family style.

Accommodations: 5 rooms with private bath. *Pets:* Not permitted. *Open:* May through November. *Mailing address:* Route 1, PO Box 310, Bryson City, NC 28713. *Phone:* (704) 488-2730. *Driving instructions:* Follow road signs to Deep Creek Campground (in the national forest). The lodge is about ⅛ mile from the campground.

Green Park Inn

A large 1882 Victorian, Green Park Inn is in Blowing Rock, an active resort area since the turn of the century, immediately north of Grandfather Mountain and just off the Blue Ridge Parkway. The inn is on the Eastern Continental Divide at an elevation of 4,300 feet, with its cocktail lounge, the Divide Lounge, positioned precisely on that spot.

Each of the eighty-five guest rooms has wall-to-wall car-

peting, color television, a telephone, a private bath, and is decorated in a contemporary style. The inn, which has served at various times as a showcase for several furniture manufacturers, has a game room, a multilevel dining room, and a large lobby and wide verandas full of latticework and old wicker furniture.

The adjacent Blowing Rock Country Club extends golf and tennis privileges to guests of the inn. A heated outdoor swimming pool is on the grounds, and meals are served to guests on the modified American Plan.

Accommodations: 85 rooms with private bath. *Pets:* Not permitted. *Open:* Late April through December. *Mailing address:* PO Box 7, Blowing Rock, NC 28605. *Phone:* (704) 295-3141. *Driving instructions:* Green Park Inn is in Blowing Rock, on U.S. 321 South.

Blue Boar Lodge

Blue Boar Lodge is actually in Nantahala National Forest, which is contiguous with Pisgah National Forest, Cherokee National Forest, and Chattahoochee National Forest in the very western part of the state. It is at the junction of the Great Smoky and Nantahala mountains, just east of the Joyce Kilmer Memorial Forest. The building, a combination of lodge and ranch styles and directly overlooking a pond inhabited by trout and wild ducks, has six guest rooms, each with private bath.

Lodge rates include all meals served family style; and guests interested in hiking, fishing, or hunting in the surrounding forests can arrange for box lunches.

Accommodations: 6 rooms with private bath. *Pets:* Not permitted. *Open:* May through October. *Mailing address:* Route 1, Robbinsville, NC 28771. *Phone:* (704) 479-8126. *Driving instructions:* Blue Boar Lodge is on Joyce Kilmer Forest Road, which is off U.S. 129, about 85 miles southwest of Asheville.

Eseeola Lodge

Eseeola Lodge, privately owned, is in the northeastern portion of Pisgah National Forest, about 50 miles northeast of Asheville and a few miles southwest of Grandfather Mountain, a 5,984-foot peak. The lodge was built between 1926 and 1936 almost entirely of chestnut lumber, with chestnut-bark siding and peeled chestnut logs supporting its gabled porches. The twenty-eight guest rooms are paneled in chestnut, and most of their furnishings are of chestnut as well. Much of the woodwork came from a woodworking shop set up by the lodge's original owners.

The grounds include an eighteen-hole golf course, all-weather tennis courts, horseback-riding facilities, a heated swimming pool, and seven cottages. The main building has a lounge and a lobby, each with a stone fireplace, as well as a card room and a television room. The dining room serves three meals a day to the public as well as guests, and rates at the lodge include all meals.

Accommodations: 28 rooms with private bath. *Pets:* Not permitted. *Open:* June through Labor Day. *Mailing address:* PO Box 98, Linville, NC 28646. *Phone:* (704) 733-4311. *Driving instructions:* Eseeola Lodge is in the center of Linville about a mile off the Blue Ridge Parkway.

364

North Dakota

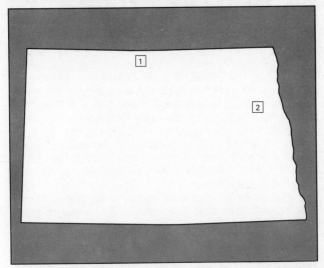

State map and tourist information: Dept. of Tourism, Liberty Memorial Bldg., State Capitol, Bismarck, ND 58505; 800-437-2077 (out-of-state); 701-472-2100 (in-state). **State parks:** *Information:* Parks and Recreation Dept., 1424 West Century Avenue, Suite 202, Bismarck, ND 58501; 701-224-4887. *Entrance fees:* $1 per vehicle. *Reservations:* Contact individual park; send $15 deposit. Accepted (and recommended) up to 1 year in advance for early June—early September. *Restrictions:* No hunting. Dogs must be leashed (not allowed in lodgings). *Facilities:* Swimming, June—October. Boating, April—October. Cross-country skiing and snowmobiling, December—March.

Lake Metigoshe State Park is in northern North Dakota, on the Canadian border about 10 miles northeast of Bottineau, 12 miles west of the International Peach Garden, and near the Willow Lake National Wildlife Refuge to the east. The 1,050-acre park is dotted with lakes and varies in terrain from sandy beaches to both marshlands and hilly areas wooded with oaks, aspens, ashes, elms, and birches. The marshlands and lakes attract migrating waterfowl by the thousands, and in spring visitors might spot squadrons of Canada geese, a wide variety of ducks, and terns, herons, bitterns, egrets, eagles, and ospreys. Wildlife includes elk, deer, moose, coyotes, mink, beavers, raccoons, and porcupines. A system of trails includes Old Oak National Recreation Trail, a self-guiding 3-mile route complete with boardwalks, nature blinds, and overlook towers, encompassing both marshlands and forested areas.

Activities include swimming at a sand beach with bathhouse; boating, with launching facilities; fishing for walleyes, perch, muskellunge, and pike; picnicking; and cross-country skiing and snowmobiling. The naturalist service offers interpretative programs including lectures, films, and guided walks.

The park has a group camp, accommodating two hundred, consisting of a main lodge with kitchen and dining and meeting facilities, an auditorium, and two dormitories that can accommodate a hundred people each. Each dormitory has log exteriors and native wood-paneled interior walls, a common room with a fireplace, and central shower and sanitary facilities.

Accommodations: Group camp, including 2 dormitories with shared bath. *Towels and linens:* Not provided. *Cooking and eating utensils:* Provided. *Stove and refrigerator:* Provided. *Pets:* Not permitted. *Open:* All year. *Mailing address:* Route 1, Box 152, Bottineau, ND 58318. *Phone:* (701) 263-4651. *Driving instructions:* From Bottineau take Route 14 north, then Route 43 east, a total distance of 14 miles.

Turtle River State Park is in eastern North Dakota, about 25 miles west of Grand Forks. Its 655 acres are in the lush, thickly wooded Turtle River valley, whose terrain of flat river-bottom land gradually rises in a series of small, rolling hills. Burr oaks, basswoods, green ashes, elms, cottonwoods, chokecherries, and wild plums are predominant in the wooded areas. Elsewhere there are sections of open prairie and wetlands. Characteristic wildlife includes weasels, beavers, woodchucks, and squirrels, and occasional deer and moose. During spring and fall migrations a wide variety of waterfowl visit—terns, great blue herons, and bitterns rest in the Turtle River, and orioles congregate in the forested areas. At one time the park was covered by Lake Agassiz, a glacial lake that, when it receded, left behind moraines of sand and gravel, sections of which remain. Archaeologists who have studied the historical significance of the park believe it to have been a part of the Arvilla Mounds complex, probably visited frequently by indigenous peoples between the seventh and tenth centuries.

There are miles of hiking trails, some of which are self-guiding; a swimming pool with a bathhouse; picnicking areas; a sledding hill; and cross-country skiing and snowmobiling trails. In winter a warming house with vending machines operates in the area where most of the trails begin.

The park has a group lodge comprising a main lodge building and six sleeping cabins accommodating twelve people each. The wood-frame main lodge, built by the Civilian Conservation Corps, has exposed-beam ceilings; its kitchen and dining facilities can handle as many as seventy-five people. An easy walk from the lodge are the sleeping cabins, just across the river. Each of these has six double bunk beds and shower and sanitary facilities.

Accommodations: 6 cabins (group camp) with shared bath. *Towels and linens:* Not provided. *Cooking and eating utensils:* Provided. *Stove and refrigerator:* Provided. *Pets:* Not Permitted. *Open:* Mid-May to mid-September. *Mailing address:* Box 9B, Arvilla, ND 58214. *Phone:* (701) 343-2011 or (701) 594-4445. *Driving instructions:* Turtle River State Park is off U.S. 2, about 25 miles west of Grand Forks.

Ohio

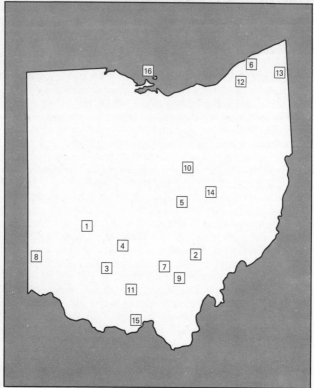

State map and tourist information: Buckeye Response Center, Suite 250, 175 S. Third St., Columbus, OH 43216; 800-BUC-KEYE; 614-462-4992 (from Alaska, Hawaii). **State parks:** *Information:* Parks & Recreation Div., Fountain Sq., Bldg. C, Columbus, OH 43224; 614-265-7000. *Entrance fees:* None. *Reservations:* Contact individual park. For 5 lodges (Burr Oak, Deer Creek, Hueston Woods, Salt Fork, Shawnee) call 800-ATA-PARK (in Ohio, Mich., Ky., Ind., Ill., W. Va., Md., Pa., Tenn., N.C., and western N.Y.); elsewhere 614-439-4406. Deposit for first night's lodgings required, check or credit card. Reservations accepted (and recommended) up to 1 year in advance. *Restrictions:* Hunting limited to selected parks. Alcohol not permitted outdoors; dogs must be leashed (not allowed in lodgings); no vehicles longer than 35 feet. *Facilities:* Swimming, Mem. Day—Labor Day. Boating, May—October. Golf and tennis, April—October. Cross-country skiing and snowmobiling, December—March.

Buck Creek State Park is in southwestern Ohio, about 4 miles east of Springfield, encompassing some 4,000 acres, 2,100 of which are water. This relatively new park grew up around the C. J. Brown Lake, created as part of a flood-control project in a fertile agricultural region that impressed early settlers because of the many springs that appeared among its meadows and fields. The wife of a pioneer named a nearby settlement Springfield.

Water sports are especially popular here. The lake has a 186-slip marina, with fueling, docking, and launching facilities, as well as a concession that rents out rowboats, paddleboats, and motorboats. There is no horsepower limitation on the lake, which has a quarter-mile long sand beach with a food concession. The lake's northernmost section is rife with waterfowl—egrets, herons, loons, canvasbacks, Canada geese, and snow geese. Winter activities include snowmobiling, sledding, ice-skating, cross-country skiing, and ice-fishing.

The park has twenty-six wood-frame cabins in a wooded area. Four of the cabins overlook C. J. Brown Lake. Each has two bedrooms, a living room with a sofa bed, a private bath, a kitchen, and a screened porch.

Accommodations: 26 cabins with private bath. *Towels and linens:* Provided. *Cooking and eating utensils:* Provided. *Stove and refrigerator:* Provided. *Pets:* Not permitted. *Open:* All year. *Mailing address:* 1901 Buck Creek Lane, Springfield, OH 45502. *Phone:* (513) 322-5284. *Driving instructions:* Buck Creek State Park is off Route 4, roughly 4 miles east of Springfield—take exit 62 off of Route 70 to Route 40 W.

On the eastern edge of the western section of Wayne National Forest, Burr Oak State Park is 3,256 acres of hilly and heavily wooded land and water in southeastern Ohio, about 15 miles north of Athens. The park contains the 664-acre Burr Oak Lake and 22 miles of hiking trails popular with backpackers, including one all the way around the lake that usually takes three days with stopovers at primitive campsites. (The park trail system connects with the Buckeye Trail which winds around the state.) The lake has a beach and is equipped with a dock and fueling facilities for boats (limited to 10-horsepower motors). Other activities include golf, tennis, and fishing.

This section of Ohio is especially appealing in the fall, when the foliage turns color. Winter attracts sledders, ice-skaters, cross-country skiers, and snowmobilers. *Park mailing address:* Route 2, Box 286, Glouster, OH 45732. *Park phone:* (614) 767-3570.

Burr Oak Lodge and Cabins

Burr Oak Lodge is a sixty-room modified A-frame built of wood and stone. Its dining room seats 140 people, and it has four meeting rooms and a banquet hall, the "Chicadee Room."

Each guest room has wall-to-wall carpeting, color television, and a telephone; about half of the rooms have views of the lake. The lodge also maintains thirty cabins in a wooded area, each with two bedrooms, a living room with a sofa bed, a kitchen, and a screened porch.

Accommodations: 60 lodge rooms and 30 cabins, all with private bath. *Towels and linens:* Provided. *Cooking and eating utensils:* In cabins. *Stove and refrigerator:* In cabins. *Pets:* Not permitted. *Open:* All year. *Mailing address:* RFD 2, PO Box 159, Glouster, OH 45732. *Phone:* (614) 767-2112. *Driving instructions:* Burr Oak State Park is at the intersection of Routes 78 and 13, roughly 15 miles north of Athens.

About 30 miles southeast of Dayton, Cowan Lake State Park comprises 1,775 acres of land and water. Cowan Lake itself was formed by a dam on the Todd Fork River, where William Smalley, Clinton County's first settler, in 1797 homesteaded a piece of land now submerged beneath the 700-acre lake. Formerly one of General Anthony Wayne's soldiers during the Revolutionary War, Smalley had spent much of his life as a captive of the Indians.

Cowan Lake has boat rentals (10 horsepower limit) with fueling, docking, and launching facilities, and a beach for swimming. Canoes, sailboats, and powerboats can be seen on the lake; though less aquatically minded visitors take advantage of the park's 11 miles of hiking trails, one of which, Lotus Cove Self-guided Tour, includes a boardwalk that overlooks a colony of American lotuses (water lilies). Another hiking trail, Emerald Woods Trail, passes through a forest of American beeches. In autumn the leaves of this tree take on the color of parchment. In winter those still clinging to the branches look beautiful against the snow. Winter activities include sledding, cross-country skiing, and ice-fishing.

The park has twenty-seven wood-frame cabins in a wooded area overlooking Cowan Lake. (Some have views of the lake.) Each has two bedrooms, a living room with a sofa bed, a private bath, a kitchen, and a screened porch.

Accommodations: 27 cabins with private bath. *Towels and linens:* Provided. *Cooking and eating utensils:* Provided. *Stove and refrigerator:* Provided. *Pets:* Not permitted. *Open:* All year. *Mailing address:* 729 Beechwood Road, Wilmington, OH 45177. *Phone:* (513) 289-2105. *Driving instructions:* From Wilmington take U.S. 68 about 8 miles south to Route 350; then take Route 350 west 2 miles.

On 8, 300 acres, 1,300 of which are water, Deer Creek State Park is in southwestern Ohio, about 30 miles southwest of Columbus. The park's terrain consists for the most part of reverting farmland, with gently rolling hills and large open fields. The area is heavily populated with deer and pheasants, and the open fields attract large numbers of hawks: sharp-shinned, red-tailed, red-shouldered, and Cooper's hawks, as well as American kestrels. Built as a flood-control project, 1,277-acre Deer Creek Lake has a beach, boats for rent, a launching ramp, and no limit on the horsepower of private boats. The park has an eighteen-hole golf course, two swimming pools, lighted tennis courts, and facilities for basketball, volleyball, sledding, ice-skating, and cross-country skiing.

Technology is at work in Deer Creek State Park, whose lodge is partially heated by solar panels and whose sewage treatment recycles nitrogen and minerals. *Park mailing address:* 20635 Waterloo, Mount Sterling, OH 43143. *Park phone:* (614) 869-3124.

Deer Creek State Park Lodge and Cabins

Deer Creek Lodge is a rustic-looking, modern stone building with 110 guest rooms as well as a 250-seat restaurant plus banquet and meeting facilities that can accommodate as many as 600.

The guest rooms, decorated in earth tones, have wall-to-wall carpeting, color television, telephones, and sliding glass doors that open onto private balconies that overlook the lake, the lodge's pool, or the park. Some of the rooms can accommodate as many as eight people. Some have Murphy-style bunk beds, and others have loft areas with additional sleeping space.

The lodge also has twenty-five cabins, each with two bedrooms, a kitchenette, a living room with a sofa bed, and a furnished screened porch that overlooks the lake.

Accommodations: 110 lodge rooms and 25 cabins, all with private bath. *Towels and linens:* Provided. *Cooking and eating utensils:* In cabins. *Stove and refrigerator:* In cabins. *Pets:* Not permitted. *Open:* All year. *Mailing address:* PO Box 153, Mount Sterling, OH 43143. *Phone:* (614) 869-2020. *Driving instructions:* Deer Creek State Park is off Route 207, roughly 10 miles south of Mount Sterling.

Dillon State Park is in east-central Ohio, about 7 miles northwest of Zanesville along the shores of Dillon Lake, a 1,600-acre
impoundment of the Licking River. The 4,000-acre park adjoins
a 3,500-acre wildlife preserve and consists for the most part of
gently rolling hills wooded primarily with oaks, maples, beeches,
dogwoods, and a few pines. Characteristic wildlife includes deer,
raccoons, opossums, grouse, and quail. The lake attracts a wide
variety of waterfowl, especially during migrations, when ducks
and geese pass through and eagles and ospreys stop by to fish
in Dillon Lake, with its large population of bass, bluegills, crappies, and catfishes. Red-tailed hawks are common here, as are
American kestrels, and the park has a nesting colony of great
blue herons.

Most activities center on the lake, which has a 1,360-foot
sand beach with a bathhouse, a marina with launching ramps,
and canoes, rowboats, and pontoon boats for rent. (There is no
horsepower limitation on the lake). Other facilities include camping and picnicking areas, interpretative programs, and 7 miles
of hiking trails, some of which connect with trails in the adjacent
wildlife area.

Dillon park has twenty-nine wood-frame "deluxe" cabins in
a wooded area, each with a fully equipped kitchenette, two
bedrooms, a private bath, a screened porch, and a living room
with a sofa bed. The cabins are heated for use all year.

Accommodations: 29 cabins with private bath. *Towels and
linens:* Provided. *Cooking and eating utensils:* Provided. *Stove
and refrigerator:* Provided. *Pets:* Not permitted. *Open:* All year.
Mailing address: 5265 Dillon Hills Drive, PO Box 126, Nashport,
OH 43830. *Phone:* (614) 453-0442. *Driving instructions:* Dillon
State Park is off Route 146 about 7 miles northwest of Zanesvile.

Geneva State Park is on 698 acres in northeastern Ohio, on the shore of Lake Erie about 10 miles west of Ashtabula. The park encompasses 2 ½ miles of Lake Erie beachfront, shaded at points by stands of virgin oaks, as well as freshwater marshes and estuaries. The area is a prime one for birders, who can watch a wide variety of migratory and permanently resident waterfowl either diving into the lake or stalking around in the marshes.

Swimming is one of the most popular pastimes here. There are no boat rentals or facilities in the park, although the general area is frequented by both boaters and fishermen. The park has 5 miles of hiking and cross-country skiing trails as well as designated snowmobiling trails.

Each of the park's twelve cabins, in a sparsley wooded area along the shore of Lake Erie, has three bedrooms, a living room with a sofa bed and a brick fireplace, wall-to-wall carpeting, a kitchen, a private bath, and a screened porch.

Accommodations: 12 cabins with private bath. *Towels and linens:* Provided. *Cooking and eating utensils:* Provided. *Stove and refrigerator:* Provided. *Pets:* Not permitted. *Open:* May through October. *Mailing address:* Pandanorum Road, PO Box 429, Geneva, OH 44041. *Phone:* (216) 466-8400. *Driving instructions:* Geneva State Park is off Route 534 about a mile west of Geneva-on-the-Lake.

In southeastern Ohio, less than 30 miles west of Athens and just west of Wayne National Forest, Hocking Hills State Park consists of six separate sections and encompasses, in all, 1,943 acres of unique terrain. Submerged at one time beneath an inland sea, this area was covered by sandstone, which over the years was uplifted, weathered, and eroded. Geological forces turned the area into a sort of rugged sculpture, with precipitous gorges, rushing streams, caves, and waterfalls. Extensive stands of mature hardwood forest sprinkled with conifers and wildflowers characterize the landscape.

Exploring the natural formations—Old Man's Cave Gorge, Devil's Bathtub, Sphinx Head, and Upper and Lower Falls—is a regular activity here; and although the park has no beach, it has two swimming pools—one at the campground and another near the dining lodge. The park has 33 miles of hiking trails but no boating facilities. Ice-fishing is popular in winter.

Hocking Hills Lodge and Cabins

Hocking Hills has forty wood-frame cabins set on a hill in a stand of red and eastern white pines. Each cabin has two bedrooms, a living room with a sofa bed, a kitchen, a private bath, and a screened porch.

Although it has no rooms for guests, Hocking Lodge has a snack bar, a dining room, a game room, a television room, and meeting and banquet facilities for as many as 450 people. The lodge also has a swimming pool, which is free for cabin guests. (There's a small fee for others.)

Accommodations: 40 cabins with private bath. *Towels and linens:* Provided. *Cooking and eating utensils:* Provided. *Stove and refrigerator:* Provided. *Pets:* Not permitted. *Open:* All year. *Mailing address:* 20160 SR 664, Logan, OH 43138. *Phone:* (614) 385-6841. *Driving instructions:* Hocking Hills State Park is off Route 664 about 10 miles southwest of Logan.

Hueston Woods State Park is on 3,596 acres in southwestern Ohio, near the Indiana border and about 25 miles north of Cincinnati. The park takes its name from Matthew Hueston, who served wth General Anthony Wayne during the Revolutionary War. Hueston bought a great deal of land in southwestern Ohio and, being something of a conservationist, left much of it as it was. The virgin forest, primarily American beeches and sugar maples, is today a designated state nature preserve, as well as a national natural landmark.

A special feature of the park is its nature center, which has a collection of live native animals, including exhibits on the natural history of the region, an outdoor pen full of white-tailed deer, a flight cage containing birds of prey, and an extensive raptor (birds of prey) rehabilitation center.

Activities include golf on an eighteen-hole par-72 course, boating and fishing on the 625-acre Acton Lake, hiking, camping, cross-country skiing, tennis, horseback riding, and swimming in the lake. *Park phone:* (513) 523-6347.

Hueston Woods State Park Lodge and Cabins

Hueston Woods Park Lodge is a large wood-and-stone A-frame style building on the shore of Acton Lake. The lodge has a restaurant, a gift shop, indoor and outdoor swimming pools, a game room, and a sandstone fireplace that's 100 feet high.

Each of the ninety-four guest rooms has wall-to-wall carpeting, color television, a telephone, and a balcony. About half of the rooms overlook the lake.

The lodge also operates cabins in the woods about a mile away. The cabins are rustic and have either one or three rooms, including kitchen facilities but no television or telephone.

Accommodations: 94 lodge rooms and 14 cabins, all with private bath. *Towels and linens:* Provided. *Cooking and eating utensils:* In cabins. *Stove and refrigerator:* In cabins. *Pets:* Not permitted. *Open:* All year. *Mailing address:* RFD 1, College Corner, OH 45003. *Phone:* (513) 523-6381. *Driving instructions:* Hueston Woods State Park is at the junction of Routes 732 and 177, roughly 5 miles north of Oxford.

Lake Hope State Park, in southeastern Ohio on 3,103 acres about 15 miles west of Athens, is adjacent to Zaleski State Forest and less than a mile from Wayne National Forest. Iron smelting was at one time a major industry here, and a stone furnace preserving this early craft is maintained in the park. The furnaces required large quantities of wood, thereby denuding large tracts of land and requiring a subsequent reforestation program. The hilly terrain is now wooded primarily with oaks and hickories, and wild orchids bloom in spring.

The park has 21 miles of hiking trails, including a backpacking trail that also passes through the state-forest land. Owing to drainage from nearby coal mines, Lake Hope is blue-green in color. Visitors can rent boats or swim from the beach. Winter activities include sledding, ice-skating, and cross-country skiing.

The park has sixty-nine cabins on a wooded ridge from which the lake can be seen in winter when the trees are leafless. The cabins are of three types—deluxe, standard, and "sleeping." Each deluxe cabin has two bedrooms, a living room with a sofa bed, a kitchen, a private bath, and a screened porch. The standard cabins, one large room with curtain partitions for privacy, have a bath and a kitchen. The sleeping cabins have from one to four bedrooms, a fireplace, and a limited kitchen with no utensils. Also in the complex is Lake Hope Dining Lodge, which has a view of the lake, oak-paneled dining rooms, and facilities for meetings or banquets, but no guest rooms.

The park also has a sleeping lodge, which accommodates 24 people and has a fireplace and a full kitchen.

Accommodations: 69 cabins with private bath. *Towels and linens:* Provided. *Cooking and eating utensils:* Provided except in "sleeping" cabins. *Stove and refrigerator:* Provided. *Pets:* Not permitted. *Open:* All year. *Mailing address:* Zaleski, OH 45698. *Phone:* (614) 596-5253. *Driving instructions:* Lake Hope State Park is off Route 278, about 4 miles north of Zaleski.

At the confluence of the Clear Fork and Mohican rivers, Mohican State Park is on 1,296 acres about 50 miles southwest of Akron. The terrain consists primarily of rolling hills and ridges, although sections of the Mohican gorge are steep, almost precipitous. The park is just northeast of Mohican Forest and shares the area's abundance of hardwoods, as well as its stands of eastern white pine and hemlock. The Mohican flows quickly, with the result that canoeing is a popular sport in the park. Many canoe liveries in the area provide rentals and services.

Twelve miles of hiking trails wind through the park, and facilities include indoor and outdoor pools, a beach for swimming, tennis courts, and ball fields. In winter the park is used by snowmobilers, ice-skaters, sledders, cross-country skiers, and ice fishermen. *Park mailing address:* Route 2, Box 22, Loudonville, OH 44842. *Park phone:* (419) 994-3965.

Mohican Lodge and Cabins

Built into a hill that overlooks Pleasant Hill Lake, Mohican Lodge is a large modified wood A-frame with ninety-six bedrooms. The building has a dining room, a lounge, a game room, and meeting and banquet facilities. Each guest room has wall-to-wall carpeting, color television, a telephone, a private bath, and sliding glass doors that open onto a private balcony that overlooks either the lake or the swimming pool.

The park also has twenty-five cabins about 10 miles from the lodge, along the Clear Fork River, with screened porches. Each cabin has two bedrooms, a living room, a kitchen, and a bath.

Accommodations: 96 lodge rooms and 25 cabins, all with private bath. *Towels and linens:* Provided. *Cooking and eating utensils:* In cabins. *Stove and refrigerator:* In cabins. *Pets:* Not permitted. *Open:* All year. *Mailing address:* Route 2, Perrysville, OH 44864. *Phone:* (419) 938-5411 for lodge, (419) 994-4290 for cabins. *Driving instructions:* Mohican State Park is at the junction of Routes 3 and 97, roughly 5 miles southwest of Loudonville.

In southern Ohio, roughly 70 miles east of Cincinnati, Pike Lake State Park consists of 613 acres, including the 13-acre Pike Lake. The wooded, rolling terrain was landscaped and developed in the 1930s by the Civilian Conservation Corps, which planted hundreds of pines among the hardwoods and built the lake. Surrounded by hills, Pike Lake has a sandy beach and a variety of sought-after inhabitants—largemouth bass, bluegills, channel catfishes, and bullheads, to name a few. Visitors can rent boats, but all motors must be electric.

Numerous trails run through the park, including a section of the 900-mile Buckeye Trail, which winds through most of Ohio. Wildlife includes white-tailed deer, foxes, wild turkeys, and ring-necked pheasants. Winter sports include ice-skating and cross-country skiing.

The park has twenty-five cabins in a wooded area a short walk from the lake, plus a group lodge that overlooks the lake. The cabins are of two types—deluxe and standard. Each deluxe cabin has two bedrooms, a living room with a sofa bed, a private bath, a kitchen, and a screened porch. The standard cabins consist of one room with curtain partitions for privacy; each has a kitchen area and a private bath but no porch.

The group lodge accommodates twenty-two and has two bedrooms, a kitchen, a dining room, and two bathrooms, as well as a dormitory on its second floor.

Accommodations: 25 cabins with private bath and a group lodge with shared baths. *Towels and linens:* Provided. *Cooking and eating utensils:* Provided. *Stove and refrigerator:* Provided. *Pets:* Not permitted. *Open:* All year except all standard and some deluxe cabins, which are open April through October. *Mailing address:* 1847 Pike Lake Road, Bainbridge, OH 45612. *Phone:* (614) 493-2212. *Driving instructions:* Pike Lake State Park is off Route 124 about 5 miles northwest of Morgantown.

Punderson State Park, in northeastern Ohio, about 30 miles east of Cleveland, comprises 990 acres, of which 840 are land. The park contains three lakes, one of which, Punderson Lake, is one of the state's few natural lakes. Formed by a glacier, the lake is popular among boaters, fishermen, and swimmers. Boats can be rented, docked, or launched here; but only electric motors are permitted.

Punderson is considered Ohio's premier winter-sports park, with facilities for snowmobiling, ice-skating, ice-fishing, and cross-country skiing. The park also has a large sledding hill. At the summit is a chalet where there's usually a fire going and refreshments on winter days. Other activities in the park include swimming in the pool, tennis, shuffleboard, horseshoe pitching, and volleyball. *Park mailing address:* Box 338, Newbury, OH 44065. *Park phone:* (216) 564-2279.

Punderson Manor House and Cabins

A Tudor-style manor house on which construction had begun in 1929 but which was never completed, Punderson Manor House was acquired by the state along with the land and lakes that comprise the park. The building was remodeled in the 1950s and again in the 1980s. Along with later additions, the lodge overlooks the lake, as do the dining room and the pub, both of which have fireplaces.

The manor house has seven guest rooms in the original style of the building, while the connecting annex has another twenty-four modern-style rooms. Each room has wall-to-wall carpeting, color television, a telephone, and a private bath. About half the rooms overlook the lake.

The park also has twenty-six cabins in a wooded area, some of which overlook the lake. Each has two bedrooms, a living room, a screened porch, a kitchen, and a private bath.

Accommodations: 31 manor-house and annex rooms and 26 cabins, all with private bath. *Towels and linens:* Provided. *Cooking and eating utensils:* In cabins. *Stove and refrigerator:* In cabins. *Pets:* Not permitted. *Open:* All year. *Mailing address:* 11755 Kinsman Road, Box 224, Newbury, OH 44065. *Phone:* (216) 564-9144. *Driving instructions:* Punderson State Park is on State Route 87, 2 miles west of State Route 44.

Pymatuning State Park is in northeastern Ohio about 40 miles north of Youngstown, along the Pennsylvania border. The park consists of some 35,000 acres, 17,000 of which are water—the Pymatuning Reservoir. The reservoir extends across the border into Pennsylvania, where there is another section of Pymatuning State Park, covering an additional 22,000 acres. These two contiguous state parks provide plenty of open space and water and complement each other. (The Pennsylvania park has a fish hatchery, a waterfowl museum, and a fish-feeding station.)

Visitors can rent boats, or fuel and launch their own (there's a 10-horsepower limit), and the most sought-after fish are walleyes and muskellunge. The reservoir has a beach with a bathhouse and a food concession. Open all year, the park is in the snow belt, which makes for excellent cross-country skiing, ice-fishing, ice-skating, and iceboating.

The park has sixty-two wood-frame cabins in two different wooded sections. The cabins are of two types—deluxe and standard. The deluxe cabins, each with two bedrooms, a living room with a sofa bed, a kitchen, a private bath, and a screened porch, are behind the park office. The standard cabins, set in the woods among hardwoods and conifers, have one large room each, with curtain partitions for privacy. Each standard cabin has a private bath and a kitchen but no porch.

Accommodations: 62 cabins with private bath. *Towels and linens:* Provided. *Cooking and eating utensils:* Provided. *Stove and refrigerator:* Provided. *Pets:* Not permitted. *Open:* 27 cabins all year; 35 April through October. *Mailing address:* Route 1, Andover, OH 44003. *Phone:* (216) 293-6329. *Driving instructions:* Pymatuning State Park is off Route 85, approximately 2 miles east of Andover.

With more than 17,000 acres of rolling terrain broken by patches of woods and almost 3,000 acres of water, Salt Fork State Park, in eastern Ohio about 80 miles west of Columbus, is the site of the northernmost confrontation between Union and Confederate troops.

Salt Fork Lake, with its 76 miles of shoreline and abundant bass, bluegills, crappies, and walleyes, is a popular spot for fishing, boating, and swimming. Park visitors can rent boats or bring their own. The park has a launch ramp, docking and fueling facilities, and no limitation on the horsepower of power boats. Other activities include golf, swimming, waterskiing, tennis, cross-country skiing, and snowmobiling. Some of the 15 miles of hiking trails, as well as the picnic areas and the campground, were specially designed for use by the handicapped. *Park mailing address:* Box 672, Cambridge, OH 43725. *Park phone:* (614) 439-3521.

Salt Fork Lodge and Cabins

Salt Fork Lodge is a stone-and-wood building with a pool in front and a lake behind. It contains 148 guest rooms, a restaurant, a lounge, and a main lobby with a fireplace. Each guest room has wall-to-wall carpeting, color television, a telephone, a private bath, and sliding glass doors that open onto a balcony overlooking either the lake or the pool. There are also six suites, each with a small bar area that can be arranged into a second bedroom.

The lodge also operates fifty-four cabins, each having a living room with a sofa bed, a screened porch, two bedrooms, a kitchen, and a private bath. Some of the cabins are immediately on the lake; others are on a hill. All the cabins have lake views.

Accommodations: 148 lodge rooms and 54 cabins, all with private bath. *Towels and linens:* Provided. *Cooking and eating utensils:* In cabins. *Stove and refrigerator:* In cabins. *Pets:* Not permitted. *Open:* All year. *Mailing address:* State Route 22 E, PO Box 7, Cambridge, OH 43725. *Phone:* (614) 439-2751. *Driving instructions:* Salt Fork State Park is off U.S. 22, roughly 8 miles northeast of Cambridge.

The 1,165-acre Shawnee State Park is in southern Ohio, about 80 miles southeast of Cincinnati and a couple of miles from the Ohio River and Kentucky. The park is entirely within the boundaries of Shawnee State Forest, 60,000 acres of heavily wooded hills and ridges. The state forest is crisscrossed by trails, including a 50-mile backpacking trail. Known as the "Little Smokies of Ohio," the region is one of mists and wildflowers, where whorled pogonias and showy orchises bloom.

Popular activities include hiking, horseback riding, golf (an 18-hole course), swimming, fishing, camping and boating. Visitors can rent boats or launch their own (only electric motors allowed) on the 68-acre lake. The park has a 136-slip marina on the Ohio River. In winter ice-skating, cross-country skiing, and ice-fishing are the favored sports. *Park phone:* (614) 858-6652.

Shawnee Lodge and Cabins

A large modified A-frame built of wood and stone, Shawnee Lodge is a fifty-bedroom facility with a restaurant, banquet and meeting facilities, a gift shop, a lounge, and a lobby with a large fireplace. The guest rooms, half of which overlook the woods, have wall-to-wall carpeting, color television, telephones, and private baths and balconies. The lodge also operates twenty-five cabins in a wooded area about a quarter of a mile away. Each of these has two bedrooms, a living room with a sofa bed, a screened porch, a private bath, and a kitchen.

Accommodations: 50 lodge rooms and 25 cabins, all with private bath. *Towels and linens:* Provided. *Cooking and eating utensils:* In cabins. *Stove and refrigerator:* In cabins. *Pets:* Not permitted. *Open:* All year. *Mailing address:* PO Box 98, Friendship, OH 45630. *Phone:* (614) 858-6621. *Driving instructions:* Shawnee State Park is off Route 125 about 7 miles west of Portsmouth.

South Bass Island State Park is a 35-acre island in Lake Erie, north of the Port Clinton Penninsula and Catawba Island. It is near where one of the most famous naval engagements of the War of 1812 was fought. The winner of the battle was Commodore Oliver Hazard Perry of the U.S. Navy, and the island houses the 26-acre Perry Victory and International Peace Memorial at Put in Bay, a national monument. The memorial, built in 1915 and the largest Doric column in the world, was erected "to inculcate the lessons of international peace.

The island is accessible by ferries that depart from either Port Clinton or Catawba, except during the winter, when the lake freezes. The truly intrepid can get here even when the lake is frozen by driving across the ice, which quite a few people do.

The most popular activities in the park are boating and fishing. Those who come in winter often do so for sledding, ice-skating, or ice-fishing. Mostly, South Bass Island State Park is for relaxing.

The park has four "cabents" on a hillside overlooking Lake Erie. A "cabent" is a hybrid, a cross between a tent and a cabin. Hexagonal wooden structures with fabric roofs, they were originally designed for the Boy Scouts. Ninety percent of the front of a cabent consists of windows. With another in the roof, the result is that with all windows open (you can't see through them when they're closed), natural convection currents cool the structure. The fabric roof also lets in natural light. Each of the cabents in South Bass Island State Park has about 450 square feet of space, a kitchenette, a bath with shower, and curtains that serve as partitions.

Accommodations: 4 "cabents" with private bath. *Towels and linens:* Not provided. *Cooking and eating utensils:* Provided. *Stove and refrigerator:* Provided. *Pets:* Not permitted. *Open:* Memorial Day through September. *Mailing address:* 4049 East Moore's Dock Road, Port Clinton, OH 43452. *Phone:* (419) 797-4530. *Driving instructions:* South Bass Island State Park is accessible by ferry (except in winter) from Port Clinton or Catawba Island. Port Clinton is on Route 163, which intersects with Route 2 about 30 miles east of Toledo. Catawba Island is a few miles northeast of Port Clinton on Route 53, which intersects with Route 163.

Oklahoma

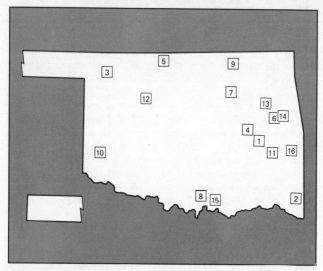

State map, and tourist information: **State parks** *Information:* Oklahoma
Tourism and Recreation Dept., Literature Distribution, 215 N.E. 28th St.,
Oklahoma City, OK 73105; 800-652-6552 (in Oklahoma and surrounding
states), 405-521-2409 (elsewhere). *Entrance fees:* None. *Reservations:* Call
800-522-8465 (in Okla.), 800-654-8241 (in surrounding states), and
405-521-2464 (elsewhere). Confirmation must be returned with a deposit
for first night, check or credit card; accepted up to 1 year in advance but
not later than 5 days in advance; recommended 2 to 3 months in advance
(minimum, 2 nights on weekends) for early June—early September; 1 month
in advance, rest of year. *Restrictions:* Hunting limited to designated areas.
Dogs must be leashed. No alcohol in outdoor areas. *Facilities:* Swimming
and interpretative programs, Mem. Day—Labor Day. Boating and golf,
all year.

Arrowhead State Park is in eastern Oklahoma, about 90 miles south of Tulsa on the shores of Lake Eufaula, a 102,500-acre impoundment of the Canadian River. The park's 2,459 acres are in Oklahoma's lush and hilly Kiamichi country near the Kiamichi, Jackfork, and Sanbois mountain ranges. Lake Eufaula, Oklahoma's largest man-made lake, with 600 miles of shoreline, is popular with boating and fishing enthusiasts, its waters filled with black bass and catfishes. A marina offers launching facilities and boat rentals, fishing docks, and fishing guides. Waterskiing and horseback riding are regular activities, as are swimming from the park's beach and in its pool, and golf on its eighteen-hole course. *Park mailing address:* Route 1, Canadian, OK 74425. *Park phone:* (918) 339-2204.

Arrowhead Resort Lodge and Cabins

Arrowhead Resort Lodge, constructed of native stone and rough-hewn timber, is on the south shore of Lake Eufaula. It

has ninety-eight guest rooms, a restaurant overlooking the pool, and a gift shop. Each guest room has wall-to-wall carpeting, color television, a telephone, and a private bath. A few suites have private balconies, and half the rooms overlook the lake.

The resort also has 101 wood-frame cabins in a wooded area overlooking the lake, each with color television, a telephone, a tiled floor, a kitchenette, and a private bath. About half the cabins sleep two (in a separate bedroom) and have fireplaces. The larger cabins sleep four, with a separate bedroom for two and a queen-size hide-a-bed.

Accommodations: 98 lodge rooms and 101 cabins, all with private bath. *Towels and linens:* Provided. *Cooking and eating utensils:* Not provided. *Stove and refrigerator:* In cabins. *Pets:* Permitted in cabins. *Open:* Most of year, except in winter; call for precise dates. *Mailing address:* Route 1, Canadian, OK 74425. *Phone:* (918) 339-2711. *Driving instructions:* Arrowhead State Park is off U.S. 69, about 20 miles north of McAlester.

Beavers Bend State Park is in southeastern Oklahoma about 10 miles west of the Arkansas border and 10 miles north of the southern section of Ouachita National Forest, which is just north of the Texas line. The most popular explanation of how Beavers Bend got its name is that the Beaver family once owned much of the land now under Broken Bow Lake, a 14,220-acre impoundment of the Mountain Fork River. An alternative theory is that it was named for the area's many beavers. The 3,522-acre park, in the foothills of the Kiamichi Mountains, is at elevations ranging from 300 to 1,200 feet. Its terrain is hilly and wooded, the most common trees being oaks, maples, hickories, sweet gums, cedars, and ponderosa pines. A relatively large population of bald eagles winters here.

Popular activities include fishing, hiking, swimming, and picnicking. Facilities on the Mountain Fork River include a beach with a bathhouse. The river is stocked with rainbow trout; anglers

also go after smallmouth and largemouth bass and crappies.

Beavers Bend State Park has forty-seven wood-frame cabins, some of which are on the river; they vary in size, accommodating from two to six. Each has a fully equipped kitchenette and a private bath. The park also has a grocery store and restaurant with a deck overlooking the river.

Accommodations: 47 cabins with private bath. *Towels and linens:* Provided. *Cooking and eating utensils:* Provided. *Sto e and refrigerator:* Provided. *Pets:* Permitted. *Open:* All year. *Mailing address:* Beavers Bend State Park, PO Box 10, Broken Bow, OK 74728. *Phone:* (405) 494-6538. *Driving instructions:* From Broken Bow take Route 259 north 6 miles, then take Route 259A east 3 ½ miles to Beavers Bend State Park.

Boiling Springs State Park is in northwestern Oklahoma about 5 miles south of the Kansas border on the North Canadian River. Its 840 acres are on fairly flat, wooded terrain, the most common trees being oaks, pines, cedars, elms, box elders, mulberries, catalpas, introduced mimosas, and cottonwoods (one cottonwood being the second largest in the state). The park was named for its springs, a few of which, though cold, seem to boil up through sand. The park has several well-marked hiking trails, including the Seven Bridge trail, which crosses a spring seven times.

A 7-acre lake is stocked with black bass and channel catfish. Activities include camping, picnicking, swimming in the park's pool (which has a bathhouse), and golf on an adjacent eighteen-hole public course.

Boiling Springs State Park has two duplex cabins—each with two separate cabin units—in a wooded area beside the lake. Each cabin unit accommodates up to six and has a fully equipped kitchenette, a stone fireplace, and a private bath.

Accommodations: 4 cabins with private bath. *Towels and linens:* Provided. *Cooking and eating utensils:* Provided. *Stove and refrigerator:* Provided. *Pets:* Permitted. *Open:* All year. *Mailing address:* Boiling Springs State Park, Box 965, Woodward, OK 73802. *Phone:* (405) 256-7664. *Driving instructions:* From Woodward take Route 34 a mile north, then take Route 34C 5 miles east to Boiling Springs State Park.

Fountainhead State Park is in eastern Oklahoma about 30 miles south of Muskogee, on the shores of Lake Eufaula, a 102,500-acre impoundment of the Canadian River with 600 miles of shoreline. The 3,401-acre park, in a hilly, wooded area, is particularly popular with anglers, who go after black bass and catfishes. Other activities include hiking, tennis, picnicking, horseback riding, boating, swimming in the park's pool, and golf on its eighteen-hole course. A full-service marina with launching ramps and fishing docks rents out boats. *Park mailing address:* Box 85, West Star Route, Checotah, OK 74426. *Park phone:* (918) 339-2204.

Fountainhead Resort Lodge and Cabins

The sleek, modern semicircular main building of the Fountainhead Resort complex has 186 lodge rooms, a large lobby, a gift shop, and a restaurant that offers, in season, lakeside-terrace dining, western barbecues, and Hawaiian luaus.

Each guest room has wall-to-wall carpeting, color television, a telephone, a private bath, and a balcony. Half the rooms overlook the lake and the pool; the other half, the woods.

The resort also has twenty A-frame cottages arranged side by side in pairs. Each A-frame has an entire wall of glass looking out on the lake, as well as wall-to-wall carpeting, a kitchenette, color television, a telephone, and a private bath. A few units have fireplaces.

Accommodations: 186 lodge rooms and 20 cottages, all with private bath. *Towels and linens:* Provided. *Cooking and eating utensils:* Not provided. *Stove and refrigerator:* In cottages. *Pets:* Permitted in cottages only. *Open:* All year. *Mailing address:* Fountainhead Resort, West Star Route, Checotah, OK 74426. *Phone:* (918) 689-2501. *Driving instructions:* Fountainhead State Park is off I-40, roughly 14 miles southwest of Checotah.

Great Salt Plains State Park, about 840 acres in northern Oklahoma, is about 125 miles north of Oklahoma City and 20 miles south of the Kansas border. It runs along the shores of the 9,300-acre Great Salt Plains Lake and is within the boundaries of the Salt Plains National Wildlife Refuge. More than 280 species of birds have been identified here, many of them during migration. (Bald eagles, for example, spend the winter fishing near the dam's spillway.) An unusual feature is a designated area for digging selenite crystals, small, diamond-shaped clusters of crystals found underground in certain areas of the salt flats.

The park has a beach with a bathhouse, boat-launching ramps, a fish-cleaning station, softball diamonds, playgrounds, and a number of trails through the woods. Predominant trees are ashes, pines, locusts, and elms. Fishing is a popular activity, with anglers going after channel catfish, stripers, and walleyes.

The park has six one-room wood-frame cabins, five accommodating four, and one accommodating six. The cabins, with fully equipped kitchenettes and open porches, are in a wooded area a short walk from the lake. The cabins accommodating four have one double bed and one double hide-a-bed. The six-person cabin has two double beds and one double hide-a-bed.

Accommodations: 6 cabins with private bath. *Towels and linens:* Provided. *Cooking and eating utensils:* Provided. *Stove and refrigerator:* Provided. *Pets:* Permitted. *Open:* All year. *Mailing address:* Great Salt Plains State Park, Route 1, Box 28, Jet, OK 73749. *Phone:* (405) 626-4731. *Driving instructions:* Great Salt Plains State Park is off Route 38 about 8 miles north of Jet.

Greenleaf State Park, in eastern Oklahoma, is roughly 23 miles southeast of Muskogee. Its 565 acres are on the shores of the 930-acre Greenleaf Lake in the Cookson Hills, thickly wooded primarily with oaks, elms, and ashes. The area supports a wide variety of birds, especially robins, bluebirds, and cardinals. In migration season, during February and early March, as many as forty-two bald eagles have been sighted at one time. On their way up north the eagles like to stop and do some fishing. For park visitors, Greenleaf Lake has sizable populations of black and sand bass, crappies, and bream.

The park has a marina with launching facilities and a heated dock where anglers can buy bait, as well as a playground, picnic areas, and several hiking trails.

There are fourteen cabins that are constructed of stone, three with views of the lake. Thirteen cabins can accommodate four people, and one accommodates two. Ten cabins have fireplaces and stone walls; those without fireplaces have wood paneling. Each cabin has a kitchenette and a private bath.

Accommodations: 14 cabins, with private bath. *Towels and linens:* Provided. *Cooking and eating utensils:* Provided. *Stove and refrigerator:* Provided. *Pets:* Permitted. *Open:* All year. *Mailing address:* Greenleaf State Park, Route 1, Box 119, Braggs, OK 74423. *Phone:* (918) 487-5196. *Driving instructions:* Greenleaf State Park is on Route 10 about 3 miles south of Braggs.

Keystone State Park, in northeastern Oklahoma about 15 miles west of Tulsa, is a 715-acre reserve along the shores of Keystone Lake, a 26,000-acre impoundment of the Arkansas River. The terrain, hilly and wooded, especially with black and post oaks, is best viewed from a trail running along the lake and through a heavily wooded area. Lake Keystone attracts many fishermen. A state "Striped Bass Locator Map" has been developed, using ultrasonic telemetry. A small group of striped bass were captured in 1977 and "marked" with small transmitters emitting traceable ultrasonic pulses. Over the years, research biologists have been able to trace the movement patterns of the fish, and now anglers can determine exactly where bass congregate: Primarily around submerged islands.

Keystone State Park's marina has launching facilites (but no boats for rent), and a retail outlet sells fishing supplies. There are several picnic shelters, with tables and grills, and a playground, but no designated swimming areas. The lake is the site of "Sailboard Madness," in which hundreds of sailboarders compete in a two-day, five-race event.

Of twenty-one wood-frame cabins in a wooded area beside the lake, sixteen are one-bedroom units accommodating four, and five are two-bedroom units that accommodate six. Each smaller cabin has a small open porch; each larger one has a deck and a patio with lawn furniture. All have fully equipped kitchenettes and private baths.

Accommodations: 21 cabins with private bath. *Towels and linens:* Provided. *Cooking and eating utensils:* Provided. *Stove and refrigerator:* Provided. *Pets:* Permitted. *Open:* All year. *Mailing address:* Keystone State Park, Box 147, Mannford, OK 74044. *Phone:* (918) 865-4991. *Driving instructions:* From Tulsa take U.S. 64 west 16 miles, then take Route 151 south 1 ½ miles.

8 *Lake Murray State Park*   **OKLAHOMA**

Lake Murray State Park is in southern Oklahoma, about 7 miles
south of Ardmore and 10 miles north of the Texas border. The
park is in Oklahoma's Lake Country, along the shores of Lake
Murray, a 5,728-acre man-made lake created expressly for recrea-

tion. The 12,496-acre park is about 15 miles south of the Arbuckle Mountains, which geologists find interesting because of the unusually wide variety of geological structures found within such a small geographical area. Popular activities in the park include hiking, horseback riding, waterskiing, scuba diving, boating, and motorcycling. The park has beaches for swimming, a marina with launching ramps and boat rentals, fishing piers, a baseball diamond, playgrounds, a nine-hole golf course, and a miniature-golf course. *Park mailing address:* Box 1649, Ardmore, OK 73402. *Park phone:* (405) 223-4044.

Lake Murray Resort Lodge and Cabins

On a peninsula jutting into the lake, Lake Murray Resort has fifty-five guest rooms, a restaurant overlooking the lake, and a lounge. Each guest room has wall-to-wall carpeting, color television, a telephone, and a private bath. A few of the rooms are in suites with balconies.

The resort's eighty-eight cabins, about half of which are along the lake, come in two sizes. The smaller size accommodates four and has wall-to-wall carpeting, color television, a telephone, and a private bath. The larger one, accommodating six, has two bedrooms, a living room with a sofa bed, wall-to-wall carpeting, color television, a telephone, and a fireplace. None of the cabins has cooking facilities.

Accommodations: 55 lodge rooms and 88 cabins, all with private bath. *Towels and linens:* Provided. *Cooking and eating utensils:* Not provided. *Stove and refrigerator:* Not provided. *Pets:* Permitted in cabins only. *Open:* All year. *Mailing address:* Lake Murray Resort, Box 1329, Ardmore, OK 73402. *Phone:* (405) 223-6600. *Driving instructions:* Lake Murray State Park is on Route 77S about 7 miles south of Ardmore.

Osage Hills State Park, in northeastern Oklahoma, is about 40 miles northeast of Tulsa and 20 miles south of the Kansas border. Its 1,199 acres are in a hilly area wooded mainly with cottonwoods, oaks, willows, sycamores, and cedars. There is a large population of white-tailed deer, and wild turkeys, coyotes, and bobcats are occasionally sighted. The park has an 18-acre lake, good for fishing, boat rentals, a swimming pool with a bathhouse, tennis courts, playgrounds, softball diamonds, and hiking trails. The main trail, primarily used for guided horseback rides, is open to hikers as well when no more than a few riders are on it. The park is usually quiet. Many of its visitors have kept coming back for decades.

Osage Hills has eight cabins built of native stone and wood on a hill among sycamores, oaks, and cottonwoods. Seven were put up in the 1930s by the Civilian Conservation Corps; the eighth, built recently, was designed to complement the others. The cabins, which vary in size, can accommodate from four to six people. Each has a fully equipped kitchenette, a living room with a sofa bed and a stone fireplace, and a private bath.

Accommodations: 8 cabins with private bath. *Towels and linens:* Provided. *Cooking and eating utensils:* Provided. *Stove and refrigerator:* Provided. *Pets:* Permitted. *Open:* All year. *Mailing address:* Red Eagle Route, Box 84, Pawhuska, OK 74056. *Phone:* (918) 336-4141. *Driving instructions:* Osage Hills State Park is off U.S 60 about 16 miles east of Pawhuska.

Quartz Mountain State Park is about 40 miles south of Elk City, in a part of southwestern Oklahoma known as the Great Plains Country. The 4,284-acre reserve is along the shore of Altus Reservoir (Lugert Lake), a 6,260-acre impoundment of the Red River with 49 miles of shoreline and a reputation for excellent walleye, crappie, and bass fishing. The area served long ago as a wintering ground for the Kiowa and Comanche. The rugged, moderately wooded mountains for which the park is named are riddled with quartz bluffs.

Activities include swimming from sand beaches and indoor and outdoor pools, tennis, golf on a nine-hole course, and boating. A full-service marina is available, as are canoe and paddleboat rentals. The naturalist service offers interpretative programs and guided hikes and walks. *Park mailing address:* Route 1, Lone Wolf, OK 73655. *Park phone:* (405) 563-2238.

Quartz Mountain Resort Lodge and Cabins

A hundred yards from the lake, Quartz Mountain Resort has forty-five lodge rooms, a restaurant overlooking the water, saunas, and a game room. Each guest room, with a view of either the lake or the mountains, has wall-to-wall carpeting, color television, a telephone, and a private bath.

The resort also has available fourteen wood-frame cabins, each with a kitchenette. Six are duplexes and will accommodate four. The other eight cabins, which overlook the lake, can accommodate six.

Accommodations: 45 lodge rooms and 14 cabins, all with private bath. *Towels and linens:* Provided. *Cooking and eating utensils:* Not provided. *Stove and refrigerator:* In cabins. *Pets:* Permitted in cabins only. *Open:* All year. *Mailing address:* Quartz Mountain Resort, Lone Wolf, OK 73655. *Phone:* (405) 563-2424. *Driving instructions:* Quartz Mountain State Park is on Route 44 about 9 miles southwest of Lone Wolf.

In eastern Oklahoma, about 50 miles south of Muskogee and 25 miles northwest of Ouachita National Forest, is Robber's Cave State Park, named for a former outlaw refuge and consisting of 8,246 acres of heavily wooded terrain in the Sanbois Mountains. The park's three lakes, with a combined surface area of 189 acres, afford good fishing. The park has a dock where paddleboats and yak-a-noes (plastic rafts with backrests) are available for rent, a beach and a pool—both with bathhouses—a miniature-golf course, as well as a nature trail, hiking and riding trails, and an equestrian campground. Other facilites include a café, a grocery store, an amphitheater, a playground, and a softball diamond.

Robber's Cave has twenty-six wood-frame one- and two-bedroom cabins with cedar and pine siding. Accommodating from four to six people, they are on a hill overlooking the lake, in an area with pines, hickories, and oaks. A few cabins have wood paneling, and each has either a fireplace or a wood stove, a living room with a sofa bed, and a completely equipped kitchenette.

Accommodations: 26 cabins with private bath. *Towels and linens:* Provided. *Cooking and eating utensils:* Provided. *Stove and refrigerator:* Provided. *Pets:* Permitted. *Open:* All year. *Mailing address:* Box 9, Wilburton, OK 74578. *Phone:* (918) 465-2565. *Driving instructions:* Robber's Cave State Park is off Route 2 about 5 miles north of Wilburton.

The 515-acre Roman Nose State Park, in western Oklahoma about 70 miles northwest of Oklahoma City and 5 miles east of the North Canadian River, is in a large canyon with walls composed of red shale and white gypsum. The park has an 83-acre lake and a series of springs, one of which—the Spring of Everlasting Waters—flows at a rate 600 gallons per minute. The area was at one time heavily used by the Cheyenne, after whose chief, Roman Nose, the park takes its name.

Activities include hiking on trails lined by cedar, fishing and boating on Lake Boecher—with rentals available—golf, and tennis. There is a natural-rock swimming pool with a bathhouse and a natural spring (where wading is popular), lighted tennis courts, and a nine-hole golf course. *Park mailing address:* PO Box 227, Watonga, OK 73772. *Park phone:* (405) 623-4215.

Roman Nose Resort Lodge and Cabins

Roman Nose Resort's main lodge has two wings housing a total of forty-eight guest rooms, each room having wall-to-wall carpeting, color television, a telephone, and a private bath. The rooms have views of either Lake Boecher or a wooded hillside. The main lodge has a restaurant that overlooks the lake, as well as a recreation room.

Along a road near the swimming pool are the resort's ten wood-frame cabins, each of which accommodates four and has a kitchenette and a private bath.

Accommodations: 48 lodge rooms and 10 cabins, all with private bath. *Towels and linens:* Provided. *Cooking and eating utensils:* Not provided. *Stove and refrigerator:* In cabins. *Pets:* Permitted in cabins only. *Open:* All year. *Mailing address:* Box 61, Watonga, OK 73772. *Phone:* (405) 623-7281. *Driving instructions:* Roman Nose State Park is off Routes 8 and 8A, roughly 7 miles north of Watonga.

Sequoyah State Park is in eastern Oklahoma, about 12 miles northeast of Muskogee and adjacent to the 19,025-acre Fort Gibson Refuge and Hunting Area. The 2,730-acre park, along the shores of Lake Gibson, a 19,900-acre impoundment of the Arkansas River, encompasses a state waterfowl refuge. The wooded and hilly area is just south and west of the Boston Mountains and north of the Cookson Hills. Wildlife include deer, wild turkeys, and foxes.

The marina has rentals, docks, and launching facilities; and Lake Gibson has a large population of sunfishes, crappies, catfishes, and largemouth and white bass. There are several hiking and nature trails, as well as a "fitness" trail suitable for runners. The park has an eighteen-hole golf course with a clubhouse and pro shop, horse-drawn stagecoach and train rides, stables and bridle trails, tennis courts, and fields for softball. Swimming is available at either a pool or a beach, both of which have bathhouses. *Park mailing address:* Route 3, Box 112, Hulbert, OK 74441. *Park phone:* (918) 772-2046.

Western Hills Guest Ranch

On a peninsula that juts into Gibson Lake, Western Hills

Guest Ranch consists of four large buildings arranged in a horseshoe shape around a swimming pool. The complex has 101 guest rooms, a restaurant, a game room, a recreation room, and meeting and banquet facilities. Each guest room has wall-to-wall carpeting, color television, a telephone, and a private bath. Rooms overlooking the pool have balconies; the other rooms have lake views.

Fifty-four lakeside cottages are also available, which vary in size and can accommodate from two to six. Each of the twenty cottages accommodating six people has a kitchenette; and all have carpeting, color television, telephones, and private baths.

Accommodations: 101 lodge rooms and 54 cabins, all with private bath. *Towels and linens:* Provided. *Cooking and eating utensils:* Not provided. *Stove and refrigerator:* In twenty cottages. *Pets:* Permitted in cottages only. *Open:* All year. *Mailing address:* Box 509, Wagoner, OK 74477. *Phone:* (918) 772-2545. *Driving instructions:* Sequoyah State Park is off Route 51 about 6 miles east of Wagoner.

Tenkiller State Park   **OKLAHOMA**

Named for an Indian family that sold some of this land to the state, the 1,190-acre Tenkiller State Park is in eastern Oklahoma about 20 miles east of Muskogee and 20 miles west of the Arkansas border. Although the park is along the shore of Lake Tenkiller, a 12,900-acre impoundment of the Illinois River, between the Brushy Mountains and Cookson Hills, its terrain is relatively flat except for a few hills and a series of bluffs beside the lake.

The landscape is moderately wooded, mainly with hickory, oak, cedar, pine, elm, maple, redbud, and dogwood trees. The area has a sizable population of deer and birds, and red-tailed hawks and bald eagles can be seen, especially in autumn and winter.

The park has a marina with launching facilities and rentals, while the beach and swimming pool have bathhouses. Anglers go after catfishes, crappies, walleyes, sunfishes, and smallmouth, largemouth, and white bass; or they may fish the Illinois River below the dam for rainbow trout.

Tenkiller Park has forty wood-frame cabins, each with a kitchenette, a small porch, and a private bath. A U-shaped "cabana" has ten sleeping rooms, each with beds and a private bath. Twenty-four one-bedroom cabins can accommodate four people each; sixteen two-bedroom units can accommodate six. Eight of the two-bedroom units have fireplaces, and all overlook the lake.

Accommodations: 40 cabins and 10 sleeping rooms, all with private bath. *Towels and linens:* Provided. *Cooking and eating utensils:* In cabins. *Stove and refrigerator:* In cabins. *Pets:* Permitted in cabins only. *Open:* All year. *Mailing address:* Star Route, Box 169, Vlan, OK 74962. *Phone:* (918) 489-5641. *Driving instructions:* Tenkiller State Park is off Route 100 about 7 miles northeast of Gore.

Texoma State Park is in southern Oklahoma about 140 miles southeast of Oklahoma City and 10 miles north of the Texas border. The 1,882-acre park is beside Lake Texoma, a 93,080-acre impoundment of the Red River, which marks the boundary between TEXas and OklahOMA—hence the lake's name. The lake has 590 miles of shoreline, about 60 percent in Oklahoma, and is popular among fishermen, for its abundance of striped bass, and among boaters, as sailboats become more common. The park has a full-service marina with launching ramps.

Other activities include hiking, tennis, baseball, and horseback riding. The park has both a beach and a swimming pool, as well as an eighteen-hole golf course. Hiking and nature trails wind through the countryside, and interpretative programs are offered in summer, when the recreation staff organizes hayrides, cookouts, and rodeos for Friday and Saturday nights. *Park mailing address:* Box 279, Kingston, OK 73439. *Park phone:* (405) 564-2566.

Lake Texoma Resort Lodge and Cabins

Overlooking the lake, Lake Texoma Resort Lodge has a hundred guest rooms, a restaurant, a bring-your-own-bottle lounge, and a gift shop. Some of the guest rooms overlook the lake, and each has wall-to-wall carpeting, color television, a telephone, and a private bath.

The resort also has sixty-eight cabins equipped with kitchenettes. Twenty-eight of these overlook the lake, and each has two bedrooms, a living room with two sofa beds, color television, a telephone, air-conditioning, heat, and a fireplace. The other forty cabins are each a single room with color television and a telephone, as well as private bath. The small cabins can accommodate four; the larger ones eight.

Accommodations: 100 lodge rooms and 68 cabins, all with private bath. *Towels and linens:* Provided. *Cooking and eating utensils:* Not provided. *Stove and refrigerator:* In cabins. *Pets:* Permitted in cabins only. *Open:* All year. *Mailing address:* Box 248, Kingston, OK 73429. *Phone:* (405) 564-2311. *Driving instructions:* Texoma State Park is off U.S. 70 about 4 miles east of Kingston.

Wister State Park is in eastern Oklahoma about 70 miles southeast of Muskogee and 10 miles west of the Arkansas border. The 3,040-acre park is a few miles north of Ouachita National Forest, between the Sanbois Mountains to the north and the Kiamichi Mountains to the south. In this hilly and wooded terrain, the most common trees are oaks, pines, cedars, hickories, and redbuds. The park is adjacent to Lake Wister, with a 4,000-acre surface area and a 115-mile shoreline, where boating and fishing are the most popular activities. Anglers can rent boats and go after largemouth and smallmouth bass, sunfishes, catfishes, crappies, and walleyes.

There are several picnic areas and a swimming pool with a bathhouse. Rest rooms and showers, sheltered picnic areas, and tables and grills are found within the park.

Wister State Park has fifteen wood-frame one-bedroom cabins in a wooded area beside the lake. They can accommodate four people—two in the bedroom and two on the sofa bed in the living room. Each cabin has an open porch, a kitchenette, and a private bath; and two have fireplaces.

Accommodations: 15 cabins with private bath. *Towels and linens:* Provided. *Cooking and eating utensils:* Not provided. *Stove and refrigerator:* Provided. *Pets:* Permitted. *Open:* All year. *Mailing address:* Wister State Park, Route 2, Box 6B, Wister, OK 74966. *Phone:* (918) 655-7212. *Driving instructions:* Wister State Park is on U.S. 270 about 9 miles southwest of Poteau.

Oregon

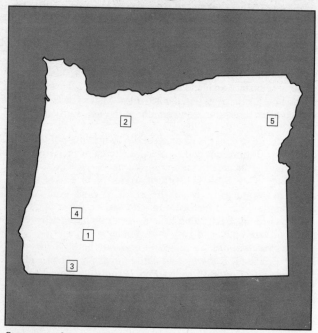

State map and tourist information: Dept. of Economic Dev., Tourism Div., 595 Cottage St. N.E., Salem, OR 97310; 503-378-6309. **State parks:** *Information:* Oregon State Parks, 525 Trade St SE, Salem, OR 97310; 503-378-6305. *Entrance fees:* None. *Reservations:* Contact individual lodgings. Deposit for first night by check; minimum stay, 3 nights. Reservations accepted beginning January 1 (recommended 3 months in advance for Mem. Day—Labor Day). *Restrictions:* Hunting limited to selected parks. Dogs must be leashed. *Facilities:* Swimming and boating, Mem. Day—Labor Day.

Crater Lake National Park, in southwestern Oregon about 60 miles north of Klamath Falls, comprises 183,180 acres and varies in elevation from 5,965 to 8,926 feet. The lake itself measures 25 miles in circumference and occupies the crater of Mount Mazama, a volcano that probably collapsed in on itself about seven thousand years ago. The lake is a deep blue, almost purple, color. There is no definitive explanation of what gives the lake its unique color, although its depth and lack of vegetation may allow only the shorter wavelengths of light—blue, indigo, and violet—to pass through the lake and pass back to its surface.

Crater Lake is the second deepest in the Western Hemisphere, going to a depth of almost 2,000 feet. Multicolored lava walls, at times as high as 2,000 feet, surround it, and a small volcanic cone in the center forms Wizard Island. Golden eagles are observed here, as are bears, deer, elk, and cougars.

Hiking, fishing, boating, and admiring the scenery are the most frequent activities. The park has a museum, and interpretative talks are given. *Park mailing address:* PO Box 7, Crater Lake, OR 97604. *Park phone:* (503) 594-2211.

Crater Lake Lodge and Cabins

Crater Lake Lodge, a huge wood-frame and stone Tyrolean-style building, has a deeply pitched shingled roof with dormer windows. The lodge, set along the crater rim at 7,000 feet, has a lobby with a large stone fireplace, a dining room with a ceiling supported by log beams, a cocktail lounge, a cafeteria, and a gift shop.

The seventy-nine lodge rooms are small but comfortably furnished and carpeted. Most share baths, and some have views of the lake. The lodge also administers twenty-two cabins. The eight ponderosa cabins have tile floors, upholstered easy chairs, and a private bath with shower. The fourteen sleeping cottages, which were built of oak, are more rustic and have hardwood floors, basic furnishings, and cold running water only (no baths). Visitors who stay in these cabins use the toilet facilities in the adjacent cafeteria building.

Accommodations: 79 lodge rooms, about half with private baths; 22 cabins, 8 with private bath. *Towels and linens:* In lodge

and ponderosa cabins. *Cooking and eating utensils:* Not provided. *Stove and refrigerator:* Not provided. *Pets:* Permitted in cabins only. *Open:* Early June through early September. *Mailing address:* Crater Lake, OR 97604. *Phone:* (503) 594-2511. *Driving instructions:* From Klamath Falls take U.S. 97 north to Route 62, which runs into the park. The lodge is about 6 miles beyond the toll station at the southern entrance to the park.

Mount Hood National Forest, in northwestern Oregon in the Cascade Mountains, has 1,077,711 acres that vary in elevation from about 4,200 feet to 11,239 feet at the summit of Mount Hood, once a volcano and now the highest point in Oregon. It is bordered on the south by the Willamette National Forest, and on the east, about half its boundary is contiguous with Warm Springs Indian Reservation. The terrain is thickly forested, mainly with pines, hemlocks, spruces, western red and Alaska yellow cedars, larches, and various species of fir—Douglas, white, Pacific silver, and alpine. The wildlife includes elk, deer, black bears, gray foxes, coyotes, cougars, beavers, otters, weasels, and Canada lynx; and bird life that ranges from wild turkeys to ravens, grouse, and great horned owls. Bald eagles winter along the Columbia River, which forms the forest's northern border as well as Oregon's border with Washington.

The forest encompasses several rivers, including the Columbia, the Hood, the White, the Salmon (famous for steelhead fishing), and the Clackamas. White-water rafting and kayacking on the Clackamas is a popular but dangerous sport, and forest rangers suggest that enthusiasts not try to run the river unless they have either a great deal of experience or a first-rate guide. The forest's hundreds of miles of hiking trails include a 100-mile section of the Pacific Crest, which runs for 2,600 miles from the Mexican border to Ross Lake on the Canadian border. Fishing for trout and steelheads, hunting for deer and black bears, camping, and cross-country skiing are other frequent activities. The downhill ski slopes are open all year. *National Forest mailing address:* 2955 N.W. Division, Gresham, OR 97030. *National Forest phone:* (503) 666-0700.

Timberline Lodge and Chalets

Built under the auspices of the Works Progress Administration and dedicated in 1937 by Franklin D. Roosevelt, Timberline Lodge is at the timberline, elevation 6,000 feet. This lodge was built largely by hand, and to this day the handmade furnishings are periodically restored by the "Friends of the Timberline" organization. Appointments range from a 400-ton chimney that stands 100 feet tall, to hand-carved newel posts and stained-glass

windows. Facilities include two bars, two restaurants, a gift shop, a sauna, a heated outdoor swimming pool, and complete base facilities for skiers.

The fifty-six guest rooms in the lodge have wall-to-wall carpeting, hand-hooked rugs, handmade bedspreads and 1930s furnishings, hand-sewn drapes, color television, a private bath, and views of either Mount Hood or the valley. Nine chalet rooms, used primarily by skiers, are furnished with bunk beds and have a shared bath.

Accommodations: 56 rooms with private bath, 9 chalet rooms with shared bath. *Towels and linens:* Provided. *Cooking and eating utensils:* Not provided. *Stove and refrigerator:* Not provided. *Pets:* Not permitted. *Open:* All year. *Mailing address:* Timberline Lodge, Timberline, OR 97028. *Phone:* (503) 272-3311. *Driving instructions:* From points west take Route 26 to Government Camp, then follow the signs to Timberline.

Oregon Caves National Monument is in southwestern Oregon, about 30 miles southwest of Ashland and roughly 10 miles north of the California border, at the northern tip of the Siskiyou National Forest. The monument is in the Siskiyou Mountains, which range in elevation here from 5,000 to 7,055 feet at Grayback Mountain. The monument centers around an enormous cavern formed by groundwater high in carbolic acid, which dissolves the marble bedrock. With walls entirely of marble, the caves are arranged essentially in four tiers connected by sometimes tortuous cave passages. The caves have fascinating flowstone formations, like the icicles beside a highway cut through rock.

The caves are electrically lighted, and guided tours are available. Children under six are not permitted. *Park mailing address:* Oregon Caves National Monument, OR 97523. *Park phone:* Ask your operator for Oregon Caves toll station #2.

Oregon Caves Chateau

Oregon Caves Chateau is a rustic wooden lodge built in 1934 on a mountainside. The six-story lodge, with its base on the canyon floor and its main entrance on the fourth floor, overlooks mountains thick with pines and marble outcroppings. The lodge has a wood-paneled lobby with two fireplaces built of marble and a picture window overlooking treetops, the canyon, and a waterfall. The lobby and the dining room have exposed-beam ceilings supported by massive peeled logs. (A mountain stream flows through the restaurant.) The lodge has a coffee shop.

The guest rooms in the lodge are furnished simply, each with brightly colored drapes and bedspreads, wall-to-wall carpeting, and a private bath. Most rooms have views.

Accommodations: 22 lodge rooms with private bath. *Pets:* Not permitted. *Open:* Early June through early September. *Mailing address:* PO Box 128, Caves Junction, OR 97523. *Phone:* (503) 592-3400. *Driving instructions:* From Grant's Pass take Route 199 south for 30 miles to Cave Junction, then go east on Route 46 (Caves Highway) for 20 miles.

Umpqua National Forest, in southwestern Oregon, immediately north and west of Crater Lake National Park on the western slopes of the Cascade Mountains, comprises some 1,029,351 acres and varies in elevation from 600 feet to 9,182 feet, at the summit of Mount Thielsen. The forest is wooded almost entirely with conifers, the most common species being Douglas fir, hemlock, ponderosa pine, and lodgepole pine. Many mountain streams, isolated lakes, waterfalls, and scenic rivers are in the forest, which has such first-rate trout lakes as Diamond Lake and Fish Lake, as well as Yasko Falls, an unusually scenic waterfall.

The mountainous and rugged terrain includes numerous "moist meadows" that appear near ridgetops and the headwaters of Little River, Jackson Creek, and the South and North Umpqua rivers. These meadows are verdant and thick with green fescue, blue wild rye, fernleaf, loveroot, false hellebore, mountain bluebells, and western coneflowers. Wildlife is widely varied—deer and bears are fairly common, and the forest is home to a large herd of Roosevelt elk estimated at about 2,500.

Fishing, hiking, sightseeing, cross-country skiing, and snowmobiling are the leading activities. Miles and miles of scenic roads and trails meander through the forest, and the North Umpqua

River has perhaps the best waters for steelheads in North America. *National Forest mailing address:* PO Box 1008, Roseburg, OR 97470. *National Forest phone:* (503) 672-6601.

Steamboat Inn and Cabins

On the banks of the North Umpqua River, Steamboat Inn is a complex that includes eight cabins, a main lodge with a restaurant, and a store selling fishing gear. The inn functions during the day as a roadside café but is transformed in the evening into a dining room, where hors d'oeuvres and carafes of wine are set out.

Behind the dining room, which has a stone fireplace, are eight wood-frame cabins, which are in a stand of firs and share a deck overlooking the North Umpqua River. They are simply but comfortably furnished and have wall-to-wall carpeting, pine paneling, and a private bath.

Accommodations: 8 cabins with private bath. *Towels and linens:* Provided. *Cooking and eating utensils:* Not provided. *Stove and refrigerator:* Not provided. *Pets:* Not permitted. *Open:* All year. *Mailing address:* HC 60, Box 36, Idleyld Park, OR 97447. *Phone:* (503) 496-3495 or 498-2411. *Driving instructions:* Steamboat Inn is on Route 138, 38 miles east of Roseburg.

Wallowa Lake State Park is in northeastern Oregon, about 79 miles east of La Grande in the Wallowa Whitman National Forest. The park is in the Wallowa Mountains along the shores of Wallowa Lake, elevation 4,500 feet, which was formed by a glacier and lies at the base of mountains that rise to 8,500 feet. The rugged terrain is wooded primarily with pines, red and white firs, tamaracks, and cottonwoods. Swimming is a regular activity (in summer), and the facilities here include a swimming area that, depending on the level of the lake, is either sandy or grassy.

The Eagle Cap Wilderness Area, which borders the park, has miles of hiking trails and is adjacent to many privately owned recreational facilities: A gondola to the summit of Mount Howard, which overlooks the lake and the mountains; marinas with boats for rent; horseback-riding facilities; even a go-cart track. Wallowa Lake Lodge, adjacent to the park, has launching facilities as well as boats, motors, canoes, and water bikes for rent. *Park phone:* (503) 432-4185. *Park mailing address:* Route 1, Box 323, Joseph, OR 97846.

Wallowa Lake Lodge and Cabins

Wallowa Lake Lodge is a large wood-frame clapboard building built in 1923 and enlarged in 1926. The lodge has a dining room that overlooks the lake, a lounge with a bar, a lobby with a stone fireplace, a small gift shop, and twenty guest rooms with adjoining baths. Two lodge rooms can be rented as a suite with a private bath, or, depending on who rents the room first, a room with a private bath and a room with a bath down the hall. The lodge rooms have hardwood floors partially covered with area rugs, wooden chairs and dressers, and a washbasin. About half the rooms have lake views; the other half overlook the mountains.

Thirteen cabins, most with a kitchen and a fireplace, vary in size, accommodating either one or two, or four to six. Eight cabins are next to the lake; the others are set back a short way. All have a bath with shower, except one, which has a tub.

Accommodations: 20 rooms with private or shared bath and 13 cabins with bath. *Towels:* Not provided in cabins. *Linens:* Provided. *Cooking and eating utensils:* In cabins. *Stove and*

refrigerator: In cabins. *Pets:* In cabins (additional charge). *Open:* Mid-June through Labor Day. *Mailing address:* Box 1, Joseph, OR 97846. *Phone:* (503) 432-4082 or (503) 426-4336 off season. *Driving instructions:* Wallowa Lake Lodge is off Route 82, 6 miles south of Joseph.

Pennsylvania

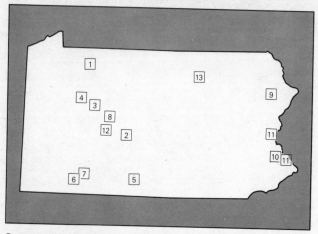

State map and tourist information: Bureau of Travel Development, 4th Floor, Forum Bldg., Harrisburg, PA 17120; 717-787-5453. **State parks:** *Information:* Bureau of Parks, PO Box 1467, Harrisburg, PA 17120; 717-787-8800. *Entrance fees:* None. *Reservations:* Write to Bureau of Parks for reservation applications. Spring reservations must be received no earlier than November 1 and no later than December 15 for mid-December lottery. Summer reservations accepted no earlier than January 1 and no later than March 15 for mid-March lottery. Fall reservations no earlier than June 1 and no later than July 15th for mid-July lottery. Full payment in advance required once confirmation is received. Minimum and maximum stay of 1 week in summer; 1 week or ½ week in spring and fall. Contact individual park to be placed on a waiting list. *Restrictions:* Hunting limited to certain parks. Dogs must be leashed (not allowed in overnight areas). No alcohol. *Facilities:* Swimming, boating, and interpretative programs, Mem. Day—Labor Day. Golf, April—October. Skiing November—March.

Allegheny National Forest is in northwestern Pennsylvania, about 90 miles northeast of Pittsburgh and adjacent to New York's 65,000-acre Alleghany State Park. At an average elevation of about 2,000 feet on the Alleghany Plateau, the forest consists of ½-million acres of densely forested terrain. There are two particularly beautiful tracts of virgin forest here—the Tionesta Scenic Area and the Heart's Content Area—where visitors can wander through mature stands of hemlocks, birches, eastern white pines, black cherries, beeches, and maples. The forest floor is rife with ferns, trilliums, forget-me-nots, wood sorrel, dwarf ginseng, spring beauties, and other flora. The area supports a healthy population of raptors, particularly broad-winged, red-tailed and red-shouldered hawks. Bald eagles have been observed during winter along the Allegheny River. Activities include hiking on hundreds of miles of trails (a 70 mile section of the North Country Trail meanders through the forest), camping, fishing, boating, and other water sports, and cross-country skiing and snowmobiling. Canoeing and kayacking are becoming more popular. *Forest mailing address:* Allegheny National Forest, Box 847, Warren, PA 16365. *Forest phone:* (814) 723-5150.

The Kane Manor Country Inn

Built in 1896, this 18,000-square foot mansion is on 250 acres. The mansion was the second homestead of the family of General Thomas Kane, who led the Bucktail Division through the battles of Gettysburg and the second battle of Bull Run. General Kane's sons were as brave as he—one, a physician, performed surgery on himself twice, and another, an industrialist, walked 1,300 miles across the arctic to rescue a fellow explorer.

The Kane Manor Country Inn has 11 guest rooms decorated primarily with antiques. There are two dining rooms, each of which seats 16, a cellar pub, and a gift shop. On weekdays guests are served a complimentary Continental breakfast, and on weekends, a full breakfast.

Accommodations: 11 rooms, 7 with private bath. *Pets:* Not permitted. *Open:* All year. *Mailing address:* 230 Clay Street, Kane, PA 16735. *Phone:* (814) 837-6522. *Driving instructions:* Take I-80 to exit 8, Route 66, go north into Kane; take Route 6 east to the edge of town, turn left at the yellow light; proceed 1½ blocks.

The 3,500-acre Black Moshannon State Park is in central Pennsylvania, about 35 miles northeast of Altoona, on a mountainous plateau and surrounded by hills. The park is 5 miles east of the Allegheny Front, where it was once feared that the rugged terrain would prohibit the area's development. Wooded mainly with oaks, maples, eastern white pines, and hemlocks, the park has a natural bog area filled with mushrooms, peat, and even sphagnum moss, which is rare this far south of Canada.

A large lake is in the center of the park, and visitors can rent paddleboats at a nearby concession. Black Moshannon Creek is stocked by the state with trout. The park also has swimming facilities, miles of trails, interpretive programs, and a small grocery store that operates during the summer months. Hunting is permitted here, the main targets being white-tailed deer, black bears, and wild turkeys. Trappers in the park harvest raccoons and beavers.

The park's thirteen mortar-and-log cabins are on a hill above the lake in a thick stand of pines that obscure the view. The cabins, in two sizes, can accommodate either four or six people. The cabins have fireplaces with inserts, and are furnished and come with electric stoves and refrigerators. Sanitary and shower facilities are in a central location.

The park frequently has firewood for the use of cabin occupants; because the pieces of wood are large, occupants are advised to bring an ax or a saw.

Accommodations: 13 cabins with shared bath. *Towels and linens:* Not provided. *Cooking and eating utensils:* Not provided. *Stove and refrigerator:* Provided. *Pets:* Not permitted. *Open:* Mid-April through mid-December. *Mailing address:* RD 1, Box 183, Phillipsburg, PA 16866. *Phone:* (814) 342-1101. *Driving instructions:* From Altoona take Route 220 north to Route 504; then take Route 504 west—it runs right through the park.

Named for the unusually clear meandering stream, Clear Creek State Park is a 1,208-acre reserve in northwestern Pennsylvania, about 80 miles northeast of Pittsburgh. The Clarion River to the northwest separates it from the 506,465-acre Allegheny National Forest, and on its southeastern border is the 10,113-acre Kittanning State Forest. The area is thick with hemlocks, eastern white pines, mountain laurels, and rhododendrons, and both river and creek are rife with fish. Anglers catch brook trout in Clear Creek, and panfish, walleye, northern pike, and smallmouth bass in the Clarion River.

A class-C waterway that flows at an average of 4 miles per hour, the Clarion River is frequented by canoeists, who can rent canoes at a concession near the park. Some 400 feet of shore of a small man-made lake is maintained as a swimming beach. Hunting is permitted on the northernmost 210 acres of the park, where hunters mainly go after white-tailed deer, black bears, wild turkeys, and grouse.

The park has a nature center with a small museum, a self-guided nature trail, a 2-acre sledding and tobogganing area, and during the summer, a nature-interpretation program that features films and hikes. Bear Town Rocks, a particularly scenic area, affords a panorama of the surrounding terrain from a tower.

The park's twenty-two cabins are rustic log buildings put up in the 1930s by the Civilian Conservation Corps. Several include a great deal of stonework, and the larger ones have stone fireplaces. The smaller cabins have stoves and most cabins are close to either the Clarion River or Clear Creek. Furnished with up to four bunks plus tables and chairs, each is equipped with a stove and a refrigerator. Although not required, the park frequently has firewood available for cabin occupants; because these pieces are large, occupants are advised to bring along an ax or a saw. Sanitary facilities are in a central location.

Accommodations: 22 cabins with central shared bath. *Towels and linens:* Not provided. *Cooking and eating utensils:* Not provided. *Stove and refrigerator:* Provided. *Pets:* Not permitted. *Open:* All year. *Mailing address:* RD 1, Box 82, Sigel, PA 15860. *Phone:* (814) 752-2368. *Driving instructions:* Take I-80 to exit 13, then go north on Route 36 to Sigel; from Sigel take Route 949 north for 4 miles.

In northwestern Pennsylvania, about 15 miles southwest of the Allegheny National Forest and roughly 80 miles northeast of Pittsburgh, Cook Forest State Park encompasses some 6,500 acres. Cook Forest has been protected because of its large stands of virgin timber, including 171 acres of virgin eastern white pines and hemlocks populated by numerous raptors—Cooper's, red-shouldered, and broad-wing hawks as well as various species of owls (look for them among the hemlocks). The many hardwoods throughout the forest, including red and white oaks, yellow, white, and black birches, and beeches and maples make for good fall foliage.

Canoes may be rented from nearby concessions for use on the Clarion River, which borders the park on the south. There is also a swimming pool, 27 miles of hiking trails, an old sawmill, an ice-skating pond, cross-country ski trails, 20 miles of snowmobile trails, and a fishing area for children and the handicapped.

The park has an interesting tradition: Each year an outdoor Easter service is held at dawn in an amphitheater in the campground. Over the years it has attracted anywhere from four hundred to three thousand people.

Cook Forest's twenty-four cabins were constructed of logs in the 1930s by the Civilian Conservation Corps. Of the twelve small cabins, two have fireplaces, and all of the larger cabins, which can accommodate up to eight, have stone fireplaces. One group of cabins is next to Toms Run, a trout-stocked stream that flows into the Clarion River; the other is on a hillside overlooking trees. Sanitary and shower facilities are in a central location.

Accommodations: 24 cabins with central shared bath. *Towels and linens:* Not provided. *Cooking and eating utensils:* Not provided. *Stove and refrigerator:* Provided. *Pets:* Not permitted. *Open:* Mid-April through November. *Mailing address:* Box 120, Cooksburg, 16217. *Phone:* (814) 744-8407. *Driving instructions:* Cook Forest State Park is on Route 36, 7 miles south of Leeper.

Cowans Gap State Park is in southern Pennsylvania about 50 miles southeast of Altoona and 20 miles north of the Maryland border. Its 1,085-acres are in a wind gap, or valley, in the Tuscarora Mountains, which range in elevation from 1,400 to 2,200 feet. The park is wooded primarily with oaks, maples, and pines, and its 42-acre lake has a sand-and-grass beach with a bathhouse and is stocked with brown, rainbow, and palomino trout. Rowboats and paddleboats are for rent, and launch facilities are available for visitors bringing their own craft. (Only electric motors are allowed on the lake.)

One of two developed trails encircles the lake, and numerous firebreaks (roads cut through the woods to prevent the spread of fire) ensure good hiking. Winter activities include cross-country skiing, ice-skating, ice-fishing, and sledding.

Among a wide variety of wildlife are deer, raccoons, foxes, black bears, and an occasional bobcat. Commonly sighted birds include grosbeaks, nuthatches, woodpeckers, grackles, and red-tailed and sharp-shinned hawks.

The park has ten wood-frame and stone cabins, two-bedroom units accommodating four people, built in the 1930s by the Civilian Conservation Corps in a wooded area. Each has a kitchenette, an open porch, and a stone fireplace with inserts. The cabins have no running water or sanitary facilities, which are available in a central location.

Accommodations: 10 cabins with central shared bath. *Towels and linens:* Not provided. *Cooking and eating utensils:* Not provided. *Stove and refrigerator:* Provided. *Pets:* Not permitted. *Open:* Mid-April through mid-December. *Mailing address:* HC 17266, Fort Loudon, PA 17224. *Phone:* (717) 485-3948. *Driving instructions:* From Fort Loudon take Route 75 north to Richmond Furnace Road, then take Richmond Furnace Road west into the park.

Kooser State Park is in southwestern Pennsylvania about 30 miles southwest of Johnstown in the Laurel Mountains. The hilly terrain, with elevations from 2,200 feet to 2,700 feet, is wooded mainly with hemlocks, white pines, beeches, birches, maples, and oaks—red and black—and rhododendrons account for a good part of the area's understory. The 170-acre park is adjacent to 51,000 acres of state forest. Kooser has a mile-long hiking trail, as well as shorter ones and cross-country ski trails, all of which extend into the state forest, as do 3 miles of designated snowmobiling trails.

The park has a small lake with a beach and a bathhouse and is stocked with trout. (There is no boating.) Other facilities include picnic pavilions, a playing field, and a snack bar.

Kooser Park has nine cabins—five of wood-frame construction and four built of logs—that are one- or two-bedroom units accommodating either four or six people. Each has a kitchenette, a stone fireplace, and an open porch. The cabins have hot and cold running water; sanitary facilities consist of outside pit toilets.

Accommodations: 9 cabins with privy. *Towels and linens:* Not provided. *Cooking and eating utensils:* Not provided. *Stove and refrigerator:* Provided. *Pets:* Not permitted. *Open:* All year. *Mailing address:* RD 4, Box 256, Somerset, PA 15501. *Phone:* (814) 445-8673. *Driving instructions:* Kooser State Park is off Route 31, about 11 miles west of Somerset.

Linn Run State Park is in southwestern Pennsylvania, about 25 miles southwest of Johnstown in the Laurel Hill Mountains. Its 612 acres are at an elevation of 1,740 feet in a small, narrow valley wooded mostly with poplars and maples and, higher up on the mountainsides, oaks. Two sides of the park are contiguous with Forbes State Forest, and visitors here often extend hiking jaunts from the park into the forest. The park has 5 miles of well-marked trails and several picnicking pavilions, one of which is rented to groups of up to forty-eight. Stream waters are a little too acidic to support a large population of fish, and the park therefore offers fishing only at the times when the state stocks the waters.

Characteristic wildlife includes deer, grouse, wild turkeys, and an occasional black bear. The park is within 30 miles of several downhill-ski areas: Laurel Mountain, Sugarbush Mountain, and Hidden Valley.

The park's ten wood-frame cabins, in a forested area near a stream, were built in the 1930s by the Civilian Conservation Corps. They vary in size from one room to two bedrooms, and can accommodate from two to six. Each has a kitchenette and a stone fireplace but no plumbing—running water is available from a pump between each two units, and sanitary facilities consist of outside pit toilets.

Accommodations: 10 cabins with privy. *Towels and linens:* Not provided. *Cooking and eating utensils:* Not provided. *Stove and refrigerator:* Provided. *Pets:* Not permitted. *Open:* All year. *Mailing address:* Box 527, Ligonier, PA 15658. *Phone:* (412) 238-6623. *Driving instructions:* From Ligonier take U.S. 30 southeast to Route 381, then take Route 381 south into Rector and look for signs to the park access road.

Parker Dam State Park is in northern Pennsylvania, at the western edge of Moshannon State Forest about 20 miles south of Saint Marys. Its hilly 895 acres reach elevations ranging from 1,500 to 2,000 feet. Trees common in the wooded terrain include oaks, maples, beeches, red pines, and spruces. Several streams run through the park, and a lake formed by Parker Dam has a sand beach with a bathhouse. Visitors can rent canoes or paddleboats, and launching facilities are available (electric trolling motors only). Activities include fishing, picnicking, hiking, snowmobiling, cross-country skiing, and sledding.

The 75-mile-long Quehanna Trail passes through numerous park habitats, running over rocky areas, grasslands, swamps, beaver dams, and at one point entering an extensive stand of white birches. Bird life is abundant, the most common species being evening grosbeaks, mallards, red-tailed hawks, and great horned owls.

Parker Dam's sixteen cabins, accommodating from four to eight, are constructed of chestnut logs and are in a wooded area near a stream. Each has a stone fireplace and a wood stove, a kitchenette area, and one, two, or three rooms. Between each two cabins is a small toilet and shower facility.

Accommodations: 16 cabins with shared bath. *Towels and linens:* Not provided. *Cooking and eating utensils:* Not provided. *Stove and refrigerator:* Provided. *Pets:* Not permitted. *Open:* Mid-April to late December. *Mailing address:* Penfield, PA 15849. *Phone:* (814) 765-5082. *Driving instructions:* From Penfield take Route 153 southeast for 2½ miles, then turn northeast on the park access road and go another 2½ miles.

Promised Land State Park is in northeastern Pennsylvania, about 30 miles southeast of Scranton in the Pocono Mountains. Wooded primarily with pines and scattered stands of oaks and maples, its 2,971 acres are on a plateau at about 1,800 feet above sea level and are surrounded by another 8,039 acres of the Delaware State Forest, whose eastern boundary is contiguous with the Delaware Water Gap National Recreation Area. The park's two lakes (450 acres and 173 acres) are used for swimming, fishing, and boating. A sand beach has a bathhouse, and visitors can rent rowboats or canoes, or bring their own boats (only electric motors permitted) and launch them here. Most of the park's numerous hiking trails—from a short, self-guided trail to one 12 miles long running through a rugged, hilly area—connect with longer trails into the state forest. Winter activities include ice-fishing and skating, snowmobiling on 24 miles of trails, and cross-country skiing. A large variety of wildlife includes deer, woodpeckers, and hawks, and an unusually large population of black bears.

The park has twelve log cabins set in a wooded area, varying in size from one to two bedrooms and accommodating from two to four people. Each has a kitchenette, an open porch, and a stone fireplace; some have wood stoves. The cabins have no running water or sanitary facilities, which are available in a central washhouse near the cabins.

Accommodations: 12 cabins with central shared bath. *Towels and linens:* Not provided. *Cooking and eating utensils:* Not provided. *Stove and refrigerator:* Provided. *Pets:* Not permitted. *Open:* Mid-April through mid-December. *Mailing address:* Promised Land State Park, RD 1, Box 96, Greentown, PA 18426. *Phone:* (717) 676-3428. *Driving instructions:* Take I-84 to Route 390 (exit 7), then take Route 390 south for about 5 miles. It runs right through the park.

Ralph Stover State Park is in southeastern Pennsylvania, about 35 miles north of downtown Philadelphia and 2 miles west of the Delaware River and the New Jersey border. Its 45 acres in the Tohickon Creek Valley are wooded primarily with ashes, black walnuts, oaks, and hemlocks. Tohickon Creek is a stocked trout stream where fishermen gather along its banks as soon as trout season opens. At one time a small dam on the creek powered a gristmill; and although the gristmill no longer exists, the dam's raceway still forms a small impoundment where visitors often go wading. High Rocks Scenic Overlook, at the summit of a 100-foot sheer rock face rising above the creek, offers sightseers a panoramic view of a horseshoe bend in the Tohickon. It also attracts rock climbers, who find the cliff ideal for practicing.

Deer, muskrat, squirrels, and raccoons are the most commonly sighted mammals in the park, and characteristic bird life includes bluejays, robins, warblers, grouse, and, along the creek, ducks and geese, especially during migrations. The principal activities here are light hiking, fishing, and picnicking.

The state park has six stone-and-wood cabins in a wooded area near the creek. Each can accommodate four people and has a small stove-refrigerator combination, a stone fireplace, and a paved patio. The cabins have no baths, and guests use a central shower facility and a central vault toilet building.

Accommodations: 6 cabins with shared central shower and sanitary facilities. *Towels and linens:* Not provided. *Cooking and eating utensils:* Not provided. *Stove and refrigerator:* Provided. *Pets:* Not permitted. *Open:* Mid-April through mid-December. *Mailing address:* RR 1, Box 209, Pipersville, PA 18947. *Phone:* (215) 982-5560. *Driving instructions:* Ralph Stover State Park is at the end of Stump Road, about 5 miles east of Plumsteadville.

Sixty miles long but only 60 feet wide, Roosevelt State Park runs in an unbroken strip along the banks of the Delaware River from Easton south to Bristol, Pennsylvania. It beautifully preserves the Delaware Canal—virtually all of whose engineering and operational structures are still intact—as both an historic and a recreational site. The canal was completed in 1833 by the state, in part to block the Lehigh Coal and Navigation Company—which owned the Lehigh Canal—from gaining control of the entire interconnecting canal system that served the metropolitan markets of Philadelphia and New York. Built during the massive public-works projects of the 1830s, its principal use was to haul coal downriver. Lehigh Coal and Navigation obtained control in 1861 and continued operation of the canal until 1932.

A good way to appreciate the canal's historical significance is to visit the Hugh Moore Park and Canal Museum in Easton (215) 258-7155; and the best way to appreciate the Delaware River is to walk along the canal towpath, which runs for miles through some of the prettiest scenery in the Northeast. The autumn foliage is outstanding, and the summer foliage is lush.

Along the towpath are interesting historic and natural sights, including many locks and aqueducts, covered bridges, tiny villages, and several natural phenomena: Hexenkopf Rock, a strange-looking promontory that pops out of an elevated meadow, takes its name from a Pennsylvania Dutch word that means "witch's head" and overlooks a scenic part of the river. Ringing Rocks, a collection of mineral deposits in an empty field, sound like bells when you tap them with a hammer.

The Pennsylvania Rivers Inventory designated the Delaware a Priority 1-A Waterway—that is, an endangered scenic river in need of protection because of its "outstanding aesthetic and recreational value." In 1983, Congress designated a 73-mile stretch of the Delaware a "wild and scenic river." The waterway is currently threatened by a plan to pump millions of gallons of water a day out of the shallows to supply a nearby nuclear power plant. Local residents opposed to the proposed pumping station—near Point Pleasant, in roughly the center of the park—have succeeded in suspending construction during the time the shad are running. *Park address:* Box 615A, RR 1, Upper Black Eddy, PA 18972. *Park phone:* (215) 982-5560.

All the accommodations below, listed from north to south, are privately owned. All are adjacent to the park and are convenient for inn-to-inn hiking or bicycling.

The Riegelsville Hotel

Near the northern end of the Delaware Canal, about 9 miles south of Easton, The Riegelsville Hotel, built in 1838, is set between the river and the canal. Several of the guest rooms overlook the river, a view slightly obscured by a large Norway maple, and the public rooms retain much of its original rough-sawn siding and stone walls. The dining room and bar are decorated with Art Nouveau stained-glass panels made by the owners' son, who works here now as head chef. The hotel has two dining rooms, both with stone fireplaces where fires are kept going when it's cold.

The twelve guest rooms are small and simply but comfortably furnished. Some have iron four-poster or walnut high-backed beds; several have Victorian floral-print wallpaper; some have water views; and some have private half or full baths.

Accommodations: 12 rooms, 7 with private full or half bath. *Pets:* Permitted. *Open:* All year. *Phone:* (215) 749-2469. *Driving instructions:* Take Route 32 to Riegelsville and turn onto River Road—the hotel is less than a hundred feet from one of the oldest surviving Delaware River bridges.

Bridgeton House

Adjacent to the Upper Black Eddy—Milford, New Jersey, bridge, Bridgeton House is a restored early-nineteenth-century roadside inn. Its brick exterior has been painted white; its shutters, a deep red. The inn is furnished with many antiques. The living room, for example, has an antique tavern table surrounded by twig chairs, braided rugs, and assorted primitive-style pieces.

One guest room has a reproduction canopied bed and French doors overlooking the river and the bridge. Several other guest rooms also have views of the river, and each is furnished with some antiques. All seven guest rooms have painted floors and exposed beams, and several have four-poster beds.

Accommodations: 7 rooms with private bath. *Children:* Not permitted. *Pets:* Permitted if well behaved. *Smoking:* Not per-

mitted. *Open:* All year. *Mailing address:* River Road, Upper Black Eddy, PA 18972. *Phone:* (215) 982-5856. *Driving instructions:* Bridgeton House is on Route 32 (River Road), about 8 miles south of Riegelsville.

Evermay-on-the-Delaware

An 1871 Victorian building painted gold and tan, Evermay-on-the-Delaware is on 25 acres overlooking the Delaware River adjacent to a county park. An elegant hotel operating from 1871 until the early 1930s, when it closed, it opened again in 1982 after an elaborate restoration.

The parlor has two fireplaces, a grandfather clock, brocade camelback settees, and a number of period antiques. Tea is served each afternoon, and sherry is put out each evening. Rates include breakfast, served each morning in a glass conservatory at the rear of the building—peacocks stroll about on the other side of the glass.

The sixteen guest rooms have antique quilts and pillows, marble-topped dressers, walnut beds, and Oriental rugs; a few of the rooms still have their original fireplaces. The Carriage House has two guest rooms on its ground floor and a two-bedroom suite with a sitting room and bath on its second story.

Accommodations: 16 rooms with private bath. *Children:*

Not permitted. *Pets:* Not permitted. *Open:* All year. *Phone:* (215) 294-9100. *Driving instructions:* Evermay-on-the-Delaware is on Route 32 (River Road), roughly 12 miles north of New Hope, Pennsylvania.

The Golden Pheasant Inn

Both of the Golden Pheasant Inn's two buildings were built to service commercial traffic on the Delaware Canal during the nineteenth century. The main building, constructed of fieldstone and dating from 1857, was entirely restored in 1967. Its six guest rooms are all furnished with period antiques and have wall-to-wall carpeting, as well as marble-topped washstands and bureaus, floral-print wallpapers, lace curtains, and carved beds. One room has a Franklin stove, and all overlook either the river or the canal. The public rooms include a greenhouse-dining room dressed up with a profusion of plants, and another dining room decorated with velvet love seats and Tiffany lamps.

Stover Mansion, an 1810 Federal brick building, has a multigabled mansard roof and gingerbread trim. It was built by the owners of a grist and lumber mill immediately across the road; its paneling and doors are of cherry, and its floors, of random-width pine. The kitchen, dining room, living room, and three of the guest rooms have a fireplace, and all guest rooms are furnished with antiques and Oriental, hooked, or braided rugs.

Accommodations: 14 rooms with shared bath. *Pets:* Not permitted. *Open:* All year except from the weekend before Christmas to mid-February. *Mailing address:* River Road, Erwinna, PA 18920. *Phone:* (215) 294-9595. *Driving instructions:* The Golden Pheasant Inn is on Route 32 (River Road), about 17 miles north of New Hope, Pennsylvania.

Black Bass Hotel

One of Roosevelt State Park's historic buildings, the Black Bass Hotel was constructed in 1745 and over the years has accommodated everyone from mid-eighteenth century fur trappers to early-nineteenth century Delaware Canal work gangs—though we're assured that George Washington never slept here. The hotel was bought in 1949 by its current owner, who filled it with antiques, including a solid pewter bar from Maxim's in Paris. The decor includes exposed beams and uprights, a display of British-royalty memorabilia, and antique lanterns. The sitting room has a fireplace and a harpsichord, the hotel's bar has a piano that is active on weekends, and its dining room has restored tables, candlelight, unobtrusive classical music, and traditional American cuisine.

Each bed in the seven guest rooms is covered with either a handmade quilt or a hand-crocheted spread, and all have antiques—a four-poster, a maple canopied bed, a heavily carved floor-to-ceiling headboard. Guest rooms on the river side have iron balconies. One suite is available, with two bedrooms, a living room, and a private bath.

Accommodations: 7 rooms with shared bath; 1 suite with private bath. *Pets:* Permitted if well-behaved. *Open:* All year. *Phone:* (215) 297-5770. *Driving instructions:* Black Bass Hotel is on Route 32 (River Road), about 7 miles north of New Hope.

Centre Bridge Inn

Dating from 1705, Centre Bridge Inn is a beautifully restored Colonial building between the Delaware River and the canal, about 100 feet or so from the bridge between Stockton, New Jersey, and Centre Bridge. Its elegant main floor is furnished with formal period antiques, and downstairs there is a dining room and bar, each with exposed beams, a fireplace, and a tavern atmosphere. Food and drink are served in warm weather on an outdoor terrace overlooking the river.

The nine guest rooms are furnished with many antiques including brass and four-poster beds; other appointments are dormer and sloping-dormer windows, handmade quilts, and period reproduction wallpapers.

Accommodations: 9 rooms with private bath. *Children:* Not permitted. *Pets:* Not permitted. *Open:* All year. *Mailing address:* River Road, New Hope, PA 18938. *Phone:* (215) 862-2048. *Driving instructions:* Centre Bridge Inn is at the junction of Route 32 (River Road) and Route 263, about 2 miles north of New Hope.

The Inn at Phillips Mill

A restored stone barn that once served as a gristmill, The Inn at Phillips Mill has five guest rooms, a small formal dining room, a lounge with leather furnishings and a stone fireplace, and a glassed-in dining terrace with a copper roof.

Each guest room has an antique bed (some are four-posters, some brass) covered with a handmade quilt and a private bath. One guest room is actually a suite with a sitting room.

Rates include a complimentary breakfast, which is left each morning outside the guest rooms. The dining room has a French menu.

Accommodations: 5 rooms with private bath. *Children:* Under 12 not permitted. *Pets:* Not permitted. *Open:* Mid-February to the first week in January. *Mailing address:* North River Road, New Hope, PA 18938. *Phone:* (215) 862-2984. *Driving instructions:* The Inn at Phillips Mill is on Route 32 (River Road), about 1 ½ miles north of New Hope.

S. B. Elliott State Park's 330 acres are in central Pennsylvania in the Moshannon State Forest, about 20 miles east of Du Bois. Although on a plateau, and with an average elevation of about 2,000 feet, the terrain in the park is fairly level and thickly wooded primarily with red and white oaks, red maples, and scattered stands of eastern white pines. Visitors are more than likely to spot deer, grouse, wild turkeys, and occasionally black bears. Numerous trails in the park link up with longer ones in the state forest. At the edge of the park, until three years ago, there was a state nursery that was developed in the 1930s by the Civilian Conservation Corps.

The park has no swimming or boating facilities, but visitors can go to Parker Dam State Park, about 7 miles north of S. B. Elliott.

The park has six log cabins in an area wooded with a stand of eastern white pines. Built by the Civilian Conservation Corps, they are either one room or one-bedroom units; three will accommodate eight, and the other three can hold four. Each has a stove and a refrigerator as well as a stone fireplace, but no plumbing. Running water is available at a spigot outside the cabin, and sanitary facilities consist of outside vault toilets.

Accommodations: 6 cabins with outside toilet. *Towels and linens:* Not provided. *Cooking and eating utensils:* Not provided. *Stove and refrigerator:* Provided. *Pets:* Not permitted. *Open:* Mid-April through mid-December. *Mailing address:* Route 1, Box 65, Penfield, PA 15849. *Phone:* (814) 765-5082. *Driving instructions:* Take I-80 to exit 18, then take Route 153 north for a mile.

The 780-acre Worlds End State Park, in northeastern Pennsylvania, is at an elevation of between 1,100 and 2,000 feet in the Endless Mountains about 50 miles west of Scranton, adjoining Wyoming State Forest. The hilly and thickly wooded terrain has mainly pines, hemlocks, maples, cherries, birches, beeches, and some oaks. Loyalsock Creek runs through the park, as does Loyalsock Trail, which is maintained by the Alpine Hiking Club for its 56 miles. The creek, a noted Pennsylvania water trail, has a swimming beach with a bathhouse. Anglers fish for trout and bass, and canoers use the park as a starting point. Deer, wild turkeys, foxes, grouse, and black bears are found in the area. The park has an 8-mile-long backpacking trail and 3 miles of snowmobiling trails. Eagles Mere, 5 miles from the park, has a toboggan run.

Worlds End has nineteen log cabins in a wooded area beside Loyalsock Creek. With either one or two bedrooms, they can accommodate from two to six. Each has a kitchenette, a stone fireplace, and a wood stove. None has plumbing—pit toilets and water pumps are outside the cabins; a wash house is nearby.

Accommodations: 19 cabins with privy. *Towels and linens:* Not provided. *Cooking and eating utensils:* Not provided. *Stove and refrigerator:* Provided. *Pets:* Not permitted. *Open:* Mid-April through mid-December. *Mailing address:* Worlds End State Park, PO Box 62, Forksville, PA 18616. *Phone:* (717) 924-3287. *Driving instructions:* Worlds End State Park is about 5 miles northwest of LaPorte on Route 154, between Forksville and LaPorte.

South Carolina

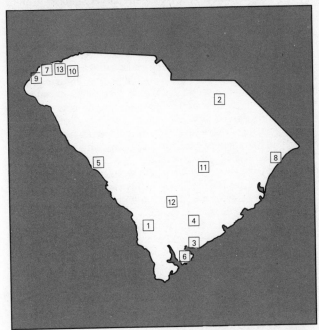

State map and tourist information: Div. of Tourism, Edgar A. Brown Bldg., 1205 Pendleton St., Columbia, SC 29201; 803-758-8816. **State parks:** *Information:* Div. of Parks, Edgar A. Brown Bldg., 1205 Pendleton St., Columbia, SC 29201; 803-758-7507. *Entrance fees:* $1 per car; $5 per recreational vehicle (June 1—Labor Day); waived for lodgers. *Reservations:* Contact individual park. Send $50 deposit for 1-week stay; $25 deposit for less than 1 week. Reservations accepted (and recommended, especially for parks in the mountains or by the beach) by October 20th for the next year (mail only). After the first Monday in November, reservations can be made by telephone. Minimum 1 week, maximum 2 weeks for June—August. *Restrictions:* No hunting. No alcohol in day use areas (permitted in cabins). Dogs must be leashed (not allowed in lodgings). *Facilities:* Swimming and interpretative programs, Mem. Day—Labor Day.

The 307-acre Barnwell State Park is in southern South Carolina about 40 miles southeast of Augusta among gently rolling hills that are thickly wooded, in the park's undeveloped areas, with oaks, hickories, sweet gums, poplars, and pines. At two small lakes (15 acres and 10 acres) visitors can rent rowboats or paddleboats or go swimming at a sandy beach that has a bathhouse. Fishing is popular, anglers going after largemouth bass, crappies, and bream. Other popular activities include hiking, camping, and picnicking. The facilities include a playground.

An attraction of note is about 5 miles north of the park: Healing Springs, a series of artesian wells where people can be seen filling containers with the reportedly curative waters.

Barnwell park has five octagonal wood-frame cabins constructed of redwood. They are in a wooded area close to the lake but have no lake view. Each has two bedrooms, a fully equipped kitchenette, a living room with a sofa bed, a private bath, and a sun deck.

Accommodations: 5 cabins with private bath. *Towels and linens:* Provided. *Cooking and eating utensils:* Provided. *Stove and refrigerator:* Provided. *Pets:* Not permitted. *Open:* All year. *Mailing address:* Box 147, Blackville, SC 29817. *Phone:* (803) 284-2212. *Driving instructions:* Barnwell State Park is off Route 3 about 3 miles south of Blackville.

Cheraw State Park is in northeastern South Carolina about 5 miles south of Cheraw and 15 miles northeast of the Carolina Sandhills National Wildlife Refuge. The 7,361-acre park is mostly undeveloped and ocupies a relatively flat area wooded primarily with oaks, sweet gums, poplars, hickories, dogwoods, and redbuds. At the 323-acre Dogwood Lake, an impoundment of Eureka Creek, visitors can rent paddleboats and go after bream, bass, crappies, and catfishes, with all of which it is stocked. It also has a sandy beach with a bathhouse, and a nature trail runs along the lake to the dam. Other facilities include an archery range, a bridle path, a playground, picnic shelters, and a miniature-golf course.

Cheraw State Park's eight wood-frame one-bedroom cabins are on a rise overlooking the lake. Each has a living area with a sofa bed, a fully equipped kitchenette, a screened porch, electric heating, and air-conditioning.

In the woods are two wood-frame group lodges which are primitive-style dormitory cabins. One accommodates 64, the other, 140. Both have central bath-shower and kitchen-dining facilities.

Accommodations: 8 cabins with private bath, 2 group lodges with shared bath. *Towels and linens:* Provided. *Cooking and eating utensils:* Provided. *Stove and refrigerator:* Provided. *Pets:* Not permitted. *Open:* All year. *Mailing address:* PO Box 888, Cheraw, SC 29520. *Phone:* (803) 537-2215. *Driving instructions:* Cheraw State Park is off U.S. 1, about 5 miles south of Cheraw.

Edisto Beach State Park, 1,250 acres in southeastern South Carolina, is on Edisto Island about 35 miles southwest of Charleston. Edisto Island actually comprises two islands: The larger one is separated from the mainland by the intercoastal waterway and from the smaller island by a brackish marsh. The terrain is marshy, relatively flat, and wooded primarily with pines and live oaks. A popular pastime on the almost 3 miles of beach is collecting shells and sand dollars. Another is birding. Between the ocean and the marsh, a wide variety of bird species appear, especially great and snowy egrets, little and great blue herons, belted kingfishers, greater yellowlegs, green- and black-crowned night herons, northern harriers, red-tailed hawks, and American kestrels.

Visitors can fish either in the ocean or in tidal creeks, swim at a beach area with a bathhouse, hike, and picnic. The park also has interpretative programs, a playground, a miniature-golf course, a boat ramp, and a loading dock.

The park has five wood-frame cabins on a bluff overlooking a marsh about a mile from the ocean. The cabins are two-bedroom units that will accommodate as many as six. Each has a fully equipped kitchenette, a living room with a sofa bed, a private bath, and a screened porch. All have views of the marsh, which will delight birders.

Accommodations: 5 cabins with private bath. *Towels and linens:* Provided. *Cooking and eating utensils:* Provided. *Stove and refrigerator:* Provided. *Pets:* Not permitted. *Open:* All year. *Mailing address:* Route 1, Box 84, Edisto Island 29438. *Phone:* (803) 869-2156. *Driving instructions:* From Charleston take U.S. 17 west to Route 174 then take Route 174 south to the park.

The 1,270-acre Givhans Ferry State Park is in southeastern South Carolina about 30 miles northwest of Charleston. It extends along the banks of the Edisto River, which is bordered by cypresses, cedars, and sweet gums and looks like the color of strongly brewed tea as a result of tannic acids released by the cedars. The terrain combines flat areas, hills, and ridges; and ash, oak, loblolly pine, and hickory trees are also common. The park's large population of wildlife includes deer, raccoons, and bobcats, and among the plentiful bird life are red-tailed hawks and ospreys, which like to fish in the river.

The river has a sandbar beach with a bathhouse but no lifeguards, and visitors swim at their own risk. Other facilities include playing areas for baseball, football, and volleyball, as well as a picnic shelter, a recreation building, and two nature trails. One nature trail runs along several of the park's ridges and crosses a few footbridges; another follows an old roadbed for 5 ½ miles.

The park has four wood-frame cabins on a 30-foot cliff overlooking the Edisto River. Each has two bedrooms and can accommodate as many as six with a fully equipped kitchenette, a private bath, a brick fireplace, and a living room with a sofa bed and a brick fireplace.

Accommodations: 4 cabins with private bath. *Towels and linens:* Provided. *Cooking and eating utensils:* Provided. *Stove and refrigerator:* Provided. *Pets:* Permitted. *Open:* All year. *Mailing address:* Givhans Ferry State Park, Route 3, Box 49, Ridgeville, NC 29472. *Phone:* (803) 873-0692. *Driving instructions:* Givhans Ferry State Park is off Route 61 about 3 miles west of Givhans.

Hickory Knob State Park is in western South Carolina, just across Clark Hill Lake from the Georgia border and about 45 miles northwest of Augusta, Georgia. Its 1,091 hilly and heavily wooded acres lie along the shores of Clark Hill Reservoir and are within the boundaries of the southernmost section of the 75,000-acre Sumter National Forest.

Hickory Knob has both resort and conference facilities. In 1982 it opened a 6,560-yard championship golf course with a pro shop where carts and other equipment can be rented. There is also a swimming pool for cabin and lodge guests, lighted tennis courts, three trapshooting ranges (of which two are skeet ranges), equestrian trails, a fishing pier, bicycles and rowboats for rent, and launching, docking, and refueling facilities, nature trails, a putting green, and playground equipment. The park's stables can accommodate fifty horses, and its kennel can hold eighty dogs. An arena is suitable for horse or dog shows.

The park's accommodations include sixty lodge rooms, as well as eighteen cabins arranged in nine duplexes. The main building contains a dining room, a coffee shop, a gift shop, and a "lodge hall" with color television, a stone fireplace facing a carpeted conversation pit, a grand piano, pool tables, and card tables. Each of the lodge guest rooms, close to the main building in a group of modern one-story buildings, has wall-to-wall carpeting, color television, a telephone, air-conditioning, and large windows. These rooms are designed so that two adjoining units can be turned into a suite.

The nine cabin duplexes are of modern design and, like the lodge buildings, are in a wooded area. Each cabin is a one-bedroom unit accommodating up to six people and has two double beds, a sofa bed in its living room, a fully equipped kitchenette, color television, a telephone, and a private bath. Nine cabins have fireplaces.

Accommodations: 60 lodge rooms and 18 cabins, all with private bath. *Towels and linens:* Provided. *Cooking and eating utensils:* In cabins. *Stove and refrigerator:* In cabins. *Pets:* Not permitted. *Open:* All year. *Mailing address:* Route 1, Box 199-B, McCormick, SC 29835. *Phone:* (803) 443-2151. *Driving instructions:* Hickory Knob State Park is off U.S. 378 about 7 miles southwest of McCormick.

Hunting Island State Park is on the Atlantic Ocean in southeastern South Carolina, about 16 miles southeast of Beaufort. Its 5,000 acres are on Hunting Island, which has large areas of brackish marsh and is wooded with willows, oaks, and loblolly and slash pines. The park includes 5 miles of Atlantic coast line. Some 200 yards up from the beach, a former lighthouse affords a fine view to those willing to climb its stairs. At the beach are swimming areas and four bathhouses. The park has a 3-mile hiking trail, a nature trail, and a boardwalk that runs through a marsh where many waterfowl congregate: Great and snowy egrets; little, great blue, black-crowned, and green herons; greater yellowlegs; kingfishers; and ospreys. At least one osprey nest is in active use and is especially popular among brown pelicans. Crabs and shrimp abound, and in the fall hungry park visitors harvest them in competition with the herring gulls. Other popular activities include picnicking, miniature golf, and ocean fishing. The facilities include a snack bar and a store that sells groceries and sundries.

Some of the park's fourteen wood-frame cabins are directly on the beach. Others are set back, but most have ocean views. Cabins vary in size from two to three bedrooms each and can accommodate from six to ten. Each has a fully equipped kitchenette and a private bath. Some have a screened porch, and some have a fireplace.

Accommodations: 14 cabins with private bath. *Towels and linens:* Provided. *Cooking and eating utensils:* Provided. *Stove and refrigerator:* Provided. *Pets:* Not permitted. *Open:* All year. *Mailing address:* Route 1, Box 668, Frogmore, SC 29920. *Phone:* (803) 838-2011. *Driving instructions:* Hunting Island State Park is at the end of U.S. 21, about 16 miles east of Beaufort.

Keowee-Toxaway State Park, 1,000 acres in northwestern South Carolina about 30 miles northwest of Greenville and 10 miles south of the North Carolina border, is 1,100 feet up in the foothills of the Appalachian Mountains, along the shores of the 18,000-acre Lake Keowee. The area is wooded mainly with oaks, hickories, pines, hemlocks, walnuts, and dogwoods. A creek, thickly lined in places with rhododendrons, runs through the northern section of the park, an area that was once a center of the Cherokee civilization. Archaeologists did extensive digging here before large stretches of the terrain were flooded to form Lakes Keowee and Jocassee. The park's interpretative center has a collection of Indian artifacts, which are also exhibited in a number of kiosks set up along a nature trail.

Another hiking trail, 5 ½ miles long, runs from high ground down to the lake. Popular activities include camping, picnicking, and fishing. There are no designated swimming areas, but visitors can swim at their own risk. The wide variety of wildlife includes deer, foxes, black bears, bobcats, wild turkeys, turkey vultures, red-tailed hawks, and quail.

The park has one stone-and-wood cabin in a wooded area beside the lake. Its two levels can accommodate a total of up to ten people with three bedrooms, three baths, a fully equipped kitchenette, a living room with sofa bed, and two stone fireplaces.

Accommodations: 1 cabin with private bath. *Towels and linens:* Provided. *Cooking and eating utensils:* Provided. *Stove and refrigerator:* Provided. *Pets:* Not permitted. *Open:* All year. *Mailing address:* Sunset, SC 29685. *Phone:* (803) 868-2605. *Driving instructions:* Keowee-Toxaway State Park is off Route 11 about 20 miles northeast of Walhalla.

Myrtle Beach State Park is on the Atlantic Ocean in eastern South Carolina about 25 miles south of the North Carolina line. Its 312 acres are 3 miles from the town of Myrtle Beach, which bustles with diversions, such as nightclubs, movie theaters, video-game arcades, restaurants, boutiques, and amusement areas. Golfers frequent the more than thirty nearby courses. The park itself has ocean beaches, as well as a swimming pool, a fishing pier, a miniature-golf course, picnic areas, playgrounds, a nature trail, and a nature center that conducts interpretative programs and campfire activities. The relatively flat terrain is wooded with lob-lolly and slash pines and a few palms and oaks. The profuse spring wildflowers include azaleas and wild lilies.

The park's five cabins are 100 yards from the beach. Each is a two-bedroom unit with a fully equipped kitchenette, a living room with sofa bed, and a screened porch. They have hardwood floors and can accommodate up to six in each. There are also two apartments in a building that was once a camp trading post, subsequently converted when a new trading post was built. Each of the apartments, which are in the campground area, has a kitchenette and a private bath. One can accommodate two people; the other, which has two baths, can accommodate eight.

Accommodations: 5 cabins and 2 apartments, all with private bath. *Towels and linens:* Provided. *Cooking and eating utensils:* Provided. *Stove and refrigerator:* Provided. *Pets:* Not permitted. *Open:* All year. *Mailing address:* U.S. 17 South, Myrtle Beach, SC 29577. *Phone:* (803) 238-5325. *Driving instructions:* Myrtle Beach State Park is off U.S. 17 about 3 miles south of the town of Myrtle Beach.

The 1,165-acre Oconee State Park, in northwestern South Carolina about 40 miles west of Greenville and 10 miles east of the Georgia border, is in the Appalachian Mountains. On a plateau between Stumphouse and Long mountains, it has an average elevation of about 2,000 feet. The thickly wooded area's mixture of hardwoods and softwoods is composed predominantly of oaks, maples, hickories, hemlocks, and eastern white and shortleaf pines. The park is flanked on two sides by a 79,000-acre section of Sumter National Forest. The popular Foothills Trail runs about 70 miles from the park through the national forest and on to Table Rock State Park. Numerous other trails wind through the park, as does a small mountain stream that empties into a 22-acre lake.

Lake fishing is a regular activity, and visitors can rent rowboats, paddleboats or canoes. The park has a grassy shoreline with a bathhouse, as well as picnic areas, a playground, and a restaurant. A variety of planned activities include square dancing, bingo, slide shows, and nature walks. Twelve miles away is the Chattooga River, popular for its trout fishing and whitewater rafting. (The movie *Deliverance* was filmed here.)

There are sixteen wood-frame cabins and three log cabins available. Thirteen are along the lake and the other six are back in a wooded area. The cabins vary in size from one to two bedrooms and can accommodate from four to eight people. Each has a fully equipped kitchenette, a screened porch, and a stone fireplace. Several have a sofa bed in the living room, and the one that accommodates eight has a sleeping loft.

Accommodations: 19 cabins with private bath. *Towels and linens:* Provided. *Cooking and eating utensils:* Provided. *Stove and refrigerator:* Provided. *Pets:* Not permitted. *Open:* All year. *Mailing address:* Star Route, Walhalla, SC 29691. *Phone:* (803) 638-5353. *Driving instructions:* Oconee State Park is on Route 107 about 12 miles north of Walhalla.

Pleasant Ridge State Park is in northwestern South Carolina, about 20 miles north of Greenville and 8 miles south of the North Carolina border. Its 300 acres are in the foothills of the Appalachian Mountains, at an average elevation of about 1,200 feet. The hilly, forested area is populated mainly with oaks, maples, hickories, hemlocks, and pines; while wildlife includes deer, wild turkeys, raccoons, foxes, a few hawks, and several species of ducks. The park has a 2½-acre lake, a sandy beach, and a bathhouse, as well as picnic and camping areas and a playground. Fishing for bream is popular, and visitors can rent rowboats or paddleboats. An easy-to-follow nature trail runs through a thickly wooded area. Visitors may take side trips to Caesars Head Mountain (elevation 3,208 feet) or to a stock-car racetrack 2 miles away.

The park has two wood-frame cabins in a wooded area back from the lake. These two-bedroom units can each accommodate six people, and each has an open porch, a fully equipped kitchenette, and a living room with a sofa bed and a brick fireplace.

Accommodations: 2 cabins with private bath. *Towels and linens:* Provided. *Cooking and eating utensils:* Provided. *Stove and refrigerator:* Provided. *Pets:* Not permitted. *Open:* All year. *Mailing address:* Box 2, Cleveland, SC 29635. *Phone:* (803) 836-6589. *Driving instructions:* From Greenville take U.S. 25 north to Route 11, then go 3 miles west on Route 11.

Poinsett State Park, in central South Carolina about 30 miles southeast of Columbia in Manchester State Forest, is a 55,000-acre nature preserve. The 1,000-acre park was named for Robert J. Poinsett, who lived in the area and introduced poinsettias into the United States after he had seen them growing wild in Mexico. The hilly terrain, surrounded by relatively flat land, is wooded primarily with oaks, hickories, maples, and pines. Several swampy areas are populated by egrets, herons, kingfishers, red-tailed hawks, and deer and foxes. A 15-acre pond has a sandy beach with a bathhouse, and fishermen go after bream and bass. Rowboats or paddleboats are available for rent.

The park's 6 miles of trails include an interpretative trail 1 ½ miles long that runs through fairly level terrain, as well as a 4½-mile hiking trail running through wooded areas at higher elevations. The park has a restaurant, a playground and picnic areas.

Four wood-frame cabins are located in a wooded area. Each two-bedroom unit can accommodate from four to six and has a fully equipped kitchenette, a living room with a sofa bed, and a stone fireplace. Two cabins have screened porches.

Accommodations: 4 cabins with private bath. *Towels and linens:* Provided. *Cooking and eating utensils:* Provided. *Stove and refrigerator:* Provided. *Pets:* Not permitted. *Open:* All year. *Mailing address:* Route 1, Wedgefield, SC 29168. *Phone:* (803) 494-8177. *Driving instructions:* Poinsett State Park is off Route 261 about 18 miles southeast of Sumter.

Santee State Resort Park, 2,364 acres, is in central South Carolina, about 50 miles southeast of Columbia along the shore of Lake Marion, which, with its sister lake, Moultrie, forms the Santee-Cooper lake complex, covering some 171,000 acres with 450 miles of shoreline. The park is across the water from the Santee National Wildlife Refuge, a 35,000-acre preserve along the Atlantic flyway. Both park and refuge are prime spots for birders, especially during the migration seasons, when many species of waterfowl pass through. The terrain is wooded primarily with oaks, hickories, sweet gums, cypresses, poplars, and long- and shortleaf pines.

Park activities center around the water. The park rents out both rowboats (visitors must attach their own motors) and paddleboats, and there are two launching ramps, a fishing pier, and a bait-and-tackle shop. (The world-record black crappie and catfish were caught here.) Elsewhere is a grassy beach with a bathhouse.

Other activities include tennis, hiking, bicycling (bike rentals available), and picnicking. Santee State Park is surrounded by numerous resort facilities, including two eighteen-hole golf courses within 3 miles. There's a restaurant open all year, as well as the hundred-seat "Village Round," a day-use meeting and banquet facility.

The park has thirty redwood rondettes, which are octagonal cabins with two bedrooms, a fully equipped kitchenette, a private bath, and a deck. Twenty of the rondettes are in a wooded area beside a creek. The other ten, each of which has its own floating dock, are on two piers.

Accommodations: 30 rondette cabins with private bath. *Towels and linens:* Provided. *Cooking and eating utensils:* Provided. *Stove and refrigerator:* Provided. *Pets:* Not permitted. *Open:* All year. *Mailing address:* Route 1, Box 79, Santee, SC 29142. *Phone:* (803) 854-2408. *Driving instructions:* From Sumter take I-95 to exit 98, then take Route 6 northwest 1½ miles.

Table Rock State Park is in northwestern South Carolina about 25 miles northwest of Greenville and 3 miles south of the North Carolina border. The 3,068-acre park is in the foothills of the Appalachian Mountains, around the base of Table Rock Mountain (elevation 3,124 feet), where, according to legend, a mythical giant Indian chief is said to have dined. The hilly terrain is wooded primarily with oaks, maples, hickories, sweet gums, poplars, hemlocks, and eastern white pines. The park's 36-acre lake has a sandy beach with a diving board and a bathhouse. Visitors can rent paddleboats, rowboats, and canoes; the anglers among them go after trout, bass, bream, and crappies.

The park has numerous trails, one of which goes to the summit of Table Rock Mountain; another, to the top of Pinnacle Mountain (elevation 3,425 feet); and a third along Carrick Creek to the lake. Foothills Trail runs for 70 miles from Pinnacle Mountain through Sumter National Forest to Oconee State Park. Table Rock has nature and interpretive programs, a playground, a miniature-golf course, and a restaurant overlooking the lake.

Fifteen wood-frame cabins are scattered around the park, most in a group near the lake, of which one cabin has a view. They vary in size from one to three bedrooms and can accommodate from four to eight people. Each has a fully equipped kitchenette, a screened porch, a stone fireplace, and a private bath.

Accommodations: 15 cabins with private bath. *Towels and linens:* Provided. *Cooking and eating utensils:* Provided. *Stove and refrigerator:* Provided. *Pets:* Not permitted. *Open:* All year. *Mailing address:* Route 3, Pickens, SC 29671. *Phone:* (803) 878-9813. *Driving instructions:* From Pickens take U.S. 178 north to Route 11; then go about 5 miles east to Table Rock State Park.

South Dakota

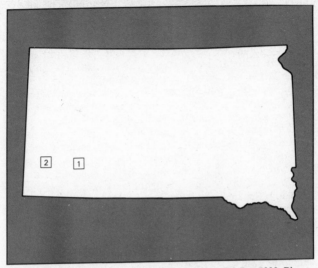

State map and tourist information: Div. of Tourism, PO Box 6000, Pierre, SD 57501; 800-952-2217 (in-state) and 800-843-1930 (out-of-state) or 605-773-3301. **State parks:** *Information:* Parks Div., Dept. of Game, Fish & Parks, 445 E. Capitol, Anderson Bldg., Pierre, SD 57501; 605-773-3391. *Entrance fees:* $12 per vehicle, annually; $6 for 3-day stay; $2 per person, daily (under 12, free). *Reservations:* Contact individual lodging. Deposit for first night generally required. (Recommended that reservations be made in early winter for mid May—September.) *Restrictions:* No hunting. Dogs must be leashed in outdoor areas. *Facilities:* Swimming, June—Labor Day. Boating, May—September. All parks limited October—April.

Badlands National Park, 243,500 acres in southwestern South Dakota, about 50 miles southeast of Rapid City, is in a corner of the state occupied primarily by the Black Hills National Forest and Buffalo Gap National Grassland. The park got its name from the Indian term *mako sica*, meaning "bad land," and its terrain is indeed forbidding, eerie and desolate. The Badlands looks as inhospitable as the moon, seemingly as lifeless and as beautiful, with myriad canyons, cliffs, precipices, spires, and rock formations. After adjusting to the barren landscape, you begin to see patches of vegetation—prairie grass and wildflowers. The predominant colors are tan and gray, although the rocks are streaked with mineral stains (primarily iron) forming bands of red and pink. About 70 million years ago the area was a shallow sea, which receded, leaving some of the shale sediments that are sprinkled in certain areas of the park. Later, volcanic ash blew into the area on winds from the west and combined with sediments left by wide, shallow flooding rivers that washed silt down from the black hills. Today, the Badlands are extremely arid, receiving fewer than 16 inches of rain a year, which, combined with melting snow, the processes of freezing and thawing, and some wind erosion, are the active forces that create the terrain.

Among the Badlands' many fossil remains, archaeologists have discovered the skeletons of three-toed horses, saber-toothed cats, and a prehistoric rhinoceros-like animal. (The Indians called them "thunderhorses" when they discovered their skeletons.) A Fossil Exhibit Trail passes by partially excavated fossils protected by glass bubbles, and the visitors' center has a "touch and feel" room where visitors can handle fossils. The most popular activity, sightseeing, can easily be done by car or on foot or horseback. Although animal life might at first seem scarce, antelope, mule deer, coyotes, golden eagles, cliff swallows, and other wildlife, especially birds, frequent the Badlands. There's also a herd of 300 to 500 buffalo, protected within one section of the park. The main visitor season is summer, when the temperature is frequently in the high nineties and the hundreds. *Park mailing address:* Box 6, Interior, SD 57750. *Park Phone:* (605) 433-5361.

Cedar Pass Lodge and Cabins

Owned by the U.S. Government and leased to the Oglala Sioux tribe, the Cedar Pass complex consists of a 1930s lodge facility, remodelled in 1985, and nineteen cabins. The early sections of the lodge were built of logs, which were stuccoed over on the exterior and left exposed inside. The cabins are also stucco outside, with knotty pine inside. They are in a flat area surrounded by tannish-gray buttes streaked with bands of red. The complex includes a large gift shop that sells souvenirs and Indian craft pieces, mainly jewelry, and a restaurant specializing in buffalo meat. (There are buffalo burgers and an open-faced "Indian taco" made from Indian fry-bread and filled with buffalo meat, lettuce, tomato, and cheese.)

The cabins, in a grove of elms, vary in size and can accommodate from three to eight people, some with single beds, some with doubles, and some with a combination. Most have wall-to-wall carpeting, some with rustic, ranch-style furnishings, others with oaken furnishings. Each has a private bath and individually controlled heat and air-conditioning. There are no telephones, no television, and no kitchens, although guests may use the picnic tables and cook on their own camping stoves.

There are no sports facilities at the complex, but running and jogging are enthusiastically encouraged by the lodge manager.

Accommodations: 19 cabins with private bath. *Towels and linens:* Provided. *Cooking and eating utensils:* Not provided. *Stove and refrigerator:* Not provided. *Pets:* Permitted. *Open:* May through mid-October. *Mailing address:* PO Box 5, Interior, SD 57750. *Phone:* (605) 433-5460. *Driving instructions:* Take I-90 to exit 131, then proceed south 8 miles to the Badlands National Park headquarters.

Custer State Park is in southwestern South Dakota about 25 miles south of Rapid City. The 73,000-acre state park (the second largest outside Alaska) is in the Black Hills and is contiguous with Black Hills National Forest. The rugged and mountainous terrain here has elevations ranging from a low of 3,700 feet in French Creek Canyon (where golden eagles nest) to a high of 7,242 feet at the state's highest point, Harney Peak. The area is wooded with ponderosa pines and white spruces, especially at the higher elevations, as well as bur oaks, aspens, and birches, which are common along the streams and drainage areas. There are four man-made lakes and such natural wonders as the Cathedral Spires—tall, thin granite needles—that attract mountain climbers. Wildlife includes bighorn sheep, deer, elks, coyotes, pronghorn antelope, and the nation's largest herd of bison.

Popular activities are hiking on many trails, several of which are self-guided; fishing; and horseback riding. Other attractions are the preserved cabin of South Dakota's first poet laureate, Badger Clark; the Black Hills Playhouse; and a park museum. *Park address:* Star Route 3, Box 70 Custer SD 57730. *Park phone:* (605) 255-4515.

Custer State Game Lodge and Cabins

A large wood-frame and stone building with hills rising in front and buffalo grazing on its grounds, the State Game Lodge and its attached motel additions have forty-seven guest rooms, a dining room, a cocktail lounge, fast-food facilities, a grocery store, and a gift shop. Each lodge room is a motel-type unit with Danish-modern furnishings, wall-to-wall carpeting, and a private bath.

The State Game Lodge's twenty cabins, of wood-frame and logs, are in a wooded meadow beside a creek. Five large cabins can accommodate up to eight people, and fourteen cabins have either one or two bedrooms. Each cabin is simply but comfortably furnished with wall-to-wall carpeting, a fully equipped kitchen, and up-to-date furniture and appliances.

Accommodations: 47 lodge rooms and 20 cabins, all with private bath. *Towels and linens:* Provided. *Cooking and eating utensils:* In cabins. *Stove and refrigerator:* In cabins. *Pets:* Per-

465

mitted if leashed. *Open:* May 15 through October 1. *Mailing address:* Custer, SD 57730. *Phone:* (605) 255-4541. *Driving instructions:* From Rapid City take Route 79 south to Route 36 West. This joins U.S. 16A, which brings you to the State Game Lodge, 2½ miles from the entrance.

Blue Bell Lodge and Resort

At an elevation of 5,000 feet, Blue Bell Lodge and Resort consists of a 1920s rustic lodge built of ponderosa pine logs and eighteen chinked log cabins. The main lodge has a lounging area and a cocktail lounge, and its dining room has a large stone fireplace, 13-foot ceilings, exposed, chinked log walls and ceilings, and pine furniture. It serves family-style meals, with buffalo meat on the menu. There is also a grocery store at the resort.

The log cabins, in a stand of pines along French Creek, vary in size and appointments. Ten of them have one room each and are equipped with a refrigerator, a hot plate, and a bath with

shower. Four cabins have two bedrooms, a kitchenette, and a bath with tub and shower (two have a fireplace and a large screened porch). Each of four "guest units" have a bath with tub and shower but no cooking facilities. All cabins have hardwood floors partially covered with throw rugs, wood paneling (the older ones have exposed-log walls), and comfortable rustic furnishings.

Accommodations: 17 cabins with private bath. *Towels and linens:* Provided. *Cooking and eating utensils:* Not provided. *Stove:* Stove or hot plate in 14 cabins. *Refrigerator:* In 14 cabins. *Pets:* Permitted. *Open:* May 15 through October 1. *Mailing address:* Custer State Park, Custer, SD 57730. *Phone:* (605) 255-4531. *Driving instructions:* Blue Bell Lodge and Resort is on Route 87, within Custer State Park, near Wildlife Loop Rd and Wind Cave National Park.

Legion Lake Resort Cabins

At an elevation of 5,100 feet on the shore of its namesake, Legion Lake Resort comprises a shingle-roofed wood-frame lodge and twenty-six wood-frame cabins. The main lodge has a restaurant, a bar, a grocery store, and a gift shop.

Secluded from each other, the cabins are on a hill wooded with ponderosa pines. Thirteen are "overnight" accommodations with tiled or linoleum floors, heat, and modern furniture. There are also housekeeping cabins, some with two rooms and some with three, which have stoves and refrigerators as well as basic cooking and eating utensils in their kitchenettes. These are furnished with modern pieces and have tile or linoleum floors. Each cabin has a private bath with shower.

Accommodations: 26 cabins with private bath. *Towels and linens:* Provided. *Cooking and eating utensils:* In housekeeping cabins. *Stove and refrigerator:* In housekeeping cabins. *Pets:* Permitted. *Open:* May 15 through October 1. *Mailing address:* Custer, SD 57730. *Phone:* (605) 255-4521. *Driving instructions:* Legion Lake Resort is on Route 16A, 7 miles east of Custer.

Sylvan Lake Resort Lodge, Cottages, and Cabins

Among ponderosa pines and white spruces and overlooking Sylvan Lake from an elevation of 6,500 feet, Sylvan Lake Resort consists of a stone-and-wood lodge with twenty-five bedrooms, plus eleven guest cabins and twenty-one housekeeping cottages. The main lodge has a restaurant specializing in such dishes as mountain trout, as well as a cocktail lounge, and a grocery store.

Lodge rooms vary in size and appointments and can accommodate from one to four. Comfortably furnished, each room has wall-to-wall carpeting, wallpaper, and a telephone. Most rooms have a lake view. The guest cabins are of modern design and have stone fireplaces, wall-to-wall carpeting, wood-paneled walls, and a private bath. A few have sofa beds, and one has a kitchenette. Four of the twenty-one housekeeping cottages are duplexes and share with the seventeen others a simple, rustic decor. Each housekeeping cabin has linoleum floors, wood-paneled walls, a kitchenette with a two-burner hotplate and a small refrigerator, and a shower.

The resort also has two "special" cottages—Honeymoon Cottage and Senators Cottage, each with a private bath. Honeymoon Cottage, secluded on a granite ridge facing the Black Hills, has a stone fireplace, wall-to-wall carpeting, a queen-size bed, and a love seat. Senators Cottage, which is also secluded, is built of logs and has three bedrooms, two sofa beds, a large living room with a stone fireplace, wall-to-wall carpeting, and a kitchenette.

Accommodations: 25 lodge rooms, all with private bath; 11 cabins and 21 cottages, all with private bath. *Towels and linens:* Provided. *Cooking and eating utensils:* Not provided. *Stove and refrigerator:* In some cabins. *Pets:* Permitted in housekeeping cottages only. *Open:* Mother's Day through September 25. *Mailing address:* PO Box 752, Custer, SD 57730. (605) 574-2561 *instructions:* Sylvan Lake Resort is at the junction of Routes 87 and 89 in Custer State Park.

Tennessee

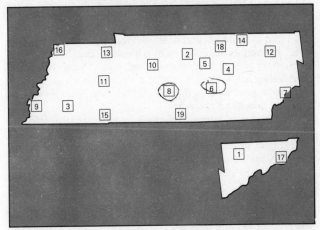

State map and tourist information: Dept. of Tourism, 601 Broadway, PO Box 23170, Nashville, TN 37203; 615-741-2158. **State parks:** *Information:* Division of Parks, 701 Broadway, Nashville, TN 37203; 617-742-6667. *Entrance fees:* None. *Reservations:* Call 800-421-6683 (in eastern U.S.) or contact individual parks (western U.S.). Deposit for first night, by credit card or check. Reservations accepted (and recommended) up to 1 year in advance for June—Labor Day; 2 to 5 months for rest of year. Rented weekly June—Labor Day. *Restrictions:* Hunting limited to certain parks. Special $1.25 fishing permit in some parks. *Facilities:* Swimming and interpretative programs, Mem, Day—Labor Day. Golf, March—November. Cross-country skiing (Roan Mountain State Park only), late November—early March.

A thickly forested 3,687 acres, Big Ridge State Rustic Park is in northeastern Tennessee, about 25 miles north of Knoxville. Its ruggedly hilly terrain is bordered on three sides by Norris Reservoir, the broadest part of which local residents call "Loyston Sea." Numerous ridges (Chestnut, Bluebird, Big, Pinnacle) run through the park, interspersed with valleys with names like Bluemud Valley, Dark Hollow, and Big Valley. Big Ridge, at 1,538 feet the highest point in the park, offers extended views of the lake and forests to the north.

The park was originally formed by a cooperative effort of the Tennessee Valley Authority and the National Park Service, who sought to demonstrate that badly eroded farmland along the TVA lakeshores could be transformed into well-forested recreation and park areas. The Civilian Conservation Corps helped in the effort to transform this once-abused land into the heavily forested area it is today.

A peninsula with a sand beach and bathhouse juts out into Big Ridge Lake and provides excellent swimming. Visitors can rent canoes, rowboats, and paddleboats, and the park has miles of hiking trails.

Big Ridge State Rustic Park has two log and seventeen wood-frame cabins, five on the shore of Big Ridge Lake and the other fourteen on a hillside overlooking the lake. Built by the Civilian Conservation Corps, they are one-room units with two double beds, a sofa-sleeper, a kitchen, and a screened porch. Each also has wood paneling, hardwood floors, a fireplace, and a private bath.

Accommodations: 19 cabins with private bath. *Towels and linens:* Provided. *Cooking and eating utensils:* Provided. *Stove and refrigerator:* Provided. *Pets:* Not permitted. *Open:* April through October. *Mailing address:* Maynardville, TN 37807. *Phone:* (615) 992-5523. *Driving instructions:* From Knoxville take I-75 north to the Norris-Clinton exit, then go east on Route 61 for approximately 12 miles.

Cedars of Lebanon State Recreational Park, in central Tennessee about 27 miles east of Nashville, comprises 10,000 acres (named for the expansive cedar forest in the biblical kingdom of Lebanon) and contains the largest remaining red cedar stand in the United States. Among its other botanical distinctions is the only patch of Tennessee Purple coneflowers to be found in the world. About the size of a carnation, the coneflower has a brilliant purple blossom. Botany groups often visit the park, which sponsors a Wildflower Weekend in early spring. The fairly flat terrain here is wooded mainly with oaks, ashes, walnuts, honey locusts, and many dogwoods and redbuds. The park also has numerous limestone sink holes, depressions eroded into soluble rock by water, and nine tenths of its acreage has been left in a natural state.

Facilities include three trails, which range in length from half a mile to 4½ miles long, tennis courts, playgrounds, an interpretative center, a snack bar, riding stables with horses for hire, a camp store, and picnicking areas.

Cedars of Lebanon Park Lodge and Cabins

The park has nine wood-frame cabins, accommodating four people, set in a wooded area. Each has hardwood floors, a fully equipped kitchenette, color television, a wood stove, a downstairs bedroom, an upstairs bedroom with an adjoining loft, a small open porch, and a private bath.

A group lodge can accommodate eighty people in two dormitory-style buildings, each of which has 2 separate chaperon rooms. The lodge, at the end of a road in the woods, has a large kitchen and a dining-meeting room.

Accommodations: 9 cabins with private bath and a group lodge with shared baths. *Towels and linens:* Provided. *Cooking and eating utensils:* Provided. *Stove and refrigerator:* Provided. *Pets:* Not permitted. *Open:* All year. *Mailing address:* Box 220, Cedars of Lebanon State Recreational Park, Route 6, Lebanon, TN 37087. *Phone:* (615) 444-9394. *Driving instructions:* The park is off U.S. 231, at the intersection of Route 10, about 7½ miles south of Lebanon.

Chickasaw State Rustic Park is in southwestern Tennessee, about 60 miles northeast of Memphis. The roughly 14,000-acre park, in the Chickasaw State Forest, is wooded primarily with loblolly pines punctuated with scattered stands of oaks, hickories, walnuts, and locusts. The hilly terrain is criss-crossed by miles of hiking trails and unimproved roads, including several that are set aside for three-wheelers. One hiking trail runs around one of the park's two lakes and then up through a hilly, thickly wooded area. The 50-acre Lake Placid has a sand beach with a bathhouse; the other lake is primarily used for fishing, the prime catches being bass, bream, and crappies. Other park activities include basketball, tennis, archery, softball, and boating, with fishing and paddleboats for rent. There are facilities for picnicking, as well as a restaurant, a snack bar, a gift shop, and a store that sells groceries, sundries, and camping supplies.

Chickasaw Lodge and Cabins

The park has eleven wood-frame cabins in a wooded area beside a lake. Several are right on the lake, and most have lake views. Each has a fully equipped kitchenette, a brick fireplace, air-conditioning, and a private bath. These two-bedroom cabins can accommodate six.

A group lodge, accommodating 40, has a central dining area and several meeting rooms, as well as two central bathhouses. The park restaurant, at additional charge, prepares all food for the group lodge guests.

Accommodations: 12 cabins with private bath and a group lodge with shared bath. *Towels and linens:* Provided. *Cooking and eating utensils:* Provided. *Stove and refrigerator:* Provided. *Pets:* Not permitted. *Open:* All year. *Mailing address:* Route 2, Henderson, TN 38340. *Phone:* (901) 989-5141. *Driving instructions:* Chickasaw State Rustic Park is on Route 100, about 10 miles southwest of Henderson.

Cumberland Mountain State Rustic Park is in central Tennessee, about 60 miles west of Knoxville and 3 miles north of Hinch Mountain (elevation 3,048). The park's 1,720 acres are part of the Cumberland Plateau, which extends from New York to Alabama and is generally considered America's largest timbered plateau. The park was originally established to provide a recreation area for 250 families chosen by the Roosevelt Administration in 1938 to homestead this sparsely populated area. (In the end, the families built their own timber and stone homes, as well as the elementary school, high school, cannery, amphitheater, and administration building—mostly providing their own labor.) Construction and development of the park were completed by the Civilian Conservation Corps and the Works Progress Administration. The CCC structures still stand, including a dam and bridge that, like most of the buildings, are made of a local sandstone called Crab Orchard stone.

The park's 40-acre lake has a sand beach and a bathhouse, and visitors here can rent rowboats, Dreamboats (paddleboats), and canoes, as no private boats are allowed on the lake. Many trails meander through the park, which also offers tennis, basketball, badminton, and shuffleboard, and a video-game room. The park naturalist service plans daily activities including movies, guided tours, and square dances.

The Cumberland Mountain Restaurant, with private meeting and banquet rooms, has a three hundred–seat dining room overlooking the dam and lake. The restaurant, which serves two meals a day, is closed from Christmas through February.

Cumberland Park Lodge and Cabins

In a wooded area beside Byrd Lake are thirty-four cabins with private baths and 2 group lodges. The three "timberlodge" cabins, directly on the lake and with a deck overlooking it, have three bedrooms, color television, hardwood floors, and a fireplace, and can accommodate ten. The seven two-bedroom deluxe cabins are gray A-frames with skylighted bedrooms, color television, a living-kitchenette area, and a patio, and can also accommodate ten. The sixteen rustic cabins with one and two bedrooms are built of pine and accommodate up to six; the one-bedroom cabins have screened porches. Eight one-room efficiency

473

cabins are in a group of four duplex units. One stone lodge (Mill House), accommodating sixteen, has a fireplace, a kitchen, and rustic furnishings; the other, Coon Hollow, is a group lodge accommodating six.

Accommodations: 2 group lodges and 34 cabins with private bath. *Towels and linens:* Provided. *Cooking and eating utensils:* Provided. *Stove and refrigerator:* Provided. *Pets:* Not permitted. *Open:* All year. *Mailing address:* Route 8, Box 322, Crossville, TN 38555. *Phone:* (615) 484-6138. *Driving instructions:* Cumberland Mountain State Rustic Park is off U.S. 127 South, about 4 miles south of Crossville.

Fifty miles east of Nashville, on the eastern Highland Rim, is the 6,100-acre Edgar Evins State Rustic Park. It was developed by the state after the U.S. Army Corps of Engineers built a dam on the Caney Fork River creating a reservoir that began to be used as a recreation area. The park, named for a Tennessee statesman instrumental in building the Center Hill Dam, has a wooded terrain characterized by bluffs and ridges.

Visitors can rent boats and fishing equipment; small- and largemouth bass are the most sought-after catches. A 1½-mile-long trail follows the edge of the lake, and a swimming pool is available for cabin guests.

The park's thirty-four cabins, built of western cedar, are arranged in clusters about 200 yards from the lake. Each cabin has wall-to-wall carpeting and a balcony off its living room. The living room, which is paneled, and the kitchen areas are on the second floor, and the bedrooms are downstairs. The cabins have no telephones but come equipped with color television.

Accommodations: 34 cabins, all with private bath. *Towels and linens:* Provided. *Cooking and eating utensils:* Provided. *Stove and refrigerator:* Provided. *Pets:* Not permitted. *Open:* All year. *Mailing address:* Route 1, Silver Point, TN 38582. *Phone:* (615) 858-2114. *Driving instructions:* Edgar Evins State Rustic Park is off I-40, about 20 miles west of Cookeville.

On the Cumberland Plateau just north of Smartt Mountain (elevation 2,142 feet), Fall Creek Falls State Resort Park comprises 16,800 acres about 80 miles southwest of Knoxville. Oak and hickory forests dominate the terrain, which has numerous streams and gorges lined with tulip trees and hemlocks. One of the park's four waterfalls, Fall Creek Falls, is the tallest waterfall east of the Rockies, cascading 256 feet into the enshadowed pool at the bottom of its gorge.

The National Park Service originally operated the park as a recreation demonstration area during the 1930s, and in 1944 the U.S. Department of Agriculture deeded it to Tennessee. The state operated it as a rustic area until the mid-1970s, when it was developed as a resort. Among the park's extensive facilities is the Village Green Complex, housing a camp store, a craft center, a launderette, a visitors' lounge, an Olympic-size swimming pool, a recreation center (Ping-Pong, pool, etc.), an amphitheater, lighted tennis courts and a ball field, horseshoe pits, basketball courts, and badminton courts.

There are also miles of hiking and horseback-riding trails as well as self-guided nature and motoring trails, a 3-mile bicycle path running from the inn to the falls, a large lake, and an eighteen-hole, par 72 golf course with pro shop, rental clubs, a snack bar, a dressing room, and gasoline carts. Horses are for hire, and bicycles, canoes, paddleboats, and fishing boats may also be rented. *Park phone:* (615) 881-3297.

Fall Creek Inn and Cabins

Fall Creek Inn consists of a seventy-three-room stone lodge and twenty cabins with two bedrooms each, all with private bath. The lodge is directly on Fall Creek Lake, and all rooms have lake views from either a balcony or a patio. All the rooms have wall-to-wall carpeting, color television, a telephone, and a private bath; seven honeymoon suites have queen-size beds; and a Governor's Suite has a separate living room, a bedroom, and a kitchenette. The lodge also has a dining room seating three hundred, a large lobby with a stone fireplace, a recreation room, and banquet and conference facilities.

The inn's cabins are clustered in two groups: fishermen's cabins and inland cabins. The fishermen's cabins have two bed-

rooms upstairs; downstairs are a living room with a free-standing fireplace and a private porch overhanging Fall Creek Lake, a kitchenette, color television, a telephone, and wall-to-wall carpeting.

Each of the single-story inland cabins, in a wooded area a few hundred feet from the lake, has wall-to-wall carpeting, color television, a telephone, a living room with a stone fireplace, and a kitchenette.

Accommodations: 73 lodge rooms and 20 cabins, all with private bath. *Towels and linens:* Provided. *Cooking and eating utensils:* In cabins. *Stove:* In cabins. *Refrigerator:* In cabins and Governor's Suite. *Pets:* Not permitted. *Open:* All year. *Mailing address:* Fall Creek Inn, Fall Creek State Resort Park, Route 3, Pikesville, TN 37367. *Phone:* (615) 881-3241. *Driving instructions:* Fall Creek Falls State Resort Park is 11 miles east of Spencer, off Route 111.

One of the nation's most popular parks, Great Smoky Mountains National Park encompasses over 500,000 acres along the Tennessee–North Carolina border, about 60 miles east of Knoxville, Tennessee, and 30 miles west of Asheville, North Carolina. The park has sixteen mountain peaks higher than 6,000 feet, more species of native trees than Europe, 1,400 species of flowering plants, 2,200 species of mushrooms, 300 streams inhabited by 70 species of fish, impenetrable stands of mountain laurel and rhododendron, and an almost ubiquitous smokelike haze that wraps itself around the mountains. The Great Smokies are one of the country's oldest range of mountains, and their enormous diversity of plant and animal life is due to the glaciers, which stopped their southern advance right before the mountains. A large variety of animals trying to keep ahead of the glaciers wound up making their home in the Great Smokies, which are in many ways a meeting point of northern and southern habitats. At one time entirely controlled and inhabited by Indians, the mountains were named after a Cherokee word that means "the place of blue smoke."

The scenery here is breathtaking at any time of year. In spring there is a profusion of flowering plants, from delicate wild lilies and orchids to expansive stands of catawba rhododendron, flame azalea, and mountain laurel; and in autumn the place is riotous with turning leaves. The park has some 800 miles of hiking trails, including a 72-mile section of the Appalachian Trail, which is fitted out with a series of shelters spaced a day apart. At several points in the park there are nineteenth-century homesteads, left standing as they were, and at Cades Cove an 11-mile road runs past old homesteads, churches, gristmills, cabins, and a cemetery.

Hiking is probably the leading activity, with any number of trails to choose from—some are short and easy, some long and strenuous. Birding, fishing, camping, and bicycling are also popular, and the naturalist service offers various interpretative programs, including two- to five-day-long workshops, which are administered in conjunction with the University of Tennessee. *Park mailing address:* Gatlinburg, TN 37738. *Park phone:* (615) 436-5615.

LeConte Lodge and Cabins

At the summit of Mount LeConte, LeConte Lodge consists of three small log lodges (two with three-bedrooms, one with two), eight cabins, and a wood-frame, shingled main lodge where meals are served. The lodge is rustic and remote, and getting here involves a 5½-mile hike. In all, five trails lead to the lodge; the longest of them is 8 miles, but the views from the summit of Mount LeConte are worth the walking.

Accommodations here are rustic. The three lodges can accommodate from eight to twelve people each and have either two or three bedrooms, a living room with a nonworking fireplace, kerosene lamps and heating, hardwood floors, no electricity, and outside cold running water and toilets. The cabins, which contain one room, can accommodate from two to five people and have the same amenities as the lodges.

Accommodations: 3 lodges and 8 cabins with privy (flush). *Towels and linens:* Provided. *Cooking and eating utensils:* Not provided. *Stove and refrigerator:* Not provided. *Pets:* Not permitted. *Open:* April through October. *Mailing address:* LeConte Lodge, PO Box 350, Gatlinburg, TN 37738. *Phone:* (615) 436-4473. *Driving instructions:* LeConte Lodge is off U.S. 441 near Gatlinburg. Guests should ask for specific driving and hiking directions when making reservations.

The home of John Oliver, the first known settler in Cades Cove.

Wonderland Hotel

Among poplars, oaks, sycamores, hemlocks, and pines, Wonderland Hotel is a 1912 rustic wood-frame building. The hotel's porch, furnished with swings and rocking chairs, spans the entire length of its facade and looks up at Blanket Mountain, which the restaurant also overlooks. The restaurant has a fireplace, and the lobby has two fireplaces where guests tend to congregate. A large meeting room is used primarily for family reunions and other gatherings.

The twenty-six guest rooms have queen-size beds, wall-to-wall carpeting, and views of either Blanket Mountain or woods. Most rooms have a private bath, many with claw-footed tubs.

Accommodations: 26 rooms, most with private bath. *Pets:* Not permitted. *Open:* Memorial Day through late October. *Mailing address:* Wonderland Hotel, Route 2, Gatlinburg, TN 37738. *Phone:* (615) 436-5490. *Driving instructions:* Wonderland Hotel is off Route 73, about 7 miles west of Gatlinburg.

A 1,135-acre reserve bordered on the northwest by the Duck River, Henry Horton State Resort Park is in central Tennessee in a picturesque area of gently rolling hills about 45 miles south of Nashville. The park's terrain is mostly fairly flat, with small hills and scattered woods. The Buford Ellington eighteen-hole, par 72 championship golf course, probably the park's main attraction, is considered one of the finer courses in the southeast. Bordered by the Duck River, it has a shape that resembles the State of Florida. The course is open all year, with complete facilities including a pro shop, rental clubs, and gasoline carts.

Another prime attraction is the multifield skeet and trap range in the park's southeast corner. Available to individuals as well as gun-club groups, the range has complete facilities including a clubhouse, rentals, ammunition and other equipment, and a manager who will provide instruction. The park's recreation center organizes such group activities as square dances, movies, archery instruction, and hayrides. There are lighted tennis courts and facilities for volleyball, basketball, and badminton.

Horton Inn and Cabins

Recently constructed of brick and wood, Horton Inn is a rustic-style lodge with a 250-seat restaurant and three private dining rooms for banquets or meetings, an Olympic-size pool and a wading pool for children, and a lobby with a fireplace.

Each of seventy-two lodge guest rooms, several of which have a private balcony, has wall-to-wall carpeting, color television, a telephone, and air-conditioning. There are also four suites with two bedrooms and a connecting living room and kitchenette area.

The inn operates four modern wood-frame cabins close to the main building. Each of the cabins, which accommodate up to seven, has wall-to-wall carpeting, color television, a telephone, air-conditioning, a kitchenette, and a bath with a shower.

Accommodations: 72 lodge rooms, 4 lodge suites, and 4 cabins, all with private bath. *Towels and linens:* Provided. *Cooking and eating utensils:* In suites and cabins. *Stove and refrigerator:* In suites and cabins. *Pets:* Not permitted. *Open:* All year. *Mailing address:* Horton Inn, Henry Horton State Park Resort, Chapel Hill, TN 37034. *Phone:* (615) 364-2222. *Driving instructions:* Henry Horton State Resort Park is off Route 31A.

Meeman-Shelby Forest State Recreational Park comprises 13,800 acres in southwestern Tennessee, about 20 miles northwest of Memphis. Bordering the Mississippi River, it consists mostly of flat riverbottom land that gives way to gently rolling hills. Hardwoods predominate—particularly oaks, hickories, maples, and ashes—and the characteristic wildlife includes deer, bobcats, and coyotes. The park supports a wide variety of bird life—wild turkeys and martins are especially common, eagles occasionally appear, hawks are plentiful, and, especially during migration seasons, many ducks and geese congregate along the Mississippi and on the park's two lakes. There are some 20 miles of hiking trails used by backpackers and hikers. Fishing is also a regular park activity, with anglers going after crappies, bass, bream, and catfishes. Facilities for water sports include fishing and paddleboat rentals, launching ramps for those bringing their own craft, and an Olympic-size swimming pool. Other facilities are bike trails, a marina, an interpretative center, stables with horses for hire, a snack bar, playgrounds, and picnicking areas.

Meeman-Shelby Forest Lodges and Cabins

The park's five wood-frame cabins, with two bedrooms accommodating six people each, are in a wooded area overlooking the lake. Each has a fully equipped kitchenette, a private bath, a brick fireplace, and a small porch.

Also available is a group lodge, accommodating 135 people in four dormitories with shared baths. Its brick-and-wood main building includes kitchen facilities and a dining room with a fireplace.

Accommodations: 5 cabins with private bath and a group lodge with shared baths. *Towels and linens:* Provided. *Cooking and eating utensils:* Provided. *Stove and refrigerator:* Provided. *Pets:* Not permitted. *Open:* All year. *Mailing address:* Route 3, Millington, TN 38053. *Phone:* (901) 876-5201. *Driving instructions:* Take Route 51 to North Watkins Road, then follow North Watkins to its end, to Bluff Road, which runs into the park.

Montgomery Bell State Resort Park encompasses 5,500 acres in central Tennessee, about 35 miles west of Nashville, in an area of rolling hills wooded primarily with oaks, hickories, pines, dogwoods, and redbuds. It was at one time the site of Laurel Furnace, a nineteenth-century iron-manufacturing operation run by Montgomery Bell, an early Tennessee industrialist. (The Bell ironworks molded the cannon balls used by Andrew Jackson's artillery during the battle of New Orleans.) The Cumberland Presbyterian Church was founded here in 1810, and the original log cabin that housed the church, the home of the Reverend Samuel McAdoo, is in the park.

The park has three lakes, one with a sand beach and bathhouse, and all with generous populations of bass, bluegills, and crappies. Other facilities include a swimming pool for lodge and cabin guests, an eighteen-hole golf course, 110 campsites, picnicking areas, a restaurant, a snack bar, a gift shop, tennis courts, rental boats, backpacking trails, and a recreation building.

Montgomery Bell Park Lodge and Cabins

Accommodations in the park include a forty-room lodge–conference center and nine cabins. The lodge consists of two motel-type buildings, one older and one newer, that house the guest rooms, two conference rooms, a restaurant overlooking the lake, a private dining room, and an arts-and-crafts gift shop. Each guest room has carpeting and color television. Those in the older wing are smaller and have a bath with shower only, but they overlook the lake. Each room in the newer wing is large and has a bath with both tub and shower.

The wood-frame cabins, with a living room and two bedrooms accommodating six each, are within walking distance of the lodge. Each has a fully equipped kitchenette, a fireplace, a private bath, and color television.

Accommodations: 40 lodge rooms and 9 cabins, all with private bath. *Towels and linens:* Provided. *Cooking and eating utensils:* In cabins. *Stove and refrigerator:* In cabins. *Pets:* Not permitted. *Open:* All year. *Mailing address:* Route 1, Box 684, Burns, TN 37029. *Phone:* (615) 797-9051. *Driving instructions:* Montgomery Bell State Park is off U.S. 70, about 5 miles west of White Bluff.

The largest of Tennessee's state parks, Natchez Trace State Resort Park, on a northern offshoot of the original Natchez Trace, is 42,000 acres in western Tennessee off I-40, between the Tennessee and Big Sandy rivers, about halfway between Memphis and Nashville. (The Natchez Trace was first an Indian trail, later used by frontier boatmen who, having floated farm products downriver from Virginia, Pennsylvania, and Kentucky, needed an overland route back up the Mississippi to Nashville and the upper reaches of the Cumberland River basin.) At one time badly abused and heavily eroded, this area was established as a "land-use-area" project by the U.S. Department of Agriculture and in 1955 was finally deeded to the state. Today the area is the most successful of Tennessee's pine planting and harvesting operations. Forests are a mixture of conifers and hardwoods, and the park contains the third-largest pecan tree in North America. (The legend goes that one of Andrew Jackson's soldiers, on the way home from the Battle of New Orleans, gave a pecan to a local settler, who then planted it.)

The park's four lakes range in size from 90 to 690 acres. Visitors can rent rowboats or pedal boats at the dock on Cub Lake (the only lake where private boats are not allowed) or launch their own at the other three lakes. Frequent catches include largemouth and rock bass, bluegills, catfishes, and crappies. The beach is a swim-at-your-own-risk affair, and there is a pool for guests at Pin Oak Lodge. Among the numerous hiking trails is an overnight trail for backpackers, as well as miles of fire roads open to motorcycles and other off-road vehicles.

The park's nature center provides guided tours, organized games, slide shows, hayrides, and square dances, and other recreation activities include badminton, tennis, archery, shuffleboard, and volleyball. *Park phone:* (901) 968-3742.

Pin Oak Lodge and Cabins

Pin Oak is a modern wooden lodge with twenty guest rooms on the shore of the 690-acre Pin Oak Lake. Half the lodge guest rooms face the lake, which from the air looks like a pin oak leaf, and the other half face the pool. Second-floor rooms have balconies; those on the ground floor have small patios. The

487

The "Big Pecan," one of the largest pecan trees in the world.

building also has a 120-seat dining room, a lobby, a recreation room with pool tables and a large television, and private meeting and dining rooms for conferences and other group meetings. Each guest room has wall-to-wall carpeting, color television, a telephone, and a private bath.

Pin Oak Lodge administers eighteen rustic cabins overlooking Cub Lake. Designed to sleep six, each has air-conditioning, a kitchenette, an outdoor grill, and lake views. Most have a fireplace, but none have television or a telephone.

Accommodations: 20 lodge rooms and 18 cabins, all with private bath. *Towels and linens:* Provided. *Cooking and eating utensils:* In cabins. *Stove and refrigerator:* In cabins. *Pets:* Not permitted. *Open:* Lodge April through November; cabins all year. *Mailing address:* Pin Oak Lodge, Natchez Trace State Resort Park, Wildersville, TN 38388. *Phone:* (901) 968-8176. *Driving instructions:* Natchez Trace State Resort Park is off I-40, about 35 miles northeast of Jackson.

Russ Rose and his wife, Nancy, make baskets from white oak splints
Museum of Appalachia

Norris Dam State Resort Park is on 4,000 acres in northeastern Tennessee, about 20 miles northwest of Knoxville, at the site of Norris Dam, the oldest of a series of dams begun in 1933, and the first project of the Tennessee Valley Authority. The dam divides the park into two sections: The eastern one was developed in the 1930s by the Civilian Conservation Corps; the western section of the park, developed by the State of Tennessee, was dedicated in 1976. Hills, ridges, and valleys form the terrain, which is abundant with streams, caves, wildflowers and extensive stands of virgin hardwood forest.

Norris Lake has numerous marinas, with good facilities for boating, waterskiing, and fishing. Also among the facilities are an Olympic-size swimming pool, a snack bar (summer only), tennis courts, and a naturalist and recreation service that plans such activities as boat tours of the lake and cave tours, movies, guided hikes, and campfires. Numerous hiking trails wind through the park.

A special feature is the Lenoir Museum cultural complex, which consists of an eighteenth-century gristmill and threshing barn, and a gift shop. (Also nearby is the Museum of Appalachia, which, with thirty reconstructed and furnished log cabins, celebrates early frontier mountain life.)

The park has twenty rustic vacation cabins (unavailable in 1984 because of renovation) and ten deluxe cabins with three bedrooms each, all with private bath.

The rustic ones, accommodating either two or four, are in the older eastern section of the park and have one large room with two double beds, a kitchenette, bath, and fireplace.

The deluxe cabins, in the newer western part of the park, are of a modern design and accommodate six. Each has wall-to-wall carpeting, color television, a front porch and a back patio, a kitchenette, a living-dining area, and a fireplace.

Accommodations: 30 cabins with private bath. *Towels and linens:* Provided. *Cooking and eating utensils:* Provided. *Stove and refrigerator:* Provided. *Pets:* Not permitted. *Open:* All year (deluxe cabins); March through Thanksgiving (rustic cabins). *Mailing address:* Route 1, Box 500, Lake City, TN 37769. *Phone:* (615) 426-7461 or 494-0518. *Driving instructions:* Norris Dam State Park resort is off U.S. 441, about 20 miles north of Knoxville, near Norris.

Named for an old steamboat stop on the Tennessee River, Paris Landing State Resort Park comprises 841 acres in northwestern Tennessee, about 21 miles southeast of Murray, Kentucky. Part of the eastern Gulf Coastal Plain, the terrain varies from almost imperceptibly rolling hills to steep and sudden ridges wooded mostly with oaks, hickories, and pines. The park is immediately west of the 158,000 acre Kentucky Lake, the second largest man-made lake in the world, with over 300 miles of shoreline. Across the lake is the Tennessee Valley Authority's 170,000-acre recreation area Land Between the Lakes, a 40-mile-long peninsula separating Kentucky and Barkley lakes.

Boating, fishing, and waterskiing are the main activities, and the park rents boats and has a full-service marina that can handle craft of all sizes. Golf is also available at an eighteen-hole, par 72 course, which includes a pro shop, power carts, rentals, and a snack bar. There are two swimming pools, one Olympic-size pool for the public and one for inn guests only, as well as an unsupervised beach. The park recreator offers organized activities, and the park includes picnic areas, a camp store, lighted tennis courts, and an outdoor game area for volleyball and baseball.

Paris Landing Inn

In the southern part of the park, beside Kentucky Lake, is a one-hundred-room, modern wood-and-concrete inn with a 230-seat restaurant that offers private dining and banquet facilities, a gift shop, and a large carpeted lobby with comfortable furniture and a fireplace.

All guest rooms have wall-to-wall carpeting, color television, a telephone, a private bath, and sliding glass doors leading onto a private balcony overlooking the lake. The inn's one suite has two bedrooms, a living room, and a kitchenette.

Accommodations: 100 rooms with private bath. *Pets:* Not permitted. *Open:* All year. *Mailing address:* Route 1, Buchanan, TN 38222. *Phone:* (901) 642-4311. *Driving instructions:* Paris Landing State Resort Park is off Route 79, about 15 miles northeast of Paris.

Pickett State Rustic Park and Forest, 11,752 acres in northern Tennessee, is about 65 miles northwest of Knoxville, just south of the Kentucky border. It adjoins the 123,000-acre Big South Fork National River and Recreation Area that preserves the scenic valleys and gorges of the Big South Fork of the Cumberland River in Kentucky and Tennessee. The park is in a remote wooded section of the upper Cumberland Mountains, where Sergeant Alvin C. York, the World War I hero, was raised. The terrain includes many interesting rock formations, such as natural bridges, caves, and ancient Indian artifacts.

The park's 12-acre man-made lake has a sand beach and a bathhouse. The targets for anglers are trout, and visitors can rent canoes or rowboats at the park dock, as private boats or motors are not permitted on the lake. Fifty-eight miles of hiking trails wind past waterfalls and extensive stands of rhododendron. Other activities include archery, badminton, volleyball, Ping-Pong, and field sports.

In the center of the park are five modern chalets, five wooden cottages, and five rustic stone-and-wood cabins. The chalets, constructed of wood, have two floors connected by a spiral staircase. All the accommodations come fully equipped for housekeeping and have a private bath and a fireplace; some have lake views.

Accommodations: 5 chalets, 5 cottages, and 5 cabins, all with private bath. *Towels and linens:* Provided. *Cooking and eating utensils:* Provided. *Stove and refrigerator:* Provided. *Pets:* Not permitted. *Open:* All year (chalets); April 1 through December 1 (cabins and cottages). *Mailing address:* Box 174, Rock Creek, TN 38556. *Phone:* (615) 879-5821. *Driving instructions:* From Jamestown take U.S. 127 (Route 28) north for about 2 miles, then turn east on Route 154 and proceed for roughly 10 miles to Pickett State Rustic Park.

When they were building Pickwick Dam in the 1930s, a village of about a thousand workers for the Tennessee Valley Authority and Civilian Conservation Corps sprang up here, 90 miles east of Memphis, on a lake formed when the dam closed its floodgates on the Tennessee River. The State of Tennessee bought the former TVA-village area in 1969, developed it, and then expanded it to include a heavily wooded area across the lake that is now used as a day-use area with primitive camping and an unimproved beach.

The developed part of the 500-acre park has a par 72, eighteen-hole golf course with a pro shop, a snack bar, and power carts. Its roughly 2 miles of beaches are unsupervised, but there is a pool for inn and cabin guests. A marina with 230 slips can handle very large craft, and visitors can rent boats as well as fishing gear. Other activities include archery, tennis, badminton, and field games.

Pickwick Landing Inn and Cabins

A 78-bedroom, three-story modern lodge is in the southeast section of the park overlooking Pickwick Lake. Constructed of Canadian cedar, the lodge also has a 135-seat dining room and a 320-seat private dining room, which divides into 3 private rooms for banquets or meetings.

Each guest room has wall-to-wall carpeting, color television, a telephone, and a private bath, and opens onto a patio or a balcony. Three suites have two bedrooms, a sitting room, and a private bath.

Close to the lodge and also overlooking the lake are ten cabins, each with two bedrooms, a complete kitchen, a living room with a Franklin stove, and a picnic table and barbecue grill outside.

Accommodations: 78 lodge rooms and 10 cabins, all with private bath. *Towels and linens:* Provided. *Cooking and eating utensils:* In cabins. *Stove and refrigerator:* In cabins. *Pets:* Not permitted. *Open:* All year. *Mailing address:* PO Box 10, Pickwick Dam, TN 38365. *Phone:* (901) 689-3135. *Driving instructions:* From Savannah take Route 128 south for about 11 miles—the park is at the intersection of Routes 128 and 57.

Divided into ten segments along 22 miles of Reelfoot Lake shoreline, Reelfoot Lake State Resort Park comprises 18,725 acres, 18,000 of which are water, in the northwest corner of Tennessee, about 5 miles southeast of the 359-degree turn the Mississippi River makes at the Tennessee-Kentucky-Missouri borders. Legend has it that Reelfoot, a Chickasaw chieftain, fell in love with Starlight, a Choctaw princess, but because of his clubfoot he was refused her hand in marriage. Reelfoot and and his colleagues kidnapped the princess, and while celebrating their prize, the earth opened up and swallowed them, causing the entire area to flood. (Geologists have their own explanation: A series of earthquakes in western Tennessee during 1811 and 1812 flooded the dense forest, creating Reelfoot Lake.)

The cypress-lined lake is home to many waterfowl and is visited by golden and bald eagles. Visitors can rent boats, dock their own at a marina with seventy-five slips, or take a ride on one of the excursion boats that operate from April through October. There is a swimming pool, tennis courts, and facilities for games including badminton, shuffleboard, archery, pool, and basketball. A museum houses wildlife displays and a collection of Indian artifacts. From December through March the park naturalist conducts daily tours of the large population of wintering bald eagles.

Airpark Inn and Restaurant

So called because of the 3,500-foot adjacent lighted airstrip, Airpark Inn and Restaurant is a modern, cypress lodge with twenty guest rooms, a gift shop, and a hundred-seat restaurant. The building is on a pier over a cypress and willow swamp filled with ferns and wildflowers.

The inn has two types of rooms—doubles and suites. In the suites is a large living area with a sofa bed and a sleeping loft overhead. Both the rooms and the suites have wall-to-wall carpeting, color television, a telephone, a private bath, and sliding-glass doors that open onto a private balcony. (When the water level is high, you can fish right from your room.)

Five additional rooms are in a motel-type unit 16 miles south at the Reelfoot Spillway. All have a private bath and accom-

The partially submerged forest of Reelfoot Lake

modate at least three; some have a kitchenette.

Accommodations: 20 inn rooms and 5 motel rooms, all with private bath. *Towels and linens:* Provided. *Cooking and eating utensils:* In some motel rooms. *Stove and refrigerator:* In some motel rooms. *Pets:* Permitted with supervision. *Open:* All year. *Mailing address:* Route 1, Box 296, Tiptonville, TN 38079. *Phone:* (901) 253-7756. *Driving instructions:* The Airpark Inn is on Route 78, about 10 miles north of Tiptonville.

Roan Mountain State Resort Park's 1,450 acres are in north-eastern Tennessee, in the Appalachian Mountains, about 30 miles southeast of Johnson City near the Tennessee–North Carolina border. This splendid park lies entirely within the boundaries of the Cherokee National Forest, on a broad, grassy plateau extending for 6 miles at an elevation of nearly 6,000 feet. The park is home to the world's most extensive natural stand of rhododendron. At the annual Rhododendron Festival held here each year in late June, you can walk for miles through the dark purple blossoms.

Seven well-marked trails meander through the park, ranging in length from less than half a mile to almost 4 ½ miles, following mountain peaks, streams, or the Doe River. In spring the park is the setting for the Carter County Wildflower and Bird Walks, and each fall there's a Roan Mountain Naturalist Rally. The park has three cross-country ski trails that total about 9 miles, as well as facilities for badminton, volleyball, horseshoe pitching, and Ping-Pong. A restaurant that seats fifty is open all year except in winter.

Roan Mountain Park has twenty cabins, accommodating six adults each, that are built of western red cedar with cedar-shingle roofs. Each has a bedroom, a complete kitchen, and a large living room–dining area running the length of the cabin, as does the porch this area opens onto. A sleeping loft overlooks the living room, which is furnished with a sofa bed, two chairs, a coffee table, and two end tables, and has a Fisher wood stove on a stone hearth. None of the cabins has television or a telephone.

Accommodations: 20 cabins with private bath. *Towels and linens:* Provided. *Cooking and eating utensils:* Provided. *Stove and refrigerator:* Provided. *Pets:* Not permitted. *Open:* All year. *Mailing address:* Route 1, Box 236, Roan Mountain, TN 37687. *Phone:* (615) 772-3303. *Driving instructions:* Take U.S. 19E to Roan Mountain, then take Route 143 south for 2 miles.

The 11,000-acre Standing Stone State Rustic Park is in north central Tennessee on the Cumberland plateau, roughly 75 miles northeast of Nashville and 15 miles south of the Kentucky border. The park takes its name from an 8-foot-tall sandstone boulder that stood on a ledge and marked a boundary between two Indian tribes. The stone, which fell one day, is preserved as a monument in Monterey, Tennessee. The land here, once badly eroded, was chosen in the 1930s by the Works Progress Administration and the Civilian Conservation Corps for development and reforestation.

A 69-acre lake is frequented by anglers and boaters, who may rent rowboats. There are a swimming pool, tennis courts, 10 miles of hiking trails, as well as facilities for basketball, badminton, volleyball, and other field sports.

Standing Stone Park Lodges and Cabins

In a wooded area a few hundred yards from the lake, which is obscured by foliage in summer, are seventeen cabins. Fourteen are constructed of chestnut logs and have stone fireplaces. Most of these have one bedroom, but one has three bedrooms. Each has a porch, a full kitchen, and a private bath. Each of three "timberlodge" cabins has three bedrooms, a fireplace, a living room, a kitchen, and a private bath.

The park also has three group lodges that can accommodate twelve, sixteen, or fifty people. Each has a full kitchen and a dining area, and one, Overton Lodge, is right on the lake.

Accommodations: 17 cabins with private bath and 3 group lodges with shared bath. *Towels and linens:* Provided. *Cooking and eating utensils:* Provided. *Stove and refrigerator:* Provided. *Pets:* Not permitted. *Open:* All year (lodges); April through November (rustic cabins). *Mailing address:* Livingston, TN 38570. *Phone:* (615) 823-6347. *Driving instructions:* Standing Stone State Rustic Park is on Route 52, about 20 miles north of Cookeville.

Tims Ford State Rustic Park, 413 acres in the Elk River Valley, is in southern Tennessee, roughly 65 miles west of Chattanooga. For purposes of flood control, the Tennessee Valley Authority built the Tims Ford Dam at the headwaters of the Elk River, whose basin was apparently populated as many as twelve thousand years ago. Before the dam was completed and the area flooded, archaeologists dug in the basin and uncovered artifacts used by ancient inhabitants.

Tims Ford Lake, a 10,700-acre reservoir, is frequented by anglers and boaters, and visitors can rent fishing and boating supplies as well as boats with a 9-horsepower motor. The park has 5 miles of paved trails for hikers and bicyclists, and its swimming pool, the largest in Tennessee, is L-shaped, with a children's wading pool and a 12-foot-deep diving pool. Other activities include badminton, basketball, and table tennis.

The park has twenty cabins on a wooded slope overlooking the lake. They are constructed of western red cedar and supported on stilts to permit a view of the water. Each cabin has two bedrooms, a sunken living room with a fireplace, hardwood floors, three balconies—one off each bedroom and one off the living room—and a private bath. The cabins come with complete kitchen facilities and color television.

Accommodations: 20 cabins with private bath. *Towels and linens:* Provided. *Cooking and eating utensils:* Provided. *Stove and refrigerator:* Provided. *Pets:* Not permitted. *Open:* March through November. *Mailing address:* Route 4, Winchester, TN 37398. *Phone:* (615) 967-3230 or 967-1952. *Driving instructions:* Tims Ford State Rustic Park is off Route 50W, about 11 miles west of Winchester.

Texas

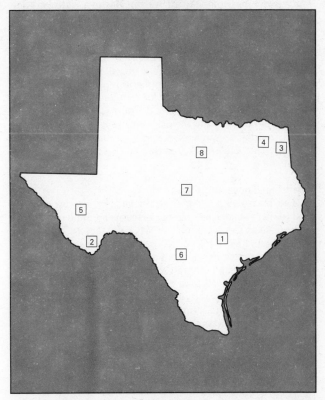

State map and tourist information: Tourist Development Agency, Box 12008, Capitol Station, Austin, TX 78711; 512-475-4326. **State parks:** *Information:* Parks Dept., 4200 Smith School Rd., Austin, TX 78744; 512-479-4890. *Entrance fees:* $2 per vehicle daily; $15, annually; waived for senior citizens. *Reservations:* Contact individual park. Deposit for first night by check. Reservations accepted (and recommended) up to 90 days in advance throughout year. *Restrictions:* No hunting. Dogs must be leashed (not allowed in lodgings). No alcohol. *Facilities:* Swimming, Mem. Day—Labor Day. Golf, all year.

Thirty-two miles southeast of Austin, Bastrop State Park is a reserve of 3,503 acres where a sprawling stand of loblolly pines—the "lost pines" of Texas—grow. They call these loblolly woodlands "lost" because they're separated by a 100-mile stretch of post oak forest from the major east-Texas stands. Loblollies are tall, straight pines whose clusters of needles look like spheres with dark centers and light peripheries.

The park contains a small lake, a swimming pool, a scenic drive, and a 3,353-yard, nine-hole golf course. The 900-acre Lake Bastrop, although not in the park but close by, has swimming, fishing, boating, and waterskiing facilities. Bastrop is contiguous with Buescher State Park, another 1,013-acre thickly wooded reserve.

Lost Pines Lodge and Cabins

The park has a "lodge" cabin and twelve rustic cabins overlooking a small lake from its northern end. Built in the 1930s by the Civilian Conservation Corps (CCC), they are constructed of either hand-hewn logs or stone, each with a stone fireplace. The cabins vary in size and can accommodate from two to six people with private bath and shower. Lost Pines Lodge, with four bedrooms, two baths, a kitchenette, and a living room, accommodates as many as eight. All cabins have cooking facilities, although cooking and eating utensils are not provided. They are furnished simply. Many still have their original wooden furnishings, carved by the CCC staff.

Accommodations: 4 lodge rooms with shared baths and 12 cabins with private bath and shower. *Towels and linens:* Provided. *Blankets:* Not provided. *Cooking and eating utensils:* Not provided. *Stove and refrigerator:* Provided. *Pets:* Permitted if leashed; not permitted in cabins. *Open:* All year. *Mailing address:* Box 518, Bastrop, TX 78602. *Phone:* (512) 321-2101. *Driving instructions:* Bastrop State Park is off Route 21 about a mile east of Bastrop.

Big Bend National Park is in southwestern Texas, about 300 miles southeast of El Paso and across from Mexico. The 740,118-acre park is named after a big bend in the Rio Grande River, which forms the southern border of the park as well as the U.S.–Mexican border. Running for 107 miles along the edge of the park, the Rio Grande passes through three large and scenic canyons, parts of which are so steep that sunlight never shines directly onto the canyon floors. Two of the canyons, Santa Elena and Boquillas, are acccessible by trails and well worth a day trip, especially for photographers and birders.

The terrain is a mixture of cactus-sprinkled desert lowlands and 7,800-foot mountains wooded with pines, oaks, and junipers. In summer, temperatures in the desert and river valley average about 100°F., while the mountainous areas average a comfortable 85°. Visitors should always check with park rangers before attempting an ambitious desert hike, for water can be scarce and high temperatures far more enervating than one may suspect. The park has many trails and a good system of paved and improved dirt roads. Primitive roads also meander through the park, but visitors again should check with park rangers about conditions on these before driving through.

Big Bend National Park supports some four hundred species of birds and more than a thousand species of plants, including some unusually delicate flowering cacti. In addition to the wide range of plant and animal life, the area also hosts some of the country's most awesome scenery. The stretches of desert, the canyons, the mountains, the sheer rock faces, and even the clouds overhead seem to change color constantly as though each angle of the sun represented a different palette.

Horseback riding and river rafting are other ways of touring the park, and the park naturalists service offers interpretative talks and guided walks. *Park mailing address:* Superintendent, Big Bend National Park, TX 79834. *Park phone:* (915) 477-2251.

Chisos Mountain Lodge and Cottages

In the Chisos Basin, at an elevation of 5,400 feet, Chisos Mountain Lodge consists of a 1966 concrete-and-glass lodge with a restaurant, a coffee shop, and a gift shop; a motel unit with twenty-eight guest rooms; and six adobe cottages. The lodge is

at the center of park activity, and the restaurant and half of the motel rooms have mountain views.

The motel rooms have wall-to-wall carpeting and private baths. The adobe cottages have flagstone floors, private baths, and can accommodate six people each. If need be, the cottages can be equipped with roll-away beds to accommodate eight adults.

Accommodations: 28 motel rooms and 6 cottages, all with private bath. *Towels and linens:* Provided. *Cooking and eating utensils:* Not provided. *Stove and refrigerator:* Not provided. *Pets:* Permitted. *Open:* All year. *Mailing address:* Big Bend National Park, TX 79834. *Phone:* (915) 477-2291. *Driving instructions:* Big Bend National Park boundary is on U.S. 385 about 45 miles south of Marathon.

Caddo Lake State Park is 480 acres in northeastern Texas about 140 miles east of Dallas and 30 miles northwest of Shreveport, Louisiana. Legend has it that the Great Spirit once warned a chief of the Caddo Indians to lead his people to high ground lest they be annihilated by earthquakes and floods. The chief ignored the warning, so the legend goes, and soon afterward a party of warriors returned from a hunt to find their village gone and an enormous lake covering the land. According to modern-day geologists, however, Caddo Lake was formed by logs that jammed up the Red River and flooded its tributaries.

Caddo Lake was at one time an important waterway, part of a water route from New Orleans to Jefferson, Texas; but when the U.S. Army Corps of Engineers cleared the river blockages, the level of the lake dropped. These days it has labyrinthine bayous and channels winding through groves of giant cypresses draped with Spanish moss. The park adjoins Big Cypress Bayou and is dotted with piney woods and hardwood bottomlands.

Activities include swimming, boating, waterskiing, and fishing. There are several hiking trails, and picnic facilities are set among the piney woods and beside the bayou.

The park has nine cabins built of pine logs and mortar, seven with fireplaces equipped with gas logs. Set in a wooded area, the cabins vary in size, accommodating from two to six people. Four have hardwood floors, and each has a kitchen, a private bath with shower, heating, and air-conditioning.

Accommodations: 9 cabins with private bath. *Towels and linens:* Provided. *Blankets:* Not provided. *Cooking and eating utensils:* Not provided. *Stove and refrigerator:* Provided. *Pets:* Not permitted. *Open:* All year. *Mailing address:* Route 2, Box 15, Karnack, TX 75661. *Phone:* (214) 679-3351. *Driving instructions:* From Marshall take Route 43 northeast 14 miles, then take Route 2198 east 1 mile.

The 551-acre Daingerfield State Park is near the northeastern corner of Texas, about 55 miles southwest of Texarkana, in a region that is heavily forested with a mixture of pines and hardwoods that the state has been managing for preservation and recreation purposes since the 1930s. The 80-acre Lake Daingerfield, popular with swimmers, anglers, and boating enthusiasts, has a boat-launching ramp, as well as a dock. (There is a 5 mph speed limit.) Paddleboats and canoes are available.

Both the road into the park and a 2½-mile nature trail encircling the lake are lined with dogwoods. The trail leads through stands of cinnamon ferns that grow up to 5 feet. Daingerfield Lake attracts migrating waterfowl and offers colorful reflections when the leaves turn color in autumn.

Daingerfield Park Lodge and Cabins

The park has a lodge and three cabins, each overlooking the lake and having a kitchenette and a private bath with shower, heat, and air-conditioning. Two smaller wood-frame cabins accommodate up to six each. The larger cabin, built of stone, can sleep up to eight. The wood-frame lodge, which can accommodate groups of up to twenty, has a kitchen, a living room, five bedrooms, two baths, and a fireplace.

Accommodations: 1 lodge and 3 cabins with private bath and shower. *Towels and linens:* Provided. *Blankets:* Provided. *Cooking and eating utensils:* Not provided. *Stove and refrigerator:* Provided. *Pets:* Not permitted. *Open:* All year. *Mailing address:* Route 1, Box 286-B, Daingerfield, TX 75638. *Phone:* (214) 645-2921. *Driving instructions:* Daingerfield State Park is off Route 49 on Park Road 17 about 3 miles east of Daingerfield.

Davis Mountains State Park, on 1,869 acres in southwestern Texas about 90 miles south of Pecos, takes its name from the Davis Mountains, which have many peaks above 7,000 feet—Mount Livermore (8,382), Sawtooth Mountain (7,748), and Black Mountain (7,550), to name a few. At an average elevation of about 5,200 feet on the Upper Limpia Creek, the park and its surrounding areas support a wide range of flora and fauna, including wild orchids (depending on rainfall), magueys, sotols, and cacti, black- and white-tailed deer, and pronghorn antelope.

North of the park are the ruins of Fort Davis, which was built in 1854 and abandoned in the early 1890s. Another nearby attraction is McDonald Observatory. On the summit of Mount Locke, 6,791 feet up, the observatory houses a 26-foot-long, 75-ton telescope that is open to the public during the day. Lectures are offered, and a limited number of people (who must apply by writing in advance) are given access to the telescope to observe the stars at night on the last Wednesday of each month. *Park phone:* (915) 426-3337.

Indian Lodge

The pueblo-style Indian Lodge is on a hill overlooking Limpia canyon. The original section of the lodge was built in the 1930s by the Civilian Conservation Corps and now houses fifteen rooms, all with handmade furniture, built by the CCC staff, and vegas (exposed beams). The 1967 addition has twenty-four more modern rooms, along with a restaurant, a gift shop, an assembly room for tours and conventions, and a huge lobby with comfortable couches and lounge chairs, color television, and a fireplace. Each guest room has air-conditioning, a television, a telephone, and a private bath. There are various accommodations, some with single beds, some with double beds, and some with a combination. There is also one suite, a heated swimming pool, and a nearby playground for children. The lodge restaurant operates from 7:30 A.M. to 9:00 P.M.

Accommodations: 39 rooms with private bath. *Pets:* Not permitted. *Open:* All year except two weeks in late January. *Mailing address:* Box 786, Davis Mountain State Park, Fort Davis, TX 79734. *Phone:* (915) 426-3254. *Driving instructions:* Indian Lodge is on Route 118 about 4 miles north of Fort Davis.

Named after former Vice President of the United States John Nance Garner, Garner State Park is on 1,420 acres in a rugged, hilly section of southeastern Texas about 75 miles west of San Antonio. The park is bordered on the west by the Frio ("cold") River, popular with swimmers and, when the water's high, with tube riders. The spring-fed Frio has grassy banks lined with pecans, oaks, elms, and bald cypresses, and affords a naturally shallow wading area for children at a point where it flows slowly over a section of rock.

The terrain—hills, canyons, and meadows crisscrossed by spring-fed streams—is inhabited by white-tailed deer, armadillos, wild turkeys, quail, and chachalacas (game birds usually found in Mexico). The park has a 75-foot-deep natural cave, plenty of hiking trails, and several lookout points with panoramic views. Parts of it are blanketed by ferns and mosses; others, with wildflowers in spring. Live oak and Spanish oak are profuse, and the shrubbery includes wild cherry and persimmon bushes. Facilities include a miniature-golf course and paddleboats, and each summer night the park sponsors a country-and-western dance.

Fourteen of the park's eighteen cabins were built of cypress and cedar in the 1930s by the Civilian Conservation Corps and have stone fireplaces. Four others, without fireplaces, are of more recent construction. Each cabin has a stove and a refrigerator, as well as a private bath with shower, and can accommodate six people with three double beds.

Accommodations: 18 cabins with private bath. *Towels and linens:* Provided. *Blankets:* Not provided. *Cooking and eating utensils:* Not provided. *Stove and refrigerator:* Provided. *Pets:* Not permitted. *Open:* All year. *Mailing address:* Concan, TX 78838. *Phone:* (512) 232-6132. *Driving instructions:* Garner State Park is off U.S. 83 about 31 miles north of Uvalde.

Lake Brownwood, actually a reservoir formed by a dam on the Pecan Bayou, a tributary of the Colorado River, has a surface area of 7,300 acres and 100 miles of shoreline. Of this, 538 acres constitute Lake Brownwood State Recreation Area, about 68 miles southeast of Abilene and 20 miles north of Brownwood. The lake's rugged shore is rocky and lined mainly with oaks, willows, and mesquites. Facilities include boat-launching ramps and docks, a lighted fishing pier, and supervised and unsupervised swimming and waterskiing areas.

The Lake Brownwood area, one of the most fertile in Texas, was extensively used by the Apache and Comanche Indians, who found here an abundance of game and water. Well-maintained hiking and nature trails run through wooded areas; there are several playgrounds.

Lake Brownwood Lodges and Cabins

The seventeen cabins and three lodges at the recreation area were all built of native stone by the Civilian Conservation Corps in the 1930s. Each cabin has a fireplace, a kitchen, a private bath, and a lake view.

Beach Lodge, close to the lake, can accommodate up to twenty-six people in a dormitory arrangement. It has a dining room, a living room, a kitchen, two baths, and a fireplace. Fisherman's Lodge has five bedrooms and can accommodate a maximum of ten people with a kitchen, a living room, two baths, a stone fireplace, and a stone patio. Group Hall has a dining room with eight group tables, a kitchenette, and four bunkhouses that sleep eight each. Bath and shower facilities are in separate buildings.

Accommodations: 17 cabins with private bath and 3 group lodges with shared baths. *Towels and linens:* Provided except Group Hall. *Blankets:* Provided except Group Hall. *Cooking and eating utensils:* Not provided. *Stove and refrigerator:* Provided. *Pets:* Permitted outside only and if leashed. *Open:* All year. *Mailing address:* Route 5, Box 160, Brownwood, TX 76801. *Phone:* (915) 784-5223. *Driving instructions:* From Brownwood take Route 279 north 16 miles, then take Park Road 15 east for 6 miles.

Possum Kingdom State Recreation Area is in north-central Texas about 100 miles west of Fort Worth. The 1,528-acre reserve is along the shore of Possum Kingdom Lake, an impoundment of the Brazos River. The lake, with 310 miles of shoreline, is stocked with striped bass and has large populations of black bass, perch, and catfishes. The facilities include a fishing pier, rowboat rentals, two boat launches for those who bring their own craft, and a designated swimming zone about half a mile away from a bathhouse.

The recreation area has no marked or designated trails, but visitors are free to hike or walk wherever they like, although in the hotter months they should beware of rattlesnakes. (Rattlesnakes are far more afraid of you than you are of them, and the chance of coming across one is almost nill; but if you do, give the creature plenty of room.) Other characteristic wildlife are deer, raccoons, opossums, skunks, and, of late, a few cougars. Resident mallards and geese are always on the lake, and during migrations all manner of waterfowl congregate. The recreation area's terrain varies from flat to hilly and rocky, and cedars and junipers are the predominant tree species.

The recreation area has six cement-and-wood cabins in an open area about 100 yards from the lake. Each has a kitchenette, a small open porch, air-conditioning, electric heating, a private bath, and a lake view.

Accommodations: 6 cabins with private bath. *Towels and linens:* Provided. *Cooking and eating utensils:* Not provided. *Stove and refrigerator:* Provided. *Pets:* Not permitted. *Open:* All year. *Mailing address:* Box 36, Caddo, TX 76029. *Phone:* (817) 549-1803. *Driving instructions:* Possum Kingdom State Recreation Area is on Park Road 33, which runs north from U.S. 180, about 60 miles west of Fort Worth.

Utah

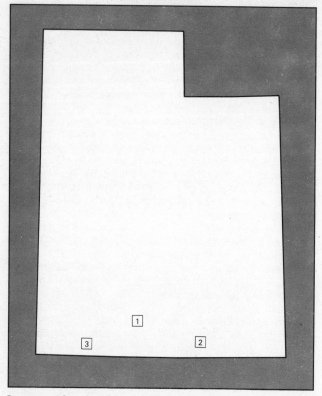

1

3   2

State map and tourist information: Travel Council, Council Hall, Capitol Hill, Salt Lake City, UT 84114; 801-533-5681. **State parks:** *Information:* State Parks Dept., 1636 W. N. Temple St., Salt Lake City, UT 84116; 801-533-6011. **National parks:** Contact park directly.

Bryce Canyon National Park's 36,010 acres are in southwestern Utah, at the southern edge of Dixie National Forest, about 80 miles east of Cedar City. The canyon consists of a series of horseshoe-shaped bowls that resemble amphitheaters cut into the Paunsaugunt Plateau, which is composed mostly of pink and ivory-hued limestone. The bowls are crowded together, their otherworldly spires, minarets, walls, and pinnacles colored in reds and shades of pink and maroon. Sections of the canyon have such names as Wall Street, Peekaboo Canyon, and Silent City. From the edge of the plateau's Pink Cliffs, the spire-filled bowls resemble a cityscape with skyscrapers.

The park varies in elevation from about 6,500 to 9,000 feet, which results in an unusual array of vegetation. In areas not dominated by pink stone castles, there are such different species as sagebrush, dwarf juniper, piñon and ponderosa pine, Douglas and white fir, and blue spruce. Although the main pastime here is viewing the scenery, other activities include interpretive programs such as guided walks; hiking and horseback riding; and in winter, cross-country skiing and snowshoeing. *Park mailing address:* Superintendent, Bryce Canyon National Park, Bryce Canyon, UT 84717. *Park phone:* (801) 834-5322.

Bryce Canyon Lodge and Cabins

Bryce Canyon Lodge, elevation 8,000 feet, has a rustic stone-and-wood lodge and 120 cabins. The main lodge has a large lobby with couches, easy chairs, and a large stone fireplace, as well as a dining room and a gift shop.

The accommodations come in two varieties, "Western" cabins and motel units. The Western cabins, built of logs, sleep five and are more luxuriously appointed, each with thick carpeting, wood-paneled walls, a private bath with tub and shower, a vanity and dressing area, a gas-log fireplace, a telephone, and a porch. Each of the 70 motel units features carpeting, a private bath, and a private porch.

Accommodations: 120 cabins and motel units with private bath. *Towels and linens:* Provided. *Cooking and eating utensils:* Not provided. *Stove and refrigerator:* Not provided. *Pets:* Not permitted. *Open:* Mid-May through September. *Mailing address:*

TWA Services, 451 North Main Street, PO Box 400, Cedar City, UT 84720. *Phone:* (801) 586-7686. *Driving instructions:* From Panguitch take U.S. 89 south about 7 miles, then take Route 12 east about 17 miles.

Glen Canyon National Recreation Area is in southern Utah, just north of Page, Arizona, and the Glen Canyon Dam. To the south of the 1,245,855-acre area are Grand Canyon National Park and the Navaho Indian Reservation; to the east is Natural Bridges National Monument; and to the north, Canyonlands National Park. The area's name comes from a description of the wooded "glens" of the Colorado River Valley by John Wesley Powell, who explored this region in the 1860s and 1870s. (The medieval Scottish word *glen* meant a narrow, secluded valley or canyon.)

Powell, a strong advocate of water reclamation, gave his name to Lake Powell, an impoundment of the Colorado River formed by Glen Canyon Dam. The 1,560-foot-long dam, rising 710 feet from its base at bedrock and consisting of 5 million cubic yards of concrete, flooded Glen Canyon and created an unusually beautiful lake, a 180-mile stretch of water bordered by precipitous canyons of red Navaho sandstone.

Boating is by far the most popular activity, followed closely by fishing, waterskiing, and swimming. Anglers go after largemouth and striped bass, rainbow and brown trout, walleyed and northern pike, catfishes, and crappies. Some record catches: a rainbow trout weighing 16 pounds 11 ounces, a 24-pound catfish, and a striped bass weighing 31 pounds 6 ounces. A variety of boats, including houseboats, are available at the marinas, and many cruise packages are available, including a "Sunset-Moonlight Dinner Cruise" that leaves from Wahweap.

Visitors should be sure to see Rainbow Bridge, the world's largest natural stone bridge. *Park mailing address:* Box 1507, Page, AZ 86040. *Park phone:* (602) 645-2471.

Bullfrog Resort and Marina

About 60 miles (by air, 295 by road, 90 by boat) north of Glen Canyon Dam, Bullfrog Resort and Marina has a fifty-room motel and sixteen "housekeeping units" that are mobile homes with either two or three bedrooms. The resort store sells food, beer, and fishing and boating supplies; and its restaurant seats two hundred and overlooks the lake.

The motel unit, next to the restaurant, is on a hill above Lake Powell, of which half its rooms have views. Each room has wall-to-wall carpeting, color television, a telephone, and

Rainbow Bridge

a private bath. Each housekeeping unit is carpeted and has a fully equipped kitchen and a private bath. These units are set back about half a mile from the lake in a desert area.

Bullfrog Resort and Marina also has available a varying number of houseboats, ranging from 34 to 50 feet, that accommodate from four to ten. Each has a fully equipped kitchen and a bath with shower.

Accommodations: 50 motel rooms, 16 housekeeping units, a varying number of houseboats, all with private bath. *Towels and linens:* In housekeeping units. *Cooking and eating utensils:* Provided. *Stove and refrigerator:* Provided. *Pets:* Not permitted. *Open:* All year. *Mailing address:* Hanksville, UT 84734. *Phone:* (801) 684-2233. *Driving instructions:* From Hanksville take Route 95 to Route 276, then take Route 276 south to Bullfrog Resort and Marina.

Hite Resort and Marina

Just north of Farley Canyon and about 100 miles (by air, 140 by boat, 250 by road) northeast of Glen Canyon Dam, Hite Resort and Marina consists of five "housekeeping units" and two stores that sell groceries, souvenirs, and fishing and boating supplies.

The housekeeping units, three-bedroom mobile homes, each with carpeting, a kitchen, and a private bath, are set back about 1 ½ miles from the lake in a desert area.

The resort and marina also rent out houseboats that are from 34 to 50 feet long and can accommodate from four to ten. Each is fully equipped with a kitchen and a bath with shower. Marina staff will show inexperienced boaters how to operate them.

Accommodations: 5 housekeeping units and a varying number of houseboats, all with private bath. *Towels and linens:* In housekeeping units. *Cooking and eating utensils:* Provided. *Stove and refrigerator:* Provided. *Pets:* Not permitted. *Open:* All year. *Mailing address:* Star Route 1, Box 1, Hanksville, UT 84734. *Phone:* (801) 684-2278. *Driving instructions:* From Blanding take U.S. 163 south to Route 95, then take Route 95 northwest to Hite Resort; from Hanksville take Route 95 south.

Hall's Crossing Resort and Marina

About 60 miles (by air, 90 by boat, 250 by road) northeast of Glen Canyon Dam and just east of Halls Creek Bay, Hall's

Crossing Resort and Marina consists of a store that sells groceries, souvenirs, and fishing and boating supplies, as well as sixteen housekeeping units set back about half a mile from the lake in a desert area. Each housekeeping unit is a three-bedroom mobile home with a kitchen and a bathroom with shower.

The resort and marina also rents out houseboats that are fully equipped, each with a kitchen and a bath. The houseboats range from 34 to 50 feet and can accommodate from four to ten.

Accommodations: 16 housekeeping units and a varying number of houseboats, all with private bath. *Towels and linens:* In housekeeping units. *Cooking and eating utensils:* Provided. *Stove and refrigerator:* Provided. *Pets:* Not permitted. *Open:* All year. *Mailing address:* Blanding, UT 84511. *Phone:* (801) 684-2261. *Driving instructions:* From Blanding take U.S. 163 south to Route 95, then take Route 95 west to Route 263, which runs to Hall's Crossing Resort and Marina.

Lake Powell

Wahweap Lodge and Marina

About 5 miles north of Glen Canyon Dam and the visitors' center and a few miles west of Antelope Island, Wahweap Lodge and Marina is a group of modern motel-style buildings with guest rooms, restaurants, and stores that sell food, beer, and fishing and boating supplies. The lodge has a sandy beach, where summer water temperatures reach seventy-six degrees.

Each of the 269 lodge rooms, half of which overlook the lake, has wall-to-wall carpeting, color television, a telephone, a private bath, and either a balcony or a patio. Of several two-room suites, some have small refrigerators. The complex's two restaurants overlook the lake, and its lobby has a fireplace.

Wahweap Lodge and Marina also rents out houseboats from 34 to 50 feet long that accommodate from four to ten. Each is equipped with a kitchen, a toilet, and a shower. Guests renting houseboats needn't have any boating skills: Marina staff will teach novices how to handle the craft.

Accommodations: 269 lodge rooms and a varying number of houseboats, all with private bath. *Towels and linens:* In lodge. *Cooking and eating utensils:* In houseboats. *Stove and refrigerator:* In houseboats. *Pets:* Not permitted. *Open:* All year. *Mailing address:* PO Box 1597, Page, AZ 86040. *Phone:* (602) 645-2433. *Driving instructions:* Wahweap Lodge is off U.S. 89 (look for signs) about 10 miles northwest of Page, Arizona.

Zion National Park, in southwestern Utah about 25 miles south of Cedar City, is some 147,035 acres of colored canyons, deep red mountain domes, sage flats, cacti, and stands of ponderosa pine, Douglas fir, and quaking aspen. The canyons are composed primarily of Navaho sandstone deposited millions of years ago by an inland sea; the major erosive force is the Virgin River, which follows a gradient ten times as steep as that of the Colorado River. The canyon walls rise precipitously, and in a very short distance can go from allowing a reasonably wide thoroughfare at their bases to closing up to form a darkened passage resembling an alley between two skyscrapers.

Just looking is definitely the most popular activity, especially at such sights as Angels Landing, Checkerboard Mesa, Bridge Mountain, the Temple of Sinawava, the Great White Throne, and The Watchman.

The park has several scenic roads and many well-marked trails. Visitors can sign up for guided backpacking trips, guided walks, trips on horseback, and interpretative talks and programs. *Park mailing address:* Superintendent, Zion National Park, Springdale, UT 84767. *Phone:* (801) 586-7624.

Zion Lodge and Cabins

Zion Lodge consists of a rustic wood-and-stone lodge and 120 cabins at an elevation of 4,000 feet in the canyon. The lodge building has an upstairs dining room overlooking rock formations sprinkled with trees, a recreation room with a stone fireplace, a lobby with comfortable furniture, and a gift shop.

The cabins come in "Western" and "frontier" styles. The Western cabins, built of logs, are more luxuriously appointed with thick carpeting, wainscoting, wood-paneled walls, private baths with tub and shower, vanity and dressing areas, and porches, and sleep five. The wood-frame frontier cabins are smaller. Each has carpeting, a private bath with shower, a small porch, and can accommodate up to three.

Accommodations: 120 cabins with private bath. *Towels and linens:* Provided. *Cooking and eating utensils:* Not provided. *Stove and refrigerator:* Not provided. *Pets:* Not permitted. *Open:* May 12 through October 11. *Mailing address:* TW Services, Inc.

PO Box 400, Cedar City, UT 84720. *Phone:* (801) 586-7686. *Driving instructions:* From Cedar City take I-15 south about 30 miles to Route 9, then take Route 9 east to Zion National Park and the lodge.

Virginia

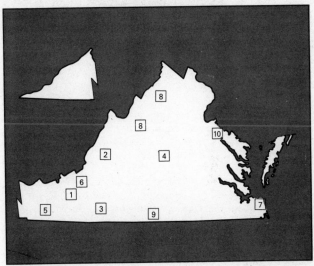

State map and tourist information: Div. of Tourism, 101 Bell Tower, Capitol Sq., N. 9th St., Richmond, VA 23219; 804-786-4484. **State parks:** *Information:* Div. of Parks, 1201 Washington Bldg., Capitol Sq., Richmond, VA 23219; 804-786-2132 or 786-2134. *Entrance fees:* $1 per vehicle daily; $15, annually; waived for lodgers. *Reservations:* Contact individual park, or call 804-490-3939. Deposit required for first night, check or credit card; mail payment for entire stay within 10 days. Reservations accepted (and recommended) up to 51 weeks in advance for most popular parks (Virginia Seashore & Douthat). Recommended up to 3 months in advance for June—Labor Day and 1 month in advance for May and September in all other parks. Minimum stay, 1 week; maximum 2 weeks. *Restrictions:* Hunting limited to certain parks. Dogs must be leashed; fee of $1 per day, not to exceed $3 per week. *Facilities:* Swimming, interpretative programs, boating ($1 launch fee), Mem. Day—Labor Day.

Claytor Lake State Park, 472 acres in southwestern Virginia about 50 miles southwest of Roanoke, is in the foothills of the Appalachians about 10 miles east of Jefferson National Forest. The hilly terrain, wooded mainly with walnuts, maples, oaks, birches, and pines, is along the shore of Claytor Lake, which is 21 miles long and was formed by a dam. The park has a sandy beach with a bathhouse, a full-service marina with launching facilities, and boats for rent. Visitors can also fish, ride on miles of bridle trails, or hike.

The park has a snack bar and a visitors' center in the historic 1879 Howe House. The naturalist service leads nature walks and offers interpretative programs at a gazebo-like amphitheater.

The park's twelve concrete-block cabins have two bedrooms each and overlook Claytor Lake. Each has a fireplace, a fully equipped kitchen, rustic furnishings, and a hot-water heater.

Accommodations: 12 cabins with private bath. *Towels and linens:* Provided. *Cooking and eating utensils:* Provided. *Stove and refrigerator:* Provided. *Pets:* Permitted ($1.00 fee per day). *Open:* May through September. *Mailing address:* Route 1, Box 267, Dublin, VA 24084. *Phone:* (703) 674-5492. *Driving instructions:* Claytor Lake State Park is off I-81 at exit 33 near Dublin.

Douthat State Park, 4,493 acres in the Appalachian Mountains, is in western Virginia about 50 miles north of Roanoke and about 30 miles west of the southern tip of Monongahela National Forest in West Virginia. The terrain is heavily wooded with oaks, maples, tulip trees, and pines, and elevations are as high as 3,050 feet. A 50-acre lake, with a white sand beach and a bathhouse, is stocked, Memorial Day through Labor Day, by the state with 100,000 rainbow trout. There is a special day-by-day trout-fishing fee, and visitors can rent boats at the park dock, which also has fishing equipment.

The park has 40 miles of wooded hiking trails, as well as a grocery store, a snack bar, and a restaurant overlooking the lake. The visitors' center has wildlife exhibits and resident naturalists during the summer months. *Park phone:* (703) 862-7200.

Douthat Park Lodge and Cabins

The park has thirty cabins and a lodge. Cabins vary in size and construction and can accommodate from two to six; the lodge can accommodate twelve. Twenty-five of the cabins and the lodge are constructed of logs, and five cabins are built of concrete block. There are five one-room, thirteen one-bedroom, and twelve two-bedroom cabins, all of which have recently been renovated. Each has a fireplace, rustic furnishings, a kitchen, and a private bath. The lodge has a kitchen, a dining-sleeping room, five bedrooms, and two baths.

Accommodations: 1 lodge with shared bath and 30 cabins with private bath. *Towels and linens:* Provided. *Cooking and eating utensils:* Provided. *Stove and refrigerator:* Provided. *Pets:* Permitted ($1.00 per day; $3.00 per week fee). *Open:* Memorial Day through Labor Day. *Mailing address:* Route 1, Box 212, Millboro, VA 24460. *Phone:* (703) 826-7200. *Driving instructions:* Douthat State Park is on Route 629 about 4 miles north of I-64 near Clifton Forge.

The story is that when news of Christ's death was brought to the foothills of the Blue Ridge Mountains, the fairies and nymphs dancing by a stream there wept, and as their tears fell on the ground small crystalline crosses, the "fairy stones," were formed. But geologists have a different explanation for this phenomenon found near the southern part of the 4,570-acre Fairy Stone State Park: The heat, pressure, and upheaval during the formation of the Appalachian Mountains created staurolite, which forms small hexagonal crystals that occur only in pairs. If these pairs intersect at right or nearly right angles, they form tiny crosses.

In addition to collecting fairy stones, visitors may swim in the 168-acre Fairy Stone Lake, which has a sand beach with a bathhouse. The park has bicycling and self-guided hiking trails, as well as horses for hire and bridle trails. Fishing and boating are also popular, with launching facilities and boats for rent. Other facilities include a grocery store, a snack bar, and a restaurant overlooking the lake.

The park has twenty-four cabins, several overlooking the lake. They vary in size from one room to two bedrooms and can accommodate from two to six people. Eight are log cabins, and sixteen are built of concrete block. Each has a fireplace, rustic furnishings, a kitchen, a water heater, and a private bath with shower.

Accommodations: 24 cabins with private bath. *Towels and linens:* Not provided. *Cooking and eating utensils:* Provided. *Stove and refrigerator:* Provided. *Pets:* Not permitted. *Open:* May through September. *Mailing address:* Route 2, Box 134, Stuart, VA 24171. *Phone:* (703) 930-2424. *Driving instructions:* Fairy Stone State Park is off Route 57 about 8 miles west of Bassett.

A 270-acre reserve with two freshwater lakes, Goodwin Lake–Prince Edward State Park is in south-central Virginia, roughly 60 miles southwest of Richmond. The park, most of which has been left undeveloped, is popular among boaters, anglers, and swimmers. Its lake has a beach with a bathhouse, and visitors can either rent boats or launch their own. There is also a snack bar.

Several hiking trails include the self-guided Twin Beech Trail, named after a twin beech tree, runs through a forest of white, red, swamp, turkey, chinquapin, and other species of oak, a stand of dogwoods, a groundhog burrow, and a place where crayfish and tadpoles may be found. The trail, passing through an area of early forest succession, finally comes to a spot where the respective understories of low and high ground may be quickly and easily compared.

The park has six cabins in a loop area at the northern tip of Prince Edward Lake. Constructed of concrete block, each has two bedrooms, a fireplace, a fully equipped kitchen, rustic furnishings, a water heater, and a private bath with shower.

Accommodations: 6 cabins with private bath. *Towels and linens:* Not provided. *Cooking and eating utensils:* Provided. *Stove and refrigerator:* Provided. *Pets:* Permitted. *Open:* May through October. *Mailing address:* Route 2, Box 70, Green Bay, VA 23942. *Phone:* (804) 392-3435. *Driving instructions:* Goodwin Lake–Prince Edward State Park is off U.S. 360, about 4 miles south of Burkeville.

Hungry Mother State Park takes its name from the legend of Molly Marley, who, along with her young son and other women and children, was taken hostage after an Indian raid and massacre. Molly and her child managed to escape and wandered through the mountains eating nothing but berries. When she collapsed beside a stream at the foot of what is now called Molly's Knob, the child followed the stream until he arrived at a cluster of houses. He was able to utter only the words "Hungry mother." A search party found Molly's body and named the stream Hungry Mother Creek.

The 2,180-acre park is in southwestern Virginia, about 100 miles southwest of Roanoke and adjacent to the southwestern extremity of Jefferson National Forest. A 108-acre lake, formed in the 1930s by damming Hungry Mother Creek, has a sand beach and a bathhouse. The park has launching facilities where visitors can also rent boats. Horses are for hire, and the park has a bridle trail as well as many hiking trails, including Molly's Knob Trail, which leads up to an elevation of 3,270 feet and a panorama of the park's mountainous terrain, most of which has been left in its natural state.

The park's twenty-five cabins vary in size and can accommodate from two to six people. There are five log cabins, eight wood-frame cabins, and twelve concrete-block cabins. Each has a fireplace, a kitchen, rustic furnishings, and a private bath with shower.

Accommodations: 25 cabins with private bath. *Towels and linens:* Provided. *Cooking and eating utensils:* Provided. *Stove and refrigerator:* Provided. *Pets:* Permitted. *Open:* May through October. *Mailing address:* Route 5, Box 109, Marion, VA 24354. *Phone:* (703) 783-3422. *Driving instructions:* Hungry Mother State Park is on Route 16—exit 16 or 17 on I-81—about 3 miles north of Marion.

The 700,000-acre Jefferson National Forest is in southwestern Virginia and southeastern West Virginia, along the West Virginia border in the Allegheny and Blue Ridge mountain ranges, bordered on the north by George Washington National Forest and on the south by the Cherokee National Forest in Tennessee. The region varies in elevation from about 900 to 5,729 feet at the summit of Mount Rogers—the highest point in Virginia—and in terrain from river bottomland to alpine meadows wooded with oaks, hickories, maples, walnuts, yellow pines, and, in a few sections, extensive stands of spruce. The forest encompasses several rivers—the James, New, Big Sandy, Cumberland, and Clinch—and seemingly numberless mountain streams. It also encompasses 9 wilderness areas totalling 47,872 acres, and the 115,700-acre Mt. Rogers National Recreation Area. More than 600 miles of trails wind through the forest, including a 300-mile section of the Appalachian Trail, which extends from Georgia to Maine. Wildlife includes deer, wild turkeys, foxes, and some black bears, along with a wide variety of bird life—hawks and eagles, many species of passerines, and—during migration season especially—ducks, geese, and other waterfowl.

Hiking and sightseeing are probably the most popular activities, followed by fishing, hunting, horseback riding, and canoeing. The James River attracts quite a few white-water enthusiasts and is, as are other rivers in the forest, stocked with rainbow and brook trout.

The Homestead

Constructed and operated in the grandest of traditions, the Homestead consists of several large buildings ranging from the original 1891 hotel to a sleek modern annex. The hotel has three golf courses, a ski slope, an indoor pool, tennis courts, an ice-skating rink, and complete spa facilities, with saunas, steam baths, mineral baths, and massage personnel. The level of service is unusual, to the point that the hotel's staff outnumbers its guests. The Homestead is particularly noted for its food, which is as bountiful as it is varied, with one hundred and fifty items on the lunch menu.

Guest accommodations vary from rooms in the modern wing,

decorated with modern furnishings, to bedrooms and parlors in the older wing, fitted out with traditional furnishings, and arranged in such a manner that adjacent rooms can be combined into suites or single rooms with parlors. Some have balconies, and others have porches.

Accommodations: 520 rooms with private bath. *Pets:* Not permitted. *Open:* All year. *Mailing address:* Route 220, Hot Springs, VA 24445. *Phone:* (703) 839-5500. *Driving instructions:* Take Route 220 south to Hot Springs and the Homestead.

Vine Cottage Inn

Five hundred yards from, and at one time owned by, the Homestead, Vine Cottage Inn was built in 1903. It now has seventeen guest rooms. The inn has a large veranda furnished with wicker and a living room with a fireplace and walnut wainscoting. Three of the guest rooms can accommodate as many as six people. There is also a ground-floor suite with a private entrance, a porch, a kitchen, and antique furnishings. Each room has a sink, and those with a private bath have a claw-footed tub. Many rooms have antique appointments, and a complimentary breakfast is included in the rates.

Accommodations: 17 rooms, 10 with private bath. *Pets:* Not permitted. *Open:* All year. *Mailing address:* Box 205, Route 220, Hot Springs, VA 24445. *Phone:* (703) 839-2422. *Driving instructions:* Vine Cottage Inn is on Route 220 in the town of Hot Springs.

Reminder: Rates and credit-card information are listed in the index.

Seashore State Park is in the city of Virginia Beach in southeastern Virginia, on Cape Henry, where the Chesapeake Bay meets the Atlantic Ocean. A designated national landmark, the park consists of 2,770 acres, most of which are being preserved as a natural area. The terrain varies enormously, with four different ecological habitats. The 27 miles of hiking trails pass through lagoons where Spanish moss grows on bald cypresses, through a semitropical forest, and over high dunes overlooking the bay. The Bald Cypress Trail runs through an area of dunes and swamps. A twenty-four–page guide to this trail is available free at the visitors' center, which also has interpretive exhibits of indigenous plant and animal life.

Popular activities include hiking, bicycling, boating—with launching facilities—fishing, and crabbing. Swimming is unsupervised and restricted to registered overnight guests, who have access to the park's beach on Chesapeake Bay.

The park has twenty cabins, each with a dining and sleeping room, two bedrooms, a fireplace, a kitchen, and a bath with shower. Six are wood-frame cabins, and fourteen are built of concrete blocks. Each has a hot-water heater and can accommodate up to six people.

Accommodations: 20 cabins with private bath. *Towels and linens:* Provided. *Cooking and eating utensils:* Provided. *Stove and refrigerator:* Provided. *Pets:* Permitted (fee). *Open:* May through October. *Mailing address:* 2500 Shore Drive, Virginia Beach, VA 23451. *Phone:* (804) 481-2131. *Driving instructions:* Seashore State Park is on U.S. 60, on Cape Henry in Virginia Beach.

Shenandoah National Park is in northern Virginia, extending roughly from Front Royal on the north to Waynesboro on the south. It is 100 miles long, varies in width from 3 to 12 miles, and encompasses 195,353 acres, of which almost 80,000 are designated wilderness. The park runs along the Blue Ridge Mountain chain (which literally looks blue when the haze and light conditions are right) and has sixty peaks, some over 4,000 feet, forming a natural border between the Shenandoah Valley and the Piedmont. Views from the mountains are spectacular in any season. Skyline Drive, easily one of the nation's most scenic roads, traverses the mountains for 105 miles, with scenic overlooks that afford sweeping views—sometimes of the Shenandoah Valley and Massanutten Mountain to the west, sometimes of the Piedmont to the east, and, occasionally, of both at the same time.

Established as a park in 1938, the area was at one time heavily farmed and logged almost to exhaustion. Since the government acquired the land, however, second-growth forest reserves have been thriving. The area is wooded primarily with oaks, locusts, pines, walnuts, hickories, and sweet gums, as well as several large virgin stands of hemlock and red spruce. The park encompasses hundreds of streams, scores of waterfalls, a labyrinth of ridges and hollows, and has seventeen species of orchids and two hundred species of birds, as well as deer, black bears, gray foxes, and bobcats, to name a few.

Activities include hiking on some 500 miles of trails (94 miles of the Appalachian Trail pass through the park), fishing—especially for trout—bicycling, and horseback riding. Backpacking is also popular, and the park's naturalist service offers interpretative programs and guided walks. *Park mailing address:* Route 4, Box 292, Luray, VA 22835. *Park phone:* (703) 999-2266.

Skyland Lodge and Cabins

Founded in 1894 by a man who was to be instrumental in establishing Shenandoah National Park, Skyland Lodge is at 3,680 feet, the highest elevation along Skyline Drive. The main lodge is a 1950s concrete-and-wood building with a restaurant overlooking the valley, a taproom with nightly entertainment, and a gift shop. The restaurant has a stone fireplace, and the main building has meeting and banquet facilities.

Shenandoah River

The complex's 156 guest rooms are in the main lodge, two smaller wood-frame lodges, motel units, and 25 cabins. All guest rooms have carpeting, and sixteen have either a porch or a terrace and a view of the valley. Each of the smaller lodges has eight rooms, two with a living room and fireplace. These lodge units have no valley views, nor do the cabins, which vary in size from two to four rooms and are uncarpeted. Although most have private baths, a few share baths.

Accommodations: 131 lodge and motel-type rooms with private bath and 25 cabins, 13 with private bath. *Towels and linens:* Not provided. *Cooking and eating utensils:* Not provided. *Stove and refrigerator:* Not provided. *Pets:* Permitted. *Open:* April through November. *Mailing address:* ARA-Virginia Sky-Line Co., Inc., PO Box 727, Luray, VA 22835. *Phone:* (703) 999-2211. *Driving instructions:* Skyland Lodge is off Skyline Drive at milepost 41.7.

Big Meadows Lodge and Cottages

At milepost 51.3 on Skyline Drive, Big Meadows Lodge is at an elevation of 3,640 feet on a high plateau overlooking the Shenandoah Valley. The complex's ninety-two guest rooms are in a rustic stone-and-wood main lodge building, three wood-frame lodges with eight rooms each, three motel units, and five cottages. The main lodge, built of wormy chestnut, has a restaurant overlooking the valley, as well as a large lounge, both with stone fireplaces. A taproom offers nightly entertainment. Also in the main lodge, with its flagstone and random-width oak flooring and a flagstone terrace overlooking the valley, are six small guest rooms on the second floor. Each has wall-to-wall carpeting, a private bath, and a private terrace with a view of the valley.

Each motel room also overlooks the valley and has either a porch or a terrace, as well as carpeting and a private bath. Of the three small lodges, two have living rooms with fireplaces and can be rented as suites. All rooms in the lodges have private baths and carpeting and are in a wooded area and, therefore, have no valley view. The wood-frame cottages, also in a wooded area, have carpeting and private baths and are arranged so that their two rooms can be rented either singly or together.

Accommodations: 92 rooms with private bath. *Towels and*

linens: Not provided. *Pets:* Permitted. *Open:* Mid-May through October. *Mailing address:* ARA-Virginia Sky-Line Co., Inc., PO Box 727, Luray, VA 22835. *Phone:* (703) 999-2221. *Driving instructions:* Big Meadows Lodge is off Skyline Drive at milepost 51.3.

Lewis Mountain Cabins

Lewis Mountain Cabins is a complex of seven wood-frame cabins in a wooded area 7 miles south of Big Meadows Lodge. The cabins are two-room units, each with a private bath, heat, electric lights, and, outside the cabin, a connecting cooking and living area with a concrete floor, an overhead shelter, a fireplace, an outdoor grill, an electrical outlet, a water tap, a storage cabinet, and a picnic table.

Accommodations: 7 cabins with private bath. *Towels and linens:* Provided. *Cooking and eating utensils:* Not provided. *Stove:* Outdoor grill provided. *Refrigerator:* Not provided. *Pets:* Permitted. *Open:* Late April through October. *Mailing address:* ARA-Virginia Sky-Line Co., Inc., PO Box 727, Luray, VA 22835. *Phone:* (703) 743-5108 or (703) 999-2255. *Driving instructions:* Lewis Mountain Cabins are off Skyline Drive, 7 miles south of Big Meadows Lodge.

Staunton River State Park, a 1,287-acre reserve of woods and meadows in south-central Virginia, is about 100 miles southwest of Richmond and 30 miles north of Roxboro, North Carolina. It is on a peninsula that juts into the 48,000-acre Buggs Island Lake, also called John H. Kerr Reservoir, which is fed on the north by the Staunton River, also called the Roanoke River, and on the south by the Dan River. Both park and river were named after a Captain Staunton who in pre-Revolutionary days patrolled a section of the waterway to protect settlers from Indian attacks. In fact, the area was once the home of the Occoneechee Indians, who were virtually annihilated in 1676 by Nathaniel Bacon and his troops, hell-bent on avenging the Jamestown massacre.

Facilities include a pool with a bathhouse, rental boats and launching facilities, tennis courts, a playground, a visitors' center with interpretive exhibits, and a naturalist program including guided walks along well-marked trails.

The park has seven wood-frame cabins, accommodating from one to six, at its eastern end, near the shore of the Staunton River and almost at the end of the peninsula. They vary in size from one-room to two-bedroom units, and each has a fireplace, rustic furnishings, a kitchen, and a private bath with shower.

Accommodations: 7 cabins with private bath. *Towels and linens:* Provided. *Cooking and eating utensils:* Provided. *Stove and refrigerator:* Provided. *Pets:* Permitted if leashed. *Open:* May through October. *Mailing address:* Route 2, Box 295, Scottsburg, VA 24589. *Phone:* (804) 572-4623. *Driving instructions:* From South Boston take Route 304 northeast about 7 miles, then turn east on Route 344, which enters the park.

Westmoreland State Park is in northeastern Virginia, about 60 miles south of Washington, D.C., on a peninsula formed by the mouths of the Potomac and Rappahannock rivers. The park is on the south shore of the Potomac, just beyond the point where it starts widening before flowing into the Chesapeake Bay. The park's 1,295 acres, like much of Tidewater Virginia, were once plantation land whose soil was depleted by overintensive farming. Under state regulation, the land here is beginning to recover and is in the early stages of reforestation.

Activities include boating, with both launching facilities and boats for rent. There is hiking, fishing, and swimming in an Olympic-size swimming pool, which has a bathhouse. The park also has a restaurant and a convenience store.

Of the park's thirty-one cabins, ten are built of logs, seven are of wood-frame construction, and fourteen are concrete block. They vary in size from one to two bedrooms and accommodate from two to six people. Each has a fireplace, rustic furnishings, a kitchen, and a private bath with shower.

The park's six "overnight" cabins have bunks, pillows, blankets, and mattresses but lack kitchen and bathrooms, which are at the park's nearby campground.

Accommodations: 31 cabins, 25 with private bath. *Towels and linens:* Not provided. *Cooking and eating utensils:* In all but "overnight" cabins. *Stove and refrigerator:* In all but "overnight" cabins. *Pets:* Permitted. *Open:* May through October. *Mailing address:* Route 1, Box 600, Montross, VA 22520. *Phone:* (804) 493-8821. *Driving instructions:* Westmoreland State Park is off Route 3 about 5 miles northwest of Montross.

Washington

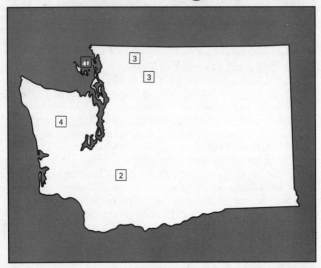

State map and tourist information: Dept. of Commerce, Washington State Travel Agency, 101 GA Bldg., Olympia, WA 98504; 800-541-WASH (out-of-state) and 800-562-4570 (in-state). **State parks:** *Information:* Park & Recreation Commission, 7150 Cleanwater Lane, Olympia, WA 98504; 206-754-2543 (out-of-state) 800-562-0990 (in-state). *Entrance fees:* None. *Reservations:* Contact individual lodgings. Deposit for the first night, check or credit card. Recommended that reservations be made 2 to 4 weeks in advance. *Restrictions:* No hunting. Dogs must be leashed (check individual park about pets in lodgings). *Facilities:* Swimming and interpretative programs, Mem. Day—Labor Day. Scuba diving, all year. Cross-country skiing and snowmobiling, December—February.

Moran State Park, in northwestern Washington in the San Juan Islands archipelago, comprises 4,600 acres on the horseshoe-shaped Orcas Island, which is about a mile wide at its narrowest and roughly four miles wide at its broadest. Most of the park property was donated to the state by shipbuilder Robert Moran; and one of its peaks, Mount Pickett, was named after a sea captain. Both park and island are for people who like the sea, and fittingly, the only way to get there is by ferry from Anacortes. The park's highlight is Mount Constitution, rising from near sea level to an elevation of 2,454 feet, from where there are vistas—weather permitting—that extend as far as Victoria in British Columbia, the city of Bellingham, the other San Juan Islands, and the Olympic and Cascade mountain ranges. Also noteworthy is Cascade Falls, 51 feet tall with a gorge surrounded by fir and spruce trees.

The park's principal activities are fishing and swimming. Visitors can rent boats and fishing supplies or use the boat-launching facilities. Hiking trails and a road lead to the top of Mount Constitution. *Park mailing address:* Star Route, Box 22, Eastsound, WA 98245. *Park phone:* (206) 376-2326.

Outlook Inn

A nineteenth-century two-story wood-shingled inn with its own private beach, a small pond, and a large flower garden, Outlook Inn was built as a general store and also served as a jail (the cells were behind the store). It began operating as an inn in the 1880s. Although not within the Park's boundaries, it's close by and parklike in its own right.

The inn's dining room, with a fireplace and a view of Eastsound, specializes in simple, home-cooked meals and farm-style breakfasts. Guests rooms have hand-carved or brass beds, flower-print wallpapers, marble-topped dressers, and period memorabilia. Six rooms have views of the sound, one has a porch, and another has a patio. All but one accommodation, a suite, share baths.

Accommodations: 30 rooms with shared bath and 1 suite with private bath. *Pets:* Permitted sometimes—check in advance. *Open:* All year. *Mailing address:* PO Box 210, Eastsound, WA

98245. *Phone:* (206) 376-2581. *Driving instructions:* From Anacortes take the ferry to Orcas, a ride of about two hours; then drive north about 8 miles to Eastsound and the inn.

Mount Rainier National Park is in east-central Washington, 56 miles southeast of Tacoma, its 235,404 acres covering 337 square miles, about 25 percent of which comprises the mountain's base. Mount Rainier, with an elevation of 14,410 feet, is the fifth-highest summit in the contiguous United States and was at one time the highest. It is an almost extinct volcano, whose last eruption, about 2,000 years ago, blew off the top 2,000 feet of rock. Steam vents still melt snow at its higher elevations, which are always covered with snow, while its base has several hot springs. Twenty-six glaciers are active, more than half of which crawl downward along the sides of the peak.

The rugged terrain varies, with thick forests of Douglas fir, western red cedar, western hemlock, spruce, Alaska cedar, and a few maples and black cottonwoods. Trees in the forested areas grow very large, and it's not uncommon to see 200-foot-tall firs and hemlocks. The vegetation changes dramatically as the elevation increases, where the mountainside's thickly wooded sections gradually give way to areas of wildflowers. The most common flowers in the subalpine and alpine meadows include trilliums, clintonias, twinflowers, devil's-walking-sticks, lupines, avalanche lilies, Indian paintbrush, asters, and valerians. More than a hundred species of birds and sixty species of mammals are native to the area.

The park has a 320-foot waterfall, Comet Falls, as well as smaller ones, and a host of streams and rivers, which in spring can become tumultuous. There are hundreds of miles of hiking trails and scenic roads, and interpretative programs are available. The most popular activities are mountain climbing, hiking, horseback riding, fishing, and skiing. *Park mailing address:* Superintendent, Mount Rainier National Park, Tahoma Woods, Star Route, Ashford, WA 98304. *Park phone:* (206) 569-2211.

National Park Inn

The property around the National Park Inn was originally developed by James Longmire following his discovery of the warm springs at the site in 1861. Longmire and his family subsequently built primitive accommodations, advertised the curative powers of the waters (as claimed by the Indians), and started taking

in guests during the last part of the century. In 1899 Congress approved the establishment of Mount Rainier National Park, and eighteen years later portions of the current lodge were built.

Among firs and hemlocks, at an elevation of 2,700 feet, the inn is a rustic wooden lodge with a peaked roof and guest rooms on the second floor. The inn has a restaurant that serves three meals daily and a country store that sells handmade Northwest Indian arts and crafts, as well as souvenirs and groceries. For guests there's a small area upstairs for relaxing, as well as the front porch, which stretches across the front of the building.

Accommodations: 16 rooms, 8 with private bath. *Pets:* Not permitted. *Open:* All year. *Mailing address* (for reservations): Mount Rainier Guest Services, Inc., Star Route, Ashford, WA 98304. *Phone:* (206) 569-2565 (hotel) or (206) 569-2275 (for reservations). *Driving instructions:* From Tacoma take Route 7 southeast to Elbe, then pick up Route 706 and go east to Longmire and the inn.

Paradise Inn

At an elevation of 5,400 feet, the first section of the Paradise Inn was constructed in 1916 almost entirely of local cedar salvaged from a forest fire that devastated the area in 1885, drawn up to the site from the canyon rim by horses. The inn's annex was completed in 1920.

The inn's steeply pitched roof is broken by gables, which, along with the many full-story windows and French doors throughout, offer unobstructed views of the Tatoosh Mountains.

Both the lobby and the dining room—built of Alaska cedar, with hand-hewn logs supporting the beamed ceilings—have cathedral-like dimensions. The lobby has a cut-stone fireplace at each end and a mezzanine with lounge chairs and game and card tables. The dining room, which seats 200, has parquet floors, an exposed-beam ceiling, many windows, and a stone fireplace. The inn has a cocktail lounge, a gift shop that sells souvenirs and Northwest Indian crafts, and a snack bar.

The Paradise Inn has two types of accommodations. The thirty-two rooms in the older sections have rustic, ranch-oak-style furniture, with a sink in each room, and share, European-style, two bath and shower facilities. The ninety-five newer rooms have wood paneling, ranch-oak–style furniture, and private baths, as well as a variety of sleeping combinations—some twin beds, some double beds, and several two-bedroom suites with connecting bath. All the rooms have carpeting and views either of Mount Rainier, on one side, or of Paradise Valley, on the other. There are no telephones or television sets in the rooms.

Accommodations: 127 rooms, 95 with private bath. *Pets:* Not permitted. *Open:* June through mid-October. *Mailing address* (for reservations): Mount Rainier Guest Services, Inc., Star Route, Ashford, WA 98304. *Phone:* (206) 569-2291 (hotel) or (206) 569-2275 (for reservations). *Driving instructions:* From Tacoma take Route 7 southeast to Elbe, then follow Route 706 east to Paradise and the inn.

North Cascades National Park is in northwestern Washington, about 90 miles northeast of Seattle and contiguous with the Canadian border. Its official size is 504,478 acres, but the park also encompasses the 61,127-acre Lake Chelan National Recreation Area and the 105,490-acre Ross Lake National Recreation Area. North Cascades National Park and the two National Recreation Areas within its borders have an aggregate of some 670,000 acres. The parklands are bordered on the east by Okanogan National Forest, on the south by Wenatchee National Forest, and on the west by Mount Baker National Forest. Altogether, North Cascades National Park and its surrounding national parks and forests make up nearly one-fifth of the State of Washington.

The Cascade Mountain Range extends from Canada's Fraser River to the northern Sierra Nevada in California, and North Cascades National Park preserves an especially rugged section of this chain of mountains. Among the higher of the many peaks are Goode Mountain (elevation 9,220 feet), Mount Logan (8,966 feet), Mount Redoubt (8,956 feet), and Mount Blum (7,680 feet). The park also includes The Pickets, a ragged series of summits that resembles a picket fence; glaciers; fir and spruce forests; alpine meadows; waterfalls; and lakes and streams. Ross Lake, 24 miles long, at one point in its varying width is almost 2 miles across; Diablo and Gorge lakes, and a few miles of Lake Chelan—which is almost 56 miles long—are in the park, all popular among anglers and boaters. Lake Chelan is fed by fifty-nine streams and twenty-nine glaciers, and, like Ross and Diablo lakes, resembles a Norwegian fjord.

Hiking, mountain climbing, horseback riding, horse pack trips, canoeing, and river rafting are the popular activities. The park rangers (at the three stations—Sedro Wooley, Marble Mount, and Stehekin) frequently organize interpretative walks and campfire programs that include talks on the history, vegetation, wildlife, and bird life of the region. *Park mailing address:* Superintendent, North Cascades National Park, 800 State Street, Sedro Woolley, WA 98284. *Park phone:* (206) 855-1331.

North Cascades Lodge and Cabins

A group of rustic wood-frame one- and two-story lodge buildings flanked by housekeeping cabins of similar design,

Lake Chelan, in the Lake Chelan National Recreation Area, is the gateway to the North Cascade mountains.

North Cascades Lodge is near the north shore of Lake Chelan in the Stehekin Valley. There are no roads to the lodge, which is accessible by boat or floatplane, both of which leave from the village Chelan, about 50 miles to the south, or by an 11-mile hiking trail that begins from a parking area off North Cascades Highway at Rainy Pass. The ferry *Lady of the Lake* runs on a daily schedule during the summer, but only four days a week the rest of the year.

The eighteen lodge rooms are wood-paneled, and the eight cabins have kitchenettes. Among other services, the lodge will arrange for float trips, horseback treks, or ski trips, as well as boat, car, or bicycle rentals. It has a dining room, a lounge, a gift shop, a grocery store, an outdoor game area, and a ski shop.

Accommodations: 18 lodge rooms and 8 cabins, all with private bath. *Towels and linens:* Provided. *Cooking and eating utensils:* In cabins. *Stove and refrigerator:* In cabins. *Pets:* Not permitted. *Open:* All year. *Mailing address:* Box 186, Chelan, WA 98816. *Lodge phone:* (509) 682-4711. *Ferry phone:* (509) 682-2224. *Chelan Airways phone:* (509) 682-5555. *Driving instructions:* The lodge is accessible only by boat or plane; guests are advised to make advance arrangements with the lodge.

Diablo Lake Resort

Diablo Lake Resort is on the northeastern shore of Diablo Lake, a 910-acre body of water about 5 miles west of Ross Dam. The resort's facilities include a grocery store that has a lounge area with fireplace, a game room, comfortable seats, and reading materials. A lounge overlooking the lake offers everything from take-out lunches and dinners to daily specials; and a marina rents out boats with or without motors.

The resort's twenty wood-frame cabins, in a wooded area, vary in size from one to three bedrooms. Each is electrically heated and has wall-to-wall carpeting, a private bath with a tub-shower, and a living, cooking, and dining area.

Accommodations: 20 cabins with private bath. *Towels and linens:* Provided. *Cooking and eating utensils:* Provided. *Stove and refrigerator:* Provided. *Pets:* Not permitted. *Open:* All year. *Mailing address:* Diablo, Rockport, WA 98283. *Phone:* Call operator and ask for Newhalem 5578 under area code 206. *Driving instructions:* From I-5, which runs along the Washington coast, take Route 20 east 68 miles to the Diablo Lake Resort.

Ross Lake Resort

Because the level of Ross Lake can vary by as much as 100 feet during the course of the year, Ross Lake Resort literally floats. At one time, guests had to hike along a mountain trail with their gear on their backs, but now the trip is easier: You can get here via a series of boat and truck rides. The entire resort—cabins, office, and marina—sits above the water on log rafts.

The resort has three types of accommodations. Each of eight "modern" units has an electric or propane stove and a refrigerator in a combination living room and kitchen area, a wood-burning fireplace, a private bath with shower, and a picture window overlooking the lake. The "modern" bunkhouse is like the modern units but will accommodate up to ten guests, all of whom must be part of the same group. Each of the two "rustic" cabins has a wood stove for cooking and heating, a refrigerator, and running water, and both share a toilet-and-shower facility on a nearby float. A marina rents canoes, as well as powerboats with small motors. The lodge was originally a remote fishing camp, and to a large extent it still is.

Accommodations: 8 cabins with private bath, plus 1 bunkhouse and 2 rustic cabins with shared bath. *Towels and linens:* Provided. *Cooking and eating utensils:* Provided. *Stove and refrigerator:* Provided. *Pets:* Not permitted. *Open:* Mid-January to late October. *Mailing address:* Lake Ross Resort, Rockport, WA 98283. *Phone:* (206) 397-7735. (This number cannot be dialed direct. Call your local operator, give the telephone number, and explain that the routing for the call is through "206026." The call will be routed through Newhalem, Washington, via the Everette, Washington, operator.) *Driving instructions:* Leave I-5 at Burlington, take Route 20 east for 65 miles, and go across Diablo Dam and on to the Ross Lake parking lot.

In northwestern Washington, west across Puget Sound from Seattle and south across the Strait of Juan de Fuca from Vancouver Island, Olympic National Park comprises 908,720 acres of extremely varied terrain. It occupies much of the Olympic Peninsula south of Port Angeles, encompassing 50 miles of Pacific coastline, a unique rain forest, perennially snow-capped mountain peaks, and more than sixty glaciers. An early British sea captain who saw the 7,965-foot Mount Olympus from a ship named it after the home of the Greek gods. In an hour, visitors can drive from an ocean beach, through a rain forest, and on to an alpine zone above the timberline.

It is hard to choose a leading natural attraction at Olympic National Park. The Pacific coastal area, separated by some 30 miles from the other sections of the park, is outstandingly scenic. From there you ascend to a rain forest with huge moss-covered trees, seven species of which grow larger here than anywhere else in the world, including a western red cedar 22 feet in diameter. The rain forest is unique, being wooded mainly with conifers—western hemlocks, western red cedars, Douglas firs, silver firs, Sitka spruces, and Alaska cedars. Ferns, mosses, wildflowers, shrubs, and vines run riot in the forest's understory, which receives as much as 12 inches of rain in a day.

The next level in the park is a heavily wooded transition area thick with silver firs, western white pines, hemlocks, and cedars. The following zone is subalpine, with wind-dwarfed junipers and mountain ashes. The really intrepid continue up and go through a series of alpine meadows with tiny plants, reaching glacial summits with majestic views that extend for hundreds of miles in clear weather.

The park is a vast wilderness area, with hundreds of miles of hiking trails, but visitors must check with the visitors' centers on current regulations governing use of the park. (For example, those wishing to camp overnight within the park must obtain permits from park service rangers.) The two main visitors' centers, open year round, are in Port Angeles at the northern end of the park and at Hoh Rain Forest, which is on a road in the western section of the park that starts from Route 101, about fifteen miles south of Forks. (Route 101 is the road that completely encircles the park.)

Hoh Rain Forest

The coastal section of the park is reached from Kalaloch, La Push, or Ozette, where there's a 3-mile hike from the parking lot at Lake Ozette to the coast. This section is a long, narrow strip which runs about 57 miles, south from Ozette, comprising some of the most beautiful and rugged coastline in Washington state. It includes some sand beaches sheltered by lagoons, although swimming is discouraged by the park service because of the dangerous currents.

The inland sections of the park can be reached from Quinault on the south, from Port Angeles on the north, and from various tertiary roads leading off of Route 101. Many concessionaires offer fishing trips and rafting excursions. Fishing, swimming, skiing, hiking, and admiring the majestic surroundings are the most popular activities. *Park mailing address:* Superintendent, Olympic National Park, 600 East Park Avenue, Port Angeles, WA 98362. *Park phone:* (206) 452-4501.

Kalaloch Lodge

Kalaloch Lodge, beside an estuary on a bluff overlooking the Pacific Ocean, is actually many buildings, including a gray-shingled, two-story main lodge, a motel, and cabins. The rustic-style lodge, built in 1952 to replace an earlier building, has eight guest rooms—four with ocean views—a lobby with a stone fireplace, and a restaurant. The newer motel unit has ten guest rooms and suites, all of which come with an ocean-view deck or a fireplace and have maid service. Of the thirty-four cabins, the twenty-two newest are built of logs, and the other twelve are on a bluff. Each cabin has a kitchenette, and the log cabins have free-standing fireplaces and brass beds. All rooms have private baths.

Accommodations: 8 lodge rooms, 10 motel rooms, and 34 cabins, all with private bath. *Towels and linens:* Provided. *Cooking and eating utensils:* Not provided. *Stove and refrigerator:* In cabins. *Pets:* Permitted in cabins only ($4 per night charge). *Open:* All year. *Mailing address:* Route 1, Box 1100, Forks, WA 98331. *Phone:* (206) 962-2271. *Driving instructions:* Kalaloch is on Route 101, about 70 miles north of Aberdeen.

Lake Crescent Lodge

Lake Crescent Lodge, on the shore of Lake Crescent, has conifers surrounding it and mountains behind. Each room in the complex has a view of the lake, the forest, or the mountains, or a combination of these.

Accommodations include relatively inexpensive rooms in the main lodge with shared bath facilities; cottages with fireplaces; and a motel unit where each room's lakeside doors lead to a private patio or balcony. Appointments vary from modern pieces in the motel rooms to rustic wooden furniture in the cottages and lodge rooms, which have hardwood floors. The cabins have no kitchen facilities, but all accommodations have maid service and the lodge has a dining room. There is also a cocktail lounge, a gift shop, and a lobby.

Accommodations: 49 rooms, 41 with private bath. *Towels and linens:* Provided. *Cooking and eating utensils:* Not provided. *Stove and refrigerator:* Not provided. *Pets:* Permitted. *Open:* May 1 through September 25. *Mailing address:* Star Route 1, Box 11, Port Angeles, WA 98362. *Phone:* (206) 928-3211. *Driving instructions:* Lake Crescent Lodge is off U.S. 101, roughly 15 miles west of Port Angeles.

Sol Duc Hot Springs Resort

South and west of Lake Crescent in the Soleduck River Valley, surrounded by virgin Douglas fir, Sol Duc Hot Springs Resort is a complex of three types of accommodations. Guests can stay in a motel unit, each of whose rooms has wall-to-wall carpeting, a private shower, a chair, a desk, and two easy chairs. Each modern cabin has a kitchenette, as well as a bath with shower; most overlook the river or the woods. Each of the rustic, unheated cabins has wood paneling, cold running water and a toilet, and limited views. A shared shower is centrally located.

Other facilities at the resort are a dining room, a coffee shop, a cocktail lounge, a souvenir shop, a swimming pool, and three hot mineral-spring pools. Groceries and sundries can be purchased, and fishing tackle and bathing suits are availabe for rent.

Accommodations: 23 rooms and cabins with private bath. *Towels and linens:* In motel units and modern cabins. *Cooking and eating utensils:* Not provided. *Stove and refrigerator:* In modern cabins. *Pets:* Permitted ($2 per night charge). *Open:* Memorial Day through September 30. *Mailing address:* PO Box 1355, Port Angeles, WA 98362. *Phone:* (206) 327-3583. *Driving instructions:* Sol Duc Hot Springs Resort is off U.S 101, about 40 miles west of Port Angeles.

Log Cabin Resort

Log Cabin Resort has no log cabins, although it does have eight vintage 1920s wood-frame cabins, as well as twelve A-frame chalets and four motel units. The resort complex was named after the Log Cabin Hotel, which burned down on this site. Lodge facilities include a restaurant, a cocktail lounge, a grocery and gift shop, a self-service laundry, and a marina with boat-launching facilities and canoe, rowboat, paddleboat, and power-boat rentals.

Two sizes of wood-frame cabins, open only in summer, are on a plateau overlooking the resort and the lake. Each of the larger cabins has a kitchen, a bedroom, a living room, and a private bath. Each of the smaller ones has one room and a private bath. The baths in both sizes contain either a shower or a claw-footed tub.

The A-frame chalets are by the water; each has a sleeping loft and, on its lower level, a combination bedroom, living room, and "convenience center" (a large work counter with a sink and a refrigerator), and a private bath with shower. The chalets have no stove, but each has a barbecue outside.

Each of the motel units, which are about 30 feet from the water, has wall-to-wall carpeting, a wet bar with a work counter and a sink, and a private bath.

Accommodations: 4 motel rooms, 12 chalets, and 8 cabins, all with private bath. *Towels and linens:* Provided. *Cooking and eating utensils:* Not provided. *Stove:* In cabins. *Refrigerator:* In cabins and chalets. *Pets:* Permitted in cabins only. *Open:* April through September. *Mailing address:* 6540 East Beach Road, Port Angeles, WA 98362. *Phone:* (206) 928-3325. *Driving instructions:* From Port Angeles take U.S. 101 west 18 miles, then turn right onto East Beach Road and go 3 miles to Log Cabin Resort on the left.

Lake Quinault Lodge

A large shingled building constructed in 1926, Lake Quinault Lodge is on the shore of Lake Quinault in the southwestern part of the Olympic National Forest. The National Forest surrounds the National Park and, at this point, borders the Quinault Indian Reservation. A crew of craftsmen and laborers had to drag the building materials for the lodge across 50 miles of dirt roads, working 24 hours a day, completing the building in less than 10 weeks. President Franklin D. Roosevelt, after a stay here in 1937, began the process that created the national park and forest.

The lodge has a large lobby with exposed-beam ceilings and a huge brick fireplace; a cocktail lounge has wood-paneled walls on which hang elk and moose heads and other hunting and fishing trophies. There is also a dining room with a picture window that overlooks the lake, as well as a recreation room.

The fifty-four guest rooms are in the main lodge building or in a recently completed annex. The rooms in the older lodge have a 1920s ambience, and some have private baths. Each annex room has wall-to-wall carpeting, a private bath, a fireplace, and a balcony overlooking the lake.

Accommodations: 54 rooms, 46 with private bath. *Pets:* Permitted in certain areas only—check in advance. *Open:* All year. *Mailing address:* P.O. Box 7, Lake Quinault, Quinault, WA 98575. *Phone:* (206) 288-2571. In Washington only, toll free: (800) 562-6672. *Driving instructions:* Take U.S. 101 to South Shore Road, then follow South Shore Road to the Lake Quinault lodge.

561

West Virginia

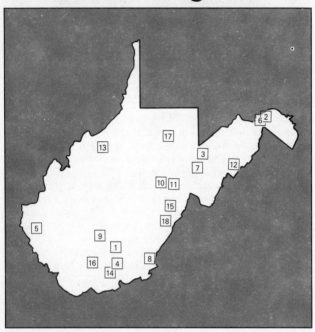

State map and tourist information: Governor's Office of Economic and Community Development, Travel Div., State Capitol Complex, Rotunda R-151, Charleston, WV 25305; 304-348-2286. **State parks:** *Information:* Dept. of Natural Resources, Div. of Parks & Recreation, 1800 Washington St. East, Charleston, WV 25305; 304-348-2764. *Entrance fees:* None. *Reservations:* Call 800-642-9058 (state residents), 800-624-8632 (surrounding states), and 304-348-2766 (all other states). Deposits (cabins) of ½ of the full rental payment (4 nights or more) or full payment (3 nights or less). Deposits (lodges) for first night; by check or credit card. State residents may reserve up to 12 months in advance; out-of-state residents, up to 10 months in advance. Cabins rented weekly, second Monday in June—Labor Day. *Restrictions:* No hunting. No alcohol in outdoor areas. Dogs must be leashed (allowed in cabins, not in lodges). *Facilities:* Swimming and boating, Mem. Day—Labor Day. Golf and tennis, April—October. Skiing, November—March.

Babcock State Park, in south-central West Virginia, about 60 miles southeast of Charleston and about 30 miles southwest of Monongahela National Forest, consists of 4,127 acres of rugged, wooded, hilly terrain riddled with gorges. A foamy trout stream rushes through one, cascading over several falls, while another shelters the native-sandstone administration and restaurant building, which can be seen from an overlook along Island in the Sky Trail. Across the stream from the administration building, there's a reconstruction of a nineteenth-century gristmill built from parts of other antique mills. The mill grinds cornmeal and buckwheat flour, which may be purchased by visitors.

The park has more than 10 miles of hiking trails, a swimming pool, tennis courts, and a 19-acre lake where rowboats, paddleboats, and sailboats may be rented. The park also has a large population of rhododendrons, primarily of two varieties that take turns blooming: The purple variety blooms from late May through June; the pink variety, the state flower, blooms from mid-June into July. *Park phone:* (304) 438-5662.

The park has twenty-six cabins available, in two types—"standard" and "economy." The standard cabins are constructed either of logs or in a wood-frame style and feature open fireplaces, well-equipped kitchens, baths with tile showers, and a separate bedroom. The economy cabins have one room that serves as a living room, bedroom, and kitchen (smaller kitchen facilities than the standard cabins), and a screened porch.

Accommodations: 26 cabins with private bath. *Towels and linens:* Provided. *Cooking and eating utensils:* Provided. *Stove and refrigerator:* Provided. *Pets:* Permitted if leashed. *Open:* Last weekend in April through fourth Monday in October. *Mailing address:* Route 1, Box 150, Clifftop, WV 25831. *Phone:* (304) 438-6205. *Driving instructions:* Babcock State Park is off Route 41 about 20 miles north of Beckley.

Spruce Knob, the highest point in West Virginia.

At the elbow of West Virginia's eastern panhandle, Berkeley Springs State Park consists of 7 acres located less than a mile from the Potomac River. The park is one of America's oldest health spas: Its mineral springs have been attracting visitors for centuries. The original users of the springs were Indians, who apparently came from as far as Canada to take the waters. Listed in the National Register of Historic Places and administered as a state park, the springs continue to attract aquaphiles.

The spa's most famous visitor was George Washington, who first came here as a young surveyor in 1748. He so enjoyed the springs' curative powers that he built his summer presidential residence here. The town had many of this country's foremost statesmen as residents. When the land was put up for sale, George Washington, along with three signers of the Declaration of Independence, four signers of the Constitution, seven members of the Continental Congress, and five Revolutionary generals, was among the purchasers.

The springs are in a narrow valley and issue from the base of a steep ridge. They discharge about 2,000 gallons of clear water per minute at a temperature of 74.3°F. The park's "curative" facilities include mineral baths, Roman baths, dry-heat cabinets, steam cabinets, massage facilities and personnel, and infrared heat. There's also a swimming pool. The Roman baths, fourteen individual tiled sunken pools filled with hot mineral water, are especially popular. *Park phone:* (304) 258-2711.

The Country Inn
A 1932 Colonial-style brick building with six large columns, the Country Inn is adjacent to the state park and includes a central living room with comfortable couches, fresh- or dried-flower arrangements, and a wood stove, as well as a lounge with overstuffed chairs, rockers, and a high ceiling. The inn has a public restaurant with wood-paneled walls that serves generous portions of such entrées as golden brown pan-fried trout or ham with red-eye gravy.

The guest rooms here are decorated individually, mostly with wood furnishings. Most have color television, and room service is available.

Accommodations: 37 rooms with private bath. *Pets:* Not permitted. *Open:* All year. *Address:* 207 South Washington Street, Berkeley Springs, WV 25411. *Phone:* (304) 258-2210. *Driving instructions:* The park and the inn are off Route 522, roughly 6 miles south of Hancock, Maryland.

Blackwater Falls State Park is in northeastern West Virginia, about 5 miles south of the Maryland border at the beginning of the state's eastern panhandle. The 1,688-acre park takes its name from the five-story-high waterfalls on the Blackwater River, which has carved out a canyon half a mile wide. The canyon below the falls is littered with huge boulders, and a system of stairways and boardwalks leads to the base of the falls. The park contains another scenic waterfall, Elakala, which is a hundred yards from the lodge and is crossed by a footbridge.

The park is within the boundaries of Monongahela National Forest and is contiguous to Seneca Rocks National Recreation Area, both of which are ideal for hikers and nature lovers. The park has a beach for swimming, and visitors can rent rowboats or paddleboats. Horses are available for hire, and the park's facilities include a playground, a naturalist service, a sled run, a souvenir and gift shop, and a restaurant. Downhill skiing and golf are available 10 miles south off Route 32, at Canaan Valley State Park.

Blackwater Lodge and Cabins

Blackwater Lodge, on the south rim of Blackwater Canyon, is a modern 55-bedroom lodge with a peaked roof, a large dining room, a lounge, a gift shop, and a recreation room. The guest rooms are furnished with modern pieces and have wall-to-wall carpeting, color television, telephones, air-conditioning, private baths, and views of the surrounding area.

Blackwater Lodge also administers 25 deluxe cabins on the canyon's south rim. Of modern design, the cabins feature native wood-paneled walls, stone fireplaces, forced-air heaters, fully equipped kitchens with built-in cabinetry and modern appliances, as well as comfortable, rustic-style modern furnishings.

Accommodations: 55 lodge rooms and 25 cabins, all with private bath. *Towels and linens:* Provided. *Cooking and eating utensils:* Provided. *Stove and refrigerator:* Provided. *Pets:* Not permitted. *Open:* All year. *Mailing address:* PO Box 490, Davis, WV 26260. *Phone:* (304) 259-5216. *Driving instructions:* Blackwater Falls State Park is off Route 32 a mile west of Davis.

On 2,146 acres, Bluestone State Park is in central southeastern West Virginia, about 70 miles southeast of Charleston. On the shores of West Virginia's second-largest lake, the 1,800-acre Bluestone Lake, the park is popular among boaters, fishermen, and swimmers. Visitors can rent canoes, rowboats, or motorboats at the park marina, while anglers go after catfish, smallmouth and largemouth bass, bluegills, and crappies. The lake has a beach, as well as a swimming pool that is open during the summer months. The park's rugged, heavily wooded, mountainous terrain has 8 miles of designated hiking trails.

The area immediately around Bluestone Park is full of recreational facilities and natural attractions, including Pipestem Resort Park (8 miles away), the outdoor musical plays performed at Grandview State Park, and the falls at Sandstone State Park. The New River, popular among white-water canoers, is close; and the 20,000-acre Bluestone Public Hunting Area is adjacent.

Bluestone Park has 25 deluxe cabins that are modern in design and have wood-paneled walls, stone fireplaces, separate bedrooms, fully equipped kitchens with modern appliances, baths with tiled showers, and forced-air furnaces. Pool fees are included in the price of cabin rentals.

Accommodations: 25 cabins with private bath. *Towels and linens:* Provided. *Cooking and eating utensils:* Provided. *Stove and refrigerator:* Provided. *Pets:* Not permitted. *Open:* Late March through mid-December. *Mailing address:* Box 3, Athens Star Route, Hinton, WV 25951. *Phone:* (304) 466-1922. *Driving instructions:* Bluestone State Park is off Route 20, about 4 miles southwest of Hinton.

"Cabwaylingo" is an acronym for four West Virginia counties—CABell, WAYne, LINcoln and MinGO. The forest comprises 8,123 acres in western West Virginia, roughly 50 miles south of Huntington and about 5 miles east of the Kentucky border. Popular activities include hiking on the numerous scenic trails, fishing, and hunting. There is a swimming pool, along with a children's wading pool and a bathhouse, which has lifeguards on duty from late May through late August. The forest has a playground, several rustic picnic sites with tables, fireplaces, firewood, drinking water, and toilet facilities.

Cabwaylingo State Forest has 13 cabins available for rent. Located in the middle of the park, the cabins feature open fireplaces, kitchens, and baths with tiled showers.

Accommodations: 13 cabins with private bath. *Towels and linens:* Provided. *Cooking and eating utensils:* Provided. *Stove and refrigerator:* Provided. *Pets:* Not permitted. *Open:* Late April through late October. *Mailing address:* Route 1, Dunlow, WV 25511. *Phone:* (304) 385-4255. *Driving Instructions:* From Huntington take Route 152 south about 52 miles.

In the eastern panhandle of West Virginia, Cacapon State Park is a long, narrow 6,115-acre reserve that extends northeastward across the panhandle from the Virginia border to just short of the Maryland border. Its rolling hills are thick with hardwoods, presided over by Cacapon Mountain, its 1,400-foot summit reachable by a paved road, as well as hiking and bridle trails. The park has a lake—popular with swimmers, fishermen and boaters—where rowboats and paddleboats are available for rent. Golf is also popular—the eighteen-hole championship course was designed by Robert Trent Jones. The park also has tennis courts, horses for hire, and a naturalist program that includes special outings and films.

Cacapon Lodges and Cabins

Cacapon State Park has 29 cabins, an older lodge, and a modern lodge. The cabins are of three types—deluxe, standard, and economy. Deluxe cabins have a separate bedroom, an open fireplace, wood-paneled walls, a completely equipped kitchen with modern appliances, a bath with a tiled shower, and electric or forced-air heat. Standard cabins have a separate bedroom, an open fireplace, a kitchen, and a bath with tiled shower. Economy cabins have a combination living room, kitchen, and dining room, a simply equipped kitchen, and a bath with a tile shower.

The older lodge is an eleven-room building constructed of hand-hewn logs. It has hand-wrought iron hardware, stone chimneys, low-ceilinged rooms paneled in chestnut and knotty pine, and a decidedly old-fashioned ambience. Its bedrooms all share baths.

The newer lodge has a lounge with black walnut paneling and a fireplace, as well as a restaurant, a gift shop, a recreation room, and fifty modern guest rooms that feature wall-to-wall carpeting, telephones, television, air-conditioning, and private baths. This lodge overlooks the golf course.

Accommodations: 61 lodge rooms, 50 with private bath; 29 cabins with private bath. *Towels and linens:* Provided. *Cooking and eating utensils:* Provided. *Stove and refrigerator:* In cabins. *Pets:* Not permitted. *Open:* All year. (The older lodge and all

but deluxe cabins closed in winter.) *Mailing address:* Cacapon State Park, Berkeley Springs, WV 25411. *Phone:* (304) 258-1022. *Driving instructions:* Cacapon State Park is off U.S. 522, roughly 5 miles south of Berkeley Springs.

The 6,015-acre Canaan Valley Resort Park is near the northwestern border of West Virginia's eastern panhandle, within Monongahela National Forest. The national forest is noted for its canyons, waterfalls, unexplored limestone caves, and Canaan Valley Resort State Park—an excellent base for exploring. The park is in a valley at an elevation of 3,200 feet, surrounded by mountains that rise as high as 4,200 feet. The *New York Times* called Canaan Valley Park "a wholesome, family type resort in a superb natural setting," with a wide array of seasonal activities.

The park has a heated outdoor pool, lighted tennis courts, hiking trails, a scenic chairlift, and a naturalist service that offers guided nature walks, hayrides, and movies. Other facilities include an eighteen-hole golf course surrounded by mountains and visited by white-tailed deer and Canada geese. For winter recreation the park has a ski slope with chair lifts, snowmaking equipment, and base facilities, as well as 20 miles of cross-country trails. There's also a lighted outdoor ice-skating rink.

Canaan Valley Lodge and Cabins

A large complex of modern buildings, Canaan Valley Lodge has two types of accommodations available. The main lodge consists of a large dining room, a coffee shop, a gift shop, a lounge, a game room, and meeting and banquet facilities for 5 to 500 people.

Buildings flanking the main lodge contain 250 bedrooms with modern furnishings, including color television and individual heating and air-conditioning. The lodge also administers fifteen cabins in a nearby wooded area. Of modern design, the cabins have wood-paneled walls, fully equipped kitchens, open fireplaces, and baths with tiled showers.

Accommodations: 250 lodge rooms and 15 cabins, all with private bath. *Towels and linens:* Provided. *Cooking and eating utensils:* Provided. *Stove and refrigerator:* Provided. *Pets:* Not permitted. *Open:* All year. *Mailing address:* Route 1, Box 330, Davis, WV 26260. *Phone:* (304) 866-4121. *Driving instructions:* The park is off Route 32, roughly 9 miles north of Harman.

Greenbrier State Forest is in southeastern West Virginia, a couple of miles south of White Sulphur Springs and just west of the Virginia border. The 5,130-acre forest is dotted with streams and hiking trails, which wind through mountainous terrain. Within its borders are Kate's Mountain, noted for its scenic overlook, and Roaring Mountain. The forest has several picnic areas with tables, fireplaces, firewood, drinking water, and toilet facilities, as well as nearby playgrounds. Visitors can rent boats, and the nearby Greenbrier River is frequented by fishermen. Also popular is the forest's swimming pool, which has a children's wading pool and a bathhouse. Hunting is permitted in the forest.

Greenbrier has 12 log cabins available in a wooded area in the west-central section of the forest. Several scenic trails pass by, or start at, the cabin area. The cabins have open fireplaces, fully equipped kitchens with modern appliances, and baths with tile showers. Two of the cabins accommodate two, six accommodate four, and four accommodate six.

Accommodations: 12 cabins with private bath. *Towels and linens:* Provided. *Cooking and eating utensils:* Provided. *Stove and refrigerator:* Provided. *Pets:* Not permitted. *Open:* Late April through October. *Mailing address:* Star Route Box 125, Caldwell, WV 24925. *Phone:* (304) 536-1944. *Driving instructions:* From White Sulphur Springs take U.S. 60 about 4 miles west, then take Harts Run Road south about a mile.

Hawks Nest State Park is about 50 miles southeast of Charleston. The 276-acre park takes its name from its position, which like the nest of a hawk, is high above the surrounding terrain. It is located at a particularly rugged section of the New River gorge, which has a length of about 60 miles and a depth, in places, of more than a thousand feet. The area is heavily wooded with a mixture of hardwoods and softwoods, and the views from the higher elevations in the park are panoramic.

Popular activities here include boating, fishing, swimming, hiking, and tennis. The park has an aerial tramway that connects the Hawks Nest Lodge with the marina on Hawks Nest Lake. Although the lake is tranquil, the stretches immediately above and below it are extremely popular among whitewater enthusiasts. A rustic museum featuring Indian and pioneer artifacts is set on high ground that overlooks the gorge.

Hawks Nest Lodge

The modern Hawks Nest Lodge is on high ground that overlooks Hawks Nest Lake. The lodge has a dining room that overlooks the lake, the marina, and the aerial tramway, and a swimming pool, which has a view that extends for miles.

Equipped with modern furnishings, the guest rooms have wall-to-wall carpeting, private baths, and television. Many have private balconies that overlook either the gorge and the lake or the swimming pool.

Accommodations: 31 rooms with private bath. *Pets:* Not permitted. *Open:* All year. *Mailing address:* Ansted, WV 25812. *Phone:* (304) 658-5212. *Driving instructions:* Hawks Nest State Park is off U.S. 60, about 50 miles southeast of Charleston.

The second-largest West Virginia state park, Holly River comprises 8,050 acres of densely forested, mountainous terrain in the east-central part of the state. The park, in a valley surrounded by 3,000-foot mountains, is noted for its heavy rainfall and wide variety of trees, ferns, and such wildflowers as flame azalea, pink lady's slipper, Indian paintbrush, wild geranium, purple trillium, and Solomon's seal. Laurel Fork, a tributary of the Holly River and a good trout stream, winds through the area. Hiking trails run past the stream and two of its scenic waterfalls—Tecumseh and Tenskwatawa, named after two Indian chiefs. Another hiking trail leads to the summit of Potato Knob (elevation 2,480 feet), which overlooks the surrounding woodlands and three waterfalls.

The park has a swimming pool and adjacent facilities for tennis, badminton, horseshoe pitching, croquet, and shuffleboard. The park also has a softball field, a restaurant, a commissary store, and a naturalist service that offers nature hikes, lectures and films, marshmallow roasts, and organized sports events.

Holly River has nine cabins available located within a stand of hemlocks and rhododendrons. The cabins are constructed either of stone, logs, or a combination of the two. Five are designed to accommodate two people, and four of them can serve up to four people. Each has a stone fireplace, a fully equipped kitchen with modern appliances, a bath with a tile shower, and rustic furnishings, including rocking chairs.

Accommodations: 9 cabins with private bath. *Towels and linens:* Provided. *Cooking and eating utensils:* Provided. *Stove and refrigerator:* Provided. *Pets:* Permitted. *Open:* Third weekend in April through fourth Monday in October. *Mailing address:* Hacker Valley, WV 26222. *Phone:* (304) 493-6353. *Driving instructions:* Holly River State Park is on Route 20 about 20 miles north of Webster Springs.

Kumbrabow State Forest is in east-central West Virginia, a few miles west of Monongahela National Forest and a few miles south of Rich Mountain. "Kumbrabow" is an acronym for the names of three prominent families who were instrumental in the early development of the forest—KUMp, BRAdy, and BOWers. Although now thick with second-growth timber, the forest used to have extensive stands of virgin spruce and hemlock before being heavily logged over. The forest has the highest elevations of any in West Virginia, ranging from 3,000 to 3,800 feet.

The forest has many hiking trails, several picnic sites, and a children's playground. Anglers go after trout in Mill Creek, a natural trout stream. Hunting is permitted in the forest, the primary game being deer, bear, turkey, and ruffled grouse.

Kumbrabow Forest has five rustic cabins in its northeastern corner, at an elevation of about 3,000 feet. Completely furnished, each has gas lamps, a fireplace, a wood-burning kitchen stove, and a gas refrigerator. Guests get water from a nearby well; sanitary facilities are located outside the cabins.

Accommodations: 5 cabins with shared bath. *Towels and linens:* Provided. *Cooking and eating utensils:* Provided. *Stove and refrigerator:* Provided. *Pets:* Not permitted. *Open:* Late April through early December. *Mailing address:* Box 65, Huttonsville, WV 26273. *Phone:* (304) 335-2219. *Driving instructions:* From Elkins take U.S. 219 south for 24 miles, then turn onto the rock-base road that leads to the forest.

Lost River State Park is in northeastern West Virginia's panhandle, about 5 miles north and west of George Washington National Forest across the border in Virginia. The 3,712-acre park takes its name from the Lost River, which flows along and then disappears underground, only to reappear. Although the area was owned by a Tory, Thomas, Lord Fairfax, until the Revolutionary War, successful American military leaders were given a chance to acquire British-owned territory, with the result that General Henry "Light-Horse Harry" Lee took title to this land and passed it on to the prominent Lee family of Virginia. Light Horse Harry's cabin is still here, preserved as a museum and listed in the National Register of Historic Places.

The park is in a heavily wooded, mountainous area that is perhaps best viewed from Cranny Crow overlook at an elevation of 3,250 feet. Miles of hiking and bridle trails wind through the park, where visitors can also rent horses. Other popular activities include swimming in the park's pool, which is overlooked by a cluster of facilities for tennis, croquet, archery, volleyball, badminton, and horseshoe-pitching. Commonly sighted wildlife includes deer, raccoons, screech owls, wild turkeys, and grouse.

The park's twenty-four cabins are of two types—deluxe and standard. Each deluxe cabin is of frame construction and has native-wood paneling, a forced-air furnace, modern furnishings, a fully equipped kitchen with modern appliances, a stone fireplace, and a bath with tiled shower. Built of logs, the standard cabins also have stone fireplaces and baths with tiled showers. They differ from the deluxe cabins in that they have less space and more limited kitchen facilities.

The park has a restaurant that serves meals during summer.

Accommodations: 24 cabins with private bath. *Towels and linens:* Provided. *Cooking and eating utensils:* Provided. *Stove and refrigerator:* Provided. *Pets:* Not permitted. *Open:* Standard cabins from the last weekend in April through fourth Monday in October; deluxe cabins from last weekend in March through second Monday in December. *Mailing address:* Route 2, Box 24, Mathias, WV 26812. *Phone:* (304) 897-5372. *Driving instructions:* Take Route 259 to Mathias, then turn onto a secondary paved road and drive 4 miles west.

North Bend State Park is in northwestern West Virginia, about 70 miles northeast of Charleston. The 1,405-acre park takes its name from a horseshoe bend in the north fork of the Hughes River, which the park lodge overlooks. The park offers a number of hiking trails, including one specially designed for the wheelchair-bound and the blind. The park has a large swimming pool, a miniature-golf course, tennis and other game courts, picnic areas, playgrounds, and a nature program that includes films, campfires, and hikes.

North Bend Lodge and Cabins

North Bend has a modern, rectilinear lodge built with a generous amount of glass. The lodge has a dining room overlooking the mountains, as well as a lounge, meeting and banquet rooms, a gift shop, and two outdoor patios. The thirty guest rooms are spacious and comfortable, and each has a private bath, color television, a telephone, air-conditioning, and two double beds. Nine are handicapped accessible.

The park also has eight cabins constructed of solid cedar logs, wood-shingle roofs, and native wood-paneled walls. Each has a stone or free-standing fireplace, an electrical heating unit, wall-to-wall carpeting, a fully equipped kitchen with modern appliances, a modern bath with a tub and tiled shower, and either two or three bedrooms.

Accommodations: 30 lodge rooms and 8 cabins, all with private bath. *Towels and linens:* Provided. *Cooking and eating utensils:* In cabins. *Stove and refrigerator:* In cabins. *Pets:* Not permitted. *Open:* All year. *Mailing address:* North Bend State Park, Cairo, WV 26337. *Phone:* (304) 643-2931. *Driving instructions:* North Bend State Park is off Route 31 about 2½ miles northeast of Cairo.

Pipestem Resort State Park is in southern West Virginia about 15 miles southeast of Beckley and 10 miles from the Jefferson National Forest across the Virginia border. The park consists of 4,023 acres near the Bluestone Dam Recreation Area, overlooking the Bluestone River gorge. Its terrain is rugged, heavily wooded, and mountainous. Scenic overlooks along miles of hiking and riding trails provide breathtaking views. Rugged as its terrain is, Pipestem is extensively developed with two golf courses, two lodges, two Olympic-size swimming pools (one indoors, one outdoors), an archery range, horse and bicycle rentals, lighted tennis courts, two restaurants, snack bars, a supper club, an amphitheater for summer entertainment, and a large local arts-and-crafts shop.

Winter activities focus on the park's sled run and miles of cross-country ski trails. Although it might appear heavily developed, Pipestem offers a nice balance of activity and tranquility, of manicured greens and heavily wooded mountains.

Pipestem Lodges and Cabins

The park has two modern lodges and twenty-five deluxe cabins. The lodges are both modern and feature a generous use of glass. Pipestem Lodge (open all year) is on a rise that overlooks the Bluestone River gorge. Mountain Creek Lodge (closed in winter) is at the bottom of a thousand-foot-deep gorge accessible only by aerial tramway. Both lodges have dining rooms, snack bars, gift shops, and banquet and meeting facilities. The rooms have wall-to-wall carpeting, color television, telephones, private baths, and modern furnishings.

There are also twenty-five wood-frame deluxe cabins with outdoor decks, wood-paneled walls, color television, open fireplaces, fully equipped kitchens with modern appliances, electric heat, and private baths with tiled showers. The cabins are in a wooded area.

Accommodations: 143 lodge rooms and 25 cabins, all with private bath. *Towels and linens:* Provided. *Cooking and eating utensils:* In cabins. *Stove and refrigerator:* In cabins. *Pets:* Not permitted. *Open:* All year. *Mailing address:* Pipestem, WV 25979. *Phone:* (304) 466-1800. *Driving instructions:* Pipestem Resort State Park is off Route 20 about 20 miles northeast of Princeton.

Within the boundaries of Monongahela National Forest, bordered on the west by the Greenbrier River, Seneca State Forest encompasses 11,684 acres in eastern West Virginia about 90 miles east of Charleston and about 10 miles from Back Creek Mountain across the border in Virginia. The Forest has miles of hiking trails. The 4-acre Seneca Lake, named after the Indian tribe that roamed and hunted in this area, is stocked with trout, as is the Greenbrier River, also noted for its bass and pike. The terrain is rugged and mountainous, with elevations that range from 2,250 to 3,631 feet.

Seneca Forest has seven rustic log cabins in its south-central section, around Seneca Lake. Three of the cabins accommodate four, two accommodate six, and two accommodate eight. The cabins have no running water or bathrooms. (Guests get water from a nearby well; and sanitary facilities are located outside.) The cabins come equipped with gas lamps, wood-burning kitchen stoves, fireplaces, and gas refrigerators. Cabin rentals include free swimming privileges at nearby Watoga State Park.

Accommodations: 7 cabins with central bath. *Towels and linens:* Provided. *Cooking and eating utensils:* Provided. *Stove and refrigerator:* Provided. *Pets:* Permitted. *Open:* May 1 through December 1. *Mailing address:* Route 1, Box 140, Dunmore, WV 24934. *Phone:* (304) 799-6213. *Driving instructions:* From Marlinton take Route 39 southeast for 5 miles, then turn northeast onto Route 28 and proceed for 11 miles.

A 3,776-acre reserve, Twin Falls State Park is in southern West Virginia, roughly 20 miles southwest of Beckley. The park, which takes its name from two waterfalls, is thickly wooded with a mixture of hardwoods and conifers. The park has an eighteen-hole golf course and clubhouse, a large swimming pool, tennis courts, and many hiking trails, several of which lead to scenic overlooks. A special feature of the park is a thoroughly restored early-nineteenth-century pioneer homestead on Bower's Ridge that is open to visitors. *Park mailing address:* PO Box 1023, Mullens, WV 25882.

Twin Falls Lodge

In a wooded area at one of the highest points in the park, Twin Falls Lodge is a series of modern, rectilinear brick and glass buildings overlooking the golf-course, clubhouse, and swimming-pool complex. The lodge also has a dining room, a gift shop, a lounge, and meeting rooms. The bedrooms have carpeting, modern furnishings, color television, telephones, air-conditioning, and private baths. All have sliding glass doors that open onto private balconies.

The park also includes thirteen cabins on a wooded hillside, secluded from each other. Trails run from the cabin area to the golf course and recreation area. The cabins feature native wood-paneled walls, stone fireplaces, electric heat, year-round insulation, fully-equipped kitchens with modern appliances, and baths with tiled showers.

Accommodations: 20 lodge rooms and 13 cabins, all with private bath. *Towels and linens:* Provided. *Cooking and eating utensils:* Provided. *Stove and refrigerator:* Provided. *Pets:* Not permitted. *Open:* All year. *Mailing address:* PO Box 1023, Route 97, Mullens, WV 25882. *Phone:* (304) 294-4000. *Driving instructions:* From Beckley take Route 16 southwest to Route 54, drive north to Maben, and then take Route 97 west to the park.

In northern West Virginia, about 15 miles east of Clarksburg and 25 miles south of the Pennsylvania border, Tygart Lake State Park comprises 1,376 acres. It takes its name from Tygart Lake, a long, narrow man-made body of water that winds for 13 miles among thickly wooded hills and valleys. Built by the U.S. Army Corps of Engineers in the 1930s as a flood-control project, it has since become a mecca for scuba divers, swimmers, waterskiers, boaters, and fishermen.

On the north shore of the lake, the park has a beach for swimming and boat-launching facilities where visitors can rent boats for waterskiing, sightseeing, or fishing. The park's facilities include playgrounds, picnic grounds, a naturalist service, and a souvenir shop. *Park mailing address:* Route 1, Box 260, Grafton, WV 26354. *Park phone:* (304) 265-3383.

Tygart Lake Lodge and Cabins

On a plateau overlooking Tygart Lake is the modern wood and glass Tygart Lake Lodge, which includes a hundred-seat dining room overlooking the lake, as well as facilities for banquets and meetings.

Each guest room has wood-paneling, wall-to-wall carpeting, color television, a telephone, air-conditioning, and a private bath. Many have lake views. The lodge also administers ten deluxe cabins along the lakeshore road about 3 miles farther south. The cabins have native wood-paneled walls, stone fireplaces, fully equipped kitchens with modern appliances, water heaters, and private baths with tiled showers.

Accommodations: 20 lodge rooms and 10 cabins, all with private bath. *Towels and linens:* Provided. *Cooking and eating utensils:* In cabins. *Stove and refrigerator:* In cabins. *Pets:* Not permitted. *Open:* May through October. *Mailing address:* Route 1, Box 258, Grafton, WV 26354. *Phone:* (304) 265-2320. *Driving instructions:* Tygart Lake State Park is off U.S. 119 about 5 miles south of Grafton.

The largest and oldest of West Virginia's parks, Watoga State Park is in the eastern section of the state in the Appalachian highlands, about 90 miles east of Charleston and 10 miles west of the Virginia border. The 10,057-acre park is bordered to the north and east by Monongahela National Forest and adjoins Calvin Price State Forest to its south. The park takes its name from a Cherokee word that can be roughly translated as "river of the islands," probably in reference to the Greenbrier River, which forms its western border. The park contains the 400-acre Brooks Memorial Arboretum.

The park has a swimming pool, as well as facilities for tennis, shuffleboard, croquet, badminton, volleyball, archery, and horseshoe-pitching, along with an 11-acre lake with boat-launching facilities. Rowboats and paddleboats are available for rent, and horses are available for hire. Numerous hiking trails wind through the park, including a short one that runs around the lake and a 6-mile path that ambles through the arboretum.

Watoga State Park has two types of cabins—deluxe and standard—and both types are fully equipped for housekeeping. The eight wood-frame deluxe cabins have wood-paneled walls, complete kitchens with modern appliances, stone fireplaces, baths with tiled showers, and forced-air furnaces.

The twenty-five standard cabins, most of which were built of logs, are smaller and less opulently appointed than the deluxe cabins, although they too have stone fireplaces. The standard cabins have smaller kitchen facilities and lack a heating system.

Accommodations: 33 cabins with private bath. *Towels and linens:* Provided. *Cooking and eating utensils:* Provided. *Stove and refrigerator:* Provided. *Pets:* Permitted. *Open:* Deluxe cabins from last weekend in March through second Monday in December; standard cabins from last weekend in April through fourth Monday in October. *Mailing address:* Star Route 1, Box 252, Marlinton, WV 24954. *Phone:* (304) 799-4087. *Driving instructions:* Watoga State Park is off a paved secondary road that runs southeast from U.S. 219 from just northeast of Hillsboro.

Wisconsin

State map and tourist information: Wisconsin Tourism, 123 Washington Avenue, Madison, WI 53702; 608-266-2161. **State parks:** *Information:* Parks and Recreation Commission, 4th Flr., G.E.F. Bldg. 2, 101 S. Webster St., Madison, WI 53702; 608-266-2181. **National parks:** Contact park directly.

Along and off the coast of Bayfield Peninsula in northwestern Wisconsin, Apostle Islands National Lakeshore comprises 68,509 acres, of which about 26,500 acres are water. Of the twenty-two Apostle Islands, twenty are part of the national lakeshore. Characterized by their abundance of beaches, clay banks, sandstone cliffs, and lush forests, the islands were formed when the last glaciers receded, carving deep gorges through the sandstone bedrock, then leaving large deposits of debris. The rock formations are complex, with grottoes, caves, and arches testifying to the glaciers' erosive effect.

Remote and ruggedly beautiful, the islands are perfect for camping, hiking, swimming, and boating; and the area is known for its outstanding fishing, particularly for lake and rainbow trout. Various concessionaires offer such services as a marina with boat rentals, excursion trips, shuttles among the islands, and fishing trips.

In addition to its twenty islands, which range in size from 2 acres to 10,000 acres, the park includes a 12-mile section of the Bayfield Peninsula. Although lovely in summer, this area can be harsh in winter, with temperatures as low as $-30°$ F. combined with an average snowfall of 100 inches.

Red Cliff Indian Reservation, adjacent to the park, operates a cultural center with exhibits and offers handcrafted items for sale. *Park mailing address:* Route 1, Box 4, Bayfield, WI 54814. *Park phone:* (715) 779-3397.

Chateau Madeline

Although Madeline Island, the largest of the twenty-two Apostle Islands, isn't, strictly speaking, part of the national lakeshore, it is an excellent base for exploring the other islands, as well as the 2,204-acre Big Bay State Park.

On a hillside overlooking Lake Superior and the Wisconsin mainland, surrounded by pines and birches on 15 acres of grounds, Chateau Madeline has a seven-room lodge and three cottages with three bedrooms each. Guest rooms have hardwood floors, wainscoting, antique furnishings, and large windows. Two rooms have a view of the lake, and the other looks out at forest. One cottage, on a beach below the main house, features pine-paneled guest rooms with views of Chequamegon Bay; another

has a private beach; and the third, a fireplace, a living room, and private decks.

Rates include all meals at the lodge restaurant. (The staff will put together box lunches for guests on request.) The dining room overlooks the lake and the mainland, and the breakfast room and living room have tiled fireplaces.

Accommodations: 7 lodge rooms and 3 cottages, most with private bath. *Pets:* Not permitted. *Open:* Mid-June to mid-October. *Mailing address:* PO Box 27, La Pointe (Madeline Island), WI 54850; off season: 4209 Country Club Road, Minneapolis, MN 55424. *Driving instructions:* From Bayfield take the ferry (15 minutes) to the town of La Pointe on Madeline Island—Chateau Madeline is 1½ miles to the right of the town dock.

Nicknamed the "Cradle of Rivers," Nicolet National Forest is in northeastern Wisconsin, just south of Lake Superior and the Upper Peninsula of Michigan, and just north of the Menominee Indian Reservation. The 656,000-acre forest has small hills, ranging in elevation from 800 to 1,500 feet, and is wooded primarily with quaking aspens and scattered stands of maples, basswoods, birches, firs, and red, white and jack pines. The forest has literally hundreds of lakes and some 600 miles of trout streams, many of which the state stocks with both rainbow and brown trout (fly-fishing aficionados consider this one of the finest trout-fishing areas in the world). One local resident claims to have caught—legally—300 trout last year. Characteristic wildlife includes deer, black bears, foxes, beavers, raccoons, squirrels, and a wide variety of bird life. The wetlands attract thousands of migrating waterfowl—ducks, geese, herons, egrets—and the forest is host to a population of about forty bald eagles.

The Pershtigo and Wolf rivers are famous for being among the best white-water canoeing rivers in the country, and for snowmobiling, the forest has 520 miles of trails. There are some 80 miles of well-groomed cross-country ski trails and many miles of hiking trails (although hiking isn't that popular because of the density of the forested sections). Lakewood, a town in the forest, is considered by some to be the snowmobiling capital of the world. *Forest headquarters:* 68 South Stevens, Rhinelander, WI 54501. *Forest phone:* (715) 362-3415.

Wolf River Lodge

By the shore of the Wolf River, Wolf River Lodge is a rustic log-and-shingle building with eight guest rooms, a central lounge, and a dining room. The lounge, fitted out with couches and easy chairs and braided rugs over a hardwood floor, is a center of activity, especially when its 10-foot-wide stone fireplace has a fire going. The menu in the dining room is limited, but trout is a house specialty.

The guest rooms vary in size and appointments and include such features as hand-made quilts on the beds and braided rugs on the floors. Some have hardwood floors, some are carpeted, and some overlook the river. Only one has a private bath—the rest share baths.

587

The lodge operates a school for white-water canoeing. The lodge's owner, George Steed, won the American Canoe Association Masters Title in the white-water slalom three years in a row. If, with no experience, you show up on a Sunday and attend the school, chances are excellent that you'll be negotiating the Wolf River's rapids by the time Friday rolls around.

Accommodations: 8 rooms, 1 with private bath. *Pets:* Not permitted. *Open:* Late April through September and Christmas through mid-March. *Mailing address:* White Lake, WI 54491. *Phone:* (715) 882-2182. *Driving instructions:* Take Route 55 north and, just past its intersection with Route 64, look for the Wolf River Lodge sign.

Wyoming

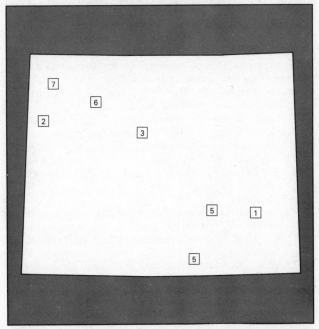

State map and tourist information: Travel Commission, Cheyenne, WY 82002; 307-777-7777. **State parks:** *Information:* Recreation Commission, 920 Thomes, Cheyenne, WY 82002; 307-777-7695. *Entrance fees:* None. *Reservations:* Contact individual lodgings. Deposit for first night, check or credit card. Reservations accepted up to 1 year in advance (recommended 6 to 8 weeks in advance, mid May—early September.) *Restrictions:* Hunting limited to designated areas and in certain parks only. Dogs must be leashed. *Facilities:* Swimming, backpacking, and boating, Mem. Day—Labor Day. Cross-country skiing and snowmobiling, November—March. **National parks:** Contact parks directly.

Glendo State Park, in southeastern Wyoming about 100 miles north of Cheyenne, encompasses 19,000 acres, of which 9,930 acres border on the 12,500-acre Glendo Reservoir, formed by Glendo Dam and the North Platte River, at an elevation of 4,675 feet. The reservoir, with 78 miles of shoreline, is surrounded by hills sprinkled with rock outcroppings and pines; and a series of dunes rises out of its eastern end. Vegetation here is a mix of grasses, sagebrush, and pine-covered hills, and the North Platte Canyon is lined with cottonwoods and willows.

Activities include swimming, fishing, hiking, waterskiing, cross-country skiing, snowmobiling, and boating. Anglers go after pike, rainbow trout, catfishes, and perch; and visitors can rent powerboats and skiing equipment. *Park mailing address:* Box 398, Glendo, WY 82213. *Park phone:* (307) 735-4433.

Glendo Marina

Glendo Marina is a complex of buildings on the shore of Glendo Reservoir. Its main lodge, with a restaurant specializing in home-cooked food, sells groceries, liquor, bait and tackle, and sundries.

Guest accommodations are in a six-unit motel overlooking the lake. Decorated in log-cabin style, each room has exposed-beam knotty-pine ceilings, two double beds, modern wooden furniture, wall-to-wall carpeting, and a private bath. There are no kitchen facilities, but linens and maid service are provided.

Accommodations: 6 motel rooms with private bath. *Pets:* Permitted if leashed—check in advance. *Open:* All year. *Mailing address:* Lake Shore Drive, PO Box 187, Glendo, WY 82213. *Phone:* (307) 735-4216. *Driving instructions:* Take I-25 to Glendo, then follow the signs to the park, which is 3 ½ miles southeast of Glendo. Glendo Marina is 2 miles into the park.

A 311,736-acre reserve, Grand Teton National Park is in northwestern Wyoming just south of Yellowstone National Park, immediately west of the Bridger Teton National Forest, and immediately east of the Targhee National Forest in Idaho. The park's highlight is the Grand Teton mountain range, majestic slate-blue snow-capped peaks rising abruptly from the sagebrush flats at their base to as high as 13,770 feet. The seemingly numberless lakes have names like Surprise, Amphitheater, Solitude; and the Snake, one of the least industrially polluted rivers in America, winds through the area.

The park includes Jackson Hole, named after a trapper, which serves as the winter range of what is part of the largest herd of elk in North America. The range of altitudes accounts for the spectrum of wildflowers, including many alpine species, that color the meadows, fields, and slopes from early spring to late summer; and the spruces, pines, cottonwoods, and white-barked aspens which form forests below the timberline. Shiras moose, bighorn sheep, bears, mink, coyotes, and many other mammals live in the park, which also sees rare trumpeter swans, as well as eagles and ospreys, among more than a hundred species of birds.

Although the majority of visitors to Grand Teton National Park probably spend most of their time gazing at the spectacular scenery, hiking, boating, fishing, rafting, backpacking, mountain climbing, cross-country skiing, and snowmobiling are all regular activities. *Park mailing address:* Drawer 170, Moose, WY 83012. *Park phone:* (307) 733-2880.

Owned by Jackson Hole Preserve, Inc., a nonprofit educational organization, the Grand Teton Lodge Company uses its income to improve its own facilities and to further conservation activities of Jackson Hole Preserve. The company offers three types of accommodations—luxury and budget log cabins, and moderately priced rooms—and handles reservations and inquiries for the first three lodging facilities listed below. *Mailing address:* PO Box 240, Moran, WY 83013. *Phone:* (307) 543-2855.

Jenny Lake Lodge

A complex of log buildings—thirty cabins and a main lodge—Jenny Lake Lodge has an award-winning dining room decorated with rustic elegance. The lounge in the main lodge has log ceilings and walls, a fireplace built of native stone, and hardwood floors covered with throw rugs.

The cabins, each named after a local flower, have such amenities as two overstuffed easy chairs, a writing desk, a private bath, and headboards adapted from original bedsteads. They are within an easy walk of Jenny Lake and the main lodge building. Among the cabins are four two-room suites with fireplaces.

Activities include hiking on the many trails, horseback riding, and fishing. Typical dinner entrées in the dining room include such items as fillet of sole meunière with almonds, duckling à l'orange, and filet mignon béarnaise.

Accommodations: 30 cabins with private bath. *Towels and linens:* Provided. *Cooking and eating utensils:* Not provided. *Stove and refrigerator:* Not provided. *Pets:* Permitted if leashed. *Open:* Early June through mid-September. *Driving instructions:* Jenny Lake Lodge is on Jenny Lake Loop Road, 25 miles north of the town of Jackson.

Jackson Lake Lodge

On a small rise overlooking Jackson Lake, Jackson Lake Lodge has a 42-room main lodge with 343 motor-lodge rooms grouped around the main building. Overlooking the lake and the Teton Range, the lodge has a lounge with a 60-foot picture window and several fireplaces; a dining room with many windows and murals depicting trappers; another dining area for light meals and snacks; and a Western-decor cocktail lounge with an 18-foot-long diorama of trappers' life. Gift, apparel, and beauty shops, and room service for breakfast, are among other full-service amenities. Each guest room has a private bath with shower.

Several rooms, in both the main lodge and the motor-lodge units, have views; and on the grounds are riding stables, a large heated swimming pool, and a service station.

Accommodations: 385 rooms with private bath. *Pets:* Permitted if leashed. *Open:* June through mid-September. *Mailing address and phone:* See above. *Driving instructions:* Jackson Lodge is 35 miles north of the town of Jackson on Route 89.

Colter Bay Village

Colter Bay Village is a complex of 209 cabins in a wooded area near Jackson Lake and the National Park Service amphitheater, the visitors' center, and the Indian Arts Museum. Jackson Lake has a beach and a boat-launching facility, and in the village are a restaurant, a grill, a coin laundry, a package store selling beer, a shower facility, a general store, a sporting-goods and tackle shop, and a service station.

Three type of cabins are available: Single-room units with a semiprivate bath; single-room units with a private bath; and cabins with two rooms and connecting bath that are suitable for families or couples traveling together and that can sleep up to six people.

Boating, swimming, fishing, horseback riding, and hiking are the principal activities at the Village.

Accommodations: 209 cabins with private bath or semiprivate bath. *Towels and linens:* Provided. *Cooking and eating utensils:* Not provided. *Stove and refrigerator:* Not provided. *Pets:* Permitted if leashed. *Open:* Late May through September. *Mailing address and phone:* See above. *Driving instructions:* Colter Bay Village is on Route 89, 40 miles north of Jackson.

Signal Mountain Lodge, Apartments, and Cabins

Signal Mountain Lodge, 17 miles north of the park headquarters and at an elevation of 6,700 feet, has several types of accommodations: one- and two-room cabins that are carpeted, heated, furnished primarily with handmade log pieces, and that have a private bath with a tub and shower; motel rooms with modern furnishings, carpeting, and a private bath with tub and shower; apartments that overlook Jackson Lake and the Grand Tetons, each with a bedroom with a double or king-size bed, a sitting room with a sofa bed, an electric kitchenette (cooking and eating utensils are not provided), a private bath with tub and shower, and a balcony or deck overlooking the lake and mountains; one- and two-bedroom family units with lake views (some of these have a kitchenette, and the units are adjoining and can be rented for groups of up to ten); a completely furnished one-bedroom house with fireplace, washer and dryer, television, and a full kitchen; and a houseboat that sleeps up to four.

Other facilities at the lodge include a dining room, a snack bar, a cocktail lounge, a gas station, a grocery store, pontoon boats, and organized raft trips.

Accommodations: 32 cabins, 16 motel rooms, 30 apartments, 1 house, and 1 houseboat, all with private bath. *Pets:* Permitted ($5 additional). *Open:* All year. *Mailing address:* PO Box 50, Moran, WY 83013. *Phone:* (307) 543-2831. *Driving instructions:* From Jackson take Route 289 north 12 miles, then turn left at Moose Junction—the lodge is 17 miles north of park headquarters.

Hot Springs State Park, about 1,000 acres in northern Wyoming at the beginning of the Big Horn River Basin, is immediately northeast of Thermopolis, a name taken from the Greek, meaning loosely, "city of heat." Thermopolis is at the foot of the justifiably famous Wind River Canyon and is about 4,000 feet above sea level. The Owl Mountains are on the south side of the park, the Big Horn range is to the northeast, and the Absarokas are to the west; 12,000-foot peaks are less than 30 miles away. Thermopolis and Hot Springs State Park both take their names and reputations for the heat from Big Spring, from which flows 3 million to 4 million gallons of hot mineral water (average temperature 135° F.) every twenty-four hours. Especially beautiful is Rainbow Terrace, formed by the minerals that precipitate out of the hot water, creating—when combined with various algae that grow at different temperatures—deposits with delicate shades of green, orange, reddish orange, and yellow.

Big Spring, along with other land, was purchased in 1896 from the Shoshone and Arapaho, and each August the event is celebrated with the "Gift of the Waters Pageant." The park, a geologic wonder marked by colorful and steep canyons, mountain springs, and an enormous variety of vegetation, has a herd of grazing buffalo. *Park address:* Superintendent, Thermopolis, WY 82443. *Park phone:* (307) 864-3848.

Holiday Inn of the Waters

On the bank of the Big Horn River, Holiday Inn of the Waters has eighty rooms and facilities that include a modern bathhouse with mineral steam baths, saunas, private soaking tubs, and full-time massage therapists, with water pumped to the bathhouse directly from Big Spring. There are two swimming pools: One is fresh water; the other, a year-round outdoor hot mineral pool. The inn also has racketball courts and exercise rooms, a beauty shop, a dining room, and a cocktail lounge.

Each guest room has air-conditioning, wall-to-wall carpeting, color television, a private bath, and modern furnishings. Rooms with waterbeds are available.

Accommodations: 80 rooms with private bath. *Pets:* Permitted. *Open:* All year. *Mailing address:* PO Box 1323, Hot

Springs State Park, Thermopolis, WY 82443. *Phone:* (307) 864-3131. *Driving instructions:* From Casper take Route 20-26 west to Shoshone, then take Route 20 north to Thermopolis and Hot Springs State Park.

The Plaza Hotel and Apartments

A short walk from Big Spring, The Plaza Hotel and Apartments is a large brick building with twelve bedrooms; eighteen one-room apartments; ten two-bedroom apartments; and one three-bedroom apartment. Its facilities include a steam bath and massage department with mineral baths (steam, tub, and sweating cot), and a staff of massage therapists. The hotel has no dining room but is across the street from a restaurant and a picnic-playground area.

The Plaza's apartments, simply but comfortably furnished, have basic cooking facilities—stove, refrigerator, and some cooking and eating utensils. Their bedrooms are carpeted, and each has a private bath.

The hotel's bedrooms are carpeted, with basic furnishings and a half bath (showers are shared).

Accommodations: 29 apartments, 21 with private bath; and 12 bedrooms with half bath and shared shower. *Towels and linens:* Provided. *Cooking and eating utensils:* In apartments. *Stove and refrigerator:* In apartments. *Pets:* Permitted if small. *Open:* All year. *Mailing address:* Box 671, Thermopolis, WY 82443. *Phone:* (307) 864-2251. *Driving instructions:* From Casper take Route 20-26 to Shoshone, then take Route 20 north to Thermopolis and Hot Springs State Park.

The four sections of the Medicine Bow National Forest are in southern and southeastern Wyoming, in the Medicine Bow and Park mountain ranges near the Colorado border. The northernmost section is in the Laramie Peak Mountains, beginning about 30 miles southeast of Casper. The two sections of the Thunder Basin National Grassland, in eastern Wyoming, are part of Medicine Bow National Forest, which comprises about 1 million acres in all and varies in elevation from 7,000 to 12,000 feet. It is wooded primarily with lodgepole pines, Engelmann spruces, alpine firs, and scattered stands of quaking aspens. The grassland areas—at about 5,000 feet elevation—are expansive, relatively level open areas covered with grass and sagebrush and lightly sprinkled with ponderosa pines.

Numerous mountain streams course through the forest, and the state stocks many with rainbow trout. There is rafting on the North Platte River, especially through its white-water areas. Characteristic wildlife includes elk, deer, antelope, black bears, and mountain lions. The forest supports a wide variety of birds, including, especially in the grassland, golden eagles. Hunting, camping, and hiking are regular activities, as is horseback riding. In winter there is cross-country skiing and snowmobiling, and the Snowy Range Ski Area has tows and downhill slopes. *National Forest mailing address:* 605 Skyline Drive, Laramie, WY 82070. *Forest phone:* (307) 745-8971.

Medicine Bow Lodge Guest Ranch

At an elevation of 8,500 feet, Medicine Bow Lodge Guest Ranch consists of a 1917 lodge constructed of logs and eight log cabins, as well as a bathhouse with whirlpool and sauna facilities. The main lodge has a lounge with couches, easy chairs, a piano, wall-to-wall carpeting, and a stone fireplace. There is also a game room and a dining room that serves from a preset-menu that changes every two weeks during the summer. The lodge overlooks Barrett Creek, which is 12 feet away.

The cabins, with log exteriors and inside paneling, are furnished with beds, tables, and chairs. The largest can accommodate nine people. Each is heated and has a private bath, although the plumbing works only in warmer months; when the weather turns cold, cabin guests use a central bathhouse.

The lodge, on 75 acres, has two trout streams on its property, and in summer horses are available for hire and pack trips on horseback are offered. Winter activities include cross-country skiing and snowmobiling.

Accommodations: 8 cabins with private bath in summer, shared bath in winter. *Towels and linens:* Provided. *Cooking and eating utensils:* Not provided. *Stove and refrigerator:* Not provided. *Pets:* Check in advance. *Open:* All year. *Mailing address:* Route 130, PO Box 752, Saratoga, WY 82331. *Phone:* (307) 326-5439. *Driving instructions:* From Saratoga take Route 130-230 south for 8 miles, then take Route 130 east for 12 miles to the lodge.

Shoshone National Forest is in northwestern Wyoming, immediately east and southeast of Yellowstone Park. Its 2,466,097 acres are rugged and mountainous, with elevations varying from a low of 4,584 feet at the mouth of Clarks Fort Canyon to 13,804 feet at the summit of Gannett Peak, the highest point in Wyoming. The forest, among the Rocky, Absaroka, and Wind River mountain ranges, has numerous summits higher than 10,000 feet, and one, Bear Tooth Mountain, does indeed resemble a bear's tooth. A varied terrain includes hardwood river valleys, sagebrush and alpine meadows, and high-elevation alpine fir forests. Lodgepole pine, blue spruce, Engelmann spruce, and alpine fir are among the conifer species, along with stands of aspens and cottonwoods in the river valleys. Three rivers, each a tributary of the Missouri and stocked with cutthroat and rainbow trout, run through the forest—Clarks Fork, the Wind, and the Shoshone.

Among the abundant wildlife are grizzly and black bears, elk, moose, bighorn sheep, mountain goats, white-tailed and mule deer, antelope, and mountain lions. Red-tailed hawks cruise overhead, and golden and bald eagles winter here. *Forest address:* Box 2140, Cody, WY 82414. *Forest phone:* (307) 527-6241.

Absaroka Mountain Lodge

About 10 miles east of the east entrance to Yellowstone National Park, Absaroka Mountain Lodge comprises a lodge with a dining room building and thirteen cabins. The cabins and the main lodge buildings are of chink-log construction, and the dining room is in the original 1904 homestead cabin. The public rooms have log and leather furnishings, exposed chink walls decorated with hunting trophies, and hardwood floors covered with handwoven Indian rugs.

The cabins, beside a creek among pines and aspens, vary in size and decor. Some have log furnishings and handmade beds, others have wall-to-wall carpeting and contemporary Western-style appointments. All have a private bath.

Accommodations: 13 cabins with private bath. *Towels and linens:* Provided. *Cooking and eating utensils:* Not provided. *Stove and refrigerator:* Not provided. *Pets:* Permitted. *Open:* June through December. *Mailing address:* PO Box 168, Wapiti, WY 82450. *Phone:* (307) 587-3963. *Driving instructions:* Absaroka Mountain Lodge is off Route 14-16-20, about 40 miles west of Cody.

Goff Creek Lodge

Along Goff Creek, Goff Creek Lodge is a group of peeled-log buildings—a main lodge with a dining room and nine cabins—built in 1910 and renovated in the 1960s. The dining room, which specializes in boneless mountain trout and which will prepare a trout for guests who happen to catch one, has a stone fireplace. Both it and the rest of the lodge have exposed-log walls and exposed-log and plank ceilings along with Navaho rugs, hunting trophies, and Indian artifacts.

The cabins also have exposed-log and plank ceilings, as well as wood-paneling and western-style furnishings. Most cabins have two guest rooms, each with a private bath.

Goff Creek was named for John Goff, who occupied the area following 1905. Goff, a buffalo hunter, was the personal hunting guide for President Theodore Roosevelt when he visited this region.

Accommodations: 14 cabins with private bath. *Towels and linens:* Provided. *Cooking and eating utensils:* Not provided. *Stove and refrigerator:* Not provided. *Pets:* Not permitted. *Open:* Mid-May through mid-October. *Mailing address:* PO Box 155, Cody, WY 82414. *Phone:* (307) 587-3753. *Driving instructions:* Goff Creek Lodge is off Route 14-16-20, about 41 miles west of Cody.

Bill Cody's Ranch Inn

Operated by the grandson of Buffalo Bill, Bill Cody's Ranch Inn is a group of log buildings in a valley about 26 miles east of Yellowstone. The main lodge, which is 70 feet long, has a dining room, a lounge, a bar, and one guest room. Its living room has a stone fireplace, and the decor throughout the building is suggested by such touches as electrified kerosene lamps, handmade pine lamps, and Indian rugs.

The inn has thirteen cabins, each with two guest rooms and appointments that include custom-made headboards, a sofa bed, a writing desk and chair, an easy chair, and a side table with a handmade lamp. There is also a three-story chalet that has a family unit accommodating up to eight, and a "honeymoon hideaway" accommodating two. It can be rented separately or as one unit.

Accommodations: 1 lodge room, 13 cabins, and 1 chalet, all with private bath. *Towels and linens:* Provided. *Cooking and eating utensils:* Not provided. *Stove and refrigerator:* Not provided. *Pets:* Not permitted. *Open:* All year. *Mailing address:* PO Box 1390, Cody, WY 82414. *Phone:* (307) 587-2097. *Driving instructions:* The ranch is off Route 14-16-20, about 26 miles west of Cody.

In the northwestern corner of Wyoming, Yellowstone National park comprises 2,221,766 acres of some of the most scenic terrain in the country. The first explorers of the area were not believed when they described Yellowstone's natural wonders—geysers that shoot water hundreds of feet into the air; bubbling mud pots; mountains of petrified trees; cliffs of obsidian, a 1,200-foot-deep canyon of yellow stone; a tumultuous river; steaming terraced cliffs, and delicately colored rimstone pools. Encompassing about 3,472 square miles, Yellowstone is surrounded by five national forests that comprise another 8,000 square miles of protected land—Gallatin, Custer, Shoshone, Bridger Teton, and Targhee National Forests—and adjacent to its southern border is Grand Teton National Park.

Yellowstone has two hundred geysers and some ten thousand other thermal features including hot springs. Old Faithful, the world's most famous geyser, erupts regularly every seventy minutes, sending a column of water an average of 130 feet into the air. Yellowstone also has falling columns of water—one, the Lower Falls of the Yellowstone River, drops 309 feet. Among scores of other scenic attractions are the Grand Canyon of the Yellowstone River, Mount Washburn, Norris Geyser Basin, Yellowstone Lake, and Mammoth Hot Springs. Abundant wildlife includes a herd of bison, elk, bears, antelope, bighorn sheep, deer, coyotes, and cougars, to name a few. (The park emphasizes that the wild animals should be viewed from a safe distance and must never be fed. To discourage bears, visitors should lock food in car trunks.) The bird life is extremely varied, and ospreys and bald eagles soar over Yellowstone Lake.

Yellowstone was the first natural area set aside as a park anywhere in the world. Yellowstone's exemplary beauty inspired Congress to pass the Park Act in 1872, creating the first national park and making the first move toward the development of the U.S. National Park System.

Activities include sightseeing, backpacking, horseback riding, hiking, boating, and fishing. The park has 1,000 miles of hiking trails and six visitors' centers. Numerous interpretative programs and guided hikes and horseback rides are available, as are scenic cruises on Yellowstone Lake and campfire programs. *Park mailing address:* Yellowstone National Park, Box 168, WY 82190.

Park phone: (307) 344-7381 (ask for Visitor Services).

TW Services, Inc., operates all accommodations in the park and handles inquiries as well as reservations and specific driving instructions for the lodgings listed below. An activities department operates and takes reservations for special activities including sightseeing tours, stagecoach trips, guided fishing trips, and so on. *Mailing address:* TW Services, Inc, c/o Reservations, Yellowstone National Park, WY 82190. *Phone:* (307) 344-7311 (room reservations); (307) 344-7901, ext. 5240 (activities reservations).

Old Faithful Inn

A quarter of a mile from the Old Faithful geyser, Old Faithful Inn is a large, dormer-windowed stone-and-log building with 325 guest rooms as well as a restaurant, a bar, a snack bar, a gift shop, an information desk, and a large lobby with a huge stone fireplace. Its interior balconies overlook the lobby, and its second-floor lobby overlooks the geyser.

The rooms vary from new, modern units to rustic ones with exposed-log doors and walls. All rooms are carpeted, 194 have private baths, and about half overlook the geyser.

Accommodations: 325 rooms, 194 with private bath. *Pets:* Check in advance. *Open:* Early May through mid-October. *Mailing address and phone:* See above.

Lower Falls

Old Faithful Lodge

The Old Faithful Lodge complex near Old Faithful includes a main lodge constructed of logs and 239 cabins. The main lodge has a cafeteria, a bar, and a gift shop.

The cabins, which vary in size and appointments, include standard cabins, family cabins, budget cabins, and budget shelters. The 147 standard cabins have carpeting, wood-paneled walls, and a private bath. The seventeen rustic family cabins have a half bath with lavatory and sink; guests use a central shower facility and bring their own towels. Sixty-four budget cabins are even more rustic and have only a sink; guests use a central lavatory-shower facility and bring their own towels. Eleven budget shelters are very basic and have a sink; guests use a central lavatory-shower facility and bring their own towels and bedding.

Accommodations: 239 cabins, 147 with private bath, 17 with half bath, 75 with sink only. *Towels and linens:* In standard cabins. *Cooking and eating utensils:* Not provided. *Stove and refrigerator:* Not provided. *Pets:* Check in advance. *Open:* Early June to late September. *Mailing address and phone:* See above.

Old Faithful Snowlodge and Cabins

Near Old Faithful, Old Faithful Snowlodge and Cabins is a group of buildings centered around Snowlodge, a rustic wood-frame building of modern design. The main lodge has thirty guest rooms, a restaurant, a bar, an ice-cream parlor, a gift shop, and a lobby with a stone fireplace. The rooms in the lodge are rustic, and guests use a central shower and sanitary facility.

There are also thirty-four standard cabins, which have wall-to-wall carpeting, wood-paneled walls, and a private bath.

Accommodations: 30 lodge rooms with shared bath and 34 cabins with private bath. *Towels and linens:* Provided. *Cooking and eating utensils:* Not provided. *Stove and refrigerator:* Not provided. *Pets:* Check in advance. *Open:* Late June to early September; mid-October through November 1. *Mailing address and phone:* See above.

Canyon Lodge Cabins

Near the Grand Canyon of the Yellowstone River, about a quarter of a mile from the rim, Canyon Lodge Cabins consists of 588 cabins, as well as a main lodge building with a restaurant, a bar with a fireplace, a cafeteria, and a gift shop.

One hundred cabins, classified as luxury, are appointed with attractive modern furnishings and wall-to-wall carpeting as well as a private bath. Each of the other 488 cabins is classified as standard and has carpeting and a private bath with shower.

Accommodations: 588 cabins with private bath. *Towels and linens:* Provided. *Cooking and eating utensils:* Not provided. *Stove and refrigerator:* Not provided. *Pets:* Check in advance. *Open:* Mid-June to late August. *Mailing address and phone:* See above.

Lake Yellowstone Hotel and Cabins

Lake Yellowstone Hotel and Cabins, along the shore of Lake Yellowstone, consists of a sprawling wooden building with 184 guest rooms and 110 cabins. The main lodge has a restaurant with a view of the lake, as well as a bar, a gift shop, and a lobby with a fireplace. For fishing and boating enthusiasts, this is the place to stay.

Of the lodge guest rooms, 105 have a private bath and the rest share a bath. All rooms are carpeted and comfortably appointed, and about half have views of the lake.

Of the cabins, seventy-six are classified as standard and have carpeting and a private bath. The other thirty-four are classified as family and have a half bath with a sink and lavatory. Guests in the family cabins use a central shower facility and supply their own towels.

Accommodations: 184 lodge rooms, 105 with private bath; 110 cabins, 76 with private bath. *Towels and linens:* In lodge rooms and standard cabins. *Linens only:* In family cabins. *Cooking and eating utensils:* Not provided. *Stove and refrigerator:* Not provided. *Pets:* Check in advance. *Open:* Late May through late September. *Mailing address and phone:* See above.

Lake Lodge and Cabins

An eighth of a mile from Lake Yellowstone Hotel and set back from the lake, Lake Lodge and Cabins includes a main lodge with a cafeteria, a bar, and a gift shop, as well as 186 cabins.

One hundred of the cabins, classified as luxury, have attractive contemporary furnishings, wall-to-wall carpeting, wood-paneling, and a private bath, many with a tub as well as a shower. The other eighty-six cabins, classified as standard and somewhat smaller than the luxury cabins, have carpeting, wood-paneled walls, and a private bath with a shower only.

Accommodations: 186 cabins with private bath. *Towels and linens:* Provided. *Cooking and eating utensils:* Not provided. *Stove and refrigerator:* Not provided. *Pets:* Check in advance. *Open:* Early June through early September. *Mailing address and phone:* See above.

Roosevelt Lodge

At Tower Junction, a mountainous area on the Yellowstone River, Roosevelt Lodge includes a rustic single-story lodge and seventy-eight log cabins. The main lodge has a restaurant, a bar, a gift shop, and a lobby with a stone fireplace. In its appearance as well as in the activities it offers, Roosevelt Lodge has a decidedly Western feel. There are both horseback rides and stagecoach rides, including horse or coach journeys to ranch-style cookouts.

The cabins vary in size and appointments, the most luxurious being seven standard cabins. Each of these has wood paneling, carpeting, and a private bath. Nine family cabins are more rustic than the standard cabins with neither carpeting nor paneling and with a half bath that has a sink and lavatory; guests use a central shower facility and supply their own towels. The fifty Roughrider cabins are quite rustic, with a wood stove for heat and a sink; guests use a central sanitary and shower facility and bring their own towels. At twelve rustic shelters—very basic cabins with wood stoves for heat—guests use a central sanitary and shower facility and bring their own towels and bedding.

Accommodations: 78 cabins, 7 with private bath. *Towels and linens:* In standard cabins. *Linens:* In family and Roughrider cabins. *Pets:* Check in advance. *Open:* First week in June through first week in September. *Mailing address and phone:* See above.

Mammoth Hot Springs Hotel

Near park headquarters and the north entrance to Yellowstone and close to the hot springs and the multicolored terraced formations, Mammoth Hot Springs Hotel includes a large rustic wood-frame building with 96 guest rooms, as well as 125 cabins. The main lodge has a restaurant, a bar, a coffee shop, and a gift shop. Of the guest rooms, sixty-eight have a private bath and about twenty-five overlook the hot springs; others overlook the mountains. The rooms are simply but comfortably furnished and have wall-to-wall carpeting. The main lodge also has two suites, each with a kitchenette and private bath.

Of the cabins, seventy-three are standard and fifty-two are budget. The standard cabins have wood-paneling and carpeting as well as a private bath. The more rustic budget cabins have only a sink; guests use a central sanitary and shower facility and bring their own towels.

Activities at the hotel include full-day bus tours of Yellowstone.

Accommodations: 96 lodge rooms, 68 with private bath; 2 lodge suites with private bath; and 125 cabins, 73 with private bath. *Towels and linens:* In lodge rooms, suites, and standard cabins. *Linens:* In budget cabins. *Cooking and eating utensils:* In suites. *Stove and refrigerator:* In suites. *Pets:* Check in advance. *Open:* Early June to mid-September. *Mailing address and phone:* See above.

Grant Village

A group of rustic wood-frame buildings on Lake Yellowstone, Grant Village has a restaurant, a bar, and a gift shop, as well as 294 deluxe guest rooms, each with wall-to-wall carpeting, contemporary furnishings, and a private bath.

Among the activities offered are full-day bus tours of Yellowstone that leave from and return to the village.

Accommodations: 294 rooms with private bath. *Pets:* Check in advance. *Open:* Mid-June to mid-September. *Mailing address and phone:* See above.

State-by-State Index
of Rates and Credit-Card Information

Rates given are for high season only and are *subject to change*. Unless otherwise specified, Hotel and Lodge rates represent the cost for two persons per day, double occupancy (dbl); Cabin and Chalet rates vary with the number of persons and length of stay. Each park is numbered for easy referral to state maps in the text.

Credit-card abbreviations:

AE = American Express	MC = MasterCard
CB = Carte Blanche	V = Visa
DC = Diners Club	NCC = No credit cards accepted

ALABAMA

1 Cheaha State Park: Bald Rock Group Lodge, $195–$270 daily (50 persons); Cheaha Lodge, $39 daily (dbl); Chalets, $53 daily (4 persons); Cottages, $37 daily (2 persons, $4 each additional). AE, MC, V.

2 Chewacla State Park: Cabins, $30 daily (2 persons); $38 daily (3 persons, $3 each additional, children under 6 free). MC, V.

3 Desoto S.P.: Lodge, $40 daily (dbl); Chalets, $55 daily (4 persons, $4 each additional); Cabins, $44 daily (3 persons, $4 each additional). AE, MC, V.

4 Gulf State Park: Lodge, $75 daily (dbl); Resort Inn, $75 daily (dbl, $5 each additional, children under 12 free), AE, MC, V; Lakeside Cabins, $324 weekly (2 persons); Rustic Cabins, $180 weekly (2 persons, $18 each additional, children under 6 free). No credit cards accepted for cabins.

5 Joe Wheeler State Park: Group Lodge, $100 daily, $600 weekly (20 persons); Cottages, $30–$38 daily (2 persons, children under 6 free); Resort Lodge, $46 daily (dbl, $5 each additional, children under 12 free). MC, V.

6 Lake Guntersville State Park: Lodge—Bluff Room, $41 daily (dbl); Parking Lot Room, $37 daily (dbl); Motel Suite, $70 daily (dbl); Cottages—Lakeview, $70 daily (4 persons); Chalets, $80 daily (6 persons, $4 each additional, children under 12 free). MC, V.

7 Lakepoint Resort State Park: Lodge, $46 daily (dbl); Cabins, $53 daily (4 persons), $89 daily (8 persons). AE, CB, DC, MC, V.

8 Little River S.P.: Cabins, $100 weekly (4 pers, $3 each additional). MC, V.

9 Monte Sano State Park: Cabins, $30 daily (2 persons, $3 each additional, children under 6 free). MC, V.

10 Oak Mountain State Park: Cabins, $50 daily (4 persons, $3 each additional, children under 12 free). MC, V.

11 Roland Cooper State Park: Cabins, $51 daily (4 persons, $4 each additional, children under 12 free). MC, V.

ALASKA

1 Denali National Park: Hotel—Luxury Rooms, $200 daily (4 persons); Economy Rooms $19–$86 daily (dbl, $9 each additional); McKinley Chalets, $80 daily (1 person, $9 each additional), MC, V; Camp Denali (NCC)—Cabins, $100 daily (4 persons); $120 (6 persons, including meals, minimum 4-night stay); North Face Lodge, $160 daily (dbl, including meals and transportation). MC, V.

2 Glacier Bay National Park: Lodge and Cabins, $46 daily (dbl); $32 (3 persons); $26 (4 persons). AE, MC, V.

3 Katmai National Park: Brooks River Lodge, $90 daily (dbl); $32 (3 persons); $26 (4 persons), MC, V, AE; Grosvenor Camp (NCC), $1,400 per person weekly.

4 Lake Clark National Park (NCC): Lodge, call for daily and weekly rates; Cabin, $75 daily (dbl, including meals). Van Valin's Island Lodge and Cabins, $150 daily (20 persons, write for family rates).

ARIZONA

1 Canyon de Chelly National Monument: Lodge, $37 daily (dbl, $2 each additional); Motel, $46 daily (dbl, $2 each additional). AE, MC, V.

2 Grand Canyon National Park: El Tovar Hotel, $67 daily (dbl, children under 12 free). AE, CB, DC, MC, V; Bright Angel Lodge (NCC), $119 daily (dbl); Bright Angel Cabins (NCC), $20–$57 daily (dbl); Thunderbird Lodge (NCC), $72 daily (dbl); Kachina Lodge (NCC), $72 daily (dbl); Yavapai Lodge (NCC), $46–$57 daily (dbl); Mushwhip Lodge (NCC), $46 daily (dbl); Mushwhip Cabins (NCC), $31 daily (2 persons, $6 each additional); Phantom Ranch (NCC), Cabins, $45 daily (2 persons), $53 (3 persons); Grand Canyon Lodge (North Rim)—Motel, $47 daily (dbl), Frontier Cabins, $59 daily (2 persons), Deluxe Cabins, $51 daily (2 persons), Pioneer Cabins, $46 daily (4 persons), AE, MC, V.

ARKANSAS

1 Buffalo National River: Cabins, $37 daily (2 persons), $45 (5 persons), $49 (6 persons, $4 each additional, children under 2 free). MC, V.

2 Crowley's Ridge State Park (NCC): Cabins, $22 daily (2 persons, $3 each additional, children under 12 free).

3 DeGray State Park: Lodge, $42–$50 daily (dbl, $5 each additional, children under 12 free). AE, MC, V.

4 Devil's Den State Park (NCC): Cabins, $35–$45 daily (2 persons, $3 each additional, children under 12 free).

5 Lake Catherine State Park: Cabins, $36 daily (2 persons), $29–$34 (6 persons, $3 each additional, children under 12 free). MC, V.

6 Lake Chicot State Park (NCC): Cabins, $34 daily (2 persons, $3 each additional, children under 12 free).

7 Lake Fort Smith State Park (NCC): Cabins, $29–$34 daily (2 persons, $3 each additional, children under 12 free).

8 Lake Ouachita State Park: Cabins, $45 daily (2 persons, $3 each additional, children under 12 free). MC, V.

9 Mount Nebo State Park: Cabins, $32–$36 daily (2 persons, $3 each additional, children under 12 free). MC, V.

10 Ozark Folk Center: $36 daily (dbl, $3 each additional, children under 12 free). MC, V.

11 Petit Jean S.P.: Lodge, $24–$28 daily (dbl); Cabins, $29–$40 daily (2 persons); Duplex, $40 (2 persons, $3 each additional, children under 12 free). MC, V.

12 Queen Wilhelmina State Park: Inn, $32–$47 daily (2 persons, $3 each additional). MC, V.

CALIFORNIA

1 Death Valley National Monument: Furnace Creek Inn and Ranch—Inn, Lodge, and Cabins, $63 daily (dbl, $8 each additional, children under 12 free). AE, CB, DC, MC, V. Stove Pipe Wells Village, Motel, $42 daily ($8 each additional, children under 12 free). MC, V.

2 Devil's Postpile National Monument: Red Meadow Motel and Cabins, call for current rates.

3 Inyo National Forest: Lodge, $30–$48 daily (dbl, includes breakfast, $6 each additional); Cabins, $40–$62 daily (2 persons, includes breakfast, $6 each additional). AE, MC, V.

4 Lassen Volcanic National Park: Drakesbad Guest Ranch—Lodge and Cabins, $88 daily (dbl, $34 each additional adult, $17 each child under 11, includes all meals); Bungalows, $102 daily (dbl, $39 each additional adult, $19 each child under 11, includes all meals); Duplex Units, $110 daily (dbl, $40 each additional adult, $20 each child under 11, includes all meals). MC, V.

5 Pfeiffer Big Sur State Park (NCC): Big Sur Lodge—Cabins, $48–$65 daily (dbl, $5 each additional); Suites, $70–$75 daily (4 persons, $5 each additional).

6 Sequoia and Kings Canyon National Parks: Giant Forest Lodge—Motel, $52.80–$66 (dbl, $5 each additional); Cabins, $41.80–$56.10 (2 persons, $5 each additional). MC, V. Bearpaw Meadow Camp Tent Cabins, $43.20 per person daily (includes breakfast and dinner). MC, V. Stony Creek Lodge Rooms,

$54.45–$57.75 daily (dbl, $5 each additional). AE, MC, V. Grant Grove Cabins, $41.80–$44 daily (2 persons, with bath), $22.26–$24.38 (without bath, $5 each additional). MC, V. Cedar Grove Lodge, $52.47–$55.65 daily (dbl, $5 each additional). MC, V.

7 Tahoe National Forest (NCC): Sierra Shangri-La—Cottages $45–$65 daily (dbl, $10 each additional); Efficiencies, $80–$95 daily (4 persons, $10 each additional).

8 Yosemite National Park: Ahwahnee Hotel, $121.50 daily (dbl, $10 each additional, $5 each child under 12). AE, DC, MC, V. Hotel Wawona, $39 daily (dbl, without bath, $6 each additional adult, $3 each child under 12), $56 (dbl, with bath). AE, DC, MC, V. Yosemite Lodge—Motel, deluxe, $66.50 (dbl, $6 each additional, $3 each child under 12); standard, $30–$57; Cabins, $41 daily (2 persons, with bath, $6 each additional adult, $3 each child under 12), $29.50 (without bath). AE, DC, MC, V. Curry Village—Motel, deluxe, $66.50 daily (dbl, $6 each additional adult, $3 each child under 12), standard, $30 (without bath) $57; Cabins, $41 daily (2 persons, with bath $6 each additional adult, $3 each child under 12), $29.50 (without bath); Tent Cabins, $17.75 daily (dbl, $4 each additional adult, $2 each child under 12). AE, DC, MC, V. White Wolf Lodge and Cabins—Cabins, $31 (2 persons, $5 each additional adult, $2 each child under 12); Tent cabins, $21 daily (2 persons, $5 each additional adult, $2 each child under 12). AE, DC, MC, V. Tuolumne Meadows Tent Cabins, $21 daily (2 persons, $5 each additional adult, $2 each child under 12). AE, DC, MC, V. High Sierra Camps Tent Cabins (NCC), $49.29 per person daily (includes breakfast and dinner).

COLORADO

1 Black Canyon of the Gunnison National Monument: Cabins, $75–$125 daily (dbl). MC, V.

2 Mesa Verde National Park: Lodge, $46–$49 daily (dbl, $3 first additional, $1 each subsequent additional, children under 13 free). AE, DC, MC, V.

FLORIDA

1 Everglades National Park: Lodge, $55–$63 daily (dbl, $6 each additional, children under 16 free); Cottages, $55 daily (2 persons, $6 each additional). AE, DC, MC, V.

2 Hontoon Island S.P. (NCC): Cabins, $8 daily (4 persons), $10 (6 persons).

3 Jonathan Dickinson State Park (NCC): Cabins, $35 daily (2 persons, $2 each additional).

4 Mike Roess Gold Head Branch State Park (NCC): Cabins, $31–$50 daily (6 persons).

5 Myakka River State Park (NCC): Cabins, $30 daily (6 persons).

6 T. H. Stone Memorial—St. Joseph Peninsula State Park (NCC): Cabins, $25 daily (4 persons), $30 (8 persons).

GEORGIA

1 Amicalola Falls State Park: Cabins, $34 daily (1 bedroom), $42 (2 bedrooms), $48 (3 bedrooms). MC, V.

2 Black Rock Mountain State Park: Cabins, $42 daily (2 bedrooms), $48 (3 bedrooms). MC, V.

3 Chattahoochee National Forest (NCC): Hotel, $25 daily (dbl, $4 each additional).

4 Cloudland Canyon State Park: Cabins, $42 daily (2 bedrooms), $48 (3 bedrooms). MC, V.

5 Crooked River State Park: Cabins, $42 daily (2 bedrooms), $48 (3 bedrooms). MC, V.

6 Cumberland Island National Seashore: Greyfield Inn, $75 per person daily (includes all meals, children under 11, 10% discount). MC, V.

7 Elijah Clark State Park: Cabins, $42 daily (2 bedrooms). MC, V.

8 Franklin D. Roosevelt State Park: Cabins, $34 daily (1 bedroom), $42 (2 bedrooms). MC, V.

9 Fort Mountain State Park: Cabins, $42 daily (2 bedrooms), $48 (3 bedrooms). MC, V.

10 George T. Bagby State Park: Cabins, $42 daily (2 bedrooms). MC, V.

11 Georgia Veterans Memorial S.P.: Cabins, $42 daily (2 bedrooms) MC, V.

12 Hard Labor Creek State Park: Cabins, $42 daily (2 bedrooms). MC, V.

13 Hart State Park: Mobile Homes, $30 daily (2 bedrooms). MC, V.

14 Indian Springs State Park: Cabins, $42 daily (2 bedrooms). MC, V.

15 John Tanner State Park: Apartments, $30 daily (4 persons); Group Lodge, $80 daily (32 persons). MC, V.

16 Little Ocmulgee State Park: Cabins, $32 daily (1 bedroom), $42 (2 bedrooms). MC, V.

17 Magnolia Springs State Park (NCC): Cabins, $42 daily (2 bedrooms), $48 (3 bedrooms).

18 Mistletoe State Park: Cabins, $42 daily (2 bedrooms). MC, V.

19 Red Top Mountain State Park: Cabins, $42 daily (2 bedrooms). MC, V.

20 Seminole State Park (NCC): Cabins, $42 daily (2 bedrooms).

21 Stephen C. Foster State Park: Cabins, $42 daily (2 bedrooms). MC, V.

22 Tugaloo State Park: Cabins, $42 daily (2 bedrooms). MC, V.

23 Unicoi State Park: Lodge, $40 daily ($5 each additional; under 13 free); Cottages, $34 daily (1 bedroom), $42 (2 bedrooms), $48 (3 bedrooms). MC, V.

24 Vogel State Park: Cabins, $34 daily (1 bedroom), $42 (2 bedrooms), $48 (3 bedrooms). MC, V.

25 Will-A-Way Recreation Area: Cabins (2 bedrooms), $32.04 daily (handicapped), $48.88 (nonhandicapped); Group Camp, $6.50 per person daily (30 to 250 persons). MC, V.

HAWAII

1 Haleakala National Park (NCC): Cabins, $15 daily (3 persons, $5 each additional adult, $2.50 each additional child under 13).

2 Hawaii Volcanoes National Park: Hotel, $37-$48 daily (dbl, $10 each additional, children under 19 free); Cabins, $14.56 (4 persons). AE, CB, DC, MC, V.

3 Kokee State Park: Cabins, $25 (3-7 persons). AE, MC, V.

4 Mauna Kea S.P. (NCC): Cabins, $10 daily (1 person) to $30 (6 persons); Group Lodges, $8 daily (1 person) to $2-$2.75 per person (32 persons).

5 Polipoli Springs State Recreation Area (NCC): Cabins, $10 daily (1 person) to $30 daily (6 persons).

6 Waianapanapa State Park (NCC): Cabins, $10 daily (1 person) to $30 daily (6 persons).

IDAHO

1 Heyburn State Park: Lodge, $20 daily (dbl), MC, V; Cabins, $15 daily (2 persons), $20 (4 persons, no charge for roll-away), AE, MC, V.

ILLINOIS

1 Giant City State Park: Cabins, $30 daily (2 persons), $35 (4 persons, $4 each additional, children under 10 free). MC, V.

2 Illinois Beach State Park: Resort, $67-$73 daily (dbl, $7 each additional, children under 8 free). AE, CB, DC, MC, V.

3 Pere Marquette State Park (NCC): Lodge and Guest Houses, $31-$33 daily (2 persons, $9 each additional, children under 6 free).

4 Starved Rock State Park (NCC): Lodge, $38-$46 daily (dbl); Cabins, $33-$35 daily (dbl, $9 each additional).

5 White Pines Forest State Park (NCC): Cabins, $31 daily (2 persons, $5 each additional).

INDIANA

1 Brown County S.P. (NCC): Lodge, $30 daily (dbl); Cabin Motel Rooms, $24-$28 daily (4 persons); Housekeeping Cabins, $45 daily (8 persons).

2 Chain O' Lakes State Park (NCC): Cabins, $35 daily (2 bedrooms).

3 Clifty Falls State Park: Inn, $30-$32 daily (dbl). MC, V.

4 Lincoln State Park (NCC): Cabins, $18 daily (2 bedrooms).

5 McCormick's Creek State Park: Inn, $26–$30 daily (dbl). AE, MC, V.
6 Pokagon State Park: Inn and Cabins, $25–$30 daily (dbl). MC, V.
7 Potato Creek State Recreation Area (NCC): Cabins, $35 daily (2 bedrooms).
8 Shakamak State Park (NCC): Cabins, $13 daily (4 persons), $14–$15 daily (6 persons).
9 Spring Mill State Park: Inn, $29.40–$31.50 daily (dbl). MC, V.
10 Turkey Run S.P.: Inn and Cabins, $28.35–$31.50 daily (dbl). MC, V.
11 Whitewater Memorial S.P. (NCC): Cabins, $35 daily (2 bedrooms).

IOWA

1 Backbone State Park (NCC): Cabins, $100 weekly (4–6 persons).
2 Lacey-Keosauqua State Park (NCC): Cabins, $100 weekly (4 persons).
3 Lake of Three Fires State Park (NCC): Cabins, $80 weekly (4 persons).
4 Lake Wapello State Park (NCC): Cabins, $100 weekly (4–6 persons).
5 Palisades-Kepler State Park (NCC): Cabins, $100 weekly (4 persons).
6 Springbrook State Park (NCC): Cabins, $80 weekly (4 persons); Group Lodge, $15 daily (per cabin), $25 daily (for kitchen), $50 daily minimum ($1 daily per person for church and school groups).

KENTUCKY

1 Barren River Lake State Resort Park: Lodge, $49 daily (dbl, $5 each additional; under 17 free); Cottages, $89.25 daily (2 bedrooms). AE, DC, MC, V.
2 Buckhorn Lake State Park: Lodge, $39.96 daily (dbl, $5.40 each additional, children under 17 free). AE, DC, MC, V.
3 Carter Caves State Park: Lodge, $42 daily (dbl, $5.25 each additional, children under 17 free); Cottages, $49.35 daily (efficiency), $57.75 (1 bedroom), $68.25 (2 bedrooms). AE, DC, MC, V.
4 Cumberland Falls State Resort Park: Lodge, $49.35 daily (dbl, $5.25 each additional, children under 17 free); Cottages, $52.50 daily (1 bedroom), $63 (2 bedrooms). AE, DC, MC, V.
5 General Butler State Resort Park: Lodge, $47.52 daily (dbl, $5.40 each additional, children under 17 free); Cottages, $56.16 daily (efficiency), $61.56 (1 bedroom), $73.44–$91.80 (2 bedrooms), $108 (3 bedrooms). AE, DC, MC, V.
6 Greenbo Lake State Resort Park: Lodge, $46.20 daily (dbl, $5.25 each additional, children under 17 free). AE, DC, MC, V.
7 Jenny Wiley State Park: Lodge, $46.20 (dbl, $5 each additional, children under 17 free); Cottages, $54.60 daily (1 bedroom), $71.40 (2 bedrooms). AE, DC, MC, V.
8 John James Audubon State Park: Cottages, $51.84 daily (dbl, $5.40 each additional, children under 17 free). AE, DC, MC, V.
9 Kentucky Dam Village State Resort Park: Lodge, $58.85 daily (dbl, $5.35 each additional, children under 17 free); Cottages, $62.06 daily (1 to 2 bedrooms), $77.44–$107 (3 bedrooms). AE, DC, MC, V. Houseboats (NCC), $1,050 weekly.
10 Lake Barkley State Resort Park: Lodge, $59.90 daily (dbl, $5.40 each additional, children under 17 free); Cottages, $91.80 daily (6 persons, $5.40 each additional, children under 17 free). AE, DC, MC, V.
11 Lake Cumberland State Resort Park: Lodge, $50.76 daily (dbl, $5.40 each additional, children under 17 free); Cottages, $54.40 daily (1 bedroom), $70.20 (2 bedrooms). AE, DC, MC, V. Houseboats (NCC), $810–$1,120 weekly.
12 Mammoth Cave National Park: Hotel and Motel, $42 daily (dbl, $5.25 each additional, children under 17 free in motel); Hotel Cottages $32.55 daily (dbl, $5.25 each additional); Woodland Cottages $25 daily (dbl, $4.20 each additional, children under 17 free). MC, V.
13 Natural Bridge State Park: Lodge, $54.46 daily (dbl, $5.25 each additional, children under 17 free); Cottages, $54.46 daily (efficiency), $57.75 (1 bedroom). AE, DC, MC, V.
14 Pennyrile Forest State Park: Lodge, $46.20 daily (dbl, $5.25 each additional, children under 17 free); Cottages $46.20 daily (efficiency), $54.40 (1 bedroom), $60.90 (2 bedrooms). AE, DC, MC, V.

15 Pine Mountain State Park: Lodge, $49.35 daily (dbl, $5.25 each additional, children under 17 free); Cottages, $57.75 (1 bedroom), $68.25 daily (2 bedrooms). AE, DC, MC, V.

16 Rough River Dam State Resort Park: Lodge, $49.35 daily (dbl, $5.25 each additional; under 17 free); Cottages, $68.25 daily (4 persons). AE, DC, MC, V.

LOUISIANA

1 Chemin-A-Haut State Park (NCC): Cabins, $25 daily (8 persons); Group Lodge, $43.20 daily (20 persons, $2 each additional).

2 Chicot State Park (NCC): Cabins, $25 daily (4 persons), $30 (6 persons); Group Lodge, $172 daily (80 persons).

3 Lake Bistineau State Park (NCC): Cabins, $30 daily (6 persons).

4 Sam Houston Jones State Park (NCC): Cabins, $30 daily (6 persons).

MAINE

1 Baxter State Park (NCC): Cabins, $9 per person daily (minimum daily charge of $25, children under 6 free).

MARYLAND

1 Elk Neck S.P. (NCC): Cabins, $75 weekly (4 persons, $15 each additional).

2 Herrington Manor State Park (NCC): Cabins, $130 weekly (2 persons), $160 (4 persons), $200 (6 persons).

3 New Germany State Park (NCC): Cabins, $136.54 weekly (2 persons), $168 (4 persons), $210 (6 persons).

MASSACHUSETTS

1 Mohawk Forest (NCC): Cabins, $8 daily (3 persons), $10 (5 persons).

2 Mount Greylock State Reservation (NCC): Lodge, $8 daily per person.

3 Savoy Mountain State Forest (NCC): Cabins, $8 daily (4 persons).

4 Willard Brook State Forest (NCC): Cabins, $56 weekly (3 persons), $70 weekly (5 persons).

MICHIGAN

1 Fort Custer State Recreation Area: (NCC): Cabins, $20 daily (20 persons).

2 Island Lake Recreation Area (NCC): Cabins, $20–$40 daily (20 persons).

3 Isle Royale National Park: Motel, $98.88 daily (dbl, includes all meals, $26 each additional adult, $20.50 each additional child under 13); Cabins, $54.08 daily (dbl, $6.50 each additional). MC, V.

4 J. W. Wells State Park (NCC): Cabins, $20 daily (18 persons).

5 Ortonville State Recreation Area (NCC): Group cabin, $20 daily (20 persons).

6 Porcupine Mountains State Park (NCC): Cabins, $20 daily (2–8 persons).

7 Van Riper State Park (NCC): Cabins, $20 daily (6–14 persons).

8 Waterloo State Recreation Area (NCC): Cabins, $20 daily (20 persons); Group Camp, $1,440 weekly (100 persons, $2.40 each additional), $1,728 weekly (120 persons, $2.40 each additional).

9 Wilderness State Park (NCC): Cabins, $20 daily (8–24 persons).

10 Yankee Springs Recreation Area (NCC): Group Cabins, $20 daily (10–24 persons).

MINNESOTA

1 Itasca State Park: Lodge, $20 daily (dbl); Motel, $26–$28 daily (dbl, $6 each additional, $3 children under 12); Group Lodge, $150–$175 daily (22 persons); Cabins, $34 daily (1 bedroom), $50 (2 or 3 bedrooms); Quadriplex Cabin, $30–$32 (dbl, $6 each additional, $3 under 12); Housekeeping cabins, $26 (dbl, $6 each additional, $3 under 12). MC, V.

2 Superior National Forest: Gunflint Lodge, suites, $395 per person weekly (includes all meals, 10% service charge, 50% discount for children 16 and under). AE, DC, MC, V. Cascade Lodge, $35–$46 daily (dbl, $6 each additional, $3 each additional child 4–6, under 4 free), Cabins, $37–$52 daily (dbl, $6 each additional, $3 each additional 4–6, under 4 free), Motel, $40–$53 daily (dbl, $6 each additional, $3 each additional 4–6, under 4 free), MC, V. Bearskin Lodge—

Cabins, $300 weekly (dbl, $35 each additional adult, $25 each additional child under 16); Apartments, $390 weekly (dbl, $35 each additional adult, $25 each additional child under 16), AE, MC, V. Borderland Lodge (NCC): Villa, $250 weekly (dbl, $40 each additional adult, $30 each additional under 18, children 3 and under free). Nor'Wester Lodge: Villas and Cabins, $285–$425 weekly (dbl, $60 each additional adult, $30 each additional under 12). MC, V. Trout Lake: $35–$50 ($5 ea. add.), MC, V.

MISSISSIPPI

1 Clarkco State Park: Cabins, $29–$44 daily (2–6 persons). MC, V.

2 George Payne Cossar S.P.: Cabins, $44.52 daily (4–6 persons). MC, V.

3 Holmes County State Park: Cabins, $32–$44 daily (4–6 persons); Group Lodge, $5 per person daily (40–100 persons). MC, V.

4 Hugh White State Park: Motel, $28 daily (2–4 persons); Cabins, $35 daily (4 persons); Group Lodges, $5 per person daily (35 persons). MC, V.

5 J. P. Coleman State Park: Motel $30 daily (dbl); Cabins, $35 daily (4–6 persons). MC, V.

6 John W. Kyle State Park: Cabins, $35–$36 daily (4 persons); Group Lodge, $5 per person daily, MC, V.

7 Lake Lowndes State Park: Cabins, $44 daily (6 persons), MC, V.

8 Leroy Percy State Park: Cabins, $22–$24 daily (4–6 persons). MC, V.

9 Paul B. Johnson State Park: Cabins, $39–$42 daily (4 persons); Group Lodge, $5 per person daily (45–110 persons). MC, V.

10 Percy Quin State Park: Cabins, $36 daily (4–5 persons); Group Lodge, $5 per person daily (45–200 persons). MC, V.

11 Roosevelt State Park: Cabins, $35–$36 daily (1 bedroom), $39 (2 bedrooms), $43 (3 bedrooms); Group Lodges, $5 per person daily (40–104 persons). MC, V.

12 Tishomingo State Park: Cabins, $34–$38 daily (4 –6 persons). MC, V.

13 Tombigbee State Park: Cabins, $26 daily (1 bedroom), $34–$44 (2 bedrooms); Group Camp, $5 per person daily (25–100 persons). MC, V.

14 Wall Doxey State Park: Cabins, $34–$44 daily (4–7 persons); Group Camp, $5 per person daily (40–96 persons). MC, V.

MISSOURI

1 Bennett Spring State Park: Cabins, $22–$30 daily (dbl, $2 each additional), $32–$52 (4 persons, $2 each additional). MC, V.

2 Big Lake State Park (NCC): Motel, $28.50 daily (dbl, $2.50 each additional); Cabins, $24.50 daily (4 persons, $2.50 each additional).

3 Lake Wappapello S.P. (NCC): Cabins, $27 daily (dbl, $3 each additional).

4 Meramec State Park: Cabins, $26 daily (1 bedroom), $34 daily (2 bedrooms), $40 daily (3 bedrooms), $74 daily (5 bedrooms).

5 Montauk State Park: Motel, $28 daily (dbl, $3 each additional, children 3 and under free); Housekeeping cabins, $31 daily (1 bedroom), $35–$41 daily (2 bedrooms); Sleeping cabins, $21–$29 daily (1–4 persons). MC, V.

6 Ozark National Scenic Riverways (NCC): Cabins $22 daily (2 persons), $28 daily (4 persons), $35 daily (6 persons).

7 Roaring River State Park (NCC): Motel rooms, $26 daily (dbl, $2 each additional); Cabins, $34–$44 daily (6–8 persons).

8 Sam A. Baker State Park (NCC): Cabins, $24 daily (2 persons), $30–$32 (4 persons), $34–$36 (6 persons).

9 Stockton: $24–$32 daily (dbl, $3 each additional, under 5 free) MC, V.

10 Thousand Hills State Park: Cabins, $30 daily (4 persons, without kitchen), $35 daily (4 persons, with kitchen) MC, V.

11 Wakonda State Park: Cabins, call for current rates.

12 Washington State Park (NCC): Cabins, $28 daily (4 persons, $2 each additional), $32 daily (6 persons).

MONTANA

1 Glacier National Park: Glacier Park Lodge, $51–$59 daily (dbl, $4 each additional, children under 12 free); Lake McDonald Lodge, $39–$59 daily (dbl, $4 each additional, children under 12 free); Many Glacier Hotel, $51–$59 daily (dbl, $4 each additional, children under 12 free); Swiftcurrent Motor Inn—Motel, $37–$41 daily (dbl, $3 each additional, children under 12 free), Cabins, $16–$28 daily (dbl, $2 each additional, children under 12 free); Rising Sun Motor Inn—Motel, $41 daily (dbl, $3 each additional), Cabins, $37 daily (dbl, $3 each additional, children under 12 free); Prince of Wales Hotel, $49–$56 (Canadian dollars) daily (dbl, $5 [Canadian] each additional, children under 12 free); Village Inn, $48–$62 daily (dbl, $5 each additional, children under 12 free). All of the above lodgings accept MC and V. Granite Park and Sperry Chalets (NCC): $40 per person daily (includes all meals, $35 per child under 12).

    2 Kootenai NF (NCC): $25 per night.

NEBRASKA

    1 Chadron State Park: Cabins, $22–$26 daily (2 bedrooms). MC, V.

    2 Fort Robinson State Park: Lodge, $16–$18 daily (dbl, $4 each additional); Cabins, $26 daily (2 bedrooms), $36 (3 bedrooms), $44 (4 bedrooms); Multiple-Bedroom Units, $72 daily (6 bedrooms), $80 (7 bedrooms), $90 (8 bedrooms), $98 (9 bedrooms); Group Facility, $400 daily (60 persons). MC, V.

    3 Niobrara S.P.: Cabins, $20 daily (1 bedroom), $26 (2 bedrooms). MC, V.

    4 Platte River S.P.: Cabins, $8–$30 daily (2–8 persons); Group Lodge, $40 daily (20 persons); Tepees and tents, $6 daily (4–6 persons). MC, V.

    5 Ponca State Park: Cabins, $26 daily (4–6 persons). MC, V.

    6 Victoria Springs State Area: Cabins, $26 daily (4–6 persons). MC, V.

NEVADA

    1 Lake Mead National Recreation Area: Echo Bay Resort—Motel, $48–$52 daily (dbl, $6 each additional, children under 6 free). Houseboats, $535–$965 (7 persons, 3–7 days), $675–$1,095 (12 persons, 3–7 days), $765–$1,375 (12 persons, 3–7 days), MC, V. Lake Mead Resort—Motel, $36.75–$44.10 daily (dbl, $5.25 each additional), MC, V. Temple Bar Marina—Rooms, $38–$48 daily (dbl, $6 each additional, children under 6 free), Fishing Cabins, $18 daily (dbl, $4 each additional, children under 6 free), MC, V. Cottonwood Cove Resort and Marina—Rooms, $47.50 daily (dbl, $5 each additional, children under 6 free), Houseboats, $535–$965 weekly (6 persons), $765–$1,375 (12 persons) MC, V. Lake Mohave Resort—Rooms, $52–$64 daily (dbl, $6 each additional), Houseboats, $561.75–$1,013.24 (6 persons, 3–7 days), $708.75–$1,254.75 (12 persons, 3–7 days), $803.25–$1,443.75 (12 persons, 3–7 days). MC, V.

NEW HAMPSHIRE

    1 White Mountain National Forest (NCC): Camp, $25.75 per person daily (includes breakfast and dinner, $13.00 per child under 10).

NEW JERSEY

    1 Bass River State Forest (NCC): Cabins, $30 daily (8 persons); Lean-tos, $10 daily (6 persons).

    2 Belleplain State Forest (NCC): Cabins, $75 daily (24 persons); Lean-tos, $10 daily (6 persons).

    3 High Point State Park (NCC): Cabins, $30 daily (6 persons).

    4 Jenny Jump State Forest (NCC): Camp Shelters, $15 daily (6 persons).

    5 Lebanon State Forest (NCC): Cabins, $20 daily (6 persons).

    6 Parvin State Park (NCC): Cabins, $20 daily (6 persons).

    7 Stokes State Forest (NCC): Cabins, $20 daily (6 persons), $40 (8 persons), $55 (16 persons).

    8 Wharton Forest (NCC): Cabins, $20 daily (4–6 pers), $40 (8–10 pers).

NEW MEXICO

    1 Conchas Lake State Park: Conchas Lodge, $35–$40 daily (dbl, $5 each additional, children under 13 free), MC, V. Conchas North Dock—Cabins, $18–$24 daily (dbl, $4 each additional), Duplexes, $41 daily (dbl, $4 each additional), Mobile Homes, $32–$48 daily (dbl, $4 each additional). Gulf credit cards.

    2 Elephant Butte Lake State Park: Damsite Recreation Area Cottages, $25–$36 daily (dbl, $3.50 each additional, children under 12 free). MC, V.

Elephant Butte Resort Marina Houseboats (NCC), $750 weekly (6 persons). Elephant Butte Inn, $39–$44 daily (dbl, $3 each additional). AE, CB, DC, MC, V.

NEW YORK

1 Adirondack State Park: Balsam House, $45–55, MAP, AE, MC, V. The Point (NCC), $300–$375 daily (dbl, includes all meals). Garnet Hill Lodge (NCC), $72 daily (dbl, includes breakfast and dinner, $22 each additional, $17 each additional under 11). Big Moose Inn, $32 daily (dbl, $3 each additional), AE, MC, V. Hedges (NCC), Rooms and Cottages, $42–$46 per person daily (includes breakfast and dinner, $14 per child under 15). Hemlock Hall (NCC)—Lodge and Motel Rooms and Cottages, $68–$92 daily (dbl, includes breakfast and dinner, $16 per child 2–8). Adirondak Loj (NCC)—Dormitory and Bunk Rooms, $17 per person daily (includes breakfast, $8.50 per child under 12), Cabins, $16.50 daily (4 persons). Johns Brook Lodges (NCC)—dormitories and rooms, $13 per person daily (includes breakfast, $7 per child under 12), Cabins, $24 daily (6 persons), $45 daily (12 persons).

2 Allegany State Park (NCC): Quaker Area Cabins, $62–$116 weekly (4–6 persons); Redhouse Area Cabins, $116 weekly (4–6 persons).

3 Bear Mountain and Harriman State Parks: Sebago Area Cabins (NCC), $116 weekly (4 persons, $5 each additional). Bear Mountain Inn, $49 daily (dbl, $10 each additional adult, $7.50 each child under 10), AE, MC, V.

4 Buttermilk Falls State Park: Cabins, call for current rates.

5 Canoe-Picnic Point State Park (NCC): Cabins, $62 weekly (4 persons).

6 Cayuga Lake State Park (NCC): Cabins, call for current rates.

7 Chenango Valley State Park (NCC): Cabins, $116 weekly (4 persons).

8 De Wolf Point State Park (NCC): Cabins, $62 weekly (4 persons).

9 Fair Haven Beach State Park (NCC): Cabins, $62 weekly (4 persons), $118 weekly (6 persons).

10 Fillmore Glen State Park (NCC): Cabins, $62 weekly (4–6 persons).

11 Gilbert Lake (NCC): Cabins, $116 weekly (4 pers), $118 weekly (6 persons).

12 Green Lakes State Park (NCC): Cabins, $116 weekly (4 persons).

13 Kring Point State Park: Cabins, call for current rates.

14 Lake Erie State Park: Cabins, call for current rates.

15 Lake Taghkanic State Park (NCC): Cabins $100 weekly (1 bedroom), $134 (2 bedrooms), $164 (3–4 bedrooms).

16 Letchworth State Park: Cabins (NCC), $62–$84 weekly (1 room), $164 weekly (3 rooms); Glen Iris Inn, $33 daily (dbl, $4 each additional), AE, MC, V.

17 Mills-Norrie State Park (NCC): Cabins, $116 weekly (4 persons).

18 Newtown Battlefield State Park: Cabins, call for current rates.

19 Robert H. Treman State Park: Cabins, call for current rates.

20 Robert Moses State Park (NCC): Cabins, $134 weekly (4 persons).

21 Saratoga Spa State Park: Gideon Putnam Hotel, $239 daily (dbl, includes all meals) AE, DC, MC, V.

22 Selkirk Shores State Park (NCC): Cabins, $116 weekly (4 persons), $118 weekly (6 persons).

23 Taconic State Park (NCC): Cabins, $116 weekly (4 persons); Cottages, $134 (2 bedrooms), $164 (3 bedrooms).

24 Taughannock Falls S.P.: Cabins, call for current rates. Taughannock Farms Inn (NCC), $40–$50 daily (dbl, includes breakfast, $8 each additional).

25 Wellesley Island State Park (NCC): Cabins, $62 weekly (4 persons).

NORTH CAROLINA

1 Blue Ridge Parkway: Bluffs Lodge, $42 daily (dbl, $5 each additional, children 8 and under free) MC, V. Peaks of Otter Lodge, $49.25 daily (dbl, $4 each additional, children under 16 free); suites, $65–$75 daily (dbl, $4 each additional, children under 16 free). MC, V. Pisgah Inn, $47.03 daily (dbl, $5.23 each additional, children under 8 free), MC, V. Rocky Knob Cabins, call for rates.

2 Hanging Rock State Park: Cabins, call for current rates.

3 Morrow Mountain State Park: Cabins, call for current rates.

4 Nantahala NF: Outdoor Center: Vacation houses, $56-125 ($5 each additional; under 12 free); Motel, $24-33; Hostel bunk, $4; AE, MC, V. Village: Lodge rooms $32-65; apartments, $30-40; cabins, $25-75; mobile homes, $40. AE, MC, V.

5 Pisgah National Forest: Blue Boar Lodge, $30 daily (dbl, all meals, $20 each child 9-12 years, $15 each 2-8 years) MC, V. High Hampton Inn, $50 per person daily (dbl, all meals, $35 each additional, $29 each child under 6), AE. Folkestone Lodge, $48 daily (dbl, $9 each additional; under 12 free), MC, V. Green Park Inn, $60-$110 daily (dbl), AE, MC, V. Eseeola Lodge, $120 per couple daily (all meals; $40 each 12-18 years, $20 each under 12), MC, V.

NORTH DAKOTA

1 Lake Metigoshe State Park (NCC): Group Camp, $2 per person daily ($80 minimum charge).

2 Turtle River State Park (NCC): Lodge, $50 daily; Cabins (Group Camp), $2 per person daily ($118 minimum charge).

OHIO

1 Buck Creek State Park (NCC): Cabins, $48 daily (6 persons).

2 Burr Oak State Park: Lodge, $49 daily (dbl, $2.50 each additional, children under 12 free); Cabins, $248 weekly (6 persons). MC, V.

3 Cowan Lake State Park (NCC): Cabins, $198 weekly (6 persons).

4 Deer Creek State Park: Lodge, $69.44 daily (dbl, $5 each additional, children under 10 free); Cabins, $352.80 weekly (6 persons). AE, DC, MC, V.

5 Dillon State Park (NCC): Cabins, $198 weekly (6-8 persons).

6 Geneva State Park (NCC): Cabins, $166 weekly (6-8 persons).

7 Hocking Hills State Park (NCC): Cabins, $198 weekly (4-6 persons).

8 Hueston Woods State Park: Lodge, $54-$62 daily (dbl, $5 each additional, children under 10 free); Cabins, $225-$298 (4-6 persons). MC, V.

9 Lake Hope State Park (NCC): Sleeping Cabins, $32 daily (1 bedroom), $34 (2 bedrooms), $42 (3 bedrooms), $50 (4 bedrooms); Housekeeping Cabins, $156-$198 weekly.

10 Mohican State Park: Lodge, $62.93 daily (dbl, $5 each additional, children under 12 free), MC, V; Cabins (NCC), $214.83 weekly (6 persons).

11 Pike Lake State Park (NCC): Cabins, $156-$198 weekly; Group Lodge, $350 weekly (22 persons).

12 Punderson State Park: Manor House, $54 daily (dbl, $5 each additional, children under 10 free); Cabins, $310 weekly (4-6 persons). AE, MC, V.

13 Pymatuning State Park (NCC): Cabins, $164.58 weekly (4-6 persons), $208.89 (6-8 persons).

14 Salt Fork State Park: Lodge, $69.44 daily (dbl, $5 each additional, children under 18 free); Cabins, $315 weekly (6 persons), AE, DC, MC, V.

15 Shawnee State Park: Lodge, $56.42 daily (dbl, $5 each additional, children under 18 free); Cabins, $323.33 weekly (6 persons). MC, V.

16 South Bass Island State Park (NCC): Cabents, $150 weekly (6 persons).

OKLAHOMA

1 Arrowhead State Park: Lodge, $45-$49 daily (dbl, $10 each additional, children under 18 free); Cabins, $45 daily (dbl, $10 each additional, children under 18 free), AE, DC, MC, V.

2 Beavers Bend State Park: Cabins, $35 daily (standard 1 bedroom), $40-$45 (new 1 bedroom or 2 bedrooms). MC, V.

3 Boiling Springs State Park: Cabins, $36.05 daily (dbl, $10 each additional, children under 18 free). MC, V.

4 Fountainhead State Park: Lodge, $49-$53 daily (dbl, $10 each additional, children under 12 free); Cottages, $45 daily (dbl, $10 each additional, children under 12 free). AE, CB, DC, MC, V.

5 Great Salt Plains State Park: Cabins, $36.05 daily (dbl, $10 each additional, children under 18 free). MC, V.

6 Greenleaf State Park: Cabins, $35 daily (dbl, $10 each additional, children under 18 free). MC, V.

7 Keystone S.P.: Cabins, $40 daily (4 persons), $50 (6 persons). MC, V.

8 Lake Murray State Park: Lodge, $45–$49 daily (dbl, $10 each additional, children under 18 free); Cabins, $25–$30 daily (2 persons), $30–$50 (4 persons), $65 (6 persons). AE, CB, DC, MC, V.

9 Osage Hills State Park: Cabins, $35 daily (dbl, $10 each additional, children under 18 free). MC, V.

10 Quartz Mountain State Park: Lodge, $44–$48 daily (dbl, $10 each additional, children under 12 free); Cabins, $50 daily (1 bedroom), $65 (2 bedrooms). AE, CB, DC, MC, V.

11 Robber's Cave: Cabins, $35 daily (1 bedroom), $45 (2 bedrooms), MC, V.

12 Roman Nose State Park: Lodge, $44–$48 daily (dbl, $10 each additional, children under 18 free); Cabins, $45 (4 persons). AE, CB, DC, MC, V.

13 Sequoyah State Park: Lodge, $53 daily (dbl, $10 each additional, children under 18 free); Cabins, $45–$50 daily (dbl, $10 each additional, children under 18 free). AE, CB, DC, MC, V.

14 Tenkiller State Park: Cabins, $26.78–$41.20 daily (dbl, $10 each additional, children under 18 free). MC, V.

15 Texoma S.P.: Lodge, $49.53 daily (dbl, $10 each additional, children under 18 free); Cabins, $55 (1 bedroom), $65 (2 bedrooms). AE, DC, MC, V.

16 Wister State Park: Cabins, $35–$40 daily (dbl, $10 each additional, children under 18 free). MC, V.

OREGON

1 Crater Lake National Park: Lodge (NCC), $40–$58.72 daily (dbl); Cottages, $21.41 daily (4 persons, without bath), $56.50 (4 persons, with bath); Ponderosa cabins, $43.41 (dbl).

2 Mount Hood National Forest: Lodge, $46.64–$107 daily (dbl, $8 each additional); Chalets, $31.80 daily (dbl, $8 each additional), AE, DC, MC, V.

3 Oregon Caves National Monument: Chateau (NCC), $40–$44 daily (dbl, $4 each additional); Cottages, $33 daily (dbl, $4 each additional).

4 Umpqua National Forest: Inn, $48 daily (dbl, $14 each additional, children under 16 free), MC, V.

5 Wallowa Lake S.P.: Lodge (NCC), $28 daily (dbl, $6 each additional); Cabins, $38–$50 daily (1 bedroom), $42–$66 (2 bedrooms), $58–$82 (3 bedrooms).

PENNSYLVANIA

1 Allegheny NF: Kane Manor, $42 dbl. (weekdays), $59 dbl. (weekends), MC, V.

2 Black Moshannon State Park: Cabins, call for current rates.

3 Clear Creek State Park (NCC): Cabins, $58–$60 weekly (2–3 persons), $66–$82 weekly (4 persons).

4 Cook Forest State Park (NCC): Cabins, $82 weekly (4 persons), $104 (6 persons), $120 weekly (8 persons).

5 Cowans Gap State Park (NCC): Cabins, $98 weekly (4 persons).

6 Kooser S.P. (NCC): Cabins, $76 weekly (4 persons), $98 (6 persons).

7 Linn Run State Park: Cabins, call for current rates.

8 Parker Dam State Park: Cabins, call for current rates.

9 Promised Land S.P. (NCC): Cabins, $76–$98 weekly (2–4 persons).

10 Ralph Stover State Park: Cabins, $50 weekly (4–5 persons).

11 Roosevelt State Park: Riegelsville Hotel, $40–$65 daily (dbl, $5 each additional) MC, V, AE. Bridgeton House, $65–$80 daily (dbl, inc. breakfast, 20% discount during the week) MC, V, AE. Evermay-on-the-Delaware, $49–$80 daily (dbl, inc. breakfast and afternoon tea) MC, V, AE. Golden Pheasant, $47.75 daily (dbl, inc. breakfast) MC, V, AE. Black Bass, $60 daily (dbl), $110–$125 (suites, 2 persons), $175 (suites, 4 persons) MC, V, AE. Centre Bridge Inn, $55–$100 daily (dbl, $10 each add) MC, V. Inn at Phillips Mill, call for rates.

12 S.B. Elliott State Park: Cabins, call for current rates.

13 Worlds End State Park (NCC): Cabins, $50 weekly (2 persons), $66–$82 weekly (4 persons), $92 weekly (6 persons).

SOUTH CAROLINA

1 Barnwell State Park (NCC): Cabins, $156 weekly (6 persons).
2 Cheraw State Park: Cabins, call for current rates.
3 Edisto Beach State Park (NCC): Cabins, $174.72 weekly (6 persons).
4 Givhans Ferry State Park: Cabins, call for current rates.
5 Hickory Knob State Park: Lodge, $30–$34 daily (dbl, $5 each additional, children under 12 free); Cabins, $270 weekly (6 persons) V.
6 Hunting Island S.P. (NCC): Cabins, $249.60–$312 weekly (6–10 persons).
7 Keowee-Toxaway S.P. (NCC): Cabins, $50–$55 daily (10 persons).
8 Myrtle Beach State Park: Cabins, call for current rates.
9 Oconee State Park (NCC): Cabins, $168 weekly (4 persons), $186 weekly (6 persons), $228 weekly (8 persons).
10 Pleasant Ridge State Park: Cabins, call for current rates.
11 Poinsett S.P. (NCC): Cabins, $93.64 weekly (4 per.), $124.80 (6 per.).
12 Santee State Resort Park: Cabins, $224.64 weekly (6 persons), $243.36 (6 persons). MC, V.
13 Table Rock State Park (NCC): Cabins, $168 weekly (1–2 bedrooms), $234 (3 bedrooms).

SOUTH DAKOTA

1 Badlands National Park: Lodge and Cabins, $28 daily (2 persons), $30.50 (3 persons), $33 (4 persons), $35.50 (5 persons) MC, V, AE, DC.
2 Custer State Park: Custer Lodge (NCC), $35–$55 daily (dbl), motel $44–$48 daily (dbl), cabins, $32–$40 daily (2–6 persons, without kitchen), $43–$50 (3–8 persons, with kitchen). Blue Bell Lodge, cabins, $36–$38 daily (2 persons), $40–$42 daily (3–4 persons), $46–$70 (6–8 persons), MC, V. Legion Lake (NCC), sleeping cabins, $25 daily (4 persons), housekeeping cabins, $35 daily (5 persons), $40 (7 persons). Sylvan Lake, lodge, $35–$50 daily (2–4 persons, $5 each additional), cabins, $48–$53 daily (4 persons), $38–$46 (2–6 persons), MC, V.

TENNESSEE

1 Big Ridge Rustic Park: Cabins, $215 weekly (4–6 persons), MC, V, AE.
2 Cedars of Lebanon State Park: Cabins, $275 weekly (8 persons); Group lodge, $125 daily (33 persons, $3.75 each additional) MC, V, AE.
3 Chickasaw State Rustic Park: Cabins, $215 weekly (6 persons); Group lodge, $64 daily (20 persons, $3 each additional) MC, V, AE.
4 Cumberland Mountain State Rustic Park: Cabins, $130 weekly (1 room), $215 weekly (1 bedroom), $275 (2–3 bedrooms); Group lodge, $275 weekly (16 persons) MC, V, AE.
5 Edgar Evins State Rustic Park: Cabins, $275 weekly (6 persons) MC, V, AE.
6 Fall Creek Falls State Resort Park: Rooms, $49.28 daily (dbl, $6 each additional, children under 11 free); Cabins, $347.20 weekly (8 persons) MC, V.
7 Great Smoky Mountains National Park: LeConte Lodge, call for current rates. Wonderland Hotel, call for current rates.
8 Henry Horton State Resort Park: Rooms, $44 daily (dbl, $6 each additional, children 12 and under free); Suites, $60 daily (8 persons); Cabins, $275 weekly (6 persons) MC, V, AE.
9 Meeman–Shelby Forest S.P.: Cabins, $275 weekly (6 persons) MC, V, AE.
10 Montgomery Bell State Resort Park: Lodge, $35–$38 daily (dbl); Cabins, $215 weekly (12 persons). MC, V, AE.
11 Natchez Trace State Resort Park: Lodge, $55 daily (dbl, inc. breakfast and dinner; $15 each additional, inc. meals, children under 12 free, not inc. meals); Cabins, $215 weekly (4–6 persons) MC, V, AE.
12 Norris Dam State Resort Park: Cabins, $275 weekly (6 persons) MC, V, AE.
13 Paris Landing State Resort Park: Rooms, $44 daily (dbl, $6 each additional, children under 12 free) MC, V, AE.
14 Pickett State Rustic Park and Forest: Chalets and rustic cabins, $230 weekly (4 persons); Cottages $294.25 weekly (4–6 persons) MC, V, AE.
15 Pickwick Landing State Resort Park: Lodge Rooms, $44 daily (dbl, $6 each

additional, children under 12 free); Cabins, $275 weekly (8 persons) MC, V, AE.

16 Reelfoot Lake State Resort Park: Inn & Motel Rooms, $38 daily (dbl, $6 each additional, children under 12 free). MC, V, AE.

17 Roan Mountain Resort Park: Cabins, $255 weekly (6 persons). MC, V, AE.

18 Standing Stone State Rustic Park (NCC): Cabins, $130 weekly (4–6 persons) $215 weekly (10 persons); Group lodges, $3 per person daily (minimum daily charge of $75, up to 48 persons), $32.50 daily (weekdays, 16 persons), $42.50 daily (weekends, 16 persons).

19 Tims Ford State Rustic Park: Cabins, $270 weekly (10 persons) AE.

TEXAS

1 Bastrop State Park (NCC): Cabins, $18 daily (dbl, $4 each additional, $1 each child under 12).

2 Big Bend National Park: Motel, $43.77 daily (dbl, $5.15 each additional); Cottages $48.92 (dbl, $5.15 each additional) MC, V.

3 Caddo Lake State Park (NCC): Cabins, $18 daily (dbl, $4 each additional, $1 each child under 12).

4 Daingerfield State Park (NCC): Cabins, $18 daily (dbl, $4 each additional, $1 each child under 12); Lodge, $64 daily (20 persons).

5 Davis Mountains State Park (NCC): Rooms, $25–$30 (dbl, $4 each additional, $1 each child under 12).

6 Garner State Park (NCC): Cabins, $18 daily (dbl, $4 each additional, $1 each child under 12).

7 Lake Brownwood State Recreation Area (NCC): Cabins, $18 daily (dbl, $4 each additional, $1 each child under 12).

8 Possum Kingdom State Recreation Area (NCC): Cabins, $18 daily (dbl, $4 each additional, $1 each child under 12).

UTAH

1 Bryce Canyon National Park: Cabins, $36.89–$61.85 daily (dbl, $5 each additional, children 3 and under free) MC, V, AE.

2 Glen Canyon National Recreation Area: Bullfrog Resort, Motel, $54–$58.50 daily (dbl, $5 each additional, children under 12 free); Housekeeping units, $49.50 daily (dbl, $5 each additional, children under 12 free); Houseboats, $675 weekly (4 persons), $925 (6 persons), $1050 (8 persons), $1350 (10 persons) MC, V, AE. Hite Resort, Housekeeping units, $49.50 daily (dbl, $5 each additional, children under 12 free). MC; Houseboats, $925 weekly (6 persons), $1050 (8 persons), $1350 (10 persons). Hall's Crossing Resort, Housekeeping units, $49.50 daily (dbl, $5 each additional, children under 12 free) MC, V, AE; Houseboats, $925 weekly (6 persons), $1050 weekly (10 persons), $1350 weekly (12 persons). Wahweap Lodge, rooms, $51.50–$58.50 daily (dbl, $3.50 each additional, children under 12 free) MC, V, AE, DC, CB; Houseboats, $925 weekly (6 persons), $1050 (8 persons), $1350 (10 persons).

3 Zion National Park: Cabins, $36.89–$54.25 daily (dbl, $5 each additional, children 3 and under free) MC, V, AE.

VIRGINIA

1 Claytor Lake State Park (NCC): Cabins, $125 weekly (4 persons).

2 Douthat State Park (NCC): Cabins, $80–$90 weekly (1 bedroom), $150 (2 bedrooms); Lodge, $360 weekly (9 persons).

3 Fairy Stone State Park (NCC): Cabins, $65–$70 weekly (1 bedroom), $125 weekly (2 bedrooms).

4 Goodwin Lake: (NCC): Cabins, $125 weekly (2 bedrooms).

5 Hungry Mother State Park (NCC): Cabins, $65–$70 weekly (1 bedroom), $125 (2 bedrooms).

6 Jefferson National Forest: Homestead, $98–$120 per person daily (includes breakfast and dinner, $20 daily for children 1–3, $39 for ages 4–9, $45 for ages 10–14, $75 for ages 15–18). AE, MC, V. Vine Cottage Inn, $41.60 daily (dbl, $5 each additional). MC, V.

7 Seashore State Park (NCC): Cabins, $150 weekly (2 bedrooms).

8 Shenandoah National Park: Big Meadows Lodge and Cottages, $27–$45 daily (dbl, $3 each additional, children under 16 free). AE, MC, V. Skyland Lodge—Rooms, $45.50 daily (dbl, $3 each additional, children under 16 free); Cabins, $22–$43 daily (dbl, $3 each additional). AE, MC, V. Lewis Mountain Cabins, $28 daily (4 persons), $48 daily (6 persons). AE, MC, V.

9 Staunton River State Park (NCC): Cabins, $65–$70 weekly (1 bedroom), $125 (2 bedrooms).

10 Westmoreland S.P. (NCC): Standard Cabins, $65–$70 weekly (1 bedroom), $125 (2 bedrooms); Overnight Cabins, $6 daily (dbl, $1.50 each additional).

WASHINGTON

1 Moran State Park: Outlook Inn, $35 daily (dbl, shared bath), $57 (dbl, private bath) MC, V.

2 Mount Rainier National Park: National Park Inn, $26 daily (dbl, without bath, $5 each additional), $39.50 (dbl, with bath, $5 each additional), Suites, $53 daily (3 persons $5 each additional) MC, V. Paradise Inn, $26 daily (dbl, $5 each additional), $45.50 (dbl with bath, $5 each additional), Suites, $60 (3 persons, $5 each additional) MC, V.

3 North Cascades National Park: North Cascades Lodge (NCC), rooms, $35–$60 daily (dbl, $10 each additional, $5 each child under 11); Cabins, $58 (2 persons, $10 each additional, $5 each child under 11). Diablo Lake Resort, call for current rates.

4 Olympic National Park: Kalaloch Lodge, rooms, $38–$50 daily (dbl, $6 each additional, $3 each child under 5); Motel rooms, $48–$64 daily (dbl, $6 each additional, $3 each additional child under 5); Cabins, $58 daily (1 room), $62 (1 bedroom), $78 (2 bedrooms) MC, V. Lake Crescent Lodge rooms, $30 daily (dbl, $5 each additional); Motel rooms, $50 daily (dbl, $5 each additional); Cottages, $30 daily (1 room), $35 (2 rooms), with fireplaces, $55 daily (1 room), $57 (2 rooms) MC, V. Log Cabin Resort, motel, $45 daily (dbl, $5.50 each additional); Chalets, $52 daily (dbl, $5.50 each additional); Cabins, $35–$39 (dbl, $5.50 each additional) MC, V. Sol Duc Hot Springs Resort, lodge and cabins, $22.50–$45 daily (dbl, $4 each additional) MC, V.

WEST VIRGINIA

1 Babcock State Park: Cabins, $170.10 weekly (2 persons), $206.85 (3 persons), $249.99 (4 persons), $298.20 (6 persons) MC, V.

2 Berkeley Springs State Park: Country Inn, $35–$50 daily (dbl, $5 each additional) MC, V, AE.

3 Blackwater Falls State Park: Lodge, $38–$85 daily (dbl, $4 each additional, children under 12 free); Cabins, $52 daily (dbl, $4 each additional, children under 12 free) MC, V.

4 Bluestone State Park (NCC): Cabins, $233 weekly (2 persons), $303.45 (4 persons), $366.45 (6 persons).

5 Cabwaylingo State Forest (NCC): Cabins, $36.75 daily (2 persons), $47.25 daily (4 persons), $57.75 daily (6 persons).

6 Capacon State Park: Lodge, $38.85 daily (dbl, $5 each additional, children under 13 free); Cabins, $170.10 weekly (2 persons), $206.85 weekly (3 persons), $249.90 (4 persons) MC, V.

7 Canaan Valley Resort State Park: Lodge, $48 daily (dbl, $6 each additional, children under 12 free); Cabins, $360 weekly (2 bedrooms), $427 (3 bedrooms), $490 (4 bedrooms) MC, V, AE.

8 Greenbrier State Forest (NCC): Cabins, $170.10 weekly (2 persons), $249.90 (4 persons), $298.20 (6 persons).

9 Hawks Nest State Park: Lodge, $38.85 daily (dbl, $4 each additional, children under 13 free) MC, V.

10 Holly River S.P. (NCC): Cabins, $42 daily (2 persons), $58 daily (4 persons).

11 Kumbrabow State Forest (NCC): Cabins, $35 daily (4–6 persons).

12 Lost River State Park (NCC): Standard Cabins, $162 weekly (2 persons, $197 weekly (3 persons), $238 (4 persons), $284 (6 persons); Deluxe cabins, $289 (4 persons), $386 (8 persons).

13 North Bend S.P.: Lodge, $37 daily (dbl, $4 each additional, children under 13 free); Cabins, $342.30 (2 bedrooms), $410.55 (4 bedrooms) MC, V.

14 Pipestem Resort State Park: Lodge, $48.30 daily (dbl, $6.30 each additional, children under 13 free); Cabins, $350.19 weekly (2 bedrooms), $427.35 weekly (3 bedrooms), $490.35 (4 bedrooms) MC, V.

15 Seneca State Forest (NCC): Cabins, $135 weekly (4 persons), $170 weekly (6 persons), $215 weekly (8 persons).

16 Twin Falls: Lodge, $38.85 daily (dbl, $4 each additional; under 13 free); Cabins, $319.20 weekly (4 persons), $387.25 (6 persons), $431.55 (8 per.) MC, V.

17 Tygart Lake State Park: Lodge, $38.85 daily (dbl, $4 each additional, children under 13 free) MC, V. Cabins (NCC), $233.10 weekly (2 persons), $303.45 weekly (4 persons), $366.45 weekly (6 persons).

18 Watoga State Park (NCC): Standard cabins, $175 weekly (2 persons), $347 weekly (8 persons); Deluxe Cabins, $303.45 (4 persons).

WISCONSIN

1 Apostle Islands National Lakeshore: Chateau Madeline, $50–$70 per person daily (includes all meals). AE, MC, V.

2 Nicolet National Forest: Wolf River Lodge (NCC), $105 per person daily (all meals, weekends), $40–$100 daily (dbl, no meals, weekdays).

WYOMING

1 Glendo State Park: Marina and rooms, $35 daily (dbl, $3 each additional) MC, V.

2 Grand Teton National Park: Jackson Lake Lodge, call for current rates. Jenny Lake Lodge, call for current rates. Colter Bay Village, call for current rates. Signal Mountain, Cabins, $38–$51 daily (dbl, $8 each additional); Motel rooms $55–$86 daily (2–4 persons); Apartments, $71–$88 daily (6 persons); House, $690 weekly (2 per.), $740 (4 per.); Houseboats, $135 daily (4–6 per.) MC, V, AE.

3 Hot Springs State Park: Plaza Hotel (NCC), Apartments, $85 weekly (1 room), $135 weekly (2 rooms), $200 weekly (3 rooms); Bedrooms, $85 weekly (dbl, $3 each additional). Holiday Inn of the Waters, $45–$56 daily (dbl., $6 each additional, children under 18 free) MC, V, AE, DC, CB.

5 Medicine Bow Forest: Cabins, $35 (4 persons, $5 each additional) MC, V.

6 Shoshone National Forest: Absaroka Mountain Lodge, Cabins, $43 daily (4 persons, $3 each additional) MC, V. Goff Creek Lodge, Cabins, $42–$45 daily (dbl., with 1 bed $5 each additional), $48–$51 (dbl, 2 beds, $5 each additional) MC, V, AE. Bill Cody's (NCC), Cabins, $52–$68 daily (dbl, $6 each additional); Chalets, $80–$100 daily (8 persons).

7 Yellowstone National Park: For all of the following: $5.20 each additional; children under 10 free; MC, V, AE. Old Faithful Inn, $29.12–$49.12 daily (dbl, without bath), $42.12–$66.56 daily (dbl, with bath). Old Faithful Lodge, Standard cabins, $37.74 daily (dbl); Family cabins, $29.12 daily (dbl); Budget cabins, $19.76 daily (dbl); Budget shelter, $16.12 daily (dbl). Old Faithful Snowlodge, lodge rooms, $29.12 daily (dbl, without bath), $42.12 daily (dbl, with bath); Standard Cabins, $40.56 daily (dbl). Canyon Lodge, Standard Cabins, $39.14 daily (dbl), luxury cabins, $52.53 daily (dbl). Lake Yellowstone Hotel, Deluxe rooms, $54.08 daily; $42.12 daily (dbl, with bath); $29.12 daily (dbl, without bath); Standard cabins, $40.56 daily (dbl); Family cabins, $29.12 (dbl). Lake Lodge, Standard cabins, $39.52 daily (dbl); Luxury cabins, $53.04 daily. Roosevelt Lodge, Standard cabins, $40.17 daily (dbl); Family cabins, $28.84 daily (dbl); Roughrider cabins, $15.97; Rustic cabins, $12.88 daily (dbl). Mammoth Hot Springs Hotel, rooms, $28.84 daily (dbl, without bath), $49.72 daily (dbl, with bath); Standard cabins, $40.17 daily (dbl), Budget cabins, $19.57 daily. Grant Village, rooms, $42.12 daily (dbl), deluxe rooms, $54.08 daily (dbl).

THE COMPLEAT TRAVELER'S READER REPORT

To: *The Compleat Traveler*
    c/o Burt Franklin & Company, Inc.
    235 East 44th Street
    New York, New York 10017 U.S.A.

Dear Compleat Traveler:

I have used your publication. I would
like to make the following ☐ recommendation, ☐ comment,
☐ suggestion, or ☐ criticism:

From (name): _____

Address: _____

_____ Telephone: _____